The Foreign Burial of
American War Dead

The Foreign Burial of American War Dead

A History

Chris Dickon

McFarland & Company, Inc., Publishers
Jefferson, North Carolina, and London

LIBRARY OF CONGRESS CATALOGUING-IN-PUBLICATION DATA

Dickon, Chris.
The foreign burial of American war dead : a history / Chris Dickon.
p.   cm.
Includes bibliographical references and index.

ISBN 978-0-7864-4612-4
softcover : 50# alkaline paper ∞

1. Soldiers' bodies, Disposition of — History.   2. War casualties — United States — History.   I. Title.
UH570.D53   2011   355.6'990973 — dc23   2011022548

BRITISH LIBRARY CATALOGUING DATA ARE AVAILABLE

© 2011 Chris Dickon. All rights reserved

No part of this book may be reproduced or transmitted in any form or by any means, electronic or mechanical, including photocopying or recording, or by any information storage and retrieval system, without permission in writing from the publisher.

On the cover: Corporal Charles Price sounding "Taps" over the graves of fallen marines at the First Marine Division cemetery at Hungnam, Korea, December 13, 1950 (National Archives)

Manufactured in the United States of America

*McFarland & Company, Inc., Publishers
Box 611, Jefferson, North Carolina 28640
www.mcfarlandpub.com*

Table of Contents

Preface and Acknowledgments 1

ONE. Seas and Shores 3
TWO. Prisons and Churchyards 12
THREE. Safe Havens and Hasty Cemeteries 20
FOUR. In Foreign Lands at Home 27
FIVE. Paris and Parral 36
SIX. Americans in Any Uniform 44
SEVEN. Decisions to Be Made 58
EIGHT. Monuments and Pilgrimage: Search for the Lost 69
NINE. Scattered from the Sky 87
TEN. Islands and Farmlands 102
ELEVEN. Expanded Families, Gracious Towns 119
TWELVE. Cold Earth and Tropical Earth 137
THIRTEEN. Remembered, Lost, Forgotten, Unknown 148
FOURTEEN. Ordinary Lives, Extraordinary Events 166
FIFTEEN. Memorial Day 182

Afterword 212
Appendices 217
Notes 277
Bibliography 283
Index 287

Preface and Acknowledgments

This book was inspired by a glint of sunlight on sparkling water in the Northwest Arm of Halifax Harbour one summer day in 2007. Quiet waves lapped up against a small promontory across the Arm from the bobbing vessels of the Armdale Yacht Club, and the feeling of the place — the moving water, the sunlight, the small piece of land and a gentle breeze — was peaceful in a way that I hadn't experienced before. It made no sense. This was not a place with a happy history. The clubhouse of the yacht club across the water had once been the warden's house of Melville Island, one of Britain's most notorious prisons of the early 19th century. And within the steep hill that rose up from the promontory were the bones of about 400 souls who had come to rest during that time as the dead of war, victims of disease and famine, and refugees from American slavery. Deadman's Island, as it was known, was covered with deep forest and bramble.

Its residents had been remembered and forgotten a number of times over the hundreds of years. Occasionally they showed up as curiosities in the form of stray bones and skulls while the promontory supported other uses. Then, in the late 1990s, a developer had gained ownership of the land and made plans to convert it into a condominium project. The residents of the Arm began to mobilize against the effort on aesthetic and environmental grounds, but they were not able to succeed in their protest until it was discovered that the hill held the remains of approximately 180 American war dead who could be identified by name, age, hometown and cause of death. The land was saved and enshrined by three nations in subsequent events that are described in the following pages. In 2007, it was a very comfortable place on a summer day in Nova Scotia.

One wondered: if almost 200 named Americans had been buried forgotten for 200 years in a hill in Halifax, where else in the world were American war dead still buried? The vast majority of them, of course, rested in the wonderful cemeteries of the American Battle Monuments Commission in ten nations from the Pacific to the Mediterranean. But it turned out that there were many more to be found.

The expedition begins in England, France and Libya before and after the turn of the 19th century. From there, it moves to Spain and Mexico. Then it pivots on the American Civil War and the Spanish American War before it returns to Mexico and then moves on to all of Europe, and finally up to Arctic Russia. It stops in prisons and prison ships, in forgotten and isolated places, and in official and unofficial cemeteries, large and small. It is accompanied by melancholy poetry and royal music. The story's arc traces the evolution of American attitudes and practices about its war dead from the days when a loved one lost overseas may as well have been an unreachable star in the sky to the current era of immediate return of the loved one's remains to a grieving family. It goes deeply, more than I expected, into the human results of war and remembrance: the seemingly endless potential of reverence for war dead, even over long measures of time, distance and hardship.

Every story has its emotional center, and it was not difficult to find the center of this one.

Others may fix it at some other point, but, for my own sensibilities as a child born of World War II, I found it in the words of historian Ton Vermeulen as we talked in the old city hall turned history museum in Zoetermeer, the Netherlands.

In the darkness of World War II, this little town seemed cut off from the world under Nazi occupation. The people felt forgotten and without any sense of what their future would hold. They feared the worst. Late in the war, however, it was the American and British planes flying in increasing numbers over their darkened landscape each night that began to give the townspeople hope. Everything else was mystery, fear and speculation; but, Vermeulen said of the planes that cast their shadows in the moonlight, "They were real." When one of them, an American B-24, fell on a farmer's field one day, one of its crew, John McCormick, was hidden from the Germans by the Dutch Resistance. McCormick then decided to join the Resistance himself, but his decision led to his death and subsequent burial in the courtyard of the town's main church. McCormick is buried there still, and his sacrifice is celebrated twice each year. He is the American embodiment of a light that fell in a darkened place.

My trip to Zoetermeer was part of a remarkable time spent in Europe in the week leading up to, and through, the American Memorial Day of 2009. The people I met there show up in these pages as the best of advocates for the Americans buried in their midst, and most have played an ongoing role in the development of this book as it has gone through continuing research and fact checking. Two of them in particular have helped me to establish the historic and emotional undertone of the story.

The city of Plymouth, England, is blessed by the enthusiasm and curiosity of historian Barbie Thompson. Plymouth's role in American history did not stop when the Pilgrims left Plymouth Sound for the new land. It figures in much of this story, as does the rest of Devon County. Barbie's continuing assistance over the last year has been invaluable.

You will meet Jerry Sheridan briefly in Chapter Thirteen and more fully in Chapter Fifteen. It was Memorial Day weekend spent with Jerry and with Laura Hoffman — both with the American Overseas Memorial Day Association–Belgium — that moved my understanding of this story into an unexpected realm. Jerry is an American professor of international relations at the Brussels Center of the American University of Washington, D.C. As vice president then (president now) of AOMDA-Belgium, he is an inexhaustible advocate for every American killed in war and buried in Belgium, a complicated European nation that he knows very well. It is his attention to the eight isolated American burials from both World Wars scattered across Belgium that defines the ethic of remembrance that you will find exemplified throughout this book, and it defined the standards by which I've tried to tell the story that follows. I give special thanks to Dr. Frances Beck and Michael Manning, my readers and proofers, who are always willing to examine my scribblings and ask, "Say what?"

CHAPTER ONE

Seas and Shores

... buried them as decently as in our circumstances we could.
— Andrew Sherburne

By the end of his life, the American naval hero John Paul Jones had become a man without a country. More than a century later, Pres. Theodore Roosevelt would demand a change in that status and open up a bizarre passage in the history of America's relationship to its military dead. But this was 1792, and a lot had transpired in the 45 years of Jones' life that mirrored both the tentative and forceful first steps of the new nation. It also seemed to predict the centuries that would follow as America formed its own identity in an increasingly complicated world and began to take a better accounting of the dead left in the wake of its history.

Jones had died in self-imposed exile in Paris. The eulogy given him by the officiating clergyman at his burial on July 20, 1792, spoke to both the impact and sadness of Jones' years. "Legislators! citizens! soldiers! friends! brethren! and Frenchmen!" he exclaimed, "we have just returned to the earth the remains of an illustrious stranger, one of the first champions of the liberty of America; of that liberty which so gloriously ushered in our own."[1]

The true name of the "illustrious stranger" was not actually John Paul Jones, but simply John Paul when he was born on July 6, 1747 in Scotland. His family had lived near the sea. As the young John Paul became familiar with the ways of the tobacco trade with America, his attraction to the world beyond the horizon brought him to an apprenticeship in the trade, and he sailed away at age 12. His first stop was the Rappahannock River in coastal Virginia, the home of an older brother who had settled there earlier.

At age 19, Jones entered the workforce of the slave trade under the British flag, but only briefly, as he found the trade repugnant. It was that experience, in some versions of his life story, that instilled in him the certain sense of the power of freedom and liberty he would pursue in following years. But if that was so, it was contradicted by the reputation he would eventually gain as a cruel and unforgiving shipmaster. His use of torture was alleged, then he was blamed for the death of an errant sailor under his command, and, in the following years, accused of smuggling. The accumulation of complaints led to his final departure from Scotland to Virginia in 1773, where he added Jones to his name and became the first man to be named first lieutenant in the Continental Navy in December 1775.

Like many who fought for America, and later in the American Civil War, John Paul

Jones was the hybrid product of more than one nation. The Revolutionary War of 1776 pitted the formerly British against the still British. The British practice of impressment, the kidnapping and enslavement of citizens of other nations into the Royal Navy, added to the confusion. The never-ending tides of immigration across the world would in war always position nationals of one country on the side of another country. The ferment of the first decades of the United States of America would extend into the individual lives of many of those who played a role in those unsettled times.

Thus, Paul Jones, as he was sometimes alternatively called, distinguished himself over and over in the Revolutionary War as a former British subject on the American side. He beat back the enemy from the Bahamas to Nova Scotia, menaced the coasts of Scotland and Ireland, and famously uttered the words "I have not yet begun to fight!" in response to a British demand that he surrender in a battle that he ultimately won. During the war he would be derided as a pirate by the British, be honored by the King of France with the title Chevalier, and receive with that title a gold medal of honor from the Continental Congress of 1787 for "valor and brilliant services" despite a difficult relationship with everyone from crew to command in those years.

That honor aside, however, he found himself virtually unemployed as an American naval hero in 1788. There was nothing for him to do in the United States, so he hired on with Catherine the Great of Russia in the Second Russo-Turkish War. He referred to himself now as Pavel Dzhones, and became rear admiral on a Russian flagship. By all accounts, he acquitted himself well in the effort. But he did not get along with his Russian counterparts, who, in Jones' view, caused his recall from service and loss of command. The problem was compounded

by a charge that Jones, who had a recognized weakness for women, had taken indecent liberties with a twelve-year-old girl. The charge was vigorously refuted on his behalf by the French ambassador to Russia and was eventually accepted as false by Catherine the Great, who allowed him to kiss her hand on July 7, 1789, and took other actions to show her belief in him.[2] He returned to Paris an embittered man and died alone on July 18, 1792. He was found lying across his bed or couch, his feet on the floor.

Two days after his death, John Paul Jones was placed in a lead coffin in the anticipation that the United States might want to claim the body of its hero; but there seemed to be no interest in doing so at the time. His statelessness was a condition of the times and would be resolved over the years. He was interred in the St. Louis Cemetery for Foreign

A portrait of John Paul Jones "drawn from nature" by J.M. Moreau le Jeunne, dated May 1780, twelve years before Jones' death. Subsequent paintings and drawings of Jones would depict him with a variety of facial structures that bore little resemblance to each other. It would become important to know what he actually looked like in 1905 (*Library of Congress*).

Protestants in Paris, the first recorded American military member, notable or not, to be buried in a foreign land. "Let never tyrants, nor their satellites, pollute this sacred earth!" exclaimed the officiating clergyman, a M. Marron. "May the ashes of the great man, too soon lost to humanity, and eager to be free, enjoy here an undisturbed repose!"[3] When the cemetery was closed six months later, it might have seemed that the cleric's plea would be honored in a way not intended. It was in a less savory part of Paris, and it eventually disappeared. Its eroded surface became the site of animal fights for wager, and then abandoned land, its dead forgotten.

But the matter of the 18th century burial of Chevalier John Paul Jones would become a national issue in the 20th century as American attitudes about its war dead began to change. And it would beg a question of fairness to the dead in the first years of the 21st century.

On the Sunday before his death, John Paul Jones had been visited at his apartment by the American minister to France, the Hon. Gouverneur Morris. He asked to speak privately with Jones in the garden, after which it was observed that the admiral was exhausted and took to his bed. The conversation was about the troubled relations between the United States and the Barbary powers of the Mediterranean. Morris told Jones that he would soon receive a commission to enter into negotiations with the dey of Algiers for the release of American Christians taken as slaves by Mediterranean pirates and that a suitable military force would be placed at his disposal to back up the negotiations. The commission, however, arrived a few days after Jones' death.

The problem of American sailors taken captive in North Africa had been much on Jones' mind over his career. In December 1788 he wrote to Thomas Jefferson about a number of matters, including the American prisoners in Algiers: "I continue to be deeply affected; the more so as I learn from the pirate [he had met] now here, who took the greatest part of them, that if they are not very soon redeemed, they will be treated with no more lenity than is shown to other slaves."[4]

Indeed, the Muslim pirates of the Mediterranean were among the most vexing problems for post–Revolutionary America. Simply put, the new nation's best economic opportunities lay in the trade of abundant resources with Europe; but whenever its ships passed through the Straits of Gibraltar they were likely to be menaced by the pirates of Algiers, Tunis, Morocco and Tripoli. And the more lucrative the potential of trade, the more dangerous things became. Pirates aside, the Mediterranean was a violent place in those days as the battle space of constant European wars first set off by the French Revolution of 1789 and extending through the Napoleonic Wars up to 1815. American opportunity lay in the selling of goods to warring nations, and, while merchant ships could thread their way through fighting ships with some success, the pirates always lay in wait. If an American ship was taken it might be converted to a pirate vessel and its sailors damned to hard lives of perpetual slavery. Christian sailors were especially prized because there would be no scruples about the treatment of infidels. Those who died were buried in Christian burying grounds beneath coastal sands and a few feet above the point of high tide.

The actions were part of an economic system that had existed in the Mediterranean for centuries. If ships and sailors could not be rescued by force — not a likely prospect for American interests — they could be ransomed at great price. In some respects, the problems the pirates presented to all nations could fall under the heading of "the cost of doing business." In a larger context, the system offered advantages to some of its victims. If the British, for example, had a greater ability to fight off pirate ships with their Royal Navy or to pay ransoms with their great wealth, they gained added superiority over other nations not as well equipped or as bountifully funded.

In its first years, America chose to accept the cost of doing business rather than fight back. Treaties were negotiated and sums were paid, but they proved to be ultimately unreliable. Over the years, Thomas Jefferson, for one, had come to the conclusion that those who took American ships and enslaved American citizens should be punished rather than paid, and that respect for America's sovereignty among nations was a paramount requirement. In 1794, Congress directed the building of six navy frigates designed primarily to fight the pirates, the founding force of the modern U.S. Navy. But it was another American fighting ship, the USS *Philadelphia*, that would gain the highest profile in the ongoing struggle with the pirates of the Mediterranean.

The *Philadelphia* had been built in her namesake city and commissioned in 1800. She would eventually cross paths with a Lt. Richard Somers, who was from a merchant seafaring family not far away in Somers Point, New Jersey. Born in 1778, Somers had taken to the sea as a boy as if by instinct. He learned to sail on Great Egg Bay and formed a friendship in boarding school with Stephen Decatur, Jr., both of them destined to become U.S. Naval heroes of a special rank.

In 1801, the ongoing saga of the United States and the pirates evolved into the First Barbary, or Tripolitan, War. On the occasion of the inauguration of Pres. Thomas Jefferson, the pasha of Tripoli, Yusuf Karamanli, demanded a tribute of $225,000. Jefferson refused, and the pasha declared war in May of that year by the act of bringing down the flag that flew above the U.S. consulate. Algiers and Tunis soon joined the battle and were met by U.S. Commodore Edward Preble, commanding a fleet of frigates, schooners and assorted other fighting craft.

The first American shots in the war were fired from the USS *Enterprise* against the corsair *Tripoli* on August 1, 1801. Richard Somers was on the nearby USS *Boston* at the time and described the encounter in a letter to Stephen Decatur, excerpted in part:

> While running for Malta, on the 1st of August, the ENTERPRISE, came across a polacca-rigged ship such as the Barbary Corsairs usually have, with an American brig in tow. It had evidently been captured and her people set adrift. [Capt. Andrew] Sterrett, who commands the ENTERPRISE, as soon as he found the position of affairs, cleared for action, ran out his guns, and opened with a brisk fire on the Tripolitan. He got into a raking position, and his broadside had a terrific effect upon the pirate. But — mark the next — three times were the Tripolitan colors hauled down, and then hoisted again as soon as the fire of the ENTERPRISE ceased. After the third time, Sterrett played his broadside on the pirate with the determination to sink him for such treachery; but the Tripolitan rais, or captain, appeared in the waste of the ship, bending his body in token of submission, and actually threw his ensign overboard....
>
> Now I must tell you a piece of news almost too good to be true. I hear the Government is building four beautiful small schooners, to carry sixteen guns, for use in the Tripolitan war, which is to be pushed actively; and that you, my dear Decatur, will command one of those vessels, and I another! I can write nothing more exhilarating after this; so, I am, as always, your faithful friend, Richard Somers.[5]

The *Enterprise* would eventually come under the command of Decatur. Somers would be successful in a number of Mediterranean encounters that would lead to the command assignment that would take him to a heroic death.

Under Commodore Preble, American forces kept the upper hand against the Barbary States. In 1802, the fleet was reinforced with the USS *Argus*, USS *Constellation*, USS *Constitution*, USS *Chesapeake* and the USS *Philadelphia*, among others. In 1803, an effective blockade was enforced against the coastal cities, and their harbors were put under attack. In the course of one of those skirmishes, the USS *Philadelphia* ran aground and was captured on a reef in Tripoli harbor. Her captain and 300 crew were taken prisoner, most to the rough cells and dungeons of the Old Castle Fort. Equally bad, in the eyes of the U.S. Navy, was that the *Philadelphia* was taken as prize and preparations were begun to convert her into a Tripolitan warship to be named *Gift of Allah*.

The actions that prevented the USS *Philadelphia* from becoming the *Gift of Allah* would bring together American military heroism, intelligence, might and cunning in an action far from the country's own shores for one of the first times in its history. It was the kind of operation that would be copied in similar situations against similar enemies over the following centuries. And it would lead to the first known burial abroad of named American military members lost in combat.

Key to success of the mission was a ketch that had served in Napoleon Bonaparte's Egyptian campaign before capture by the British and eventual appropriation into the Tripolitan navy. She was under that flag when Stephen Decatur and the *Enterprise* found her on a course to Constantinople with a cargo of female slaves. She was easily taken prize and soon renamed the USS *Intrepid*. It was a fortuitous capture on Decatur's part because the plan that emerged to save the *Philadelphia* from her captors required the participation of a small Tripolitan sailing ship in an audacious charade.

Commodore Preble had determined that the *Philadelphia* could not be recaptured and had to be destroyed. The inclination of his young officers was to blast it out of the water with their own battleships, but Preble had a more subtle plan and he gave Decatur the assignment to carry it out. Once commissioned as the USS *Intrepid*, the little ship was refitted to take on the appearance of a small coastal trader of no military importance. Decatur and his crew took on the clothes and demeanor of worn Muslim sailors, and approached the *Philadelphia* on the night of February 16, 1804. Hailing the U.S. frigate's Muslim crew, they claimed to be a Maltan ketch made anchorless by recent storms and in need of the shelter of a larger ship to ride out the hours until morning.

As the Tripolitans finally determined that they would be allowed to do so, the crew of the *Intrepid* mustered its incendiary cargo and began its operation. As the frigate sent out a boat with a fasting line, the *Intrepid* sent out its own boat toward the frigate. By the time the ruse was discovered by Turkish forces holding the frigate, it was too late. The *Intrepid* and the *Philadelphia* were linked, and, with little resistance, the Americans were fully on board within ten minutes. Each man set fire to a designated part of the *Philadelphia* and she was fully engulfed in less than half an hour. Without a casualty, the *Intrepid* sailed away as the American frigate presented a spectacular show of fireworks in Tripoli harbor, each of her cannons exploding when overheated by the fire. Tides and winds turned the burning ship so that some of the cannons aimed themselves at the city, which was already in turmoil because of the brazen attack.

Stephen Decatur sailed the *Intrepid* to Syracuse in southern Italy and became an American naval hero for the ages. Even the British naval warrior Lord Nelson was taken by what had been accomplished, "the most bold and daring act of the age," he was said to have exclaimed. But it was another heroic act of the Tripolitan War that brought an end to the life of Decatur's friend Richard Somers.

By the late summer of 1804, Commodore Preble was implementing what might, in another day, be called guerrilla tactics against the Tripolitans. In August, he summoned the *Intrepid* back from Italy for a mission that would turn her into a floating incendiary to be sailed into the midst of the enemy's navy and exploded. Lt. Somers volunteered to command the mission, which was to use two fast rowing boats and crews to remove Somers and his crew before detonation. Naval historian James Fenimore Cooper described the events of September 4, 1804, in his classic *History of the Navy of the United States of America*, published in 1841:

> The sea was covered with a dense haze, though the stars were visible, and the last that may be said to have been seen of the Intrepid, was the shadowy forms of her canvas, as she steered slowly, but steadily, into the obscurity, where the eyes of the many spectators fancied they could still trace her dim outline, most probably after it had totally disappeared. This sinking into the gloom of night, was no bad image of the impenetrable mystery that has veiled the subsequent proceedings of the gallant party on board her.[6]

The exact cause of the premature explosion of the *Intrepid* would never be agreed upon. Commodore Preble took the view that she had been boarded by Tripolitan sailors, prompting the crew to blow up the ship so that her valuable munitions would not fall into enemy hands, thus sacrificing their own lives. Capt. William Bainbridge of the *Philadelphia* would find their bodies the following day. Though a prisoner, he was allowed enough freedom to manage the situation in which the Americans found themselves. James Fenimore Cooper quoted from Bainbridge's private journal:

> Was informed that the explosion that we heard last night, proceeded from a vessel (which the Americans attempted to send into the harbour,) blowing up; which unfortunate scheme did no damage whatever to the Tripolitans; nor did it even appear to heave them into confusion....
>
> On the 8th, by the Bashaw's permission, went to the beach of the harbour, and there saw six persons in a most mangled and burnt condition, lying on the shore; whom we supposed to have been part of the unfortunate crew of the fire-vessel, the bottom of which grounded on the north side of the rocks near the round battery. Two of these distressed-looking objects were fished out of the wreck. From the whole of them being so much disfigured, it was impossible to recognise any known feature to us, or even to distinguish an officer from a seaman. Mr. Cowdery, who accompanied us, informed me that he saw six others yesterday, on the shore to the southward, which were supposed to have come from the same vessel.[7]

The *Philadelphia*'s surgeon was able to make better identification of the 13 bodies eventually recovered, and they were buried in Tripolitan earth outside the Old Castle Fort on the harbor. The U.S. Congress expressed its sympathy for the families of those lost, and the war came to an end. A treaty and a final ransom of $60,000 was paid to retrieve the *Philadelphia*'s crew in 1805.

Lt. Richard Somers and the crew of the USS *Intrepid* would become the first named Americans killed in combat and buried abroad. If their graves were marked upon burial, those markings soon disappeared, in part because Christian symbols were not welcome in a Muslim nation. They would be forgotten until the 1930s, then forgotten again until the following century when a small town in New Jersey began to pose provocative questions about equality in the way America remembers its war dead.

In 1831, a veteran of the Revolutionary War of 1775–1783 published the book *Memoirs of Andrew Sherburne: A Pensioner of the Navy of the Revolution, Written by Himself*. In the preface, Sherburne begged the reader to forgive his lack of education and limited way with words, but the book that followed was a remarkable first-person account of a young man's journey through the War of Independence, most of the time spent as a prisoner of the British. He offered a telling glimpse into the slim line between life and death navigated by those at sea during times of war. On a prisoner's march somewhere near Placentia, Newfoundland, his group came to a place Sherburne called Distress Bay,[8] and the wreckage of a sailing ship:

> It was supposed that this vessel must have gone entirely to pieces, several miles from the shore. We supposed her to have been a brig, and we knew her to have been an American built, for on

the forehead of some of her carved images, the letters U.S.A. were carved. She might have been captured by the English, and in their service. There was no doubt but that she had been to the West Indies, for we found several hogsheads of rum upon the shore, and some of them not much injured.... The remains of this vessel were scattered a mile or more on the shore. We picked up fourteen men and a boy about twelve or fourteen years old. We dragged them up on the bank, (for the shore here was low,) and with staves dug a grave two or three feet deep, and buried them as decently as in our circumstances we could.[9]

The deceased may have been British sailors who had taken over an American ship, but if they were American merchant sailors, they were likely to have been enlisted in the revolutionary cause under letters of marque extending military rights and duties to merchant ships in time of war. Sherburne's story may have been the first written account of American military personnel buried abroad, and it included two touchstones of the war years to come: the deaths and burials of navy dead in tidal lands near the sea, and the practices of the British in regard to American captives.

From the Revolutionary War through the War of 1812, the most dreaded destination for anyone unfortunate enough to be captured by the British was one of the prison hulks anchored in American and British harbors. The most notorious of them in the Revolutionary War was the HMS *Jersey*, mired in the mud of New York's East River at the site of the future Brooklyn Navy Yard. Andrew Sherburne would come across the *Jersey* in his adventures, and his account is restrained compared to some others:

> I entered the Jersey towards the last of November. I had just entered the eighteenth year of my age, and had now to commence a scene of suffering almost without a parallel. The ship was extremely filthy, and abounded with vermin. A large proportion of the prisoners had been robbed of their clothing. The ship was considerably crowded; many of the men were very low spirited; our provisions ordinary, and very scanty. They consisted of worm eaten ship bread, and salt beef.... [A]t night the hatches were shut down and locked, and there was not the least attention paid to the sick or dying, except what could be done by the convalescent; who were so frequently called upon, that in many cases they overdid themselves, relapsed and died.[10]

In the fall of 1780, Capt. Silas Talbot, a future commander of the USS *Constitution*, was imprisoned on the *Jersey*. His writings describe 1100 nearly naked prisoners with no berths for sleeping or places to sit. The ship was run by brutal guards and made lethal by dysentery and fever. Talbot estimated the death toll at ten per day in the cool fall months, but a much higher number in the preceding summer. He reported that the bodies were seen buried in the banks of Long Island, with stray bones and skulls scattered on the shore.[11] The observation would be in keeping with what little is known about the outcome for dead American prisoners held in England. The prisoner Andrew Sherburne arrived in Plymouth, England in November 1781.

In the rich history shared by America and Plymouth the departure of the Pilgrims who would form Plymouth Colony, Massachusetts in 1620, was only a single event. One hundred fifty years later and in the years following, the prison hulks, land bound prisons and hospitals of Plymouth would become an American colony of another sort. More than 300 years later, Plymouth would look to America as one of its saviors in World War II. Over all of those centuries, Plymouth remained a place of sharp hills, windswept harbors and roiling waters at the edge of the North Atlantic.

Andrew Sherburne's reaction upon entering the harbor was confused: "It excited some peculiar sensations to lift up my eyes and behold the land of my forefathers. I must confess I felt a certain kind of reverence and solemnity that I cannot well describe. Yet when reflecting

The interior of the British prison hulk *Jersey* during the Revolutionary War, showing prisoners and guard (*Library of Congress*).

on my situation, and bringing into view the haughtiness of her monarch and government; their injustice and cruelty to her children; felt an indignant, if not a revengeful spirit towards them."[12]

At this point in his travels, Sherburne had not yet had the experience of the *Jersey* in New York, but all imprisoned American sailors knew that their every endeavor should be to end up in a land bound prison instead of the third level of hell in one of the prison hulks. It was a matter of luck, negotiation and a determination of one's status. To be a prisoner of war was good, but to be a traitor against the British homeland was bad. And in the first years of the war the American revolutionaries were considered traitors.

In Plymouth, the plum assignment for a captured soul was Old Mill Prison located on a windswept promontory in the bay. It was there that Sherburne eventually found himself heading: "I was then pressing the soil of Old England, in a walk of about a mile and a half.... I had not walked so much on the land before since my tedious march through the dreary wilderness of Newfoundland. I felt a high degree of animation that my prospects were so flattering. It was indeed a peculiar gratification to think of entering Old Mill prison. At length we came to the outer gate, which groaning on its hinges, opened to receive us into the outer yard."[13] Old Mill was its own small city, good and bad, and a place where residents died on a regular basis. Its population was a mix of all nationalities at odds with the British for various reasons, and Sherburne estimated 800 to 1000 Americans to be in residence. The Royal Naval Hospital in Plymouth, deemed a benevolent place for prisoners, also contained an American population and experienced associated deaths.

In 1779, the British philanthropist John Howard embarked on a tour of the country's military prisons, noting conditions and taking a census of American, Spanish and French prisoners. At Pembroke Prison in Pembrokeshire he found 37 Americans living in filthy conditions and mostly without shoes and socks. Two hundred fifty-one Americans were found in Forton Prison in Portsmouth, most of them in good health, probably because they were the recipients of charity assistance from residents of the city. Howard found just 298 Americans at Old Mill Prison two years before Sherburne's estimate of up to 1,000. Howard's figure included Americans in the prison hospital, which he determined to be an unhealthy place. Over three years at Old Mill, by Howard's count, 734 Americans had resided in the prison, of whom 102 escaped, 114 joined British forces and 36 died.[14]

It was probably the case that Old Mill saw the least death among British prisons. The full number of American deaths in England during the Revolutionary War can't be known. It included those from the land bound prisons, those who had died in the prison transports that came from America — many of those ships as bad as the prison hulks — and from the hulks themselves. The hulks in America, Great Britain and other locations saw the deaths of Americans beyond all scale. In 1908, the Prison Ships Martyrs Monument was constructed in Fort Greene Park, Brooklyn, New York. Inspired by the offense of the prison ship *Jersey*, which had moored nearby, and drawing from the consensus of history, it asserted that 11,500 Americans had died in the hulks in the U.S. and abroad during the Revolutionary War.

The total death toll abroad was supplemented by the creation of a diaspora of American prisoners sent into the world by the British, as far away as Africa and Asia and as near as Antigua in the West Indies. In 1782, the narrative of an unnamed crew member of the captured American privateer *New Broom* gave this account of casual death and burial:

> We were all put on board of a prison-ship, which lay in a cove on one side of the harbor, where the heat was so severe as to be almost insupportable. We were allowed here but barely enough to sustain nature, and the water they gave us was taken out of a pond a little back of the town, in which the cattle and negroes commingled every sort of impurity, and which was rendered, on this account and from the effect of the heat upon it, so nauseous that it was impossible to drink it without holding the nostrils. I soon found that life was to be supported but for a short time here and set myself therefore about contriving some way to effect my escape from this floating place of misery and torment. The doctor came on board every morning to examine the sick, and three negro sextons every night, to bury the dead.... Early one morning I swallowed tobacco juice and was so sick by the time the doctor came, that I obtained without difficulty a permit from him to go on shore to the hospital. I was soon ready to disembark, for I had been previously robbed of everything except what I had on. After arriving at the hospital, I was conducted into a long room where lay more than two hundred of the most miserable objects imaginable, covered with rags and vermin. I threw myself down on a bunk and after suffering extremely for some time from the effects of the tobacco, went to sleep, but was soon waked by a man-nurse, who told me that there was physic for me and immediately went off to another. I contrived unperceived to throw my dose out of the window and was not again disturbed, except during the following night, when I was waked several times by the carrying out of the dead.

The prisoner was eventually able to escape with two others to Guadeloupe, in the Leeward Islands.[15]

Except for Andrew Sherburne's writing of bones seen lying on the beaches near the prison hulk *Jersey*, there were no accounts of where all of the dead from prisons on land and sea and the far-flung reaches of the British Empire were buried. The War of 1812 would both confirm the worst speculations and offer the first efforts by all sides to follow acceptable practices and keep records.

Chapter Two

Prisons and Churchyards

All sleep unknown; their bodies rot / By all, save distant friends, forgot.
—Anon.

One day in 1814, another prisoner in another war looked out from another British prison hulk and saw a sight that was similar to that noted by Capt. Silas Talbot, prisoner of the *Jersey*, in 1780. The young Benjamin Waterhouse, whose narrative as a prisoner in the War of 1812 would mirror that of Andrew Sherburne in the Revolutionary War, watched events unfold as two fellow prisoners attempted to escape from the *Crown Prince* in the Medway River near Chatham, England. One of the men turned back. "The sentry heard him breathing," wrote Waterhouse, "and said, 'Ah! Here is a porpoise, and I'll stick him with my bayonet,' and only the crying out of the poor would-be refugee saved him. The ship's officers on examining the hole [used to escape] were amazed, and one of them remarked that he did not believe that the Devil himself could keep these fellows in hell if they made up their minds to get out. The next day the other poor chap was seen lying dead on the beach, and to the disgust of the prisoners was allowed to remain there two days before he was buried."[1]

A Journal of a Young Man of Massachusetts (1754–1846) by Benjamin Waterhouse, M.D., is a thorough and curious autobiographical account of a sailor's hard journey through the War of 1812. Far from being the unfortunate sailor depicted, though, the actual Dr. Waterhouse was one of the first faculty members of the Harvard Medical School and an initial developer of a smallpox vaccine that would go on to solve one of the world's most pressing health problems. Common wisdom holds that the autobiography under his name is actually a collection of the accounts of a number of other people. No matter his true identity, the subject of the autobiography travels through the core of the story of Americans buried abroad in an important but mostly forgotten war. And the War of 1812 was, in some interpretations, a conflict started because of a miscommunication between the United States and Great Britain. Other views hold it as a defining second revolutionary war between the two nations. From the American perspective, it was the result of continued bad behavior on the part of the British after the Revolution.

When the British lost America in 1783, they also lost its seagoing workforce of 10,000. The Royal Navy made up for the loss through the practice of impressment. If a British ship arrived in almost any port in the world when they were in need of crew members, a thuggish press gang would simply go into town and grab any able-bodied man they might find and put him under a form of slavery on the ship. After the war, British ships still showed up in

American ports for supply and repair, and seemed to be able to impress American men with ease. The problem was compounded by the British notion that many of those so impressed were thereby British subjects. The determination of true nationality was further confused by the escape of actual British sailors from their harsh lives aboard Royal Navy vessels. Most would then assume Americans identities, and in turn sign on to American ships.

Thus it was that on the bright summer day of June 22, 1807, the American frigate USS *Chesapeake* set out from Norfolk, Virginia, on what was to be an uneventful trip to the Mediterranean, but quickly found herself confronted by the British frigate HMS *Leopard* not far off the Virginia Capes. The Chesapeake was not prepared for any kind of confrontation, its decks not yet organized and cleared, and its crew working at the task of beginning a trans–Atlantic voyage. The *Leopard* signaled that it would like to send a party aboard the *Chesapeake*, not an unusual request; but when they arrived, the *Leopard*'s officers insisted that four Royal Navy deserters were among the *Chesapeake*'s numbers and demanded that they be produced.

Commodore James Barron of the *Chesapeake* insisted that no such men would be found in his crew and that, in any case, the British would not be allowed to search for them, let alone take them away. The officers of the *Leopard* bid a polite farewell, returned to their ship and promptly let loose upon the *Chesapeake* a series of broadsides at very close range. Under surprise attack, the *Chesapeake* managed to fire back just once — that shot the work of Lt. William H. Allen, who had served on the USS *Philadelphia* and would go on to become the first American military casualty to be buried abroad ceremoniously five years later. In less than fifteen minutes, the *Chesapeake* was dead in the water. The four suspect crew (three of whom were originally Americans who had been impressed into the Royal Navy) were rounded up to begin a journey north to Halifax, Nova Scotia. The *Chesapeake* was left to limp slowly back into Norfolk in disgrace.

The event had the effect of reminding Americans, rudely and with force, that the Revolutionary War was only a beginning step in gaining sovereignty and self-determination in the larger world. It led to near riots in the streets of Norfolk and Portsmouth, angry editorials in newspapers up and down the East Coast, resolutions against the British passed by town councils as far west as Kentucky, and the banning of all British ships from American waters by Pres. Thomas Jefferson. It played a role in the continuing discussion of how best to defend America against its enemies. And it was a first step leading to the War of 1812.

Officially, the second named conflict between the U.S. and Great Britain was caused by another form of British abuse. As America continued to seek its place in world trade after 1807, the problems of impressment were compounded by the ongoing Napoleonic wars and the insistence by the British that American ships would not be allowed to trade with France, a stance codified under British Orders in Council. The Chesapeake Affair, as it was called, was settled in 1811 with reparations paid and apology from the British. But the Orders in Council led to a congressional resolution of war against the British on June 18, 1812. No matter that the British had rescinded the offending orders two days earlier in London. Communications in those days weren't instant, and the war was on. It was a war that some Americans wanted to undertake in any case, with the hopes that it might allow expansion into British Canada.

The War of 1812 was fought from Louisiana to the Canadian frontier and in the Atlantic Ocean. It was not expected that the small American navy would do well against the powerful resources of the Royal Navy, but the first year of the war found American ships prevailing against their British counterparts much to American surprise and British disbelief. English morale became dismal and in need of a victory. That finally came on June 1, 1813, when the

USS *Chesapeake* set out to sea once again, this time from Boston, with the goal of defeating the HMS *Shannon,* which had been blockading Boston Harbor. James Lawrence, captain of the *Chesapeake*, was confident of his ability to defeat the *Shannon*; but he miscalculated, and the *Chesapeake* was forced to surrender in less than 15 minutes. It was as he lay mortally wounded that Lawrence uttered, "Don't give up the ship!" or similar words. The admonition was to no avail. The ship and its wounded were taken north to Halifax, England's base of naval operations in North America.

Whatever the animus between American and British forces at sea, the death of officers of opposing forces often brought forth a response that was profoundly civil. The death of James Lawrence offered a first example and the first recorded ceremonial burial abroad of an American lost in combat. Lawrence, born into a family of lawyers in Burlington, New Jersey, but drawn to the sea, had been second in command under Stephen Decatur in the destruction by fire of the USS *Philadelphia*. He was known on all sides as a decent and compassionate man, and no less so when it came to those he fought at war. Commanding the USS *Hornet* early in 1813, he had sunk the HMS *Peacock* in a classic battle between sailing frigates, and had shown a concern for the safety and well being of the *Peacock* crew that had been noted by the British.

Thus, when the body of James Lawrence was brought into Halifax Harbour draped in the American flag on the top deck of the defeated *Chesapeake,* the reaction of the Haligonians was quiet and respectful. On June 8, under meticulous instructions from the garrison's command, the coffins of Lawrence and two other American officers were moved from their ship. An eyewitness gave this account:

> The procession was very long, and everything was conducted in the most solemn and respectful manner; and the wounded officers of both nations, who followed in the procession, made the scene very affecting. I never attended a funeral in my life where my feelings were so much struck. There was not the least mark of exultation that I saw, even among the commonest people. All appeared to lament his death; and I heard several say they considered the blood shed on the Chesapeake's deck as dear as that of their own countrymen.[2]

Lawrence and the others were buried with honors in the hallowed Old Burying Grounds on Barrington Street. Perhaps twelve others of the crew who were already dead or severely injured were buried in the cemetery of the naval hospital.

Many of the surviving *Chesapeake* sailors were marched over Citadel Hill to the site of the British prison on Melville Island. They may have spent some time on a prison hulk anchored off the island. Their eventual entrance into the prison was noted just briefly by another of its inmates, Benjamin Waterhouse. "Early in the month of July," he wrote, "we were not a little disturbed by the arrival of the crew of our ill-omened, ill-fated Chesapeake."[3]

In total, *A Journal of a Young Man of Massachusetts* was intended by Waterhouse as an indictment of the inhumanity of British prisons. "Our new prisons in the United States," he wrote, "reflect great honour on the nation. They speak loudly that we are a considerate and humane people; whereas the prison at Halifax, erected solely for the safe keeping of prisoners of war, resembles an horse stable, with stalls or stanchions for separating the cattle from each other."[4] Waterhouse's descriptions of Melville Island, and those of others, were similar to the descriptions of Old Mill Prison in Plymouth, worse in some respects and better in others. But Melville Island was distinguished by two characteristics that set it apart in some respects. Over some of its years, it was a setting for social life in Halifax. Its inmates were allowed to work in the city at the trades they had practiced before the war, and the prison was often a destination for weekend life in the city, where prisoners sold crafts or offered

Two. *Prisons and Churchyards* 15

Melville Island prison on the northwest arm of Halifax Harbor, circa 1800s. Its cemetery, Deadman's Island, is at the promontory facing the prison building across the water. *J.E. Woolford, c. 1818 (Library and Archives, Canada)*.

entertainments, while picnics were held on the island. Most important, the prison at Melville Island had a dedicated cemetery, of a limited sort, for its inmates.

The first American prisoner of the War of 1812 to die on Melville Island was James Newell, age 27, of Boston, on August 10, 1812. His ship was the USS *Gossamer*, a privateer-brig surrendered to the HMS *Emulous* without a shot on July 30. Seaman Newell died of typhus while in prison. His body was taken by skiff across an inlet in the Northwest Arm of Halifax Harbour and buried without ceremony or marker in nearby Target Hill, so called because it had been used for shooting practice since the British had first used Melville Island for French prisoners in 1803. A poem, put forth by Benjamin Palmer, another diarist of imprisonment in the War of 1812, as written by an unnamed inmate, predicted that the dead would be forgotten:

> Go view the graves that prisoners fill
> Go count them on the rising hill
> No Monumental marble shows....
> Whose silent dust does there repose
> All sleep unknown; their bodies rot
> By all, save distant friends, forgot.[5]

The lamentable prophecy was correct up to a point. Less than 200 years later, the dead prisoners would return to the conscience of a modern Halifax and bring together the representatives of three nations to remember who they were.

James Lawrence would not long remain the first naval officer lost in combat and buried with honors abroad. Eventually his body was disinterred from the Old Burying Ground above

Halifax Harbour, as were those of his two officers, and removed to the Trinity churchyard cemetery on lower Broadway in Manhattan. But not long after the defeat of the *Chesapeake*, a similar fate would fall to another U.S. frigate with a much-respected commander.

William H. Allen was born in Providence, Rhode Island, in 1784. His father was a major in the Revolutionary War and his uncle a governor of Rhode Island. Educated to a life in politics, he was called instead to the sea and joined the navy against his parents' wishes in 1800. He worked his way up the chain of command on various ships, including the USS *Philadelphia* and USS *Constitution*, until he arrived as a third lieutenant on the USS *Chesapeake* early in 1807. In the Chesapeake Affair of that year he improvised a way to get the only shot off at the HMS *Leopard* before the American ship surrendered. The first year of the War of 1812 found him on the USS *United States* under Stephen Decatur when it captured the HMS *Macedonia*, one of those naval outcomes that surprised America and bewildered England.

Appointed commander of the brig *Argus*, Allen sailed into the heart of the War of 1812 with orders to menace the commerce, shipping, light cruisers and harbors of the enemy from Ireland to the Mediterranean. This he accomplished with precision and the taking of 20 enemy prizes. But in all instances he, like James Lawrence, conducted himself with grace and compassion and with respect for the needs and rights of civilians caught in the cross fire. In his last letter to his sister, he wrote, "When you shall hear that I have ended my earthly career, that I only exist in the kind remembrance of my friends, you will forget my follies, forgive my faults, call to mind some little instances dear to reflection, to excuse your love for me, and shed one tear to the memory of Henry."

The end of Allen's career came on the morning of August 14, 1813, when the *Argus* was approached by the HMS *Pelican*, a larger ship with orders to destroy the *Argus* at all costs. Allen could have escaped, but he chose to take on the fight and lost. Mortally wounded, he was taken to the (by now named) Millbay Prison in Plymouth, England, and died in the hospital, as did one of his officers, Richard Delphy (born perhaps in 1795 in Washington). As with James Lawrence, Allen and Delphy were buried with full British honors. The ship's doctor, James Inderwick, wrote the following in his book *Cruise of the U. S. Brig "Argus" in 1813*:

> The funeral took place on Saturday, August 21st. The procession left Mill Prison at noon. On the coffin was a velvet pall, over which was spread the American ensign, and on it were laid his hat and sword. As the coffin was being removed to the hearse, the guard saluted; when deposited, the procession moved forward, the band playing the "Dead March in Saul." Upon arrival near the church, the guard halted and clubbed arms, single files inward, through which the procession passed to the church, into which the corpse was carried and deposited in the centre aisle. The funeral service was read by the vicar, after which the recessional took place, passing through the guard as upon entrance, and the body was interred in the south yard of St. Andrew's on the right of his midshipman, Richard Delphy, who had had both legs shot off at the knees, and whose interment had taken place only the preceding evening.[6]

St. Andrew's Church had existed on what would become Plymouth's Royal Parade since the eleventh century. But, at some point in time after 1813, its south yard would disappear beneath the surrounding streets of the growing city.

On October 5, 1813, Benjamin Waterhouse arrived in Portsmouth Harbour on his way to continuing imprisonment in England. At the time, there were 1700 Americans held in the prisons and hulks of Plymouth, Portsmouth and Chatham. They were described as living in filth and rags. By mid–1814, Britain held an estimated 75,000 military prisoners of all nationalities under conditions not much changed since the Revolutionary War. Death was inevitable, and if Portchester Castle in Portsmouth was an example, there seemed to be no place or plan for systematic burial of the deceased. Anecdotal history describes bodies lightly buried in nearby mud flats and the use of a coffin with a sliding bottom to remove the deceased with some dignity but a larger measure of practicality. Stray bones would surface in the tidal waters for years afterwards.[7]

Upon arrival in Portsmouth, Waterhouse's ship was placed in quarantine, fumigated, and whitewashed, the last task performed by its passengers because, as Waterhouse noted in his journal, "it was always customary in America, as we left a house, or a room we hired, to leave it clean, and it was ever deemed disreputable to leave an apartment dirty." Their ship declared free of contagion, the prisoners were moved to another ship with lack of space and breathable air, the full aroma of diarrhea, and only stone ballast on which to rest. "God of mercy cried I [Waterhouse], in my agony of distress, is this a sample of the English humanity we have heard and read so much of from our school boy years to manhood? If they are a merciful nation, they belong to that class of nations 'whose tender mercies are cruelty.'"[8]

Eventually, Waterhouse and his fellows were moved to the hulk *Crown Prince* on the River Medway at Chatham. He found his time there to be not unpleasant in the larger scheme of things. He saw the river as a willow-lined respite in a beautiful countryside, and the treatment he received was the best in all of his travels. That changed for the worse when the prisoners were moved to the hulk *Chatham*, which held a less savory and less healthy population of Danes and Americans. Eighty-four of the Americans were said to have died of typhus and buried in the river marshes, probably joining those who may have died in a smallpox epidemic on the *Crown Prince* in the summer of 1813.

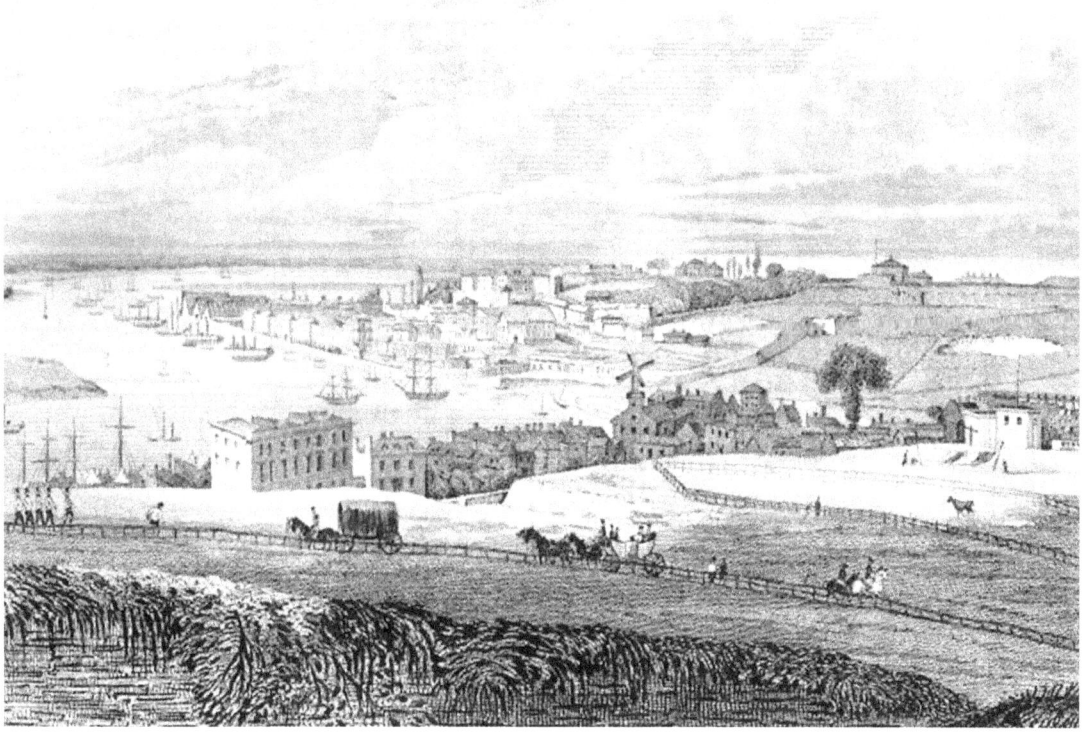

The Medway River at Chatham, England, ca. 1820. (*Engraving of "Chatham Dockyard from Fort Pitt" from Ireland's* History of Kent, *fol. 4, 1831, facing p. 349. Drawn by G. Sheppard, engraved by R. Roffe.*)

With all of their travails, one word inflicted mortal fear in the minds of all prisoners of the British in England: Dartmoor. As the War of 1812 wore on, an increasing number of prisoners were moved to the large, dark prison a day's forced march uphill and inland from Plymouth, near Princetown. Benjamin Waterhouse took the journey to the ugly prison in a desolate place. Of its setting he wrote, "This highland receives the sea mists and fogs, and they settle on our skins with a deadly dampness. This moor affords nothing for subsistence or pleasure. Rabbits cannot live on it. Birds fly from it, and it is inhabited, according to the belief of the most vulgar, by ghosts and demons; to which will doubtless be added, the troubled ghosts of American prisoners."[9]

The interior of the prison was no better, dark and cold, overcrowded with men and sickness. Death was almost a daily occurrence, in some years more so than in others. The first American to die at Dartmoor was Horace Bisley of Rockhill, Connecticut. Less than eighteen years of age, he had probably contracted pneumonia in the prison hulks at Plymouth, then been marched, like others, with scant clothing and shoes through the snows up to Dartmoor, 1500 feet above sea level. Bisley, prisoner no. 202 of the 250 Americans first brought to Dartmoor, died April 11, 1813. He would most likely have been covered with his shirt for a shroud, carried to a small building near the prison's gasworks, and, when a certain number of fellow deceased had been accumulated, buried in a common, shallow grave without ceremony.[10]

The number of those so buried was increased by the Dartmoor Massacre of April 6, 1815. By that time, the inhabitants of Dartmoor were no longer prisoners of a war that had been

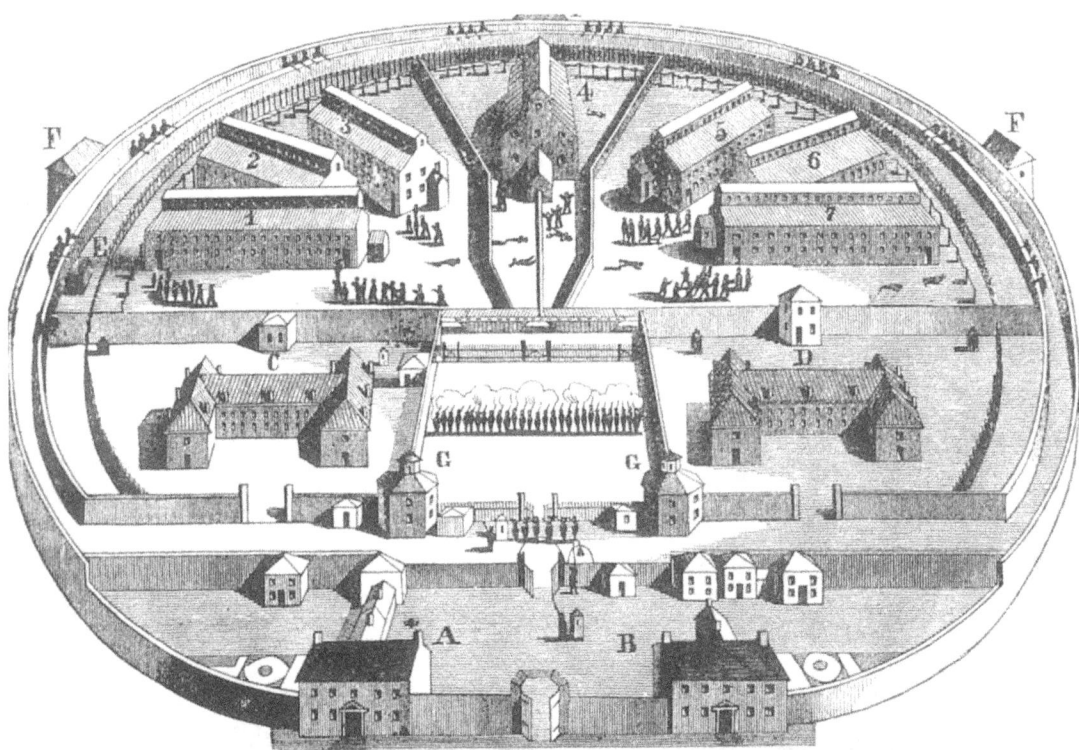

This drawing of Dartmoor Prison depicts the Dartmoor Massacre of April 6, 1815. The guards can be seen firing their guns at the center; the five dead Americans are lying in front of cell block 4. The cemetery was located behind the same cell block and outside the perimeter wall. Benson John Lossing, *Pictorial Field-Book of the War of 1812* **(New York, Harper and Brothers, 1868), 1068.**

ended by treaty on February 16 of that year. It would take months and years for all combatants to sort things out and return to peaceful lives. While awaiting repatriation, the Americans at Dartmoor tried to sketch out a more pleasant life, though they were still under guard. History offers countless accounts and interpretations of what happened on the rare pleasant April day. A contemporary account is given by one of those perhaps most angry about the event almost 200 years later, Ron Joy, a retired guard of the prison that still operated in the 21st century and its unofficial historian:

> Some Americans were playing football in our marketplace inside the prison compound, and they kicked the ball over the wall. One of them was a sixteen-year-old boy, and they asked for the ball back. So the sentries brought it back and they kicked it over again, and the sentries said they wouldn't bring it back. So they said if you don't kick it back we'll come and get it. The armory was there, all the rifles in racks. They knocked a hole through the wall, the Americans, but they weren't out to get the rifles, they went to get the ball. But they were heading toward a row of rifles, so the army was called in and told them to get back, but they refused to go. So they fired some shots over their heads to warn them to get back. Somebody said "false alarm, they're blanks," and they refused to go back. Then they said go back or we'll fire a volley right into you. They refused to go and they fired a volley straight in. There were sixty wounded, and seven killed.

Asked why he thought the Americans were so obstinate, Ron Joy replied with a smile and with great respect: "Well they always were, weren't they." He supported the quip with the information that when the French were force-marched to Dartmoor it required few British troops to keep them in line, but Americans required one soldier for each prisoner.

The War of 1812 concluded as ambiguously as it had begun. It seemed, in retrospect, to have been fought for no clear stated reason. The Orders in Council had been canceled two days before its start, the practice of impressment had long since ceased, and any dreams of American expansion into Canada had not been realized. The person known as Benjamin Waterhouse arrived back in New York on June 7, 1815. "Tears gushed from my eyes," he wrote, "and had I not been ashamed, I should have kneeled down and kissed the earth of the UNITED STATES."[11] The real Benjamin Waterhouse had retired from the practice of medicine in 1812, become medical supervisor of the nation's military posts in New England, and died in Cambridge, Massachusetts, in 1846.

An unknown number — probably in the thousands — of American parolees and freed men at war's end stayed in England, presumably to die and be buried in cities and towns across the land. The records — if not the gravestones — of two of them managed to survive into the 21st century: Benjamin Elwell and Abraham Burnham, both parolees who died in March 1815 and were buried in Ashburton Parish.

The war was forgotten, as were those who had died and been left behind. But in the fullness of history, it could be seen by many as among the most important of wars. It closed the breach between the U.S. and Great Britain so that they could go on to become the strongest of friends and allies. It set enduring boundaries between the United States and Canada, giving Canada a first step in gaining its own independence from the British starting in 1867. And it would turn out that many of those buried and forgotten in its wake would eventually be remembered, some in remarkable ways.

Chapter Three

Safe Havens and Hasty Cemeteries

With sorrow we leave you alone / And sigh our farewell o'er the billow
—From the gravestone of Adam Gillis

In the mid-nineteenth century, the America that had wrenched itself from British domination in two wars was now a confident player in the world, mostly through its naval forces. The continuing problems with the Barbary pirates had been conclusively settled by Stephen Decatur in an example of gunboat diplomacy against the dey of Algiers and a treaty between the two antagonists in 1815. The end of the War of 1812 in that year led to the Convention to Regulate the Commerce between the Territories of the United States and of His Britannick Majesty, though enmity on the water between the two naval forces would continue. The Monroe Doctrine of 1823 had asserted the rights of the Americas against European colonization.

In 1826, the United States was party to an international agreement with Algiers that a protective wall would be constructed around the European Cemetery in that city, "where the bodies of Europeans are exposed to insults by the public and to damage by the sea." Disrespect was a problem for Christian graves in Muslim countries. It would figure in the ongoing story of the graves of Richard Somers and his shipmates of the USS *Intrepid* in Tripoli.

In the 1820s and 1830s, various treaties were concluded with Brazil, Chile, Austria-Hungary, Venezuela and Morocco, and a 1797 treaty with Tunis was improved for American interests. A representative of American international history of these years would be found in the travels of the 74-gun ship-of-the-line USS *Delaware*. Though launched from the Gosport Shipyard at Portsmouth, Virginia, in 1820, there was no need for her use until 1828, when she set out for the Mediterranean in service of American commerce and diplomacy. In the 1830s, she was decommissioned twice for lack of a mission in a relatively placid world. In 1841, she was recommissioned to represent American interests during a war between Brazil and Argentina. In 1843 and 1844 she cruised the Mediterranean.

The U.S. naval base of operations in the Mediterranean for a time had been Gibraltar, shared with the British. But lingering feelings from the War of 1812 led to an unmanageable outbreak of duels over the smallest of slights, and in 1820, American operations were moved to Port Mahon on the island of Menorca, off the Mediterranean coast of central Spain, a place of good food and cultural entertainment. With that relocation, the navy's Mediterranean Squadron became a duty station of choice described by one sailor as "a perpetual yachting party."[1] A popular navy song of the time included these lines:

> I lost my hat at Cape de Gat
> And where do you think I found it?
> Behind a stone at Port Mahon,
> With three pretty girls around it.[2]

Its delights aside, Port Mahon also became the de facto training base for the U.S. Navy before it was moved officially to Annapolis, Maryland, in 1845. Some saw the port as the "cradle of America's modern, professional navy." As a naval base during peacetime, Port Mahon did not have to deal much with death. But it had a cemetery, surrounded by a wall and set right at the edge of the sea, which dated back at least to the British occupation of the island from 1798 to 1802. It was known as the English Cemetery, perhaps not so much for the nationality of those buried there as for a tacit diplomacy regarding cemeteries that allowed Protestant foreigners to be buried in Catholic countries without being labeled heretics.[3] When the USS *Delaware* arrived from Rio de Janeiro for her last visit in April 1843, the base had a doctor, G.R.B. Horner, one of the fathers of U.S. naval medicine. When *Delaware* sailor Robert Alberger slipped from the spars stowed on deck and into the main hold eighty feet below, striking a cross beam on the way down, he fell into Horner's care.

Dr. Horner's classic book, *Seamen: With Remarks on Their Enlistment, Naval Hygiene and the Duties of Medical Officers*, published in 1854, narrated Alberger's demise in painful detail (he was a large man, strong and active):

> Stout as he was, the spine was so completely fractured that a curvature of three or four inches backwards was produced, and immediate paralysis, with loss of sensation and motion, occurred in the lower extremities. The bladder lost the power of contraction, the bowels became torpid, perfect prostration of strength followed, and yet his mind was not impaired. By the use of internal and external stimulants already mentioned, reaction was induced in eight hours. Cups, blisters, issues, pills of calomel and colocynth, blue mass, magnesia and rhubarb, were subsequently employed as indicated. In a few days his urine, from being bloody, became mucous, next purulent and foetid; he suffered much pain in the loins and abdomen, took the extract of stramonium, acetate of opium and infusion of buchu leaves, had a cataplasm and cups put over the abdomen, and when his strength permanently failed, was given a bitter infusion. No remedies were of durable utility; he became weaker and weaker, gradually wasted away.[4]

Alberger was buried in the cemetery at Port Mahon along with at least twenty-two of his fellow Americans who had arrived there over the years. They ranged from David Horton of the USS *North Carolina* in 1825 to Mary Griffith Hunter, the wife of a sailor, in 1875. In one respect, Horner's account of Alberger's death was the most that could be known about those Americans buried at Port Mahon, though the ages and hometowns of some of the others were inscribed on their tombstones, along with melancholy remarks. Adam Gillis of the USS *Delaware*, died October 21, 1843:

> Far away from your friends and dear home
> You sleep on a cold earthen pillow
> With sorrow we leave you alone
> And sigh our farewell o'er the billow

James Smith of the USS *Brandywine*, died February 4, 1826:

> He who lays here, was much loved,
> By all his shipmates round;
> But he's no more, 'twas an accident,
> The unfortunate man was drowned
> Alas he's gone, the debt is paid,
> He owed for a short time:
> Mourn not for him, he's better off,
> He sails with more divine.[5]

With the move of naval training to Annapolis in 1845, Port Mahon gradually lost importance to the U.S. Navy, although it was regularly used by other nations as a port of call, as reflected in the nationalities of those who ended up in the English Cemetery. The last recorded burial was that of Lt. Karl von Bunsen in 1890. He was from a prominent family, a member of which invented the Bunsen burner. The lieutenant's grave was visited in 1904 by Kaiser Wilhelm II of Germany, who directed the construction of an elaborate black marble tomb wrapped in wrought iron for it, by far the most ostentatious in the cemetery.

In the larger frame of history, the full arc of American attention to the island of Menorca would follow the lifetime of the navy's first named admiral, David Farragut, the preeminent naval hero of the U.S. Civil War, with origins in the Menorcan city of Ciudedala, where his father was born in 1775. Jorge Ferragut Mezquida traveled to the Spanish colony of Florida in his late teens. Inspired by family stories of the British occupation of Menorca, he joined the Revolutionary War, in which he served as a naval lieutenant, then as a major in the cavalry. James Farragut, the true name of David Farragut, was born in 1801. When his mother died and Jorge fell into ill health, James was taken under the wing of navy commander David Porter. Porter introduced James to friends mistakenly as David and the name stuck.

The burial of Adam Gillis of the USS *Delaware* in the cemetery at Menorca on October 21, 1843, artist unknown (*James Maps Collection*).

The young David embarked on a naval career at age 10. It took him to Menorca a number of times, though his career was generally undistinguished. But living in Norfolk, Virginia, at the outbreak of the Civil War, he could not accept Virginia's secession from the Union, moved north, and was given the assignment of commanding the forces that would blockade southern ports. In that command, he took New Orleans from the Confederates in 1862, a turning point in the war. That was followed by the Battle of Mobile Bay, during which he exclaimed, "Damn the torpedoes, full speed ahead [or a variation of those words]!" and captured the last major port held by the Confederacy on the Gulf of Mexico.

Farragut was the first American to attain the rank of admiral, and among the many honors that would follow was a return trip to Spain, where he was received by Queen Isabella in Madrid, and to Port Mahon, where he returned to his father's birthplace the day after Christmas 1867. Celebrations were held across the island, but Farragut's subsequent departure in the first week of 1868 marked the final glory for Menorca's relationship with the U.S. Navy.

David Farragut never returned, nor did the ships of his navy in any meaningful way. The English Cemetery came increasingly to sit alone and untended at the edge of the sea. In 1970, the historian Capt. Edgar K. Thompson, USN (Retired), would conclude a description of the old cemetery at Port Mahon with a lament often stated over the centuries and in various ways: "Many times the writer has seen English naval work parties engaged in cleaning and repairing headstones in various ports in Central and South America. The United States Navy has no similar provision in its Regulations and it is no wonder our older naval graves reflect the lack of interest of those in Washington."[6] The observation, and its related questions, especially as they applied to Port Mahon and those buried in Tripoli, would come up again in following years.

At the time that the United States pulled out of Port Mahon, the nation's place in the larger world was pretty much settled and easily defended. Yet to come was conflict over the place of the United States within its own continent, and within its own self-concept. By 1846, the border between the United States and Canada was almost fully in place, settled in part by the War of 1812, though a few squabbles were yet to be settled with Great Britain. And the nation beneath the border was on the move. The technology of steam power was revolutionizing transportation (and would bring change to the way the country would deal with its fallen abroad). Railroads and population were expanding dramatically. Some cities had doubled in size. "Manifest Destiny" was the operating principle of the day: that the future was limitless, to be found not just in the cities, but in the new frontiers of the West and the ports that would expand trade into the Pacific. Though unnamed yet as such, Manifest Destiny had also been part of the psychology of the War of 1812 as it applied to thoughts of expansion into Canada. And it was sometimes as much about spreading the American ideal as it was about acquiring land. Like many such ambitions, however well or ill intended, it would lead to death in war, and, in this case, to the beginning of a new era in practices that dealt with the bodies of those lost.

The last matter that needed to be settled in this era of growth, it seemed, was the southern border with Mexico, a nation that seemed always to be on the brink of manifest implosion. Its war of independence from Spain in 1821 had obtained its goal, but destroyed its economy and left it with conflicting notions of how to proceed. Those conflicts played out in a failed monarchy for a few years, then factional struggles of a constitutional republic for many more.

The first popular use of the term Manifest Destiny came in the writing of newspaper columnist John L. O'Sullivan in 1845 concerning the republic of Texas, which sat between two nations heading in opposite directions. It was, O'Sullivan wrote, "our manifest destiny to overspread the continent allotted by Providence for the free development of our yearly multiplying millions."[7] Texas had been part of Mexico since the revolution of 1821. But, away from the population centers of Mexico, it was sparsely populated until Americans were allowed to settle by the Mexican government. Those settlers, in turn, undertook their own revolution in 1835 and were rewarded with their own republic, which was then annexed by the United States ten years later. It was the right thing to do, according to John L. O'Sullivan and those higher up the chain, including Congress and Pres. James Polk. Right or not, it resulted in the Mexican-American War of 1846–1848.

This was not a war that anybody really wanted to have. Both Britain and France attempted to mediate the dispute without success. Various financial approaches that would compensate Mexico and enhance a secondary American goal of obtaining California and access to the Pacific Ocean were rebuffed. Political turmoil in Mexico through 1846 wasn't helpful. The first skirmishes of the conflict took place in April and May of that year. The U.S. Congress declared war on May 13, and the Mexican congress returned the challenge on July 7. It was ended with the signing of the Treaty of Guadeloupe Hidalgo on February 2, 1848, which gave the U.S. control of Texas and the land that would become California, Nevada and Utah. Parts of Colorado, Arizona, New Mexico and Wyoming were added for good measure.

It was a good result for the United States, but at the very high cost of 13,283 American fatalities. Fought in parts of Mexico that were yet to become U.S. territory, and deep into the Mexican south, there were no plans for the dead except to bury them in place. Any extraordinary effort that was made was likely to be problematic.

The battle of the San Pasqual Valley, outside of San Diego, California, on December 6, 1846, left nineteen Americans dead. At the time, San Diego was in American hands, but too far away. Afraid that if the Americans were buried in place their bodies would be disinterred and stripped of clothing, their fellows tied them to mules and headed to San Diego for proper burial. Events intervened and the effort proved futile. In his 1849 book, *A Complete History of the Mexican War: Its Causes, Conduct, and Consequences,* author Nathan Brooks voiced a reverence for the dead of war that would be heard increasingly as the century progressed: "As night closed in, under a willow that grew beside the battlefield, were laid to rest, in all possible silence and secrecy, the departed brave. Thus to lay down for ever in the strange land, far away from kindred and from home, those whom a march together of two thousand miles, common hopes and hardships, common dangers, enjoyments and privations, had familiarized and endeared, was to the survivors of this little band of brothers no common grief."[8]

Deeper into Mexico there could be no hope of taking American bodies to safe havens. They were buried quickly in place to escape the accelerated decomposition of heat. If possible, they were buried near a battlefield hospital or in the proximity of a Mexican cemetery. As in past conflicts in foreign lands, American Protestants could not be buried in cemeteries of another religion. Those American dead who were returned home often went to the wealthiest of families, who could afford a cost that would not be borne by the government. The United States did not repatriate its war dead as a matter of policy.

In his official report to the secretary of war of March 6, 1847, American general Zachary Taylor concluded an account of the American victory at the Battle of Buena Vista with a bland description of a transaction with Mexican general Santa Anna. "A staff officer was dispatched to Gen. Santa Anna, to negotiate an exchange of prisoners, which was satisfactorily completed on the following day. Our own dead were collected and buried, and the Mexican wounded, of which a large number had been left upon the field, were removed to Saltillo, and rendered as comfortable as circumstances would permit."[9] The burial of approximately 500

The Mexican-American War was visualized by a series of Currier & Ives prints. "The Night After the Battle: Burying the Dead" was one of a number of prints with that title. The battle depicted was not specified (*Library of Congress*).

American dead from the Battle of Buena Vista took place in a hastily laid out two-acre site surrounded by a crude adobe wall. The cemetery was soon forgotten, at least until the end of the century, as the war moved to its conclusion.

That conclusion was hastened by the Battle of Molina del Rey, outside Mexico City on September 8, 1847. It cleared the way for the storming of Chapultepec Castle, also known as the Halls of Montezuma, on September 13, 1847. Chapultepec was the Mexican capital's last defense on its west side, and the castle sat atop a 200 foot hill. American forces attacked from all directions. Huge ladders that allowed the soldiers to come over the wall and eventually raise the American flag accompanied guns and mortar. American troops, under Gen. Winfield Scott, entered Mexico City a day later. The battle added a victory for the first line of what would become the Marine hymn. "From the Halls of Montezuma to the Shores of Tripoli" wrapped up the first American victories abroad in a single line, the shores of Tripoli being the site of decisive battles with the pirates of the Mediterranean. Its tune was taken from the French composer Jacques Offenbach.

The battles of Molina del Rey and Chapultepec resulted in 246 Americans killed and 47 missing. But the weeks of fighting around Mexico City had led to countless more American deaths, many of their bodies buried hastily and without records, as in the rest of Mexico. If ever they were looked for, they were never found. In the case of the Mexico city battles, however, an incremental step was taken in the development of American sensibilities about its fallen abroad. An act of Congress of September 28, 1850, authorized "the purchase of a cemetery near the city of Mexico, and the interment therein of the remains of the American officers and soldiers who fell in battle or otherwise died in or near the city of Mexico."[10] It would also be used as a burial place for those American citizens who would die in Mexico City in the years to come.

Two acres adjacent to the English Cemetery were purchased for $3,000. Site improvements at a cost of $1,734 were undertaken in July of 1852, and by the following year, some 750 Americans were officially buried. The number was an estimate based only on a collection of bones found at the surrounding battle sites four years after the war's conclusion. All were listed as unknown, although casualty lists for the two battles of Mexico City were available.

As the first dedicated American military cemetery abroad, and a model for what was to follow, it would always be a source of small controversy and skeptical observation, perhaps most caustic in an unsigned article in *The Nation* magazine of March 29, 1866. The author noted that on the other side of the obelisk which contained the engraving "To the memory of the American soldiers who perished in this valley in 1847," another engraving said, "The Remains of 750 Are Here Interred Under an Act of Congress," to which he asked, "750 what?"[11]

By his reporting, the author asserted that a Mr. C.C. Goss had been sent to Mexico to superintend the opening of the cemetery. "He soon began to dredge the chief battle-fields of our national glory, and had the mournful pleasure of amassing a formidable heap of bones. Many of these, however, were appended to be frames of mules and other beasts of burden who had perished on the fields—the more especially as Mr. Goss's accredited terms of contract with the teamsters who raked together and garnered the bones were 'so much a load.'" It was further speculated that the second engraving was craftily written to suggest, but not actually say, that the bones were human (and there was also some discussion about 750 Americans being buried underneath an act of Congress). But the author's larger concerns about the cemetery went more to what grew on top of it than what lay beneath.

The cemetery's keeper, a man named Schneider, was paid only six dollars for each grave he might dig. But since the initial burial of 750, there had only been 110 internments in two years, which the writer figured was not a living wage. Schneider was saved, he noted, by an agreement that allowed him to grow vegetables on any piece of land not nourished by the dead. It was very fertile land in hardscrabble Mexico City, and his crop of choice was cabbage. Cabbages grew in abundance and all about. They lined the cemetery's main procession road. And the locals, who never liked the cemetery of their victors and never would, referred to the place as the American Cabbageground. Worse, Schneider made and sold sauerkraut from his cabbages, perhaps the only sauerkraut to be found in all of Mexico. "At all events, it is the most celebrated, and everybody is loud in praise of Schneider's sauerkraut."

The Nation article went on in a similar vein for some hundreds more words, but concluded that the cemetery might more respectfully represent the United States if the federal government would invest more in its upkeep and Schneider's compensation.

In May 1872, Congress approved an annual salary for the cemetery keeper of $1,105. In January 1873, the American Cemetery in Mexico came under the protection and funding of the administration of all military cemeteries within the United States—an auspicious event.[12]

Chapter Four

In Foreign Lands at Home

It is indescribable! It was sickening, distressing and shocking to look upon!
—Lemuel Abbott

On the morning of April 21, 1865, the funeral train of assassinated Pres. Abraham Lincoln pulled out of Union Station in Washington to begin a twelve-day journey through seven states that would end in the president's birthplace of Springfield, Illinois. In many ways, the slow journey would be symbolic of the evolution in methods of disposition of the dead who had fallen over the course of the American Civil War.

Lincoln's death came at the time of the early stages of the modern era of the practice of embalming. The art and science of preserving human bodies for viewing and mourning stretched back to antiquity, but it was the unceasing and seemingly endless production of bodies in the Civil War — estimated at 620,000 to 700,000 — that brought the practice to the fore in America. The embalming of Lincoln was the first that most people had heard of the process. It was a curiosity that added to the outpouring of observers and mourners that greeted the funeral train along the way.

The beloved president was dead, yet he could be seen. "His face was calmed and peaceful," wrote train conductor William Gould. "He looked as if he was asleep in pleasant dreams."[1] As he lay in state in the capitol building in Harrisburg, Pennsylvania, an observer noted that "the whole face still indicating the energy and humor which characterized the living man."[2] At Independence Hall in Philadelphia an estimated 130,000 mourners filing past the open casket kicked up so much dust that Lincoln's face had to be cleaned by the attending embalmer before it was moved back to the train. When Lincoln was reburied in a more secure crypt in 1901, persistent rumors that the body had long ago been stolen led to an opening of the coffin. He was found to be totally recognizable, a reported lingering, melancholy smile on his face.[3]

Such was the power of embalming. And in Lincoln's case, as in others much less notable, such was the power of the developing railroads to move bodies about the nation with relative ease. These circumstances were echoed in the power of the sentiment that the dead should be returned to their homes. And the power of "home" was a driving force in outcomes for the dead of the Civil War. Many Americans would die in what might be called the foreign lands of their own country. Many who arrived from Europe and Asia in the waves of immigration would be recruited into the war as a point of citizenship, and die even further from home. Some of those still living after the war would move on from America in disillusionment or in search of new adventures. In all respects, the Civil War would develop philosophy and practices to be applied to the dead of foreign wars that were to come.

The creation of the American cemetery in Mexico City had been an important step in the civilization of war death, but the anonymous bones it held were still jumbled together as they were in previously established American cemeteries in England and Canada.

With the anger and violence of the Civil War, however, came a balancing notion of the value of the individual soldier. He was, after all, closer to a citizen fighting for a cause than a soldier or sailor fighting in the name of a nation. More poetically, perhaps, the war over slavery was at its core about the worth and value of the individual. Over the course of the war, though, those who advocated for the dead, and those who prepared to die, would have to fight for their good treatment every step of the way.

The first battles of the war brought about little change in procedure, or non-procedure. The dead were buried near where they fell, often by burial squads made up of prisoners of war and those on the low end of the battle scale. Graves were often haphazardly marked and recorded. Burial sites could quickly disappear with the passage of time and recording errors made under battle duress could not be overcome. Of the 1500 killed in the battles of Wilderness and Spotsylvania Courthouse, for example, just a fourth could be identified. And, though this was a battle close to home for its participants, newspaper ads placed by families of the region seeking information about their lost members went largely unanswered. The problem of identification was further compounded by the new technologies of this war that damaged, or made unrecognizable, bodies with more devastation than in previous wars. The sheer numbers of those killed made battlefields of the Civil War more desperate than most of those that had come before.

"Death is nothing here," wrote the American poet and chronicler of the Civil War, Walt Whitman, in his diary of December 26, 1862. "As you step out in the morning from your tent to wash your face you see before you on a stretcher a shapeless extended object, and over it is thrown a dark gray blanket. It is the corpse of some wounded or sick soldier of the regiment who died in the hospital tent during the night. Perhaps there is a row of three or four of these corpses lying covered over."

In 1864, Lemuel Abijah Abbott, an officer of the Tenth Regiment Vermont Volunteer Infantry, kept a diary of most of his twenty-second year. "The rattle and roar of musketry and artillery is dreadful," he wrote on May 12, 1864, "and may continue all night. I am about to lie down perhaps for my last sleep, but I'm too exhausted to have the thought keep me awake for seldom has sleep, sweet sleep, been more welcome."[4] Abbott saw a lot of death as he fought through Virginia under Ulysses S. Grant:

> This breastwork is filled with dead and wounded where they fell, several deep nearly to the top in front, extending for forty feet more or less back gradually sloping from front to rear, to one deep before the ground can be seen. The dead as a whole as they lie in their works are like an immense wedge with its head towards the works. Think of such a mass of dead! hundreds and hundreds piled top of each other! At the usual distance in rear of these breastworks — about ninety feet — are two more complete dead lines of battle about one hundred feet apart, the dead bodies lying where the men fell in line of battle shot dead in their tracks. The lines are perfectly defined by dead men so close they touch each other.[5]

The Civil War was not expected by either side to last very long, and plans to deal with battle deaths were well intended. Burials for the most part were to take place near field hospitals. Each Union hospital, for example, was required to have a morgue and to keep careful records. Burials were to be respectful, and, where hospitals stayed in place, gravesites were to be main-

FOUR. *In Foreign Lands at Home* 29

African American Union troops bury white Union troops in Fredericksburg, Virginia, on May 19 or 20, 1864. The military custom of white burials made by black soldiers would follow into World War II (*Library of Congress*).

tained. The Confederate army hired locals to build coffins and dig graves. But the sheer numbers of continuing deaths overwhelmed the systems.

The first Battle of Bull Run in July 1861 produced more than 800 Union and Confederate deaths. The retreating Union forces did not have time or inclination to bury their dead, and the job fell, as it did to most winners at war through the ages, to the victorious forces. But

Confederate soldiers are buried by Union soldiers following the Battle of Antietam on September 17, 1862 (*Library of Congress*).

their first responsibility was to their own dead. And so it went through much of the Civil War.

But in the Civil War, one was more likely to die of disease than to be slain. Lemuel Abbott narrated one of the causes of disease in his travels with Gen. Grant:

> Many of the bodies have turned black, the stench is terrible, and the sight shocking beyond description. I saw several wounded men in the breastworks buried under their dead, just move a hand a little as it stuck up through the interstices above the dead bodies that buried the live ones otherwise completely from sight. Imagine such a sight if one can! It is indescribable! It was sickening, distressing and shocking to look upon! ... Was there ever before such a shocking battlefield? Will the historian ever correctly record it? No pen can do it. The sight of such a horror only can fully portray it.[6]

Death led to disease, which led to death. The environment of the war was the environment of measles and smallpox, dysentery and diarrhea, contamination and sepsis, typhoid and malaria. In the medical history of mankind this was a time when medical practitioners were first showing up with force on the fields of war, and just barely so in the Civil War. The work of Florence Nightingale in Europe, for example, helped to bring a turning point in the mindset of war. In Turkey, her attention to hygiene, food quality, exercise and sewage problems during the Crimean War (1853–1856) led to the beginning of international standards and the establishment by others of the International Red Cross in 1864. But it was not in time to have much of an effect on the war in America. The hospitals could not keep up, and the graveyards, large and small, could not adequately meet the demand.

"Could anything in Hades be any worse?" asked Lemuel Abbot of his diary. And he articulated an uncertainly about death that would drive the actions of many of his fellows: "But I have never thought I should be killed in battle. It's delightful to have perfect faith— the faith of a child in such a way. It helps one to go into battle, although I dread being wounded, it shocks the system so. I never go into a fight or take a railroad journey, though, without feeling reconciled to yield up my spirit to Him who gave it if it is His will. This gives one calmness and reconciliation unspeakable. God be praised for giving me such peace. This is my prayer."[7] Every soldier planned to live, but worried that he might die. And with each soldier's observations of the chaos of death and burial and record keeping — in some cases his own growing indifference to the death all around — he wondered if his body would be properly returned to dust, his identity would be maintained, his whereabouts made known to his family. There were no requirements that record keeping, such as it was, extend to the notification of the families of the dead. It fell to the individual soldier to prepare himself for the possible anonymity of death in his own way.

In his memoir, *Campaigning with Grant*, Gen. Horace Porter, aide to Gen. Ulysses S. Grant, recounted preparations for the battles of Northern Virginia in May 1864:

> As I came near one of the regiments which was making preparations for the next morning's assault, I noticed that many of the soldiers had taken off their coats, and seemed to be engaged in sewing up rents in them. This exhibition of tailoring seemed rather peculiar at such a moment, but upon closer examination it was found that the men were calmly writing their names and home addresses on slips of paper, and pinning them on the backs of their coats, so that their dead bodies might be recognized upon the field, and their fate made known to their families at home.[8]

It was, for Gen. Porter, just a glimpse into another problem of identification he would undertake to solve at the turn of the next century.

The pre-identification of individual soldiers became more institutionalized with printed parchment tags passed out to the troops, personal information to be filled in. That evolved to individually and commercially made pieces of wood strung around the neck with rope, then to metal discs that contained more comprehensive information. *Harper's Weekly* began to advertise mail order "Soldiers' Pins" of various designs, metals and costs. Their use was expanded through the sales of itinerant merchants who traveled from battle to battle to sell their wares, especially as each battle loomed. But despite the individual and commercial effort, 42 percent of Civil War deaths remained unidentified. The army would not order mandatory use of metal identifying tags until 1906.

Death without identification, especially in the heroism and tragedy of war, was, in the American mind of the time, as bad as another feature of the war in a nation set apart within its own borders: death far from home and without the witness of loved ones. Last words were important to the continuity of family. They could be the utterances of truths that might otherwise never be known. Upon hearing them, the family could endorse the further good travels of the soul. And the power of family accounted for the many bodies found with pictures of children or wives still within their grasp. In preparation for possible death, the soldier kept them accessible for a last expending of energy. Or his fellows, still living, made sure that they were with the body of his lifeless person. If the body could be identified, the best that could be done was to send it home to family. The disparity between the ability of officers and the rank and file to reach that destination began to ease up through the work of the same pack of traveling merchants that sold identifying tags. As the war progressed and science improved, professional embalmers set up their own tents near battle sites, and, like identification tags, their services were sometimes purchased in advance of a possible need by those who could afford them. One of the most notable of embalmers was Dr. Thomas Holmes of New York. A graduate of the medical school at Columbia University, his journey through the Civil War gave him the opportunity to develop his art and its chemical tool kit in a harsh, real world. He charged seven dollars for preparing an enlisted man's body for return home, embalming and coffin included, twelve dollars for the body of an officer. After an estimated 4,000 Civil War embalmings, Holmes went on to become a distinguished practitioner whose services were used in the upper reaches of society. Many of those who sold embalming services in the latter years of the war, however, were not so savory, and embalming remained mostly a curiosity, enhanced by the death of Pres. Lincoln, into the next century.

The footings of policy that would endure into the foreign wars of the following century were seemingly midwifed out of the chaos of the Civil War. They built upon each other and pushed new procedures in record keeping, science and transportation. After the First Battle of Bull Run, the Union issued orders requiring its commanders to bury their dead, keep records and submit reporting up the line — the first impulses toward the concept that would eventually be called "Graves Registration." The following year saw requirements that commanders anticipate the laying out of land for burials that might be required and include with each burial a headboard with as much identifying information as was known. Whether those orders were fully observed in the chaos of war was quite another matter. And there was little

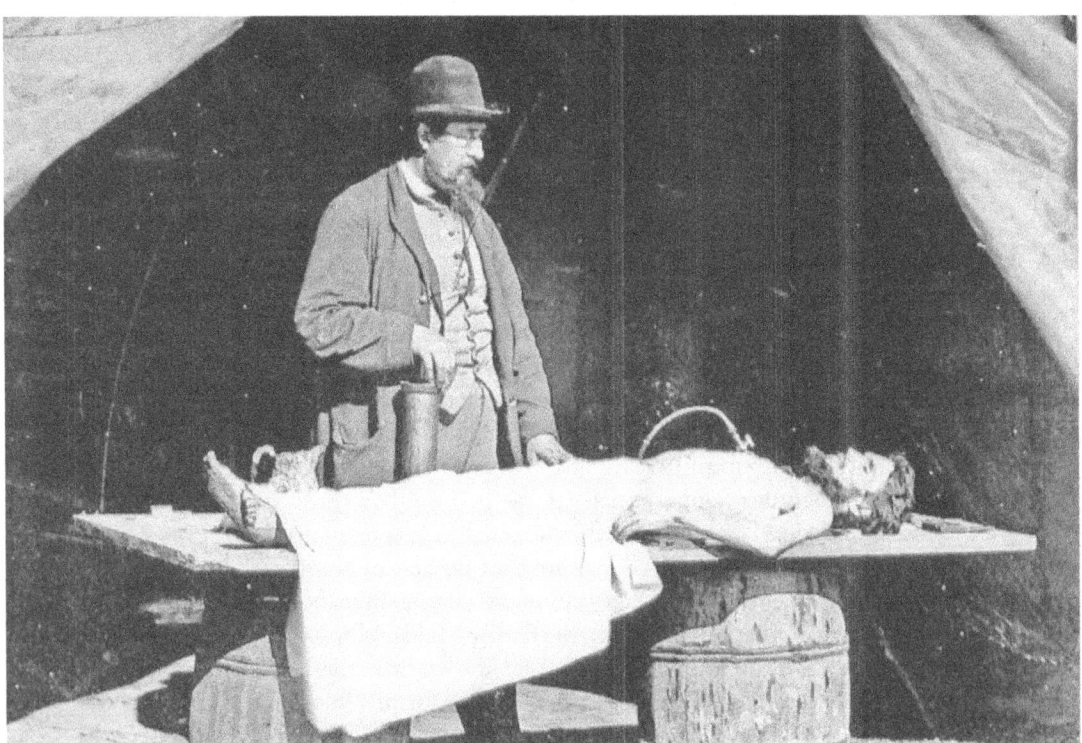

Believed to be Dr. Richard Burr of Philadelphia, appointed as embalming surgeon of the Union army in October 1862, embalming an unidentified corpse, time and location unknown (*Library of Congress*).

structure in place — burial teams, record keepers — to fulfill them. Confederate forces had even less to go on in terms of orders and resources.

Further, the two sides could not easily accomplish the kind of back channel negotiations required to give each other time and space to bury their dead. In addition, the social contract that encouraged the victors to attend to the bodies of the vanquished was weak at best. When it was grudgingly fulfilled it was often with an expediency that led to lost and torn bodies and common pits of the anonymous dead, sometimes accompanied by markers that were more disparaging than informative. As a further insult, bodies buried in shallow graves or in natural declivities in the land would often reappear in heavy rains.

It was not that the impulse to create properly designed cemeteries for military dead was lacking. A congressional act of July 17, 1862, had set in place the American determination to bury those who had died in service to their country in protected national cemeteries. But as with much legislation, good intentions had to be backed up with appropriations and continuing consensus among politicians. The demands of the Civil War worked against stabilizing the process, but the movement led to creation of national cemeteries. They were intended to bring together in hallowed grounds those previously buried in the environs of particular battles, as well as veterans who had died of natural causes long afterward. Structure was not fully in place to move a soldier buried underneath a tree, for example, to a designated cemetery during the war and often those cemeteries were filled only after the war's conclusion. The cemetery at Chattanooga, Tennessee, for example, was ordered created in November 1863, but the largest portion of its population was not in place until 1866, with inclusion of bodies buried along Union general William Sherman's march to Atlanta and bodies collected from other battle sites in Tennessee and Alabama. It was designated a full national cemetery in 1866, and by 1870 included almost 13,000 inhabitants, 4,189 of those unknown.

National cemeteries were most firmly established with the Act to Establish and to Protect National Cemeteries, approved February 22, 1867. It established standards of land use, design, individual graves, inspections and chains of command. It was required that all of those interred be buried equally, regardless of race or standing. By 1881, the cemeteries interred, according to quartermaster general Montgomery Meigs, "318,850. All soldiers' graves have been marked with marble or granite headstones as provided by law, and neat marble slabs will be erected at the graves of other than soldiers yet remaining to be permanently marked as fast as means will permit."[9]

Montgomery Meigs was one of those lesser known in American history without whom the nation might have been much different. The job of quartermaster general at the time of the Civil War was the marshalling and use of resources, and the development of logistics and strategy to support the military mission. Meigs was an engineer and graduated fifth in his class from the U.S. Military Academy at West Point. His imprint was placed on the bridges, aqueducts and buildings of Washington, including the capitol building and its dome, and the post office. He was appointed quartermaster general under Abraham Lincoln. He marshaled supplies and logistics that supported the major military campaigns of the war, and he brought forth the purchase of land from the family of Confederate general Robert E. Lee that would become Arlington National Cemetery (where Meigs himself is buried).

After the war and his own retirement, Meigs continued to work on the architecture of Washington, D.C., and played leadership roles in the development of the Smithsonian Institution, the American Philosophical Society and the National Academy of Sciences. His work in all cases was determined and professional, and it set the tone for the role of the quartermaster general in the disposition of the dead abroad in the wars that were to follow.

"The dead, the dead, the dead," wrote Walt Whitman of the Civil War, "our dead — or South, or North — ours all (all, all, all finally dear to me), or East or West, Atlantic Coast or Mississippi Valley — somewhere they crawled to die alone — in bushes, low gullies, or on the sides of hills. (There, in secluded spots, their skeletons, bleached bones, tufts of hair, buttons, fragments of clothing are occasionally found yet.)"[10] Whitman's view of the nation was always expansive and specifically geographic. In 1882, he published *Specimen Days and Collect*, a book of wandering through American history, landscape, spirit and future possibilities. Not remembering a lesson of the War of 1812, he exulted in an expansionist's dream.

> Long ere the second centennial arrives, there will be some forty, to fifty great States, among them Canada and Cuba. When the present century closes, our population will be sixty or seventy millions. The Pacific will be ours, and the Atlantic mainly ours. There will be daily electric communication with every part of the globe. What an age! What a land! Where, elsewhere, one so great? The individuality of one nation must then, as always, lead the world. Can there be any doubt who the leader ought to be?[11]

In that year, Canada was well into its history as a self-governing colony of the United Kingdom and, just as in 1812, it was not destined to become part of the United States. But Cuba was another matter entirely. It had struggled unsuccessfully to gain independence from Spain from 1868 to 1878, and freedom for Cuba had been a growing American cause since then. Walt Whitman saw that independence coming with benefits to the U.S., but it would not be until three years after his death in 1892 that the next steps were taken in the Cuban revolution against Spain, under Jose Marti.

American sympathy for Cuba turned to resolve when the USS *Maine*, sent to Cuba to show an American presence, blew up in Havana Harbor on February 15, 1898. The already anti–Spanish sentiment of the time was fueled by the certain belief that the cause of the explosion was a Spanish mine. On April 20, Pres. William McKinley signed a resolution demanding Spanish withdrawal from Cuba. On April 25, Spain declared war on America, to which Congress responded with a declaration that a state of war had already been in place since April 21.

The Spanish-American War lasted just four months, and it was fought intensely from Asia to the Caribbean. At its conclusion, the U.S. had gained control over Cuba, Puerto Rico, the Philippines and Guam. The judgment of history about the war, however, was never resolved. Was it a true fight against Spanish imperialism or the creation of American commercial interests? Did a mine blow up the *Maine*, or was it more innocently an explosion in the ship's coal bunkers? Or, more conspiratorially, did U.S. forces blow it up as an excuse for war? Whatever its cause, 2,446 Americans were killed in the conflict. Another 4,196 were casualties of the following Philippine War by which the U.S. attempted to take control over the Asian islands it had won from Spain. It was the lessons learned in the Civil War that led to the first instances of systematic return of American war dead from distant lands to familiar shores. And in the view of quartermaster general Marshall Ludington, speaking of the return of the remains of 1,122 dead from the West Indies in 1899, it was another example of American leadership in the world. "It seems proper to remark here," he said, "that this is probably the first attempt in history where a country at war with a foreign power has undertaken to disinter the remains of its soldiers who ... had given up their lives on a distant foreign shore, and bring them by a sea voyage to their native land for return to their wives and friends, or their reinterment in the beautiful cemeteries which have been provided by our government for its brave defenders."[12]

The Civil War had demanded the development of planning for the disposition of the dead, and effective record keeping to back it up. It had brought about the cycle of interment and disinterment that brought bodies from hastily dug graves to transitional burials to national cemeteries. It had used the fast growing technology of transportation to bring the dead home on steam-powered trains. All these developments were applied to the Spanish American War, and railroads were supplemented by refrigerated steamships.

New procedures were particularly put in place in the Cuban theatre under orders of Pres. McKinley. The lag time between death and final burial in the Civil War had led to an untenable number of unknown bodies, in his view. The Quartermaster Burial Corps was created, with the inclusion of civilian morticians whose job was to move bodies home as quickly as possible. The work moved on to Puerto Rico, then to the Philippines where the establishment of the United States Army Morgue and Office of Identification at Manila gave foundation to the Graves Registration Service that would bring proactive efficiency to the wars that would follow. Graves Registration and the Burial Corps worked simultaneously to expedite returns. In 1901, just 9 of 1,384 remains returned from Manila were left unidentified.

Returns were channeled to the Arlington or San Francisco national cemeteries, family burial plots, or national cemeteries close to home. Nearly all were accounted for and the bodies kept as safe as possible. Further, the developing national cemeteries would take the veterans of those wars as they died in old age. Some went to the already existing cemetery in Mexico City, or the Corozal Cemetery in Panama that was established in 1923. Other veterans of both the Civil War and Spanish American War would take themselves to far-flung parts of the world before their deaths, but they would not be forgotten in the fullness of time.

The twentieth century would open with a sensational example of a nation's new determination to bring home its dead. And the two world wars to follow would show how difficult it could be to fulfill that goal in its entirety.

Chapter Five

Paris and Parral

Slime, mud, and mephitic odors were encountered, and long red worms appeared in abundance.

—Horace Porter

One day in May 1864, Gen. Horace Porter, aide to Gen. Ulysses S. Grant, caught a moment's glimpse into one of death's small ambiguities. Union forces in the Civil War had just taken several hundred casualties in Northern Virginia.

"A staff-officer," he wrote, "passing over the ground after dark, saw in the vicinity of the Fredericksburg road a row of men stretched upon the ground, looking as if they had lain down in line of battle to sleep. He started to shake several of them, and cried out: 'Get up! What do you mean by going to sleep at such a time as this!' He was shocked to find that this row consisted entirely of dead bodies lying as they fell, shot down in ranks with their alinement perfectly preserved. The scene told with mute eloquence the story of their valor and the perfection of their discipline."[1]

On a day in April forty-two years later, Gen. Porter found himself at the U.S. Naval Academy in Annapolis, Maryland, with Pres. Teddy Roosevelt, military dignitaries of the United States and France, and crowds numbering in the thousands. He had arrived at the pinnacle of his personal achievement in life: the awakening of the dead to participate in the affairs of the living, the discovery and return to America of the body of John Paul Jones.

It was 1906. The United States was by now, or was about to become, the preeminent world power. Roosevelt, a naval historian and enthusiast, had the further development of the American navy on his agenda. Who better to symbolize American naval might than its first hero? And it was no longer the case that American military buried abroad were forever lost from the earth of their own nation. A year earlier, Roosevelt had spoken to "the National sense of gratitude for the service done by [Jones] toward the achievement of independence, and the sentiment of mingled distress and regret felt because the body of one of our greatest heroes lies forgotten and unmarked in foreign soil."[2] The search for John Paul Jones was given the authority of presidential sanction, and the work of Horace Porter was about to enter into previously uncharted precincts of the dead.

There had been something almost melancholy about Jones' death and burial in 1792 that had haunted the minds of a few patriots for decades to follow. In 1876, former Virginia congressman E.W. Hubbard wrote a summary of Jones' contribution to American history and its sad conclusion: "His subsequent career, when his services ignored by his country, he wandered first to Russia, then to France, eating bitter bread, broken-hearted, in his exile dying in poverty and want, is the record and shame of history."[3]

The first attempt to return John Paul Jones to his adopted country had taken place over six years starting in 1845. It was a confident plan undertaken by Civil War colonel John Sherburne, by now an author and Jones biographer, and presented to secretary of the navy William Graham. The author would simply travel to Paris, obtain the body, return with it on an American frigate and see to its interment in the Congressional Cemetery in Washington.

Graham responded with his agreement that "in no event must the remains of the Chevalier Jones repose anywhere save in this country. America, which is the legatee of his fame, should be the guardian of his ashes. I guarantee to you a most glorious reception, an honorable and public interment for them."[4] Similarly, American ambassador to France, Richard Rush, offered his gracious assistance, but with one caveat: "I have no knowledge of the place of his interment, of which, perhaps, you may know something."[5] And therein lay a problem that would not be solved for decades: the burial place of John Paul Jones had been lost. Sherburne thought he knew where it was; but it turned out that he did not, and the remains were not found. In any case, when John Paul's family in Scotland heard of the plan they protested: Best to leave him at rest.

Publicity about the failure of the plan evidently did not reach all interested parties. In a long article about John Paul Jones in the April 1870 edition of his magazine, *All The Year Round*, the writer Charles Dickens asserted that "in 1851 the remains of Paul Jones were removed from Paris, and sent to America in the United States frigate, *St. Lawrence*, to be interred in the Congress Cemetery at Washington."[6]

In a letter dated January 17, 1895, acting navy secretary William McAdoo responded to a historian's query on the matter. He recounted the 1845 plan to return the remains: "All efforts, however, to trace them have been unsuccessful as it was ascertained upon investigation that the cemetery where he had originally been buried had been sold and all the bones therein collected and placed in a pit, or carried to the Catacombs, as usual at the time. The purpose, therefore, of those interested in having the remains of the illustrious naval hero rest in this country had to be abandoned."[7]

By 1905, the St. Louis Cemetery for Protestants had fully receded into the history of a growing city. A tracing back through the years of development revealed it to lie deep beneath a block of one- and two-story buildings, business and residences, warehouses and gardens in the northeast part of the city. Also by 1905, Gen. Horace Porter had been U.S. ambassador to France for eight years, much of that time consumed with a passion to find John Paul Jones and return him home. His work was worthy of a sleuth. He methodically overturned rumors that Jones had not, indeed, been buried in St. Louis Cemetery, but in various other cemeteries throughout France and Scotland. The common names John, Paul and Jones left open a world of possibility. He searched city records and found none that would indicate the bodies of St. Louis had ever been moved elsewhere. He found untrue, as expected, a story that the lead coffins of Saint Louis had been dug up during the Revolution to be converted into bullets.

When Porter determined the validity of Saint Louis, he learned a supposed history of its land. Staged fights between animals had long since ceased, but it had moved on to become a burial place for other dead dogs and livestock of the city, the home of commercial laundries and their liquid waste, living quarters with cesspools, and for a time the final resting place of the neighborhood's night soil and rubbish. The plot of land sat on the Rue Grange aux Belles, the "Street of the Beautiful Barn."

Porter's excitement in France was matched in the United States. In November 1903, Congress took notice of the matter with a resolution directing the secretary of state to locate, disinter and return Jones to the United States, and appropriated $10,000 for the job. In their national meeting of April 1904 the Daughters of the American Revolution, after discussion of $25,000 raised for the Prison Ships Martyrs Monument in Brooklyn, appointed a committee and began to raise funds to support the repatriation of Jones.

The owners of the sad buildings, sheds and barren ground at the edge of Rue Grange aux Belles quickly determined that their properties were worth much more than previously thought. With utmost patience, Porter dropped the matter to let speculation subside, and restarted his work quietly two years later. "At the end of that time," wrote Porter, " negotiations were quietly opened upon the basis of purchasing the right to explore the abandoned cemetery by means of subterranean galleries, provided that all damages to houses should be repaired, any victims of disease caused by foul emanations from the disturbed soil indemnified, and the property afterward restored to its former condition."[8]

The city's chief quarrier was loaned to the effort, and he directed the building of timbered shafts into the deep soil. "The drainage was bad in places and there was trouble from the water," wrote Porter. "The walls of one of the buildings were considerably damaged. Slime, mud, and mephitic odors were encountered, and long red worms appeared in abundance."[9] The first shaft reached a depth of eighteen feet, and traveled past skeletons embedded in the soil, often in pairs, one atop the other. Their lack of coffins indicated the low station of many of the deceased. Four more shafts were burrowed into the soil, some with airshafts to the surface, and those traveled through fields of skeletons fallen akimbo into the mire. Porter's research led him to the conclusion that numbers of them might be Swiss military members killed in the Revolution.

Gangs of workers labored night and day. Iron rods were pushed between shafts to detect the lead coffins that could not be seen, one of which was believed to contain John Paul Jones. It wasn't until two weeks after the work had begun that the first lead coffin was found broken open, the body within dismembered at the neck. It proved not to be that of Jones. It was another month before a second lead coffin was found, and another week until a third revealed itself, but without a label to identify its occupant. It was opened after a ventilation shaft had been dug to take off the odor that would result. Porter described what was found:

> The body was covered with a winding-sheet and firmly packed with hay and straw. A rough measurement indicated the height of Paul Jones. Those engaged upon the work had been furnished some time before with copies of the admiral's Congressional medal showing his bust in profile. I had found in the Paris mint the die from which this medal was made and had had a number of copies struck from it. Half a dozen candles were placed near the head of the coffin, and the winding-sheet was removed from the head and chest, exposing the face. To our intense surprise the body was marvelously well preserved, all the flesh remaining intact, very slightly shrunken, and of a grayish brown or tan color. The surface of the body and the linen were moist. The face presented quite a natural appearance, except that the cartilaginous portion of the nose had been bent over toward the right side, pressed down, and disfigured by its too close proximity to the lid of the coffin. Upon placing a medal near the face, comparing the other features and recognizing the peculiar characteristics of the broad forehead, contour of brow, appearance of the hair, high cheek-bones, prominently arched eye orbits, and other points of resemblance, we instinctively exclaimed, "Paul Jones"; and all those who were gathered about the coffin removed their hats, feeling that they were standing in the presence of the illustrious dead, the object of the long search.[10]

As distinguished scientists and anthropologists performed an examination of the corpse, excavation of the cemetery continued with the discovery of two more lead coffins. Then everything was replaced, and the dirt, which had had to be stored as much as two miles away, was returned to refill the shafts and related caverns.

The final judgment of science, seemingly confirmed by a comparison to the head dimensions of a life-sized bust of the admiral by Jean-Antoine Houdon, was that this was, indeed, the body of John Paul Jones. Importantly, the autopsy itself was seen as a milestone in the history of forensics. After one hundred thirteen years preserved in alcohol, the body was supple and strong. It could be determined that Jones had died of "dropsy" (edema born of congestive heart failure), and that he had suffered other disorders that could have been specific to the places in which it was known that Jones had traveled. The admiral was known to have suffered no wounds, and the body had none. Identification confirmed, John Paul Jones was taken to the American Church of the Holy Trinity on April 20, 1905, where his coffin rested beneath a draped American flag to await its return to a grateful nation.

Doubts were immediately raised in the minds of some that the body found could actually be that of a man buried more than a century previously. In a letter to the editor of the *New York Times* on May 21, 1905, a writer identified only as M.K.S. insisted that "while expert anthropologists in Paris have given opinions which are interesting as coincidences, they may have felt the same enthusiasm and been as sanguine of the result of their examination as Ambassador Porter seems to have been about finding the body and Columbus was when he thought he had found India because the land he discovered looked like it!"[11] It was a low-grade controversy that would continue for a century.

On June 30, the cruiser USS *Brooklyn*, which had distinguished herself in the Spanish-American War and was now performing the first experiments in seagoing telegraphy, led a

The shaft within the St. Louis Protestant Cemetery where the body of John Paul Jones was found, taken at a time when the use of flash photography underground could be problematic. Gen. Horace Porter sits at the left, and a workman on the far right pinpoints the site of the coffin with his axe. *John Paul Jones commemoration at Annapolis, April 24, 1906 (Government Printing Office).*

small fleet of U.S. ships into the harbor at Cherbourg to formally retrieve Jones from France. Twenty-one-gun salutes were exchanged all around between the forces of the two nations. "The aspect of the harbor today," reported the *New York Times* on July 1, 1905, "was strikingly beautiful as the sun came out and the many me[r]chantmen, steam yachts and other pleasure craft in these waters strung out their full complement of colors, in which the American flag predominated."[12]

On July 6, all of ceremonial Paris was in full dress and the people were in the streets in the hundreds of thousands as military personnel, dignitaries and diplomats of America and France came together around the coffin at the American Church on l'Avenue de l'Alma in the afternoon. Its setting in a bower of flowers and flags had been a gift of the French. The body was formally given by Gen. Porter to the United States through an assistant secretary of state and passed on to the care of the U.S. Navy for transit home on the USS *Brooklyn*. "This day American claims her illustrious dead," he said of the event, "to testify that his name is not a dead memory, but a living reality, to quicken our sense of appreciation, and to give assurance that the transfer of his remains to the land upon whose arms he shed so much luster is not lacking in distinction by reason of the long delay."[13]

It would be almost a year before John Paul Jones would be formally put to rest in his adopted country. As his coffin sat in limbo, a war of words began among the cities and cemeteries of the nation over which was most deserving of his mortal presence. The State Department argued that he should be buried at Arlington, the navy that he should rest in the National Sailor's Cemetery in Annapolis. New York, Philadelphia and Fredericksburg, Virginia, made claims, the latter two because he had lived in those cities at one time. Some suggested that the decision should be left to Gen. Porter for obvious reasons. But in the end, it was Teddy Roosevelt who chose Annapolis, though not for burial in the common cemetery.

Roosevelt's instinct about the usefulness of the return of John Paul Jones to his desire for a stronger navy was voiced full force in a speech to ten thousand citizens and sailors of two countries at the naval academy on April 24, 1906. He presented the admiral as the exemplar of resolve and courage in the face of overwhelming odds. He bitterly lamented those times in American history when the country was not prepared to meet its enemies, particularly in the War of 1812. "This nation was guilty of such short-sightedness, of such folly, of such lack of preparation, that it was forced supinely to submit to the insult and was impotent to avenge it," he said, followed by a command that each military individual and organization be fully prepared for all outcomes. Courage was not enough, he warned: "Remember that no courage can atone for lack of that preparedness which makes the courage valuable."[14]

The Spanish-American war had given firm footing and method to the idea that American dead should be

The French sculptor Jean Francoise Houdon (1748–1821) was a friend and portraitist of Benjamin Franklin. He spent part of his training dissecting corpses in Rome, and his statuary was thought to be very true to life. This bust of John Paul Jones was made from a life mask in 1781 and was compared with the corpse thought to be that of Jones in 1905 (*U.S. Naval Academy*).

Pres. Teddy Roosevelt delivering the keynote address at the commemorative ceremony held in honor of John Paul Jones at the U.S. Naval Academy on April 24, 1906. Jones' flag-draped casket rests before the speaker's stand (*Naval History and Heritage Command*).

returned home. The dramatic return of John Paul Jones over distance and time set the example of how far a nation would go to complete that task. The wars that were to follow would see the prescription doggedly fulfilled, though with notable exceptions, the first of them in a mostly forgotten prelude to World War I.

In 1910, the Mexican Revolution was begun with the overthrow of dictator Porfirio Diaz by the liberal forces of Francisco Madero, who promised democracy, agrarian and labor reform. The struggle between opposing forces filled out the rest of the decade as Madero was assassinated in 1913 and succeeded by a dictator, Gen. Victoriano Huerta. Among the results was increased tension between Mexico and the United States and the rise of the murderer, cattle rustler and bank robber José Doroteo Arango Arámbula, otherwise known as Pancho Villa, a heroic figure in Mexican-American history. Reminiscent of Robin Hood, Pancho Villa and his men fought against oppression of the rural poor, then became revolutionaries with Francisco Madero. As commander of the División del Norte, Villa put together a strong army, parts of which included recruited Americans. Based in Chihuahua, he raised funds and guns by stealing cattle and trading with the American side of the border. His lifestyle became operatic and eventually entered the popular culture of both nations in movies, stories and song.

When the United States took up common cause with revolutionary forces that opposed him, Villa began to attack U.S. border towns. America became less enamored with him; but to the people of northern Mexico his heroism increased as he took on the big nation to the north. It was his raid on Columbus, New Mexico, and its Thirteenth Cavalry detachment on March 9, 1916, that caught the full attention of Pres. Woodrow Wilson. Eighteen Americans had been killed. Guns, merchandise and cattle were stolen and the town was badly burned.

Pres. Wilson demanded the capture of Pancho Villa, and on March 15 Gen. John Pershing led 7,000 men and reconnaisance airplanes into northern Mexico on what was called variously the Pancho Villa Expedition, the Mexican Expedition or, most commonly, the Punitive Expedition. It was carried out with the guarded support of the Mexican government of Venustiano Carranza, but regular clashes occurred between Americans and Mexican forces and civilians when it was perceived that the Americans were overstepping their license. The most notorious of those conflicts came in the town of Parral, 300 miles due south of El Paso, Texas, in the state of Chihuahua. The town was the base of Villa's operations, and the eventual place of his assassination in 1923. His tomb in the municipal cemetery may or may not actually have been the final resting place of his bones which, by some accounts, were removed to a national cemetery in Mexico City.

The true particulars of what occurred in the event known as the Parral Affair would never be fully determined. A synthesis of various American and Mexican accounts tells a basic story. At a time when an edgy Mexican government had demanded an immediate withdrawal of the Punitive Expedition, American forces were gathered outside of Parral. Townspeople believed that they were intended to be an occupation force. A number of American soldiers, reported as either 2 or 150, entered the town, ostensibly to purchase supplies, and were set upon by an angry mob of citizens or bandits. The altercation was advanced by a gunshot from an angry townsperson and escalated beyond control with the American use of a machine gun. The Americans were finally able to retreat with the help of Mexican forces, and the loss of life on both sides was reported as minimal to extensive.

The end of the expedition in January 1917 did not resolve matters between Mexico and the United States. At the same time, World War 1 was in its third year without official American involvement, though goods in support of the European Allies were coming out of American ports. German spies had infiltrated Mexico as a base for sabotage against American trade with

Europe, and to provoke diversionary hostilities between the U.S. and Mexico. Then, in January, a message from German foreign secretary Arthur Zimmerman to the German ambassador in Washington, Johan von Bernstorff, was intercepted and decoded by the British. It directed that if it appeared the U.S. would enter the European war, the German ambassador in Mexico was to make an offer of a military alliance between the two nations and offer German support in the reopening of old wounds:

> We intend to begin unrestricted submarine warfare on the first of February. We shall endeavour in spite of this to keep the United States neutral. In the event of this not succeeding, we make Mexico a proposal of alliance on the following basis: make war together, make peace together, generous financial support and an understanding on our part that Mexico is to reconquer the lost territory in Kansas, New Mexico and Arizona. The settlement in detail is left to you.
>
> You will inform the president [Carranza] of the above most secret as soon as the outbreak of war with the United States is certain and add the suggestion that he should, on his own initiative, invite Japan to immediate adherence and at the same time mediate between Japan and ourselves. Please call the president's attention to the fact that the unrestricted employment of our submarines now offers the prospect of compelling England to make peace within a few months. Acknowledge receipt.[15]

The telegram, known historically as the Zimmerman Telegram and intended to keep America from entrance into the European war, had the opposite result. Public uproar was one of the influences on the American declaration of war on Germany on April 6, 1917. And later in the month the German proposal was declined by Mexico as unrealistic and unworkable.

America would now enter the Great War in Europe. Nothing much had been accomplished by the Punitive Expedition, but valuable lessons had been learned about the use of aerial reconnaissance and motor transport. New prophylactic measures had been developed related to soldiers and the traveling brothels that accompanied the troops. Both Gen. Pershing and then Lt. George Patton found their careers advanced by the action, and 11,000 troops trained under Pershing in Mexico moved with him to France.

Following on the success of Graves Registration in the Spanish-American War, all American dead were returned home from Mexico — with a handful of exceptions that would engage the nation's interest ten years later.

Chapter Six

Americans in Any Uniform

But I've a rendezvous with Death / At midnight in some flaming town.
—Alan Seeger

The first American serviceman to be killed in World I was sailor John Eopolucci. He was part of a navy guard on the merchant steamship *Aztec* as it collided with a mine, or was torpedoed, off the coast of Brest, France, on April 1, 1917. He had attempted to help a lifeboat clear the sinking ship, but he fell into the sea. The second navy death was Osmand Ingram. As he watched a German torpedo coming toward his ship, the USS *Casin*, on October 16, 1917, he tried to release the ship's depth charges to lessen the explosion. But he was blown overboard by the torpedo. Lost at sea, 23 miles south of Mind Head, Ireland, he was posthumously awarded the Medal of Honor for an effort that, had it succeeded, would have lessened the loss of life of his fellow sailors.

The first three members of American armed forces killed on land were Pvt. Thomas Enright of Pittsburgh, Pennsylvania, Corp. James Bethel Gresham of Evansville, Indiana, and Pvt. Merle Hay of Glidden, Iowa. Enright and Gresham had moved from Mexico to France with Gen. Pershing, and Hay had joined them in the First Infantry Division, known as the *Big Red One*, from a clerk's job in a farm implement store. All three were described as quiet, unassuming young men who, caught in the trenches of the Western Front near Barthelemont, Lorraine, France, were nearly decapitated by German trench knives on November 3, 1917. They were buried where they fell in a ceremony with a French honor guard and a lengthy speech by a French general.

A monument in their honor was constructed in the spring of the following year, according to the *New York Times* of May 26, 1918, "in one of the little valleys of Meurthe-et-Moselle, at the foot of a slope on the summit of which rise the ruins of the town of Barthelemont. It is a rolling green country—where the war has not actually torn it to pieces—not actually mountainous, but full of little hills and sudden valleys, with beautiful meadows here and there on the hillsides."[1] The monument was the grateful contribution of French citizens, from the department's capital city of Nancy to the smallest village of the region. It was made of local granite and designed by Louis Majorelle, a leading decorator and designer of the time. It read:

> As worthy sons of their great and noble nation,
> They fought for Right, for Liberty, for Civilization,
> against German Imperialism, curse of the human race.
> They died on the Field of Honor.

Gen. Pershing would eventually visit the site and observe a moment of silence. Some years after the war, the bodies of Enright, Gresham and Hay would be returned to their families. The monument would be destroyed by the Germans in World War II. But the story would point to the power of a certain European reverence for American fighting men in the two world wars. It would accompany those soldiers to their graves in the large official cemeteries yet to be laid down upon the rolling green country, hillsides and sudden valleys, particularly of France, Belgium and the Netherlands. It would take some of them to the little known, isolated cemeteries of small towns and churchyards where they would rest alone without their countrymen. And it would energize the small rituals and ceremonies of European community life into the 21st century.

Gresham, Enright and Hay of the U.S. Army, and Eopolucci and Ingram of the U.S. Navy, were not actually the first Americans killed in the war. Many had preceded them, but would not be counted as American casualties. A few were extraordinary individuals whose remains would never be returned to American soil.

"Life is only beautiful if divided between war and love," Alan Seeger was quoted as saying by an Egyptian friend, Bif Bear, as they walked in the Thiescourt Woods of Oise, northern France. Seeger had just returned from a short leave amid the pleasures of the Latin Quarter of Paris. "They are the only two things truly great, fine and perfect, everything else is but petty and mean. I have known love for the last few weeks in all its beauty and now I want to make war ... but fine war, a war of bayonet charges, the desperate pursuit of an enemy in flight, the entry as conqueror, with trumpets sounding, into a town that we have delivered! Those are the delights of war! Where in civil life can be found any emotion so fine and strong as those?"[2]

It was July 1916. Seeger and Bear were members of the French Foreign Legion, drawn to France by the certainty of what must be done to fight German aggression in Europe. Alan Seeger was a young American writer and poet whose work would mature as he moved toward what he predicted as his inevitable death. After graduation from Harvard University in 1910 and two years spent in New York's Greenwich Village, he had moved to Paris, all the while writing poetry that the *New York Times* would posthumously describe as "visualizing both material beauty and human emotion and clothing them in sumptuous and opulent language."[3]

He was in Belgium when the German army crossed the Belgian frontier into France, and then he traveled by ship to Paris. The Foreign Legion had been created in 1831 to turn those who had led undisciplined and often criminal lives into fighters for France. Eventually, the Legion took on the yet-to-be-reformed rabble-rousers of other countries. By the time of the First World War it was a legendary force, including men of all nations with a sense of adventure, often in pursuit of lofty ideals — a description of Alan Seeger. He exchanged letters with his mother and kept a diary. And he descended from the sunlight into the dark trenches of war, describing the journey.

The beginning of his journey was in Toulouse: "The stir of leaves, noise of poultry in the yards nearby, distant church bells, warm southern sunlight flooding the wide cornfields and vineyards."[4] Marching through the villages of Marisain and Bergères he saw that "the first was completely destroyed, not a house on the main street escaped the fire. Nothing but blackened walls and here and there the inhabitants standing with sullen faces in their ruined doorways."[5]

Then there were the terrors and boredom of the battlefield: "Darkness would hardly begin before a fusillade would start from the lines nearby, the cry 'Aux armes, aux tranchées!' would run from door to door and we would hasten out into the night to wait in the muddy ditches while bullets whistled about. But these fusillades would always die out, provoked probably only by the German patrols seeking to discover our position. At first I felt a little uneasy, but in the end only bothered. In the daytime we slept, oblivious to the shells that burst around us."[6]

Alan Seeger wrote to his mother: "You are quite wrong about my not realising what I was going into when I enlisted. I had not been living for two years in Europe without coming to understand the situation very well, and I was under no illusion that the conflict which was to decide the fate of empires and remake the map of Europe would be a matter of a few months. I knew that it would be a fight to a finish."[7] He predicted his finish in one of the signal poems of World War I, "I Have a Rendezvous with Death" (excerpted):

> But I've a rendezvous with Death
> At midnight in some flaming town,
> When spring trips north again this year
> And I to my pledged word am true
> I shall not fail that rendezvous.

It was not long after their walk in the Thiescourt Woods that Seeger and Bear found themselves confronting the enemy near the village of Belloy-en-Santerre. It was the opening days of the Battle of the Somme, which was intended by Allied Forces to draw down German resources and divert their attention from the battle of Verdun, near Paris. "Suddenly a word of command," wrote Bear, "an order of deliverance, passes from mouth to mouth. 'Forward! With bayonets!'"— the command that Seeger had awaited so long. "In an irresistible, sublime dash we hurl ourselves to the assault, offering our bodies as a target. It was at this moment that Alan Seeger fell heavily wounded in the stomach. His comrades saw him fall and crawl into the shelter of a shell hole. Since that minute nobody saw him alive."[8]

The next day was July 4, 1916: "Seeger was found dead. His body was naked, his shirt and tunic being beside him and his rifle planted in the ground with the butt in the air. He had tied a handkerchief to the butt to attract the attention of the stretcher bearers. He was lying on his side with his legs bent. It was at night by the light of a pocket electric lamp that he was hastily recognized. Stretcher bearers took the body and buried it next day in the one big grave made for the regiment, where lie a hundred bodies. This tomb is situated at the hill 76 to the south of Belloy-en-Santerre."[9]

The Battle of the Somme would not end until November. With the line against the Germans advanced just seven miles at its furthest, more than 310,000 would be lost on both sides. In death, Alan Seeger would become a historic figure in American literature, and his descendants would expand the creative force of American folk music. But, a lover of France, his remains would finally come to rest no more than ten miles south of Belloy-en-Santerre.

Of those Americans who entered the war through the Foreign Legion, a number were drawn to the growing use of airplanes in battle. Some were able to move from the Legion to the Service Aéronautique as pilots and copilot observers. That led to the development of an American flying corps in France. The aerial help of the Americans was welcomed, to say nothing of the public relations benefits that would accrue as Americans watching from overseas could gain an identification with the European war through the heroic exploits of their own nationals. An "Escadrille Américaine" under French command was created in 1916, but the German enemy complained that Americans were not officially in the war and should not be named as combatants. The complaint was acceded to and the name of the group was changed to the Lafayette Escadrille, in honor of the Marquis de Lafayette, a French hero of the American

Revolution. Escadrille pilots became precision acrobats of the sky, in daily engagements with the best of the German Imperial Air Service, including Manfred Albrecht Freiherr von Richthofen, known as the Red Baron. As the Escadrille evolved into the larger Lafayette Flying Corps, almost 200 Americans saw combat under French leadership.

Among those eventually drawn into the French air service was Charles Wesley Chapman of Waterloo, Iowa. The Chapman men were of Scotch-Irish ancestry, stocky and resolute, though of a gentle nature. Charles Wesley's grandfather had come to Dubuque in 1856, at a time when the city was becoming an important commercial outpost on the western edge of the country's expansion. He worked in hotels and railroads, and Charles Wesley's father entered the thriving lumber business of the region. It was as a student at Amherst College that Chapman made the decision to enter the faraway conflict with an initial ambition of joining the ambulance program of the American Field Service (AFS), just at the time that America was entering the war. In letters and telegrams exchanged with his parents in April, 1917 he assured them that the ambulance service would be safe, got their help in assembling documents, asked if they might be able to take care of his dog, Chap, thanked them for the occasional check for spending money, and explained that he would be working in a local Ford factory for a few weeks "and try to pick up some knowledge of the Ford."

The force behind the AFS at the time derived from members of the academic community of Boston who determined that the work to be done could no longer rely on the donated cars used in Europe up to that point. They would be replaced by converted Model T Fords. The vehicles were sent in wooden boxes from Detroit, and the wood was then used to build ambulance bodies to be attached to each chassis. Charles Chapman set off for Europe with a gained expertise in Fords and an expectation of saving lives; but, learning that he would only become a common truck driver, he enlisted in the Lafayette Flying Corps. His older brother would later attempt to join the U.S. Army Air Corps after official American entrance into the war, but he could not meet visual requirements. A later descendent would serve as a pilot in World War II and the Korean War.

Chapman enlisted in the French air service in June 1917 and received training through February 1918. As the United States entered the war, the Lafayette Flying Corps evolved into the 94th Aero Squadron of the U.S. Army Air Service, an establishing unit of the eventual U.S. Air Force. Its pilots were seen as hybrids of the French-American flying liason, and Chapman became second lieutenant, Escadrille Américaine no. 94, still named Américaine rather than Lafayette by some accounts.

If it seemed unlikely that a lumber clerk from Iowa would volunteer to risk his life in the skies over Europe, Chapman's first months of training only compounded the curiosity. In his first acrobatics instruction at Pau, France, he was able to accomplish his spins and somersaults with grace on the first attempt; but upon landing, his gait was staggering and his face pale. That evening, he revealed to his friends that he had been made to feel deathly ill by the experience. The sky had swum about him and he had come close to fainting in the confusion. Given the suggestion that he limit himself to two-seater flying that was not acrobatic, he persisted against continuing faintness until the problem had been licked.

On patrol over Autrepierre on May 3, 1918, he attacked a group of four enemy monoplanes and one biplane. He was able to shoot one of them from the sky, but it would be in exchange for his own life, which was extinguished in a fiery plane falling rapidly to the Earth. Charles Wesley Chapman, in the words of a fellow flyer, "died as he had lived, cleanly and gamely fighting till he was shot down within the enemy lines."[10] Posthumously, he was given both the American Distinguished Service Cross, and the French-Belgian Croix de Guerre. His remains would never be returned home from that limbo between three nations, though they would not be lost and forgotten.

As Pres. Woodrow Wilson, Gen. John Pershing and American forces searched for Pancho Villa in 1916 Mexico, World War I was two years old and very much a part of the national life of Canada to the north. Great Britain was threatened by Germany, and in August 1914, Canada declared that it had 40,000 volunteer troops ready to cross the Atlantic if needed. The full course of the war involved 619,000 Canadian forces serving in Canadian and British battalions, 22,000 of those in the Britsh Royal Air Force.[11] The Canadians would distinguish themselves in the war, particularly in the Battle of Vimy Ridge in April 1917. Vimy Ridge had been a German stronghold in Nord-Pas-de-Calais, France, since 1914. Its geography above the surrounding area made it strategically important, and attempts to regain it from the enemy had been unsuccessful. The task was then given to 26,000 Canadian forces, who succeeded on the strength of meticulous planning, preparation and courage in a wartime event that would become a marker in Canadian history. By war's end, Canada was seen less as a lingering colony of Great Britain and more — finally, in the minds of many Canadians — as a strong and sovereign nation.

Sixty thousand Canadians were killed in the war, but a portion of those killed as Canadian were actually American in origin, as were some of those identified as British in the final accounting of the war and the listings of its dead. On May 28, 1916, the *New York Times* reported at length on a historic event in Toronto, Ontario: "A Unitarian clergyman and citizen of the United States in the uniform of a British lieutenant colonel, addressing a meeting of Canadians and Americans in a Methodist church in Toronto and urging them to enlist in the war in Europe — such was the blending of nationalities and beliefs in one great purpose that seemed to focus more definitely than anything else the story of the American Legion in Canada, the overseas organization of citizens of the United States who are going to fight in Flanders as a separate unit."[12]

The clergyman was Maj. C. Seymour Bullock. A native of New York state, he had served as a chaplain of the First Illinois Cavalry in the Spanish-American War and gone on to become a chaplain of the Church of Our Father in Ottawa. It was his idea to recruit Americans living in Canada into the Canadian forces, and he did so successfully through centers in Vancouver, Winnipeg, Toronto, and, eventually, Halifax. His effort met with great success and soon began to bring in Americans from within the United States. Of the first 875 to enlist in what would become the 97th Battalion, almost half came from the Canadian border states of New York and Michigan. They were presumed to be motivated by both the spirit of adventure and crusade and Canadian recruitment efforts that talked of German forts on the American-Canadian border if they weren't stopped on the battlefields of Europe.

Maj. Bullock reminded everyone that 48,000 Canadians were estimated to have fought with Union forces in the American Civil War. Eighteen thousand of them were killed, and there was a debt to be repaid. By the time of the Toronto meeting, 16,000 Americans were fighting with Canadian and British forces. Without renouncing their American citizenship, and with the tacit approval of the American government, they had made an oath to "be faithful and bear true allegiance to his Majesty King George V." They would enter the Commonwealth Forces and "defend his Majesty in person, crown, and dignity against all enemies and ... observe and obey all orders of his Majesty and of all the generals and officers set over" them. "It won't do to dismiss them as a lot of boys or adventurers or soldiers of fortune, certainly not as vagabonds," wrote the *New York Times*. "Many of them are over forty. The average age is about thirty. They surely know that trench warfare in Europe is not a lark."[13]

One of those who Americans who went to World War I as a defender of the crown was Lt. Philip Comfort Starr, a graduate of Harvard College in 1914. His father, Merritt Starr, wrote matter-of-factly in a later Harvard publication: "Our son, Lieutenant Philip Comfort Starr (Harvard, 1914) went over to Canada in June 1916; became naturalized as a British subject, and enlisted as a private in the Canadian artillery."[14] Starr was perhaps atypical of Americans in the Canadian military, but not extraordinary in his hard work for the war or in the manner of his death. He had grown up in Winnetka, Illinois, and had taken college prep in California. Studying mathematics and engineering, he went first to Cornell and then to Harvard. After graduation, he became restless and briefly changed his profession from engineering to scientific farming. In 1915, he began to study the war in Europe and determined that he had a human duty to be part of it. One month after the recruiting event in Toronto, he went to the city and enlisted in the Canadian Field Artillery as a private. His skills and resolve took him to the rank of sergeant, then to further training in Kingston, Ontario, from which he emerged as a lieutenant. In England, he developed his engineering skills with the design of temporary bridges for use in battle.

"Arrive France today. On the job at last!" he cabled home on December 15, 1917. Two months later Philip Comfort Starr found himself at Ypres, Belgium. The Ypres Salient, also called "No Man's Land," had been one of the most consistently tragic battlefields of the war. Its dangers included the illnesses that lived virulently in the trenches, and Starr was hospitalized for ten days with the flu before returning to Ypres. It was there, while inspecting artillery emplacements, that he was shot through the helmet on February 20, 1918. He was one of 185,000 members of the Commonwealth Forces who would lose their lives on the Salient over the course of the war.

Members of the American forces would also die at Ypres, and many of them would eventually be buried in the nearby American cemetery at Flanders Field. But the bodies of American Philip Comfort Starr and many of his fellow countrymen of the Commonwealth Forces would seem to disappear in the record keeping, only to emerge years later in cemeteries across Europe that most Americans would never really know about.

The enlistments of Alan Seeger, Charles Chapman and Philip Comfort Starr, and thousands of others like them, in the cause of a free Europe, spoke of a growing desire in America to enter a war that, in its first years, had seemed the problem of someone else in another part of the world. The same German arrogance that had assumed Mexico could keep the United States out of the war during the Punitive Expedition carried through in other German actions that began to interfere with American trade in Europe and escalated to the sinking of American ships with callous disregard for those on board. A German submarine's destruction of the British passenger liner *Lusitania* on May 7, 1915, killed 1,195 innocent passengers, including 124 Americans.

On land, the same breech of Belgium's declared neutrality that had energized Alan Seeger became symbolic of all German intransigence. Atrocities committed in war, the use of chemical weapons, sabotage committed on American soil, and, finally, the cynicism of the Zimmerman Telegram turned the military determination of the United States from minor skirmishes on the Mexican border to full throated war on the European continent.

In a speech to Congress on April 2, 1917, Pres. Woodrow Wilson seemed to capture the spirit of those Americans who had gone to the war before it would be declared: "We have no selfish ends to serve. We desire no conquest, no dominion. We seek no indemnities for ourselves, no material compensation for the sacrifice we shall freely make. We are but one of the champions of the rights of mankind." War was declared against Germany four days later. Gen. John Pershing was recalled from Mexico and given his next mission.

On April 20, an extraordinary event took place in London. It brought full circle the relationship between the United States and Great Britain that had begun before the Revolutionary War. And, in its way, it made the point that April 6, 1917, was not so much an entrance of the United States into the war as a continuation of the sacrifices already made by some of its citizens. This event was America Day in England, a celebration of the decision made in Washington and the success that was now sure — and finally to come. The American Stars and Stripes was hung beside the Union Jack on Victoria Tower at the southern end of Westminster Palace. Those in attendance ranged from the king and queen, through the royal retinue, and American dignitaries and officers, and plain citizens overflowing into the streets of the city. Airplanes circled overhead. At St. Paul's, Bishop Charles Henry Brent, an American humanitarian and religious leader of the time, took all listeners into his "clear tones that rang like trumpet notes through the great cathedral," according to the *New York Times*:

> America has found her soul! America, which has stood for democracy, the cause of the plain man, must fight for that cause at all costs. Democracy means peace, and that is what America, with the allies, is fighting for. Democracy places ballots before bullets. We are at war today that we may destroy war, and, please God, we will achieve our purpose. That is the duty of democracy.[15]

The American and British flags hung equally within St. Paul's. "Overhead in the dim arches," continued the *Times*, "hung the dust-weighted and battle torn flags of the famous British regiments, some of which had been carried in the American War of Revolution, while among the tombs and memorials of famous soldiers ranged about the walls were the names of those who fought against the colonies in that war."

Among those attending in honored roles were those Americans who had already long been fighting in the war through Canadian and Commonwealth forces, including seventy privates and thirty officers convalescing from wounds in hospitals around London. For them, and those they represented, the war would continue. At the ceremony's close, all in attendance stood as one to sing "The Star Spangled Banner." Even the lips of King George could be seen moving with the words.[16]

Among those who followed Gen. Pershing from Mexico to Europe was Kenneth Gow of Summit, New Jersey. His journey through World War I was notable for his membership in what came to be known as the Silk Stocking Regiment of the sons of the wealthy of the New York City area. More notable was a 457-page narrative of his experiences left behind upon his death.[17]

Gow was described by his childhood minister as "a little singing boy," cheerful and manly. In his twenties, he was a near-sighted book salesman in Brooklyn, but he volunteered into the Punitive Expedition in May 1916. Eventually he entered the Seventh New York Militia Regiment, whose historic armory sat on Park Avenue near East 67th Street, at the heart of "upper crust" New York. The regiment had a proud history, though it always had to overcome the view that its soldiers were idle members of the "silk stocking" crowd. As America entered the war, the Seventh moved aggressively to be sure that it would be among the first units sent to the front in Europe. Its numbers included Van Rensellaers and Rhinelanders, and some of lesser station. Kenneth Gow was of Scotch heritage and had come to know the well-off of New York through their summer stays in Summit, a health resort of the region and a center of silk manufacturing.

Lt. Gow became a natural leader in the regiment and was put in charge of transport, which at that time was animal-based. He set a tone that would eventually give him the identity as the spiritual leader of the regiment. "You fellows can swear all you want to at the mules," he told his men, "I know they are exasperating at times; but if I catch one of you calling another an obscene name, into the guardhouse you go."[18] He arrived in France in May 1918 and, like Alan Seeger before him, was enchanted: "Ridges of hills rising one after the other, a quaint picturesque old city nestling among them and running down to the water's edge. Beautiful green fields, all with hedges running around them, giving a peculiar symmetry to the landscape."[19]

He moved with his horses and mules to Oudezeele near the Belgian border, where he found fellowship with soldiers from Belgium to New Zealand in rustic taverns. He took up residence in an old farmhouse where one night, as he wrote to his mother, he found a young girl playing Chopin nocturnes on a piano. He listened for an hour. His first encounter with the enemy came in the trenches of Flanders, near Ypres, where his regiment had the job of delivering horses and mules to the front and bringing bodies back to the burial officer. The bodies were sewn up in burlap and placed in small graves with cross markers.

At the outset of the American entrance into the war, it was decided that all dead would be buried abroad and returned home when practical, probably after the war had ended. As a culmination of all the experience of previous wars, the Graves Registration Service was initiated in August 1917. Its job was to establish and care for cemeteries as needed in battle, quickly establish identities of the dead, and keep records — and to do so with reverence. Chaplains were to be present at all burials, battlefields were to be thoroughly searched for bodies, and isolated burials out of the line of sight of record keeping were to be avoided. Injured soldiers were often assigned to burial details and for the most part saw it as work to be done in honor of their fallen comrades. Identifying the locations and identities of temporary burials was an ethic of the work, even if all that could be done was to note on a report that Pfc. John Smith of Anytown was buried three feet west of the oak tree on the northeast corner of the intersection of two named country roads. A result was that the identities of just less than 3 percent of American bodies in the war would go unknown. The whole system would enable the effort that followed the war to bring all bodies home or to American cemeteries in Europe. But some would still end up in limbo.

Another of those who had traveled with Gen. Pershing from Mexico to Europe was Lt. James A. Pigue. Pigue was born in Nashville, Tennessee, in 1884 and trained at the Virginia Military Institute in 1903 and 1904, with subsequent time spent at the Annapolis Naval Academy. His extraordinary career would cover all the bases of American military history in the first years of the century. He was one of six chosen to assist army surgeon general William Gorgas in preparations for construction of the Panama Canal. His next major assignment was as second in command of the government pier of the 1907 Jamestown Expedition in Norfolk, Virginia, after which he saw another two years of naval service in the Mediterranean and North Atlantic. In 1909, he was discharged from the service at his own request.

In 1916, Pigue reenlisted to join the Punitive Expedition as a first lieutenant, won two medals for excellence and mustered out when his regiment returned to Nashville. He rejoined the service as America entered World War I, arrived in Belgium on May 20, 1918, and was given command of the British and American artillery effort. The service, according to the observations of a friend, "Revealed a new, regenerated Jim, full of that great soul-spirit often developed by the fire and iron of War." Pigue would express his own view of life at war in a letter home: "We all can't be heroes and wear medals and get our names in the dispatches, but we can do our full duty, and wear our medals on our hearts."

On July 15, James Pigue took command of a battalion of the 117th Infantry and led it into action near Ypres, Belgium. On July 18 he was shot through the heart by a German sniper. Word of his death reached Nashville quickly. A memorial service was held at his church, First Baptist of Nashville. The *Nashville Banner* of August 2, 1918, wrote that "he was one of the most popular young men of Nashville, and his death will come as a shock to his many friends." His father, Edward, said, "My boy's heart was in the service of his country." Edward Pigue would make a decision that would touch the hearts of those who came to honor his son as he continued to rest in the fields of modern Belgium almost a century later.

James Pigue, Kenneth Gow, Thomas Enright, James Gresham and Merle Hay were five of 4.7 million who served in the official American forces of World War I. Of that number, 53,402 of them would die in battle, and 63,114 of other causes.[20] The plan of the Graves Registration Service was to use temporary burial grounds as a step toward the establishment of the permanent American cemeteries in Europe that would eventually come under the purview of the American Battle Monuments Commission.

The effort to gain an understanding of the range of individual and small mass burials of Americans all over France, and to bring them together for more official burial or shipment home, began to become more apparent in the lives of the still living in the spring of 1918. In February of that year, Gen. John Pershing had ordered the regular publication of *Stars and Stripes*, a newspaper for Americans fighting in France. During its continued publication, until June 1919, its reporting about death was uninhibited and often poetic.

On February 28, 1919, the newspaper told of the beginning stages of an effort directed by Congress to find and protect 70,000 of the dead in France. It was still probable that final disposition of the bodies would have to wait until after the war, it reported, but "in the meantime the A.E.F is gathering its dead together, that in death they may be as they were in life— in serried ranks, shoulder to shoulder, comrades. From frozen dugouts, from old ruins, from those hastily improvised and now sunken openings in the ground that were shell holes and battle graves, from wheat field and river bank and meadow knoll, from all of the thousands of places of isolation and great loneliness, the dead are being tenderly lifted and borne to take their places in the ordered ranks of the army."[21] Not everyone, however, would be brought into the system that led from temporary burial to an American cemetery or a home.

In the fall of 1918, the trench system in Flanders had become so complex that it was easy to get lost while walking from one point to the next and possible to venture into enemy territory with the taking of a wrong turn. The well-tended graves of fellow soldiers, buried where they had fallen, had become the route markers of the system. Kenneth Gow wrote home about the assault on the eardrums committed by German arms and the games that had been made out of the problem of cooties in the trenches. When coming out of the trenches, the men would throw coins in a common pot, then examine themselves to find whose body harbored the largest louse, the winner taking the purse. "They are all colors and sizes," he wrote, "and bite like a fiend incarnate. The only consolation one has when they make a sortie on one's person is the knowledge that they are no respecters of rank, file or station in life."[22]

Gow and his regiment moved on to Douellens, 75 miles from the midpoint of the Hindenburg Line. Preparation for the battle that would breach Germany's last best defense against Allied forces was underway. Gow arrived by train in Douellen at nightfall and moved his horses and mules through a dark land with only a compass to lead him. Days later, he wrote of a run with his horse across the French countryside as the sun broke through a cloudy morning. He saw France as he had first seen it upon arrival in May. "I love the country and its people," he wrote.[23]

At the end of September, Kenneth Gow took his last long ride with his horse — over three nights beneath a clear, cold moon — toward Tincourt near the Hindenburg Line. After that journey, his natural optimism seemed to take on the burden of unceasing warfare. "If it is my fate to go this time," he wrote to his family, "remember you have given a son to a great cause. Pray not for my welfare, but that I may have the strength and courage to do my duty and not fail those who depend upon me."[24] In his subsequent actions, and letters to friends, he began to say good-bye, while at the same time he described the beginning of the end of the war with the breaking of the Hindenburg Line: "[W]e smashed it, and smashed it into a shapeless ditch. We went over the top with the Australians, the cream of Britain's fighting men, behind us, and when our objective was reached they went through us and carried on what we had made possible."[25] Once inside the line, he wrote to his mother that she had never been so close: "I feel as though I wanted you as I never have in all my life before."[26]

The Silk Stocking Regiment moved on through St. Souplet in pursuit of the retreating German army. Gow nursed his injured horse as they moved and was saddened by the terror the regiment found there in the huddled townspeople after the use of chemical warfare, even the German soldiers scattered about and lying dead where they had fallen from their own poisonous gas. The next move in pursuit of the Germans would be the crossing of the Selle River, and on the evening of October 17 Gow wrote to a friend that he was the last officer of his unit still alive. Thus, on the next day he stood in command of the machine gun company for which he had supplied the horses and mules. Wearing a trench coat, he sought out the best emplacement for his guns. He reminded a friend that if necessary, the maps and instructions for what was to be done could be found in his coat pockets. When his men finally looked up after an incoming barrage, they found him lying on the ground, killed instantly by shrapnel behind his left ear. His men carried his body back to the line and laid him in the care of his horses and mules. He was wrapped in canvas, and, for whatever reason, he would never make it back to the company of his fellows nor to home.

The effort to retrieve bodies from the wide sweep of war to concentrated transit points and temporary cemeteries continued through the period between the armistice and the Treaty of Versailles. By December 1919, noted an official publication of the War Department, 70,552 bodies had been registered in France; 2,519 in the British Isles; 1,207 in Germany; 1,015 in Belgium; and 154 in Luxembourg.

Near the bottom of the list of dead by country was a notation reflecting an almost inexplicable anomaly of World War I: 111 American dead were registered in Archangel, North Russia.[27] The controversy over the movement of American Expeditionary Forces to Archangel, Russia, in September 1918 would continue into the following century. In some interpretations, it almost seemed to be a case in which a small portion of the American war machine had been freelanced into a situation not directly related to the war. In another view, it had been a trick perpetuated against a group of American fighting men by their own government, and for a cause that was muddled at best.

Russia's course through the war, and its defense against Germany, had taken the largest toll on the condition of its own society. As its economy collapsed, the anger of the people was countered by increased oppression by the government. As the war progressed, soldiers were eventually sent to the front without weapons and told to forage among arms of the dead for what they could find. Divisions between the people and their government erupted in the Revolution of February 1917. The revolution could only further detract from Russia's ability to fight off German aggression, and when Vladmir Lenin began to energize the Bolshevik Party from exile in Switzerland, Germany provided him safe transport to Russia. As social and economic deterioration continued, the Bolsheviks rose in power, culminating in the October Revolution of 1917. The Russian Civil War of 1918 followed. It was fought between the Red Army, fueled by radical communism, and the White Army, more moderate liberals and socialists who did not seek radical change.

The Bolsheviks had signed an armistice agreement with Germany at the end of 1917. As the Allied Forces found themselves succeeding against the Germans in 1918, they feared that Russian arms would fall into German hands just as Germany could now afford to focus solely on the Western Front of the war. Britain and France began to support a continuing effort against the Bolsheviks that would require continued German attention to Russia. Seven thousand British troops were sent to guard Allied war materiel in Northern Russia, but more help was needed, and, in the closing months of the war, U.S. Pres. Woodrow Wilson succumbed to Allied pressures and those of his cabinet. The burden of his unannounced decision to place American troops under British generals fell most heavily on the Dearborn, Michigan, headquarters of the army's Eighty-Fifth Division.

The group had been in training for conventional warfare in Europe, and was moved to England with that expectation. But, once across the Atlantic, they were told that 5,000 of them would instead be going to Arctic Russia. Common wisdom would hold, but records would never confirm, that they were chosen for two simplistic reasons: as Michiganders, they would, of course, be able to deal with snow and cold, and as they were mostly from the industrial melting pot of Detroit they already had ethnic and cultural ties to that part of the world.

Pres. Wilson intended that their mission be only defensive, but once in place they were split into three battalions and sent on offensive missions against the Red Army deep into the Russian interior, based loosely in Archangel on the Northern Dvina River near the White Sea. Though the armistice was signed on November 11, 1918, the men of the American North Russia Expeditionary Force (ANREF), soon to be called the Polar Bear Expedition, continued to fight under the most difficult of conditions. The first division was herded into coal ships for transport up the Dvina River. "What a rotten hole they have us dumped into now," wrote Pvt. Clarence Schue of Detroit. "Coal dust 2 inches thick, damp, filthy dungeon. We are sleeping on the bottom of the scow no light, ventilation or anything."[28] Half of the battalion was sickened, and it was not until mid–November that it received cold weather gear. The boots provided could not gain traction in the arctic snow and could only be replaced by those taken from the bodies of dead Russians.

The matter of Michigan boys sent on a questionable mission to Russia just as the war was ending quickly became controversial in Detroit and its newspapers. Their fates and fortunes were followed as closely as possible, and their letters home were published for all to see. Corp. Joseph Babinger of the 339th Infantry wrote to his brother after a difficult battle with the Bolsheviks of September 29, 1918:

> We were camped in a heavy wood just outside of a burg, when a heavy artillery fire was opened on us. The Bolos thought they could take the town, but they were badly mistaken. They did not know they were fighting Americans, as they were told we were not. When they saw the different style of battle we put up, they just turned and ran....
>
> The enemy in France was in front if us, but here they are on four sides of us so you can imagine what we are up against. Our casualties are heavy in proportion to our numbers, and we believe most of the time that we are forgotten. We have no reinforcements and a big hospital list that is staring us in the face all of the time. We really don't know how long we can hold out.
>
> It is very cold here, 40 to 50 degrees below zero. Tell the people in the states not to send their boys any money orders as they will not cash them for us. Hope that the government will soon send us help.

There would be no help to send. The only bittersweet consolation was a tacit understanding by all involved that a mistake had been made in sending American men to be led by British generals in Arctic Russia as the war was drawing to a close. But winter was closing in on the men, and the shipping season was giving way to the ice floes of the north. The battles with the Bolsheviks continued, the troops left mostly to fend for themselves. Imprisoned by the environment in life, the bodies of the fallen looked as if they would stay imprisoned in death. A letter from the army's chief surgeon in Russia to the parents of Lt. Ralph Powers of Amherst, Ohio, killed on January 22, 1919, stated the problem bluntly: "Owing to the conditions of the country here, which is mostly swamps, I believe it would be inadvisable to think of removing any bodies of our American soldiers."

According to the account of 1st Lt. Arthur Collar, Lt. Powers had been in charge of a battle hospital at Vicorko Gora. When the hospital was set afire by enemy shells, he finished dressing wounds, wrapped his patients in blankets and spirited them out of the village on sleighs under heavy fire. He returned to Vicorko Gora the following day and set up a wound dressing operation. When Powers was mortally wounded in another shelling, Collar moved to help him. The letter to Powers' parents continued, "As I did so, he said, 'Never mind me Collar there are others hurt worse than I am.' He was placed to one side of the room and from there he gave instructions as to the best ways to dress the wounded. He would not let us dress him until all the wounded had been properly cared for." He died of wounds to the arms and hips a day later.

Pfc. Alfred Schuck of Company A, 339th Infantry, 85th Division, stands at the most advanced American outpost in Russia on January 7, 1919. The village in the distance is Pagosta, held by the Bolsheviks. The church is a source of daily machine gun fire aimed at American troops (*U.S. Army Signal Corps, Bentley Historical Library, University of Michigan*).

A reindeer team used to move Polar Bear members around Archangel and its environs in the foreground of a local church on March, 17, 1917 (*U.S. Army Signal Corps, Bentley Historical Library, University of Michigan*).

The body of Lt. Powers would be lost for years, but not forgotten. He might have been buried in a military cemetery that had become out of reach behind enemy lines as the winter progressed, or he may have been one of those buried where fallen, or perhaps one not buried at all because of the frozen ground.

By February 1919, anger and editorials in Michigan over their trapped husbands and sons began to go national. On February 10, the *Chicago Tribune* published a lengthy and condemnatory report from its unnamed correspondent in North Russia. It was seething with accusation:

> Developed into a pitiful failure ... cesspool of jealousy, hatred, mistakes ... American troops were put under an absolute imperialistic command ... complete lack of spiritual leadership ... beautiful faith of the Russians for America is breaking under the manhandling by our forces under the foreign [British] command ... suffered from a complete lack of spiritual leadership....[29]

The article asserted that the Americans had been sent to guard war supplies that did not, in fact, exist: "This old, hard ridden theory of guarding the supplies at Archangel lasted through hundreds of columns of propaganda, even long after the American troops had landed a month later." It had been expected, said the writer, that "the Russians would flock to the Allies' colors by the thousands." Instead, the growing American hatred for their mission under British command had made them angry and arrogant: "They carried on in a half-hearted way, riding rough-shod over the feelings of the natives, and acting much more like conquerors than invited guests."

Six. *Americans in Any Uniform*

In March 1919 rumblings of mutiny began to filter out of Russia. They weren't denied by the War Department and were roundly defended in the Michigan press. "These mutinous troops," exclaimed an editorial datelined Grand Rapids, April 12, 1919, "are not traitors to America. They are not lacking one iota of devotion to their country and their flag. They are splendid, loyal soldiers. But they have been treated shamefully. They have been shunted to the roof of the world and left to their own devices."

It was eventually determined that the men of the Polar Bear Expedition would be brought home from North Russia, though they might yet be replaced by other forces. But it was predicted that the earliest they would be able to return through the ice that separated them from home would be in early summer. It was not until June 30 that the Polar Bears were delivered to the American shore at Camp Merritt, New Jersey. By the Fourth of July they were celebrated on Belle Isle in the Detroit River. Upon their return, the stories of mutiny were vehemently denied. "I have heard more bunk about this mutiny than could be written in a dozen books," said Maj. J. Brooke Nichols of Detroit. He attributed the story to a misunderstanding between a sergeant and a private that had been blown out of proportion.

Perhaps more celebrated than the living in this particular case, it was the dead who gained the most attention. The welcome home that they received seemed to arise from a sense of apology for the tragedy that had befallen them in Russia. In November, those whose bodies could be found began a journey back to Detroit on the transport ship *Lake Daraga*, which was herself built by American Shipbuilding of Detroit in 1917. Their travel from Archangel to Brest, France, and across the Atlantic was followed in the national news. Their arrival at Pier Four, Hoboken, just before midnight November 12 was met with flags and bunting. In attendance at a funeral service the following morning were members of Congress, the State Department, the U.S. military and the American Legion, officials of the state of Michigan and the city of Detroit, and attaches of the Russian embassy. One hundred three coffins were laid side by side on the pier, each covered with a flag and floral wreath.

It turned out that these last of American soldiers sent off to World War I had become the first to return under a policy that guaranteed that the dead would be brought home if possible and if it was the wish of the family. "Today," intoned Senator James Wadsworth, Jr., of New York, "we meet the first company of the dead. The mother country receives into her compassionate arms all that is mortal of her gallant sons who died worthily upholding her honor by their unswerving devotion to duty."

The funeral procession moved west to Detroit and down Woodward Avenue. Fifty-one army trucks carried two coffins each, accompanied by three marching soldiers on each side. The crowd was six to twenty people deep along the way. At parade's end the sound of Taps was heard. "It came from the depths of the city hall piazza," wrote an unnamed observer. "A more blood curdling, death signifying sound I never heard. The cold chill raced up and down my spine. The trucks bearing the caskets had all halted for the token. I could not eat any dinner for the pent up emotion that kept that lump in my throat."

At the time, it was estimated that more than 200 Americans had died on the Archangel front, but just 103 came home to Michigan. The rest of them seemed lost forever, or out of reach.

Chapter Seven

Decisions to Be Made

Had they been left in France they would have been cherished as long as France endures.
—Owen Wister

On the American Memorial Day weekend in 1922, lively services in honor of American dead took place all over Europe. At Belleau Wood in France, Maj. James G. Harbord, Gen. Pershing's chief of staff, spoke of the continuing American allegiance to France going back to the Revolutionary War. American ambassador Myron Herrick spoke of the tender care given by the French to American graves. "Those gracious deeds repeated as Spring returns," he said, "revive each year memories of so many deeds accomplished, so many hopes realized, so powerful an example placed before the whole world by our two great peoples, united in age-long confidence and affection."[1]

Also in France, several million schoolchildren were taught the American role in their country's recent history and took flowers to nearby graves. At the Suresnes American Cemetery, French orphans sang "The Star Spangled Banner." "The Battle Hymn of the Republic" was sung in the church of the House of Commons in London, and the sermon was a reading of Abraham Lincoln's Gettysburg Address. A wreath was laid at the feet of a Lincoln statue nearby, as Sir Harry Lauder, the most popular Scottish singer of the day, said, "I deposit these flowers on behalf of those Americans whose forebears and relatives gave their lives in all the wars of American history."[2]

The Brookwood American Cemetery south of London was dedicated. Citizens of the town who had cared for the American graves laid flowers and tokens where the dead lay buried. Battalions of American sailors could be found in Portsmouth Harbour where all British ships joined in celebration of the day. Wreaths were laid in Plymouth, Princetown and Dartmoor Prison in honor of the dead of the War of 1812 and those who lay in the prison burial ground. Memorial Day services were also reported in Warsaw and Copenhagen and in the military cemetery at Coblenz, Germany.

In the 1900s Europe, particularly France, Belgium and the Netherlands, would assume the caretaking of the American dead of two wars almost as an ethic of the 20th century. It would begin with a massive restructuring of the geography of burial after World War I and find perpetuation in the continuing search for recovery of those lost, if only in spirit. European reverence for American dead in their midst would diminish through postwar generations, but in the following century, it would still bring grown men to tears, small towns to annual remembrances, and school children to the singing of the American national anthem. A starting point for the era might be found in a letter to the editor of *Stars and Stripes*, November 29, 1918, excerpted:

> [P]ermit a simple French woman to express her gratitude and admiration for the country which has saved us. I know with what sublime abnegation, with what disregard of danger, those brave children delivered us from the Boche at the time when they were so near Paris. One of my nephews told me about it. He said, "There were ten thousand American who fought like lions. They made a rampart for us that stopped the Boche reaching Paris....
>
> Before leaving France, please remember that there are French people who esteem and admire you, and who will never forget what you have done for their native land.
>
> I visit the cemetery every week to greet those who have fallen so valiantly in defending us, and I am really grieved not to be able to strew all their graves with flowers.
>
> Pardon me for writing this; I am but expressing all my feelings.
>
> Veuve A. Jale[3]

The sentiment was confirmed by *Stars and Stripes*, reporting on December 20, 1918, of a visit by Pres. Woodrow Wilson's daughter, Margaret, to a cemetery of 64 Americans near Bordeaux: "On her unannounced arrival, she found about a score of French women and children decorating the graves with flowers. On behalf of the women of America, Miss Wilson thanked the women of France."[4]

The Bordeaux cemetery would only be temporary, like hundreds of such places near the scenes of battle. Other small cemeteries would derive from special circumstances. In Toulouse, for example, George "Daddy" Ford, an American expatriate since 1872 and a dentist in the town, had turned his office into a place of rest and fellowship for American forces. When the first American died in a Toulouse hospital, Ford started a cemetery two miles outside of town. It would eventually hold six American bodies and Daddy Ford's daily attention. His effort was honored by the *Journal of the American Dental Association* in an article entitled "For the Stranger in a Strange Land." "If there is one thing above all else that a mother wishes for a dead son," the medical journal ventured, "it is that his resting place shall be marked, and that he shall lie in surroundings pleasant to remember, and where some distinguishing mark shall point him out as an American and as a soldier."[5]

At war's end, 79,531 American soldiers had been killed in battle or died in hospitals of wounds and illness. They could be found in approximately 2,400 large and small burial places and cemeteries across England, France, Belgium, Germany, Italy and Russia. American law now required the offering of options to the families of the dead: allow their loved ones to remain buried where they lay, to be brought to a national cemetery in Europe, or to be brought home for private burial or in a national cemetery in America. The national discussion about those options was influenced by the death of Quentin Roosevelt, the youngest son of Pres. Teddy Roosevelt, in an air fight over Chamery, France, on July 18, 1918. Behind enemy lines, the German military gave him a burial with full military honors, the cross marker made of wood from his airplane. The burial was then pictured on a postcard and used in German propaganda. With the Allied victory, Roosevelt's grave became a sacred place marked by both French and American memorials. Teddy Roosevelt was practical and direct when it came to war. Though he mourned the loss of his son heavily, he adhered to a dictum that derived from biblical sources: "Where a tree falls, let it lie."[6]

American public opinion during and after the war could be found largely in that spirit, and when the tally of family wishes for their loved ones was eventually drawn up by the War Department, 45 percent asked that they be left where they lay. Or *near* to where they lay, as the War Department struggled to gain control of a diaspora of the fallen across Europe. Those 2,400 burial places could not possibly be maintained to the standards required by America's moral law for its war dead. They needed to be consolidated, and before the war had ended the process was put in place. It fell to the Graves Registration Service to find individual bodies and gather them into temporary burials. "Five hundred here, 150 there," reported *Stars and Stripes* on March 31, 1919, "thousands of bare, sodless mounds, each with its wooden cross and metal tag, with here and there a stupefying funeral wreath laid there by some French friend, or perhaps a cluster of pansies, planted by French hands on the grave of 'An unknown American,' buried along the Paris highway he died defending."[7]

Gen. John Pershing felt that the consolidation should end within French borders and that the bodies should not be sent home to America. Talking with reporters in his Paris apartment, the *New York Times* reported on August 1, 1919, he "spoke with emphasis, saying that he felt that as the men had fought and died in France they should lie in France. He said he believed the French felt the same as he did, and that the presence of the American dead in their soil would always be a reminder of how the two nations had fought together."[8]

With all due respect to Gen. Pershing, said a growing number of parents and wives after the Treaty of Versailles, they wanted their boys and men home, and without delay. The matter became the subject of congressional hearings in November 1919. One of those testifying before the House Committee on Foreign Affairs on November 13 was George Wayne Anderson, assistant city attorney of the city of Richmond, Virginia, representing his own loss of a son now buried in France and 125 other Richmonders in similar straits. Despite the coming of winter, his group wanted the men returned immediately:

> [W]e parents ... are being compelled to look forward to some indefinite time in the future when our sons' bodies will be brought back to us, and we will have a funeral in our families. It is a matter we want to get behind us. Our wives want those bodies. They want to visit those graves....
>
> Our boys went to France knowing of the Government promise that their bodies would he returned, and we do not and can not believe that one American boy out of 10,000 would have failed to say, if asked, that he would prefer to rest in his native land. To them France itself was almost an abstraction. The love in their hearts was for America, and the crusaders' spirit was mused in them by German atrocity and inhumanity. Many had never left their native states, and we feel sure that their desire would be to find a resting place in America.[9]

The Richmond group, and others, felt that they were up against a president who was unresponsive, an indifferent Congress, and a secretary of war giving mixed signals. The government would eventually honor the commitment of law to bring bodies home, they heard the president say, but just not now; and they believed that he was only biding time until the clamor for returned bodies died down. He would not involve the War Department in such reclamations, nor would he allow any private attempts by families to return a loved one to go forth.

A large part of the problem was found in postwar French politics. Legislation was going forth in the French Chamber of Deputies that would prohibit the removal of American bodies from French soil until the early 1920s. It was the view of the Richmond petitioners that

> the reason for this was the inability of the French Government to comply with the request of French parents who were demanding the return of their sons to their home localities, and it was thought the morale of the French people would be destroyed if the French Government should undertake the return to such localities of the 1,700,000 French dead, with consequent funerals in every hamlet of France lasting through a probable period of six months, thereby causing a renewed outburst of mourning and withdrawing the attention of the people from productive employment so necessary at present to the life of France:

That to consent to such removal by America of Americans would lead to similar demands by England, Italy, Belgium, and other nations, and that no French Government could stand which granted such privileges to other countries and refused them to the French.[10]

A letter that appeared in the *New York Tribune* of September 19, 1919, compounded the problem. It was set off with the boxed title "Neglected Graves. The Letter of a Mother Who Saw." It had been sent from France by Eleanor Bradley Peters after visiting her son's grave at Thiaucourt. Though gracious in tone, it charged that the caretaker at Thiaucourt was "lonely" and had not received orders, rations or pay for three weeks; that wreathes could not be placed at individual graves because of French laws against discrimination; that names on markers were misspelled; that officers' graves seemed to be set apart from those of lesser rank; and that American cemeteries appeared to be "less beautiful" than French cemeteries.[11]

The letter gained the immediate attention of the War Department Purchase, Storage and Traffic Division and was cabled back to France for investigation. It came quickly to the attention of Maj. Gen. Fox Connor, chief of operations for the American Expeditionary Force in France, who seemed to give it his full attention. On October 9, the War Department News Bureau issued a full response in Connor's name.[12] It reported that new orders would allow private wreathes on individual graves; that incorrect spelling of names was a result of battlefield conditions and would now be corrected on a grave by grave basis; and that the planned schedule for attention to the caretaker at Thiaucourt had always been monthly. He was also found to be "homesick" and was replaced.

Discrimination in burial was explained in a sentence that offered little clarity, even when read more than once: "There is no discrimination between officers and men in the concentration of bodies. In some cases those of officers were grouped together and the enlisted men were similarly grouped."

The news release spent the most attention to the charge that American cemeteries fell short in appearance. The response was probably an accurate description of a difficult time between war and remembrance:

> Concerning the appearance of our cemeteries, practically all of them have been created during the past summer, one of the driest seasons for many years in France, and as a result they still have a new and unfinished appearance, which will disappear when grass and flowers have a chance to grow. Our permanent cemeteries have white fences around them, paths are graveled and grass sown or will be as soon as weather conditions warrant. It will be some time, of course, before American cemeteries may have the shrubberies and trees which are usually found in older cemeteries. In all our burial places the crosses will have to be straightened from time to time until the ground is thoroughly settled. Most of the American cemeteries are in the battle areas, where working conditions and living conditions still remain primitive and difficult.

Those of the ca. 1919 cemeteries that would become permanent would take on a profound beauty as the years progressed.

In the meantime, bureaucracy and bill paying had become the daily pursuit of an American quartermaster overseeing the burials of Americans dying in French hospitals. A bill from the mayor of Eclaron, Haute Marne, for example, for burial of American privates Hines Ponopy and Kretcher Alvinza in the town cemetery would be paid in the amount of 155 francs. The matter of the movement of the body of PFC Harry W. Smith from a Paris hospital to the city morgue, however, resulted in five pages of paperwork back and forth to determine cost and responsibility for the short ride. Payment of 43 francs was approved though it was noted that quartermaster transportation had been available at no charge. It was disapproved at a higher level with a note that another authority in the process had not first approved it. That authority denied the claim, saying that it had already vouchered payment for Pvt. Smith's coffin, and the bill moved on to another level of Quartermaster Corps. It had no authority to pay bills incurred by the Chaplain's Corps, as this one had been. "This office," wrote Col. C.E. Wheatly on October 22, 1919, "has supply of coffins one of which should have been used for the burial of this body. It has authority however to pay the 16 francs charged for the coffin and will do so." The eventual outcome of the bill for Pvt. Smith's travel between hospital and morgue cannot be known.

When Philip Comfort Starr and thousands of other Americans entered World War I through Canada and the United Kingdom, they came under the potential care of Sir Fabian Ware. Ware, born in Bristol, England, in 1864 and educated in London and Paris, was at various times an educator, government official, journalist and mining entrepreneur. At the outset of the war he was too old to fight and became, instead, the commander of a mobile Red Cross unit in France in 1914. He came quickly to understand what America had begun to learn in the Civil War, that mass casualties of war required practiced registration and organization of the dead. England's War Office agreed with him and saw that the perception of caring attention to the dead would also be helpful to the morale of soldiers and their families. Ware went on to enlist the leading architects and horticulturists of the day in the design of cemeteries and memorials. When the Imperial (eventually Commonwealth) War Graves Commission was founded in May, 1917, Ware was appointed its vice president under the Prince of Wales. He believed that practiced remembrance of the dead was sometimes the only thing that people could agree upon in the countervailing winds of war. He was twice knighted after the war and would play a similar role in World War II.

The commission was intended to be the best expression of the former British Empire in the concern for its fallen. The writer Rudyard Kipling was hired as a literary advisor to counsel on the language of memorial inscriptions. The director of the British Museum coordinated design. Equality of treatment of the dead was made an ethic of the work. An agreement by all members of the Commonwealth — Australia, Canada, India, Newfoundland (until its incorporation into Canada in 1949), New Zealand, South Africa, and the United Kingdom — held that no bodies would be repatriated from where they fell. The logistics of return from faraway places would be problematic, and it was believed that men who had fought in brotherhood at the front should remain that way in death.

The first three commission cemeteries were experimental and intended to find the best design for those that were to follow. The cemetery at Forceville, France, was chosen as the model for the future, a walled enclosure with uniform headstones in a "homely garden setting." By 1921, 1,000 cemeteries had been prepared to receive bodies, and in 1923 the cemeteries were taking in 4,000 newly inscribed headstones each week. By 1927, more than 450,000 dead were either finally buried or memorialized as missing in action in the commission cemeteries. Though their participation in the war before it had been officially entered into by the United States seemed to meet the tacit encouragement of their country, those Americans buried in the new cemeteries would be forever identified as Canadian or British, and sometimes Australian or New Zealand nationals.

In 1920, the American effort toward final resolutions for its dead in Europe began to gain momentum. At the beginning of the year, France gave its permission for the disinterment of 20,000 Americans buried in its soil. They would be limited to those found in 600 large and small nonmilitary cemeteries from Le Mans to Brest, where 5,500 Americans lay dead of influenza contracted before they could join the fighting. Most would be returned home as per

SEVEN. *Decisions to Be Made* 63

A contemporary view of the World War I Commonwealth War Grave cemetery at Bucquoy in Ficheux, Pas-de-Calais, France. It is located in farmland between Arras and Ayette. Many of those interred were casualties of the Battle of Arras of April and May 1917. After the armistice, it became the final resting place of those who had been buried in the smaller cemeteries of the region. It held 1,901 burials and commemorations of World War I and took on 136 burials and commemorations early in World War II. It contains the remains of 29 Americans killed in World War I (*Pierre Vandervelden*).

the wishes of their families, but the work in France would have to stand in line behind disinterments already under way in England and Germany.

In the meantime, the development of those final places of rest for American dead who would lie near to where they fell moved quickly across Europe. As completed, they are described:

- The Brookwood American Cemetery, located adjacent to a private civilian cemetery on a rail line twenty-eight miles southwest of London would contain 411 known dead and 42 unknown on 4.5 acres. Those buried here were mostly those who had died in transit to Europe and around London of various noncombat causes.
- The Flanders Field American Cemetery at Waregem, Belgium, near Ypres would contain 347 known and 21 unknown dead on 5 acres.
- The Meuse-Argonne American Cemetery, Romagne-sous-Montfaucon, Meuse, about 128 miles from Paris, would contain 13,724 known and 458 unknown dead, most lost during the Meuse-Argonne Offensive of 1918. The largest and deadliest battle of the war, it was credited with breaching the Hindenburg Line and hastening German capitulation. The 130-acre cemetery sat on land captured by the American 32nd Infantry.
- The Aisne-Marne American Cemetery, Belleau, Aisne, about six miles from Chateau-Thierry and sixty miles from Paris, would hold 2,019 known and 252 unknown dead on 42.5 acres. It was first the temporary cemetery number 1764 at Belleau Wood, holding those who lost their lives in the Belleau Wood and Marne Valley in the summer of 1918.

Above and opposite: The Memorial Day Service at the Suresnes American Cemetery near Paris on May 30, 1920 (*Library of Congress*).

- The Suresnes American Cemetery, Suresnes, Seine, in metropolitan Paris, would contain 1,528 known and 6 unknown dead on 7.5 acres, most of whom had died in Paris hospitals. It was placed on Mt. Valerian, which had been a place of pilgrimage for 16th-century Christians who saw it as a representation in France of Jerusalem and the site of the crucifixion. In the late 18th century its guesthouse was a favorite visiting place of American ambassador Thomas Jefferson, and between 1811 and 1815 it was planned first as the site of an orphanage and then a fort, the latter by Napoleon Bonaparte.
- The Somme American Cemetery, Bony Aisne, 90 miles north of Paris, would contain 1,699 known and 131 unknown dead on 13 acres. It was first temporary cemetery number 636 of the Somme Offensive in 1918.
- The Oise-Aisne American Cemetery, Seringes-et-Nesles, Aisne, sixty miles northeast of Paris, would contain 5,391 known and 619 unknown dead on 36.5 acres. It was first established by the 42nd Division as a temporary battle cemetery in August 1918 after battles south of the Oise River and in the environs of Paris.
- The St. Mihiel American Cemetery, Thiaucourt, Meurthe-et-Moselle, about twenty miles from Metz, would contain 4,034 known and 117 unknown dead on 30 acres. It was first established as a temporary cemetery in 1918 after the battle of St. Mihiel in defense of Paris.

In 1923, the U.S. Congress established the American Battle Monuments Commission to oversee the maintenance and use of military cemeteries created abroad beginning with the American Cemetery in Mexico established in 1851. The ABMC was placed under the Executive Department and its first chairman, serving as such until his death in 1948, was Gen. John Pershing. The action had a two-edged effect. It placed an official imprint on the American determination to care for its war dead as individuals from 1851 onward. By the same token, it seemed to officially disavow interest in war dead buried abroad in the years preceding 1851. These dead would have no official recognition and care.

The determination after World War I that families of those killed be given workable options for the outcomes of their loved ones' remains was matched by the growing ability of science to determine identities through laboratory work that could get beyond the destruction of fingerprints and dental clues. The increasing speeds allowed by transportation technology, and the addition of the airplane, could deliver bodies to almost any place on either side of the Atlantic. In the United States, national cemeteries were prepared to accept the bodies of

those whose families had requested burial in cemeteries filled with their peers, but a larger number of those were returned fully to the church and town cemeteries of their families. Not every American, though, would be brought home, or to a final rest with his comrades in Europe or America.

On Decoration Day 1916, the American writer Alan Seeger was to have read a poem before the statue of Lafayette and Washington at Place des États-Unis in Paris, "Ode in Memory of the American Volunteers Fallen for France," excerpted:

> Ay, it is fitting on this holiday,
> Commemorative of our soldier dead,
> When — with sweet flowers of our New England May
> Hiding the lichened stones by fifty years made gray —
> Their graves in every town are garlanded,
> That pious tribute should be given too
> To our intrepid few
> Obscurely fallen here beyond their seas.

Unfortunately, Seeger was not able to obtain leave to attend the event, and the poem was published posthumously on the fourth of July near Belloy-en-Santerre. A man of the French Foreign Legion, Seeger's body was simply placed in a mass grave with his comrades, and his bones found permanent rest in an ossuary of the cemetery at Lihons, less than ten miles away and 25 miles east of Amiens.

After his death on October 17, 1918, 1st Lt. Kenneth Gow was awarded the American Distinguished Cross and the French Croix de Guerre:

> For extraordinary heroism in action near Ronssoy, France, September 29, 1918. While supply officer for his company he personally took rations forward with a pack mule, through continuous shell and machine gun fire. When all officers of his company were either killed or wounded he assumed command and led it forward through heavy shell and machine gun fire until he was killed.[13]

His burial took an unexplained turn. American and British forces each built a cemetery, set side by side on the road from St. Souplet to Vaux-Andigny. The American cemetery held 371 American and 7 British graves, while the British cemetery was much smaller. After Armistice, all Americans were moved to the Somme American Cemetery, save one. Apparently Kenneth Gow was moved with the seven British burials to what would be known as the St. Souplet British Cemetery. There his journey would finally end. Less likely, though possible, is that he came to St. Souplet from an initial burial in the Bohain British Cemetery. In either case, Kenneth Gow was the only member of the American forces to remain buried at St. Souplet, all of his comrades being moved to the Somme American Cemetery, where, fittingly, there would be a single, unexplained British burial, its marker reading "Lieutenant T R Hostetter, 3rd Sqdn, Royal Air Force who died on Friday 27 September 1918."

It can't be known why Kenneth Gow remained in St. Souplet, but a surmise about money and influence might be made about T.R. Hostetter. An American who entered the Royal Air Force, probably through Canada, he should have been buried in a Commonwealth War Graves cemetery. But Theodore Rickey Hostetter of Locust Valley on Long Island was a scion of a family that had accumulated great wealth and influence, first in the sales of a patent medicine dating back to the Civil War, Hostetter's Bitters, then in oil and gas. Upon his death in action over the skies of France, he left behind an estate of $2,261,056. Half of it went to his sister, Greta. His death had occurred on her birthday, and her own death, of illness, occurred just a month later.

On the day of his death in July 1918, Lt. James Pigue's unit was responsible for defense of the trench lines of the East Poperinghe line near Ypres, Belgium. He was initially buried at the nearby Gwalia British Cemetery, and in the due course of the movement of bodies toward home, he was reinterred in the American section of the Lijssenthoek Commonwealth War Graves Cemetery in June 1919. The village of Lijssenthoek sat just far enough behind the front lines that it could not be reached by enemy howitzers but close enough that it became an important transit point of men and supplies going forward and the safest place to triage casualties returning from the front before sending them on to hospitals and other medical units. Death was a by-product of the process. The cemetery at Lijssenthoek was opened by the French in 1914, shared with the British beginning in 1915, and by war's end was a permanent or temporary resting place for men of all nationalities, including James Pigue among several hundred Americans. As time went by, they would either be sent home at family request or moved to the large American cemeteries as they came on line.

James Pigue had left behind a wife and son. When his wife was asked by the War Department whether she wished that his body be returned, she replied that she wanted it to stay in Europe until further notice. At some point shortly thereafter, she and her son seemed to fall out of the picture. It could be presumed that she quickly remarried. The matter of the disposition of James Pigue fell to his father, Edward Hicks Pigue.

By 1921, Mr. Pigue was a retired shoe merchant, 64 years old, a widower living alone, with a servant, on Belmont Boulevard in Nashville. On June 17, 1921, he swore allegiance to the United States as required and applied for a passport. The application stated that he would be gone for less than a year with travel planned to "England, Belgium, France, Italy, Switzerland and all countries necessary thereto to locate the body of my son, a United States soldier." A clerical correction on the typed application crossed out "all countries necessary" and covered the words with "Gibraltar" in a heavy pencil script. And, in perhaps a bureaucratic sentiment that World War I was a thing of the past, the words "to locate the body of my son, a United States soldier" were overwritten in the same heavy pencil with the single word "Travel." In his passport picture, Mr. Pigue had the appearance of a tall southern gentleman of means, with a thick crop of white hair above his forehead, two triangles of mustache beneath his nose, and a bowtie in the vee of a fine vest and jacket.

He set off from New York on the Cunard ship *Albania* on July 12, 1921, arriving in Liverpool ten days later. By the time he left, the army had given him useful assistance in finding the grave at Lijssenthoek. James had been dead for three years, and the view from America of the movement of bodies either home or to the large cemeteries of Europe was confused, unsettled, and still controversial. The plea of parents for the return of their boys that had begun in 1919 had grown as a movement. The Bring Home the Soldier Dead League, formed at that time, would grow in influence, and conspiracy theories would abound, especially in relation to continuing French prohibitions against disinterring Americans from their soil. "I think the whole matter can be summed up in a few words," League president J.D. Foster had asserted before Congress in November 1919. "So far as the French attitude is concerned, it is a desire to commercialize the graves of the American soldier dead. I can not see any other reason. I understand that they are building a large hotel near the Komagne Cemetery to accommodate American tourists who will be going over. They will not be the mothers, fathers, and widows of the soldiers buried there, but they will be tourists, sightseers, souvenir hunters, etc."[14]

As Edward Pigue set off on his journey two years later, the question about leaving the dead where they fell or bringing them home was still a dilemma for individual families, as well as the larger society. The writer Owen Wister, as an example, was a controversial figure of the time. His book *The Virginian* would become a classic American Western novel. He shared a fascination with the West with his friend and fellow Harvard classmate Teddy Roosevelt (but he would oppose Franklin Roosevelt's New Deal near the end of his life). During the war, he was an advocate for, among other things, the stronger use of music in motivating and easing the way of American soldiers. Indeed, the army and navy used "song leaders" to encourage expression through music of the frustrations, fighting resolve, unity of purpose, even the homesickness and differing ethnic roots of the soldiers. He noted that in France the Americans were called "the silent army," and he felt they needed to be taught and encouraged to sing out the basic songs of American spirit in the same way that the French broke into singing of "La Marseillaise" with every challenge.[15]

After the war, Wister was an advocate for the dead. In an open letter to the American Legion in April 1921, he charged that unclaimed bodies of dead soldiers, "piles of these poor fragments of human beings,"[16] were stacking up on the Graves Registration piers at Hoboken, some of them headed toward burial in potter's fields. The accusation met with strenuous objection from the Legion and the Graves Registration Service, each insisting that every effort was made to identify every body. Efforts to find families to receive returned bodies were sometimes hampered by the disappearance of relatives who had requested the return. But, in all such cases, the few bodies unclaimed would eventually be interred in national cemeteries with full honors. On April 16, 1921, the *New York Times* reported that forty-eight unclaimed bodies sat on the Hoboken pier as of that date.

Owen Wister's charge played into the larger questions of return. The same open letter included a vivid description of his visit to the Oise-Aisne American Cemetery: "In smooth turf and among white crosses gaped ugly holes. Out of these holes were being dragged — what? Boys whom their mothers would recognize? No! Things without shape, at which mothers would collapse.... Such as are claimed and taken to some family graveyard will soon be forgotten. Those who mourn them will be dead, too. Had they been left in France they would have been cherished as long as France endures."

"Cowardly propaganda," wrote the national president of the Bring Home the Soldier Dead League to the *New York Times*. The "worst illustration of heartlessness yet published," he continued. "Only last week I attended the funeral of one of those returned heroes and the relief it brought to the soldier's father was almost akin to joy. Who can be so heartless, so unkind, so cowardly as to even suggest the thought of depriving a parent of this relief for his aching heart?"[17]

Others disagreed. The Rev. Paul Moody of the Madison Avenue Presbyterian Church, a former pastor with the American Expeditionary Forces, confirmed Wister's observations with descriptions of his own experiences. He had stood with Gen. Pershing in Memorial Day ceremonies in 1919. "I saw the love and care with which the French treat the American graves. They [ ] those graves, rich and poor, Catholic, Protestant and Jew as they lived, fought and died, brothers animated by a common purpose. Now they are being brought back and separated as they were never separated in life, in Catholic and Protestant and Jewish cemeteries. All for what is called sentiment. But what about the worthier sentiment which remembers where and why these men died?"[18]

The debate raised profound questions. Were the dead more of the world than of country or faith? Was death for the dead, or for the living they left behind? Who, if anyone, had provenance over those who had ceased to live? It might be presumed that Edward Pigue had these questions in mind when he set off from Liverpool in search of his son. As far as can be determined, it appears that James had been abandoned by his widow, and a new father found for his young son. The names of the widow and son were not even mentioned in his obituary in the *Nashville Banner*. The army told Edward, however, that James' widow had requested that he stay in Lijssenthoek. It is not clear whether Edward had the opportunity to override her wishes. The trip that was planned through six nations came to a fairly quick end in Belgium. Edward arrived at Lijssenthoek sometime in July and found his son's grave in rows of similar tombstones in the American section. James was at rest with his brothers in a common purpose, and the decision that he would stay there was affirmed. Other families had made the same decision, some upon learning that their loved one had come to rest in a grave that was handsome and well-tended, others as a statement to those of other nations of the sacrifice made on their behalf.

Edward returned to America on the French liner *Chicago* less than a month after he had arrived. James Pigue would eventually be left very much alone and without his American comrades at Lijssenthoek. But he would not be forgotten.

Chapter Eight

Monuments and Pilgrimage: Search for the Lost

...our gallant ship tugged at her chains as if impatient to bear her precious freight on its last journey.
— Anon.

On October 25, 1921, American major general Henry T. Allen stood beside a closed coffin draped in an American flag on a pier at Le Havre, France. In one long paragraph he seemed to summarize the reason for the war that had just passed, its place in the context of a larger history between two nations, and the underlying sentiment that would drive the memorials, reclamations and pilgrimages of the decade to follow:

> We of far away America, thrilled by the amazing stand of our ancient ally against the terrific onslaught in the early years of the Great War, recognized that the tenets of our constitution — even the very foundations of our political institutions — were threatened. The ruthless treatment of Belgium with an imminent repetition of the same acts on the soil of our time honored friendly Republic and the barbarities at sea, brought forth such a wave of indignation throughout the United States as to produce an hitherto unknown solidarity of sentiment and action. The spirit of this sleeping comrade dominated from the Golden Gate to the Atlantic seaboard and from the lakes to the Great Gulf. It accompanied and inspired not only the flower of our youth, who saw with clear vision their duty on the agonizing battle fronts, but it made possible the super efforts of fathers, mothers, sisters and brothers, who did the impossible at home that their blood might be victorious abroad.

Gen. Allen then turned to address the casket that was about to be carried aboard the USS *Olympia*: "Whoever you be, your gallant deeds are indelibly inscribed in the pages of history to the glory of your nation, and as long as these free states endure will your exploits be sung. In leaving hospitable France, who has so fondly cherished you, another voyage is prepared and further honors await you in the land of your birth."

This was the Unknown Soldier, continuing on a journey that had begun four days earlier. On October 21, four unknowns had been disinterred, one each from the cemeteries at Aisne-Marne, Meuse-Argonne, Somme, and St. Mihiel and brought to the Hotel de Ville at Chalons sur Marne. There, and in Paris, all records that linked each coffin to its original interment were destroyed, making each even further unknown as to battle or resting place. The identical caskets were placed in a room with the flags of the United States and France between each. As a French band played a hymn, Sgt. Edward F. Younger, chosen for the task because of his uncommon valor in the war, entered the room and walked among the caskets. By whatever instinct given him, he lay a spray of French roses on one of them and came to attention.

The other three caskets were taken for burial at the Meuse-Argonne cemetery as graves 1, 2 and 3, Row 1, Block G. The casket of the Unknown was moved under heavy ceremony to the train station and carried to Le Havre with the accompaniment of distinguished officers of the two countries. There, schoolchildren showered it with flowers as it traveled through streets described as twenty deep with cheering citizens. The drums and bugles of the 129th Infantry of France led the way, playing funeral dirges by Chopin and Mendelssohn. Eight American sergeants, including Sgt. Younger, accompanied the casket. The parade continued with French troops, carrying their arms reversed, and a platoon of French orphans of war, each carrying a single flower. At the pier, by one description, "The cruiser Olympia, with the American flags at half-mast and the French flag hoisted half-way up the foremast, was anchored between her escorting ships. All steam was up; our gallant ship tugged at her chains as if impatient to bear her precious freight on its last journey."[1]

That same account by an unnamed writer, found in the archives of the U.S. Army Quartermaster Foundation, returned the Unknown home with the same imagery. "Safely the blue Atlantic bore him across its broad bosom and then the placid Potomac received him as the Olympia steamed up past Mount Vernon, George Washington's home, to the Nation's Capital, which bears the name of the First Great American. There, under the white dome of the lofty Capitol, the chosen here lay in state while the people paid him silent homage until Armistice Day, November 11, 1921, the time set for the last ceremonies and farewells."

On Armistice Day, a procession that seemed to include all of elected and military Washington, and including Pres. Warren G. Harding walking alone, delivered the Unknown to a sarcophagus at the Memorial Arch in Arlington National Cemetery. Ten years of minor turmoil would follow. And it would reflect the questions about the rights and ownership of the dead that derived from the questions of where they should lie.

The placing of the Unknown Soldier at Arlington on November 11 was intended by Pres. Harding as the opening event in the nine-nation Conference on the Limitation of Armaments, also known as the Washington Naval Conference, which would begin the following day. The event, said the president in an opening speech, was "not the conference of victors to define the terms of settlement. Nor is it a council of nations seeking to remake mankind. It is rather a coming together from all parts of the earth, to apply the better attributes of mankind to minimize the faults in our international relationships."[2]

The interment of the Unknown Soldier on the preceding day would become popular with the public, and a discussion had begun about how to make the tomb more representative of its underlying sentiments. Pres. Wilson had predicted that World War I would be the "war to end all wars," but some were thinking ahead to future wars, and the effect the Tomb might have on those wars. An internal memo of the Military Intelligence Division of War Department, dated December 11, 1923, and addressed to "The Chief of Staff," sought to open up a tricky question, excerpted:

The problem presented.
How can the Tomb of the Unknown Soldier be made more an inspiration of patriotism rather than sadness.

Facts bearing upon the problem.

1. The burial of the Unknown Soldier and the Conference on Limitation of Armaments were so closely connected in thought and time that they since have not been disassociated by the public. Unless steps are taken to counteract this impression, the Unknown Soldier will continue to personify a policy of disarmament to avoid the cost and sacrifices of war.

2. On the two Armistice Days which have followed the burial, the president, accompanied by the secretary of war and the secretary of the navy, has placed a wreath upon the tomb without a spoken word. Patriotic, Veteran, and other associations, meeting in the National Capitol, have followed this practice. Pictures of these ceremonies have conveyed the idea of mourning rather than patriotism. As a result, Armistice Day, tends to become a second Memorial Day in which the Unknown Soldier typifies regrets rather than glorious achievement.[3]

The memo went on to note that clergymen were now using the Unknown Soldier "as the text for idealistic peace sermons or as the basis for advocating some form of internationalism," and suggested that previous discussions about the building of a more substantial tomb be advanced by a formal appeal from the secretary of war to the artists of America to engage in a competition to design the current tomb into "a permanent National Shrine which would reflect credit upon the War Department and be an inspiration to the public." Whatever the motivation for the creation of such a shrine based on an unknown American soldier brought home from France, the path toward its eventual completion in 1932 would be tortuous.

When Edward Pigue decided to leave his son in Belgium in 1921, he could not know that James would fall under the care of an institution with origins in the Hotel Valitanoise in Passy, France, during the American Revolutionary War. As the disposition of American bodies that would remain in Europe after World War I fell into a structured process with developing cemeteries, another need presented itself. Those who would rest in European soil, whether in the American cemeteries or non–American cemeteries, like James Pigue, would not have family nearby to tend to their graves and conduct the ceremonies of death and memorial. The administration of the American cemeteries could not take on those individual responsibilities beyond burial and grounds keeping, to say nothing of attention to those individuals buried elsewhere.

One December Sunday in 1777, at 3:00 P.M., the American ambassador to France, Benjamin Franklin, called a few of his countrymen to dinner at his hotel. The weather that day was described as sunny and bracing and the dinner as sumptuous, lubricated by an array of Franklin's favorite French wines and champagnes. But the mood was not good. Franklin intended the meal to be the first of weekly gatherings of Americans in Paris to share fellowship and keep up spirits during the early discouraging years of the American Revolution. The Sunday dinners continued, and after the French Revolution they were maintained by other ambassadors and officials, giving birth to what would become the American Club of Paris.[4]

During World War I, the club, and its regular luncheons, served a necessary social function as a meeting place of the leading citizens of two countries allied in war. After the war, and in the following occupation of Germany, the mix of Americans and Europeans was intense in the cities, where the formation of "American Clubs" became essential, particularly in Antwerp and Brussels where they were formed in 1920 and 1921. The Paris club was a model, and in 1920 it was a parent, along with other American groups in Paris, of the birth of the American Overseas Memorial Day Association (AOMDA). A sketchier history exists of an AOMDA in London in the 1920s. It was led by the U.S. ambassador to England, Alanson Houghton, with a stated mission of "decoration of soldiers' graves in France, Belgium and England."[5] By 1929, the geographic reach of the mission was changed to "Great Britain and Ireland," presumably focused solely on the Brookwood American Cemetery and graves that may still have existed in Ireland.[6]

The American Memorial Day holiday was an important event in European life at the time, as it would remain into the 21st century. AOMDA-France, with assistance from the Graves Registration Service, took on the job of staging Memorial Day Services in the American cemeteries of that country. In 1923, AOMDA in Belgium took the step of moving the focus of an American Memorial Day observance from a church service in Brussels to the Flanders Field cemetery near Waregem. The Memorial Day ceremony at Flanders Field included about 350 Americans, but on the following Sunday, a larger, spontaneous, celebration among Americans and Belgians came together at the cemetery. Out of that experience, the American Club of Brussels instituted the collection of ten dollars from every American living in the vicinity of Brussels to create a perpetual fund for use by AOMDA-Belgium to memorialize the graves of 368 Americans buried in its soil.

As the decade proceeded, the events at Flanders Field seemed to take on more importance even as the war receded in memory. In 1927, the nation's most prominent architects were asked to submit proposals for the design of Flanders Field and its chapel, and the job went to the French-American architect Paul Phillipe Cret. Cret had come to the United States in 1903; but he had served in the French army during the war and had been awarded the Croix de Guerre. As an architect and designer in America, his imprint was placed on all aspects of the country's design environment over a forty-year career. It started with the (now) Organization of American States building in Washington, continued through the Folger Shakespeare Library in that city, to the Union Terminal at Cincinnati and the tower of the Main Building of the University of Texas at Austin. His work included countless bridges, government buildings and memorials, culminating in the design of the passenger cars of the Santa Fe Railroad's *Super Chief* in 1936.

Flanders Field would be a small cemetery of six acres, its headstones laid out in four symmetrical areas surrounding the chapel at its center. The annual ceremonies of memorial were to take place on the Sunday closest to each American Memorial Day. In 1927, however, that schedule was opened up to reflect the result of an extraordinary world event. The American aviator Charles Lindbergh had completed the first solo flight across the Atlantic Ocean with his landing in Paris on May 21. After days of celebration in France, Lindbergh flew to Belgium by invitation of the American Club of Brussels. While he was in the country, the usual Sunday afternoon Memorial Day ceremony took place at Flanders Field. But as Lindbergh flew to London on the true Memorial Day the following day, a larger crowd assembled at Flanders Field. Timed to the ceremony, Lindbergh diverted the *Spirit of St. Louis* from the route to London and dropped a large bouquet of flowers among the white crosses.

The creation of the American Battle Monuments Commission set a line of division between those Americans military buried abroad who would fall under the protection of the government and those who would not. Though it was set up to administer the cemeteries of World War I, it also took in the 1851 cemetery in Mexico City and its 750 anonymous residents of a common grave. If the previous cemeteries and burial places of Americans in England, Canada, Libya and Spain were known, they were perhaps deemed of a less important era.

The Americans in Mexico had not been forgotten, however. In 1897, the *New York Times* reported on an observation of the American Memorial Day in Mexico City. It was initiated by American residents and diplomatic officials, with the full support of the Mexican government, and Mexican military officials decorated the American graves.[7] Three years later, the first recorded effort to recover American bodies buried abroad took place in Buena Vista, Mexico.

Charles Lindbergh flies the *Spirit of St. Louis* over Flanders Field and drops a bouquet of flowers on May 30, 1927 (*American Overseas Memorial Day Association–Belgium*).

After American success in the Battle of Buena Vista on February 23, 1847, the need to move on quickly had allowed only a minimal cemetery to be built for American casualties. By 1900, that part of Mexico near Saltillo had become home to an American colony of a sort, and increasing American interest in the region had led to a discovery of a cemetery that had almost been lost. It was described by the *New York Times* on July 16, 1900:

> It is situated at the foot of a narrow and dirty street, lined with Mexican jacales, which is transformed into a well traveled road just before the cemetery is reached.... There is not a particle of vegetation on the cemetery plot. The graves of the dead heroes of fifty-four years ago were shallow, and in many years of absolute neglect that have passed over them, many of the bones have found their way to the surface and the ground is literally strewn with them. Femur, thigh and other bones are protruding from the ground in all parts of the cemetery, and it will be a difficult matter for the contractor to exhume and transfer the remains in anything like complete condition.[8]

An arroyo, or gulley, that originally formed a boundary of the cemetery had since changed course into the cemetery itself, washing away bones and bringing skulls to the surface, some of which had been taken as souvenirs by the surrounding residents. An original plan to invest in the improvement and beautification of the place was finally deemed impractical by the U.S. Congress, and the bones were removed to what would become the San Antonio National Cemetery.

In 1925, the U.S. Army returned its attention to the Punitive Expedition to Mexico that had preceded American involvement in World War I. Though its leader, Gen. John Pershing, believed postwar that American bodies should lie where they had fallen, the War Department authorized a second expedition, this one to find and retrieve the bodies of eight who were killed in 1916. Among those to be found were Pvt. Hobert Ledford and Sgt. Jay Richley.

Hobert Ledford was described as a gentle man who had taken on a small, white dog as a sidekick while riding his horse toward what would become a major battle at Parral in Chihuahua state. As troop M of the Thirteenth Cavalry was met by an angry mob and nervous soldiers fearing an American occupation of the town, Ledford was shot through the chest and fell from his horse. He implored his comrades to press on without him, but was quickly killed with a second shot.[9]

In the same encounter, Sgt. Jay Richley of Detroit, Michigan, was riding with Maj. Frank Tompkins. On April 12, 1916, a bullet intended for Tompkins missed its target and passed through Richley instead. He fell dead immediately, but his body, and that of Hobert Ledford, could not be retrieved in the rush of a retreat to a ranch at Santa Cruz de Villegas.[10] A truce of sorts was declared between the two sides, and under its cover a small platoon returned two miles into the path of the retreat. There they found a small, white dog guarding the body of Ledford; they returned to Santa Cruz with both safely in tow. Also under the truce, the body of Sgt. Richley was returned by the Mexicans in a coffin. At dusk on April 13, Ledford was wrapped in a blanket and laid to rest in the ranch cemetery at Santa Cruz. Psalm 23 and the Lord's Prayer were recited as the sun disappeared in the west, and taps was played. The following evening, Richley was buried in his Mexican coffin with similar ceremony.[11]

Thirteen years later, the expedition of reclamation that set out to Chihuahua from Fort Bliss, Texas, was able to recover six of the eight bodies it sought. They were returned to families in Rhode Island, Maine, New York and Texas and to the national cemeteries in Chattanooga and San Antonio. Hobert Ledford and Jay Richley were left behind in the ranch cemetery of the Villegas family, as per the wishes of their families. Richley's parents had preceded him in death, and it was the decision of his brother and sister to leave him where he lay.[12]

By the end of 1924, the status of the Tomb of the Unknown Soldier at Arlington Cemetery was still muddled as to its purpose and design. On July 31, 1923, an internal letter had passed within the War Department from H.C. Bonnycastle, quartermaster supply officer, to QM Gen. William H. Hart. Bonnycastle had been a colonel in the army and a veteran of the Spanish-American War and the Pershing expedition to Mexico in 1916. The tone of his letter was direct:

1. Your attention is invited to the apparently unfinished condition of the Tomb of the Unknown Soldier in Arlington National Cemetery, also to the fact that though nearly two years have elapsed since its formal dedication there is nothing to indicate that it is the Tomb of the Unknown Soldier, except a small neat sign bearing the words "tomb of the Unknown Soldier" placed in front of this national shrine, by this office.

2. This sign owes its existence to the fact that visitors upon being accused of sitting on the Tomb, became indignant and claimed immunity from blame because there was nothing to indicate where the remains of the Unknown Soldier had been placed. This sign, as is known to your office through at least one complaint, is subject to criticism by the public and is merely temporary.

Points 3 through 7 of the letter strongly urged the completion of a design and an attempt to get the Congress to overcome a reluctance to fund its implementation, or, failing all of that, the creation of a stopgap design to better demark the Tomb as a shrine worthy of respect, rather than a place to sit.[13]

The problem was compounded by a dispute between the War Department and the architect Thomas Hastings. Hastings had put an imprint on American architecture that would be enduring. His work included the New York Public Library, the Frick Mansion and Museum in New York, the Jefferson Hotel in Richmond, the Russell Senate Office building in Washington, hotels in Florida, mansions on Long Island and theatres on Broadway. He was also the architect of the Memorial Amphitheater, setting for the Tomb of the Unknown Soldier, at Arlington Cemetery. He was often incorrectly noted as the architect of the Tomb itself, but he was not, and that was a problem for him.

Hastings apparently believed that, following his design of the Memorial Amphitheater, his work was to continue on to the finalization of the Tomb of the Unknown Soldier. He was supported in the assumption by an acceptance of his plans by the federal Fine Arts Commission. But the War Department had another view. Though his design for the base of the Tomb had been used, with the result that visitors confused it for a resting place, there was no inclination by the War Department to continue the relationship. On February 1, 1924, the *Washington Star* reported that department secretary John Weeks had rejected the Hastings plan for a final design that seemed to go against the tone of eloquent simplicity to be found in the cemeteries and memorials that had developed in previous years. "It consisted," he wrote, "of a shaft about thirty-five feet high rising from the top of the tomb. It was decorated with several carved symbolic figures near the apex and inscribed with tributes to the unknown hero on the sides. It is understood that Secretary Weeks and his associates have suggested a smaller and less elaborate memorial."[14]

Charles Hastings seemed to restrain himself for a few months before composing a letter to Secretary Weeks, dated November 17, 1924. If it did not demand reconsideration, it did demand payment for work already done:

> While I fully appreciate your conscientious feeling or objection in the matter, at the same time realizing your sense of justice, I would like to remind you of the fact that those in authority at the time requested me to make designs of the monument....
>
> I quite realize that differences of opinion exist in matters of taste and the sense of fitness of things architecturally but it is difficult to know what to do when the point of view that a layman may take in a matter of this character is so completely different from what was authorized and now partly executed in place. It hardly seems right that we should stand for the expense of this undertaking....[15]

The Secretary responded on December 15, 1924, in a letter not couched in the language of conciliation. "[T]he following results of an investigation of this matter are given: There is no record of any contract between you and the War Department engaging, for compensation, your services for any of the work in connection with the plank for the sarcophagus of the unknown soldier. It does appear that a part of your plans were utilized by the War Department in the construction of the base." Weeks pointed out that the appropriation period for paying for that work had long since passed, and, the bill not having been submitted, there was no longer an obligation to pay it.[16]

The unresolved nature of the Tomb continued, but two years later, the notion of simplicity was given a forum in two deliberations by Congress. They seemed to bring together a full range of human sensibilities toward war dead in an attempt to determine a particularly American sensibility. At that time, an ornate Hastings type of design for a towering monument was still favored by some, but the army, now joined by the navy, still objected to it. Under consideration were resolutions directing that the secretary of war be authorized to complete the Tomb with the erection of "a suitable monument, together with such inclosure as may be deemed necessary, and a sum not to exceed $50,000 is hereby authorized to be appropriated for this purpose."[17]

The paraphrased and excerpted conversation followed this progression in the House on March 15, 1926.

Representative Thomas Blanton of Texas (thought that the thing that appealed most to the American people about the current version of the Tomb was its simplicity):

> I do not believe if you were to spend $500,000,000 you could build a monument more appropriate to our unknown dead than the one that exists there.... What is the use of spending $50,000 more? It is complete now. Will we add anything to the luster of the service of our dead in France, in whose memory this single monument is now a fitting memorial. I think not. I think that just as it stands now it does honor our unknown dead [Applause].

Representative Martin Barnaby Madden of Illinois:

> When I went over to England, in walking through Westminster Abbey, what did I find? I found the English Unknown Soldier buried under the floor of Westminster Abbey with a simple slab over his burial place. What do you find in France? You find the Unknown Soldier buried there at the foot of the Arc de Triomphe without any other monument than the Arc de Triomphe. What greater monument could be erected to the dead of the great World War than the mere fact that he died for the preservation of his country? [Applause].

Others:

> The unknown soldier of Belgium lies at the foot of a monument on the bank of a river, no monument erected to him.
>
> The unknown soldier of Italy lies at the foot of the steps of the Victor Emanuel Monument in Rome.

Representative Robert Luce of Massachusetts, and others:

> MR. LUCE: I am told that only two or three weeks ago, when there was a convention of men of the greater part of whom we would expect greater consideration and from nearly all of whom we would get greater consideration than this incident would indicate, nevertheless one among their number stood his little daughter on the tomb and tried to take a photograph of her standing there.... I am also told that it is no infrequent thing for thoughtless young people, who have not yet learned the conventions of life, who do not understand their dignity and solemnity in such matters as this, to seat themselves irreverently on the tomb.
> MR. BLANTON: Does the gentleman know that that is true?
> MR. LUCE: I am told by those who are stationed there.
> MR. BLANTON: Why do they not stop it?
> MR. HILL [of Maryland]: Why do they not attend to their business and stop it?
> MR. BLANTON: If they are stationed there they surely could not be attending to their business if they do not stop such things.[18]

Ten days later, orders emerged from the War Department directing the placement of an armed military guard at the Tomb during daylight hours. It was noted that too many people were using it as a picnic table.

Discussion in the Senate took place on June 7, 1926. Secretary of war Dwight F. Davis took part by letter to the Senate: "The War Department continues to be opposed to a shaft or monument not in keeping with the surroundings of the cemetery." Perhaps a design competition among the nation's leading artists was in order. Senator Joseph Taylor Robinson of Arkansas hoped that whatever the monument, it "suitably and effectively typify the courage, the daring, the splendid sacrifice that characterized and marked the services of the men who bore our arms to victory in the great World War."

Senator Clarence Dill of Washington State noted that a line of trees had been planted on a highway near Seattle, each of them to represent a named soldier and one of them to represent an unknown: "I shall not at this time attempt to discuss the propriety of having memorial trees, other than to say that there is nothing more appropriate as a memorial than a growing tree, for trees are the oldest and biggest living organisms on this earth today." He then quoted from a speech given at the dedication of the Memorial Highway by retired Washington State supreme court justice Stephen J. Chadwick. The Unknown Soldier represented by a tree was:

> The child of a mother, who quickened in a mother's womb, had love even before he had birth. / He was a boy trusting a mother's arms; he walked; he talked; he was a boy. / He loved all the things a boy loves — the mountains, the streams, the valleys; he played Indian; he dug caves; he enjoyed life. / And racing down the years to meet him came manhood, the fruition of a mother's dreams when her child should assume his place in the destiny of his mortal sphere. / He stepped forward to meet it, loving life as much as you or I. This much we know. / And now we speculate.
>
> Did he in 1917 still have and love that mother, or had she gone on before? / Did he have a sweetheart or perhaps a new young wife? / He might have been a father — who knows; he was the unknown soldier. / His country called in a great war. Loving life, I say, as you and I, he answered to his country's call. Casting his hopes, his plans, his ambitions for the future — yes; his life — in the balance to be weighed with all in America's cause, he answered the call of duty.[19]

A resolution was passed on July 3, 1926 authorizing a commission to conduct a competition among architects for a design that would complete the Tomb of the Unknown Soldier. The

War mothers observe Mother's Day at the Tomb of the Unknown Soldier at Arlington National Cemetery on May 9, 1937. The services involving families from all parts of the country were an annual event of the group American War Mothers, founded in 1917 to support the personnel and families of all who served in the U.S. military (*Library of Congress*).

methods and criteria for choosing the winning design were immediately criticized and picked over by competing interests, but the plan was able to go forth.

During those same years in France, another monument was under development, and there was no disagreement over the purpose of its design.

When Charles Wesley Chapman of Dubuque, Iowa, fell from the sky during his service in the Lafayette Flying Corps on May 3, 1918, he was buried by the Germans behind their lines, near the village of Remoncourt.

After the war, an American member of the Flying Corps, Edgar Guerard Hamilton, was engaged by the Allies in the search for the scattered bodies of American aviators. In the course of that work he convinced American and French public and private officials of the need for a memorial in honor of the Lafayette fliers who had sacrificed their lives for France. Eventually, the American lawyer and philanthropist William Nelson Cromwell took up the cause. (Cromwell had been controversially involved in the building of the Panama Canal. The first plans for a Central American canal from the Atlantic to the Pacific had been focused on Nicaragua, where a longer canal would be more easily accommodated by less difficult engineering through the presence of two large lakes. In 1902, the House of Representatives approved a Nicaraguan canal. Cromwell was hired as a lobbyist by those, including J.P. Morgan, who had an interest in the building of the canal in Panama. By August, the Senate had rejected the House bill and voted to fund a Panamanian project. Cromwell's tactics were not seen as completely aboveboard, but he received $800,000 for the work.[20])

On February 27, 1926, a model of a memorial to American flyers of the Escadrille was unveiled at St. Cloud, outside of Paris. "They gave a great example to the world, lighting in America the flame of that just crusade," declared French marshall Ferdinand Foch. American ambassador Myron Herrick spoke of the foreign volunteers who had figured heavily in American wars of the past, and now many American boys "are going to lie here in France, always an inspiration for the youth of France." William Nelson Cromwell promised financial support of the monument in perpetuity: "The memorial will give undying testimony in the coming years to the brotherhood of America and France in the days of battle as in times of peace."[21]

The monument would be 75 feet high — visible from Paris — and 250 feet wide on eleven acres of forest donated by France halfway between Paris and Versailles. It would contain the bodies of the dead American flyers in a sunlit crypt that would be, appropriately, open to the sky. "I have not made a funeral monument," said Alexandre Marcel, the French government's chief architect. "There are too many such already; too many reminders of death. I have made, rather, an expression of the beauty and high adventure in which the men of the Escadrille Lafayette lived, and a memorial to the glory, above all the victory, which they won."[22]

The monument comprised planned crypts for 68 American men killed in France, though not all would be filled. By mid 1928, 48 bodies, including that of Charles Chapman, had been found in the cemeteries and isolated places of France, Belgium and Italy, and one had been returned from burial in the United States. The French government waived all passport and visa fees, steamship lines offered discounted fares, and by July 4, 300 American Escadrille flyers and their families were in place for a dedication ceremony. Visitors were led down stairs to a large semicircular crypt to find seventeen rows of four marble sarcophagi, the dead buried in the order in which they had died. On November 4, 1930, the fiftieth sarcophagus gave a final home to Wallace Charles Winter, of Chicago; his body had rested in the vault of the American Cathedral in Paris, the Church of the Holy Trinity. The Memorial Crypt was then sealed in a solemn ceremony.

In that year, the Lafayette Escadrille Memorial Foundation was formed by William Nelson Cromwell and endowed with one million dollars of his own money to assure the permanent upkeep of the memorial and the continuation of appropriate religious observances, and to educate the youth of France and America about their common history.

In the same year that the Escadrille Memorial was opened to accept the bodies of gallant airmen, an older cemetery for men of the sea was found to have been forgotten and in weeds. On September 15, 1928, VAdm. John H. Dayton, commander, Naval Forces Europe, set out from Norfolk, Virginia, on the USS *Raleigh*. The mission was to take the following year for diplomatic calls in the ports of European allies. One of its first stops after crossing the Atlantic was Port Mahon, Menorca, off the coast of Spain. By that time, after the visit by Kaiser Wilhelm in 1904 and the ensuing ravages of World War I, the cemetery there was mostly a rumor in naval lore, and Dayton determined to see it for himself.

Nobody seemed to own it, much less to have authority over its care. The British vice-consul in Port Mahon had attempted to gain that authority by default, but the passing years had further obscured its origins. The U.S. Navy continued to operate in its culture of looking forward rather than backward into its own history. Shown the cemetery by the vice-consul, Dayton found the graves dilapidated, their inscriptions fading away and irretrievable as wind, rain and sun broke down the stone. Dayton directed his aides to transcribe those inscriptions that could still be read.

The visit appeared to be just in the nick of time. The inscriptions that remained were saved for history. Dayton learned that the municipal authority was beginning to talk about taking over the land for other uses and removing the bones of the dead to a common ossuary, and he vowed that the American government would step up to its obligations. The vow was supported by German and English interests that still watched over the remains of their nationals in the cemetery. A future written history of the cemetery, however, would record no results of the vow and would describe the graveyard in 1933 as in total disrepair. The British consul set upon a fundraising course toward rehabilitation, but it was put aside with the outbreak of the Spanish Civil War in 1936. The elements would continue to take their toll.

One evening in April 1816, in Norfolk, Virginia, Stephen Decatur, naval hero of the Tripolitan and 1812 wars, held forth at a dinner party in his honor and raised his glass in a toast that would echo through the following centuries in one form or another: "Our country! In her intercourse with foreign nations, may she always be in the right, and always successful, right or wrong."

It was in the conscious spirit of that sentiment that Michael Macalla found himself in the outskirts of Kadish, Russia, near the edge of the Arctic Ocean on August 22, 1930. Macalla had been there before as part of the ill-fated Polar Bear Expedition of 1918–1919. His task now was to unbury the dead. He had been in the precincts of death before. As a sergeant on March 16, 1919, he had arrived in Gabach, Russia, with his comrade, Sgt. Edward Young. Young had been wounded in previous action at Karpogora, and the wounds would not properly heal. As Macalla slept, Young shot himself to death with his service revolver. It fell to Macalla to get his corpse to distant Archangel, and he set out in a sleigh through subfreezing temperatures. When Young's body froze, he wrapped it in blankets to shield it from view. On the second night of his journey he was given refuge in a barn, but the sleigh, horse and corpse were required to spend the night outside. On the third night he was given refuge in a village morgue and slept between Young and the cadaver of a villager. On the fourth night, he became disoriented in a snowstorm and, fatigued, could only find refuge beneath a tree. He removed the blankets from Young's corpse with mumbled apologies to his friend and burrowed into them as a matter of survival. On the fifth day he delivered the body to medical offices in Archangel.[23]

Now on a warm summer day outside of Kadish eleven years later, he was searching for the grave of 2nd Lt. Clifford Ballard of Cambridge, Massachusetts, killed in action on February 7, 1919. Ballard was believed to have been buried with five others on a road just north of Kadish. Macalla noted the following in his diary:

> This Russky told us that the people around Kadish complained about finding six bodies on a path which they used often. The bodies were laying out in the open for nearly two years after [ ] left the vicinity and were pretty much nearly decayed except for bones. After many complaints to the military officer of that village ... he ordered this same Russky who gave us the info to go and bury them. He said that there were no means of identification because there were nothing left but bones. They had no clothes no tags nor anything. We decided that it was useless to try. Same Russky that took us around trenches while looking for Ballard told us of seeing two crosses in about the spot that our records show Ozdarski [Joseph S. of Detroit] and Christian [Arthur D. of Atlanta, MI] were buried.[24]

The 1930 search for the bodies of Ozdarski and Christian, and approximately 100 others left behind after the Polar Bear Expedition was the result of an anger about the expedition that would not die among the people of Michigan, particularly the people of Detroit. It was still seen as an unnecessary sacrifice by their sons, brothers and husbands, and the desire lingered through the 1920s to try to right the wrong, if only by trying to bring the dead home. The Polar Bear Association had been formed in 1922 with precisely that main objective. It took seven years of political maneuvering in the United States and Soviet Union, but in 1929 a commission of five former Polar Bears set out on a second expedition to Russia underwritten by state and federal funding.

The second journey was almost as treacherous as the first. Armed with crude maps, assorted notes and various surmises, the Michigan Commission met in Bremen, Germany, in July 1929 with a representative of the Veterans of Foreign Wars and members of the Graves Registration Service detailed to do the exhumation and identification work of the mission. Michael Macalla and Polar Bear Association president Walter Dundon went on ahead of the group. They flew uneventfully to Koenigsburg, where they changed to a small Russian plane that ran out of fuel near Smolensk. After landing in a grove nowhere near a military airfield, they were kept imprisoned in the plane under intense questioning from military and civilian officials. Finally allowed to proceed, they arrived in Moscow and waited through five days devoted to the cutting of red tape. Then they rode for five days on a broken-down train to Archangel, where ten more days were spent on red tape. Other members of the group set out from Archangel on the Dvina River where their small government cabin cruiser was rammed by a freighter in the middle of the night. The boat sank immediately and its passengers had to swim for their lives in their pajamas. The freighter picked them up, but the government demanded reparations for its lost cabin cruiser before the commission could leave the Archangel area in search of the lost graves.

"We have done everything humanly possible," wrote Macalla in his diary, but Joseph Ozdarski and Arthur Christian could not be found as the exploration continued. In his own diary, Walter Dundon asked a question of no one in particular at 9:44 P.M. on September 23: "Did you ever hike through a swamp in a strange country at midnight in rain and dark as hell. (Sept 24 Tues) up and off at 7A hiked to [ ] arr at 9:40 to find two crosses 3 [ ] So. of Permilova think they are French but am having one opened. Last night at Permilova was quite exciting about 200 inhabitants, saw mill burnt down, man murdered his wife."

The experience for Dundon and Macalla, and others on the expedition, was one of muck and mire, freezing rain, long hikes in wrong directions, unfriendly villagers, bad food, and fruitless digging. They met with unwillingness by some Russians to give up the dead. In one case, the cooperating Russian government had to threaten to blow up a small town to gain access to a grave. In another, a Russian nurse who had fallen in love with one of the soldiers while caring for him before his death first tried to misguide them, then pleaded with the searchers to leave him where he lay. Remains of 84 Americans were found in various stages of decomposition, some completely down to the bone. Positive identification could be made of all except two who were identified as American by their uniforms.

Seventy-five of the reclaimed were returned to America on the SS *President Roosevelt*, arriving in New York harbor in cold and blustery December weather described in *Time Magazine* as "a balmy breeze ... compared to the blasts of the North Russian winter of 1918–19 when these U.S. soldiers died fighting the Red Army." The same Hoboken piers that had welcomed home the dead of previous wars echoed the sounds of military ceremony, but, ten years after the fact, there were no crowds or congressional delegations. Some of the returned were sent home to families for private burial around the country, and the rest traveled to Detroit where they were welcomed during the throes of a blizzard by the governor of Michigan and a state funeral. In a summary of the Expedition of 1929, Michael Macalla described the end of their journey.

> Fifty-four were buried in a donated plot known as the Polar Bear Plot in White Chapel Memorial Cemetery, located in Troy, Michigan, at east Long Lake and Crooks Road. The remains lie buried around the beautiful Polar Bear Monument, the base of which is black granite mounted by a beautifully carved polar bear in white marble. On the base is a plaque on which these famous words of Stephen Decatur are inscribed: "Our country in her intercourse with foreign nation, may she always be right, but our country, Right or Wrong."

A wreath is laid at the Polar Bear Memorial at White Chapel Memorial Cemetery in Troy, Michigan, on Memorial Day 1930 (*Bentley Historical Library, University of Michigan*).

In 1934, twelve more of the dead were returned from Leningrad after American recognition of the Bolshevik government. They were met in New York by a contingent of officials from Detroit and returned to Michigan on a special train. After ceremonies in front of Detroit city hall, they were taken to join their comrades at White Chapel Cemetery. But the matter of the reclamation of all those killed in the fateful expedition to Archangel, Russia, was by no means closed.

On the evening of April 15, 1930, the quartermaster general, Maj. Gen. J.L. Dewitt, stood before an audience of his staff at the Pennsylvania Hotel in New York City and delivered a stern lecture about the practice of compassion. DeWitt was a veteran of the Punitive Expedition to Mexico and had risen through quartermaster ranks during World War I. In World War II, he would become the instigator and administrator of the move to strip 116,000 Japanese-Americans of their property and constitutional rights as they were moved to internment camps.

One of the results of the policy of asking families whether they wished their loved ones to be brought home or left where they lay was that thousands of families would never have the resources to visit their graves in Europe. In 1929, Congress enacted legislation directing the War Department to create a series of pilgrimages that would take Gold Star — so called because of the gold stars that hung in the windows of their homes — Mothers on tours to the cemeteries where their sons and husbands lay at rest. It was a plan that was grand in scope and intricacy, and it had fallen to the quartermaster general to make it succeed. In his long speech to staff, DeWitt seemed both to summarize the family and social origins of American men who had fought and died in the war and to indulge in the kind of stereotyping that would direct his actions against Japanese-Americans after the attack on Pearl Harbor in 1941:

> You must remember that these women will be from all classes of society and will be just as true a cross section of the country as was the draft during the war. Some of them will be highly refined educated women, some of them will be illiterate. Some of them will not be able to speak English. Some of them will be absolutely poverty-stricken and will be dependent on you and the government to pay all of their expenses. Many of them cannot read or write. I know from correspondence we have received. Many of them will be invalids. The average is over 65. One is 88 and one is 91. They will have to be handled individually, carefully, courteously and will require constant attention. The majority of them will be in an environment in which they are utterly unfamiliar. Many of them are from small towns and farms. They will depend absolutely on you. Very few of them will be able to speak French. All in all, it will demand of you the most meticulous performance of duty and attention. You must consider the temper of the women and take that into consideration with the object of the pilgrimage, which does not tend to calm mental condition. Many of them will become hysterical, I have no doubt, upon the least provocation.

Eventually, the pilgrimages would extend to mothers and widows of those who were lost at sea and those whose bodies had never been found but were memorialized on the walls of American cemeteries. And they would attempt to overcome racial segregation among the mothers of the dead without complete success, but with interesting results in some cases. Of the estimated 18,000 women deemed eligible, just 7,000 would opt to join the pilgrimages over the years 1930–1933. They would be drawn, in the most part, from the ranks of the Gold Star Mothers.

When the United States entered World War I, George Vaughn Seibold of Washington, D.C., enlisted with the desire to serve in aviation. He was sent to Canada, where he was trained for the Royal Air Force, and then sent to France. When his regular letters home stopped, his mother, Grace, tried to find out why, but she could get no information from the British government. Hoping that his disappearance was only a bureaucratic problem, Grace spent her days visiting those who had returned as wounded to Washington hospitals. Then, without warning or notice, George Seibold's wife received a box of his effects in Chicago. He had been killed on August 26, 1918, shot down by German Fokkers just outside the British lines. The family did not receive official notification of his death until December, and his remains were never identified.

Grace Seibold continued her work with the wounded and formed an informal group of mothers in similar circumstances that grew to become the American Gold Star Mothers, named for the Gold Star that hung in the windows of homes of the fallen. The organization was incorporated in the District of Columbia in 1929. As groups of Gold Star mothers in other states and communities became aware of the Washington group, a national federation was formed. African American women were members of the Gold Star Mothers. However, in keeping with the racial sensibilities of the times, although it was the intent of Congress that "colored" women would be included in the pilgrimages, the journeys would be segregated. Fathers of the fallen were not deemed as important in the equation, not nurturers to the extent that women were, and so they were not included.

The United States Lines was chosen as the steamship company of the pilgrimages. The best hotels of Europe were reserved for the American women. The military and political brass of England, France and Belgium were prepared to receive them in great ceremonies at national shrines. Gen. Dewitt's warnings about proper treatment and respect for physical and emotional frailty were respected down the line.

The first pilgrimage set out from the same Hoboken piers that had seen the comings and goings of new soldiers and returned dead. Two hundred and thirty-one women had been brought to the city directly from their homes in towns and cities across the land and by Pullman cars to New York. On May 7, 1930, the SS *America* set off from Pier Four, crowded with well-wishers playing music and shooting streamers. Ships in the harbor blasted their horns, fireboats sprayed streams of arcing water and military planes flew overhead. The mothers — 100 of them in their sixties, and 30 in their seventies — were introduced to comfortable cabins and given specially designed medals produced by the United States Lines. (For the record, ship stewardess Erna Weidlich reported that the mothers required far less attention than her usual customers who expected special service.)[25] They were met with great ceremony at Cherbourg, France, on May 15, and were taken by special train to the Gare des Invalides in Paris. A second group of 300 mothers followed on the SS *Republic* to Southampton, where they were taken to London for visits to Brookwood Cemetery.

Each of the trips followed a set formula, using Cherbourg sailings as an example:

DAY ONE: Rest in Paris.
DAY TWO: Wreath laying on the French tomb of the Unknown Soldier. Reception with French war mothers, prominent officials and civilians.
DAY THREE: Travel by bus to relevant cemeteries.
DAYS FOUR THROUGH NINE: Traveling and sightseeing in the environs of a son's grave, including some battlefields.
DAYS TEN THROUGH FOURTEEN: Sightseeing and events in Paris.

There were occasional exceptions to the itinerary. One of the first trips, for example, included Cora Willis Ware of Chicago. Her son, Edward, had joined the American Field Service in 1917 and become an ambulance driver with the French army. Then he joined the [Herbert] Hoover Food Commission, which sought to alleviate famine among European children during the war years. The work took him to Bucharest, Romania, where he died of smallpox on May 7, 1919. Lauded by his peers as a man of unflinching character and broad generosity, he was buried with full honors in the military cemetery at Bucharest. Mrs. Ware was received in Romania by Queen Marie. Of a lineage that included King George V and Tsar Alexander II, the queen had become a Red Cross nurse during the war and engaged with the needs of her subjects in ways that were considered fearless.

Others in the scattered royalties of Europe enhanced the missions of the pilgrimages. The French Countess Constance of Caen had become known during the war as "The Little Mother of American Troops" for her efforts during the war to bring messages from men she had nursed in France to their mothers in America. In France, she gave small boxes of dirt taken from the gravesites of three men to mothers to take back to mothers in their communities who could not make the trip. Her cousin, the Countess of Freycinet, had paid particular attention to the 11,000 Native Americans who had fought in the war. She gave soil from Native American graves in France to a mother from Mayetta, Kansas, to be taken to the chief of the Kickapoo Indians there, who would in turn take it to the only Indian American Legion post, in Ponca, Oklahoma. Similar parcels were sent to the Sioux and the Blackfoot.

The pilgrimages were not as fraught with peril as QM Gen. DeWitt had predicted to his staff in New York. There were fewer cases of hysteria, illness and death than might be expected in a given number of older women. Other than the odd refusal by some to enter the Roman Catholic Notre Dame Cathedral in Paris, there were few cultural collisions. It was the story of the "Negro" mothers, however, that would resonate in the American experience of the years that would follow.

In May of 1930, a group of 52 such mothers and widows signed a petition to Pres. Herbert Hoover, demanding that their trips to Europe not be segregated. The National Asso-

A group of Gold Star Mothers arrives at the Suresnes American Cemetery in France on July 26, 1930 (*National Archives*).

EIGHT. *Monuments and Pilgrimage* 85

Mrs. Catherine Gorman stands at the grave of her son James Gorman at the Suresnes American Cemetery. Pfc. Gorman, of Illinois, was with the 59th Infantry Regiment, 4th Division, and was killed on December 31, 1918 (*National Archives*).

ciation for the Advancement of Colored People took up their cause. Black and white men had fallen together in battle, it was reasoned, and they were buried in the same cemeteries. Their bereaved families should be treated with the same equality. Nothing was changed by the protest. Whereas the first white mothers had traveled to France on the luxury liner SS *United States*, the first colored mothers arrived in France on the lesser SS *American Merchant*. Negro military officials and bands led the ceremonies at either end of their voyage. They were accommodated in lesser hotels. But the people of France did not have the American experience of racial separation, and they received the black women with friendliness and fascination, mixed in with a bit of stereotyping.

"A well known colored restaurateur of Paris," wrote the July 21 Paris edition of the *Chicago Tribune*, "reports that a special consignment of watermelons has been ordered from Algeria and that all the chicken yards about Paris have been decimated in order that these American mothers may not feel themselves too much in a foreign land." *Le Paris Matin* of July 22 described for its French readership a "stirring and strange ceremony" upon the arrival of the women at the Gare des Invalides:

> 55 women were there on the platform, with childish and tired faces, hesitating on that platform where everything seemed so strange to them.
> One by one, dressed in black or bright colors, they walked up the steep stair which leads to the esplanade. Some colored people handed them flowers, and all of a sudden a jazz band of colored musicians started to play the first notes of a moaning song. Then we saw that strange band, led by an enthusiastic man, start to play the American National Hymn and then the Marseillaise.
> Stirred, and amused at the same time, the mothers who came on that sad pilgrimage agitated their small flags.

It was a lengthy dispatch to America's black newspapers by Joel Augustus Rogers, however, that seemed to place the black mothers of World War I in the larger context of the world beyond America. Rogers was an intellectual force in the understanding of black history and the black experience of his era. He noted that, segregation aside, "to which we will be forever unreconciled," the effort of the government to give all war mothers and widows the experience of the pilgrimages was a magnificent gesture. But he believed that the black women had the better experience. The attention given to them by the greatest black singers and musicians of France, and with the enthusiasm of all Paris, had brought them to a new place in their lives. The trips were perhaps the first and last touches of luxury in the lives of many of the women, white and black:

> But to the colored women it has meant something more. It has given them their first real taste of freedom. Many of them are seeing in reality what they had undoubtedly felt; that human beings, so far as color is concerned, can live in the same hotels, eat in the same restaurants, travel in the same conveyances, and get along when they will with the same tranquility as the colored and the white dead lying side by side in the cemeteries they visited.[26]

Chapter Nine

Scattered from the Sky

We would have done anything for them — even given up our lives — that wasn't too high a price.

—Andree de Jongh

"I thought of myself as the discoverer of a hidden secret, a secret of heroic death," wrote Mustapha Burchis of his frame of mind in May 1938. "I dreamed that the American government would take me to America, and I would be a great man. America was a dream to me, a dream of wealth and freedom, and now I had my big chance of having it come true."[1]

From an old Moslem Family, Burchis had fought against Italian colonization of Libya as a young man, and been put to work as a prisoner in the harbor at Tripoli. In better years, he rose to become harbormaster of the port and marshal of all who were employed by the Italian government through the Tripoli Port Authorities. He had no formal education, but he was smart and fluent in Arabic and Italian. In 1938, his dream of America was brought to life by the curiosity of the naval historian and American Pres. Franklin Delano Roosevelt. In March of that year, for a reason that was not immediately apparent, Roosevelt ordered the State Department to cable the American embassy in Rome. "Any reasonable means available" were to be used to find the graves of the first named Americans to be buried abroad in combat, Richard Somers and his crew of the USS *Intrepid*, left behind in Tripoli after the failed attempt to blow up the warships of the harbor in 1804. Mustapha Burchis was deemed the best man available and was offered the job.

"I discussed the problem with my family, relatives and friends. They all thought that I was crazy, and asked the same question, 'How can you find the graves of people who died and were buried in 1805 [sic]?' 'Yes, how?' I asked myself, and I had no answer. However, against everyone's advice I decided to take a chance and try." His wife, however, perhaps in her own dreams of America, supported him fully.

Over nearly 135 years, the story of the *Intrepid* and its men had disappeared into the tides and sands of Libyan history. Burchis knew nothing about the subject, but he was dogged. His research started in the libraries and went into the private collections of princes and pashas, municipal records, the memories of stories heard by wise old Bedouins, and then to the records of the dead held by the Christian churches of the city. "During this time," wrote Burchis, "the brothers told me about Christianity and its greatness and way of life, trying to convert me to their religion. It was the first time I had heard about the infidel's religion. I admired it and saw how near it was to ours because we also believed in one God and a moral life. The differences, I thought, were not important and I remained a good Moslem."

His research continued in Italian and Arabic newspapers and into the remembrances of stories heard in Egypt by a well-traveled sheik that American sailors might be buried in the English Cemetery on the eastern shore of the harbor. The British consulate could offer no help, but the suggestion was made that the answers might be learned from the historians of Benghazi, three hundred miles to the east. It would be an expensive journey and his wife sold her jewels to finance the trip, which only took him to more old stories. Back in Tripoli, he was led to the elders of the Jewish community who had heard stories of bodies buried on the beaches of the eastern shore. Birchus determined that he would find his answers in the street folklore of the city and began to spend his afternoons sipping tea and smoking in the traditional gathering places for socializing and the telling of old stories. A hundred-year-old man recounted his father's stories about the harbor explosions and city fires of 1804. The old man told him that many American sailors were killed and were buried where they lay on the eastern shore of the harbor. He gave him introduction into the elder Jewish community where the currency of friendship was the telling of fortunes and old stories, from which emerged more old men telling their fathers' stories.

Birchus was finally led to the conclusion that the bodies were indeed buried in the Old British Cemetery. He learned that the cemetery had been started in 1830 with the burial of the wife of the British consul of the time, it being chosen because of the belief that there were already five Christian burials there from the beginning of the century. With the woman's burial, the cemetery was walled off, to be maintained as a Protestant cemetery and was sometimes, indeed, called the Protestant Cemetery.

Mustapha Birchus wrote the report of his findings in 1939, but by then time had passed him by. Word War II had started and Libya would become one of its most dramatic battlegrounds. Italy and America were enemies. Embassies were abandoned and records were destroyed, among them Birchus' answer to the question originally asked by Franklin Delano Roosevelt, who could no longer concern himself with the fates of five sailors from a very distant past.

By the beginning of World War II in 1939, the United States had arrived at the final dispositions of the dead of World War I and reorganized its bureaucracy to deal with the dead of the war to come. The American Battle Monuments Commission (ABMC) listed 33,717 buried or memorialized in its overseas cemeteries, just a fraction of 116,516 known casualties of World War I.[2] By 1934, the responsibility for those cemeteries had migrated from the American Graves Registration Service to an organization named American War Memorials in Europe, both agencies of the War Department and the quartermaster general, then to the ABMC, reporting directly to the president. Development of national cemeteries within the United States was pursued with thoughts of the probable need for expanded capacity. The American Legion played a strong role in the process, determining, for example, that the criteria for site selection should include the proximity to urban centers from which most soldiers would likely enlist and be recruited.

The planning was well timed. In round figures, estimated by Graves Registration as of 1953, World War II had call 15,000,000 American men to service. Of that number, 359,000 would be killed and 281,000 of those would be recovered; 171,000 would be returned to the United States, and 134,000 of those would be interred in private cemeteries. The families of 37,000 would choose interment in national cemeteries; 97,000 remained buried abroad (including at the time 14,000 in Honolulu, Sitka and Puerto Rico); 10,009 unknown remained buried abroad.³ Those vast numbers, however, could not encompass every American lost and buried abroad. World War II was truly a war of the full planet; and it was played out, among other new conditions, beneath the wings of airplanes that traveled long distances.

The flying workhorses of the American war were Boeing B-17 and B-24 bombers. B-17s usually carried a crew of ten: pilot, copilot, navigator, bombardier/nose gunner, flight engineer, radio operator and four gun operators at various points in the plane. It was 74 feet long, with a wingspan just short of 104 feet. Its maximums were a 2,000–mile range, 287 miles per hour in speed and 35,600 feet in altitude. Its strength was strategic bombing in daylight hours. It seemed to be virtually indestructible and able to return home in almost any condition; it gained the nickname of Flying Fortress. Perhaps more than any fighting airplane, the Fortress entered the American popular culture as a symbol of the best aspects of American power. Its role in movies long after the war included *Twelve O'Clock High*, released in 1949, about American bombing flights from England to France and Germany.

The B-24 was a later version of the B-17, often called the Flying Boxcar because of its square fuselage. It was 67 feet long with a wingspan of 110 feet, and its maximums were a 2,100 mile range, 290 miles per hour and 28,000 feet in altitude. Its strengths were in long range flying, particularly in Atlantic and Pacific operations, but in the minds of many aviators it was not as easily handled as the B-17 and not as indestructible.

In June 1943, a crew led by Lt. John P. Bruce of Albany, Georgia, met at Kearney Air Force Base in Nebraska and picked up a brand new B-17. They flew it to Bassington, England, near Cambridge, with stops in Greenland and Iceland. It may have been the same Flying Fortress, nicknamed "Man O War," that Bruce piloted out of the 323rd Squadron of the 91st Bomb Group on a fateful bomb run to Kassel, Germany, on July 30, 1943. The run required a loop over Nazi-occupied Holland.

Though occupied, the small farming village of Opijnen, near Utrecht, had not had much experience with the ravages of war. It was harvest time, by all accounts a beautiful day, and as most farmers took a break for lunch, they heard an unfamiliar noise approaching from the east. They saw that a B-17, part of its right wing blown away, was caught in a web of Luftwaffe fighters. It had dropped out of its formation, still trying to claw its way back to England. As the plane began to fall, the order was given to bail out, but flames behind the cockpit prevented normal bailout procedures. Pilot Lt. Keene McCammon, copilot Lt. John Bruce, and bombardier 2nd Lt. Daniel Ohman left through an escape hatch in the nose. The others could not escape before the crash. Ohman's parachute failed to open.

Town burgomaster Bart Fromijne witnessed its fall. Years later, he described the event in his own written English:

> It was about eleven o'clock in the morning of July 30th, 1943 that the population of my parish got alarmed by a terrible noise. A few minutes later, we heard an awful smack. I was at the Town hall, and ran outside and saw a burning aircraft of which the cannons were still firing. In the air we saw two white things, which were slowly coming down. These things were parachutes. At the same time, we saw two German aircraft still circling above the burning plane.
>
> During the time the plane was burning and firing, I couldn't get near enough to see exactly what had happened. Looking around, I saw a hole in a thatched roof of a nearby farmhouse. I went so quick as possible there, climbed upstairs, and between the hay I found an American pilot [Bomardier Ohman]. He couldn't speak and was still groaning. The doctor came soon, but couldn't do more anything; the fall had been too heavy.
>
> When the burning had ceased, I went to the plane and saw under it two corpses of American soldiers. In the neighborhood, between potatoes and beetroots, I found five other corpses. After this very sad view, I went home to search help to transport the eight bodies to the mortuary.⁴

Pilot McCammon and copilot Bruce survived. McCammon fell into the nearby Waal River and was taken by a fisherman to burgomaster Fromijne, with a detour to the farmer's house to pick up dry socks for the visitor. Before he was grabbed by Nazi soldiers, McCammon was only able to tell Fromijne his name, hometown of St. Paul, Minnesota, and occupation of motor policeman.

Bruce fell in the nearby town of Varik, fracturing his knee. "I did get a ride," he wrote in a 1983 letter, "from where I landed on the handlebars of a young man's bicycle with a young lady on her bicycle as an escort. With the assistance of a Dutch policeman whom we encountered, I found myself in a doctor's office (in his home) where my injuries were attended to. While there I learned from the policeman that the Dr. was a sympathizer of the Nazis, whom he had called to his house."[5] McCammon and Bruce sat out the rest of the war as German prisoners of war. Lt. John Bruce would return to Opijnen many years later, in 2004.

With the abrupt appearance in their community of a fallen American bomber, the people of Opijnen demonstrated a caring for those Americans killed in the fight against German dominance of Europe that was heartfelt, and that would remain so for decades after the war's conclusion. Burgomaster Fromijne gathered up the men of the village to retrieve the crew of the fallen plane from the places where they fell. He remarked to others how young they seemed to be (the oldest just 28 years). They found one with his finger still wrapped around the trigger of his machine gun, the others, shot by the Germans as they drifted earthward beneath their parachutes, in the surrounding fields. The bodies were loaded on a horse-drawn carriage and taken to the mortuary.

The burgomaster obtained German permission to bury the eight airmen in the village. A place of great honor was chosen for their resting place, at the center of the walled cemetery next to the village's 17th-century Dutch Reformed church. The Germans at first insisted that the funeral take place at 11:00 P.M. two days later so that the villagers would have to break curfew to attend. But it was eventually moved up to 9:00 P.M., and the small cemetery grounds were filled with villagers. The next morning found flowers strewn on the new graves as both a memorial, and a poke in the eye of the Nazi occupiers. It was reported that Dutch women then planted tulip bulbs along the perimeter of the burial place, which produced flowers of red, white and blue the following spring. The farmer in whose fields the dead airmen fell, Hendrick de Koch, would spend the rest of his life attending to their care.

The story of the American flyers who fell on Opijnen represented a particular human dynamic that arose out of the comings and goings of disparate people involved in a common pursuit. In the case of Opijnen, the doctor who treated Lt. Bruce would be seen as a Nazi collaborator, one of many throughout Europe during the war. And where there were collaborators, there were also members of the Resistance. The two groups worked against each other's aims and in varying degrees of visibility. In between were the civilians, some heroic and principled like Burgomaster Fromijne, others ambivalent. A fourth participant in these shifting equations were the occasional airmen who fell from the sky.

By 1940, Belgium, like the Netherlands, had fallen beneath the relentless German advance across Europe. The king surrendered the country to Nazi occupation on May 28. A 24-year-old Belgian woman, Andrée de Jongh, saw her father weeping over the loss. She had never seen him cry. "I said to my father," she later told a reporter for the BBC, "you'll see what we'll do to them. You'll see, they are going to lose this war. They've started it but they'll lose it."[6]

Mlle. de Jongh, soon to be nicknamed "The Little Cyclone," led the formation in 1941 of what came to be called the Comet Line. Its purpose was to give refuge to downed Allied flyers and return them to the Allies so they could continue their work. In most cases they were brought to Brussels where they were taken into families of the Resistance, given false identity papers, and hidden in basements and attics. As it became possible, they were then moved through France to nonbelligerent Spain, then to British controlled Gibraltar and home. Though the Line was based in Belgium, it would accommodate flyers who had fallen in the Netherlands brought to Belgium by the Dutch Resistance. A network of a thousand volunteers did the risky work. Those who were caught could expect death, or incarceration in a concentration camp at best. De Jongh's father, Frédéric, was turned in by a collaborator and executed in 1943. She herself was captured and tortured in that year as she prepared to lead a group of airmen over the Pyrenees Mountains. It was reported that she broke under torture and admitted her role as organizer of the Comet Line, but she was not believed by the Germans. Her life was spared, and she was eventually sent to the Mauthausen concentration camp in Austria. After liberation by Allied forces in 1945, she was awarded the highest of civilian awards by the United States, Great Britain and France. She was made a Belgian countess in 1985. "I loved them like they were my brothers, my children even," she said of those served by the Comet Line. "We would have done anything for them — even given up our lives — that wasn't too high a price."[7] In her last years she worked in the leper colonies of Ethiopia and Senegal.

Out of the Comet Line came relationships between airmen and Resistance members that would resound in the subsequent generations of their families. When Staff Sgt. Gerald Sorenson jumped from his B-17G to Gibecq, Belgium, on May 1, 1944, he was quickly found by the Comet Line and taken to a succession of family homes for hiding over the following month. Jerry Sorenson was a resident of Pocatello, Idaho, born in 1919. On leave from the Air Force on May 18, 1942, he had married his longtime girlfriend, Nora Lee. Two years later he was ball turret gunner on a flight that successfully bombed the railroad yards at Metz, Germany. One of the plane's engines failed on the way to Germany, followed by a second taken out by antiaircraft fire over the target. An attempt to nurse the aircraft across the English Channel by jettisoning excess weight failed, and the crew was ordered to bail out. Sorenson was the designated jumpmaster. His own jump resulted in a twisted ankle and entrance into the Belgian Resistance.

After a month of movement through various hiding places, Jerry Sorenson was brought to the family of Arthur Abeels in Ganshoren, a part of metropolitan Brussels, on June 2, 1944. He followed by a day the arrival in the household of another flyer supported by the Comet Line, TSgt. Bernard McManaman of Lapeer, Michigan. McManaman, known as Mac, had been flight engineer and gunner on the planned last mission of the B-24 Liberator *Baby Shoes*. Damaged by German fire, the plane was close to the Belgian border at an altitude of 1600 feet, close enough to the ground that when Mac was ordered to bail out, the fall injured both his ankles and wrenched his back. He was taken in and hidden by a German farmer until he was able to walk, then taken to the underground where he was given a German passport under the name of Sels Corolus.

Eventually Mac was taken to two subsequent Belgian farms, then to the Abeels family home in Ganshoren. Abeels was president of the Ganshoren veterans association, and his son, Roger, was a member of the Secret Army, one of a number of Belgian resistance groups. Roger's dream, never fulfilled, was to become a flyer for the Royal Air Force, and the three young men became fast friends. Arthur soon came to feel like a father to each of them, and his fourteen-year-old daughter, Janine, extended her role as sister to Jerry and Bernard, who called her Jenny. That relationship would stay with her after both had died and bring the return of one of them in the form a daughter.

Instead of moving further toward freedom in the Comet Line, Sorenson and McManaman joined Roger Abeels in the Secret Army as American flyers taking an oath to work in the Belgian Resistance. Mac's handwritten statement survives, excerpted:

> I, Bernard McManaman ... voluntarily offer my services for action in a common cause in case of the invasion of Belgium by the United States Forces or our allies. I will take arms and fight under orders of the leaders of the underground movement. In case of my death, you must understand that all of my actions were voluntary & was not obliged to make any [ ] of opposition. The reason for my actions are to show my gratitude to the people of Belgium who aided me after I parachuted in Belgium March 9th 1944.[8]

The military training and aviation experience of Sorenson and McManaman brought strength to the Resistance at a time when Germany was beginning to lose the war, and the two men spent the month of August involved in tasks ranging from sabotage to the gathering of intelligence. By September 3, German forces were in full retreat across Belgium and the Secret Army was given the order to hinder their movement. Sorenson, Abeels and McManaman headed by bicycle to the village of Marcq-les-Enghien, where they would interfere with German troops on the main road through town. As they approached the village, Sorenson and Abeels had to stop to fix one of their bicycles while the others went on ahead. While working on the bicycle, the two friends saw what they thought was a single German vehicle and opened fire. The vehicle was at the head of a column, however. Under returning German fire they sought a hiding place in a rabbit hutch but were found. Their two submachine guns were no match against those of the Nazi column, and a German hand grenade finally killed them side by side in the same moment.

Bernard McManaman and the others engaged the Germans at first, but realized that they were badly outnumbered and retreated. Soon, a line of British tanks appeared. "I hopped on the British lead tank," McManaman said later. "At that time, we were 65 miles from Brussels, but we were on our way. We stopped almost every half-mile to shoot Germans in cold blood and we enjoyed it. We took a lot of prisoners."

Mac rode the tanks into the liberation of Brussels, and on the following day he returned to learn the fate of his friends Sorenson and Abeels. The British Army had taken their bodies to Marc-les-Enghien. They were recovered by Arthur Abeels and brought back to Ganshoren, where they were buried side by side, with honors, in the communal cemetery. A Belgian minister read a eulogy to Jerry Sorenson that would predict a feeling in Europe that would endure for decades, excerpted: "You died for the liberation of Belgium, for the liberty of the world. You'll never see the United States again — but lie in peace. Belgium will never forget you and ever and ever honour your glorious memory. Farewell, dear friend of our free Belgium. Farewell and thank you." Bernard McManaman returned to Brussels, where he was feted in the Hotel Metropole. There he drank copious amounts of champagne, and later reported "I wanted to drink until I could float out of the hotel." He returned home from war, but would be called to conflict again, this time with the advent of the Korean War.

As the Boeing planes ranged over the world, their crew members fell longer distances from the center of the European war. Attempts to retrieve their bodies were no less determined; but some would inevitably be left behind, and many of those would be adopted by families in the towns where they fell. In 1985, Pres. Ronald Reagan took the occasion of a state dinner for the prime minister of Denmark, Poul Schluter, to tell the story of one of such relationship:

> Natalia and Nels Mortensen, both in their eighties, live in a small town of Marstal on the island of Aero in Denmark. For the last 40 years, they have been tending the gravesite of a young man

they never met. They dig the weeds out, they place flowers — red, white, and blue ones — on the grave, and always there is a small American flag, and when it gets too worn, they replace it with another.

They're watching over the final resting place of U.S. Air Force Sgt. Jack Elwood Wagner, who died when his plane was shot down off the coast of that island, fell into the sea after a bombing raid over enemy territory on June 20th, 1944. Jack Wagner's body washed up on shore in occupied Denmark 18 days after his bomber crashed, and the word spread quickly. When the Nazi occupation troops finally arrived to bury the young American, they found nearly the whole town of 2,000 had been waiting at the graveyard since early that morning to pay tribute and homage to the young American flyer. The path had already been lined with flowers. And when the enemy troops — they, incidentally, had removed his identification before the troops had arrived — when the troops had laid him in his grave and left, then the townspeople placed two banners of red, white, and blue flowers on the grave. They conducted a funeral service. One of the banners had a ribbon which read, "Thank you for what you have done."[9]

Wagner, of Selinsgrove, Pennsylvania, was tail gunner on a B-24. The mission was to bomb a synthetic oil refinery in Politz, Germany (now Police, Poland), and another target in Ostermoor. The formation was hit by heavy flak en route to Germany, and in one burst one of the B-24s was sent into the prop wash of another. They collided and fell. Many flyers were lost at sea, and some were captured by the Germans. Jack Wagner was unable to escape from the tail of his plane as it fell. His body was found by a Danish fisherman almost three weeks later and was buried with minimal honors by the German army in a churchyard cemetery in Marstal on July 11.[10] The town's full funeral service followed.

As in World War I, many Americans in the fight were early volunteers in other national forces before their country's official entrance into the war. Some would eventually end up being transferred to American fighting units — and to be buried in American cemeteries if it came to that — while others lost in battle would rest in the care of the Commonwealth War Graves Commission. As the storms of World War II were gathering in Europe, the CWGC was putting the finishing touches on the cemeteries of the previous war. In 1939, it became necessary to evacuate its labor forces out of harm's way and shift the focus to planning for what was to come. It was a given that the need would be larger than before. There were more countries involved, and airpower would bring higher numbers of new kinds of casualties spread over larger distances and on more continents. The CWGC determined that civilian forces that worked closely with military forces, like nurses and ambulance drivers, would also fall under its care on an equal footing with soldiers, sailors and airmen of all nationalities.

By the time of American involvement in December 1941, approximately 7,000 Americans were already serving in the Royal Canadian Air Force, and in British forces by extension. As in the previous war, it seemed to be acceptable to volunteer through Canada although the United States was officially neutral. One of those who did so was Roger Wallace Hayden, whose war journey would take him from Malden, Massachusetts, to a grave in Algeria.[11]

Roger's childhood had been difficult. His mother became mentally ill after his birth, and he was raised more by a maiden aunt than his father, and in the shadow of an older brother who seemed more firmly planted in life. At age sixteen he entered the traveling masses of the Depression, finding work and food where he could, returning home occasionally. He was slight of build, but strong, and a good worker. But it was important to him to be free to travel as he wished, and to take his chances with fortune. He joined the Civilian Conservation Corps at age 17, working in a camp at Lake George, New York. There he formed a strong relationship with his supervisor, and was taken into the supervisor's Adirondack family, which, though not wealthy, was active in the social life of the region, and in the tasks of compassion that brought out the best in people during the Depression.

Roger had become more fully formed, but he still had the soul of a traveler when Germany invaded Poland in September 1939. The event was just one of a succession of steps that would eventually lead America into the war, but for many young men raised in the Depression it pushed open the door to their involvement in the fortunes of a larger world. In August 1940, Roger took the northbound bus from Lake George to Montreal to enlist with the RCAF. The war, he wrote in a letter, "was something personal to me as it was messing up my life." Just as he was putting together his future, his future could not be determined. For an American, enlistment in the RCAF was not a sure thing. Not everyone was accepted, and the process was rigorous. Roger's supervisor wrote a letter of recommendation: "I have never known him to be anything but a gentleman either on the job or off and feel that he has exceptional initiative and ability in a mechanical direction. I am proud of him trying to make the R.C.A.F." He was accepted into service a year later, but was soon deemed not to be pilot material and did not do much better in wireless training. He seemed still to be a drifter in life.

On December 7, 1941, Roger's older brother Edward was stationed on the USS *Medusa* at Pearl Harbor and did not survive the attack by Japanese warplanes. Roger was moved to a new determination with the death, and, in April 1943, he received his commission as Flying Officer Wireless Air Gunner from the Macdonald air station in Manitoba. The commission took him to the closing months of the air war over North Africa.

By mid–1940, German domination of Europe was nearly complete. The island nation of England fought on, but its crucial supply lines of oil and materiel from the Middle East and Suez Canal were jeopardized by Axis dominance of the Mediterranean. The Allies needed to protect Egypt, and when Italian forces invaded that country on September 13 a back and forth struggle was begun from French Morocco to Libya, focusing on Libya and Egypt. It culminated in the Axis surrender of North Africa on May 13, 1943. The Allied effort in the accompanying air war hadn't started to become effective until October 1941 and was strengthened in August 1942 with the arrival of more modern aircraft to be put up against the German Luftwaffe. In November, 29 Allied squadrons were in the air to give cover and support to the desert war below.

As aerial gunner for a Royal Canadian Air Force crew flying a Lockheed Hudson, built for the Royal Air Force, Roger Haven arrived for a second tour in the skies over North Africa in early May. The work included covering convoys in the Mediterranean and supporting the ground war that was by then squeezing German and Italian forces into Tunisia from all directions. Though the battle for North Africa had come to a conclusion, there was still a need to defend shipping in the Mediterranean, and on the evening of May 14 Haven's plane took off for submarine patrol on its 57th sortie from Blida, just southwest of Algiers. It was a quiet and uneventful flight. But as it attempted to return to Blida at 3:00 A.M. the following morning, it came to a low ceiling along the coast, four miles west of Algiers. The pilot descended into the clouds and sought a weather report from the base. While waiting for the report he turned the plane north and ascended toward a holding pattern. Suddenly, out of a cloud, the rocky ground of the Atlas mountain range was just beneath them and a large tree in front of them. The Hudson hit the ground at 200 miles per hour. The crash could not be explained except by speculation that the plane was not where the pilot thought it was in relation to the mountains, or that secret equipment it carried was probably navigational and had failed. No matter. Roger Wallace Haven and his crewmates were buried ceremonially on May 17, 1943, in El Alia Cemetery in the city of Algiers, where they would forever remain.

With the American entrance into the Pacific war after the Japanese bombing of Pearl

Harbor, the tracking of airmen killed in the various types of missions required for the effort was often impossible. Asia, with its islands, jungles and a more vengeful enemy was not Europe with its small town mores, cemeteries and some measure of honor to be practiced between combatants. And the distances were vast.

At the time of Pearl Harbor, Japan had already been fighting the Chinese for ten years. The path from India through neighboring Burma to China had been the lifeline of the Chinese struggle, and soon after the attack in Hawaii, Japanese air forces began to shut down the Burma Road. Described by *Life* magazine in October 1941 as having been scratched out of the mountains by the fingernails of the Burmese,[12] it was made nearly impassable two months later. Part of the new American mission in the World War became the supply of the Chinese from bases on the other side of Burma by air convoys from Assam, India, to Kunming, China. Keeping the Chinese supplied would make them more effective in draining off the Japanese effort in other places, and Burma itself was a treasure trove of needed oil, rice and tin. The airman's task soon came to be called "flying the hump." The "hump" was a 500-mile trek over the Himalaya Mountains — in regional Sanskrit, the mountains of "The House of Snow." In the valleys at the feet of the mountains were dense jungles populated by wild animals and barely civilized human tribes. The flight needed to be undertaken at very high altitude, often in violent weather, and in the face of the very effective Japanese air forces and their long-range fighters, Mitsubishi Zeroes.[13]

One of those who fell in the flight over the Hump was the American journalist Eric Sevareid. His description of the event, for the Associated Press in August 1943, was both harrowing and heartening in respect to the dangers of the flight and the unexpected benevolence of those who lived in the jungle beneath. The flight carried 21 passengers and crew, including diplomatic and military officials of the United States and China. At 9:00 A.M. on August 2, engine trouble developed and as the plane lost altitude baggage and excess weight was jettisoned. At 9:15, the passengers were told to jump. Sevareid left the plane at an altitude of 500 feet just before it crashed into a mountain. Only a last instant gust of wind prevented him from landing in the resulting fire. Upon landing uninjured, his immediate panic was that he had no idea where he was and might be the only survivor, armed only with a penknife. The copilot, Lt. Charles William Felix of Compton, California, was killed as his parachute became tangled in the tail assembly, but all the rest survived with a few broken limbs and were able to find each other. As they tried to help the injured with crude splints, they feared the native population that might find them. They were thought to be "some of the world's most primitive killers" as far as Sevareid knew.

But when the natives arrived, they carried food and drink and led them back through the foliage to their village for a party of goat and pig in their honor. The relationship between the aborigines and the strangers who had fallen from the sky was immediately friendly, and by sundown, the scene was spotted by a search plane. Three rescuers floated down to earth, and Sevareid and the others were told that, although there was an American outpost just 100 miles away, it would probably take weeks or months to reach it by foot. A British officer who had hacked his way to the site from the India side of the Hump met the group, and the following journey to civilization took three weeks. The aborigines helped to find the way, and they carried the wounded in litters and a sedan chair improvised by the Chinese passengers of the plane. Daily overflights kept the group supplied with necessities and trinket gifts for the natives. All arrived safely, except, of course, for Lt. Felix, the copilot. The natives had found him under the plane's wreckage when it stopped burning. Eric Sevareid described the funeral: "We wrapped the body of Felix in one of our parachutes and buried him there under a mountain crest, with military honors. The following Sunday we erected a cross over the grave and held services in his memory."[14]

The successes of the convoys to China were remarkable and were seen as an important factor in the Japanese defeat. By the end of their work in late 1945, the convoys had made 167,285 flights over the Hump, for the most part in C47 cargo planes, a version of the Douglas DC3 aircraft, and in C87 Liberator Express transports, a version of the B-24. A total of 3,026 pilots had delivered 721,000 tons of cargo. But the cost had been high. Six hundred planes had been lost, and more than twice as many crew members. At war's end, 345 would be missing, a number that could not be significantly reduced in following years.[15]

As important as the Hump of Burma to the Allied effort in the Pacific were flights over the mountains of the large island nation of New Guinea. By the middle of 1942, Japan had gained dominance over most of the Pacific. In May, it had fully captured Burma and the Philippines, and now it sought the full capture of New Guinea as a gateway to Australia and an attack on American lines of communication. In July, the Japanese landed on the north coast of New Guinea and began to work their way south toward strategic Port Moresby on the other side of the Owen Stanley Range (named after a British explorer in 1849). But the range was dense and soaked by constant rains. Supplies could not be replaced, ground could not be gained, and tropical disease took charge.

The Japanese were met in the struggle for New Guinea by American and Australian forces that became similarly bogged down. The American casualty rate became higher than in any other Pacific battle, and the Graves Registration Service was fully at work in the difficult terrain. Whenever it was possible, the dead were buried in group cemeteries, as well as in isolated graves as necessary. Some were noted by markers at least fifteen feet high to make them more easily found by those who would later gather them for reburial or return. Many sites quickly disappeared beneath fast-growing vegetation and undergrowth, and many New Guineans could not be hired to help because of cultural taboos against digging up bodies.[16]

The air war over New Guinea invariably involved flight over the mountain range, especially supply flights from Australia. One of those American pilots who survived a crash in coastal New Guinea was 1st Lt. George E. Morgan. In her later years, his daughter, Mary Morgan Martin, would try to learn more about his experiences in New Guinea:

> For almost two years, the Owen Stanley Mountain Range with its mostly unmeasured high peaks stood between these men and their targets. Each mission for each aircraft meant successfully crossing the range twice with the high peaks often hidden in cloud. The unmeasured peaks took their toll with aircraft tumbling completely out of sight back into the dark, thickly canopied jungle below. Those that fell into the swampy coastal areas were quickly hidden by the tall grasses. With a critical shortage of aircrew and planes, crippled aircraft could not expect an escort back to their airbase. Their buddies had to press on to the target or return "home" to prepare for the next day's mission. They could not slow down for the straggler, and so he fell unobserved by anyone able to report it. On occasion, his descent was seen by other aircrew, but the New Guinea landscape was often indistinguishable one area from another and only a general location could be reported. Early in the war when Japan held air superiority, search aircraft could not be sent. Later on when the Allies had control, they could, and were sent in search but were mostly unsuccessful. For the first two years of the war, and possibly longer, ground-based navigational aids such as radar to guide the pilots did not exist in New Guinea. The pilots had to depend solely on their knowledge of the terrain below and hope it would be visible. As one pilot stated, their only navigational aid was to "fly to the coast and hang a left."

In a report dated May/June 1946, the quartermaster general detailed the problem of grave registration in New Guinea. The identification and retrieval of ground forces was difficult enough, but the challenge faced in finding aviators seemed as insurmountable as the mountain range in which most were lost: "Expeditions have been sent out from all bases to locate crashed aircraft and transport the bodies back for burial in military cemeteries. These expeditions into the densely forested, mountainous interior of the country sometimes cover great distances and must be accomplished on foot with the aid of native carriers. Steep native trails winding over mountain peaks are the only means of access to this country, parts of which have seldom been traversed by white men."[17] Though Mary Morgan Martin would be able to see her father properly buried in the national cemetery at Memphis, Tennessee, she, and many others, would never stop thinking about those beyond the reach of steep trails over mountain peaks.

Among the pilots lost or missing in the Pacific war was the great grandson of the Confederate general Thomas Jonathan "Stonewall" Jackson, Thomas Jonathan Jackson Christian, Jr. But, fulfilling the allusion to the staying power of his great-grandfather's nickname, T.J.J. Christian, Jr., would not stay missing for long. Like his great-grandfather, Christian had been an achiever in his class at West Point. After graduation, he moved through the Army Air Corps Primary Flying School at Love Field, Dallas, and the Advanced Flying School at Kelly Field, San Antonio. He was assigned to fly B-17s based in the Philippines, his mission in the 19th Bombardment Group expanding to Mindanao, Guadalcanal and Australia after the attack on Pearl Harbor. The flying was treacherous, moving supplies from point to point, attacking enemy aircraft, installations and shipping as the Japanese moved toward the Philippines in 1942, defending Burma and fighting off Japanese Zeroes. Christian was shot down at one point and listed as missing in action. But he had fallen alive into a South Pacific jungle. He lived among the natives until he could find a way to return to his group, now based in Australia. From there, he participated in the capture of Guadalcanal, from which he flew sixty hours of combat missions and was awarded the Silver Star for gallantry.

Granted brief leave, Christian returned to Texas to be married. A daughter was conceived, though he would never meet her. In 1943, he was assigned to lead the creation of the 361st Fighter Group at the Richmond, Virginia, Army Air Base. The tool of the 361st was the Republic Aircraft P-47 Thunderbolt, the first piston engine fighter to be able to exceed 500 mph. The P-47 would fly 546,000 combat missions in the last two years of the war.[18]

In January 1944, Christian's group was in place at the air base in Bottisham, Cambridgeshire, England, and began its work over France and Germany, extending to German submarines at sea. The work was brutal in the following months. Successes seemed balanced by an equal measure of loss of men and planes. The 391st contribution to the D-day Invasion of June 6, 1944, was six bombing and strafing missions that destroyed one full ammunition train, 15 locomotives, 23 trucks and armored cars, and two aircraft on the ground. The cost was three airplanes and pilots lost. Beyond D-day, the accounting of gain against loss would become larger in numbers, and necessarily without sentiment. The group's official history for August 12, 1944, was informative and direct: "Four dive-bombing and strafing missions were carried out against rail transportation targets in France with the loss of Lts. John E. Engstrom and Merle C. Rainey of the 375th, Lt. Clarence E. Zieske of the 374th and the group commander, Col. Thomas J.J. Christian, Jr."[19]

The mission had been to bomb the rail marshalling yards in Arras, France. Before the flight, Christian had told his flyers that he was concerned with the poor dive-bombing accuracy of the group and would demonstrate how to make an improvement. Now flying a P-51 Mustang, Christian was the first of the 24-plane sortie to drop through the smoke and haze covering Arras; but he was unable to recover from the high-speed dive. It was believed that Christian had dropped two bombs at low altitude and was not able to ascend quickly enough to escape their blast. Civilians on the ground found a plane missing a left wing and with a shattered canopy. The pilot's head and arms hung lifelessly outside the cockpit. Eventually, the Germans were seen putting his body on a truck and driving off in the direction of the military cemetery at Arras. What became of the body then would be an enduring mystery.

By the first months of 1945, Allied forces in both theatres of the war were beginning to turn the tide toward victory. In mid–February, British and American bombers were on the offensive in Germany, Russian forces had liberated Budapest, and enough of Poland had been liberated to cause the government to issue commemorative postage stamps. On February 19, the American landing at Iwo Jima led to some of the most vicious and decisive fighting of the Pacific war and the iconic photograph of the raising of the American flag four days later. On February 21, Allied forces broke through the Siegfried Line that had protected Germany all the way from Switzerland to the Netherlands, and Corregidor Island was liberated in the Philippines.

On February 22, B-24 #42-95241 of the 392nd Bombardment Group set out from Wendling, Norfolk, England, toward the marshalling yards at Northeim, Germany. Among the nine-man crew was John McCormick of Scranton, Pennsylvania. McCormick had enlisted in the Army Air Corps in April 1942. He was not able to fulfill his wish of becoming a pilot, nor a navigator or bombardier. Instead, he became expert at aerial gunnery, and soon thereafter beloved as a symbol of America in the small Dutch town of Zoetermeer.[20] The mission to Northeim was fated, and for years afterward it would retain the wisp of a cloak of mystery. There have been differences in the specifics of its telling through various historic sources since 1945, even a controversy as to whether the plane had the nickname of "Jolly Duck," as some maintained. A good synthesis of the story is possible, relying largely on an official history written by the 392nd BG's contemporary historian Annette Tison.

The bombing of Northeim required a descent to 350 feet from a cruising altitude of 22,000 feet. Although the bombing was a successful hit, it would later be believed that the quick regaining of cruising altitude consumed more fuel than expected, perhaps compounded by flak damage to the fuel tanks. As the plane headed home, its fuel gauges registered too low for the return journey, and the goal became to get at least as far as liberated Antwerp. Over the North Sea, pilot Joseph L. Walker turned abruptly south to hug the Dutch coast. One engine quit, followed by another, as crew tried to lighten the plane by jettisoning all nonessential weight. Finally lowering the landing gear in a sign of surrender, the B-24 aimed for a ground landing, but it was set upon and further damaged by German fighters.

As farmer Martinus Janson looked out of a window in his farmhouse near German occupied Zoetermeer just past 3:00 P.M. that day, he saw the crippled B-24 clawing the air for a slow descent. The fall was inevitable, and the plane first clipped past a dike, losing its nose wheel. After a last hundred yards it set down on a field, losing its wing landing gear. To keep the nose lifted, the pilots stood up to leverage as much force as they could against the yoke. They managed to get around a farmhouse, though the plane's right wing cut through the tops of some fruit trees. An abrupt halt to the flight from England to Germany and back again came in a collision with a heavy clay meadow close to the other side of the farm. The plane's propellers were bent, but it was otherwise still intact, as were its nine crew members. The worst injury seemed to be a sprained ankle. Their fortunes after the crash would be determined by the interplay between civilians, German collaborators and members of the Resistance.

As the crew emerged from the plane through its ruptured bomb bays, farmer Janson motioned for them to run away from the scene quickly before the inevitable arrival of German soldiers. They split up into groups of 2 and 3, and moved away from the plane, trying to gain distance from the crash. Four were captured as they held back in trying to help one of their number with the sprained ankle. They were held as POWs until liberation two months later by the U.S. 14th Armored Division under Gen. Patton. Two found refuge with another farmer and were taken to a safe house in Rotterdam by the Dutch Resistance. Two more were saved for the Resistance by another farmer. They were dressed as Dutch farmers, down to the wooden shoes, by members of the Resistance, and led on a bicycle ride to Den Haag where they were transferred by ambulance to another civilian home. They were liberated by Canadian forces in May and were back home in America by June.

Farmer Martinus Janson, and other witnesses, also maintained that a woman in a hat and dress, carrying a suitcase, was seen emerging from the fallen plane and running into the nearby woods. It was an observation by credible people that would be puzzled over for years and conflated with postwar suspicions about the true identities of collaborators in Zoetermeer, but it would never be resolved.[21]

Of the whole experience, one of those hidden by the Resistance and eventually liberated, 2nd Lt. John Donahue, wrote in the early 1990s:

> Obviously, we always will hold the Dutch in high esteem. Many risked their lives and freedom in aiding us. A farmer got us started from a haystack with bikes, bandages and clothing; a family with small children took us in to their apartment; doctors tended us at night; couriers ferried us from safe place to safe place (including an abandoned house battered by V-2 failures and Spitfire bombings); a police inspector took our photos for identity cards; a mother provided food, etc.; a husband and wife (British gal) and daughter provided months of hiding.... At this age the near misses and close calls seem nerve shattering but at "that" age it seemed routine.[22]

For whatever reason, John McCormick ran from the plane by himself and into the nearby meadow, eventually ending up in the farmer's haystack. The plane itself was then stripped, first by farmers who siphoned off fuel and took a tire to be turned into the soles of shoes, then by German soldiers who took all essential and strategic materials and mechanisms. A guard was posted at the plane, but curious villagers were allowed to examine up close one of the American bombers they had seen pass overhead so many times. Tragically, and in keeping with practice, an RCAF fighter soon arrived overhead to further destroy the fallen plane and keep its secrets from enemy hands, but its pilots did not see the civilians examining the plane. Four were killed in the strafing, including farmer Janson, two small children, and probably the German guard.

With the other survivors of the crash already escaped or captured, the focus of the local Dutch Underground fell on the flyer found in the haystack. Underground sub-commander Wim Olivier immediately obtained clothing and a bicycle that would get him to a safe hiding place 8 miles away. McCormick, however, hadn't ridden a bicycle in years and the trip was difficult. The safe house was a hunting lodge on the Rotte River. McCormick was welcomed graciously and presented with two options by Dr. Joseph Kentgens, commander and local dentist of Zoetermeer, who was hiding there. McCormick could not be hidden in this way for too long, and he could probably surrender to the Germans without fear of harm until his release at war's end. Or he could join with them in the Resistance. The choices rose out of the particular problems faced by the Resistance at the time. In the view of Johann Teeuwise, a 21st century historian in Zoetermeer, Dr. Kentgens and his deputy, Jacob van Rij, a police sergeant with an abiding hatred for Nazis, had the advantage of gained wisdom; but others in the regional underground were young and inexperienced. There was not much of a plan in place, as there had been with the Comet Line in Belgium, to deal with Allied pilots who might fall from the sky; their presence was a big deal in some respects, something to brag about too easily. And Zoetermeer was exhausted in its ability to accommodate the refugees and fallen of the war. People came regularly from the broken cities of Den Haag and Rotterdam through the main road of the town in search of food that could not be found. It was not possible to move an American airman to the safety of Belgium, and perhaps to the Comet Line, in the last frantic weeks of the war. And the underground's need for effective assistance in those weeks was dire.

John McCormick readily agreed to join the Resistance, and by any measure, his participation was generous and without caution. He led the group in Air Force fitness exercises to build their strength. He helped to steal ration cards that could be used by the Resistance and those it protected, and he had a talent for making false passports and identification cards. He wore guns on underground missions, and at one point participated in the holdup of a group of German soldiers, robbing them of guns, money and jewelry. In April, he managed to exchange letters with some of his fellow crewmates now hiding in Den Haag:

> Yes, I was a little banged up. Couldn't walk very well but now I'm fine. All traces gone except a little scar on my forehead. I remember Walker's nose all cut up & bleeding like hell. You know I still can't remember how the hell I even got out. Don't get too pissed off like I was but Jerry found 600 damn gallons of gas before the Spits blew her up. How about that?
>
> I get lonely as hell at times but I shouldn't kick because I'm treated swell but I sure miss the Chesterfields & even a damn Cinc would taste good.
>
> I'll do that little phone job when & if I ever hit God's Country but I think we will all be home around the same time. I know the vicinity of your home & I'm not too far from you.
>
> As far as the women are concerned all I see are the wives & girls of the men here so I'll really be all keyed up.
>
> They speak English here too so my Dutch is no good either. What a language to even pronounce let alone learn.[23]

It was not known whether it was because of an informant, or a mistake by the Resistance, but on April 29, the residents of the hunting lodge found themselves surrounded by twenty German soldiers. Their demand of surrender was returned by gunfire from within, countered by a hand grenade from the Germans. Various versions of the story all say that John McCormick's actions at that point inevitably led to his death. In one he made an attempt to escape that had been preplanned by the group. In another, he emerged from the house firing a Sten gun and killed several of the Germans. A third holds that he came to the assistance of Jacob van Rij, who had become enraged when his wife was shot in the encounter and took them on single-handedly. In either case, John McCormick was killed by a single shot to his head. Jacob van Rij was shot unconscious and fell into the Rotte River, where he drowned.

The German soldiers prevailed and after the twenty-minute encounter they asked about the identity of McCormick's body. They were told only that he was a stranger who had come to Zoetermeer from Den Haag. Accepting that explanation, the soldiers gave the Dutch permission to attend to their dead. John McCormick and Jacob van Rij were laid to rest side by side in the village of Zevenhuizen on May 4. On the following day the German high command surrendered in the Netherlands. Members of the underground then assembled in a schoolyard in Zoetermeer wearing their uniforms, but they were sprayed with fire by passing German troops who had not been made aware of the surrender, or were enraged by the sight of the underground. Two were killed.

It wasn't until July 12 that McCormick's family in Altoona received word of his death, the last of the crew member families to be notified of the individual outcomes of the crash. On October 31, McCormick and van Rijn were reburied with two other members of the

NINE. *Scattered from the Sky*

John McCormick was buried in the courtyard of the Dutch Reformed Church at Zoetermeer, the Netherlands, on October 31, 1945. Buried with him are Resistance members Jacob van Rij, Cornelis van Eerden and Jan Hoorn. In attendance are Dr. Joseph Kentgens and other members of the Resistance, American and English soldiers, and the people of Zoetermeer. *Historisch Genootschap Oud Soetermeer (Zoetermeer, Holland).*

Resistance in the courtyard of Zoetermeer's Dutch Reformed Church. The burial was with full military honors and with the participation of many of the adults and children of Zoetermeer for whom John McCormick had become a beloved figure and fellow townsperson. In the following year, and in the face of the American process of registration and reclamation, the people of Zoetermeer wrote to his father, also named John, to ask if it might be possible that the son remain with them and under their care. The father agreed and wrote to the army that he "would like my boy's body to remain where it is." The army replied that "the willingness of the present inhabitants of this small town to care for [the] grave does not guarantee in any way permanent care." John McCormick replied: "I considered that it was very nice of the people of Zoetermeer, Holland to subscribe for a monument to be erected over my boy's grave; and that they wanted his body interred there; and they stated that his Grave would be taken care of. So I had no other alternative but agree with them. Hence my decision for stating to them that I would like the body of my boy to remain there. Therefore under these circumstances — I would not like to alter my decision."[24]

Graves Registration still counseled caution and the father turned to Dr. Joseph Kentgens for assistance. Kentgens met with the army and accepted full responsibility for the care of the remains. The elder McCormick's confidence in Dr. Kentgens and the people of Zoetermeer was very well placed, and the postwar era in the life and death of the young McCormick was begun.

CHAPTER TEN

Islands and Farmlands

The Path of our Forces is marked by The Graves of Our Fallen.
—Graves Registration Service in the Mediterranean
Zone of World War II

In August of 1943, the long-range capacities of the B-24 Liberator were put to their most difficult test of the war. The target was Ploiesti, Romania, where nine refineries pumped out, by some estimates, 40 percent of the petroleum used in the German war effort. Both Russian and American bombers had made runs against Ploiesti before, and the Axis powers understood the importance of placing strong German and Romanian defense forces around the city. To succeed, the flights over Ploiesti would have to be at low level to enhance surprise and accuracy. The B-24s were equipped with extra fuel tanks, and their bomb-sighting equipment was recalibrated to lower levels. The bombs they carried used time-delay fuses so that the planes could fly out of range before detonation.

On the first of August, 177 planes of five USAAF bombardment groups left Benghazi, Libya, traveling north across the Mediterranean to Corfu Island, then northeast across Albania, Yugoslavia and Bulgaria to Ploiesti. The expedition, called Operation Tidal Wave, was to be 2,400 miles round trip, requiring the B-24s to spend 13 hours in the air. But the weather over the mountains between Albania and Yugoslavia would not cooperate with the low level plan, and the flight formations began to break up. Navigation errors were made and the resulting chaos over Ploiesti put planes over unassigned targets and in each other's flight paths. Anti-aircraft gunnery surrounding the refineries was fierce and effective. The attack had little long-term effect on refinery output. The exact number of planes lost varied upwards from 53 through differing accounts, and the given number of American airmen killed on what came to be called "Black Tuesday" ranged from 300 to 500.[1]

One of those was 1st Lt. William K. Little of the 409th Bomber Squadron, 93rd Bombardment Group; he was a native of Tennessee. Despite the strong defense of Ploiesti, the tide of war was beginning to change against the Axis powers. A year later, Romania would exchange the shackles of the Nazis for the shackles of the Russians, becoming part of the Allied effort. When Lt. Little fell from the sky, the Romanian people were already disposed to that change and, as an example, his body was treated with a respect explained by an unnamed Romanian general: "Even at the time when you were attacking us, we did not hate you. We know that you did it as your holy duty for the liberty of the people; also, our liberty." American dead in Romania were often accorded a full burial service, and records were kept that could be used postwar by Graves Registration. Lt. Little's last breath was expelled in the military hospital at Sinaia, and he was buried there on August 10. The service was given by a Romanian priest, with honors performed by the Romanian military. American POWs were allowed to attend.[2]

Lt. Little's story was briefly told in a typewritten, unpublished history, "Graves Registration Service in the Mediterranean Zone of World War II." The front material included a motto: "The Path of our Forces is marked by The Graves of Our Fallen."

The course of the European war would allow record keeping and respect for fallen enemies when practical. And the presence of the fallen of previous wars in European soil was not forgotten. In Belgium, for example, harsh Nazi occupiers took a pass on Flanders Field, locking its gates and leaving it alone, perhaps ignoring the occasional memorial service held by Belgians who managed to break through the perimeter.

On the other side of the world, treatment by an even more cruel enemy was exemplified by the Bataan Death March of American and Filipino forces over 60 miles of Philippine terrain in April 1942. The initial success of Japanese forces in the Pacific was crowned by their fight to gain control of the Philippine Islands and thus the southwest Pacific. In the days after Pearl Harbor, Japanese planes met little resistance from undermanned American ground and air forces. Even fortified by almost 70,000 well-trained Filipino troops, the defense was no match for the final assault by Japanese air, ground and naval forces on December 22, 1941. American general Edward P. King had no choice but to surrender despite orders from Gen. Douglas MacArthur and Pres. Roosevelt not to capitulate. His troops were outnumbered and exhausted. Food was running short. In some interpretations of history, MacArthur's leadership as commander of the U.S. Armed Forces in the Far East was to blame for the inability of his troops to fight back, and Gen. King's surrender was deemed courageous.

All related statistics can only be estimates. The surrender delivered approximately 12,000 American, 64,000 Filipino and an uncounted number of Dutch and English troops to the unrestrained brutality of the Japanese. The captors pulled men randomly from the lines and decapitated them. They laughed as they bayoneted others. Any small challenge to their dominance would be met with instant death. Then the 76,000 were set upon a 60-mile march from Mariveles on Corregidor Island to prison camps like Camp O'Donnell and Cabanatuan. The terrain was rough and dusty beneath a broiling sun with little shade. Water and food for the marchers was not a concern of the Japanese, and any effort to go to natural water like an artesian well — even to accept a cup from a local observer of the march — led to bayoneting and summary execution, often for the compassionate Filipino as well. The men were herded into abandoned buildings at night and made to stand in their own wastes, still without food. They witnessed the rape and mutilation of civilians along the way, but they could not intervene.

As the marchers died of exhaustion, bayoneting, disease and lack of water, they were left where they fell, often to be consumed by the earth and elements over the war's remaining four years. Fortunately, some of the dead were taken by villagers from the path of the march and buried in surrounding swamps and rice paddies, sometimes with effective markers and sometimes not. It was impossible to know how many died or escaped during the six-day march. Estimates put escapes in the thousands and deaths in the hundreds, but approximately 54,000 of the group that left Mariveles arrived in the camps to the north.

Death in the camps accelerated after the arrival of Americans and Filipinos, not leveling off until later in 1942. In August, 801 men were buried at Cabanatuan, 248 in October, 73 the following January, and a normal amount for the population size in April. A Memorial Day

First Lt. William Little was buried at Ploeisti, Romania, on August 10, 1943. Though Romania was still enemy territory, the American airman received full honors from the Romanian Military, and American Prisoners of War held in Ploeisti were allowed to attend the ceremony (*National Archives*).

ceremony was held at Cabanatuan in 1944 for 2,645 Americans buried in mass graves without identification. It was believed that 1,462 were buried at Camp O'Donnell.[3] Each burial was accompanied by a Japanese death certificate attributing the death to disease, but most were due to malnutrition or execution, sometimes after torture. The census of the dead could not account for those prisoners of the Japanese who died at sea in the airless holds of "Hell Ships" and those who died in the slave labor camps and mines they were taken to all over Asia.

Not since the War of 1812 had the topographical feature of a simple beach been as important as it was in World War II. In the Pacific Theater it was the beaches of the islands and island nations that became points of sometimes the most deadly battles, and, by their nature, the immediate burial place of those who were lost. The controversy over the Battle of Tarawa in November 1943 would never be resolved. At that time, the Allied push was to gain control of the Central Pacific as a stepping-stone to the Philippines and air access to Japan. It seemed to military leaders that key to that strategic acquisition was the small island of Betio in the Tarawa Atoll of the Gilbert Islands.

The Japanese were already on Betio with heavy armament and a force of approximately 5,000, one fifth of them Korean slave laborers. The island was fortified by pillbox gunsights, and trenches lay between strategic points so that troops could move without detection. The commander of the island garrison claimed that "it would take one million men one hundred years"[4] to wrest control from his troops. And any landing on Betio would have to approach through a lagoon that was ringed with pillboxes and machine gun emplacements.

The American battle force assembled for the invasion on November 20 included 17 aircraft carriers, 12 battleships, 12 cruisers, 66 destroyers and 36 transports. Thirty-five thousand sailors and marines were drawn from the 2nd Marine Division and the 27th Army Infantry. A lengthy opening naval bombardment seemed to destroy all defenses of the lagoon and the landing was begun. But it was hampered by a miscalculation of tidal levels that hung up landing craft still off the beach and a resurgence of Japanese troops into the damaged fortifications. The American loss of life was extensive, but by the end of the day a line of Marines and tanks managed to secure a line near the island's only airfield.

The following morning, the goals were to create a bulge near the runway that would divide Japanese forces, and to take the beach that lined the full western edge of the island. A platoon of war dogs, trained in enemy search and essential players in the Pacific war, was sent in to help clear out enemy hiding places in the terrain, followed by naval bombardment that secured the beach. Other operations did not go as easily, but, after a day of intense fighting, control had been gained of the island's western end and a portion near the airfield. The Japanese commander had been killed in the fighting, and on the third day Japanese forces labored under command shortcomings that gave the advantage to the Americans, though their gains were hard won. At 4:00 A.M. on November 23, a final Japanese assault in defense of the island failed, and full American takeover of Betio was accomplished by November 28.

By estimates, 4,700 Japanese and enslaved Koreans were killed. Nearly 1,700 Americans lost their lives, and 2,300 were wounded. Unfortunately, the quick violence of those four days upended all ability to keep records and to know who lay where. Some were buried hastily where they fell, with minimal markers. Some markers properly placed were destroyed in subsequent fighting, but who and where? Some were lost at sea or more officially buried at sea, but who was who? Some were missing in action, but could they be distinguished from those killed in action and buried with some kind of notation that might have become lost? The immediately following years would serve only to confuse the issue. Eventually they would all be forgotten, then eventually remembered again, though they will probably never be fully found and sorted.

Even in the larger context of death during World War II, the public reaction to the battle for Betio was angry. The loss of life seemed too high for such a small island. The belief by some military leaders that it had been a bad mistake poorly executed began to come to the surface. Perhaps the goal of the invasion could have been attained by other, less costly means. The preliminary intelligence had been woefully inadequate, especially in regard to the schedule of the tides. Actions and subsequent actions did not follow one upon another in a fluid way.

A scathing judgment was given immediately postwar by Marine Corps general Holland Smith: "From the very beginning the decision of the Joint Chiefs to seize Tarawa was a mistake and from their initial mistake grew the terrible drama of errors, errors of omission rather than commission, resulting in these needless casualties."[5]

The military dogs used in the battle for Betio were drawn from platoons of American dogs trained in the United States and sent overseas during World War II. Dogs had been used successfully by all sides in World War I, and, as the second world war approached, Germany set up a large training center in Frankfurt. It was estimated that early in the war Germany had approximately 200,000 military and police dogs in place and had given 25,000 to Japan. The United States, however, came into the conflict without that preparation.

It was the quartermaster's job to provide dogs for battle, and public appeals for dogs during the war through efforts such as "Dogs for Defense," conducted in collaboration with the American Kennel Club, yielded 20,000 dogs volunteered for service. Of that number, approximately half were deemed trainable for the difficult tasks they would be asked to perform,

The graves of U.S. Marines buried with wooden temporary markers on the beach at Betio after successful occupation of the island in November 1943. Many of these markers, and the bodies they represented, may have been lost as Tarawa was quickly converted to an offensive outpost (*National Archives*).

which at first were projected to be as sentry animals in the United States and overseas. But their roles quickly expanded, and they were trained also as scouts, sled dogs, messengers and mine detectors. Other crucial skills seemed to evolve out of that training, often performed heroically in the eyes of those with whom they worked. In addition, they were found to increase morale considerably among the troops. Despite their considerable value, just 1,894 dogs were sent overseas. They were found to be more effective in the Pacific war where the environment of jungles, thickets and caves offered perfect staging for surprise Japanese attack and offered an even better environment for a dog's ability to see, hear and smell while practicing stealth.

The number of American military casualties buried at sea during World War II was 6,043; of those, 4,600 were members of the U.S. Navy. The actual number of Americans lost or buried at sea in all wars is difficult to determine because of a conflation of "lost at sea" and "missing in action" figures. On April 7, 1945, a single Japanese Kamikaze attack on the aircraft carrier USS *Hancock* near Okinawa caused an explosion that killed 62 of her crew. They were buried at sea on April 9, 1945 (*National Archives*).

In the attack on Betio, the dogs, mostly German Shepherds and Dobermans, could use their senses to detect the enemy in caves and other hidden places. Their method was to approach slowly and silently, making decisions based on senses, and looking back over their shoulders, or pricking up their ears, as a signal to their handlers. As mine detectors, they could place themselves on a landmine without setting it off because of their lower weight. Some would immediately go into hiding when they heard the outbreak of gunfire and immediately go to work when it ceased. They could capture injured Japanese to prevent them from escaping. When a dog was part of a mission, there was a greater sense of security, allowing forces to work more efficiently over greater distances. The feeling of security was born out in the quartermaster's assessment of their value. As an example, over two months of fighting in late 1944 on Morotai Island in the Netherlands East Indies, dogs accompanied more than 100 patrols with infantry units ranging from 5 to 200 members in size. Not one was reported to have failed to alert against trouble less than 75 yards distant, and not one human casualty resulted from 100 patrols.[6]

As the Allied effort to work across the Pacific toward the Philippines and Japan continued, its focus fell on Guam in July 1944. The largest of the Marianas Islands, Guam's size and harbor would support a large staging area for all forces. On July 21, bombardment began by planes from an offshore carrier and the bases of the Marshall Islands, followed by shelling from surrounding battleships. The infantry forces pitted 36,000 Americans against half as many

Private First Class Rez P. Hester, 7th War Dog Platoon, 25th Regiment, takes a nap while Butch, his war dog, stands guard on Iwo Jima, February 1945 (*National Archives*).

Japanese. Among the American forces that began to cross the beaches at the Orote Peninsula were two dog platoons with their handlers. Upon landing, approximately 350 dogs, mostly Dobermans trained for jungle warfare, were distributed within the 3d Marine Division. In addition to the skills used at Betio, they ran messages and stood guard over foxholes, allowing Marines the chance to sleep with a sense of security.

No less so than their human comrades, the dogs were killed and wounded by gunfire and mortars, and no less so were they moved quickly to the rear when wounded, where veterinarians waited to give them care. By August 10, 3,000 American men and 25 dogs were killed, but the island was secured. So valued were the war dogs of Guam that as the dead were returned to the beach on which the invasion had begun, one was buried at sea and 24 were each buried in a section of the temporary cemetery created for the men with whom they had fought. At some point, they were each given a small headstone with a single name. At the end of the war, among all of the dogs in service, six were awarded Silver Stars, seven received Bronze Stars and 40 received Purple Hearts. In 1946, the awards were rescinded as an assault to the dignity of their human counterparts. And when the human dead of Guam were eventually exhumed for return to national cemeteries and their families, the residents of "War Dog Cemetery Guam" were left behind. In the decades to come, their resting place would almost disappear into the nearby sea and the overgrowing jungle.[7]

Just a few months earlier, another beach on the other side of the world had become the setting of another tragedy similar to the Battle of Tarawa, and it would lead to the war's most enduring mystery about the disposition of the dead. It was April 1944, just weeks before the planned invasion of the Normandy beaches of France. The French beach that would be called Utah was a virtual duplicate of Slapton Sands, across the English Channel in the county of Devon and 30 miles west of Plymouth.

The city would be a major point of embarkation for the invasion, and for Plymouth it would be an act of vengeance against the enemy. Because of its strategic location and naval importance, Plymouth had been the objective of 59 bombing runs by the German Luftwaffe up to that time. The Plymouth Blitz was devastating to the city. Although the main target was the dockyards, important in the Atlantic war, the bombers seemed to have no reluctance to destroy the civilian life of the city. Over four years nearly 1,200 British citizens would be killed and 4,500 injured. Many of the city's buildings would be destroyed, including St. Andrew's Church, custodian of the 1813 graves of William Allen and Richard Delphy. By 1944, nearly 3,800 homes, most civic buildings, 26 schools and 41 churches were gone. Many more were seriously damaged. The city's commercial life was severely curtailed.

The American role in the war against the Nazis was particularly appreciated by the citizens of the beleaguered city that had assisted in the birth of the United States. But America's help in maintaining the lives of the people was perhaps even more so. In 1941, said 21st century city historian Pat Luxford, "whole families had to camp out at the roadside. I have a picture of a mother and two boys camped by the side of the road. Nothing. They have nothing. The Americans were sending us food parcels, and particularly clothing, because clothing was always lost. And there were all sorts of little stations where you could go and get children's clothes. All sorts of clothes."

In one night of the Plymouth Blitz, according to city historian Barbie Thompson, over 37,000 incendiary bombs were dropped to illuminate the targets and to destroy them by fire. One night, her mother, Dorrien Peake, looked outside: "There was a huge crater outside the front door, an enormous crater full of water. But the horrific thing was that there were so many fires around, reflecting in the water, that it looked like a great, big pond of blood. And that's the way she described it. She's never forgotten it."

American military personnel were all over Plymouth in the months before the Normandy Invasion. "I met a man the other day who was age eight when the Americans were here," said Pat Luxford. "He remembers Americans with their vehicles on Phoenix Wharf. They used to service them there, and he was asked by one friendly American to help service the vehicles. I think he held the tools and things like that. He has these wonderful vivid memories of the Americans to the point that he now belongs to an association here in England where people have got the old American vehicles, and they take them around to different shows."

If the Normandy invasion were to succeed, it would need practice and rehearsal. Thus, on April 28, Slapton Sands, aka the hypothetical Utah Beach, was prepared for a mock landing by American troops. Both settings shared gravel beaches leading to a piece of land beside a lake on the other side. Landing exercises on various beaches had been taking place since the previous year. But this one, named Operation Tiger, on the roiling Devon coast east of Plymouth, would be most important — and fraught enough with danger. It was to be a live ammunition exercise held under complete secrecy. Three thousand villagers had been evacuated from their homes in the surrounding area, though they weren't told why.

On April 27, 30,000 Americans in nine tank landing ships (LSTs), sailing out of Plymouth and Dartmouth and protected by destroyers and torpedo boats of the Royal Navy, successfully passed their first exercise and repaired for a second go-round, about 1:00 A.M. the following day. Unfortunately, a nearby flotilla of German torpedo boats heard the mysterious increase in radio traffic off the Devon coast and turned in that direction. Finding eight destroyers, they went immediately on the attack, and, beyond the destroyers, they came upon eight LSTs on their practice run to Slapton Sands. Two were destroyed and sunk, and one was severely damaged but managed to make it ashore. The true tragedy was that those on the sunken LSTs were not prepared to be shot at from the sea. Many were trapped in lower decks, and many did not know how to properly wear life jackets. Many jumped in panic into the sea, only to be pulled down to the depths by their heavy combat packs and overcoats. There were few lifeboats to be used, and many died of hypothermia.

By the time the German torpedo boats took their leave, 749 sailors and soldiers had died. More problematic, one of the enduring controversies of the event would be the question of how many were killed on the beach by friendly fire from "German defenders" who had, unaccountably, been given live rather than dummy ammunition. It was the largest loss of life in a training exercise in World War II, and it jeopardized the planned Normandy invasion. The two lost LSTs were necessary for the invasion and irreplaceable, and it was not known if officers had been captured who might be coerced into revealing plans for the most important invasion of the war. It was later determined that all of them had drowned.

Nearly as devastating was the interpretation of what had gone wrong. There had been only two escort ships assigned to the protection of the exercise, but one of them, a World War I destroyer, was actually undergoing repairs in Plymouth. The corvette that remained had seen the German boats, but the Americans were not notified, either through dereliction or use of the wrong radio frequencies.

It fell to the American dead, however, to give rise to a controversy that would never be fully resolved for all students of Operation Tiger: where did they go? The importance of maintaining the secrecy of the exercise and the wish not to let the Germans know what they had accomplished on April 28 meant that the dead could not be acknowledged, let alone glorified. Those who survived were sworn to secrecy. When surrounding villagers returned, they knew something of what had occurred, but not all. Out of their discussions there arose "eyewitness" accounts of mass graves made hastily in the fields of Devon and just as quickly camouflaged. More official accounts pointed to removal of the dead for temporary burial in a World War I cemetery, before interment at the Cambridge American cemetery or return to families in America. But tragic stories kept secret, even if only in this case until after the Normandy invasion the following June, are never fully defused of their mystery. The story of the dead of Slapton Sands would reemerge 40 years later.

The secrecy surrounding the tragedy at Slapton Sands was just a small part of a cat and mouse game that had been going on since a determination by Allied forces in 1943 to strike at the heart of Germany in a way that would collapse its hold on all of Europe. The strike would start at various places on the Normandy shore, rather than at one or two larger port areas, and move forward to Berlin. In August 1943, its opening stage was named Operation Overlord, and in 1944 it fell under the commands of American general Dwight D. Eisenhower and British general Bernard Montgomery. Everyone seemed to know that it would eventually take place, even the Germans. The questions were when, how and where.

Operation Overlord was preceded by Operation Bodyguard, named from an observation by British prime minister Winston Churchill that for truth to be preserved it must be surrounded by a "bodyguard of lies." The goal was to make Germany think that the expected invasion would take place later than planned, and in altogether different locations. To that end, the Germans were led to believe that invasions were planned at Pas-de-Calais, France, in the south and Norway in the north so that they would split their defensive forces in those directions. Fake radio traffic and double agents were used to convince the enemy of the existence of a fictitious army division poised to attack Pas-de-Calais, its bases made visible to

Luftwaffe intelligence in the form of dummy equipment and camps fabricated of cloth and tarpaulin. Actual aerial bombings and naval bombardments north and south of the Normandy coast were intended to deceive the enemy into believing that those areas were being softened up for invasion.

On June 6, 1944, 7,000 Allied naval vessels and 195,000 soldiers, marines and sailors set out from the coast of Britain toward the Normandy beaches. Gen. Eisenhower gave them their mission:

> You are about to embark upon the Great Crusade, toward which we have striven these many months. The eyes of the world are upon you. The hopes and prayers of liberty-loving people everywhere march with you. In company with our brave Allies and brothers-in-arms on other Fronts, you will bring about the destruction of the German war machine, the elimination of Nazi tyranny over the oppressed peoples of Europe, and security for ourselves in a free world.[8]

From the invasion of Normandy to the ultimate European victory in Berlin in May of the following year, the number of casualties during the sweep across Nazi-occupied Europe would be immense. At its start, the 611th Quartermaster Graves Registration Company, as an example, waited for returned dead in three of the British ports that had sent out invasion forces, Southampton, Weymouth, and Plymouth. From that starting point, it would follow the war all the way to Germany, beginning with the bodies quickly returned from the invasion on its first afternoon. Good English caskets with silk linings had been stacked and were waiting, but there would be no time for the niceties of embalming and cleaning. Most important was the registering of identification and the gathering of personal effects from pockets that were quickly ripped open with sharp knives. That work done, the caskets were loaded on trucks and taken to the American cemeteries at Brookwood and Cambridge. Funeral services were less hurried and appropriately formal.

In France, corpses found in the water or still in naval vessels at sea were taken back to England. But those on the beaches were placed in mattress covers rather than coffins. Burials were either in temporary cemeteries near the battle or, when possible, at the nearest already existing U.S. military cemetery. Paratrooper groups buried their own dead in a military cemetery at Blosville. Thousand of others were buried in cemeteries at Cambe and St. Mere Eglise. Identification came through dog tags or pay books, with more difficult cases saved for forensic methods.

Leading toward Paris, parts of the 611th traveled with the 5th Infantry Division to the Loire River, while other parts headed toward the Belgian frontier. With the liberation of Paris on August 25, the goals of Operation Overlord had been met, and it was officially concluded. More than 37,000 American soldiers and airmen had been killed, and 10,000 were missing in action. Based in St. James, France, the Graves Registration Division swept the surrounding battlefields for the unburied dead and those temporarily interred, so that they could be taken to more permanent cemeteries. Moving on to Brittany, the assignment was to find soldiers, buried fliers, and American spies. In Montfort, members of the 611th were fed by the villagers, were given access to their own burial records kept during the war, and were assisted in the digging up of graves.

In the sights of those who planned the retaking of Europe was the harbor at Brest, France. Brest had become a strategic base for German submarines, its port hardened against previous and unsuccessful Allied attacks. It was also a supply port for whatever forces held France at a given time. The battle to take it back from Germany would start August 7, 1944, and not be concluded until September 19. It would be one of the most difficult and deadly battles of the war. Aside from its hardened defenses, Brest was now occupied by German forces that had been pushed into the city by Allied victories from Utah Beach. The city had become a German fortress. The Americans brought naval, ground and air forces to the fight, and the Germans waited in hard fortifications with all caliber and type of guns and ammunition. The fighting was one-on-one and house-to-house. At the end, the medieval city was reduced to rubble and the port destroyed.

At Brest, the 611th began the process of sending American bodies to the St. James base. But it also fulfilled a stated rule of Graves Registration, generally followed by opposing forces, that "enemy dead will be buried in separate sections apart from regular burial sites of members of our own allied armies within the cemetery. Such graves will be properly marked and registered and will remain the custody of and be cared for by the Quartermaster Corps."[9] The order applied to civilian dead where possible.

The head officer of the 611th was Capt. James J. Shomon. His book *Crosses in the Wind*, published in 1947 under the rank of lieutenant colonel and updated and republished in 1991, told the story from which some of the present narrative is taken.[10] He described the world of enemy and civilian dead after the Battle of Brest:

> Zeke [a subordinate] took me down to the shattered submarine pens and showed me how his men fished German bodies out of the water at low tide. The dead had rocks wired to them and were difficult to drag to the surface. This kind of fishing did not appeal to me.
>
> Then we went into one of the abysmal pits beneath the shattered city of Brest. Here we found a nightmare of hell. Our lanterns hardly gave us good light, but we saw that the walls of the inner tunnels were charred black from a terrible fire. We descended a winding stairway littered with hundreds of dead French people. They were in crawling positions, headed for the main exit. The dead on the stairs were so that we had to slide on top of them in order to descend. Some of the charred and burned women had reached the very exit before they were caught in flames. Their faces were horrifying.
>
> Where the tunnel leveled off, about 200 feet below the surface, we saw a ghastly spectacle. Branching off in several directions were hospital corridors, warehouses, storerooms, all ruined by terrific fire, all filled with dead bodies. Our lights, faint against the black walls, showed us thousands of French dead.

Shomon went on to describe the smell, bodies melted into steel bed frames, and figures caught praying or reaching "heavenward." The sight would inform the very hard work that was yet to come for his group. From Brest, the 611th moved on to the Netherlands. Nearly attacked by friendly fire when mistaken for a German division, and seen by an actual German division as a harbinger of another offensive, it arrived at a potential site for a new cemetery near the village of Margraten. The region had been liberated in September, and the 65½ acre site was chosen as the site of the Ninth Army Military Cemetery. It would be one of the first to be used for American soldiers retrieved from German soil. And its development would offer the story of the creation from bare land of one of the great American military cemeteries of Europe.

In *Crosses in the Wind*, Lt. Col. Shomon described the development of what would officially be called The Netherlands American Cemetery and Memorial as a fine collaboration between American soldiers and Dutch citizens. The description was accurate up to some of the fine points. In 2009, Dutch authors Mieke Kirkels and Jo Purnot conducted an oral history project with Margraten residents and American soldiers of the time. Together, Shomon's book and the book that resulted from the oral history project, *From Farmland to Soldiers Cemetery*, tell a nuanced story of a small European village overtaken by a large American cemetery at the end of the war.

As American airmen had found in Opijnen and Zoetermeer, the people of Margraten welcomed the Americans to their town. They were led by the town clerk, Joseph van Laar, a leader of the Resistance who had given many Dutch Jews identity papers that would keep them from the German concentration camps. He also spoke very good English, and he and Shomon became fast friends. The enlisted men and staff of the division were housed in three town schools. Mess was set up in a separate building, an American bakery was created, and local butchers donated space in their own refrigerators. An African American work force of the Quartermaster Service Company was moved into an old fruit or auction warehouse that Shomon described as cold and drafty, not suitable for the group that would contribute tirelessly to the building of the cemetery.

The 960th QMSC were gravediggers for the three months they were there and in *Crosses in the Wind*, Shomon's description of them came under the heading "Negroes and Corpses." The former were described as likeable chaps, most of them from the southern United States, who worked hard when they had an incentive to do so: "The boys ate all the time. If it wasn't regular chow, it was turnips in the field, apples, pears, even raw potatoes and cabbages. It didn't matter what the food was, just so long as there was plenty of it." Shomon's narrative sank further into stereotypes in his description of their response to the corpses they were charged with burying: "They looked and looked; then suddenly a few made a break for the latrine. Back they came, however, and looked again." I heard one mutter, 'Gruesome, ain't it? Sho' is gruesome. Ah can't stand working hyar. Ah's gonna dig graves. Yassuh, give me a shovel. You kin handle him. Ah's gonna dig graves.'" It was acceptable writing for the 1940s perhaps, but it was not changed in the 1991 update; and in 2009 it would return one of those African-American gravediggers to painful memories of the true stress of the wartime gravedigger's job.

The site of the cemetery between Margraten and Cadier en Keer was chosen by visual inspection of available spaces. It had been used previously by American forces as a small landing field for reconnaissance aircraft, and it was otherwise some of the most productive farmland in the region. Lt. Col. Shomon's account holds that the land was given over for the American cemetery happily, but those who farmed the land described initial shock on first seeing the Americans digging up their land. One of them, Rich Prevoo, was walking on his land when he suddenly saw unexplained piles of dirt at some distance. He went to have a look and found Americans digging trenches with some sort of machine and filling them neatly with bodies laid side by side.

Prevoo could not communicate with the Americans across two languages and went to see the mayor. "Nothing can be done about that, it's war," said the mayor, "They just started doing it here." "Yes, but here I am with six horses and six boys," said Prevoo. "I have no fodder for the horses, and no work for the boys."

The mayor could only advise him to look for new land right away: "The Americans will probably pay you very well."[11] The speculation was not entirely correct. Eventually, every farmer displaced by the cemetery would receive some form of compensation, and there seemed to have been no lingering hard feelings. Shomon is reported to have said to Laar, "The best soil is not good enough for our boys." The recently liberated Dutch were not disposed to disagree, but the lives of many of the displaced families would be changed for following generations.

Perhaps it was not known to Shomon and Laar that the site was also historically significant. It had seen centuries of fighting men pass it by on the Cologne-Boulogne highway first built by the Romans and used by Caesar in 54 and 55 BC. Others who had probably passed by the site were King Charlemagne of the Franks in the late 8th century, Holy Roman Emperor

Charles V in the early 16th century, Napoleon in the early 19th century, and Kaiser Wilhelm II in World War I. In World War II it would be a key route of both advance and retreat for German forces.

An initial 10-acre site was surveyed and divided into plots that would contain 300 graves placed in 12 rows of 25 each, numbered left to right from bottom to top. The first digging of graves was accompanied by cold, endless rain. Graves dug five feet deep, two feet wide and six feet long were immediately filled with water that turned to clay. A planned road through the land was to be built in two days, but as the rain got heavier the equipment became more deeply mired in mud. The problem became notorious in the region and officers of an increasingly higher rank would come to examine, exclaim and order about, but the work still could not get done. Endless truckloads of gravel were brought to the site, but the gravel just sank beneath the surface. "They brought in rocks, huge rocks," wrote Shomon. "These disappeared. Then they tried poles—which turned up at the ends and broke in two under heavy trucks. Bulldozers were kept busy pulling the trucks out of the mud, and couldn't do their own work. Bigger poles were brought in, and finally, great logs from the battered Hürtgen Forest." The two-day road was finally finished in two months.

The first bodies arrived in November. In various states of decomposition and damage, they were placed in a "stripping line" in which all personal effects, ammunition and clothing were removed. Personal effects were put in a process that would return them to families (the money taken from bodies to be returned to next of kin would total nearly a half million dollars by VE Day); identification tags were placed in mouths, or in hands if mouths did not exist. A second dog tag was nailed to a white wooden cross. Bodies were placed in the mattress covers to be carried to open graves. The rain and fog did not lessen the stench.

The first burial took place on November 10. The service was led by Father Heynen of nearby Groot Welsden; he arrived by bicycle and read from his prayer book. The ceremonies continued each day in the months that followed, attended by local priests and army chaplains who conducted services specific to their own faiths. Each day's work by the 611th was concluded with its own service, accompanied by a bugler and a firing squad. But the growing routine did not lessen the simmering near horror of the work. The war was continuing not far away, and the arrival of bodies was relentless, several hundred a day. "German bodies came too," wrote Shomon, "great truckloads of them, wet, messy, and horribly battered."

Tracks of blood through the streets of Margraten would follow the trucks of bodies from the battlefront. When a truck had to stop in place for too long a time, the land on which it stopped was sprinkled with gasoline and set afire after it had moved. The stripping line continued around the clock, and the chemicals used brought the beginning stages of blood poisoning to many workers. Rubber gloves would quickly break down and fall apart; bare hands made the work easier on wet, putrefied corpses. The number of unknown bodies increased, requiring tooth charts and fingerprints where possible. The processed bodies needed time to dry in special tents, and the graves they would occupy continued to fill up with water before they could be closed. Some days the digging of one usable grave was considered a success, and it was regularly necessary to disinter some of those successfully buried because of new information about their identities. Buzz bombs flew overhead 30 to 40 times a day.

Almost invariably, the villagers of Margraten who saw any of the process, or did some of the work themselves, described a dignified treatment of the dead by the American workers, with occasional exceptions. The people of Margraten and the enlisted American soldiers were discouraged from interacting with each other. But relationships were formed in any case, often based in hospitality and home cooked food exchanged for supplies like soap, and a black

A Dutch farm building served as the first collection point for Americans killed in battle. From there, they were moved to a more central collection point, then by truck to the cemetery at Margraten (*U.S. Army Quartermaster Museum, Fort Lee, VA*).

market that turned shoes of the dead into shoes of the living Dutch, even the mattress slips used to bury bodies being turned into good clothing.

For a short time in late November, the 611th was able to catch up with the work and take a limited break. Then things got worse. The developing winter froze the water-filled cemetery, and the soil became nearly impermeable. In December, the Germans launched what would become their last counteroffensive in the Belgian Ardennes, which came to be known as the Battle of the Bulge. The pressure on Margraten increased. Graves needed to be dug with the help of blowtorches and axes. Reinforcements brought in to do the work often didn't have sufficient clothing for the cold and had to take lined boots from the corpses.[12]

The Americans and the people of Margraten settled in for a shared Christmas. At the onset of Midnight Mass on Christmas Eve, German bombers were in the air and American antiaircraft guns were fighting back. The church was filled to its limited capacity with children, nuns, Americans and people of the town. The sounds of war were ignored, and the choir was led by an accordion in the singing of hymns and carols. James Shomon remembered an atmosphere of "indescribable spiritual uplift, an exalted feeling of great splendor," and Father Heynen's sermon, given in English, excerpted:

> My friends, we gather here tonight to pay homage to Him for His divine goodness. We pray that this terrible war may soon end and give back to us the blessings of liberty and freedom which we have so long cherished. We do not know the full fury of God's wrath upon our enemies for their wickedness; we do know that he is infinite and just.
>
> Pray hard, my friends, for only through prayer will come good weather for battle. Only through prayer will come airplanes, tanks, courage to hurl the invader back into his scheming, turbulent world of evil and lawlessness....
>
> Be stout of heart, be courageous, be prayerful, my beloved, for the Almighty is with us. The free people of the world will march to victory and trample down the heathens.

The worst was yet to come, however. The sounds heard Christmas Eve were those of the Battle of the Bulge. The German goal was to push into Allied defenses along an 85-mile line from Belgium into Luxembourg. It was the bloodiest battle of the war, fought under the worst of conditions in a historically harsh winter. German troops were ordered to use extreme brutality and take no prisoners, but by the end of January they were defeated. There were 19,000 American deaths. As Allied forces moved forward in success, Graves Registration followed behind picking up corpses by the thousands.

At Margraten, which was also a temporary cemetery for German dead, more land was needed, along with a larger labor force. The blowtorches and axes continued to struggle against the frozen ground. Graves could not be closed because the unearthed dirt had frozen nearly into rocks. The corpses were frozen and warm places needed to be found to thaw them out before they could be stripped and their joints loosened for horizontal burial. The winter winds blew down tents and spread small fires. Crosses became frozen in the ground, and attempts at their disciplined alignment were abandoned. And the demand for graves continued, as well as the need for Graves Registration work as the Allies worked toward the crossing of the Rhine River. The crossing would be the real and symbolic event signaling eventual German defeat. As it approached, a quiet debate took place among American officers and Graves Registration officials over what would be done with the expected dead on both sides of the fight. It was felt that temporary cemeteries in Germany for American soldiers and fliers, while practical, would be offensive to the families of the dead. In the understanding of James Shomon, American dead would be quickly brought back to Holland, while new enemy dead, also the responsibility of Graves Registration behind a fast moving front, would be buried in Germany. Units of the 611th were sent ahead from Margraten to prepare for the work in Germany.

The return of bodies from the crossing of the Rhine was overwhelming. With 17,000 dead, the cemetery at Henri Chapelle was nearing capacity. Two days after crossing, 1,000 American bodies arrived at Margraten. Overwhelmed, Shomon appealed to the mayor of the town:

> Can you help us? We need men. We need men with shovels. Can you issue a call to all able-bodied men of Margraten to report to the cemetery at once? We have more than a thousand bodies that must be buried.
>
> The Burgomaster took off like a shot for the town hall. "Just leave it to me, Captain," he called, "just leave it to me. The men will be there."
>
> In two days the thousand dead were buried and we had more than enough fresh graves open to put us back on a normal schedule. All of us were tired from digging. One colored chap dug a grave in fifty-five minutes; it took me ninety-five.

But the supply chain of American dead back to the Netherlands remained overwhelmed, and, despite well-intentioned plans, bodies had to be buried in Germany. The administration of those temporary burials and their subsequent reburials, as well as responsibility to the enemy dead, led to a lot of traveling by 611th personnel. On one occasion, a convoy moving

American bodies approached another apparent convoy of Americans in American trucks. The trucks were driven, however, by Germans carrying American bodies they were obligated to bury. Overpowered by the Germans, the American Graves Registration personnel were ordered to bury their comrades and happily complied. The task completed, they were imprisoned in a barn for three days and awoke on the morning of the fourth day to find the Germans gone. The work continued, only to be impeded by a shortage of labor and trucks. Trucks not well suited for carrying bodies were pressed into service. Trailers were added, and in some cases, a truck carrying live troops would also pull a trailer full of the dead.

Berlin was surrendered on May 2, and the official end to the war came on May 8, VE Day. A two-day holiday was proclaimed in Margraten. Americans and Dutch visited from house to house. They sang songs of their two nations, and the French "Marseillaise." The cemetery that they had worked together to create was closed for a day, but on the following day they had to absorb another growing accumulation of bodies. The effort to bring back bodies temporarily buried in Germany increased. Units of the 611th moved out to assist in the work of the airborne divisions in registering downed fliers. They discovered a concentration camp at Ludwigslust, Germany. It was a small camp with a strained capacity of 5,000, mostly American prisoners of war and people of France, Poland, Czechoslovakia and Russia. On the same day that Berlin fell, Allied forces found 1,000 dead in the camp and hundreds more on the brink from starvation and disease. Those dead that could be identified as members of the Allied forces were returned to Margraten wrapped in blankets. It was probable that a number of unidentifiable Americans were buried in the town's churchyard. The German citizens were made to provide their own soap for cleaning bodies and sheets to serve as shrouds. And they were made to dig the graves, working on their knees.

The bodies that came back to the Netherlands were often brutally mangled and were laid with difficulty in the formerly unyielding earth that James Shomon now called the "holy" soil of Margraten.

A few months before VE Day, the people of Margraten and the 611th had held a meeting about the cemetery's future. Both the end of the war and the coming of spring were highly anticipated; even before the war had ended, pansies transplanted to the cemetery from a local garden were in full bloom. Trees were transplanted from nearby hills, and foliage brought from a nearby nursery in Munster, Germany. Two hundred truckloads of gravel were brought from the Maas River to cover the roadways, and rocks were brought from Aachen, Germany, to line the plots.

Still, the bodies were piling up, and, in the warmer weather, the smell was drifting into the town. Memorial Day was approaching and civilians were hired to finish the beautification. The pay was much needed, and Shomon's narrative of the time offers a tacit admission, without comment, that it was necessary for the men of Margraten to find work wherever possible because the increasingly large cemetery had taken up usable farm land. Approaching Memorial Day, and with the burden of war lifting, people came to the cemetery from far beyond Margraten. The concept of adopting graves was begun in which local families took responsibility for the care of individual graves, and in some cases the opening of relationships with families in the United States.

The dawn of the American Memorial Day 1945 in Margraten brought twenty trucks full of flowers gathered from sixty villages. The emotional end of the horrible war would come to the Netherlands in a celebration of the Americans who had given their lives to its ending. By now, with nearly 19,000 graves, Margraten was the largest military cemetery in the world. "They came from across the Maas," Shomon wrote, "from Sittard, from Heerlen, from Valken-

The Netherlands American Cemetery, completed for services on Memorial Day 1945. At the time, it was the world's largest military cemetery (*U.S. Army Signal Corps*).

burg, from Vaals and Gulpen. They came on foot, on bicycles, in carriages, on horseback, in automobiles." Outnumbering the dead by two to one, an estimated 30,000 to 40,000 of the living bordered the cemetery on all sides. An international pool of journalists included those on airplanes flying overhead, ready to speed pictures back to the wire services in Paris and London.

An even more elaborate Memorial Day service was held at Margraten in 1946. The *New York Times* described a Memorial Day observance "that must in many ways seem unique." The tide of humanity, it reported, included friends of Americans killed in the Netherlands, Belgium and Germany. Each grave held a flag and a flower or bouquet of some sort. Thousands knelt in prayer.

> Every person asked why he came so far to lavish such care on the graves solemnly explained that he was grateful to these dead Americans, who were, moreover, the Netherlander's friends....
>
> The demonstration today, believed to be without parallel in a foreign country, was accepted by the Netherlanders as proof of their devotion to the men who lost their lives in liberating the country. "This feeling is hard to put into words," Mrs. Van Kennenich [leader of the graves adoption movement] said. "Oh, if only your people could be here on this beautiful afternoon."[13]

Decades later, and into the next century, the American Memorial Day would continue to fill the American cemeteries with large crowds of the later generations of the people of Europe, and in ceremonies just as solemn and celebratory.

CHAPTER ELEVEN

Expanded Families, Gracious Towns

By moonlight, too, have we stood by our son's cross and looked down the long glistening rows of his comrades' crosses bathed in the mystic light.
—Edwin P. Booth

As the world began to emerge from war in 1945, life could return more freely to its ceremonies and routines. In Zoetermeer, the Netherlands, the wedding of Bill van Niekirk and Wilhelmina van den Berg was planned for June 19. Van Niekierk had been one of the first of the Dutch to run to the downed B-24 in farmer Janson's fields the previous February 22. As he arrived at the plane, tail gunner Elmer Duerr emerged carrying his parachute. He tossed it to van Niekierk as he ran to a hiding place. When things had calmed down, the young man gave it to his girlfriend to hide beneath her bed. After liberation, he made her a proposal of marriage, which she accepted. But in the immediate postwar period there was no cloth to be found in the shops suitable for a wedding dress, and the fortunate gift of the parachute was remembered. The bride made her own silk dress, and in some versions of the story, the bridesmaids' and flower girls' dresses, as well as a pair of silk boxers for her husband-to-be. Four children were born of the union, each with a christening dress sewn of parachute silk. Life eventually took the van Nickicrks to Calgary, Alberta, Canada, and, when they were in their eighties, they donated the wedding dress to the Calgary Aerospace Museum.[1]

The ceremonies of transition would not come as easily for the American dead. They were all over the world, often difficult or impossible to find, and not all had died in the service of official United States armed forces. In his book *Crosses in the Wind*, James Shomon posed the questions about American forces that remained for him after the building of Margraten Cemetery: "Now that the war is over, we must face the facts impartially. Overseas are more than a quarter of a million dead. What are we going to do with them? Where should the final burial be—overseas or at home? How much will it cost? Will the next of kin get the right body? What is the government doing to locate the still missing? Will the overseas cemeteries be taken care of?"[2]

The challenge that lay ahead was deemed a work of "monumental proportions." Soon after the war in 1946, Graves Registration estimated the number of American World War II dead was 286,959, and 246,492 had been found and identified in 359 military cemeteries and

7,655 isolated graves. As of March 31, 1946, of the 40,467 who were unidentified 18,641 had been located by Graves Registration units. The remaining 21,826 were yet to be found.[3]

As in World War I, the wishes of next of kin as to overseas, national cemetery or home burial would direct the actions of the quartermaster general, which would be undertaken without differences of any kind "shown because of rank, color or creed. No priorities will be granted and activities will follow an orderly process beginning with a complete verification of the burial records, now underway at temporary cemeteries overseas, as well as in higher field headquarters and the Office of the Quartermaster General."[4] The decision as to the number of permanent American cemeteries to be built overseas would be determined by the number of bodies relatives wished to be maintained there. Similar to World War I, 44 percent of loved ones were to remain overseas as per the wishes of their families. In a few cases, however, new families had been created around the fallen of the war. This was a development the quartermaster general hadn't anticipated and was hard pressed to deal with in a less than bureaucratic way. A number of conflicts played out in postwar Belgium, where, as in World War I, the American Overseas Memorial Day Association in Brussels would become the keeper of the stories of the dead and the caretaker of isolated graves.

After SSgt. Gerald Sorenson had fallen from the Belgian sky, he had been taken into the Comet Line, lived with the Abeels family of Ganshoren and then killed as a member of the Dutch Resistance. He had been buried in the communal cemetery, side by side with his friend Roger Abeels. Perhaps more than friends, Jerry and Roger had become like brothers, and the young Jenny Abeels like a sister they had in common.

Indeed, Jerry had become a fully realized member of the Abeels family, and after his death, the Abeels family of Belgium and the Sorenson family of Idaho began to correspond. Arthur Abeels wrote to Sorenson's wife, Nora, in November, 1945: "They were brothers together. It is for that reason that they stayed together, and they died You can't understand, dear Nora, how much we love you. You are the dear wife of our beloved Jerry. We have loved him the first day he came at home. We have never met a better boy than him. When he called us Pa and Ma, we were so happy. Roger and Jerry were like together."[5]

Nora stayed with the Abeels for three months in 1947. During that time, Ganshoren and Marcq-Lez-Enghien, where he had fallen, held commemorative services in his honor, and a street was given his name near the Abeel's home. And when the process of the quartermaster general eventually arrived to remove the American body buried in the communal cemetery at Ganshoren to one of the military cemeteries in Belgium, Sorenson's family asked that he be left in place. It would not be until 1949 that the matter was finally resolved in favor of the wishes of the blended family, and that family would retain its ties well into the next century.

Not all conflicts between the wishes of new postwar families and the quartermaster's well-intentioned drive to bury the dead in proper places went as smoothly. When the body of 2nd Lt. Robert Lee Garrett of the 466th Bomber Group was disinterred by the Army from a small cemetery in Queue-du-Bois and moved to Margraten in March 1946, two families on either side of the Atlantic were put into shared distress. Garrett, of Norman, Oklahoma, had been piloting his B-24, *Shoo Shoo Baby*, from England to a target in Germany when it collided in formation and in bad weather with another B-24, *Dark Rhapsody*. Garrett survived the plane's crash near Vollenhove, the Netherlands, and was turned over to the Comet Line by the Dutch Resistance. Eventually he arrived at the farm home in Queue-du-Bois of Joseph Bourdouxhe and his son Jean. The end of the war was on the near horizon, and the Comet Line made the decision to keep those pilots hidden in soon-to-be-liberated territories rather than risk continued travel down the Line. Like Jerry Sorenson in Ganshoren, Robert Garrett formed a family bond with the Bourdouxhes and planned to wait out the rest of the war helping on the family farm. On September 7, while the German army was in retreat across Belgium, Garrett was dressed in the clothes of a Belgian farmer and working in an orchard. As a retreating SS vehicle drove by, he was shot gratuitously, and the vehicle moved on. Three days later, Queue-du-Bois was liberated, and on the following day the Bourdouxhes laid him to rest in their family tomb.

Correspondence between the families in Belgium and the United States began immediately. Garrett's brother, John, still fighting in the Pacific Theatre, joined in the letters back and forth: "May the war end here soon so that we can be with our wives and children once more.... God bless all of you and it would make me very proud if you would consider myself as part of your family."[6] Garrett's mother, Hazel, told of the ease of heart she had been given by the Bourdouxhes: "Last year, during the anxious months of waiting each nite when I prayed for his safety, I prayed too for the protection and guidance of those who were taking care of him; for I always believed he was alive and with friends. Now I know that some of my prayers were answered.... I am so very grateful to all of you who helped care for Bobby, who made those months a little happier for him. I am grateful also to your city and country."[7]

Despite the protocol that asked for family wishes on the matter, the reinterment at Margraten had taken place without the knowledge or consent of the Garrett family. The Bourdouxhes, without power to intervene in the process, wrote to the Garretts, who began a campaign of protest against the Office of the Quartermaster. In addition, the burgomaster of Queue-du-Bois wrote to the U.S. embassy in Brussels, offering to assume all costs for reburial and a place for Bobby Garrett in the town's veterans' cemetery. In March 1949, his body was returned from Margraten and reburied with full honors. But, by a feature of Belgian law and custom, it would not be guaranteed that he could rest in perpetuity.

Neither could the living be certain that their last wishes would be granted without difficulty. When PFC Joseph G. Farina was shot through the head by a German bullet at the height of the Battle of the Bulge, he had a plan in place for the burial of his remains. Farina, of Highwood, Illinois, was the son of Italian immigrants and a devout Catholic. His path through the war started out atypically for a private first class. His assignment was to the 526th Armored Infantry Battalion and into the immediate secrecy of the development of a new piece of weaponry. Canal Defense Lights (CDLs) would blind and disorient the enemy during a full infantry attack. But after months of training in Wales, the weapon was deemed useless in Operation Overlord because of thick foliage on the Normandy coast. When the 526th finally landed on Utah Beach in August 1944, it was determined that the CDLs would not be effective in the terrain of the projected path towards Berlin. The weapon was abandoned, though its existence would not be declassified until 1958.

The 526th was then sent to Belgium to be turned into a counterintelligence force, and some of its members were taken in by families in the village of Comblain-la-Tour. Joe Farina seemed to come full circle to his Italian heritage with an assignment to the home in Comblain-Fairon of Joseph and Madeleine Pacchiotti. The Pacchiottis' son, Louis, a member of the Belgian Resistance, had been captured, tortured and killed by the Nazis six months previously, and Joe quickly began to replace his role in the family, which included a sister, Jeanninne [sic]. Joseph Pacchiotti and Joseph Farina became very attached to each other, and the younger man wrote instructions that if he were killed he wanted to be buried in the Pacchiotti family plot in the churchyard at Comblain-la-Tour. Soon thereafter, the Pacchiotti family suffered its second grievous loss of the war.

On December 17, the German Panzercorps of Col. Joachim Peiper came in contact with an army field artillery observation battalion on a march from the Netherlands to Luxembourg. The American battalion was unprepared for heavy combat and was quickly captured. Peiper's unit was called the "Blowtorch Battalion" because of crimes committed against captured Russian villages and their residents. It would fulfill that nickname with the American POWs. They were placed in a snowy field along with American POWs captured earlier. At a German order, first a tank, then small arms and machine gun fire tore into the assembled prisoners. It sought out those who attempted to escape, and German soldiers ran after others. They set fire to buildings used for hiding. When the firing was done, soldiers moved into the bloody field shooting and bludgeoning anyone who appeared to be still alive. Approximately eighty were killed.

On that same day, Joe Farina's company left at night on three hour's notice. Their task was to assist in the blocking of Peiper's advance. The mission was successful up to a point as the fighting continued in place, and the 526th sought to survive the extraordinary cold. On Christmas Day, its C rations were replaced by a turkey dinner, but the meat turned out to be so badly preserved that all of those who ate it contracted dysentery. The following week, the unit was on the move again, under orders to capture a strategic hill. But the Germans and their machine guns waited atop the hill. Though the Americans prevailed by capturing the hill, 65 of them were killed, including Joe Farina. And, with the growing efficiency of Graves Registration, his body was placed in the process that took him to burial in the American Cemetery at Henri-Chapelle on February 25, 1945.

It was not Joe Farina's wish to be buried there, and in the following year, the Farina family began to demand of the army that he be removed to Comblain-la-Tour, but without success. In 1947, Farina's mother and sister visited the Pacchiottis in Belgium and a friendship begun in correspondence was cemented in person. This friendship led to a more forceful demand, this time with the support of the American Legion, that their son and brother be returned to the Pacchiotti family. He was finally laid to rest in the family plot on August 5, 1948.

A similar story played out in France, though it involved an American mother and a French mayor's wife, supported by some of the heavy hitters of the just concluded war. John Rahill was a second lieutenant from Caldwell, New Jersey. Barely 20 years old, he had already written his last will and testament, and in January 1944 he set out upon his last journey from home. From Ft. Meade, Maryland, he and his fellow soldiers traveled to Newport News, Virginia. From there, they zig-zagged across the Atlantic in a 5,000 man troop transport. Arriving in Casablanca, Morocco, they were placed on a long freight train of old cars that were called "40 and 8s" because of their design capacity for 40 men and eight horses. After a three-day trip across the Sahara Desert to Oran, a smaller group, including Rahill, was placed on a small freighter headed for Naples. From there he was moved to France, arriving in the Seventh Army as a first lieutenant.

The Seventh would eventually be the first to reach the crossing of the Rhine the following spring; but in the winter, it was stopped in a grinding battle in Alsace Loraine. In his last letter to his parents, Rahill wrote of his upcoming birthday on New Year's Day: "Just think folks, in January I will be a man." But on the evening after Christmas his family received the telegram from the War Department telling them that he had been killed in action on December 2 near Grandvillers, France. His company commander had been wounded in action and Rahill had assumed command before his own death.

Near the end of 1944, the intensity of fighting on the way to Germany had exceeded the ability of Graves Registration to properly accommodate the dead. John Rahill and more than

1,000 of his fellows were buried in a cemetery intended to be temporary, less than a mile west of Hochfelden, France. With no more information than that, Rahill's mother, Clara, sent off a letter after VE Day addressed only to the mayor of Hochfelden, asking for details of her son's burial. It was opened by the mayor's wife, Lilly Haag, who responded immediately that John was being well cared for by the grateful people of Alsace in a beautiful piece of land on the outskirts of the town.

A quick bond was formed between the two women, and when it was learned some years later that the quartermaster general would be moving those still buried in Hochfelden to the Lorraine American Cemetery near Avhold, they worked together against the Graves Registration process to be sure that John would stay in place. To overcome the essentially benevolent but relentless focus on American cemetery burial by Graves Registration, Mrs. Rahill and Mrs. Haag began a letter-writing campaign to key military leaders of their two countries, and they were not reluctant to approach American general Dwight D. Eisenhower on the matter. Their effort succeeded and, though it had taken eight years, the responsibility of care for John Rahill was transferred to the people of Hochfelden.

By the anniversary of D-day in 1953, Pres. Eisenhower deemed it important to remind the United States and France of their long and textured friendship. On June 7, a monument to Americans soldiers lost in France was dedicated at the site of the Hochfelden Cemetery and at the grave of John Rahill. In attendance were the Rahills and the Haags, the people of the town and the American ambassador to France, Douglas Dillon. The ambassador read a message from Pres. Eisenhower: "I am grateful for the ceremony at Hochfelden in honor of American Lt. John Rahill and I wish once again to express on this occasion my feelings of friendship for the French people."[8]

Just as remembrance for the isolated graves in Belgium would become the focus of the American Overseas Memorial Day Association in that country, those of John Rahill and others would fall into the arms of Benjamin Franklin's creation, AOMDA-France.

SSgt. Abie Abraham, was a first-generation Syrian-American from Lyndora, Pennsylvania. Like many American soldiers, he was not a great fan of Gen. Douglas MacArthur. There was a prevailing feeling that he had not prepared well for an inevitable Japanese invasion of the Philippines, then managed to escape the battle on a PT boat bound for Australia, promising to return at some point in the future and leaving his men vulnerable to what would come next. For Sgt. Abraham and 75,000 American and Filipino troops, that would be the Bataan Death March and years of brutal imprisonment. Then one day after the liberation of the Philippines, the sergeant was summoned to the offices of Gen. MacArthur in Manila. He was brought to headquarters by staff car and introduced to the general. He recalled MacArthur's words in his 1971 book, *The Ghost of Bataan*:

> "I know I'm asking too much of you. I know the hardships you endured in prison camp."
>
> "How could he know?" kept popping through my mind. He was safe in Australia all the time, away from the stench and death and cruelty....
>
> "I know that thousands of your friends are dead.... I would like for you to recover the graves of the Americans who died.... I need a man," MacArthur went on in slow, well modulated words, "who was in the Death March," and as though he read my thoughts, he added, "You owe it to your friends, and especially to their loved ones back home."
>
> "Sir," I said, "I will stay and do the job. I will find all of the bodies and the graves along the March and in the prison camps."[9]

It was May 1945. What had occurred on the Bataan Death March was still not fully understood, nor were there good records of who its victims might be. But there were bodies of Americans,

Dutch men, Filipinos and Englishmen to be found, identified and reburied, and the job fell to the 601st Graves Registration Company. A very practical decision was made that the search would be helped by a survivor of the march. Abie Abraham was the only one of those still known to be in the Philippines. His acceptance of MacArthur's assignment was gallant, but he had his doubts: "All night I tossed. 'Was it fear, or was it the thought of seeing the bones of my many friends?' I still don't know the answer, but I spent a long, miserable night. When I heard the rooster crowing, I knew that daylight was near, and climbed out of bed. Something forced me to my knees and I prayed, asking God to give me the strength, and show me how to carry on throughout the long tough way."[10]

The problems to be solved by Graves Registration were daunting. This was not Europe where the weather and the help of the people of closely knit small towns gave a benefit to preservation and identification. This was a place of heat and the erosion of tropical rains, and, in the brutality of the march, hastily dug and often hidden graves. Good information was critical. At the town of Balanga, as an example, public officials and priests were asked to gather their people for a public meeting. Sgt. Abraham was introduced and told them of the full brutality of the march they had seen pass by. He shared his own memories of death and burial he had witnessed near the town, provoking the memories of others.

The meetings along the path of the march became increasingly productive. At first, they seemed to the townspeople too similar to meetings they had been forced to attend by the Japanese at the points of bayonets. Abraham and the 601st were sensitive to the problem, but they found the challenge even more difficult than they had expected it to be. In the wake of the March, they learned, whole frightened towns had moved themselves into the hills, leaving behind the care of those they had buried. Many were buried in hidden places now forgotten, and for those that could be found identification was made more difficult by the attraction of the Filipino people to trinkets, such as the bars and insignias that might be found on uniforms. Finally understanding this, Graves Registration promised that those items would only be examined and returned.

The graves that were found were marked with white crosses for further attention, but if their tenants could not be identified, they would not be disturbed. Sgt. Abraham was able to identify a number of them through recollection of the person and the cause and place of death. While imprisoned at the Cabanatuan camp, he and others had been able to preserve records of 1,035 dead on the backs of milk can labels. Each of the deaths was fully described and the paper signed by a prisoner physician, serving as an official death certificate. That information, and the work left behind by a Graves Registration captain, also imprisoned there for a time, was used to identify many more.[11]

Abie Abraham's role in the Pacific war then came full circle. In January 1946, he was summoned once again to Manila, this time to the war trials commissioner's office where he was asked to be a witness against the Japanese general Masaharu Homma. It was Homma who had accepted the American surrender on the Bataan Peninsula, encouraged the brutality of his troops and instigated the Bataan Death March:

> "Do you know the accused?" Lt. White asked me. I looked at the shrinking Gen. Homma. He gazed at me for a moment then turned very pale. "Yes, I know him."
> "Did you see him on the Death March?" "No, I did not see him, however, I knew that he was in Bataan."
> "How many bodies have you disinterred on the Death March route?"
> "To date, three hundred, and I know where many more of their graves are."
> "About how many would you say are yet to be disinterred?"

"Hundreds—"

"And you know where the graves are?"

"Yes, and it will take time, perhaps years, to recover them all."[12]

As the Pacific war had worked to a conclusion, the American air force firebombed the city of Yokohama on May 29, 1945. A third of the city was turned to rubble. After the war, two air force mausoleums constructed in Yokohama became the focus for much of the Graves Registration work in Asia, particularly as a resting place for the cremated remains of American pilots and prisoners of war.

In postwar Japan, the American occupiers under Gen. Douglas MacArthur were quickly seen as a benevolent force, not that of an evil enemy about which they had been constantly warned. The people were exhausted and disillusioned with their leadership. Hiroshima and Nagasaki had been destroyed and left toxic by atomic bombs, and other cities were not much better off. The Americans offered relief and structure, and they were met with a measure of gratitude. As Graves Registration began its work, many of the American dead were found in urns of cremated remains. Cremation was a Japanese ritual of death, and when American airmen fell from the sky, or in some cases of dead prisoners of war, their bodies would be cremated in keeping with the respect of Japanese custom.

The *Quartermaster Review* of January–February 1946,[13] for example, told of an unspecified American plane shot down over Honshu Province in May 1945. Two of its crew parachuted safely to earth and were taken prisoner. The plane, however, fell in another location near the village of Kamiomi, just northeast of Tokyo. This was not quite a new experience for the people of Kamiomi. Sometime in the spring of 1913, a meteorite had fallen in a local farm field, and it would eventually become listed in the world's meteorite database. This time, it was an American bomber, in which the villagers found six mangled bodies in the fuselage, one in the wing assembly, and two more clear of the wreckage; all of them burned beyond recognition. All were gathered up respectfully and given full cremation ceremonies. Their remains were placed in individual urns and saved in the Temple of Kamiomi for whatever the outcome of the war would be. Eventually they traveled to the Mausoleum at Yokohama, for possible identification.

At the beginning of 1945, the Mausoleum contained the cremated remains of 931 Allied dead. Just 236 of them were American and the rest English, Dutch, Canadian, Australian, Norwegian, and Chinese. Most of them were prisoners of war cremated by their captors. Their remains had been given to the care of other prisoners who managed to hold on to them or pass them on to others, until the end of the war, when they were given to the American Occupational Army. And, in the pro–American spirit of postwar Japan, Graves Registration was able to gain the help of the Japanese in finding other preserved urns in the small towns and temples of the country.[14]

But those small successes of a few hundred found here and there could not begin to make a dent in the numbers of those lost, perhaps forever. More than 80,000 Americans had given their lives in Asia. Thirty thousand of those could be accounted for in 201 temporary cemeteries; but the rest lay scattered by airplanes or by the best intentions of Filipino villagers or lost in impenetrable jungles. By spring 1947, the American Graves Registration Service of the India-Burma Zone had virtually given up the search. A restricted memo to the adjutant general of the War Department dated April 30 made what appeared to be a second assertion that the search should be ended. It noted that between August 31, 1945, and the current date just 230 remains had been found in Burma with an estimate that only 50 percent would be identified as individual or the grouped remains of a given aircrew. Fifty-three sets of remains had been found in the Assam region of India, of which 70 percent might be identified, and 66 sets had been found on Borneo Island, of which 80 percent would be identified.

Eight to ten sets each of remains *might* be found in Assam and Borneo with further search, but the numbers were so few that "it is again recommended that area search of Assam, North Burma and Borneo be discontinued as of May 1947. Searches for individual remains and airplane crashes when supported by sufficient and detailed information will of course continue to be made."[15] But the search for bodies in the Pacific Basin would never really come to an end.

With the Manila American Cemetery in the Philippines and the Punchbowl Cemetery in Honolulu, the 201 temporary cemeteries were reduced to two that were permanent. The Manila cemetery would eventually accommodate 17,206 of the dead, about 40 percent of those who had been known and unknown in the temporary cemeteries, the rest returned to families or national cemeteries. The subsequently dedicated Hawaii cemetery would hold 13,767 bodies. Tens of thousands would remain missing in action, presumably dead and buried, or left where they fell.

In 1947, the Graves Registration operations in the Mediterranean began to work toward the recovery of the dead from the furthest reaches of Europe and into the process of return home or burial in defined American cemeteries on European soil. The unpublished history of that effort, located in the National Archives, tells the story in immaculately typed pages with pasted-on snapshots that speak of the strong simplicity and ethic of both process and design. Each cemetery was to be built and maintained "to present a scene of simple reverent beauty as compatible as possible with the surrounding terrain and landscaping. Each cemetery receives equal meticulous attention."[16]

Alphabetical card files with pertinent information on one card per person were to be kept in standard cabinets at each location. Cemetery ledgers were to be able to easily direct a visitor to a given deceased and include full information about that person down to religious preference. Each cemetery was to include a small brick or stone reception house with an office, a supply room and a bathroom for use by visitors only.

The code of conduct for employees included resistance to black market activities prevalent at the time: "Let's not be accused of being willing to sell our government for a cheap five cents." Commanding officers were to "give an employee a specific job to do and let him know that he alone is responsible for it and he will work a full eight hours each day to obtain his mission...."[17]

The process of transfer from temporary cemeteries was begun. The dead of the temporary cemetery in Sofia, Bulgaria, for example, were moved to what would become the Sicily-Rome American Cemetery in Nettuno, Italy, in November 1946. The bodies in Cappuccini, Malta, would move to Nettuno in March 1947. Those disinterred from a temporary cemetery in Vis, Yugoslavia, were moved forward to another temporary cemetery in Belgrade in December 1946. Transfers from cemeteries in Bulgaria, Greece, Corsica, Sardinia and Malta were accomplished by C-47 aircraft, others by rail. In some cases, bodies were reburied with the same plot, row and grave locations that had located them in previous cemeteries. Each movement was preceded by careful planning conducted, according to the typed history, in an ethic of utmost care and dignity.

And, though they were temporary, it seemed important in the document to point out that the cemeteries in which the dead were first buried had not been lightly planned. The Cemetery at Athens was "situated in the ancient shadows of the Acropolis along the road to the ancient Greek Fort of Piraeus." Its dead, mainly members of the Air Corps, were removed

ELEVEN. *Expanded Families, Gracious Towns* 127

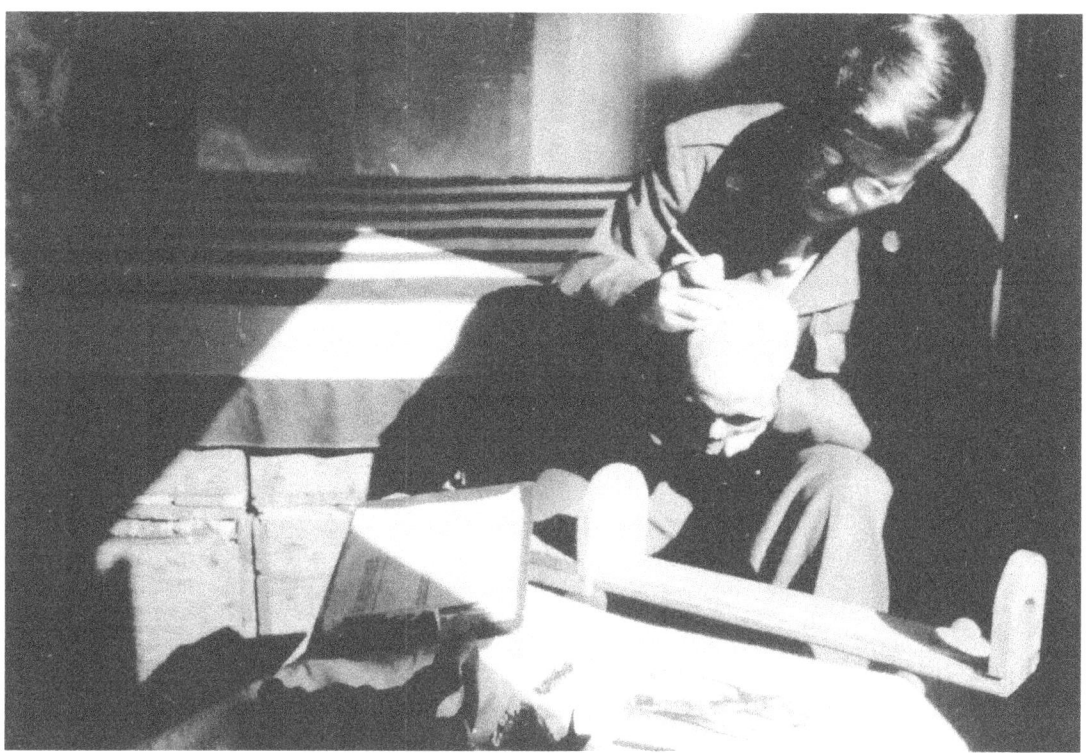

Preparation of a tooth chart was one of the most effective tools in helping to identify unknown bodies that were often recovered from isolated burials. In the Mediterranean Zone, the work was done by Central Identification Points (CIPs) in Sicily and southern Italy. The process included measuring of bones to determine height and a thorough examination of clothing for other indicators of identity (*National Archives*).

to Nettuno in January 1947. The cemetery at Caronia, Sicily, "was on the shores of the Blue Mediterranean Sea, nestling in an olive grove, with a beautiful triangular entrance and a large concrete star, the site of the Volcanic Islands of Vulcano and Stromboli, whose craters are continually active, provided a scenic memorial for the Americans buried here shortly before the fall of Sicily in August 1943." Its 658 remains were removed to another temporary cemetery at Paestum, Italy. At that time, the cemeteries at Nettuno and Paestum, and many others, had not yet been determined to be the permanent American military cemeteries of World War II. Decisions of size and location of permanent cemeteries all over Europe had to wait as the larger process of honoring the developing wishes of the families of the dead were played out.

On Thanksgiving Day of 1946, one of those families set foot in the American cemetery at Margraten in search of their son and brother. Sgt. Edwin Bray Booth of the 513th Parachute Infantry Regiment, 17th Airborne Division, had been killed in action on March 24, 1945, and awarded the Purple Heart. His father, Edwin P. Booth, was a professor of Church History at Boston University School of Theology and an author of books about Martin Luther and the relationship between religion and science, among other things. The purpose of his family's trip was to finally visit Edwin where he lay and to make the decision as to whether to ask that he be disinterred and brought home. Intending it to be helpful to the thousands of other families faced with that dilemma, Mr. Booth published his observations in the *New York Herald*

After full processing, ideally with identity determined, remains were wrapped in a clean, carefully pinned cloth for storage in a temporary burial box before repatriation or movement to an American cemetery in Europe (*National Archives*).

Tribune of February 20, 1947, and they were republished in church notices across the country.[18]

Capt. James Shomon, his men, and the people of Margraten had left the father a bittersweet gift.

> [The] approach road is through a farm, and in the field to our right the farmer followed his horses along deep furrows in rich soil. On the opposite side some winter planting was in, and a fresh green growth covered half of the furrowed acres. My heart was quiet with the expectancy of unbelief for just a moment, and then I caught my first real glimpse of the cemetery itself. A fine white-gray light, it seemed to me, took the place on the crown of the hill of the dark earth plowed and the green growing grain.
>
> Over my consciousness crept the realization, slowly, that this light was formed by thousands of small white crosses in perfect symmetry upon the hilltop. At the head, as it were, of this field of white, quietly, from a tall white pole, flew the American flag.
>
> We did not speak to each other much, and each knew only what was in his own mind. But I had come to stand in tribute at the grave of my son, and so had his mother and his brothers. It was a thing of awe and majesty to see the quiet peaceful field of crosses. Row upon row, they lie as they marched. Side by side, they sleep in death as they had slept in camp....
>
> They face a little south of west, looking toward the homes they loved so much and never more shall see.
>
> We followed the broad gravel walks through the plots and came finally to stand by a cross with

our own beloved name upon it. To stand in simple dignity and "bear what men must" was all that was left for me to do. There, by his cross, I looked upon the landscape all around me and saw it to be much like the hills of his home in New England. Far off to the north, high on a hill, a single windmill stood guard as though it would symbolize all of Holland.

Booth found the cemetery nearly perfect for its purpose. He thought that the chapel should be more prominent and better attended to. He wished that its natural surroundings would never change. What better to surround his son and the others than the growing grain of the spring and the stacked harvest of the fall. He and his family returned to Margraten over several days to see it in all types of weather: "On stormy days the full sweep of fresh, strong winds cleans the hilltop and puts a snap into the air. Under warm and sunny skies it is bathed in light and the wind is lazy. The sunsets are exquisite, with the western valley to catch the soft reflected afterglows. By moonlight, too, have we stood by our son's cross and looked down the long glistening rows of his comrades' crosses bathed in the mystic light."

Finally, Booth wrote of the constant attention of the people of Margraten, Maastricht and the surrounding countryside to each individual grave with prayers and flowers. Each grave, he realized, was receiving personal attention. He did not recommend what other families should decide about the final rest of their boys, though his family saw fit to leave Edwin Bray Booth where he lay. But the cemetery would be changed over the following years by the wishes of those who wanted their boys returned.

As beautiful as it was, as treacherous as it had been to build, and as beloved as it was by the people who lived around it, Margraten would not be exceptional among the American cemeteries of Europe. As with those of World War I, the cemeteries of the second war would be conceived and designed to place their inhabitants reverently in the lands they had helped to save from what could only be seen as evil. Those who lived on those lands would carefully attend them to for generations to come.

The work of Mediterranean Graves Registration continued. Beyond the recovery from known temporary cemeteries, the effort fanned out from central points in Naples, Rome, Mirandola and Belgrade in search of isolated burials. By October 1947 that work had been concluded in nations and islands of the Tyrrhenian and Adriatic seas, though with just 1,525 remains found. From regional processing units, they were sent to Rome for final determination of identity, if possible, and a case-by-case finalization by a board of review. As in the India-Burma Zone, the effort was closed, with the condition that individual searches based on credible information would continue.

Some temporary cemeteries had developed out of specific needs. Most of those interred in the cemetery at Naples, Italy, as of October 1947 were victims of a single bomb set off in the Naples post office four years earlier. Many more were rare burials of merchant marines not lost at sea. Gradually, burials would concentrate in the larger cemeteries that would develop into permanent places of rest. Nettuno became a particular destination for casualties of the Battle of Anzio. Though deemed successful in breaking enemy lines in Italy and clearing the way for an attack on Rome, 7,000 Allied soldiers and sailors were killed in the action, and thousands more were missing and injured. And Nettuno became a temporary resting place for 2,724 enemy dead before they could be moved to cemeteries in Germany. Named originally for the Roman god of the sea, Nettuno would become the permanent Sicily-Rome American Cemetery, though not completed until 1956.

The necessary work of Graves Registration in the Balkan countries of Albania, Bulgaria, Yugoslavia, Hungary and Romania proved more difficult than it had been in Mediterranean Europe. The American dead were more likely to be scattered by airplanes and harder to find.

Graves Registration expected that they would be found in unrecorded and isolated graves, if they had been buried at all. Delay, as always, meant loss of identifying information or loss of bodies altogether. And the countries not occupied by American forces put up bureaucratic barriers to American access, if they chose to respond to requests at all.

It took diplomatic effort to allow the first trickle of registration units, and searches of the smaller countries were slowly concluded. A temporary cemetery was set up in Belgrade, though it would at first have to struggle for necessary travel permits for search and retrieval and permission to use the necessary kinds of trucks and equipment. The difficulties culminated in a conference held in May 1947, after which the Yugoslavian government offered full cooperation and assistance. By the following September, 317 American bodies would be recovered, and 426 remains would be buried in the Belgrade cemetery by the following month. Although it was a small number, it was considered a success.

As of September 1947, the Graves Registration Mediterranean Zone oversaw 15 temporary cemeteries holding 37,427 deceased. Seventy-seven of them were members of other Allied forces, and 3,948 were enemy dead. During the years of recovery and reburial, Memorial Day services were held at each cemetery. The cemeteries and their ceremonies offered a platform for most parties in the just concluded war to reacquaint themselves with their distinctions, commonalities and previous histories. Participants in the 1946 Memorial Day service at Nettuno included representatives of U.S., British, Polish, French, and Italian forces, the American Red Cross, Daughters of the American Revolution, and the Overseas Memorial Day Association.

Recovery took place over time from all of the approximately 60 countries involved in the war. It was not until 1948, for example, that the effort to retrieve the bodies of 133 American airmen reached Denmark. In most cases, memorial stones were left behind in the cemeteries in which they had lain, and five bodies were left in place. Jack Wagner, mentioned in the remarks of Pres. Ronald Reagan at a state dinner for Denmark in 1985, was one of them. The others stayed behind for reasons lost to history, but probably by family wishes that they not be disturbed.

Decisions to bring loved ones home would cause the cemetery at Margraten to devote its immediate postwar years to the reduction of its population by 57 percent, from approximately 19,000 to 8,302. The difficult process of its development seemed only to have been reversed, and almost equally as gruesomely.

The methods and challenges of all of the search, identification, disinterments and reinterments of those years were pretty much kept from the public. It seemed enough that so many people had to make hard decisions about their loved ones, and no value could be seen in letting them know the details of what their corpses might undergo if returned home. Bodies were found in all stages of decomposition, often depending on the location and the weather they had endured over several years. But their uniforms and burial shrouds were generally intact. Once disinterred for the first time, the shock of fresh air created odors that could be intolerable.

At Margraten, as elsewhere, the whole cemetery was dug up by a mostly civilian workforce. Bodies were taken to the morgue where all flesh and clothing was removed and burned. Skeletons were cleaned and sterilized and placed in hermetically sealed coffins after identification was checked and rechecked. Those to be sent home were reserved in one location and those to be reinterred in another.

With the cemetery fully cleared, it was redesigned to accommodate sixteen burial plots. The acreage freed up by the return to America of more than 10,000 dead would be repurposed to accommodate a center mall, flagstaff, "Walls of Memory" for those missing in action, memorial tower and chapel, museum, reflecting pool, headquarters building, outside restrooms, parking and access roads, and a superintendent's house. The Netherlands American Cemetery was not fully dedicated until 1960. One of the streets in Margraten was named Shomonstraat after Lt. Col. Joseph James Shomon.

During the last years of the war, the people of Margraten had begun to take on yet another task for the cemetery that had become so much a part of their lives, one that would continue into the next century. It started when an American soldier involved in the building of the cemetery asked the town clerk, Joseph van Laar, to watch over the grave of a nephew who had been buried there. The idea was taken up by a civic group in the town, which produced a register of all burials that was quickly filled with the names of citizens who would take responsibility for individual graves. At the very least, each grave would receive flowers on days of memorial and some tidying up. But in many cases, an adoption became a family responsibility handed down through generations; and in some cases, families came together from both sides of the Atlantic toward the common purpose of caring for a dead child or husband.

Just as World War I led to the development of eleven cemeteries abroad that would fall under the purview of the American Battle Monuments Commission, World War II created fourteen. As completed, they are described:

- The Ardennes American cemetery and Memorial, located near Neuville-en-Condroz, Belgium, twelve miles south of Liege, contained 5,329 dead on 90 acres. Most were lost in the Battle of the Bulge. The cemetery also served as a Central Identification Point (CIP) for the Graves Registration service.
- The Brittany American Cemetery and Memorial near the eastern edge of Brittany, France, held 4,410 dead on 28 acres. Most lost their lives in the Normandy and Brittany campaigns of 1944.
- The Cambridge American Cemetery and Memorial sat three miles west of Cambridge University in England. Its 30.5 acres were donated to the United States by the university. It contained the remains of 3,812, most killed in the Battle of the Atlantic or in the strategic air bombardment of northwest Europe.
- The Epinal American Cemetery and Memorial in France sat above the Moselle River in the foothills of the Vosges Mountains, and contained the graves of 5,255 on 48.6 acres. Most were killed in campaigns across northeastern France to the Rhine and into Germany.
- The Florence American Cemetery and Memorial seven miles south of Florence, Italy, held 4,402 American dead on 70 acres. Most were casualties of battles that took place after the capture of Rome in June 1944.
- The Henri-Chapelle American Cemetery and Memorial near Henri-Chapelle, Belgium, held 7,992 dead on 57 acres. Most were casualties of the advances into Germany that would bring the war to a conclusion.
- The Lorraine American Cemetery and Memorial at the town of St. Avold, France, was the largest World War II cemetery in Europe. The 10,489 American dead lay in 113.5 acres, most killed in battles to break the Siegfried Line and cross the Rhine River.
- The Luxembourg American Cemetery and Memorial was located three miles east of Luxembourg City. Most of its 5,076 dead on 50.5 acres were casualties of the Battle of the Bulge and the crossing of the Rhine River. The city served as the headquarters of the U.S. Third Army of Gen. George S. Patton, who was buried there.
- The Manila American Cemetery and Memorial in metropolitan Manila, the Philip-

The beginning of a repatriation program to return American war dead for permanent burial at home was marked by a solemn ceremony in the port of Antwerp, Belgium, on October 4, 1947. Five thousand, six hundred bodies from the Henri-Chapelle American Cemetery were moved to the port and celebrated by an estimated 30,000 Belgians before being returned across the Atlantic (*American Overseas Memorial Day Association–Belgium*).

pines, was the largest World War II cemetery in terms of the dead. The 17,202 casualties, most from operations in the Philippines and New Guinea, rested in 152 acres.
- The World War II Netherlands American Cemetery and Memorial was the official name of the cemetery at Margraten. It was near the town of Margraten and six miles east of Maastricht. It held 8,301 dead on 65.5 acres.
- The Normandy American Cemetery and Memorial in France was located on a cliff overlooking Omaha Beach and the English Channel, east of St. Laurent-sur-Mer. It was the first American cemetery in Europe and remained a popular representative of all of them. The 9,387 dead rested in 172.5 acres, most lost in the Normandy invasions and subsequent operations.
- The North Africa American Cemetery and Memorial in Tunisia sat close to the site of Ancient Carthage and ten miles from the city of Tunis. The 2,841 fallen lay in 27 acres. Most were killed in an area ranging from North Africa to the Persian Gulf.
- The Rhone American Cemetery and Memorial was in Draguignan, France, 40 miles from Cannes. It held 861 dead on 12.5 acres, most lost in the liberation of southern France in August, 1944.
- The Sicily-Rome American Cemetery and Memorial was near Nettuno and 38 miles south of Rome. It held 7,861 American dead on 77 acres, most lost in the liberation of Sicily, the beach landings of southern Italy from September 1943 to May 1944, and subsequent battles northward.

- The Suresnes American Cemetery and Memorial just outside Paris, France, was the only cemetery to hold the dead of both world wars, a decision meant to be symbolic of the tragedy of two successive wars. The 1,541 World War I dead rested with 24 unknown World War II dead on 7.5 acres.

At the same point in the war that a foreseen conclusion could allow the beginning development of cemeteries for American dead, the Commonwealth War Graves Commission had been able to return to the care of some of its World War I cemeteries and begin the establishment of those for the present war. The numbers behind the CWGC effort were more daunting than those faced by the U.S. Graves Registration. The toll of recovered dead American forces was more than 281,000 plus almost 114,000 service workers related to the battlefields. The CWGC total was 600,000. And, because the CWGC philosophy was to build or use already existing cemeteries where the fallen lay instead of the American method of consolidation, the number of 14 new European cemeteries of the American Battle Monument Commission was more than dwarfed by 559 new cemeteries of the CWGC. They existed in almost every country in which the war was fought, in approximately 23,000 separate burial grounds from Albania to Zimbabwe. Approximately 800 American members of the Commonwealth Forces were buried in 30 countries abroad.[19]

Roger Wallace Haven of Massachusetts (Chapter Nine), shot down over Algeria and buried in the El Alia cemetery at Algiers, was one of them. Another was James Daniel Lawrence

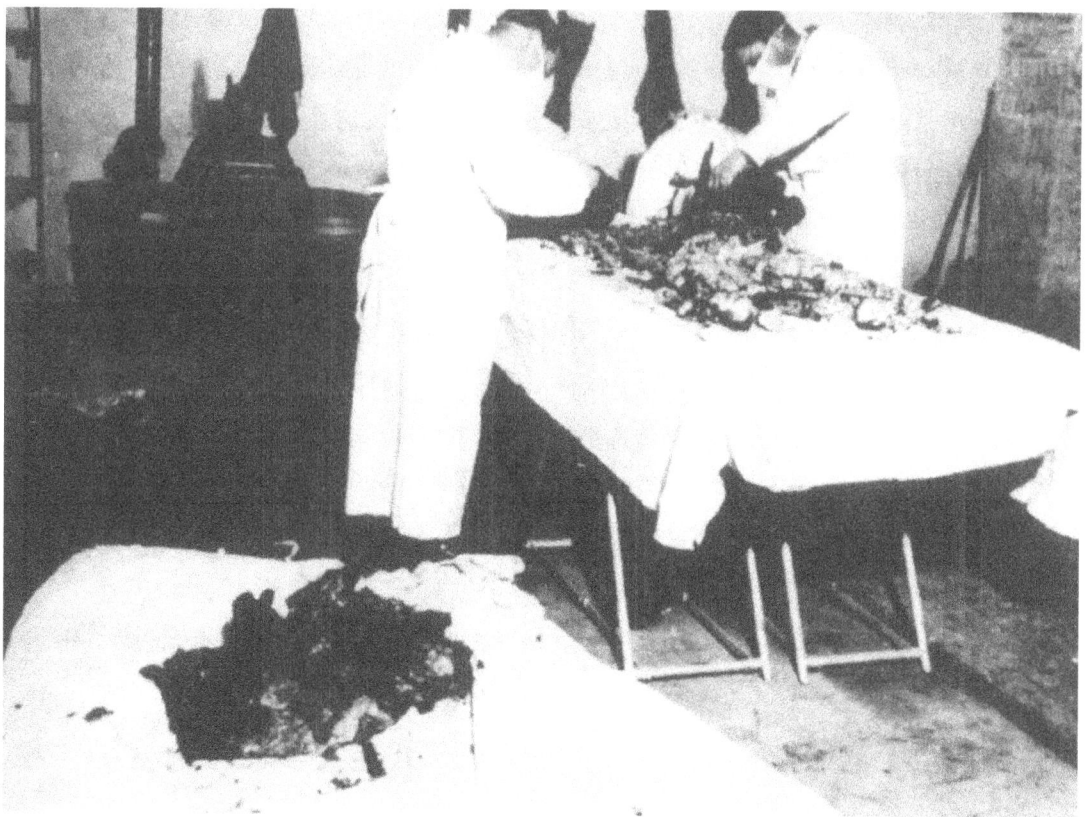

Remains interred at the Netherlands American Cemetery during World War II are prepared for reburial postwar. (*From Farmland to Soldiers Cemetery by Mieke Kirkels and Jo Purnot; Adr. Heijnen, 's-Hertogenbosch NL*).

Pablo of Emo, Montana, a pilot in the Royal Canadian Air Force. Flying in a formation of 479 aircraft from Stratford-upon-Avon, England, to Dusseldorf, Germany, on September 11, 1942, his was one of 33 aircraft lost over the target. He was buried in the Reichswald Forest War Cemetery, Kleve, Nordrhein-Westfalen, Germany. Charles Dewitt Gellatly joined the RCAF from Beaumont, Texas, and was killed in a crash northeast of Cloppenburg, Germany, on April 8, 1942. He was buried in the Sage War Cemetery, Oldenburg, Niedersachsen, Germany.

A number of American women also joined overseas forces, many of them in the Women's Auxiliary Air Force. Though they did not serve as aircrew, their work with large barrage balloons designed to protect buildings and cities from aerial attack and in meteorology and reconnaissance could be just as dangerous. Lili Stefania Bankier of Brighton, Massachusetts, was a meteorologist killed in action, at age 23, over Palestine on July 28, 1945. She was buried in the Vaad Hakehilla Cemetery of Jerusalem, but the location of the grave was lost in postwar years. Though her body probably remained somewhere near Jerusalem, only her name was given on a memorial at the Ramleh Memorial Cemetery beneath the hills of Judea.[20]

As if the ongoing march of history could not be stopped by war, the Tripolitan harbormaster Mustapha Burchis found himself having drinks with friends in a local café on June 6, 1948, the fourth anniversary of D-day. By his account, he picked up a local newspaper and read that the Americans would soon be opening a consulate in his city. "Here is a chance again," he thought. "This time I will deal directly with the representative of the United States

The Netherlands American Cemetery on a Memorial Day, probably in the early 1950s. "The girls wear ribbon on top of their heads," said Mieke Kirkels, coauthor of *From Farmland to Soldiers Cemetery*, of the custom at that time. "The clothing doesn't look as poor as it was the first years after the liberation" (*Samenwerkende Heemkunde Organisaties Margraten*).

ELEVEN. Expanded Families, Gracious Towns

The North African American Cemetery and Memorial in Tunisia holds 2,841 dead, most from the North African campaigns of World War II. Its memorial wall holds the engraved names of 3,724 missing in action. The cemetery's location is near the ancient city of Carthage and ten miles from the capital city of Tunis (*American Battle Monuments Commission*).

Government."[21] He had not been able to put aside all of the work he had done, at the indirect direction of Franklin Roosevelt, in finding the burial places of five American sailors killed in the explosion of the USS *Intrepid* in 1804.

On December 20 he sent a letter to the consul general telling of his investigation nearly a decade earlier: "I am at the disposal of the United States Government in order to let you know the fate of these heroic sailors." The letter was vetted through diplomatic channels and, in March 1949, he was invited to the consulate to put all of his work on the table. It was accepted as correct and hailed by the U.S. Navy as a new and dramatic discovery. Immediately, naval commanders from all over the Mediterranean region traveled to Tripoli, where Burchis took them to the Old Protestant Cemetery on the outskirts of town and pointed out the five graves in the northeast corner. The USS *Spokane* was ordered to head to Tripoli for appropriate ceremonies. The *Spokane* had operated mainly out of Plymouth, England, and Norfolk, Virginia, after the war, often in postwar ceremonies, including a "Full Dress" presence in recognition of the marriage of Princess Elizabeth of Great Britain and visits by the royalty of Greece and the Netherlands. As the ship approached Tripoli, its onboard newspaper, *The Spoke*, exclaimed upon the mission:

> History awakens! The graves of five unknown American sailors have been found in Tripoli. The men are believed to have been crew members of the ketch INTREPID, which was responsible for the brazen burning of the PHILADELPHIA at Tripoli, February 16, 1804.

A Commonwealth War Graves Cemetery within the larger Amsterdam New Eastern Cemetery, northern Holland, holds the bodies of three Americans who flew with the Royal Canadian Air Force in World War II (*Author photograph*).

> Out of the past — out of the pages of history, the memory of these "American Plank owners" rise to be known to the world, through a memorial to be presented by the USS Spokane.[22]

The ceremony on April 2, 1949 was full bore and full dress. A band of Scottish Camerons played martial music as they marched with a unit of the British Army, then in control of Tripoli, from the town to the cemetery. All sorts of admirals, captains, consuls and chaplains offered their thoughts and prayers. The mayor of Tripoli, a direct descendant of the same bashaw who had frustrated Thomas Jefferson to the point of war, was in attendance with 50 other local dignitaries. A memorial plaque was put up, and individual plaques were placed at each grave.

The event was deemed "a worthy tribute to the courageous sailors of the Navy of yesterday from the sailors of the Navy of today."[23] But as time would pass, a discovery of the graves of the *Intrepid* sailors would be made at least once again, leading only to frustration on the part of a small town in New Jersey.

CHAPTER TWELVE

Cold Earth and Tropical Earth

...the French and British are finished here, and we ought to clear out of Southeast Asia.
—Lt. Col. Peter A. Dewey

After TSgt. Bernard McManaman finally floated out of the Metropole Hotel in Brussels in September 1944, he arrived home in Lapeer, Michigan. He did not talk much about his experiences, and it was only in the course of the writing of a newspaper article that members of his family fully learned about his time in Belgium. It was obvious that his short time held in the heart of the Abeels family of Ganshoren remained an undercurrent in the following years. He maintained a scrapbook of his time with them. When he married, his daughter was named Janine after the young Jenny Abeels, who had been the "sister" of both Bernard and Jerry Sorenson, as well as the real sister of their friend Roger Abeels.

When Janine McManaman was just less than six months old, her father was called up for the growing Korean War. He did not want to go. On the day that he left, he kissed his mother, Edna, good-bye and walked out the door of her home. Then he turned around and walked back in, hugged her again, and said, "Mom, I have a real bad feeling about this. I know I'm not coming back."

Bernard flew with the third wing of the 13th Bombardment Squadron (Light-Night Intruder). The job of the Light-Night Intruders, in an operation sometimes called "Hoot Owl," was to fly with attack planes, finding and illuminating targets of opportunity. Though used in World War II, it was an experimental procedure for Korea. At first, the method was to search for headlights on the ground as indicators of a target. But it seemed that Koreans had a custom of night driving without the use of headlights. In one practice, reconnaissance aircraft would drop parachute flares over targets that would then be attacked by B-26 bombers, but targets like truck convoys would move away too quickly. Another method was to use a seven million candlepower light attached to the reconnaissance aircraft, but it could not be lit for more than a minute and turned the aircraft itself into an easy target. And the B-26s were often without precise radar, to say nothing of being too lumbering to move nimbly through the mountains and valleys of Korea.

By September, almost 19 sorties were being flown each night. Though the missions had their occasional great successes, the loss on all such missions between August 3 and September 30, night and day, included forty-five F-51 aircraft, eight F-80s and three B-26s. One of those B-26 aircraft was modified to include a glass nose, and two machine guns were mounted in the bombardier's compartment. On the night of September 3, 1951, it was flying at 800 feet responding to a target lit by flares near Inchon. It was hit by ground fire and crashed into a hillside. Among the three crewmen lost was Bernard McManaman.

The war into which McManaman fell, and the land on which it was fought, was the most challenging that Graves Registration had ever confronted. The fighting was cold and brutal. The battle kept changing contours, doubling back and lunging forward. The land was craggy and sharp. The weather could be fatal. The best roads were widened trails and often not wide enough for two-way traffic. The mountains could not be easily overcome, and the valleys were patches of rice paddies and soggy earth. There could be little systematic burial of the dead as they fell. Any piece of soft earth or abandoned foxhole would have to do, and any marker could quickly blow away or be destroyed when fighting returned to the spot or be stolen by the enemy. And formally laid out temporary cemeteries were subject to the same conditions.

The Korean War had begun on June 25, 1950, the result of a disputed division of Korea into north and south after the end of Japanese rule there in 1945. After an attempt by the north to invade the south with the goal of reunification, the United States and United Nations intervened on behalf of the south, while the People's Republic of China took the side of the north. The action was seen by U.S. Pres. Harry Truman as a firm stand against the beginning steps of Communist expansion. The first significant fighting involving American forces was on July 5, and by late September it became apparent that the processes of Graves Registration, so well developed in the previous world wars, needed to be rethought. It seemed the best practice would be to try to remove the dead immediately home to America or to temporary cemeteries that could be protected. At the outset of the war, the only Graves Registration unit in the region was based in Japan; it was tasked with a continuing search of the isolated graves of Americans there and the day-to-day work required in support of the occupation force.

A new identification unit was put under intense training at Fort Lee, Virginia, an accelerated acquisition of caskets and other materiel was begun, and by mid–December all principals were assembled in Tokyo with an eye toward establishing a working mortuary operation in Korea. The need was made more urgent by Communist successes from the north that were overtaking the locations of temporary United Nations cemeteries already in place. Most had been established by individual combat divisions. The work was done by the same men who would fight the enemy and trained Graves Registration personnel following behind as the fighting moved north. When the fighting was turned back southward by December, those cemeteries had to be evacuated in haste. At the United Nations cemetery at Inchon, for example, the process was begun on Christmas Day 1950; the remains of 864 dead sailed out of the harbor three days later, hours before the arrival of North Korean troops. Those bodies, and the remains in other temporary cemeteries, were moved to Camp Kokura in northern Kyushu, Japan, where the dead could be kept in temporary mausoleums pending a more substantial effort at processing. A trained workforce of 62 working in 16-hour shifts began that operation on January 2, 1951.

In the first weeks of January, the urgency of evacuating cemeteries still in control of United Nations forces increased the speed of deliveries to Kokura. But by the end of the month, the southward movement of northern forces was stopped, and a new temporary cemetery on the outskirts of Pusan was deemed probably safe. The decision was fully made, however, that it would not be advisable to think beyond temporary in Korea. There would be no attempt to build permanent cemeteries like those created abroad after World Wars I and II. Virtually all American casualties would be returned home.

The basic process of identification of remains was not much different from that practiced by Graves Registration in World War II; but by 1950, it was enhanced by developing postwar technologies. Bones, teeth, clothing and personal effects, height, hair color, shoe size, and fingerprints, when possible, were the primary sources of information. If serial numbers and other identifying marks could not be found on clothing, however, it could be subjected to chemical analysis; failing that, there was infrared photography. Precision photography preserved tattoos, scars, dentures, and strange bone and tooth formations. Fluoroscopes found additional bone fragments in removed clothing. X-rays found previous and potentially identifying injuries. It was not uncommon to find unexploded grenades and ammunition in remains, adding danger to the task.

For the first time, physical anthropologists were brought into the process. Their expertise could help determine age, race and distinguishing physical characteristics when other methods had failed. And they could help to separate intermingled remains, always a problem with the dead of war, into distinct individuals. Each set of remains was finally accompanied by a complete case history intended to establish identity beyond doubt, which was then considered by a final board of review.

With full authentication, remains were passed on to licensed embalmers for final casketing and preparation for return to America. The first shipment resulting from the process took place on March 11, 1951, when 51 caskets arrived in Yokohama, Japan, for full ceremonies that would send them on their way east across the Pacific. As the numbers of dead grew, the ship-

On August 28, 1950, a grief-stricken American infantryman whose friend has been killed in action in the Haktong-ni area of Korea is comforted by another soldier. In the background a corpsman methodically fills out casualty tags (*U.S. Army*).

A young Korean girl places a wreath of flowers on the grave of an American soldier while Pfc. Chester Painter and Cpl. Harry May present arms in the United Nations Cemetery at Pusan on April 9, 1951. Thirty-six Americans would remain buried in the cemetery after the war in fulfillment of their own wishes (*National Archives*).

ments proceeded with the same ritual on an every-ten-day or bimonthly schedule directly from Kokura. A number of Americans had been buried at the United Nations Memorial Cemetery at Pusan with the dead of all eleven nations that had fought on behalf of South Korea. They, too, were eventually disinterred and returned home, although 36 Americans who died in postwar work in Korea were permanently interred in the cemetery in fulfillment of their own wishes.

In 1952, the development of a new registration technology first used in World War II came to full effective use in Korea. The method had been derived out of the American census of 1880, which wasn't actually completed until 1887 because the number of people in the nation had overwhelmed the effort to count them. For the 1890 census machines invented by Herman Hollerith finished the count in one year, sorting punch cards into usable tabulations. Hollerith would eventually go on to found the International Business Machine Company (IBM).

At the outset of World War II, Gen. George C. Marshall foresaw the need for something more than written ledgers to keep track of the large number of servicemen that would be required, and he created a number of mobile Machine Records Units (MRUs). The MRUs traveled the war, and, indeed, were among the first to land on beaches stretching from Normandy to the Pacific. The units often included two truck trailers full of tabulating machinery and administrative operations pulled by six-wheel trucks, followed by a generator and staff car where terrain permitted. In Korea, cards with identification of remains were tabulated with cards related to casualty reports and other clues to identification. Where the cards could not solve identity problems, they gave significant help to human resources who might. Or they could hasten the conclusion that the location of an individual's remains would likely never be found. The tabulating machines ran 24 hours a day.

By April 1952, a total of 16,000 American dead had been returned home. Armistice negotiations between October 1951 and February 1952 gave Graves Registration a surge opportunity to undertake increased search and recovery operations. A goal was to convert lists of missing in action to killed in action, giving immediate pain but longer-term ease to families at home. In mid–1952, an unknown number, which could only be estimated in the thousands, were missing in action. It was not known how many were held prisoner of war, and there could be no target for numbers of missing yet to be found. It was estimated that the search area for the missing was 85,246 square miles in size, although only 40,000 of those square miles were under United Nations control, terrain that was good for hiding bodies in places that were nearly inaccessible. Search teams were sent into areas deemed most promising for results based on previous discoveries of casualties and from interviews with the population. The landscape of the dead yet to be found was described by battle maps and narratives of what had occurred, along with lists of the missing and individual information about each that might be helpful.

Graves Registration put itself in the media business through leaflet drops and the use of radio and newspapers where possible. Search teams visited schools and met with police and local officials. As in most wars worldwide, farmers were primary sources of information and advice. Specific leads were followed, and the identifying characteristics of the missing were studied in the context of the battles in which they had been lost. Battle spaces were divided into grid squares of approximately 3,000 square feet of often difficult terrain that could hold hidden explosives. A full week might be taken for examination by a team of five or six examiners with an operations truck and a Korean interpreter. They worked back and forth ten feet apart in search of anything extraordinary. As many as 400 foxholes could be found in one grid square, and each had to be excavated down to hard ground to be sure it contained no burials.

Bunkers and gun emplacements received similar treatment. Found explosives were marked and mapped for the further attention of demolitions teams. Similar efforts were undertaken in coastal areas and islands by landing craft units. Reports from all grid squares were combined into reports of map units of approximately 185 square miles. When each search was complete, the area was deemed closed for further exploration, exceptions to be made with the presence of new information.

The easier effort took place in the free area of South Korea, and the problems of North Korea waited until a full year after armistice on July 27, 1953. Graves Registration, the army and the United Nations developed a proposal for exchange of the dead to be taken to North Korea, and on July 30, 1954, an agreement was made for a period of exchange between September 1 and 30 October or longer if necessary. The American part of the exchange was given the name Operation Glory. In continuing meetings with the North Koreans up to September, the two sides agreed on processes of authentication, ceremony, media coverage and transportation. They did not agree, however, to allow each other access for search and recovery on their own territory. The results were lopsided, and differing accounts offered differing figures. But it was probably most nearly accurate to say that by mid–November the number of dead returned to the north was 14,074, while the number returned to the south was just 4,167, and only half of those American.[1]

On New Year's Eve 1953, the U.S. Army and the U.S. Air Force began sending telegrams to more than 3,600 American families telling them that their loved ones had been missing in Korea for more than a year and must now be presumed to be dead. The determination increased the official American death toll of the Korean War to 30,000, but it still did not include final determinations for 2,900 army members, 420 air force fliers, 490 Marines and 78 navy sailors.[2] On September 1, 1954, what was seen as the last delivery of bodies from North Korea took place in a highly choreographed procedure at Panmumjon. A procession of two white American jeeps and four Russian jeeps, all carrying representative forces, led eight North Korean trucks carrying 200 Allied bodies, 151 of them American. They stopped at an area of tents that would receive the bodies, with the flags of South Korea, the United States and United Nations flown at half-mast. Six hundred bodies found in South Korea were placed in the trucks for return, accompanied by an exchange of papers. The Allied dead were placed in trucks and taken to a rail station for shipment to Pusan, then by boat to the facility at Kokura where they would be identified and sent home or to a national cemetery, as per the wishes of family.

American deaths in Korea totaled 36,576; of those 33,741 were in battle while missing in action or while prisoners of war.[3] Americans unaccounted for totaled 8,176, most of them presumably buried somewhere on the Korean peninsula. The telegrams of New Year's Eve 1953 would not settle the matter, and the search for the dead would never end. Among those who had been notified of the irretrievable loss of a loved one was the family of Bernard McManaman in La Peer, Michigan. His wife would eventually move on to another marriage. His mother would insist for years that her son had not been right in his words to her as he left, and would soon return from the mists of the missing. His daughter, Janine, would never know him, and she would awake from a troubling dream nearly 60 years later.

The first American military man killed in the Vietnam era was Lt. Col. Peter A. Dewey, on September 26, 1945. The events that led to his death had been put into action with the Japanese invasion of Vietnam in September 1940 and the return to the country of the communist revolutionary Ho Chi Minh in 1941 as leader of the Viet Minh, or Viet Independence League. At that time, and in following years, American interests were focused on the retrieval of American airmen who had fallen over Vietnam, and the Viet Minh were helpful in recovering them, dead or alive.

At the time of the Japanese invasion, Vietnam was, and would remain for some time, under rule of the French, dating back to the mid 19th century. Peter Dewey had been one of those Americans who had served in World War II under another flag. The son of a congressman, he was a reporter during the German invasion of France and was inspired to join the Polish military as an ambulance driver. Later, he became an agent of the Office of Strategic Services (OSS), an earlier version of the Central Intelligence Agency (CIA). His missions in Vietnam were to support the Viet Minh American recovery effort and to find American prisoners thought to be held by the Japanese in Saigon, most of them slave laborers used in Burma to build a railroad crossing of the River Kwai. He met both goals.

As Dewey drove his jeep to the Saigon airport on September 26, he became involved in a small verbal altercation with some Vietnamese at the side of the road and exclaimed at them in the French language. Mistaken as a member of the French oppressors, he was immediately killed by machine gun fire, and his jeep careened into a ditch. A firefight broke out that would last three hours, and his body disappeared. His death by "friendly fire" could serve as a portent of the Vietnam War that would engage the United States in the early 1960s. Among his last words in Vietnam: "Cochinchina [the region of Saigon] is burning, the French and British are finished here, and we [the U.S.] ought to clear out of Southeast Asia."[4]

The remains of Lt. Col. Peter A. Dewey were never found, and his name is listed on the Tablets of the Missing at the Manila National Cemetery in the Philippines.

Arguably, the first formally recognized American deaths at the hands of the enemy of the Vietnam War occurred July 8, 1959. It was a quiet and sultry night at Bien Hoa, just north of Saigon, and a handful of American advisors were in residence at the base camp for the Vietnamese Seventh Infantry Division. A lot had occurred since the death of Peter Dewey in 1945. In the aftermath of World War II, the Allied powers had determined that Vietnam should be returned to the French. But as the French regained strength in 1946, they came into increasing conflict with the Viet Minh and evicted the revolutionary group from Saigon in November. The Viet Minh began a guerrilla war against the French, officially declared as the First Indochina War on December 19, 1946. As the war spread to Laos and Cambodia, the postwar alliance between its western powers and the Soviet Union began its conversion into the Cold War between western democracy and eastern communism. In 1949, the Viet Minh began to receive arms from communist China, and in 1950, China recognized the Viet Minh as the legitimate government of Vietnam. The noncommunist nations had other ideas about that, and with the advent of the Korean War, concluded that communist expansion was afoot in Asia, directed by the Russians.

Concurrent with the Korean War, the responsibility for maintaining a shield against northern expansion began to shift from France to the United States, and, in May 1954, the French finally exited Vietnam after the loss of a decisive battle with the Viet Minh at Dien Bien Phu. The result was a division of the country between north and south, and the following years of governance in South Vietnam was assisted by American advisors and support. It was Pres. Dwight D. Eisenhower who first enunciated the Domino Theory in April 1954. It held that if one state were allowed to fall to communism, adjacent states would also fall. The presumption served as a powerful raison d'être for American policy for a full decade.[5]

Thus it was that on that evening in July 1959 at the base camp at Bien Hoa, Maj. Dale Buis of Imperial Beach, California, was showing off pictures of his three sons, and MSgt. Chester Ovnand of Copperas Cove, Texas, was finishing up a letter to his wife. The men then cranked up a movie on a projector in the mess hall (*The Tattered Dress* with Jeff Chandler and Jeanne Crain). As Ovnand got up to change the first reel, the building was ambushed on all sides by guerrilla machine guns. Maj. Buis was the first to be killed, followed quickly by Sgt. Ovnand. Both bodies were easily recovered. The following decades would bring information to suggest that they were actually the third and fourth Americans to die in Vietnam, though it would never be asserted that Peter Dewey was the actual first, in 1945.[6] He was, though, the first whose body would be lost.

In 1961, an optimistic American president began a confrontation with a determined Vietnamese revolutionary that would not end well for the United States. It was in his inaugural speech on January 20, 1961, that Pres. John F. Kennedy asserted that "we shall pay any price, bear any burden, meet any hardship, support any friend, oppose any foe, to insure the survival and the success of liberty." In the case of Vietnam, that would mean the fighting of a limited war in pursuit of a political settlement of the country's divisions. North Vietnamese president Ho Chi Min enunciated a resolve of total war to fight for the sovereignty of all Vietnam "whatever the sacrifices, however long the struggle … until Vietnam is fully independent and reunified."

In the first years of the war, the size of an American force of advisors grew only in small increments and the number of deaths was limited. The remains of those killed were prepared at the Tan Son Nhut air base in Saigon for shipment to civilian morticians under contract to the U.S. Air Force at the Clark Air Force Base in the Philippines. By 1963, the northern enemy had become more effective, and, as the southern government had begun to fall apart, its American ally had involved more of its own people in the conflict. In November of that year, Pres. Kennedy was assassinated in Dallas, Texas, and his successor, Pres. Lyndon Johnson, inherited a war that was quickly growing out of control. He declared that Vietnam would not be lost. By the end of the year, 16,300 American advisors were in place, and the mortuary capacities at Tan Son Nhut and Clark were expanded.

As the situation only deteriorated for South Vietnam and the Americans in 1964, official American resolve took on the mantle of a necessary stand against the expansion of communism and the prophecies of the Domino Theory, and the number of American advisors rose to 23,000. Over the course of 1965, nearly 200,000 American combat troops would arrive in the country, and 1,863 would be killed. The American mortuary effort was upgraded to full force. Trained Graves Registration forces were brought into the process for the first time, and, as American army deaths began to exceed air force deaths, the responsibility was shifted to the army in 1966. The Tan Son Nhut mortuary was expanded and, in 1967, with the deaths of 11,153 Americans, another facility was put online at the Da Nang Air Force Base.

With the Vietnam War, the almost 200-year history of American military members left buried abroad came nearly to a close. The processes, policies and technologies of the three preceding wars were improved upon and perfected. Whereas bodies in the previous wars could be continually reburied in theater until family wishes were known, this time they were removed as quickly as possible by helicopter to mortuaries at Saigon and Da Nang and could be processed in half a day for flights to Oakland, California, or Dover, Delaware. There they were prepared and casketed for return to families or shipment to national cemeteries.

Nineteen sixty-eight was the worst of the war's 14 years. Political and social disarray had been building within the United States throughout the sixties, with sometimes violent protests against the war and the shifting political fortunes of those who supported or opposed it. American support of the war was thought to have tilted to opposition with the pronouncement in February by a trusted journalist, Walter Cronkite, that it would be unwinnable. Pres. John-

Specialist 4 Ruediger Richter, left, and Sergeant Daniel Spencer, right, watch over the remains of a comrade fallen on August 14, 1966, in a battle at Long Kahn Province, Vietnam. A helicopter has been called to evacuate the body (*National Archives*).

son decided in March not to seek reelection. At the beginning of the year, 463,000 American forces were in place, and 16,000 had already lost their lives.[7]

Especially in tropical Vietnam, refrigeration was an important part of the process of recovery of the dead. Those bodies not recovered close to the time of death, and especially those found in water or monsoons, could swell to double their original size as part of the process of decomposition. Aside from the transportation and storage problems created by increased size, flesh became very difficult to work with. Twenty-two collection points were placed around South Vietnam, most with 10 to 20 refrigeration units, though a few with capacities in the low hundreds. A central identification laboratory was put into operation at Tan Son Nhut in August 1968, and its work was more difficult than it should have been. Though soldiers were, as always, required to carry specific identification and markers, less than half of the remains recovered wore tags, and less than 10 percent had identifying markers on boots and clothing. Almost three-quarters of the bodies were identified by fingerprints, but the most productive method was the use of dental records.

By the end of 1968, the size of the American force had climbed to 495,000, and 30,000 had been killed.[8] As Pres. Richard Nixon renewed a mix of military and diplomatic effort in 1969, including a secret expansion of the effort to North Vietnamese supply lines in neighboring Cambodia, another 11,616 Americans were lost. The death toll in Vietnam now exceeded the figure for the Korean War, and the morale and discipline of a mostly drafted force continued to decline. By some estimates, half of American troops had taken up the use of illegal drugs as an unfortunate tool of endurance. With continuing enemy success, American opinion began to turn solidly against the war. An incremental withdrawal of troops was begun, along with a reduction in the draft. By the end of the year, the American force was reduced by 115,000 and the total of those killed in action was 40,024.[9]

A cease-fire was signed in Paris, to take effect on January 28, 1973. Pres. Nixon declared neither win nor loss, only "peace with honor in Vietnam and southeast Asia." The last American combat troops exited the country by March 29, leaving a corps of advisors still in place, while South Vietnamese troops continued the fight. A little more than 2 years later, on April 29, 1975, the war was finished. In panic, 7,000 key American and South Vietnamese officials, their families and some civilians were evacuated by helicopter from the grounds of the U.S. embassy. As the helicopters disgorged their passengers on offshore American aircraft carriers, they were pushed overboard and into the sea to make room for those yet to arrive. On April 30, the last American marines left the embassy as North Vietnamese forces flooded into Saigon and the president of South Vietnam broadcast words of surrender.

Less than two weeks later, on May 12, what many considered to be the last actual battle of the Vietnam War took place as Cambodian Khmer Rouge gunboats (American swiftboats captured in the war) seized the American container ship SS *Mayaguez* in the Gulf of Thailand. Sailing in international waters, the ship carried commercial and military cargo; it was forced to an anchorage at the small island of Kaoh Tang off the coast of Cambodia. When diplomatic efforts to secure her release failed, U.S. Pres. Gerald Ford ordered military action. Having just suffered the humiliation of the retreat from Saigon, the United States was anxious to reassert its military might, and the order was given to the air force to seize the *Mayaguez*, occupy Kaoh Tang, bomb the port of Kompong Som and a nearby airfield, and destroy all small craft in the harbor. The planning and intelligence that underlay the order proved lacking, however. It was not known whether the *Mayaguez* crew actually remained aboard the ship, and there was disagreement about the ability of Kaoh Tang to defend itself.

On the morning of May 15, full force accompanied a Marine boarding of the ship, only to find her completely deserted. At the same time, four helicopters brought a force of Marines to Kaoh Tang, but they were met with defenses that were heavier than expected. The first helicopter managed to deliver its Marines, but was then was forced to ditch in the sea. The second was forced by artillery to land in Thailand, and did not deliver its human cargo. The third landed on target with all forces delivered to the island, but was not able to fly again. The fourth helicopter was forced to land in the surf with the loss of one airman, two sailors and ten Marines.

Those Marines who had landed were able to secure a beachhead of sorts, while two more helicopters were able to deliver more troops. Soon thereafter, and without a gun fired, a fishing boat approached an American ship involved in the action with the full *Mayaguez* crew alive and well. They, as well as their ship, had been safely rescued, but the landed forces were not aware of their success and engaged Cambodian forces in fierce combat that only escalated into the afternoon. Finally, a strategic withdrawal of the Americans was assisted by more helicopters and was concluded by nightfall. Though the mission was technically a success, 41 Americans were killed or missing. All were recovered except for three Marines, who would be seen alive in subsequent days before disappearing from view. Years later it would be confirmed that they were buried somewhere in the soil of the island of Khao Tang, the last of 58,178 Americans to die in the Vietnam war.[10] An always-changing figure in the vicinity of 2,000 would count those missing in action and presumed dead, mostly in North Vietnam, Laos and Cambodia.

From that point on, only a handful of Americans yet to die abroad in war would remain missing and presumed dead in foreign soil. But the nation was 200 years old by now and the wars of its past had accumulated approximately 130,000 of the dead still buried beyond its borders, not including those missing in action. They rested in Australia, throughout the Pacific Rim, across Canada and Mexico to Coastal Spain, in the north of Africa, up to and across England and Europe, and, finally, into Arctic Russia. Many were unknown, forgotten or forever lost. Some were yet to be discovered or rediscovered after the years had lost track of them. Whatever their status, the care and search for them would go on with new resolve, new technologies and continuing reverence.

Chapter Thirteen

Remembered, Lost, Forgotten, Unknown

Dim rays filtering in through tiny windows gave the only light. The door closed behind me. I was alone with the dead.
—Edward F. Younger

The town of Waregem, Belgium, first shows up by name in the year 826, though tendrils of its origins can be found in the Roman Empire. As it grew up from the banks of the Leie River and in the midst of the surrounding forests it developed into a place known for the raising and training of horses. In 1847, a horse race was run in the village, and, by 1855, the annual race had been transformed into what would be called in the annals of equestrian history the Grand Steeplechase of Flanders, named after the Flemish region of north Belgium, which included Brussels. The steeplechase became an important event on the European equestrian calendar, with participation by the horses of kings and other royalty, including Napoleon Bonaparte III of France. In the 21st century the race is known as the Waregem Koerse. Its most difficult jump is considered to be over the Gaverbeek brook at a width of nearly 25 feet, and the brook gave its name to the Gaverbeek Horse Track and Hippodrome in Waregem. The Koerse still draws an international crowd each August, and on other days from May to September the Gaverbeek track is the setting for trotting races.

Waregem is a hardworking town of 35,000. The identity that it takes upon itself, and presents to the rest of the world, is found largely in its important history with the horse, and its relationship to the World War I Flanders Field American Cemetery and Memorial on its southeast border. Thus it was that on Sunday, May 24, 2009, the American Memorial Day weekend, the crowds at the Gaverbeek Horse Track were entertained between trotting races with pageantry out of the old American West. On the field between grandstand and track, a parade of Belgian citizens in red, white and blue versions of chaps and vests and broad brimmed hats of American cowboys rode tall and handsome horses in formations through tall grass as the traditional music of American patriotism played over loudspeakers. The horse reins were spangled with stars, and each foreleg was wrapped in red, white and blue tape. Each cowboy and cowgirl carried aloft a large American flag. In a VIP tent near the exhibition, Americans and Belgians, ambassadors, generals and admirals, and others of those who pay attention to the memorial of Americans still buried in Belgium ate corn on the cob and steak, washed down with flutes of champagne.

As straightforward and obvious as it was, the event was a delicate mix of the forces still at play more than sixty years after the American military had fought to liberate Belgium in World War II and almost a century after their participation in World War I. Nearby Flanders Field was a moral responsibility of the people of Waregem and the surrounding countryside. Except for the war years of 1940–1944, the schoolchildren of the region had sung the American national anthem at Flanders Field and placed flowers on the graves each Memorial Day since 1924. Waregem mayor Kurt Vanryckeghem was one of those children when he was growing up. He said that the cemetery was very crude in its first years, but there was an attempt to give it grace: "[O]ur town fathers at the time thought that having our children learn and sing the anthem of the country would be a fitting way for us to repay, in our small way, the debt we owed to these Americans."[1]

In 2009, the annual preparation for the singing of the anthem by the children of Waregem began in April. The children who would sing were visited by Capt. Brian Sansom and 1st Sgt. David Giddens of the U.S. Army Garrison, Brussels; James Begg, president of the American Overseas Memorial Day Association (AOMDA), Belgium, and Christopher Sims, the Belgian assistant superintendent of Flanders Field. The four visited three Waregem elementary schools where the 120 children who would particpate in the ceremony were also in the first year of English language courses. In a mix of Belgian French and English, they thanked the children for their participation. On May 24, the children sang the American National Anthem at the old cemetery just as they had for almost ninety years. Beneath a very hot sun, they worked through some of the more problematic melodic twists and turns of the anthem with studied determination.

This was the first year that the Flanders Field ceremony would be followed by the Memorial Day celebration at Gaverbeek Horse Track. The goals were manifold. Up to the 20th century, Waregem's chief industry had been its textile mills, but it had pretty much lost that identity in modern times. For the political and economic leaders of Waregem this Memorial Day was an attempt to blend its association with Flanders Field and horses into a unique and marketable profile to the rest of the world. For the Gaverbeek Horse Track and Hippodrome, it was an effort to increase its own business and potential as a tourist destination, especially for Americans.

There seemed to be nothing mercenary about those goals. The people of Waregem had been good caretakers of the American dead at Flanders Field for almost a century, and the involvement of the children through successive generations was designed to foster continued thoughtfulness about the cemetery in their midst. And a portion of the financial profits from the American Memorial Day at Gaverbeek would be contributed to the AOMDA for its continuing oversight of all American military buried in the great American and small communal cemeteries all over Belgium. Although it was the smallest of the American cemeteries to grow out of the battles of World War I, the burial ground at the edge of Waregem would become, early in the 20th century, a lasting symbol of the melancholy of war.

Among those Canadians and Americans who went early to the war was John McCrae, born into a military family in Guelph, Ontario, in 1872. His educational career in the two countries and England blended military training, medicine, and letters, and he was admitted to the Royal College of Physicians in London in 1905. He served residencies in both the United States and Canada before going on to professorships at the University of Vermont and McGill University in Montreal. Immediately upon the British declaration of war on Germany, Dr. McCrae, already a member of the Canadian military, was appointed a field surgeon and put in charge of a field hospital in Belgium. The hospital caught the casualties of the Second

A pageant of the American West held between races at the Gaverbeek Horse Track in Waregem, Belgium, on Memorial Day 2009 (*Author photograph*).

Battle of Ypres, in which the Germans began their experiments with chemical warfare. Many were lost, and after McCrae attended to their dying he would officiate at their burials. More than half of his own brigade was killed, including a student of McCrae's who had followed him from Ottawa. The remains of the young man were placed in two sandbags and buried by McCrae in total darkness on the night of May 2, 1915.

The following day, as he rested in the back of an ambulance and looked out at a field of crosses dotted with the red poppies of Belgium, he wrote a poem:

> In Flanders Fields
>
> In Flanders fields the poppies blow
> Between the crosses, row on row,
> That mark our place: and in the sky
> The larks, still bravely singing, fly
> Scarce heard amid the guns below.
>
> We are the Dead. Short days ago
> We lived, felt dawn, saw sunset glow,
> Loved and were loved, and now we lie,
> In Flanders fields.
>
> Take up our quarrel with the foe:
> To you from failing hands we throw
> The torch: be yours to hold it high.
> If ye break faith with us who die
> We shall not sleep, though poppies grow
> In Flanders fields.

In retrospect, McCrae was not fond of the poem and threw it away. But it was caught by one of his senior officers and sent to England's *Punch* magazine and was published to great acclaim in December. Three years later, as the war was coming to an end, the poem was published in the *Ladies Home Journal* in the United States and inspired the enduring choice of paper red poppies as a symbol of those who fight and die in war. John McCrae would never know about that, or about the place of his hastily written poem in the unceasing reverence, search for, attempt to recover or at least properly memorialize the dead in the generations that would follow. On January 28, 1918, he died of pneumonia and meningitis near Boulogne, France, and was buried in the Commonwealth War Graves Cemetery at Wimereux in Nord-Pas-de-Calais.

Among the casualties of World War I were the church bells of France, taken by the German forces as prizes of war. In honor of its fallen soldiers, the American Committee for Devastated France undertook to replace a number of them, and one was donated through the Poetry Society of America by Mr. and Mrs. Charles Seeger, parents of another poet of the war, Alan Seeger. On May 22, 1922, the Seegers attended ceremonies at the church in Landricourt-Sous-Coucy where the bell was given in their son's name. Each of 200 residents of the village passed it by and gave it one ring with a hand-held clapper before it was placed on the steeple.[2] The bones of Alan Seeger would finally come to rest in Ossuary Number One, dedicated to the French Foreign Legion, at the Lihons CWGC cemetery 90 km west of Landricourt-Sous-Coucy. For the new generations of a creative nature, he would always be a known presence, though not much dwelled upon. In a 2001 interview on National Public Radio, peace activist and folk singer Pete Seeger recited Alan's "I Have a Rendezvous with Death" with great feeling though the poem seemed to be an affirmation of the kind of war that Pete Seeger would decry. He spoke of a piece of wisdom that had come up through the family since World War I, that Alan Seeger, the eager enlistee in the foreign war, "saw the seeming terrible realities of war before he was killed in 1916, mowed down by machine gun while charging up a slope."[3]

During World War I, the city of Plymouth, England, served as a naval base for troop movement, a naval shipyard and manufacturer of munitions. It also received the first flying boat of the U.S. Navy to successfully cross the Atlantic, though the flight was not nonstop. The Curtiss N/C 4 arrived on May 31, 1919, in the same harbor once overlooked by the Old Mill Prison, and from which the pilgrims had departed for America 299 years earlier. Plymouth fared well in the war, and, a few years after the war's conclusion, a group of Plymouth citizens, American expatriates and members of the American group Daughters of 1812 came together in an effort to acknowledge the alliance between the two countries and the human wartime sacrifices of each. The Daughters of 1812 had been formed in 1892 as a version of the Daughters of the American Revolution and sought to preserve the history, honor and patriotic feeling of the years between the end of the Revolutionary War through the War of 1812 and its aftermath. Plymouth and its environs, of course, were a strong center of focus for the group, especially the old St. Michael's church at Princetown, near Dartmoor Prison.

During the Napoleonic Wars and the War of 1812, the French and American prisoners who endured Dartmoor were used as a labor force for a task that was said to give them some satisfaction and payment of six pence a day.[4] While the prison was full of strong men in need of occupation during that time, it was determined that a new church should be constructed in Princetown. Its foundation and walls were largely built by the French, and they were followed by the Americans, who finished its roof and interior. Its first service was held on January 2, 1814, but it was closed and locked two years later, perhaps because of the departure from Dartmoor of liberated prisoners and the reduction in the town's labor force. It was reconsecrated for use in 1831, and on June 4, 1910, various state chapters of the American Daughters of 1812 raised a considerable sum of money to build a new and very large circular stained glass window for the eastern wall facing the main road. It was installed amid great ceremony in honor of the prisoners held at Dartmoor and those who had died there.

On Memorial Day 1928, a retinue including the Daughters, crew and officers of the USS *Detroit*, which had sailed to Plymouth for the event, the U.S. commanding officer of Naval Forces in Europe, and other dignitaries of both nations descended on Dartmoor to place a memorial arch at the edge of the American Cemetery. And in 1930, the Daughters and others focused their effort to commemorate the British and American sacrifices of World War I on a 15th-century abbey adjacent to St. Andrew's Church. It had been first a monkery; then it served as the home of the priest of St. Andrew's, and was sometimes called the Priest's or Prysten House. From the mid 16th century it had been privately owned, eventually becoming a wholesale grocery in the late 19th century. The effort to return the building to church ownership was begun in 1919 with the construction of a church hall and a place of remembrance for those Plymouth residents lost in the war. Its restoration was completed in 1925.

Much had transpired in Plymouth since the War of 1812. The city had grown, accompanied by the conversion of land from rural to urban. Perhaps for that reason, the cemetery at St. Andrew's underwent a major transformation in 1871 that reduced its size and replaced much of its architecture of walls and portals. An unknown number of bodies was moved to the nearby Westwell Street Burial Ground.[5] That may have been the time that the burial places of American captain Willam Allen and midshipman Richard Delphy of the 1812 cruiser USS *Argus* were lost. Buried with great ceremony on August 21, 1813, all that could be found of them at the turn of the new century was the tombstone that had demarked each burial.

Memorial Day 1930 was an occasion for celebration across England. Every known American military grave was decorated with flags. The American ambassador placed a wreath at the Tomb of the Unknown Warrior in Westminster Abbey. The London post of the American Legion placed tributes at the British Memorial to the War Dead at Whitehall. And the American consul general joined others at the Prysten House in Plymouth to dedicate the Door of Unity. With a ceremony similar to the one that William Allen and Richard Delphy had received in 1813, their tombstones were cemented next to the doorway of the outer wall of the old abbey. Another proof, said the consul general, of the friendship between the two nations and the linking together of their two great navies.[6]

In November 1945, the writer William F. McDermott published an account of an encounter with an old World War I army sergeant in the magazine *Rotarian*. McDermott knew how to tell a story, bring it forth from an unlikely setting and make it surprising. He described the newsroom of a metropolitan newspaper long after the paper had been put to bed: dusky and quiet, littered wastebaskets and empty chairs. McDermott was finally able to talk to the old man who had sought him out and who told him his story:

> I had fought through the world war and got a couple of wounds. At Vaux, I caught some shell fire and in the St. Mihiel drive some machine gun slugs. On November 11, 1918, we crossed the Meuse

Opposite: A contemporary view of the Prysten House at St. Andrew's Church, Plymouth, England. The gravestones cemented into the wall to the right of the door are those of William Allen and Richard Delphy of the USS *Argus*. Buried ceremonially in 1813, their remains disappeared but the stones survived and were placed at the Prysten House in 1930 (*Author photograph*).

Thirteen. *Remembered, Lost, Forgotten, Unknown*

River before orders came to cease firing. I went into Germany with the Army of Occupation, and returned to the United States the following August.

An orphan, I felt at loose ends back home, so I enlisted again and was sent back to Germany. Strangely that was the land of my parents' birth. Army life ran easily, until the morning of October 23, 1921, when I received orders to report to my commanding officer.

"You are to go to Coblenz where you will meet five other soldiers from different outfits. Together, you will serve as pallbearers for the Unknown Soldier."[7]

Edward F. Younger continued his story. The major in charge at Coblenz told the men that the next day one of them would be selected to choose the Unknown Soldier. He then quizzed each about his battle experience. None of them slept well that night, for fear, Younger claimed, of being the man chosen for the imponderable task. When he was told the next morning that he would be given the job, he thought it, according to McDermott, more difficult than any past experience on a battlefield. But he took the bouquet that was to be placed on the chosen casket and entered the chapel in Chalons-sur-Mer:

Dim rays filtering in through tiny windows gave the only light. The door closed behind me. I was alone with the dead.

Instinctively I knelt in prayer on the petal-strewn floor. Then I began to walk slowly around the caskets, over each of which lay a beautiful American flag. Touching each box, I tried to picture the battles the boy who slept within it had been through, and I reflected whether I might have fought with him or known him.

I was still far from a choice when gradually something began to draw me to the casket second on the right as I had entered. As I moved toward it, the mysterious pull grew irresistible; I could not have turned back had I tried. "This," I murmured, "is the one!" Saluting, I raised the bouquet, and it seemed as if God himself guided my hand as I placed the flowers on the coffin.[8]

Like many veterans who had been part of extraordinary events, Younger's choice was a story he did not easily share. He married, but did not tell his wife for six years. He worked in the post office, but did not tell his coworkers for a decade. In 1930, he visited the Tomb of the Unknown quietly, wearing his sergeant's uniform. Once again, he placed a bouquet on the casket of an unknown young man. He had dreamed, according to McDermott, of doing the same for the unknown soldier that would be chosen from World War II, but he died before that could happen.

In 1958, at the direction of Pres. Dwight D. Eisenhower, the unknowns were chosen from both World War II and the Korean War. Through a process similar to the first, an unknown from the European Theatre of the Second World War and another from the Pacific theater were placed on the guided missile cruiser USS *Canberra* as it sat off the Virginia Capes. The choice was given to Master Chief William Charette of Ludington, Michigan, a hospital corpsman and the navy's only Medal of Honor recipient on active duty at the time. One was chosen and the other was buried at sea. The Korean unknown was chosen from four bodies exhumed from the Punchbowl National Cemetery in Hawaii, and, in 1984, the unknown from the Vietnam War was buried in a ceremony presided over by Pres. Ronald Reagan. By 1998, the use of DNA technology had become so effective in identification of the dead that the decision was made to disinter the Vietnam unknown for identification. Lt. Michael Joseph Blassie was returned to his family in St. Louis, Missouri, and reburied on July 11, 1998.

Late in the 1950s, an American Air Force veteran of the Pacific War, Jim Maps, sought out a quiet retirement in Spain. He settled on the island of Menorca. One day he took off on an exploration of his new home. An amateur historian, he knew that the island was the home of various strains of the naval history of a number of nations, and he had heard rumors of a cemetery that was almost hidden and forgotten. He stepped carefully along the craggy edges of the land at Port Mahon. The path was rocky, sheer in some places, and a bit treacherous. Eventually he came to an overgrown graveyard with the appearance of a jungle. From what he had heard of the cemetery, he had expected it to be a place of rest for British sailors. "But when I walked in, I looked down at the first stone and there was the USS *Constitution*, USS *North Carolina*, USS *Congress*, USS *Delaware*; it was a very strange English cemetery."

Many of its stones were toppled over, their inscriptions more illegible than they had been when last visited by the U.S. Navy in 1928. And the best intentions of the 1930s to preserve the cemetery had come to naught with the advent of the Spanish Civil War in 1936, followed by World War II. Maps set out to see what could be done to bring it back to life and obtained a monthly pledge of fifty dollars in aid from the closest American consulate, culminating in a $1,300 sum given in 1960 to hire local labor to cut back the vegetation, put down walkways, repair and whitewash the walls — in short to bring order out of the chaos of its neglect. As it happened during this time, two American destroyers, the USS *Forrest Sherman* and USS *Charles Roan*, visited Port Mahon and volunteer parties were put together to do more ambitions preservation work that could not be accomplished by the locals.

Jim Maps published an article about the old cemetery for the July 1965 edition of the *American Neptune*.[9] The article showed before and after pictures of the restoration and offered perhaps the most thorough written history of the cemetery ever available. It came to a con-

Master Chief William Charette selects the Unknown Serviceman of World War II during ceremonies onboard the USS *Canberra* off the Virginia Capes on May 26, 1958. The other World War II Unknown Serviceman candidate's casket is at far left, and the Unknown Serviceman of the Korean War is in the middle. The Unknown of World War II not chosen by Charette was buried at sea (*Naval Historical Center*).

clusion that could not be proved, that if its title could be researched, it would probably be found to be fully owned by the United States. And the article concluded with a note of despair. At the time of writing, said Maps, nature was once again trying to reclaim the cemetery with overgrowth. In addition, a recent visit by sailors of the USS *Farragut*, namesake of the old admiral so important in Menorcan history, had shown the key to its gate to be lost. Breaking it down, they could not fully put it back in place, making it vulnerable to the damage of stray goats munching on its weeds. It was Maps' hope that the article would awaken U.S. Navy interest in the cemetery beyond the occasional ship visits to Port Mahon, but that did not come to pass. A classified message of April 1975 from the commander of the Sixth Fleet to the commander of the U.S. Navy, Europe, spoke to the continuing problem of funding cemetery maintenance at a level of $75 per ship visit for needed materials. It noted that the Spanish navy sometimes provided the whitewash, brushes and foliage cutting equipment, but that when it did not, funds were taken from the visiting ship's operating budget. It suggested that funding come, instead, from the COMREL, or community relations budget of Navy Europe at the level of $300 per year.

During this time, the Madrid Council of the Navy League of the United States (NLUS) took up advocacy for the cemetery. Pres. Teddy Roosevelt had created the Navy League in 1902, and, like the effort to retrieve the body of John Paul Jones from France, it was intended to advance public acceptance of the navy. Under the motto "Citizens in Support of the Sea Services" it was a civilian, nonprofit, educational association dedicated to offering services and support to the personnel and families of the U.S. Navy, Marine Corps, Coast Guard, Merchant Marine and related services. The Madrid Council was formed in 1965 to serve as an interface between American and Spanish military and contractors, and a social meeting place for military, civilian, business and diplomatic interests of the two countries. In 1970, it collaborated with the city of Ciudadela in the creation of a statue and plaza in honor of the city's native-born American naval hero, Adm. David Farragut.

Jim Maps and the council continued to press the navy for better attention, and in 1977 an official memo reinforced directions that ships stopping in Menorca must attend to the cemetery. It noted that a recent visit by the USS *Portland* had revealed that the markings on many gravestones were indiscernible, and it directed that the needed information be researched for the placement of informational plaques near the withered stones for "long term identification of and due respect of these early servicemen."[10] There was no indication of an awareness of the probable availability of gravestone inscriptions that had been preserved as of 1928 by order of a previous commander of Naval Forces Europe.

Also in 1977, and several hundred miles to the southeast of Menorca, another run-down and forgotten cemetery was discovered yet again. It was described in the May edition of the *American Legion* magazine:

> From the modern asphalt highway, weathered stone steps made their way towards the sea. On one side was the whitewashed wall of the British Rod and Gun Club; on the other side was a well-repaired stone wall. The steps turned abruptly and clung to the cliff. The rocks below were green from the dampness of the Mediterranean.
>
> The stone steps stopped at a small opening in the wall. Inside, the vaulted doorway framed a picturesque seascape. A tanker rode on the blue-purple sea. White birds floated in and out of view. The walls enclosed an area not larger than half a city lot. On top of the stone floor were positioned stone burial crypts about the size of a coffin. Markers noted the deceased....
>
> In the northeast corner of the room-like cemetery, a gnarled olive tree spread its limbs over five stone coffins. On each crypt a bronze marker has been placed: "Here lies an American sailor who gave his life in the explosion of the U.S. ship Intrepid in Tripoli harbor Sept. 4, 1804."[11]

The article, by a New Jersey writer, went on to acknowledge all five of the *Intrepid* sailors buried in the small Christian cemetery at the edge of the sea, one of them Richard Somers of Somers Point. Its revelation resounded upwards, starting in an American Legion post in Leonia, New Jersey, and ending in the precincts of international diplomacy. Though Richard Somers was the only of them known to be from New Jersey, all 13 *Intrepid* sailors buried in Tripoli were made honorary citizens of Bergen County.

The Atlantic County Historical Society, based in Somers Point, took up their cause with New Jersey representatives in Congress. The rationale was simple and the goal was direct: U.S. Marines have never left their men behind, and these must be repatriated to Arlington Cemetery. At the end of 1980, the will of those people of New Jersey who cared about such things was wrapped up in a bill by Representative Harold Hollenbeck of East Rutherford calling for direct action by the secretary of the navy. Some thought that the navy could act on its own authority and without the support of legislation; others urged that the administration of Pres. Jimmy Carter directly order the action. Libya was now deemed not a friendly nation to U.S. interests, but the State Department indicated to Rep. Hollenbeck that it might be able to work with the navy and the Libyan government toward a good end. Some thought that repatriation would revive "a suffering Navy tradition" regarding the attention paid to its dead. The national American Legion pledged its support with a resolution at its national convention.

The mission was logical, and hopes were high. No headway was gained in Congress, however, or in the administration of Pres. Carter. Supporters then looked forward to the incoming administration of Pres. Ronald Reagan.[12] But on August 12, 1981, Pres. Reagan, citing Libya's involvement in international terrorism, directed air attacks on Libyan targets. By the end of the year, all Americans were asked to leave Libya, and their passports were revoked.

Though Richard Somers and the sailors of the *Intrepid* would continue their long rest in North Africa, one of the six navy ships that would carry Somers' name was returned from her own death in 1986. The first USS *Somers* had been a schooner in service on the Great Lakes in the War of 1812. Upon capture by the British, she was converted to the HMS *Somers*. The second *Somers* was a fast brig launched in 1842. On duty in the Mexican-American War, she was capsized by a freak accident of wind against sail in the harbor at Veracruz, with 32 lost. She was not seen again until 140 years later when an American archaeologist working for the Mexican government found her by chance in the waters off Veracruz. After a joint study and charting of the wreck by the two countries, she was left where she lay.

One day in the 1970s, a retired British policeman came across a similar finding of an American tool of war at rest in offshore waters. After his retirement, Ken Small had moved to Devon, just south of Plymouth, and opened up a small guesthouse near Slapton Sands. He became happily engaged in the quiet business, but at one point he suffered an inexplicable nervous breakdown. As therapy, he took to beachcombing, and over a few years found what he thought to be an extraordinary number of things lost and left behind: rings and coins, live and dead bullets and shells, other military shrapnel and parts of vehicles. Eventually, and with the help of old timers in the area, he came to learn about Operation Tiger. Since its tragic occurrence in 1944, there had been a sense that it was not something that the American military wanted anyone to know about. Indeed, more than 25 years after the fact, not many people did. And there was an underlying belief, held by some, that not all of the dead had been retrieved from Slapton Sands and its environs.

Small's interest in what he was finding in the sand was enhanced when a local fisherman told him that an object of some sort lay at the bottom of 60 feet of water, three-quarters of a mile off the beach. The fisherman helped him to locate the object, and a group of divers were sent down to see what it was. They emerged from the deep to describe an American Sherman tank. Whatever had occurred at Slapton Sands, Ken Small determined that the tank should be retrieved from its watery grave and turned into a monument to the loss of American life in the fateful exercise. His first actions were to attempt to gain ownership of the tank, an effort that seemed to bewilder military agencies in the UK and the US. The office of the U.S. Defense Property Disposal Service in Wiesbaden, Germany, finally gave him a contract of sale. The cost was fifty dollars, and the deal was closed on November 25, 1974.

Receiving no assistance from either the U.S. or the UK militaries, a salvage contractor from Portsmouth raised it to the surface with the use of inflated air bags over the course of five days. It was pulled ashore as thousands watched nearby and on television, and put in place on the beach, where it was cleaned and painted. Then, as a purely local effort, the tank was blessed by a service at the Slapton Village Church on November 9, 1984. It was not until three years later, by Small's persistence and House Resolution 314, January 6, 1987, that the tank was recognized as a memorial by delegations and dignitaries of both nations. He received a subsequent letter of appreciation from Pres. Ronald Reagan.

News of the ceremony brought Operation Tiger to a new exposure in the press of the United States and the United Kingdom, accompanied by accusations from some quarters that the whole, sad event had been covered up by authorities since 1944. At that time, it was necessary cover-up to withhold knowledge from the enemy, but it seemed that no effort had been

A Sherman tank used in Exercise Tiger and returned from the sea off Slapton Sands, Devon, England, in 1984. The recovery of the American tank was accomplished solely by British civilians, but was eventually recognized as a memorial by the United Kingdom and United States (*Wikimedia Commons*).

made since then to tell the story. And in that apparent silence, stories, from that time, of American bodies secretly buried in the fields of Devon had been allowed to linger. Out of the talk of conspiracy and cover-up there emerged the story — told by Dorothy Seekings, a baker's daughter who had helped to feed the troops — that she had seen truckloads of American corpses buried in farmland near the village. There were inconsistencies to her stories, but they were seemingly backed up by other accounts. One of them was that of dairy farmer Francis Burden, who said he had seen a two-acre wide pit dug up by U.S. troops and stacks of boxes large enough to hold bodies nearby. The same piece of land came into the ownership of farmer Nolan Tope after the war. It was reported that he had said that the field held a secret that he would take to his grave.[13]

The army response to the talk of cover-up and bodies left behind was swift and even angry. In the June 1988 edition of *Army* magazine, Charles MacDonald, once a deputy chief historian of the army's Center of Military History, pointed out a number of books and publications about Operation Tiger in the 1940s and 1950s. He reminded readers that the army had placed a memorial at Slapton Sands in 1954, though he did not mention that its dedication was only to the people of the region and not to American soldiers. And he said that full, unclassified accounts of the event were available to anyone in the National Archives: "For anybody who took even a short time to investigate, there clearly had been no cover-up other than the brief veil of secrecy raised to avoid compromise of D-day. Yet, in at least one case — WJLA-TV in Washington — the news staff pursued its accusations of cover-up even after being informed by the Army's Public Affairs Office well before the first program aired about the various publications including the official histories that had told of the tragedy."

Mentioning Dorothy Seekings by name, MacDonald pointed to a change in her story from the witnessing of mass burials to a new story that they had been buried one by one. "At long last, somebody in the news media — a correspondent for BBC television — thought to query the farmer on whose land the dead are presumably buried. He had owned and lived on that land all his life, said the farmer, and nobody was ever buried there." And, MacDonald insisted, there was no need for an American memorial to its losses at Slapton Sands. Those men were presumably included in monuments to the D-day dead both on Omaha Beach and in the American cemetery at Cambridge.[14] But the matter of where the Slapton Sands dead were buried would never be fully resolved in the minds of some.

In the early 1980s, another group of citizens of a country helped by the United States in World War II began to memorialize the American war dead buried in their soil. As in European countries like Belgium, the presence of Americans in Australia during the war had generated an appreciation for American popular culture. Barry Crompton remembered growing up in the 1950s and 1960s in Melbourne being immersed in cowboy movies and television shows like *Rin Tin Tin* as much as any American child of the time. In 1972, Crompton combined that interest in the United States with another Australian fascination and formed the American Civil War Roundtable. Australian interest in the American Civil War was no different than that in most any other country, and the Australian group interacted with a number of similar efforts in a range of nations from Japan to Sweden. But Australia had its own historic touchstone with the war.

The War Between the States was not limited to the North American continent. In Europe, for example, it played out in an extraordinary event in the harbor at Cherbourg, France. American commerce and diplomacy with the rest of the world had not ceased with the Civil War, and both the Union and the Confederacy found it necessary to be out on the oceans to interfere with international alliances made by the enemy, to engage in, or to interrupt, trade that yielded money and materials for one side or the other. The Confederate cruiser CSS *Alabama* was one of the best at damaging European trade with the Union. Built specifically for the Confederate navy in Liverpool, England, she carried three masts, two engines and a deck full of guns and cannons of various sizes. She never set anchor in waters of the American south, but she managed to attack and destroy 65 Union fighting and merchant ships from South America to South Africa and coastal New England to Western Europe. A vicious ship-killing machine, her policy was to treat all captured crewmen of the other side with care and respect until they could be safely put ashore.

On June 11, 1864, the exhausted ship put into the harbor at Cherbourg for refitting and dry-dock maintenance. Three days later, the USS *Kearsarge* arrived at Cherbourg and set up a blockade outside the harbor. The fierce fighting captain of the *Alabama* could not countenance the notion that his ship could be so easily put out of action. He completed most of his repairs and set off on June 19 to blow the *Kearsarge* out of his way. The *Kearsarge* was in better shape for the battle and quickly sank the *Alabama*. Three fatalities among the crew of the *Alabama* were recovered and buried in "an ancient hillside cemetery"[15] overlooking the harbor. George Appleby was a British citizen who had signed on with the ship's launching in Liverpool, James King was from Savannah, Georgia, and William Robinson, born in Massachusetts, had joined the Confederate Navy in Louisiana. In 1984, the wreckage of the CSS *Alabama* was discovered in 200 feet of water off the coast of Cherbourg. She was left where she lay as a protected wreckage and an archaeological treasure. Appleby, King and Robinson also remained in the ancient hillside cemetery overlooking the harbor.

The Civil War in the Pacific was much the same, with the added dimension of the need to control the whaling trade. Whale oil was in its declining years as a fuel source, but still important in the 1860s. A Pacific equivalent of the CSS *Alabama* was the CSS *Shenandoah*. Also a product of British shipyards, she began life as the troop transport *Sea King*. She was spotted in port in Glasgow by a Confederate agent and deemed a potential trade raider. An implicit understanding that the British would not sell war materiel to the Confederacy led to the playing out of a subterfuge in which the *Sea King* was secretly purchased by the Confederates and set to sail on a trade journey to India. Instead, she was sailed to Funchal, Madeira, converted into the *Shenandoah* and charged with destroying Union commerce from the Cape of Good Hope to Australia. Her propeller was damaged in a storm, and she made way to Melbourne on January 25, 1865. There, she was refitted to fight Union whalers in the North Pacific and subsequently put 24 of them out of commission. Many of those kills, however, took place in the four months after the surrender of Confederate general Robert E. Lee on April 9, 1865. Her travels had taken her as far north as the edge of the Arctic Circle where the news of current events often arrived months behind the fact.

The *Shenandoah*'s visit to Melbourne was a notable event in Australian history. Thousands of sightseers came from afar and by train to look at her, and her crew members were involved in community festivities, including a royal ball in their honor. The ship's presence in Australia took on larger implications, however. The American consul demanded that she be confiscated and her crew charged as pirates. Newspaper editorials agreed. The government, however, still part of the British Empire, allowed the Confederate ship safe harbor, and after the war Britain was made to pay reparations to the United States in the amount of twelve million dollars. The easy landing of a large fighting ship in Melbourne also revealed to some Australians how vulnerable to attack their country and its harbors might be, and a new effort was made at strengthening coastal defenses.

In 1983, Barry Crompton of the Australian Civil War Roundtable traveled to the United

States to meet with similar American groups and tour the battlefields. At the time, he was vaguely aware of perhaps a dozen American born veterans of the war buried in various places in Australia. Further discussions with his American counterparts led to the realization that there were probably more than that. The question was joined by an expatriate U.S. Air Force captain who flew for an Australian aviation company and had access to much of the country. His explorations, combined with Crompton's research and the increasing use in the late 1980s of the Internet as a generator of information, led to a growing list of Americans who had fought in the war and emigrated to Australia for various reasons. Upon death they were buried in community and family cemeteries, often without notation of their American past.

The actual number of such veterans was not large and through the following years ranged as high as 450 in Australia and New Zealand. Still, it excited the interests of the Civil War community in both Pacific countries. The search and the creation of verifiable, accurate lists of the dead became competitive and controversial among groups with different interests. The most conservative list holds 140 veterans who are named and located. They were men who did not fight for Australia and died in a country not their own, long after their combat experiences. But they are taken care of. "We try to do whatever we can to be sure that their graves are well maintained," said Barry Crompton. As in Europe, those burial sites are the places of ceremonies on the American Memorial Day.

The search for American Civil War veterans in Australia is open-ended, and a similar effort is underway for veterans of the Spanish-American War whose fortunes after the war also took them to life and death in foreign lands. The National Spanish American War Gravesite Recording Project is an Internet effort administered by those who feel that the conflict is largely forgotten. "We believe," said its director, Patrick Sherry, "that the Spanish American War was one of the most significant conflicts in American history in that the U.S. became a recognized world power as a result of the conflict. Since it was quite successfully carried out in a short time, and its losses were greatly overshadowed by the losses in the Civil War before it and World War One after it, the sacrifices of the men who fought in the Spanish American War are overlooked." The effort is intended to remember them through a constantly developing interactive database. In 2010 the base included just over 100 buried abroad, most of them in ABMC cemeteries after service in World War I. Two among them had started their military careers on the USS *Merrimac,* later the CSS *Virginia,* in the Civil War; one is buried in Scotland and one in Canada.

The Cuzco Beach Cemetery at Guantanamo Bay, Cuba, holds a gravestone for American sailor William King, presumed to be a veteran of the Spanish-American War. His dates are May 1884–April 22, 1906, the death eight years after a Marine landing in Cuba. He is one of only two Americans known to be buried at Cuzco Beach (the other is a civilian secretary, Gertrude Myers Russell, who died in 1922), and nothing more is known about him.

In the last years of the 20th century, history was abruptly reeled back to the War of 1812 as the American dead of that conflict seemed to rise to the surface of Canadian soil. The two events were about decisions related to the future use of that soil, but otherwise unrelated. Both became emotional reminders of the shared history of the two North American neighbors.

Almost inarguably, the most deadly battle of the War of 1812 had taken place at Fort Erie, Ontario, just across the Niagara River from Buffalo, New York. The Americans had captured the strategically located fort on July 3, 1814, and quickly moved to enlarge it and strengthen its defenses. The British badly wanted to get it back and first attempted to cut off supply lines at Buffalo, but the effort failed. As they prepared a siege on the fort, they were menaced by three offshore American schooners, one of them the first USS *Somers*. The British were able to capture the *Somers* and her sister ship, the USS *Ohio*. Encouraged by the success, the British fired their first shots at the fort on August 13, without effect. Two days later, they approached the fort in full force in a driving rain and were thoroughly repulsed by firepower from within. The action back and forth continued in that vein until September 17 when the British retreated.

One hundred seventy-three years later, as the land on which the fiercest fighting had taken place was prepared for building construction, a backhoe unearthed human bones from the sandy soil of a small rise known as Snake Hill near Lake Erie. Work was stopped, and an archaeological study identified the distinct remains of 28 American soldiers. They ranged in age from the mid-teens to the forties. Most had been brutally killed, with shot-off limbs and crushed bones.

At that point in the history of the United States and Canada, Fort Erie and Buffalo had long been celebrating the annual International Friendship Festival to commemorate good feeling between the two countries since the War of 1812. The 1988 festival was opened with a ceremony of repatriation from Canada to the United States. The dead were placed in 28 aluminum caskets, and, as a crowd of 500 looked on, they were saluted by American and Canadian forces, spoken over by ambassadors and colonels, and placed in 28 hearses. They passed across the Peace Bridge between the two countries as a missing man formation flew overhead; they were driven southeast to the national cemetery at Bath, near Elmira.

Among the words that flowed in the event was an attempt by an American speaker to characterize the war as only a conflict between America and England, with Canada caught in the middle. A Canadian historian, Carl Benn, took immediate exception. "That was a pretext," he said. "What really drove this thing was the Americans and their sense of Manifest Destiny. If they'd succeeded, at least Ontario, and perhaps all of Canada, would be part of the United States today." One of his countrymen took a more sanguine view. "We're all Americans really," said veteran Hugh Lyrea, "North Americans. That border really doesn't mean that much."[16]

Ten years later, another effort to develop land led to a similar reaffirmation of shared history and friendship between the United States and Canada, but with a different result for American dead. When the USS *Chesapeake* was captured by the HMS *Shannon* in 1813, a few of her badly injured crew were taken to the naval hospital in Halifax, Nova Scotia, and those who died were most probably buried in the hospital's cemetery. But another few members of her crew were taken to the prison on Melville Island on the Northwest Arm of the harbor. There they joined a population of hundreds of American prisoners of the War of 1812.

By the end of the war, as many as 8,000 American prisoners of war had passed through Melville Island, and about 188 of them had stayed behind in the prison cemetery on Deadman's Island. Without time for the dust to settle, the cemetery was pressed into service by the immigration of runaway American slaves who arrived in Halifax at a time of a smallpox epidemic. The prison was converted to a hospital for their care, and 107 of those who died were taken to the island. In the 1840s, they were joined by refugees, from troubled countries and economies across the Atlantic, who arrived in Halifax only to die of disease. Then the cemetery was forgotten for the most part. Occasional skulls and bones rose to its surface or made their way to the low sands of the waterfront, but they were treated as curiosities.

In 1997, Deadman's Island was acquired by a developer with a plan to build 60 waterfront condominiums. The prison had long since disappeared, but the old warden's house had been converted to the clubhouse for the Armdale Yacht Club. It was there that residents of the neighborhood came together in February of the following year to join forces in opposition to the condominiums. Their reasons were aesthetic and environmental, but they weren't able to make headway until it was realized that the property was an old cemetery. Even then, the developer asserted that, though they planned to build a garage into the hill, they could work around whatever old bones might show themselves.

Among those leading the neighborhood effort were a retired professor of history and vice president of Dalhousie University, Guy MacLean, and a local historian and genealogist, Iris Shea. They were able to gain momentum through continued understanding of the cemetery, and when it became apparent that there were Americans buried in the hillside the tide began to turn more quickly. Iris Shea sent a casual e-mail about the find to a military friend in the U.S. who was activated by the information but not able to find much interest in the problem from others in the military community. Guy MacLean's argument became one of fairness. There were Nova Scotian dead buried in Boston, for example. "How would we feel if they were disturbed in this way? Would we dig up the Titanic graves for a housing project?" he asked, referring to the many dead from the sinking of the HMS *Titanic* on April 15, 1912, who were buried in Halifax.

Then a remarkable fluke of history occurred. Quite independently of the controversy in Halifax, a document emerged from the dusty bins of admiralty archives in London, made its way to the National Archives in Washington and came to the attention of a professional acquaintance of Iris Shea. It contained the names, ranks, army or navy units, hometowns,

A color guard marches past Target Hill on Deadman's Island, Halifax, on June 23, 2000, while officials of three nations gather to memorialize Americans who had died in the prison at Melville Island. The hill is believed to hold the remains of approximately 400 soldiers, sailors, refugees and runaway slaves buried in the first half of the 19th century, including 188 named Americans of the War of 1812, several of whom may actually be buried at the naval hospital cemetery in Halifax (*Jack Hartnett*).

ages and causes of death of 195 Americans killed in the War of 1812 and buried in Halifax, an estimated 188 of them on Deadman's Island. The historian Guy MacLean knew immediately that, now that they could be named, the dead could exert the final push against the condominiums. And indeed, the developer quickly backed out. The city purchased the land and promised that it would be forever preserved.

That might have ended the matter. But the *New York Times* published an article about the events in Halifax, and it eventually ended up in a Memphis newspaper that was read by a Memphis fire chief, Henry Posey.[17] His first reaction was one of gratitude to the people of Halifax, but as he thought about it further, the true impact of the story became clear. "Here were some people from Canada trying to save something we had forgotten: 188 prisoners of war," he said. "Here they were forgotten, no markers on their graves, and they were trying to save it."

In another happenstance of history, Posey was also a senior master sergeant of the 164th Civil Engineering Squadron of the Tennessee Air National Guard, and his group would soon be holding joint exercises with Canadian forces not far from Halifax. Late one night, he found Guy MacLean by telephone and asked if he and his men could visit the cemetery while there. MacLean readily agreed, and the next day the mayor of Halifax agreed to bring the city's support to the American visit.

The Arabian Gulf War, from August 2, 1990, to February 28, 1991, left just one American buried abroad. U.S. Navy pilot Scott Speicher was the first American casualty of the war when his F/A/-18 Hornet fighter was shot down 100 miles from Baghdad on January 17, 1991, the first night of Operation Desert Storm, which sought to remove invading Iraqi forces from neighboring Kuwait. Speicher's plane and body could not be found, and the mystery of his whereabouts became increasingly controversial through the 1990s. After the United States invasion of Iraq in a second war starting on March 20, 2003, it became possible to search more freely for Speicher's body in Iraq; but it was not until August 2009 that it was determined he had been buried by Bedouins after dying in the 1991 crash. His burial place was found with the help of local civilians, and his body was recovered on July 28, 2009, by a U.S. Marine recovery task force (*U.S. Marine Corps*).

As they planned the visit, Henry Posey and his men thought they would hold a small memorial service. But when Posey was first brought to the small piece of land, he was surprised at the force of his own reaction. He was overwhelmed with the possibility of what the men from Tennessee had been given the opportunity to do. These were Americans killed in war and left in foreign soil who had probably not been thought of in almost 200 years. If the spirit of their times while they were alive didn't value American war dead abroad enough to try to bring them home, even to tend to their graveyards abroad, the ethic of the current times required that each and every American man and woman killed in war be sought out and brought home; if not brought home, buried in beautiful spaces with his fellow countrymen; if not buried with others, taken care of in their single places; if not found, at least memorialized with others of solemn wars.

The plan was put in place for the afternoon of June 23, 2000, and it was quickly joined with support from the city of Halifax and the governments of Canada, Great Britain and the United States. The city spent $100,000 to make the cemetery more accessible to the media and for broadcast in parts of Canada and live coverage by Peter Jennings of *ABC News* in America. Programs were printed, a flag was sent from its flight above the White House in Washington, military and diplomatic officials from the three nations prepared to give speeches. Music and marching was provided by color guards of Canada and Great Britain; a lone bagpiper, invisible in the wooded graveyard, played "Amazing Grace." It was a cool, gray day. "It starts to mean so much to you," said Henry Posey. "You realize that they had families, they had homes, they had wants and needs that were never fulfilled. When you think that they have been here for 188 years and nothing has been done, it hurts in the heart."

Five years later, on Memorial Day 2005, another ceremony was held at Deadman's Island. A fully landscaped path from a residential street, down through the woods to the cemetery, had been built by the city. Informational placards were put in place, along with benches on which to rest and look out at the sparkling water of the Northwest Arm. A monument from the U.S. Veteran's Administration was installed on the land between the water and hill of graves. Its bronze tablet rising from a marble base contained the names of the 188 Americans believed to be buried in a cemetery that was no longer forgotten.[18]

CHAPTER FOURTEEN

Ordinary Lives, Extraordinary Events

And she kept saying "I can't find him. I can't find him."
—Bernard McManaman's mother in Janine Parker's dream

As the injured War Dogs of Guam were passed to veterinarians in the rear during the successful capture of the island in July 1944, many fell into the care of Dr. William Putney. Putney had been one of the leaders of the effort to engage the dogs as full partners in the work of finding and killing the enemy. He developed training programs that conditioned them to the violent sounds of the battlefield and taught them to replace a barking response with the pointing of their bodies or the pricking of their ears. Immediately after the war, he led dog-guided platoons in search of Japanese soldiers still in hiding. Then he was made chief veterinarian of the Marine Corps and devoted much of his effort to saving from euthanasia those dogs that could not reenter society.

It was Putney and his fellow veterinarians who had built the small cemetery on the beach, and when he returned to Guam in 1989, he could not easily find it. He learned that it had been scrambled by a typhoon in 1963 and moved hastily inland. Directed to its new location he found it in disrepair and overgrown with weeds, a place of "disgrace and dishonor." He began an effort to have the dogs properly and permanently reburied. "These dogs lived in foxholes with their men. They went on and led over 350 patrols. Their handlers killed 301 enemy soldiers with the loss of only one of my men on patrols. So the fact that these dogs were killed instead of us and kept us from ever being ambushed or surprised at night makes them heroes in my mind."[1]

The National War Dog Cemetery was opened ceremonially at the U.S. Naval Base at Orote Point on July 20, 1994, the 50th anniversary of the invasion of Guam. William Putney, who had been nominated for, but never received, the Silver Star for bravery in 1944, was finally given that medal at ceremonies commemorating the end of World War II the following year.

The continuing attention paid to 25 American dogs still buried on Guam was a simple matter compared to the larger human realm of those lost in the Pacific during three wars. Like much of the warfare, the loss was assymetrical, unconventional, without basic rules of conduct between enemies and in the name of some governments that had little capability or interest in tracking or honoring the enemy's dead.

Fourteen. Ordinary Lives, Extraordinary Events

U.S. Navy petty officer 2nd class Blake Soller and his military working dog, Rico, pay tribute at the National War Dog Cemetery on Naval Base Guam on October 27, 2006. The memorial is dedicated to the war dogs killed on Guam in World War II (*Department of Defense*).

Similarly, in the 36 years that had passed since Operation Glory brought 151 sets of American remains to Panmunjon in 1954, not much else had occurred. Then between 1990 and 1994, sets numbering 242 were repatriated from North Korea through the United Nations Command at the border between North and South Korea. In 1994, former American Pres. Jimmy Carter traveled across the Demilitarized Zone between the two Koreas as part of an American effort to normalize American relations with the north in general and to reach nuclear arms agreements in particular. The visit eventually led to agreements allowing Joint Field Activities (JFAs) so that American investigators could enter North Korea to search for bodies. Altogether, 499 sets of remains had been recovered from North and South Korea, China, and Japan and disinterred from the Punchbowl Cemetery in Hawaii through mid–2010. Just 131 of them could be identified.[2]

The continuing work presently falls under the purview of the Defense Prisoner of War/Missing Personnel Office (DPMO) of the Department of Defense, which is charged with working with defense agencies, the State Department and foreign embassies and emissaries to develop and follow through on strategies for the full accounting and recovery of the military dead starting with World War II. The Joint POW/MIA Accounting Command (JPAC) performs the search and forensic work required to support those strategies.

The aftermath of the Vietnam war has proved almost as problematic as Korea except for an important difference found in current relations between previously warring nations. The United States and North Korea have been in a state of tension with each other since their conflict. But good relations have developed between the U.S., Vietnam and Laos since the 1980s, and efforts to find lost Ameicans have been generally cooperative. A good number of American remains were found in Laos in the middle of that decade, and Vietnam allowed American search teams into the country in 1988. Eventually, those teams were allowed into Cambodia, and, since then, cooperation has included the sharing of records and other documentation. As in Asia after World War II, interviews with potential witnesses of events are an important part of the process, as well as forensic research of crash sites and battle spaces. Special effort is placed on determining the final outcomes for Americans who were believed to have survived a specific potentially fatal incident. Known as "Last Known Alive" (LKA) cases, they have helped to solve some of the mysteries of those still missing in action, but not as much in helping to find and repatriate their remains.

Though the yield from this fully cooperative effort between formerly warring nations has been slim in some cases, it has been remarkably thorough and precise. The journey of Heinz Ahlmeyer, Jr., as an example, began when he was a high school football player at Pearl River High School in New York state. Described as athletic and rugged, Ahlmeyer was one of hundreds of thousands of young men who would end up in Vietnam as volunteers or conscripts. He enlisted in the Marines while he was a student at the State University of New York at New Paltz. On the first day of his tour, May 10, 1967, he was on a reconnaisance patrol in Quang Tri province and came under enemy fire. He and three others with him were presumed to have been killed, but their bodies could not be recovered and the truth of the matter remained unknown until 2004. His sister, Healea, was asked to submit a DNA sample to military investigators. The rest of her family had died, her mother in July of that year, and she did not expect anything to come of the DNA request. But in the first days of 2005, Healea received a call telling her that her brother's remains had been found and identified at the JPAC facility in Hawaii. He and the spare fragments of others presumed to have died with him were buried with full honors at Arlington National Cemetery on May 10, 2005, the 38th anniversary of his death.

Healea was in attendance. "What came home physically was one tooth," she said. "But what really came home was his embodiment and his spirit."[3]

By 2010, just 926 of the 2,646 missing in Vietnam, Laos, Cambodia and China had been found and repatriated, leaving 1,720 still lost on Asian soil, their bodies reduced to the smallest pieces and sometimes scattered to the winds.

One night in the fall of 2009, Janine McManaman Park of Pennsylvania awoke at 4:30 in the morning. "I was just shaking. I had this dream ... my grandmother and my father were in the dream. I had never dreamed of them before. She's been gone for 25 years or so. And she kept saying 'I can't find him. I can't find him.' And it made no sense to me because he was in the dream. I just couldn't stop shaking. And I thought 'Where is this coming from?' And so I thought maybe there's some information about him somewhere."

Prompted by the dream, Park entered into the almost parallel world of Internet search and the sharing of information about veterans. Her father was Bernard McManaman of the U.S. Air Force, the Comet Line, the Belgian Resistance and was later lost in a night intruder flight over Korea. She typed his name into a search engine and discovered a whole community of people also trying to find out more about him. It was not that he was a particularly extraordinary subject of research, but just that the Internet was alive with an ongoing search for many who had been lost in war and were never found. Each month, it seemed, another layer of information was laid upon the last: oral histories, lost archives, military documents, photographs recovered from the bottoms of old boxes, old battalions and bomber groups brought back together on common Websites.

Within days of traveling from link to link and exchanging e-mails with new acqaintances and veterans from her father's era, she arrived at a picture of the woman after whom she had been named by her father, Janine Abeels in Ganshoren, Belgium, who now called herself Jenny. The discovery provoked memories from her childhood. She had been six months old when he had died in Korea. As a little girl she thought that he was probably alive in a village somewhere. Somebody would find him sometime and he would come home. All that she really knew of him was what her grandmother had told her. Her mother had not been able to talk about it and had eventually remarried. "The only thing I ever had from him was my name" Janine said. "It had always been a dream to somewhere find the person that I was named after, because that was the closest connection that I had with him."

The discovery of Jenny Abeels led Janine to a man in Belgium who, it could be said, held the story of her father, her father's fellow aviator Jerry Sorenson and the Abeels family of Ganshoren in his heart as a continuing act of reverence. Jerry Sheridan was an American working in Belgium as director of the Brussels campus of the American University of Washington, D.C. He was also a vice president of AOMDA-Belgium, and the biographer of the seven Americans, including James Pigue, Joe Farina and Jerry Sorenson, who rested in isolated graves across Belgium. Each of Sheridan's biographies was open-ended, always in search of new information and derived from personal relationships with men he had never known. In the case of Jerry Sorenson, he had also formed a lasting relationship with Jenny Abeels. During a working visit to Washington, D.C., he was able to meet with Janine Parker near her home in Pennsylvania and facilitate an exchange of information between the two women. Jenny had not been aware of her American namesake. She had never married and lived mostly in the past. Her eyes lit up with a letter from Janine. She recalled that Bernard MacManaman had visited her after the war and that they had had great times together. As a result of her dream, Janine planned to give her DNA to the effort to reclaim those still lost in Korea. If his bones were found, she said without hesitation, "I would want him home right away."

Among the territorial losses suffered by the Japanese in World War II were the Micronesian Islands of the Western Pacific, among them the island of Yap. Not far west of Guam, Yap was strategic enough for military and communications needs (its location enabled the laying of the first trans-Pacific cable) that it had been fought over by the United States and Japan as a spoil of World War I. It was a diplomatic war in full fury that was eventually resolved in the favor of Japan, who then lost the island in World War II.

Fighting for possesion of Yap was constant in the summer of 1944, and on June 25 Gen. Douglas MacArthur sent a formation of bombers to cover it with 45 tons of bombs. As part of the raid, they bombed islands fromNew Guinea to Saipan, and at Yap they took out a strategic number of Japanese planes parked on the ground while losing just one B-24 Liberator. After releasing its bombs, aircraft number 528 was shot down by Japanese fighters. Fire was seen raging in the cockpit and bombardier station as the plane made a single loop that evolved into a spin and crashed into the ocean two miles off the coast. There could be no survivors, and among the ten crew lost was assistant radio operator John R. McCullough.[4]

When he was a child, McCullough's nephew, Pat Ranfranz, became fascinated with family stories about his uncle. The radio operator had died decades before the child had been born, but Ranfranz had taken up the habit of spinning the globe in his geography class, always bringing it to a stop by resting his finger on Yap Island. In college, Ranfranz changed his major from applied math and technology to history and obtained the missing aircraft report from air force archives. After he had started his own family and settled himself professionally, he began the effort to find his uncle, a "lifelong quest." He and his wife flew to Yap: "It was

A B-24 Liberator withdraws from Yap Island after a formation bombing run over Japanese military facilities and personnel areas (undated) (*National Archives*).

an overwhelming sensation. When we first arrived we were coming in for a landing on Yap, coming through the clouds at the same altitude that they would have been shot down. It was a surreal experience. And when I'm diving in that area — I've done hundreds of dives out there — there's a huge powerful force, almost like I'm talking to John out there."

In return trips he brought others who had lost relatives in the waters off Yap. Though they could not find the planes in the depths, they held memorial services and scattered flowers above presumed crash sites. Eventually, Pat Ranfranz's continued trips to Yap overcame the reluctance of its people to interact with him. They have become friends and keepers of John McCullough. In return, Ranfranz has helped them to gain an understanding of their own place in the history of World War II, and, not incidentally, to use that history in the development of tourism.

The attention given to McCullough, and other fliers fallen on and around their island, was not new to the people of Yap. As Graves Registration moved through the Pacific in 1947, there was discovered what would be called by the Associated Press "one of the loneliest American graves in all the Pacific."[5] The unknown airman had been found by the natives and buried in 1944. "The grave is lonely, but it is not forgotten. Each day the natives place fresh flowers at the base of a crude cross and push back the encroaching jungle growth." Graves Registration was able to identify the skeleton as that of First Lt. Girvis Haltom, Jr., of Stephens, Arkansas, shot down on October 24, 1944. He was returned home for burial.

Still not found in 2011, John McCullough remains unresolved for a nephew with whom he shares a resemblance. "He was a kid who never left his home, let alone to find himself flying over a Pacific island he had never heard of until the mission started," said Ranfranz. "There's never been a grave for John. There's never been a funeral for John. There's never been a closure for who he really was." Many of those shot down over the Pacific, as Ranfranz has come to understand the problem, fell into a similar limbo. They were not at first declared dead, only missing. Over the following years, those they had left behind would often move on with their lives. Wives would remarry, parents would die, children would grow up. During the last years of the war and in its aftermath, the records of their military lives and deaths were packed up in boxes and moved from ship to ship, ending up far distant from the times and places of their deaths. "They never had a chance to make an impact," said Pat Ranfranz. "That's one of the things I want to do, but they never had that chance. They were all very interesting people, but they were kind of lost, and time forgot them."

Ranfranz's search for his uncle was patient, methodical and informed. It overcame what he feels was bad record-keeping at one end of the process, made use of new technologies at the other, and it was expanded to include other airmen lost in the waters off Yap. Over the years 2005–2009, he and others uncovered/discovered over twelve American crash sites on Yap Island alone. In its initial stages, what the research needed and did not receive, according to Ranfranz, was interest and assistance from JPAC, Though JPAC's mission statement described "investigating leads and recovering and identifying Americans who were killed in action but were never brought home" with the help of "veterans, outside historians, private citizens, families of missing Americans, and amateur researchers,"[6] the response to Ranfranz was "indifferent," in his word. In June 2011, however, JPAC announced that it would spend a month interviewing eyewitness families, and using data received from others, including Pat Ranfranz, to search for the remains of as many as 30 fallen airmen in and around Yap as a prelude to recovery efforts. Ranfranz welcomed the effort, but did not expect that it would lead to the discovery of his uncle.

Whatever the truth of the matter, or the realistic extent to which the U.S. government could go to find those previously declared lost, the effort to find and retrieve the American dead of the Pacific at the beginning of the 21st century increasingly became a pursuit of private individuals and nonprofits. One of those formed an alliance with the effort to find the airmen of Yap as part of its broader focus on the whole Pacific. History Flight was a 501c3 organization based in Florida. Its director, Mark Noah, was a historian and former airline captain who was determined to bring science and expertise to the challenge of finding the missing in the Caroline, Marshall, Palau and Gilbert islands. The financial underpinning of the organization was the selling of flights in vintage World War II aircraft on a traveling circuit through much of the United States. Its pilots and researchers were drawn from a mix of air force officers and commercial pilots some of whom brought necessary academic experience in history and forensics to the work.

The science of finding the lost takes men and equipment to former battle spaces on land or sea with surface detection equipment and ground penetrating radar, combined with the tools of research and the correlation of files from previously disconnected sources. In this case, they need to be matched to the particular demands of the Pacific. Europe had the infrastructure and customs of past behavior to assist in tracking war dead. But the full breadth of the wild Pacific was without those luxuries. The mission was clear.

"For us," said Mark Noah, "it's all about the people. Sometimes people who are interested in this kind of thing are interested because of their jingoistic view of military history, or a sense of super-patriotism or something like that. Not so for us. It's just an incredible human story where the brothers and the sisters, the children of the World War II missing are still alive today." His view was that nothing much had been done to find the dead in the 1950s through 1970s, and part of a natural human process had been interrupted, only to be put back in motion by the Vietnam War.

At the time of the Vietnam War, and increasingly in the following years, it was seen by many as a misadventure, or, at worst, a national tragedy. Many years after its conclusion, even one of its chief architects, secretary of defense (1961–1968) Robert McNamara, would admit his own mistake, in a 2003 interview:

> We are the strongest nation in the world today. I do not believe that we should ever apply that economic, political, and military power unilaterally. If we had followed that rule in Vietnam, we wouldn't have been there. None of our allies supported us. Not Japan, not Germany, not Britain or France. If we can't persuade nations with comparable values of the merit of our cause, we'd better re-examine our reasoning.
>
> War is so complex it's beyond the ability of the human mind to comprehend. Our judgment, our understanding, are not adequate. And we kill people unnecessarily.[7]

The anger and disillusionment that arose in much of the American public during and after the war seemed to change the nation's usual sensibilities about war in profound ways. Distrust and anger about government spilled, unfortunately, into attitudes about those who had fought in the war. Many returned as damaged men in body and spirit, scorned by the public for their participation in a nightmare that had led to the defeat of America by a third world communist nation. And those who supported the veterans through compassion, friendship or family ties became increasingly angry at a perceived unwillingness by the government to take care of those who had survived, let alone to seek out and retrieve the dead and missing with as much determination as in previous wars.

Mark Noah's reading of history suggested that the anger over the Vietnam War, and failures in the concluding treaty between Vietnam and the U.S., led to a reassertion by those affected that American war dead had to be found, returned and honored. As part of that trend, governmental and nongovernmental efforts were increased. In 1976, the Department of Defense established the U.S. Army Central Identification Laboratory in Hawaii (CILH). Its first efforts were in New Guinea where an estimated 2,000 airmen were yet to be found. More than 30 years later, according to Mark Noah, lost aircraft and sometimes their crew can still be found. His organization, other organizations, and JPAC find individual bodies regularly: "That's fairly common. The lost graveyard thing is not that common. But outside of some of the Japanese POW camps in the Philippines, in Borneo, in Papua New Guinea where they starved Americans to death, in some cases executed them, those bodies are still out there in unmarked graves." The kind of recovery effort that was expended along the route of the Bataan Death March after the Pacific war, for example, was productive as far as it went, but it did not have the use of technologies available in the 21st century. Those technologies and funding from nongovernmental sources were used to support Pat Ranfranz's search for his uncle in the waters off Yap. In the course of that search, History Flight discovered other wrecked airplanes and the bones of three fliers who could be identified and returned home.

By far, the largest single Pacific challenge faced by History Flight, JPAC and the Department of Defense lay beneath the soil of Tarawa Island. The U.S. National Defense Authorization Act for Fiscal Year 2010:

(1) reaffirms its support for the recovery and return to the United States of the remains of members of the Armed Forces killed in battle, and for the efforts by the Joint POW-MIA Accounting Command to recover the remains of members of the Armed Forces from all wars;

(2) recognizes the courage and sacrifice of the members of the Armed Forces who fought on Tarawa Atoll;

(3) acknowledges the dedicated research and efforts by persons to identify, locate, and advocate for the recovery of remains from Tarawa; and

(4) encourages the Department of Defense to review this research and, as appropriate, pursue new efforts to conduct field studies, new research, and undertake all feasible efforts to recover, identify, and return remains of members of the Armed Forces from Tarawa.

Mark Noah asserts that there are 500 Americans still buried on Tarawa. Their names, causes of death and initial burial locations are found on identification cards generated during the battle. They disappeared after the battle as the island, now captured by the United States, was quickly converted to offensive use. The markers of the dead were removed from the land and replaced by a military base. Descriptions and locations of burial places no longer applied. After the war, Graves Registration was able to find the graves of less than half of the dead. The military base disappeared over the following years, but the unmarked dead remained.

"When you really look into it," said Noah, "the [military] terms FUBAR or SNAFU were coined to describe something just like that," he said of the acronyms that used vulgarisms to describe chaos and incompetence. He believed that the effort initiated by Congress, set to begin in 2010, would be intense and earnest. "They're going to be looking under shanty towns, and I doubt that they're going to find everybody, but they're going to find a lot." History Flight submitted its own 400-page summary of findings on Tarawa in support of the effort.

The effort at Tarawa, and Pat Ranfranz's search for a lost uncle that had led to the discovery of others, would continue. And there was something else that Mark Noah's group had begun to do successfully: researching the identities of those buried as unknown in the American cemeteries in Hawaii and the Philippines. The immediate postwar work of Graves Registration was as thorough as it had been since World War I, but fresh eyes sixty years later were able to draw new connections out of old records. One Missing Air Crew Report (MACR) might have information that shed light on the mysteries of another. Records that noted lack of positive identification because of entanglement of bones could be updated with the use of DNA testing.

The renewed search for Americans in the West and South Pacific was almost open-ended at the beginning of the 21st century. The place of Americans buried at the edge of the East Pacific, however, was pretty much settled business, though controversial in some respects. Under the headline "U.S. heroes are villains at cemetery in Mexico,"[8] the May 24, 2007, *Arizona Republic News* published a pre–Memorial Day story that was not meant to be portentous, but was nonetheless provocative. While ceremonies celebrating the defense of freedom were about to take place in American cemeteries from the Philippines to Europe, the events at the American National Cemetery in Mexico City would be low-key. "Unlike other U.S.-run war cemeteries in Europe and the Philippines," the newspaper reported, "it's the only place where the buried Americans are considered villains." Though American dignitaries would honor their countrymen within the cemetery walls, many of those on the outside thought of the dead as invaders in a war that had stolen much of northern Mexico, turning it into California, Nevada, Utah, Arizona, and parts of New Mexico, Colorado and Wyoming.

Many of those Mexicans who even knew of the cemetery's existence felt that the bodies should be dug up and returned north. And in any case, the cemetery seemed to attract few American visitors. Approximately 763,000 Americans had traveled to Mexico City in 2006, but the cemetery had only 2,500 visitors during that year, most of them curious Mexicans. While the reporter was there, however, a Mexican college student entered the cemetery's gate and began reading its tombstones. ""I don't see anything wrong with them being here," he said. "In the end, we're all human beings, and it doesn't matter who's buried where. Eventually, we all go into the ground."

In northern Mexico, two more Americans who had rested in the earth, probably without visitors in several decades, became the subject of a search by an American from Arizona who had built a second home in Chihuahua state. Ron Bridgemon's affection for Mexico had led him to a fascination for the Mexican Revolution (1910–1920). The home that Bridgemon built was in the midst of the revolution's first historic battlefields. In the course of his investigation, he began to hear sketchy stories of the burials of Pvt. Hobert Ledford and Sgt. Jay Richley in a ranch cemetery near Parral. The two had last been officially tended to in 1929, when they were left behind by an American recovery expedition at the request of their families.

In 2009, a new research tool was available to those who sought out forgotten burial places all over the world. The Internet search company Google had developed a view of the global terrain derived from satellites. Using descriptive information generally available about the site, Bridgemon went to Google Earth and found the cemetery at GPS coordinates 27° 07′ 48″ 44° N, 105° 38′ 41″ 69° W: "I knew that it was about 12 miles out of town. So you mark out your distance and you start looking in that area. There's a bridge and the river, and you go a bit further where you turn left on a dirt road going to the west. You go just half a mile and it turns into a whole ranch area. There's a church just further to the west, and a cemetery near that church." Ron Bridgemon and his son, Ron Jr. followed the visual cues given by satellite and drove up to the cemetery. "It's quite old and there's a lot of stuff there.

FOURTEEN. *Ordinary Lives, Extraordinary Events* 175

The graves of Hobert Ledford, left, and Jay Richley, right, at Santa Cruz de Villegas, Mexico. Standing left to right are Ron Bridgemon, Jr., Sue Bridgemon and Jon Gentile. In 2009, an attempt was begun to find an American source of regular upkeep of the gravesite (*Rondal R. Bridgemon, Sr.*).

It got filled up and they made a little expansion area to the west of the main cemetery, and that's where these two are buried, right inside the gate."

On his first visit to the graves of Ledford and Richley, he was just happy to have found them and to be able to take pictures of their markers. Eventually, he and his son wanted to know more. "What were their personal stories," said Bridgemon Jr. "What were they thinking in that battle. What was their motivation for joining the military, just their life stories." He thought that the lives of those whose names were found written in stone on cemetery markers were made more intriguing by relating them to specific wars and battles.

Ron Bridgemon, Sr., expanded his research on an Internet genealogical site and connected with a woman in Michigan who was researching Jay Richley's father, John. They were able to exchange information and pictures, and Bridgemon gained new information about Richley's family history and his death in Parral.

On their second visit to the cemetery at Rancho Santa Cruz de Villegas, the Bridgemons found it to be overgrown and unkempt, and they did what they could to clean it up. Ron Bridgemon, Sr., knew that the families of the men had wanted them to remain in Mexico, but it seemed to him that more could be done to maintain the site: "As Americans on foreign soil, it would be nice to have a little better maintenance for them." His plan was to try to enlist historical organizations in a program of scheduled maintenance, or perhaps find interest in the graves at the closest American military bases in Texas and Arizona.

As late as 2003, there were still discoveries to be made of old, forgotten cemeteries. In that year, two American attachés found themselves on the Atlantic coast at San Juan Del Norte, Nicaragua. Army colonel Mike Rhea, and Marine major Carlos L. Olivo had been told of two American sailors of the USS *Sabine* buried in 1859. The *Sabine* was a steam and sailing frigate used as part of an expedition to Paraguay seeking redress for a Paraguayan attack on a U.S. surveying ship in 1855. That result was achieved with no shots fired.

Rhea and Olivo were taken by boat up steamy rivers and across fetid swamps to an old wooden pier at the foot of a path leading 300 yards into a triple canopy forest. At the end of the path they found what natives called the English Cemetery. It was divided into three sections, one each for the British, Catholics and the USS *Sabine* sailors, which contained only the graves of John Burgess and Charles Smith. By some accounts, the two were crew members on a second journey to Paraguay in 1859. Burgess was killed instantly in a fall from the mizzentop. On another day, Smith was killed in a similar fall. The USS *Sabine* went on from her Paraguayan expeditions to play a creditable role in the Civil War. The 2003 discovery of two of her crew in Nicaragua was unremarked upon and forgotten in the following years.[9]

In the same year, another English and American cemetery across the Atlantic and through the Straits of Gibraltar was continuing a struggle that had started in the mid 1800s. In a letter dated June 18, 1981, navy vice admiral Ronald J. Hays agreed with the Madrid Council of the Navy League of the United States that "we must ensure that the Port Mahon Cemetery in Menorca is maintained in a manner that reflects favorably upon our country, and is indicative of the respect we hold for our deceased shipmates."[10] The new formula for doing so would be to consider the cemetery as a naval plot through the Navy Bureau of Medicine (BUMED). It expressed the wish that the Madrid Council would continue its annual "pilgrimage to Port Mahon to memorialize the twenty-some American sailors buried there, and continue the fostering of good will with the Spanish."

The council did, indeed, continue its attention to the cemetery, but the navy never followed up on the promise, concluding that the cemetery was just not in its purview. Few, if any, port calls of Navy ships were seen until a single visit in 2000. Ultimately, it would be the fostering of good will with the Spanish that would rescue the old cemetery from the worst day in its history, yet to come. In the meantime, the council paid to maintain the cemetery on an annual basis, to clean it up, pull the weeds, keep the goats out, cut the grass and whitewash the walls in preparation for Memorial Day ceremonies.

In 2004, George Mahl, a founder of the Madrid Council, sent a memo to its then president Tom Denegre, an American businessman: "I hope I'm not beating a dead horse, but it seems to me that our Navy should be doing more to help us maintain the grounds at Mahon Cemetery." Notwithstanding the contemporary pressures on the navy in the Gulf and Iraq wars, he said, the commitment of care had been made years earlier. "It would appear that their involvement is practically engraved in stone but over the years it has deteriorated."

"That was him," said Tom Denegre "[placing his boot in a strategic location] to see if I could shake something loose within the Navy, which no one else had been able to do. I, frankly, was not able to do that. We did not get any ship calls." Denegre, however, was able to get Adm. Harry Ulrich, then commander of Naval Forces Europe, to send a crew to prepare the cemetery for Memorial Day 2006. It had never been in better condition, in Denegre's opinion, but the following year it was virtually destroyed.

The cemetery sat just at the edge of Menorca Bay and in a depression surrounded by steep, foliage-covered hills. During heavy rains in the fall of 2007, water breached its back wall and filled the four-walled site to a depth that eventually exploded through the front wall so that it could drain into the bay. Stones of the broken wall could be found thirty feet off the small beach, and the bones of its single Spanish resident, buried there because he was Presbyterian, were washed to the surface. As the cemetery was always in need of protection from

FOURTEEN. *Ordinary Lives, Extraordinary Events*   177

The Port Mahon cemetery at Menorca, Spain, before its repair by the Spanish Army in 2008. The cemetery contains the bodies of 22 Americans, 2 Britains, 1 German and 1 Spaniard, buried from 1820 to 1890 (*Tom Denegre*).

marauding animals, the need to repair the walls was urgent. The Madrid Council appealed to the Spanish military for assistance.

"Because this is a burial ground for foreign nationals on Spanish Army grounds," wrote Denegre in a letter to the commanding officer of the Spanish Army, "we are requesting that the funds necessary for the repairs to the Cemetery be provided under those regulations of patrimony dealing with such matters." The regulations of patrimony were related to Spain's membership in the European Union. It required of its member nations the protection and restoration of cultural heritage, and Spain had taken on responsibility for all foreign cemeteries as a matter of policy in 2008.[11] Past confusions about the actual ownership of the land on which the cemetery sat were answered with a clear determination that the land was owned by Spain. It helped, too, that it held a Spanish national, and that the Madrid Council had long nurtured a relationship with the military community. Unlike the U.S. Navy, the Spanish army gave the project immediate priority. All of the walls were rebuilt, drainage systems were put in place to prevent flooding, and the army returned in 2009 as a follow-up. For the foreseeable future, and perhaps until the next unpredictable turn in the history of nations, the cemetery of Americans and other nationals is protected by Spain.

Southeast across the Mediterranean from Spain, and down the coast of North Africa, a less protected group of American sailors still rested in the soil of Tripoli, Libya. Decades had passed since the failed effort to retrieve Richard Somers and the crew of the USS *Intrepid* in 1981. Those efforts had always been vulnerable to the twists and turns of geopolitical events like wars, and to the antagonistic relations between the United States and Libya since the time of the Barbary Coast pirates.

In 2006, times were relatively good for the United States and Libya. Rapprochement was in the air with Libyan leader Muammar Gaddafi, and it was time to renew the effort to retrieve and return the body of Richard Somers, if no one else, from the 1804 burials at the edge of Tripoli harbor. Thus, on September 4, 2006, a group assembled at the Somers Mansion in Somers Point, New Jersey, to honor Richard on the 202nd anniversary of his death. They felt the breezes of nearby Great Egg Harbor Bay on the Atlantic coast and heard the resolve of writer and activist historian William Kelly. Kelly had grown up in nearby Camden. Among his causes was the seeking of expanded government transparency in the archiving and investigation of tragic events like the assassination of Pres. John F. Kennedy in 1963 and the attack on the World Trade Center in New York on September 11, 2001.

In the matter of Richard Somers, he was resolute:

> It is quite remarkable that we are standing today in the yard of the home of Richard Somers' grandfather, where Somers grew up as a boy, from where we can see the bay where he learned to sail, and from where he left to fight pirates, yet to return. And someday soon he will be laid to rest nearby....
>
> The efforts to repatriate Richard Somers have thus far taken over 200 years, so it's not an easy task. Besides the desires of the extended Somers family and the efforts of the citizens of the Somers Point, I think it is now time for the American military veterans to get involved and educate people about this issue and to try to convince the political administration and the U.S. military that Richard Somers and the crew of the first USS *Intrepid* can not and will not be the only exception to our long standing policy of never leaving anyone behind enemy lines. We don't have to convince the Libyans to return the remains of our men, we have to convince our own administration and our own military that now is the time to repatriate these heroes.

By that time, the New Jersey legislature had declared September 4 Richard Somers day in the state and passed a resolution in 2004 asking the U.S. State Department to "open negotiations with Libyan leaders for the repatriation of Richard Somers and his crew before September 4, 2004, the 200th anniversary of their deaths." Along with Bill Kelly, the effort was shared in Somers Point by Mayor Jack Glasser, the president of the Somers Point Historical Society, Sally Hastings, and U.S. representative Frank LoBiondo of New Jersey's Second District.

A diplomatic opening with Libya on the matter had not occurred, but Kelly was still optimistic. He recalled that the country's first popular naval historian, James Fenimore Cooper, had prophesied Somers' return as he described the burial place of the officers of the USS *Intrepid* in 1842: "Here, then, lie the remains of Somers, and his two gallant friends; and it might be well to instruct the commander of some national cruiser to search for their bones, that they might be finally incorporated with the dust of their native land. Their identity would at once be established by the number of the skeletons, and the friends of the deceased might find a melancholy consolation in being permitted to drop a tear over the spot in which they would be finally entombed."[12]

That place of final entombment was already marked out on the grounds of the Somers Mansion in New Jersey. It remained only for him to be disinterred from Libya and brought home. Others of those still buried there had their own American advocates in other places, but the focus of Somers Point, New Jersey, was full bore on its native son. The U.S. embassy in Libya had received grave flags from the group in New Jersey and placed them on the graves of five unnamed sailors of the *Intrepid* at the Protestant Cemetery rediscovered by Mustapha Burchis in 1939. Those sailors, according to contemporary research by Kelly and his group, might have been more easily found by Burchis if other records had been available to him at the time. It was Kelly's belief that the bodies had actually been placed in the cemetery sometime in the early 1930s, after they had been found by Italian road crews in the process of laying down a new street in Tripoli.

Kelly was able to open up what he believed would be a helpful contact with the ruling family through the Gaddafi International Charity and Development Foundation, which described itself as "an international non-governmental organization, [which] carries out developmental and humanitarian activities in the social, economic, cultural and human rights fields." In 2010, according to William Kelly, that relationship was yielding results in bringing Libya to the table. Also at that seating was the U.S. State Department, for which the small matter of American dead in 1804 might offer an opportunity to build more ambitious accords with the Libyans. A congressional research report on Libya dated December 3, 2007, placed contemporary relations in the context of the Barbary Wars. It told the story of the USS *Intrepid* in 1804 and reported that "efforts to repatriate the remains of U.S. personnel killed in these early 19th century military engagements with Tripoli are ongoing."[13]

Another necessary seat at the table would have to be taken by the U.S. Navy, and in trying to gain its interest Kelly invoked the story of the dogged attempt by Teddy Roosevelt and Gen. Horace Porter to find and return the body of John Paul Jones from the soils of Paris. "I'm saying that if this is important enough, people will do it," said Kelly. In 2010, the attitude of the navy about Richard Somers seemed to be something more productive than its consideration of the cemetery at Menorca, Spain, but it was still noncommittal about repatriation.

In a letter to Kelly from the chief of Naval Operations, Adm. Gary Roughead, dated March 11, 2010, Roughead told of his personal interest after a visit to Tripoli as a young man, matched with reports from a site visit by the Defense Prisoner of War/Missing Personnel Office in 2004. "Honoring the final resting place of Sailors and Marines is a long standing naval tradition," wrote Roughead. But he pointed out that there had been no documentation of the remains recovered after the explosions of the *Intrepid* and no usable record keeping of the reburials of those bodies over the centuries. However, he continued, the navy, State Department and Libyan government had held 1949 ceremonies in honor of the *Intrepid* sailors at the Presbyterian Cemetery. Thus, the cemetery "has been officially recognized by the Department of the Navy as the final resting place for her crew. My staff is working with the Department of State and the American Embassy in Libya to ascertain the condition of the graves and what actions can be taken towards their long-term care."[14]

Repatriation was not mentioned, and William Kelly understood that to bring Richard Somers home, the navy and other organizations like DPMO and ABMC would have to contravene long-standing policies that supported return of the dead only from World War I forward — John Paul Jones being a notable exception. A further complication was the lack of consensus among parties as to where Richard Somers was actually buried after two centuries of nonexistent record keeping and probable reburials. Though he represented the full *Intrepid* crew in the lore of Tripoli, no one believed that he was among the five unnamed dead in the Protestant Cemetery. The decades of investigation, research and attempts at reclamation in Somers Point, New Jersey, had resulted in a firm knowledge of the precise place. "It's 520 feet from the west gate of the Old Castle Fort," said Kelly, "and when we do an excavation of that site, we'll find him right where he was originally buried." Those officers and crew not in the Protestant Cemetery are buried nearby, in his view, under the grass of what is called Green Square. "If he is retrieved," said Kelly, "he will have an official repatriation ceremony. The captain of the [mothballed] USS *Intrepid* aircraft carrier in New York City said that they would like to have a ceremony, too." In 2011, the difficult history of Libya took another turn as revolution against repressive governments began to spread from Tunisia to neighboring

In 2010, the Protestant Cemetery on Tripoli Bay was visited by American representatives, left to right, military attaché Brian E. Linvill, U.S. ambassador to Libya Gene Cretz and his wife, Annette Cretz. The American flags mark five unknown crew members of the USS *Intrepid*, killed as the ship tried to set fire to Tripoli Harbor in 1804 (*United States Embassy, Tripoli, Libya*).

countries. In February of that year, the so-called "Arab Spring" brought turmoil to Libya in the form of a civil war. By mid-year, just half of the country was still held by the forces of Col. Muammar Gadaffi, including Tripoli. It seemed safe to presume that previous friendly arrangements with the Gaddafi government and family were in jeopardy, but the people of Somers Point, New Jersey, remained optimistic that their effort would soon be back on track on the Libyan side of the equation, though still with the challenge of finding assistance from the U.S. Navy.

When 103 coffins were brought from the expedition to Archangel, Russia, at the end of World War I to Pier Four in Hoboken on November 12, 1919, they were no doubt fully identified. They were among the last killed and the first American dead of the war to come home under the policy of return, and they were met with great fanfare as they were taken off the *Lake Daraga*. But who were they? There had most certainly been a record keeping of their names and hometowns. But those records seemed to be lost in the archives of the war, and the inability to find them was a befuddlement to Mike Grobbel as he stood in the small Michigan's Own Military and Space Museum at Frankenmuth in 2009. He and the museum's director, Stan Bozich, had been working for years to maintain the collective memory of the Polar Bear Expedition, its complicated questions of what a government can ask its men to do in war, and the fate of those still buried in Russia.

After the last of the Polar Bears were returned to Michigan and buried in the White Chapel Cemetery in Troy, their surviving comrades determined that the mission would never be forgotten. They formed the Polar Bear Memorial Association and, to be sure that the story would be transferred to the following generations of their families, they instituted a club called the Polar Bear Cubs for their children. They kept meeting with each other and sponsoring various events, including the annual Memorial Day ceremony at White Chapel.

Stan Bozich, a Royal Oak firefighter with an ethical determination that those who fought in war should be honored and remembered, became friends with the Polar Bears in the last years of their lives. In the 1970s, they had devised a plan called "Last Man Standing," which would leave an endowment of $5,000 upon the death of the last of them to be used to support continued Memorial Day observations and education about their expedition. As each died, his family was likely to donate his memorabilia to Bozich for the museum he had opened in 1983. When the last of them had passed away, Bozich was made administrator of the endowment. But the attempt to retain the memory of by-gone times and events became more difficult in modern times. "The Cub thing didn't work," he said. It was gone in 5 or 6 years. "Many of their sons fought in World War II and I knew a number of them as well. But today the Legion and VFW posts around the state are closing, because World War II people are still running them. The younger people have not stepped up and taken over the chair. So we've got a bunch of flags between the restrooms where the posts are closing and turn in their charter, they're bringing their flags and weapons to us."

Mike Grobbel's grandfather, Clement Grobbel, had been one of the Polar Bears, and he maintained an extensive Website that tracked and developed available information about the expedition. It was largely agreed by all parties that there remained between 25 and 30 Americans in the soils of arctic Russia, but it was impossible to name them. Grobbel knew the names of all of those in the ANREF forces in Russia, and he knew the names of those dead who had been returned in 1929 and 1934. But without the names of those who had been returned in 1919, he could not use the process of elimination to learn who still remained overseas.

Stan Bozich and Mike Grobbel, working with others to find an end to the journey of the Polar Bears, spoke as one for two conflicting realities. Even if they could be named, said Grobbel, those left behind could never be found. They had probably and truly turned to dust. But "we don't leave our bodies behind," said Stan Bozich. "The Marines are adamant about that. They will not leave their Marines behind. When they came out of Chosin [Korea] they came out with truckloads of Marine bodies, frozen stiff, they were like logs. But they brought them out."

In other parts of the world, the efforts of organizations like JPAC and DPMO and individuals like Mark Noah and Pat Ranfranz were still ongoing, but the Polar Bears were probably fully lost. There was no organization lobbying for the search, and it was pretty much over for the families of the Polar Bears, in Bozich's view. But he still mourned for them in his no-nonsense way, as he did those still in Korea and Vietnam. His museum's manifesto reads differently from the mission statements of similar organizations: "The displays at Michigan's Own reflect American military adventures and tragedies of the last century through the personal histories of people who, in the inexorable press of day-to-day life, might have otherwise been forgotten."

"You have to admit it was a tragedy," said Bozich. "This was a tragedy. This was a fiasco. There are a number of things that we've been involved in, our allies have been involved in, that we shouldn't have done. It was just airheads who were making the decisions." The manifesto of Michigan's Own Military and Space Museum continues:

[I]t is not a museum of war, nor an archive dedicated to the strategies or the killing machinery of battle. It is instead, a shrine to ordinary lives caught up in — sometimes ended by — the extraordinary experience of war. It is also an eloquent statement about the passing of time, and the debt subsequent generations owe to those who preceded them to preserve our Freedoms.[15]

CHAPTER FIFTEEN

Memorial Day

The equivalent of the American Memorial Day in Europe varies in meaning from country to country. In France there are two Memorial Days, each on the closing date of World War I, November 11, and World War II, May 8. They are legal holidays. In the Netherlands, May 4 is Remembrance of the Dead Day in honor of all members of the armed forces and civilians of the Kingdom of the Netherlands who died as a result of war or peacekeeping missions from World War II up to the present day. It is not a legal holiday. Liberation Day, on May 5, celebrates the capitulation of Germany in World War II and is observed unofficially every year, except every fifth year when it is an official holiday. In Belgium, Armistice Day on November 11 is a public holiday. In Great Britain, two minutes of silence are observed at 11:00 A.M. on November 11, Remembrance Day, and the official observance of the day is usually the second Sunday of the month. It is the occasion for solemn ceremonies in cemeteries and churches, the laying of wreaths and wearing of the poppies made symbolic by the poem "In Flanders Fields." In addition, the UK celebrates Armed Forces Day, usually on June 26 or 27, in honor of all military forces, including veterans and service families. The American Memorial Day is honored in each of those countries, not officially or widely, but in ceremonies attended by some of their citizens in the large and small cemeteries and isolated burial places that hold American war dead from the two world wars.

The week leading up to the American Memorial Day of May 25, 2009, found England and Western Europe under weather that was constantly changing within a range from windy rain to hot sun, but always refreshing, the best expression of a late spring. At the beginning of the week, Plymouth, England, was in its usual May confusion of cutting wind and driving rain, beautiful sunlight, mist and fog. From the stone walls along the Hoe, at the edge of the English Channel, Drake's Island appeared and disappeared in the fast changing fog. The wind made conversation impossible, and a spraying mist exploded from the waves that crashed on the rocks below. The many hills of the city were power-washed, dried in the sun, and washed again.

Knowing its place in the turmoil of history at the edge of England, one can imagine that if an X-ray of the city's soil could be devised, all sorts of skeletons and bones would show themselves. City historian Barbie Thompson agreed that it would be accurate to say that people were buried all over the place. She cited an article she had found from the mid–1800s: "It stated that not a workman could put a spade in the ground without digging up some bones. It was all in this area, and it still goes on now." The story was well known of an old

TV studio in the city that was hampered in its original construction. "They just kept digging up more bones." When the site was recently redeveloped, more bones appeared. "When you were there on the weekends," said fellow historian and genealogist Pat Luxford, "it was very eerie." "I've got so many stories about that," said Barbie Thompson. In the 1980s, those who worked in the television station became accustomed to the presence of a ghost. "Even the security guards, who are normally quite sensible people, ex-military people who do security work, they referred to this being as George. And they reckoned it must be someone from the French, or Napoleonic, period. That's what they reckoned."

There is little doubt that the remains, or dust, of an unknown number of Americans lie hidden in the marshes and hills of Plymouth, perhaps as far up the Tamar River from Plymouth Sound as the town of Saltash. But there is no definite place to find them. Some may have ended up in the Stray Park Burial Ground of the Royal Naval Hospital, which ostensibly accepted only the bodies of the French in 1813 and 1814. Dr. John Salvatore, Plymouth's Historic Environment officer, however, knew the names of two Americans buried there in October 1814, John Rose of the HMS *Leyden* on the 4th, and [ ] Robinson of the HMS *Akbar* on the 31st, both of the British ships presumed to be either prisoner transports or prison hulks. The hospital's later burial ground was called No Place Field. It accepted bodies only from 1824 onward, but, as with Stray Park, there may have been some anomalies yet to be determined by investigation still going on in 2009. By that year, Plymouth was actively researching its own archaeological history going back several hundred years, as it still sought to rebuild from the Plymouth Blitz of World War II.

A more promising excavation of the history of Americans buried in England might have been found 250 miles east of Plymouth. It was on the Medway River at Chatham that the American prisoner Benjamin Waterhouse had looked from the hulk *Crown Prince* in 1814 and seen a beautiful river and countryside. At the beginning of the 21st century, the sights that he had seen had become places of residential development, much of it of a luxury category on the water. Peter Boreham, curator of the Guildhall Museum in Rochester, Kent, had gained a knowledge of the sometimes tricky, even political, question of prisoner burials since the time of Benjamin Waterhouse.

During the Napoleonic Wars, in Boreham's reading of history, French officers who were prisoners of the British were often treated benignly and with respect. The behavior had shown itself at Melville Island Prison in Halifax, where all stripe of French prisoners were often taken within the society of the city and led relatively easy lives out of a British prison. The same conditions applied to the French on the Medway hulks. Though they shared the prison hulks with nationals of other countries, including Americans, they seemed to have been buried and memorialized over the years with special care and honor. The Medway prison hulks during the War of 1812 were places of massive death from disease. The *Crown Prince* had suffered a smallpox epidemic from the summer of 1813 into the spring of 1814. Some of its prisoners refused what limited treatment was available to them, perhaps to hasten the end of their miserable lives on the ships. Then as smallpox decreased on the Medway hulks, it was replaced by typhus, also known as gaol fever. The upper decks of the hulks were turned into sick bays, and the hospital ships were overfilled. All who died were buried in the marshes, some covered with quick lime to hasten their decomposition.

A project begun in 1869 sought to disinter all French deceased from the marshes of St. Mary's Island in the middle of the river. Hundreds were exhumed. Each was given an oak casket and buried with honors in a site behind St. George's Chapel on Dock Road, Chatham. British and French officials have held memorial services there each year since. There is no evidence that any of those reinterred at St. George's were American, but Peter Boreham strongly suspects that some of them were. The rate of death and burial during the War of 1812 was fast and often haphazard, subject to mistakes and anomalies. Boreham was quick to point out that, suspicions aside, the memorial on Dock Road is officially and solely dedicated to the French, and therein may rest a feature of international commerce and diplomacy. The towns of the Medway have long-standing sister city or twinning relationships with the commune of Valenciennes, France, as do the navies of the two nations.

As the Medway towns continued development from 2007, necessary archaeological excavations, especially in an area called Rochester Riverside, continued to reveal stray bones believed to be those of the prisoners of the hulks. Peter Boreham believes that "there could still be significant numbers of bodies buried on riverside sites in and around the Medway towns. A lot of redevelopment work is planned for the Medway towns during the next twenty years (mainly in the development of former riverside industrial sites). This should provide further details for more systematic and scientific archaeological excavation." The future promises to hold more information.

Traveling by bus north of Plymouth, the route to Yelverton, just inside the perimeter of Dartmoor National Park, follows the march taken 200 years earlier from the docks of Plymouth to the cells of Dartmoor Prison. From Yelverton, Ron Joy, age 80 and a former guard at the prison, took visitors in his truck along the continuation of the march. The highway rolled gently up and down the moors, occasionally reaching an elevation from which the horizon on all sides was endless. The road rose through Princetown, passed St, Michael's Church, and came to a simple swing gate into the prison grounds. From the outside, Dartmoor looked no different than it had ever looked. Its main building was dirt-dark granite, rising high above the ground, and seemingly without windows. Often challenged as dangerous and troubled in the first years of the 21st century, it had been converted in 2008 to a low security home for nonviolent and white-collar offenders. Asked if it was as unpleasant on the inside as it looked on the outside, its former guard Ron Joy responded, chuckling, that he hoped so, but, in fact, it was not: "It's been modernized. They've got a toilet in every cell. They've got televisions, and they've got iPods and all sorts of stuff I don't understand."

"It's a very forbidding looking place," said Barbie Thompson of Plymouth, "and the weather can be so bad up here. It can change so suddenly, can't it?" Joy said with pride that it had once been in the Guinness Book of Records for the deepest recorded 24-hour snowfall in the world, 72 inches in 1914. Even in late May, the weather on the moor blew a brutal wind under constantly changing skies above the American cemetery. "You are walking on bodies wherever you walk," said Ron Joy. "Because there's no individual graves. They used to get a dozen dying in a week, and they used to dig one pit and put them all in."

The record keeping from the years of the War of 1812 was immaculate, with about 20 different pieces of information noted for each decedent, up to the color of his eyes. Since his days as a prison guard, Ron Joy had become the fervent steward of the cemetery and advocate for its residents. The effort had taken him to America a couple of times and created relationships with families there who still felt attached to their ancestors buried on the English moor. The work had led him to the certain belief that there were more Americans buried here than named in the original records; and with the collaboration of War of 1812 interests in the United States, he had changed that number from its usual 218 to 271. He was a resource by e-mail, for a weekly handful of requests from the States for more information about individuals who might have met their ends at Dartmoor.

Even in 2009, the American cemetery at Dartmoor Prison seemed to be still in a state of development, or at least a transition from the damages of its age and the quality of the information it provided to visitors. At some point in its history it had acquired an obelisk dedicated to the Americans buried in the field from "1809 to 1815." But the correct years were 1813–1815, and the inscription had never been changed. In the late 1990s, the cemetery received visits from U.S. sailors in British ports who, using their own time, worked with prison inmates to restore the gates and walls and the archway installed by the Daughters of 1812 in 1928. That work was sporadic and often limited by the harsh weather of the moor. Later, an effort was begun to create a monument with the names of all of those buried beneath the green grass of the place, accompanied by Ron Joy's development of an accurate list in association with the American naval historian Ira Dye. Fund-raising in the United States and by American army, navy and air force groups in England provided a new monument with the names of all who lay beneath; money left over was used to create an American section of the history museum in Princetown. It was just one step in the work that Ron Joy had been doing for 30 years, and an indirect result of the Dartmoor Massacre of 1815: "I think it's a big injustice. We treated them abysmally, food wise and other treatments. We made them work at the quarries. As far as I'm concerned, they were treated badly by the English, and it should never have happened. Why do we shoot unarmed prisoners in a massacre? Six people dead, 13 seriously wounded with limbs off and all stuff like that. I mean why shoot unarmed prisoners who refused to back off. So I was anti the shooting of unarmed prisoners, and that started me off on my research."

On the way back to the bus stop at Yelverton, Ron Joy stopped at St. Michael's Church. Its graveyard was overgrown with the first weeds of spring and many of its tombstones were bent at random angles to the ground. The church was locked up and dark, but the round stained glass window presented in 1910 by the Daughters of 1812 was still in place. The church and its window were still very much in the minds and caretaking of people on both sides of the Atlantic, supported by ongoing fund-raising and maintenance.

As the Brookwood American Cemetery south of London prepared for its Memorial Day ceremonies on May 24, 2009, its chief groundskeeper, Bryan Smith, was pushing a power mower across the grounds nearest the Commonwealth War Graves Section of the larger cemetery complex. Brookwood had been a community cemetery before it was expanded for military use with both an American and CWGC section, the latter holding 73 Americans of both world wars who had served with Canadian, British and other forces. Introduced by the American Cemetery's British Associate Director, Derek O'Dell, Smith looked every bit the hardworking man that he was. After 41 years at Brookwood, starting at age 15, his knowledge of the stories of many buried there was familial. Indeed he had met the families of most who had come from America in search of an ancestor killed in World War I.

They had come to an immaculate place. Each blade of grass stood up straight at a uniform height. Each stone was surrounded by an equal square of bare soil. Each tree and bush was shaped and symmetrical. Of many of the Americans he had met over the years, he said, "They expected to see it overgrown and when they come in the see it all kept tidy, and they're stunned. When it's been many years they've been trying to trace a grave, they've just found him, the casualty, on the Internet after all of these years, and they come and find like a brother or a father, I'll take them to the grave, and they'll just break down in tears."

Smith was trained as a young man by many of the men who had dug the graves he now tended. As they passed their responsibilities on to the younger men, the old workers passed down their stories of those they had buried. And over the years, Bryan Smith had met the presidents and prime ministers of a number of countries as they came to Brookwood for various ceremonies. He had taken Prince William on a history tour, finding him to be genuinely interested in what the cemetery represented. In a recent year, Smith had received an award of the British honours system. Summoned to Buckingham Palace, he had been taken in a black limousine to meet Queen Elizabeth II: "She said 'Hello, what do you do?' and I just went 'ach, argh.' I couldn't talk to her."

Ten to fifteen thousand visitors came through Brookwood every year. Many were visitors to the community cemetery closest to the railroad station who had wandered into the American and CWGC sections, often surprised to find those sections there. In Derek Odell's estimation, just 5 to 10 percent of them were Americans. Generations after World War I, there were few relatives left even aware their ancestors were buried in foreign places. And the dead were very young. "The American headstones give the date of death," Smith said. "The Commonwealth headstones give the age at death. You walk along these very orderly lines and see 'Private somebody, eighteen years old,' and then somebody twenty-four years old. And so it goes on. Anybody between eighteen and thirty. So many of them so young."

Their sacrifice was known to a dwindling few, but not forgotten among some. According to Smith:

> We get people here, and they see all these crosses, some of them almost fall on their knees at the sight of so many Americans who lost their lives in these two wars. It's relatively rare that that happens. But we get an enormous number of visitors who bring their young children, age ten or twelve or something like that. And they walk them around and they tell them this is the result of something called the First or the Second World War, perhaps they're learning about in school or

Plymouth historian Barbie Thompson and Dartmoor historian Ron Joy stand at a distance in the American cemetery at Dartmoor Prison. The peaceful lawn covers the remains of an estimated 271 Americans. The gate to the right was placed by the Daughters of the War of 1812 as a memorial arch in 1928. Further right is the roof of one of the prison's cell blocks (*Author photograph*).

St. Michael's Church sits in Princetown, Devon, England. The bottom level was built by French prisoners at Dartmoor, and the church was completed by American prisoners. The stained glass window at the front was presented by the Daughters of the War of 1812 in 1910 and was maintained financially by that group into the 21st century (*Author photograph*).

maybe there's something on the television. And they go around and they have a look first-hand to see that these are the burial sites of these people, and that we all have a great debt to them.

In France, the week leading up to the American Memorial Day 2009 included the packing of flags to be sent to the mayors and other officials of 123 towns, villages and isolated cemeteries across the country. At the Paris offices of the American Overseas Memorial Day Association (AOMDA-France) the American Wives of Europeans (AAWE) were the chief volunteers. Two-foot tall American and French flags were rolled up into mailing tubes and sent on their way. One of the American wives recalled conversations with her French mother-in-law about the commitment of the United States in World War II and the losses suffered in the Normandy invasion. "You just can't understand what that represented to us," said the older woman, as she recalled the friendliness of the GIs during a perilous time for France. The flags were to be placed by local officials at the isolated graves of 182 Americans killed in both world wars. Among their recipients would be Kenneth Gow of the Silk Stocking Regiment, killed while leading his men near Ronssoy and now buried at Le Chateau Cambresis. Another would go to Lt. John Rahill, killed in Alsace in World War II and still buried at Hochfelden.

In addition to giving attention to the isolated graves of France, AOMDA-France collaborated with all participant groups, both American and European, in preparation for ceremonies that would be coming on the weekend in the ABMC cemeteries of France, England, Luxembourg, the Netherlands, Italy and Tunisia. The flow of donations from the United States and

The civilian and military Brookwood Cemetery in Brookwood, Surrey, is easily accessed by a 45-minute train ride from Waterloo Station in London. A selling point for the civilian cemetery when it opened in 1854 was that of exclusive train service for family members of the deceased, from a terminal near Waterloo Station specifically dedicated for cemetery service. The cemetery train was stopped during World War II and never reinstated (*Author photograph*).

the involved nations would purchase the flags and wreaths that would decorate the graves and monuments of the American cemeteries.

In Paris, AOMDA would also bring about one of the most important celebrations of its charter, the ceremony at the Lafayette Escadrille Memorial on Saturday, May 23. Since 1930, the memorial had lagged behind the vision of its founder, William Nelson Cromwell, that it be a place of rest for the American Lafayette flyers and a source of education about French-American history. By the turn of the 21st century, most accounts held that the memorial had fallen into disrepair to the point of disrespect to its residents. On June 17, 2001, a group ranging from American congressmen to French and American businessmen gathered at the memorial to recognize the 85th anniversary of the founding of the Lafayette Escadrille. Among the speeches given was that of USAF European commander general Gregory S. Martin:

> Frankly, the condition of the monument does not meet the standards expected. These airmen deserve our respect and care. The problem is, as time marches on, the trust funds and the people who are conversant with the sacrifice, begin to disappear. We are finding that out with the Lafayette Escadrille Memorial.
>
> These men were our pioneers. They were not just the forerunners of the Army Air Corps of World War II, but of the Air Force today. This is where America first learned to fly aerial combat; they gave us our aviation war wings. The bottom line is, we want the people who visit the Lafayette Escadrille Memorial to feel just as proud about the contributions of the airmen that rest here as they do about the contributions of those who rest back in the States.[1]

The 2007 Memorial Day service at the Lafayette Escadrille Memorial near Marnes-la-Coquette, France. The monument is one-half the size of the Arc de Triomphe in Paris, and holds the inscribed names of the dead American pilots of the Lafayette Escadrille and the Lafayette Flying Corps during World War I (*Peter Van Metre*).

A restoration effort was completed in 2003. But the crypt continued to be plagued by water problems and, in 2007, an effort was begun to make it watertight in a project funded by French and American military and diplomatic sources. In 2009, restoration was estimated to be 90 percent completed and the Memorial Foundation was developing a program of long-term care.

One of the pioneers referred to by Gen. Martin had been Charles Wesley Chapman of Dubuque, Iowa, shot down near Remoncourt on May 3, 1918. Despite its lapses, the memorial had held Chapman safely over the years, and his niece, Lucy Van Metre, and her son Peter visited him in 2007. Lucy had grown up thinking of the uncle she never met as a military idol in the family, defined by his death and burial in Europe as part of a great cause. "She was extremely touched," said Peter of his mother's reaction to the memorial. "She had tears in her eyes ... feeling this pride and wonderful warmth at the care they had taken in building and preserving the memorial, and pride in having a family member be a part of that." His mother's fear had been that they would be met by some gruff, French-speaking person who would grudgingly give them entrance. But instead they were met by Gaëlle Lemair, assistant to American attorney Van Kirk Reeves, president of the Foundation and AOMDA-France. The assistant spent an afternoon with the family of Charles Wesley Chapman.

When asked if he would feel the same attachment to his great uncle if his body had been shipped back home after his death, Peter Van Metre recognized the place of memorials in the way that the fallen are remembered. "Probably not," he said. "I think a little bit of the attachment, especially when you're younger, of the exciting Hollywood kind of story that it is.... The beautiful setting makes me feel special indirectly, that he's in that place and he's memorialized that way. It's a real tribute to Americans and what they stand for to many people all over the world. The fact that there are still people in those European countries who take our forebears' contribution to their freedom to heart is very special."

One American flyer who would not be acknowledged in American Memorial Day ceremonies in Europe was the great-grandson of Confederate general "Stonewall" Jackson. When Col. Thomas J.J. Christian, Jr., was shot down behind enemy lines near Arras, France, on August 12, 1944, his body was seen to be loaded on a truck and taken away by the Germans. In the sorting out of the dead that could be found or not found after the war, the body was found to be buried in the Faubourg d'Amiens Cemetery, in Arras, Pas-de-Calais. Or perhaps not.

Faubourg d'Amiens was a Commonwealth War Graves cemetery and should not have held an American fighting with U.S. forces. Officially, Christian was declared missing in action in 1951, but unofficially the declaration would remain dubious in the following years. In 1995 a conventional grave marker was created by the 361st Fighter Group and leaned against an inside wall of Faubourg d'Amiens:

> Believed to be buried in this cemetery.
> Col T.J.J. Christian Jr.
> 12 Aug. 1944
> 361st Fighter Group
> USAAF

At the same time, a large memorial to him rose from the earth of the Texas State Cemetery in Austin with the notation that his body had never been recovered. Still another monument dedicated to Christian, "et à tous les membres de l'U.S. AAF tombés dans notre region (1942–44)," sat surrounded by flowers in the town of Boisleux-au-Mont.

Late in the 20th century, Col. Christian gained an official biographer in the person of

The tombstone, center, for American colonel Thomas J.J. Christian, believed to be buried in the CWGC cemetery at Faubourg d'Amiens, France. The photograph is by Pierre Vandervelden of Peruwelz, Belgium, who maintains an Internet project photographing war cemeteries and tombstones in France and Belgium. It is an attempt by Vandervelden to extend Belgian respect for war dead buried in their ground by establishing a photograph database that can be accessed by families around the world who would not otherwise be able to see their family member's grave. His Website, In Memory, is developed in cooperation with similar Internet efforts. Of his work, Vandervelden said, "I put my little stone on the wall of remembrance" (*Pierre Vandervelden*).

Laurent Wiart of the Municipal Library of Arras. It often happened that Americans buried in the stray places of Europe were informally adopted by those made curious about who they were and how they had died. Wiart's interest was more personal, however. His grandmother had seen the crash of Christian's fighter plane, an event that stayed with her throughout her life, so that Laurent Wiart stated simply in 2010, "I think Jack Christian is part of my family history." His attempt to understand the puzzle of Christian's burial became a personal challenge, and his research was the most thorough of any.

The first part of the puzzle was the action of the Germans who had recovered the body. There were already three cemeteries nearby that could accept the airman, but the evidence seemed to indicate that he was taken to a mortuary at the Collège de Jeunes Filles in Arras, Pas-de-Calais, before anonymous burial in Faubourg d'Amiens. The cemetery was dedicated as a World War I resting place for Commonwealth soldiers, but at the end of World War II it contained eight new graves, seven of named British flyers and soldiers, and one unknown. German records showed that he was thought to be a high-ranking officer killed in a plane crash.

In 1946, a member of the Christian family in Texas initiated a search for the colonel through the Paris offices of a Texas oil company. The investigator was led to Faubourg d'Amiens

Cemetery, where he was shown the eight graves; but he was told that Christian was not believed to be the unknown. An official investigation by Graves Registration followed, and after a couple of dead-ends it, too, arrived at the eight graves in Arras, where it was learned that the British had recently exhumed the body of the unknown. The dental chart that resulted from the exhumation did not match that of Col. Christian, but a theory that would explain the discrepancy was beginning to develop. The original grave markers may not have been synchronized with the bodies that rested beneath them, and the unknown might actually be British lieutenant Francis Simpson. Evidence accumulated that the records of which body lay where had changed twice from original notations, but the CWGC eventually refused a request that all eight bodies be exhumed for sorting out. In 1951, American Graves Registration declared that without those exhumations the case would be closed.

In 1993, Laurent Wiart brought the matter up with the CWGC, asking questions about the record keeping anomalies in the late 1940s, but he received no response. In the following year, the CWGC declared the matter fully closed but allowed that it could be said Christian was probably buried in Faubourg d'Amiens. The ambiguous marker was placed in 1995. The attempt by Laurent Wiart to understand the fate of the member of his family would continue.

A few days before Memorial Day 2009, the contents of a number of old cardboard boxes were laid out on the dining room table of a canal house on the Prinsengracht in Amsterdam. Lucy Correll was an American expatriate who had lived in Amsterdam since 1973 and a member of the American Women's Club of Amsterdam (AWCA). She had recently become the club's liaison with the people of Opijnen in relation to the burials there of eight American airmen whose B-17 had crashed on July 30, 1943. True to the words of the people of the town, the cemetery they had created for the men had been a focus for community life for decades. Town officials had conducted gracious correspondence with the American families of the Opijnen airmen. They encouraged the families to accept their hospitality in Opijnen at any time and to feel free to ask any question or for any consideration. In addition, it became a tradition of the American consulate in Amsterdam to write each American family a letter describing the year's Memorial Day ceremony. A letter to all dated May 31, 1963, from Consul Byron Blankenship is excerpted below.

> On Memorial Day, yesterday, as has been the custom for many years, the people of Opijnen and a good many Americans gathered in the churchyard of the village in memory of the sacrifice that your (brother/son) made on behalf of all of us, twenty years ago....
> Yesterday 107 school children of the village of Opijnen placed flowers on the graves of the eight airmen. Dutchmen and Americans, as the attached program indicates, participated in the offer of thanks to the valiant Americans.

A letter was sent in reply to the consul by Mrs. F.R. Dick of New York City, the mother of navigator Lt. Robert Urquhart Duggan.

> We are always inspired to hear of the devotion of the Burgermeister and the people of Holland to the graves of the airmen. It is indeed a tie between Europe and America that we wish more people could know about. I am always especially touched by the participation of the schoolchildren. Last year I sent a little Christmas check for them, and the Burgermeister wrote me he had purchased a moving picture projector for the school. My appreciation is very deep for the people of Opijnen.

The Women's Club had formed an alliance with the people of Opijnen in support of the small American cemetery in 1949. Because the town had acknowledged its full responsibility to the men, it was not eligible for assistance from the United States government. The AWCA took on some of the burden and was itself assisted by the royalties of a curious book. In 1945, author Betty MacDonald wrote *The Egg and I,* the story of a young housewife's acclimation to life on a chicken farm on Washington's Olympic Peninsula. The book became a national rage, selling 2 million copies over 2 years, and eventually moved on to publication in Europe. Ten thousand copies were sold in the Netherlands, but national law forbade the movement of guilders out of the country. As a result, the Betty MacDonald Foundation was established and the book's Dutch royalties were used by the AWCA to support the Opijnen cemetery. The funds were also well invested and used for the town's schoolchildren into the 1980s.

In 1962, a complicated dance between the American quartermaster general, the Dutch War Graves Commission, the people of Opijnen and the families in America led to the production of proper gravestones by the Green Mountain Marble Company in West Rutland, Vermont. All parties followed the path of their delivery to Brooklyn, across the Atlantic to Antwerp, Belgium, by rail to Rotterdam and by U.S. Air Force truck to Opijnen. The stones replaced the white wooden crosses that had been built and maintained by the village since 1944.

By the turn of the 21st century, most of those on both sides of the ocean who played a role in the perpetuation of the cemetery at Opijnen had long since fallen away. The ceremonies had become more sparsely attended, with a reduced involvement by the AWCA, and had been shifted to the Dutch Remembrance of the Dead Day of May 4. On that day in 2001, celebrants

A Memorial Day ceremony in Opijnen, the Netherlands, undated. In 1962, the wooden crosses marking the graves of the eight American airmen who fell over the town in 1943 were replaced by stone markers (*American Women's Club of Amsterdam*).

gathered at the communal hall before moving on to the town's Dutch Reformed church where the cemetery, beneath an American flag, sat on the other side of the low hedges separating it from the quiet sidewalk and street that passed it by. Among those in attendance, as he had been each year since the plane had crashed in his farm fields in 1943, was Hendrik de Koch. He could no longer spread the flowers at the grave site as he had done for more than half a century. He was assisted by his granddaughter, Anoeska, who had assumed increasing responsibility for the site in recent years. That year, a new neighborhood had been developed nearby, and its streets had been named after the American flyers: McCammonplein, Brucestratt, Kruegerstraat, Ohmanpad, Polingstraat, Cianfichipoort, Sparkstraat, Blackwoodstraat and Perrottastraat.

A 21st century excursion into small towns like Opijnen could be a time-travel back to the darkness that had fallen across Europe under Nazi occupation. Only a few young people gave it much thought, but the elders sought to keep the memory of terror and eventual salvation alive. The old cemeteries and isolated graves of the fallen of any nationality were the keepers of the memory of that time. In the Memorial Day ceremony at Opijnen in 1957 there had been a long reading from the narrative of Bart Fromijne, witness to the crash and burgomaster at the time. He described the resolve of his townspeople, despite the constant threat of retribution from their Nazi occupiers, to set the dead American airmen right:

> Somehow the people of the village continued to bring flowers to the precious graves — the crocus of early spring, and tulips and lilacs, the roses of summer, and anemones, and the dahlias and asters of fall.
>
> What did these people talk about when they were shut safely into their cottages at nightfall? Did they wonder about the young men whose bodies they had saved and given decent Christian burial? Did they think of themselves as foolhardy or courageous, as defying the Nazis or honoring God? Did they look upon the devastated aircraft as a thing of defeat or a thing of hope? Did they think the war would ever end, that other Americans would come to avenge the death of the eight who had fallen and to set Opijnen and all of Holland free?

In 2009, a young historian in Zoetermeer, 80 kilometres to the northwest of Opijnen, asked the same question and told the same stories passed down from a time long before his own birth. In the town's handsome history museum, Ton Vermeulen talked near a large display devoted to the story of an American Liberator that fell into the fields of farmer Tinus Janson on February 22, 1945. A portion of the plane's landing gear anchored the display. The body of John McCormick, the crew member who joined the Dutch resistance, still rested in a churchyard a few blocks away. Vermeulen spoke of the situation:

> When the Germans came here in 1940, most people believed they wouldn't go away for many, many years, or maybe never. After 1942, it became clear that the German army wasn't that strong, and so they started to lose. A lot of planes flew over Holland to Germany, and especially to Hamburg and Berlin, and people got hope. Hope was the most important thing to have, to look into the future and to live further on. I think that was the most important psychological factor of the planes. They were thought of as liberators, and therefore when they crashed people tried to help.
>
> It was very dark. It wasn't allowed to have any lights during the war, so every window was closed, and cars didn't turn any lights on at night, so it was a very dark country. So if you looked to the sky at night, you could hear the planes, and with the moon and stars you could also see them. And you could also see the lights of the Germans from the ground, the searchlights. If it happens every night, it becomes more hopeful, and then hundreds of planes came over every night. People thought that they had to be important. If they weren't there, there was no proof of any hope. Because there were some illegal newspapers that were spread around in which you could read the advances of the armed forces. And there was illegal radio from England, Radio

Orange. But it was the real thing, the planes coming over in which you see, Ah! there's really something happening, that was the proof, because what the Germans said or the Allies said, you'd never know which was true. But the planes were real.

John McCormick was in one of those planes, and, with its crew, it had fallen into the care of the people of Zoetermeer. After giving his life on behalf of the Dutch resistance, McCormick had given the town another cause, the burial and memorial of an American who had come to them at a difficult time. The immediate postwar years had been difficult for Zoetermeer and many other small European towns. Food and materials were scarce, and among those who had endured the war together there was some accounting to be done. Some of the girls of the town who had consorted with German soldiers had their heads shaved, then disappeared. Other disappearances included a whole German family in 1948. Rumors of collaboration implicitly shunned this person or that whether or not they were true. It was only in later decades, often near death, that some people talked about their experiences during the war, "wanting to get even with it before their time," in Ton Vermeulen's assessment, especially before grandchildren began to get curious.

The solemn celebration of John McCormick each year was a spot of light. On April 29, the anniversary of his death, members of the underground gathered at the grave. Every May 4, the church bells rang between 7:45 and 8:00 P.M., and a long line of people passed the grave on their march to the war memorial site behind the church, in Wilhelmina Park. Then for two minutes everyone fell silent to commemorate all who had fallen in wars. They sang the American national anthem over John's and other graves as bands played. Flowers carried by Boy Scouts were placed on both memorial sites.

In February 2005, a city park was turned into "Camp McCormick" for a day and an elaborate reenactment of the events of the crash and its aftermath was staged as thousands watched. A memorial was placed near the site of the crash, dedicated to the "innocent Dutch victims of war," and to John McCormick and the men of the airplane known anecdotally as the Jolly Duck. "I know," said one of the reenactors, "it will continue to remind your children and mine of this ordinary man who carried out extraordinary deeds to defend his country and help liberate Europe. God bless John McCormick and God bless the United States of America."

By 2009, Zoetermeer was a city of 120,000 people, and many did not know about John McCormick, according to Vermeulen. But the city makes sure that its children know about war. In the higher grades they are visited by living soldiers and veterans who tell them of even more recent wars, and each year Bernhard Elementary School looks after the graves of John McCormick and three other members of the Dutch Resistance buried beside him. The children keep the gravesites clean and flowered and join in the May ceremonies.

The 2009 Memorial Day ceremony at the Netherlands American Cemetery at Margraten took place on Sunday, May 24. Among the Dutch and American civilians, military and diplomatic officials and family members of the dead were many of those Dutch citizens who had taken responsibility for each individual grave through adoption. The adoption process at Margraten had started during its construction and had rarely flagged in the more than six decades after the war. In 2008, all of Margraten's 8,301 graves were adopted, and a waiting list held the names of those who wished to take responsibility for adoptees that might yet become available. Most of the European ABMC cemeteries had adoption programs, but the Margraten effort had derived from the relationships formed during its construction and retained its strength through the efforts of various organizations. At the very least, an adoption required attention to the grounds around the grave and minimal decoration on holidays like Memorial

Day and Christmas. Often, the adoption led to relationships formed by families on both sides of the Atlantic.

One of the adopters present in 2009 was Robin Huijnen. In 2006, he had read an article in the local newspaper about the grave adoptions. This was new information for him and it fit with his growing interest in World War II, especially as it was fought in his home region of the Ardennes and Hürtgen Forest. Being a relatively young man, he had no direct experience with the war; but he believed that it was "important to remember this war and especially the men and women who fell for our freedom." He resolved to adopt a grave at Margraten, and, in doing so, he was set upon an odyssey into the complicated history of his own family.

Before starting the process, Huijnen told his father of his plans. His father remembered that his sister, Huijnen's aunt, held an adopted grave at Margraten. The adoption had first been committed to by her father, and it passed along to her upon his death. She had moved to Brussels years previously and was no longer able to give it attention; she was eager to transfer the adoption to her nephew. The necessary papers were signed, and Robin Huijnen became the guardian of the grave of Pfc. Glenn Campbell, buried in Plot F, Row 21, Grave 1. His grandfather long dead, it fell to Huijnen to learn who Glenn Campbell was, and he began with the Internet.

Campbell had entered the service from Virginia, served in the 680th Field Artillery Battalion, 17th Airborne Division, and died on April 3, 1945. He was awarded a Purple Heart. Huijnen was eventually led to a Website devoted to the 17th Airborne that was able to provide him with more information and send him on to other sources that helped to complete the circle with Campbell's family address in Norfolk, Virginia. But letters to the address went unanswered, and the trail went cold.

Over the next two years, Huijnen fed a new fascination with America by traveling through American Websites. At one point, it occurred to him to find the site for the city of Norfolk on the chance that it might link to a veterans group in the city. Instead, he was led to the Norfolk Public Library and a historian in its Sargeant Memorial Room, who sent him an e-mail. Norfolk was among the oldest of American cities, and historian Robert Hitchings, himself a descendant of the British royal family, knew the nooks and crannies of the library department devoted to its history. He was quickly able to find pictures and information related to Campbell's childhood in the city. He learned that the family had moved to Texas after the war. Finding their contact information, he attempted to talk with them, but without response. Just as Huijnen in the Netherlands and Hitchings in Virginia were about to give up the search, Hitchings was contacted by Campbell's nephew, David. It was then that the same kind of intertwining of families that had come about with the Abeels family of Brussels and the Sorenson family of Idaho, and thousands of other postwar family pairs in the United States and Europe, revealed itself in the story of the aftermath of Glenn Campbell's death.

It had been Huijnen's grandmother who had adopted Campbell's grave, in 1946. A correspondence soon opened between the two families. The Campbells talked of their grief and the Huijnens wrote of the difficult times in Holland. The Campbells sent occasional packages of material goods that could not yet be found in much of Europe. The Huijnen's sent words of assurance about the care of their boy. They shared pictures and information about their families, until things abruptly changed. Said Robin Huijnen:

> My grandmother had died early, in 1947, my father, his brother and sisters still being children. Their mother, my grandmother Mary, must have been an angel. Always caring about the others, giving away everything just to help another. Same with the adoption of the grave, in those days

quite a "burden" as they had to pay something and had to tend to the grave, keeping in mind that there was a shortage of just about everything.

When she died, her daughter wrote to the Campbells for a little while. But then my grandfather married again, and in comes a stepmother who tried to erase any memory of the real mother. Nothing was left, just one picture of grandma Mary, and the memory of her. I suspect that she also broke off the contact to the States.

With the reconnection between the two families in 2008, the Campbells returned to the Huijnens letters from the forgotten grandmother written in 1946 and 1947. In them, she told about her life and expressed her feelings about many subjects. Sixty years after her death, she was rediscovered by her family. "I cannot describe the impact it had on my father and his sister," said Robin Huijnen. "She has erased this period from her mind, because of the really bad time they had with this stepmother. So she didn't remember anything about the adoption. My father was put in a boarding school shortly after losing his mom, also losing his home."

In 2009, the common experience shared at Margraten by Americans and Dutch during and after World War II seemed no less compelling than it had been six decades earlier. In January, the Fields of Margraten Foundation was founded in the Netherlands as a result of an oral history project over the previous two years devoted to eyewitness accounts of the cemetery's construction. It resulted in a documentary broadcast on Dutch television in 2010, and the publication of the book *From Farmland to Soldiers Cemetery*,[2] both including the memories of 14 American soldiers of the time. One of those interviewed was Jeff Wiggins. He had been one of the 260 African-American grave diggers described in the book *Crosses in the Wind* by Lt. Col. James Shomon.

Like many who participate in the worst events of war, Wiggins had returned home and closed a door to his experiences, preferring not to think about them or share them with others. His three months as a grave digger at Margraten had been traumatic. He had banished them from memory and gotten on with a life that had started in a sharecropper's family in Alabama and brought him to retirement as a distinguished educator in Connecticut. As a child, he had experienced the Ku Klux Klan; as a teacher and high school principal, he had championed diversity training and multicultural education.

One day early in 2009, he received a telephone call from Mieke Kirkels, coauthor with Jo Purnot of *From Farmland to Soldiers Cemetery*. She wanted to know if he would participate in the oral history project about the cemetery as the only African-American grave digger at Margraten who could be found. He was not amused by the sudden intrusion in his life of a time he had tried to forget. "Who the hell does she think she is," he exclaimed to his wife, Janice, "65 years later, trying to jog my memory about something I had vowed I would never talk about again."

Kirkels convinced him, however, that if he didn't tell his story it would probably never be told, and he eventually agreed. His memories offered one of the few available accounts of the grave digger's experience in war, complicated, in Wiggins' case, by the status of the black soldier in World War II. Wiggins' anger at Mieke Kirkels subsided, but it was replaced with an even greater anger at James Shomon. He had known Shomon at Margraten and thought him to be a good man, especially in relation to the African-American troops of the 960th Quartermaster Service Company. He had not heard of Shomon's book, however, until Kirkels introduced it to him. There, he read Shomon's description of "Negroes" who would eat anything and spoke in the "sho' nuff" language that was a demeaning stereotype of the time.

It had been bad enough that white and black soldiers were encouraged to avoid each other socially, and that, in this case, the people of Margraten, who had never seen black people before, were not discouraged from looking at them at first in fear and from a distance, a separation that broke down over time and through a natural Dutch friendliness. With small exceptions, the black American soldiers were socially isolated. Perhaps more important, the work they did gave them a view of war that couldn't be shared with others and needed to be forgotten. Wiggins did speak of it, in part:

> Our job was to dig the graves, place the body in a mattress cover and lower them into the grave and cover them. The worst part of it for me was watching all these young Americans who weren't even old enough to vote, seeing them ... in many cases their bodies mutilated and mangled, and had to be put in the mattress cover. That was the hardest part for me.
>
> I recall a conversation with the others that once you're dead, you're dead, and color doesn't mean anything. Our job was to be as respectful and bury these soldiers with as much dignity as they deserved. Someone said to me "How the hell do you bury a guy with dignity when you're burying him in the uniform he was killed in, you're placing him in a mattress cover, and many times the grave is filling with water while you're trying to bury him.
>
> Forget about race. That's what we were trying to do. We weren't burying a white soldier, but we were burying an American soldier.

At age 19, Jeff Wiggins was the first sergeant of his company. At night they would talk about another difficulty of their work: "A number of times, the conversation came up of what more could have been done in World War II if the American Army had used the black soldier as we felt we should have been used. Would it have contributed to a shorter war? We didn't know. And we were very, very resentful that the work we were doing was work that no other soldier in the United States Army wanted to do. But when you're ordered, you're ordered."

In September 2009, Wiggins was the only African American to return to Margraten. The call from Mieke Kirkels had brought a productive use to his banished memories, and a friendship between the two. Upon his return, he discovered for himself the reverence that some Europeans still hold for the Americans who fought with them in the two world wars. "We spent two weeks in the Netherlands," he said, "and it seemed as if the whole country turned out to hear us. National television, radio, the newspapers, and I still get email from reporters who say that our interview with them was one of the highlights of their reporting life. You don't get that here [in the United States]."

Of all the people that Jerry Sheridan had to think about on Memorial Day weekend 2009 in Belgium, Jenny Abeels seemed to be the most important. Young daughter of a family in the Belgian resistance, sister to Roger Abeels and nominal sister to Jerry Sorenson and Bernard McManaman, namesake of Bernard's daughter, Janine Parker, Jenny had become a stewardess for Sabena Belgian World Airlines after the war and never married. Now elderly, she lived alone in the family home in Ganshoren. It was a three-story city rowhouse on a quiet street where the cars parked in the large median beneath very old trees.

Jenny's house had been tightly closed, metal shutters rolled up in front of the ground floor windows, and it took her some time to answer the bell. Jerry Sheridan and Laura Hoffman, both of AOMDA-Belgium, helped her to restore some of the lost tendrils of her memory and talked with her gently about the event of the day, the laying of a wreath at the nearby communal cemetery in which Jerry Sorenson and Roger Abeels were buried side by side. She needed to take her time to prepare for the visit, and, while waiting in the first floor of the old home, one could reenter the time long past of postwar Belgium. It was not so much the old stuffed furniture or the terrace visible through the dining room doors that was hidden in the overgrowth of a yard not tended in years, but in the pictures and mementoes on every wall and surface.

All of Jenny Abeel's most accessible past seemed to be held on one wall in the living room. Hanging against the faux marble wallpaper was the portrait of a young man, probably Roger Abeels, in full dress uniform, within the gilded inset of a large wooden frame. His white-gloved hand rested on the ornate, sculpted back of a wooden chair that might have come from the throne room of the king. A tall, stiff hat in the colors of the Belgian flag rested on its seat. A painting of Christ on the cross hung crookedly beneath it, and on either side of the two paintings were framed documents. One was a lithograph, a posthumous citation *de l'Armée Secrète* with the Abeels name written in large letters against a smaller text. A soldier looked sadly down upon a gravestone in the form of a cross, planted in the earth and hung with garlands. On the opposite side of the crucifixion, a document of the appreciation of the American people for Arthur Abeels' role in saving the lives of Allied soldiers was signed by Pres. Dwight D. Eisenhower. The glass-doored cabinet beneath held all of the artifacts, pictures, old watches, bullet casings, paper poppies, banners and albums of a hybrid family in time of war. Belgian and American flags hung from the cabinet's top, beneath statuary of a naked man reaching upward, every sinew of his body seeking release from oppression.

The weekend in Belgium had been uncharacteristically warm, beneath a deep blue, cloudless sky. On Saturday morning, an assembly of Belgian and American military, diplomatic and political figures had gathered at a breakfast held for AOMDA-Belgium by the mayor of Neupré, Arthur Cortis. Following that, the visitors walked to the town square where they were entertained by a small band playing the popular American dance band songs of the 1930s and 1940s. When all had arrived, the band switched to the national anthems of both countries, and wreaths were laid at the monument outside the church. A marker on the church wall noted the following in French and English: "The high altar of this church has been erected to the glorious memory of the American soldiers buried at Neuville en Condroz. Their courage and their military valour safeguarded justice and liberty."

A motorcade formed by the cars of all parties at Neupré would spend the next two days moving across Belgium under police escort. The Cadillac in the lead held the American chargé d'affaires, Wayne J. Bush, and U.S. vice admiral William D. Sullivan of the NATO Military Committee. At the nearby Ardennes American Cemetery and Memorial, the large, square marble facade of the cemetery's entrance glistened in a morning sun that had already made shadows of the wings of the large eagle hung at its center. The celebrants approached the amphitheatre above the burial grounds in black suits. Many of the Belgians wore berets. More casual citizens of the U.S. and Belgium stood at the wall overlooking 5,329 crosses so perfectly placed upon the land that one could choose to see them in the perspective of straight lines or gentle curves. They radiated out from the proscenium to the low woods at the cemetery's furthest edges.

The full ceremony was led by James Begg, president of AOMDA-Belgium, and began with an invocation by the bishop of Liège and a flyover by the U.S. Air Force. The flyovers of Memorial Day weekend in England, Belgium, France, Luxembourg and the Netherlands were aerial dances of split-second timing and communications — not in the playing out of formations above each cemetery but in the scramble over Europe to deliver each flyover on cue. Most of nineteen ceremonies would receive a flyover in the missing man formation that weekend, each planned to occur at a different point in ceremonies that basically started at the same times of day. To accomplish that, the jets, piloted as volunteer duty, would stay in the air for the most part, to head off to a given cemetery minutes before a planned flyover to be announced by the ceremony moderator. In the three events in Belgium that weekend, all three arrived within a minute of their introduction, though the flyover of Flanders Field was conducted by a single, vintage plane because all others were too busy.

The ceremonies were lengthy and followed a format of flyover, invocation, three tribute speeches — by an American diplomat, the mayor of the nearest Belgian town and an American military official — and the laying of wreaths sponsored by organizations of the two countries. Each held the singing of the Belgian and American national anthems by school children as its central event and offered Christian and Jewish prayers as exclamation points. The spoken theme of the ceremonies at the Ardennes and the Henri Chapelle American cemeteries was the lighting of the darkness placed upon Europe by the Germans. Of the American buried at Ardennes, Wayne Bush said the following:

> They did not die in vain, because Europe was reborn in peace, and freedom, and in unity. They did not die in vain because across this continent democracies have replaced dictatorships. They did not die in vain because succeeding generations of Europeans and Americans have learned an indelible lesson: that when the right of free people is threatened, we did not pretend to be isolated from it by geography; that even as we offer reconciliation to our adversaries, we must confront tyranny despite distance and difficulty, despite fear, despite every obstacle. They did not die in vain because in the winter of 1944, here in the Ardennes, the Nazis retreated. The tyrant never achieved his hope to defy the Allies. And none ever will.

From the Ardennes, the motorcade moved on narrow roads through farmland to Henri Chapelle. The parking lot and entrance seemed to sit at the top of Belgium. Down the gentle hills all around, farms distinguished themselves with fields in various shades of green and yellow. Cows lived their lives on the hillsides. The church steeple at Froidthier gathered the rest of the village beneath it. The horizon seemed to be endless, perhaps into the Netherlands in

A ceremony honoring American dead and American-Belgian friendship is held at the center of Neupré at the beginning of Memorial Day weekend 2009. The statue at the crossroads of a Belgian town is that of an American soldier (*Author photograph*).

Belgians and Americans gather at the Ardennes American Cemetery and Memorial near Liege on the morning of May 23, 2009. The stone memorial building contains a chapel and inlaid marble maps explaining the battles, predominantly the Battle of the Bulge, in which most of the cemetery's 5,329 souls were killed (*Author photograph*).

the north. All of it had been a battlefield. With great clatter, the large army helicopter of Gen. Bantz J. Craddock, supreme allied commander in Europe, pulsed through the silence of the countryside, landing on the other side of a retaining wall. Bantz gave the military tribute of the afternoon, and, after the ceremonies, Belgians and Americans lined up to take a tour of the giant helicopter

Hundreds lingered among the graves, among them a young man, Greg Busch, his wife and two small daughters from Wisconsin. They stood at the grave of Busch's great-uncle Pfc. Victor Busch, killed on Armistice Day, November 11, 1944. The little girls danced in place and did somersaults. Though Greg Busch had never known his great-uncle, he was moved almost each year to bring his family to the ceremony at Henri Chapelle. "I'm very proud," he said, "because my grandfather is very proud. He speaks highly of him. He misses him a lot. He just grew up on a farm in Wisconsin."

Greg Busch's favorite family story was about the time when his grandfather was one year old and Victor was eight: "He just decided he was going to get in the family car with my grandfather, who was still in diapers, and take him down to meet their parents. And he made it once around the house without hitting anything, and everybody came to stop him." The simple story resounded in the family history; the great-uncle was killed when the grandfather was eight years old.

Greg Busch did not know how the family had made the decision to have Victor's body

Catherine Busch, left, and Annabelle Busch, of Wisconsin, stand at the grave of Victor J. Busch, their father's great-uncle, on Memorial Day 2009 at the Henri Chapelle American Cemetery in Belgium (*Greg Busch*).

left in Belgium rather than returned home. He had asked, but no one could remember and there was no correspondence remaining that would tell him the story. "From the way things look around here," he said, "the farming community, and just the general landscape, it was a good choice to leave him here. It was a good decision." His grandfather had come to Henri Chapelle once in the 1980s and still remembered and talked about it. Greg Busch hoped to bring him over one more time. As for his own visits, they were "to honor Victor and his memory, and show my children that a member of our family died in service for our country. It just fills me with pride coming here."

After the ceremony at Henri Chapelle, the motorcade moved on to the village of Plombieres for a wreath-laying at the war memorial outside of the school, then to the village communal hall. It was there that the proof of all the words of sacrifice and liberation spoken in the ceremonies at Ardennes and Henri Chapelle could be found in this most traditional of Belgian events.

The gathering was a coming together of the forces of youth and age, dark memories and victories shared, and an appreciation for America that was both political and deeply felt, even melancholic. Those who sat together around the edges of the dance floor were the oldest of townspeople, many of whom had known the war firsthand. They had suffered it, fought in it, perhaps worked in the Resistance. The younger people and children, who knew only handed-down stories, mingled on the dance floor. The counter at the edge of the kitchen held overflowing glasses of beer and tall glasses of wine. The hors d'ouevres were small and simple. The town's young mayor and other officials mingled on the stage.

Like Jerry Sheridan, Laura Hoffman of AOMDA was an American who had lived in Belgium for a number of years. She had developed her own marketing agency there and gained a good understanding of a complicated country. Weekends in Belgium were a time to go to the communal hall and sit together. "You go and you drink a beer together, be that at parish halls or local cafés. It's not untypical to see lots of people sitting alongside each other in a line, very often on the same side of the table, drinking beer and talking or just watching the comings and goings. This is what certain generations do on a Sunday." Belgians concluded every event and ceremony with the sharing of beer. "You can't just have a ceremony and go home," she said, but on the one day of the year celebrating the Americans buried near their town the experience was deeper. The people shared the common experiences of their families 60 years earlier. The older residents of Plombières seemed to her "transported back in time to the world they had lived through then." The children who played among them in the communal hall brought them back to the present. The old men danced with the little girls, who pirouetted and jumped about.

From the stage, the mayor introduced the officials from the ceremony at Henri Chapelle, including the American diplomat and navy commander. Their speeches were short, and those of the Americans were roughly translated into Belgian French. Jerry Sheridan, more formally Dr. Jerome Sheridan, professor of international relations, NATO and the European Union to students of the American University's (Washington, D.C.) Brussels Center, saw the important place of the United States in this small village gathering. The young, progressive mayor of Plombières, standing before his electorate, was the agent of the U.S. presence in their communal hall, and of fellowship shared with its top diplomats and military leaders. "For this one day a year," said Sheridan, "America, which is still over here a very powerful, distant place, pays attention to you. And so from the standpoint of the mayor, this is very good for Plombières. It's got that connection with the United States" that would continue to enhance the fortunes of the village near the large American cemetery.

On a larger scale, Sheridan saw the presence of the three American cemeteries in Belgium as a potential bridge between the country's historic divisions of language, culture and purpose. The small nation was in most respects a federation of three disparate regions. The language of the Flemish region bordering on the Netherlands was a version of Dutch called Flemish. The language of the Walloon region, bordering France to the south, was French. The Brussels-Capital region spoke both languages and reflected the tensions between north and south, while carrying on Belgium's interaction with the commercial, diplomatic and military activities of the rest of the world. The two languages had always driven cultural conflicts in the nation, and in 2007 serious doubts began to arise in the international community that Belgium could even survive as a unified nation. An economic divide had opened up between what many saw as the forward-looking Flemish region and the mired-in-the-past French region. In its edition of May 9, 2007, the newspaper *La Libre Belgique* quoted a professor of the Belgium Free University: "It appears that the final hour of the Belgian State has drawn a little closer. French-speaking Belgians are dreading this moment, especially as, unlike the Flemish, they have no substitute homeland. While the Flemish nation is building itself, the French-speaking nation is still seeking an identity."[3]

The talk of secession of the Flemish was in the air, and, even if they could find a common language, it was felt that the two sides did not talk with each other in a way that could sustain a healthy democracy. By 2009, the crisis had been averted, but the divisions were still in place. Jerry Sheridan, however, had observed a small but important feature of the Memorial Day ceremonies at the two American cemeteries. An official from the Flemish town of Waregem had attended the ceremony in the Ardennes cemetery of the Walloon region. "That hardly ever happens," he said.

It had never happened in Laura Hoffman's memory, even though such cross regional celebration had been a part of the agenda of AOMDA-Belgium for many years. The American cemeteries, and what they represented in Belgian history, had always been something all Belgians had in common. "James Begg," said Laura Hoffman of the president of AOMDA, "does do a lot of sort of PR. He never ceases to try to get one group to the other's ceremony. He had been trying to get the folks from Waregem to go down to the ceremony in the Ardennes year after year after year. There was always polite refusal, saying thank you and maybe, but it never happened. And this particular school director [from Waregem] finally said yes. And everyone was shocked and pleased." A divide like that could be overcome if it was about Belgian national interests and not about the regions. The American cemeteries in the heart of Western Europe were powerful places.

As a vice president of AOMDA-Belgium, and part of the motorcade that traveled back and forth across Belgium on Memorial Day Weekend, Jerry Sheridan was an organizer of the large and small details of the events at the large cemeteries. A coming together of political, civilian and military forces on an international scale, they were lubricated by good attention to nuance, perception, and the proper order of things. The car was his office and his cell phone the most important tool.

It was the isolated graves of Americans, however, that seemed to draw his most personal attention. There were seven of them (an eighth, World War I second lieutenant Gilbert Malrait of Rhode island, would be added as a result of research for this book), and they seemed as much in his mind as if they had held the closest members of his own family. Perhaps it was, in part, because he had been the son of an undertaker and had grown up with an ethic of responsibility to the dead. Perhaps it was because he was an American living well in an adopted European nation. And it was certainly because he was an academic accustomed to investigation, understanding and writing.

Jerry Sheridan knew each of the isolated graves intimately, and his seeking of knowledge about each man within was open-ended. He was always searching for new information. He had developed their biographies on the AOMDA Website, stories that attempted to get beyond what was known and into the subjective courses of their lives that had brought them to rest in Belgian soil. It was the responsibility of AOMDA to give these men as much attention on Memorial Day as was given through elaborate ceremonies to those at Henri-Chapelle, Ardennes and Flanders Field. On this weekend, each received a personal visit from Sheridan and Laura Hoffman, occasionally joined by Hoffman's young son, Austin, and a handful of others. Among the first to be visited was Lt. James Pigue.

Upon the visit to his son's grave at Lijssenthoek Military Cemetery near Ypres in 1921, Edward Pigue had seen James' tombstone surrounded by a field of stones for his fallen American comrades. He determined that James should rest where he lay, and the responsibility for the grave fell to the Commonwealth War Graves Commission. He did not foresee, however, that in the following years all of the others would be reinterred at home or in the cemetery at Flanders Field. Eventually, James Pigue rested alone in the American section of Lijssenthoek. So isolated was he from the rest of the cemetery that his grave could be seen now in satellite photos taken from space.

As he drove about Belgium, Jerry Sheridan kept the car trunk full of floral wreaths and small flags of Belgium and the United States. A boom box held a tape of the anthems of both nations. At Lijssenthoek on a brilliant Sunday morning, Sheridan and Austin Hoffman cleaned up the gravesite, replaced weathered flags with new ones, and laid a wreath. All in attendance, including Laura Hoffman, Sandrin Coorevits, archivist for the city of Waregem, and this writer, already knew the story of James Pigue. But, as a tribute, Sheridan recited all that was known about him and his death above the grave. The Belgian and American anthems were played in order as hands were held above hearts.

A Belgian citizen watched from nearby. He told Laura Hoffman that he came to the cemetery often in honor of his wife's grandfather, who had fought in World War I, and because it was such a beautiful place to walk, think and remember. It was the sight of Laura's son, however, that gave him the most pleasure this morning. Austin was ten years old and wore the uniform of the Boy Scouts of America (BSA). One of several Brussels-based BSA troops abroad, the group included not only Americans but also welcomed boys of other nationalities. For as long as anyone could remember, the Boy Scouts had volunteered their services on Memorial Day weekends. "Youth must never forget, youth must not forget what happened here," he told Hoffman. It was an important admonition for Europe in 2009. The older generations with connections to the wars were passing away, and it was important that their attentions be taken up by youth. It was almost a marketing proposition for Hoffman as she led a youth outreach effort for AOMDA-Belgium. "You don't see kids out here," she said. "They will have heard stories from their own parents or grandparents about either of the wars. But for Austin's generation, this is now a hundred years ago. What does it mean?"

In the three-day weekend, and despite the strenuous work required by the three large ceremonies, the six other graves would be visited and given the same quality of attention. The farthest away was that of Pfc. Joseph Farina, killed in the Battle of the Bulge of World War II and buried in the Pachiotti family plot at Comblain-La-Tour, halfway between Brussels and Bonn, Germany. Off the A3 highway, the route descended into a valley, curving sharply from town to town until it arrived at the small church atop a hill overlooking the village. Thunderstorms had begun to fill the darkening sky of southeast Belgium, and lightning chattered in the horizon to the west. In the late afternoon a funeral was ending inside the church, and the single bell rang a repeated sharp crack through the air. The cemetery at its side was a jumble of stones made pitch black by time. Some held pictures of the dead that had faded to ghostly images. Sheridan was met at Farina's grave by a member of the Pachiotti family; Farina's descendants in the United States had shown little interest in him. The grave was cleaned up, flags were planted and a wreath was laid. Sheridan told Farina's story in English and French, and the national anthems were played.

Returning to Brussels, Sheridan stopped at the grave of Bobby Garrett in the communal cemetery at Queue-du-Bois. Returned to the cemetery from Margraten at the insistence of his family in America and the Bourdouxhe family that had given him shelter in Belgium, Garrett now rested precariously in Queue-du-Bois, as did Joe Farina in Comblain-La-Tour. Under Belgian custom, graves were rarely permanent, but leased for periods of time. If leases weren't renewed, bones would be disinterred and moved to a communal ossuary. Sheridan was afraid that Garrett's bones might succumb to that fate with the death of the one remaining member of the Bourdouxhe family. But Garrett, buried in a section of honor for fallen soldiers in a community cemetery, was perhaps not as vulnerable as Joe Farina, buried in a family plot in a churchyard cemetery. If succeeding generations of the Pachiotti family failed to pay the rent, Farina could be removed. "The body being taken away?" Sheridan asked. "That would greatly disturb me. I would think that at some point in the future if that event should occur, the AOMDA would establish a new mission." He chuckled at the notion, but it did not seem to be an idle speculation.

Among the visits to isolated graves, it was the trip to that of Jerry Sorenson that required the most planning and effort. It had taken some time for Jenny Abeels to prepare herself, and more time for her to be sure that the doors of her home were firmly locked before she got into the car with Sheridan and Laura Hoffman. The drive was across her Brussels neighborhood, through tree-lined streets to the communal cemetery. The three were met at its entrance by James Begg and an elderly couple, former members of the Belgian Resistance and formally dressed for the occasion. Begg took Abeels by the arm and walked with her slowly down the small cemetery's main sidewalk, past its narrow, shaded rows of old gravestones, and beneath the three flagpoles that held the Belgian, French and American flags in a light breeze. The branches of wildly growing trees and lilac bushes spilled over the cemetery walls, and at the back wall the group came to the Abeels family plot. Large stones in the shape of a cross marked the graves of Roger Abeels and Gerald Sorenson, and a smaller cross between marked the grave of Jenny Abeels' father, Arthur.

The inscription on Roger Abeels gravestone read simply *Mort Pour La Patrie*. Jerry Sorenson was noted as of the U.S.A., *Mort Pour La Belgique*. Attached to the staff of the cross was a stone tablet placed there by Sorenson's wife, inscribed *In Loving Memory Nora and Mom*

Jerry Sheridan and Laura Hoffman of AOMDA-Belgium honor American James Pigue at the Lijensthoek Military Cemetery at Poperinge, West-Vlaanderen, Belgium. Unseen are Sandrin Coorevits, archivist of the city of Waregem, and Laura Hoffman's son, Austin. Lijssenthoek is a Commonwealth War Graves Cemetery and includes the remains of 48 Americans who fought with commonwealth forces. As a member of the U.S. Army, Pigue's burial was meant to be temporary, but he was left there at his father's direction. The empty ground around his grave once held fellow Americans, since moved to Flanders Field or returned home. In one case, however, that of U.S. Army Pfc. Harry King, the body was moved from the temporary burial site near James Pigue to the CWGC part of the cemetery to be buried next to his brother Reginald, who was a commonwealth forces casualty (*Author photograph*).

A member of the Pachiotti family, left, and Jerry Sheridan of AOMDA-Belgium honor American Joe Farina at his grave in the church cemetery at Comblain-la-Tour. The boom box is playing the Belgian and American national anthems (*Author photograph*).

Sorenson 1947. In the foreground of the gravestones, another stone rose from the earth with well-preserved photographs of Abeels and Sorenson.

As Jerry Sheridan told the story of Sorenson and the Abeels family, Jenny stared at the site before her as if unhearing and in her own world of memory. Then, Sheridan and Begg helped her with firm but gentle hands to set a wreath down upon the grave. The two national anthems were played and she stared at the pictures of her two brothers for the duration.

Driving from Brussels to Flanders Field on Sunday May 24, 2009, Laura Hoffman talked about the dilemma faced by organizations like AOMDA as they seek to continue the remembrance of American war dead. It was, again defaulting to the challenges of her own occupation, almost a marketing proposition. It needed to cross generational differences, bridge eras of history, even find its own standards of decorum. The ceremonies of memorial would seem to require suits and ties, respectful dresses and demeanors. "Then you see others come," said Hoffman, "with Go USA T-shirts and cut off denim jeans, sport shoes and a baseball cap. And the retired general I sat next to yesterday was extremely upset that so many people, certainly Americans included, don't even remove their hats at the playing of the National Anthem. But what do you really want? Do you want people to show up in the ceremony, paying their respects, regardless of what they're wearing? It's the important thing that they come and they bring their friends and they're there. Or is it important that they get dressed up in their Sunday finest and pay their respects?"

Jenny Abeels of Ganshoren, Belgium, remembers her Belgian brother Roger Abeels and her American brother, Jerry Sorenson, pictured left to right on a small monument and buried beside each other nearby. The gravestone of her father, Arthur, stands against the wall of the communal cemetery at Ganshoren (*Author photograph*).

The authoritative answer to the question probably could not be found. "From a PR point of view," said Laura Hoffman, "the job is to get people to come in the first place." In Belgium, at least, it seemed harder to get Americans living in the country to come to the ceremonies than it did Belgians. That may have been because the American role in the wars was more closely felt by the people of the countries in which the war was actually fought. Whatever the answer, said Hoffman, she had seen some touching images in the pictures taken the previous day at Ardennes and Henri-Chapelle: "Dads with their kids, holding them by their hands, walking among the gravestones. I mean some of what they're wearing is absolutely atrocious, but the point is that somebody out there is talking to their kids about what it all means."

Perhaps because it was the smallest of the ABMC cemeteries in Europe, so beautifully designed and the subject of poetry, the afternoon Memorial Day ceremony at Flanders Field was an exquisite blend of old and young, melancholy and optimism, nature and humanity. "They are the last proof," said the cemetery's assistant director, Christopher Sims, of the 368 buried within its walls, "that Americans were over here fighting in World War I. They tell the story actually that there was a war here, that the USA was part of it."

Sims was a student of the men buried here and knew many of them well. A Belgian, he had recently spent time with fellow historians at the National Archives in College Park, Maryland. At the time of World War I, by his research, one-tenth of the American population was immigrant or first generation American. Many of them fought for their new country in the

In 2008, AOMDA–Belgium began an initiative that would engage children in the continuing maintenance of memory about the two wars that had devastated Europe. As part of the effort, fourth through sixth grade schoolchildren in Waregem were invited to enter an art competition that would address the question "why should we remember them?" The second-prize winner captured the dark time of World War I and its remembrance beneath a warm sun. In 2010, AOMDA extended its effort with children through the development of an awards program that encourages visits to the cemeteries and memorial of Belgium, and the development of understanding about what they represent (*American Overseas Memorial Day Association–Belgium*).

war, and many of those now rested in Flanders Field. As he walked among the graves in his charge he saw real people that he could talk about.

"I think there is still this strong feeling of appreciation from the prisoners of the continent," said Christopher Sims, "because the Allies liberated them. Out of respect, they keep coming back here. You'll see that on the faces of the crowd today.... [I]t's our duty now to be sure the younger generation still has a connection with what happened, to get history back, because once we forget —"

The afternoon was hot. Before the ceremony, the celebrants walked languidly down the shaded gravel path past the cemetery office. Some were dressed formally, some in wheelchairs. They were very young and very old, black and white, Belgian and American, all dressed within the bounds of decorum for the event. Loudspeakers played American dance band songs of the 1920s and 30s, like "Dancing Cheek to Cheek." The music seemed very appropriate, evocative of a time and American optimism, even of the overflight by Charles Lindbergh in 1927. Laura Hoffman's son, Austin, and his fellow Boy Scouts passed out programs and bottled water. They helped the most elderly to find seats in the shade.

Jerry Sheridan led the ceremony on behalf of AOMDA. The motorcade had brought the same diplomats and military officials that had officiated the previous day. The VIPs sat in suits and ties beneath a broiling sun. One of the schoolchildren waiting to sing the national

The people of Waregem and the surrounding region arrive for the Memorial Day ceremony at Flanders Field on May 24, 2009. The cemetery's chapel, seen at the end of the gravel walkway, is at the center of the cemetery's burial ground (*Author photograph*).

anthems fainted in the heat but was revived. There was a reading of the traditional poem dedicated to the cemetery given by a high school student chosen, by custom, from the international community of Waregem:

> In Flanders Fields the poppies blow
> Between the crosses row on row,
> That mark our place; and in the sky
> The larks, still bravely singing, fly
> Scarce heard amid the guns below—

Wreaths were laid on the steps of the octagonal chapel at the cemetery's center, colors were presented and bands played. The late afternoon began to cool. At the conclusion, the VIPs walked and drove to a nearby restaurant for a reception given by the mayor of Waregem. It was the communal gathering at the end of a ceremony, with flutes of champagne and bottles of Belgian beer.

"There is a little bit of the United States in Waregem. It's part of our daily life," said the secretary of Waregem, Guido de Langhe, drinking beer with an American writer. "I don't know how it is in the United States, but history is an important curriculum for the children. The children who sing here at the cemetery are children from the primary schools. They are ten, twelve years old. So they come with their parents and grandparents, and they know that there was a time many years ago that we were occupied, twice, and we were liberated. I think I speak for the people in Belgium, and Waregem in particular, they know what it means. They came from overseas to liberate us, and you never must forget this effort that they made."

The celebrants then moved on to the racetrack at Waregem. The cowboys of the Old West entertained on their beautiful horses, and each American flag rose and fell in the wind of their movement. The fireworks after dark could no doubt be seen above Flanders Field.

Afterword

It is impossible to know how many Americans killed in war outside of the United States have returned to dust or are still buried abroad. Whatever the number, it is constantly changing by continuing efforts to find them, by controversies over the fates of prisoners of war, and by the agendas of the many organizations devoted to finding — or at least honoring — them. A standard for MIA statistics from World War II to the present day might be the Defense Prisoner of War/Missing Personnel Office,[1] which puts the figure at 84,070. Estimates from various sources of World War I missing in action hover around 3,400. Before that, into the past, are varying estimates. One can find MIA statistics for the War of 1812, for example, ranging from zero to 4,000, and it can't be known how many of those would be inside or outside American borders.

The author's conclusion is that there are still many to be found, in part because the research for this book kept turning up more as it went along and because there seems to have been no central effort to find these dead before the research that underlies this book or to bring forth information that is otherwise obscure. The 2003 discovery, for example, of two American sailors buried in Nicaragua since 1859, described in Chapter Fourteen, was an isolated event, never before considered in the context of the larger topic. The addition of an eighth burial, that of Gilbert Malrait, to the isolated graves of Belgium and the attention of AOMDA-Belgium, mentioned briefly in Chapter Fifteen, came about because the author was able to make a connection between two interested parties.

The appendices that follow will be the first placement in one central reference of all known American war dead buried abroad since 1805, with the exception of those already known to be buried in ABMC cemeteries. But it won't be complete by any means. The effort to find these people continues in the largest of affinity groups centered around the missing and imprisoned, and by single individuals in small villages who have an instinct about the dead in their midst yet to be found.

The research for this book kept coming across mysteries that couldn't be solved despite good effort. Here are three:

(1) Page two of *Stars and Stripes* of May 24, 1918, carries an article headlined "French Will Join Memorial Day." The article led the author to information about the dead of the battle between the CSS *Alabama* and the USS *Kearsarge* in Cherbourg harbor during the Civil War, described in Chapter Thirteen. But it also went on to say that many might not be aware that there were 100 American military already buried in France. "[A]t Nantes are the graves

of several of John Paul Jones' men. There are American graves at Villefranche, Versaillies, St. Germaine and Asnieres." If, indeed, such graves existed as of 1918, the author was not able to find any record of them through basic research. Perhaps there is someone in France who knows about them or someone in France willing to search them out and report back to the rest of us. (See below.)

(2) Despite a friendly and helpful e-mail relationship with a representative of AOMDA-France, the author has not been able to learn anything more about a claim on its Website: "For graves in Denmark (120), Norway (120) and Sweden (12), the AOMDA sends flags to the American Embassies. The Embassies decorate the graves in Denmark and Norway, while the local American Legion Post places the flags in Sweden [and Germany]." Repeated efforts to learn more about that assertion have gone unanswered by AOMDA, the embassies, and the American Legion in Sweden.

(3) Most important, the subject of American women in war has been the topic of many books, academic studies and occasional newspaper features. But information about those women buried abroad is difficult to find. A good deal of the author's effort, without much success, went into following up on an article published in the *New York Times* of November 11, 1922. Its headline was "161 American Girls Died in World War."[2] Its subheads went on to assert that most were buried in France, but others were known to be buried in Siberia, Armenia, China, Manila and England. The women were, for the most part army, YMCA or Red Cross nurses.

Under the criteria set down in the formation of the American Battle Monuments Commssion, all nurses, secretaries, ambulance drivers, entertainers and other civilians killed in the course of war abroad are equally considered, buried and memorialized with those who died in combat. Of the 161 women listed by name and hometown in the *New York Times* article, just 20 can be found to be resting in ABMC's World War I cemeteries in England and France. The article was prompted, in part, by an attempt of the Women's Overseas Service League at that time to learn more about the burial status of the women on its list. Said Helen C. Courtenay, founder of the memorial movement: "There is a handsome bronze tablet in the Army and Navy building in Washington, memorializing the mules and horses who died in the war, but nowhere in Washington is there found a record of the women who died — except Army nurses — until we compiled it."

The author was not able to find any information about events and discoveries subsequent to the publishing of the list. Much can be learned, however, about some of the women named. Two of the most tragic, for example, are twin sisters Dorothea and Gladys Cromwell. Joining the Red Cross, they served in hospitals and canteens in France until January 1919. But, in an example perhaps of what would now be called post-traumatic stress disorder, as soon as their ship, *Loraine*, left France for their return home to New York, the sisters left a suicide note in their cabin and jumped into the Gironde Estuary. The bodies of both were recovered and rest near each other at the Suresnes American Cemetery.

A more intriguing example is that of Nettie Grace McBride. We know that she succumbed to typhus on December 23, 1918, while a nurse at the American Red Cross Hospital in Tumen, Siberia. "Six American soldiers carried her body to its last resting place, in a small Russian cemetery in which the Czech soldiers who had died in our hospital, [sic] are buried. It is a beautiful place, like a small woods. She was buried in her Red Cross uniform, with a small American flag across the casket."[3] Is she still buried in Siberia? The author was unable to make the journey nor to enlist anyone there who might search out an old burial place in Tumen.

This book would not have been possible without the Internet, and the Internet can support a continuing discovery of American war dead abroad. It can reach Siberia, for example, to those who might be inclined to look for the cemetery in which Nettie Grace McBride was buried. It can bring together those who might be interested in following up on the fates of all of those women in the *New York Times* article. Others can knock on the door of the U.S. embassy in Norway, for example, and ask to see the list of 120 American war dead who are said to be buried in that country. It can offer a central point for the collection and verification of this kind of information. A Website related to this book will be in place at the time of its publication, and those readers who are interested in joining that process of discovery are encouraged to seek it out through search engines using keywords related to the book and author. The constantly growing and changing nature of the Internet might make any Website URL address given in 2011 obsolete in 2012 and thereafter; search engines will always find their targets.

"Is any of this really very important?" The question was posed to Jerry Sheridan, who became president of the American Overseas Memorial Day Association–Belgium after the 2010 American Memorial Day observances in that country. Since traveling with Sheridan and Laura Hoffman of AOMDA the previous Memorial Day, this author produced a book that almost seemed to write itself on the energy of remembrance for American war dead as practiced and pursued over 200 years, and all over the world. It is a serious and profoundly important endeavor by a lot of people, and for very good reasons, but is it ultimately important in the larger scheme of things?

Sheridan's Memorial Day Weekend in 2010 had been almost exponentially more active than it had been in 2009. One reason was that he had been accompanied by a group of U.S. Air Force officers in the visits to isolated graves. Most of what they learned on the journey with him was new information. None, for example, knew about the Comet Line, which had rescued so many of their forebears in World War II. And, while the American cemetery observances of the weekend were as well attended as always, the isolated visits brought out new handfuls of people from the Belgian communities in which they were buried. James Pigue, for example, was honored by a small contingent at Lijssenthoek. At Ronse, airman Second Lt. Gilbert A. Malrait was honored by a group of about 40 air force officers, town officials, businessmen and citizens.

Most gratifying for Jerry Sheridan was the accompaniment that was received by Jenny Abeels as she was taken, now in a wheelchair, to visit the graves of her father, Arthur, brother Roger and American brother, Jerry Sorenson, at the Ganshoren communal cemetery. The American ambassador to Belgium, Howard Gutman, helped Jenny to lay the wreath on the memorial of her loved ones, as Belgian veterans, U.S. Air Force members and 75 schoolchildren of Ganshoren looked on. The children had been visited by Sheridan and Jenny Abeels beforehand, and she was able to answer their many questions. After the ceremony some of them lingered to have their pictures taken with her.

By anyone's measure, the children are the answer to the question "Is any of this really very important?" Sheridan recalled that at the service for James Pigue he had asked himself, "Why would this American man from Tennessee allow himself to be brought down by machine guns?" He finds the answer in a poem by Archibald MacLeish, "The Young Dead Soldiers Do Not Speak," excerpted:

> They have a silence that speaks for them at night
> and when the clock counts.
> They say: We were young. We have died.

> Remember us.
> They say: We have done what we could
> but until it is finished it is not done.
> They say: We have given our lives but until it is finished
> no one can know what our lives gave.
> They say: Our deaths are not ours: they are yours,
> they will mean what you make of them.
> They say: Whether our lives and our deaths were for
> peace and a new hope or for nothing we cannot say,
> it is you who must say this.
> We leave you our deaths. Give them their meaning.
> We were young, they say. We have died; remember us.

The challenge resonates in a line from "In Flanders Field" by Robert MacRae: "To you from failing hands we throw The torch." "This is what defending freedom is all about," said Sheridan. "Even today, if you're not careful and you don't defend your values, you will lose them. And these people paid that price for us." And so, the story must be taken to the children. It's a fascinating story to tell.

Appendices

Appendix 1: American Sailors Buried in Tripoli, Libya, since 1804 • **Appendix 2:** American Navy Officers Still Buried in Plymouth, England, since 1813 • **Appendix 3:** Americans Still Buried in the American Cemetery at Dartmoor Prison in England since the War of 1812 • **Appendix 4:** American Sailors and Infantry Still Buried in Halifax, Nova Scotia, Canada, since the War of 1812 • **Appendix 5:** American Sailors and a Family Member Buried in Port Mahon, Menorca, Spain, from 1825 to the Mid–19th Century • **Appendix 6:** American Sailors Buried in Nicaragua since 1859 • **Appendix 7:** American Civil War Casualties Buried in Cherbourg, France, since 1864 • **Appendix 8:** Punitive Expedition Casualties Buried Near Parral, Mexico, since 1916 • **Appendix 9:** American Flyers in the Lafayette Escadrille and the Lafayette Flying Corps Buried near Paris, France, 1928–1930 • **Appendix 10:** Americans Buried or Memorialized in Commonwealth War Grave Cemeteries since World War I • **Appendix 11:** American Armed Forces Members Still Buried in Isolated Graves in France since World War I • **Appendix 12:** American Armed Forces Members of World War I and World War II Still Buried in Isolated Graves in Belgium • **Appendix 13:** Americans Buried or Memorialized in Commonwealth War Grave Cemeteries since World War II • **Appendix 14:** Isolated Burials of American Airmen in the Netherlands since World War II • **Appendix 15:** Isolated Burials of American Airmen in Denmark since World War II • **Appendix 16:** American War Dogs Buried in Guam

These are lists of all known American war dead who remain buried abroad, from 1804 through the present day. They do not include the approximately 130,000 who are interred in the cemeteries of the American Battle Monuments Commission. ABMC burials can be searched by name on the ABMC Website at www.abmc.gov.

Because they are compiled from different sources, with different identification criteria over 200 years, they can't be fully standardized. Many originate in handwritten records that have been sometimes illegible to subsequent transcribers, and many are inconsistent in the fullness of information provided, presumably because that information was not known or valued at the time of burial. As an example, Appendix 4 can be considered state of the art in record keeping of the dead ca. 1812. It is derived from a document developed by the British Admiralty at the time of the War of 1812 and is set down in perfect handwriting. Nevertheless, some notations are illegible to modern transcribers, and much information about named individuals is not given. Similarly, Appendix 3 is sometimes vague as to specific home origin of the named individual. In many cases, towns are named without states. The author has chosen not to presume to know those states where they are not given and no other information is available. Other differences are explained in notes to each appendix.

Maps and satellite photography of each of these burial places are accessible from this book's Website.

Appendix 1: American Sailors Buried in Tripoli, Libya, since 1804

These American officers and seamen were buried in Tripoli, Libya, after the explosion of the USS *Intrepid* on September 4, 1804. They were members of a crew assembled from three navy ships and their names follow that of their ships:

USS *Intrepid*: Master Commandant Richard Somers, Lieutenant Henry Wadsworth, Midshipman Joseph Israel (14 years old);

USS *Constitution* (all believed to have the rank of seaman): William Harrison, Robert Clark, Hugh McCormick, Peter Penner, Issac Downes, Jacob Williams;

USS *Nautilus* (all believed to have the rank of seaman): James "Bos'n" Simms, Thomas Tompline, James Harris, William Keith.

It is believed that ten seamen were buried on the beach, and three officers were buried together on land above the beach. Known and possible reburials since 1804 have resulted in five unnamed *Intrepid* crew being buried in a Protestant cemetery near the beach and the belief that five crewmen are buried at one location under what is now Green Park. Richard Somers and two other officers are believed to be buried in another location beneath Green Park, approximately 500 feet from the west gate of the Old Castle Fort.

Appendix 2: American Navy Officers Still Buried in Plymouth, England, since 1813

Commander William H. Allen, Midshipman Richard Delphy. Andrews and Delphy of the USS *Argus* were buried in the south yard of St. Andrew's Church on August 21, 1813. Reorganization of the church property in 1871 led either to a loss of knowledge of the burial site location or to anonymous reburial in the nearby Westwell Street Burial Ground. The tombstones of Allen and Delphy were recovered, however, and are now cemented into the doorway of the old St. Andrew's Prysten House.

Appendix 3: Americans Still Buried in the American Cemetery at Dartmoor Prison in England since the War of 1812

Contemporary research by former Dartmoor guard Ron Joy and the late American author and historian Ira Dye names 271 Americans buried in the American cemetery at Dartmoor Prison near Princetown, Devon, England, 1813–1815. They are listed, as given, by name; ship or other military source; and home origin. Where a town is named without a state, the author hasn't presumed to know the state, even if it is obvious:

Adam, William; *Africa*; Massachusetts
Adams, James; *Greyhound*; North Carolina
Adams, John; *Ida*; Boston, Massachusetts
Adams, Robert; *Herald*; Not given
Adams, William; *Hawk*; North Carolina

Addigo, Henry; *Argus*; New York
Allan, Asha; *Herald*; New Bedford, Massachusetts
Allen, Archibald; *Harpy*; Massachusetts
Allen, John Baptist; *Herald*; Africa
Almeno, Jose; *President*; Carthagena

Amos, Peter; *Invincible*; Martha's Vineyard, Massachusetts
Anderson, Jacob; *Hussar*; Portland, Maine
Andrews, Joshua; *David Porter*; Ipswich, Massachusetts
Appleton, Daniel; *Frolic*; Ipswich, Massachusetts
Archer, Daniel; *Grand Turk*; Salem, Massachusetts
Aubury, Martin; *President*; Carthagena
Babb, Benjamin; *Victory*; Barrington
Badson, Jacob; *Young Dixon*; Boston, Massachusetts
Bailey, Moses; *Scorpion*; Pennsylvania
Baker, Charles; *Atalante*; Virginia
Baldwin, John; *Fox*; Boston, Massachusetts
Barnett, James; *Busy*; Pennsylvania
Baron, Thomas; *Argus*; Norfolk, Virginia
Barry, Peter; *Jalouse*; Salem, Massachusetts
Bateman, John; *Chasseur*; Baltimore, Maryland
Bean, William; *Malta*; Virginia
Beck, William; *Royal*; William, New Hampshire
Belloa, Darius; *Frolic*; Rhode Island
Birch, Peter; *Prosperity*; Philadelphia
Bisley, Horace; *Star*; Rockhill, New Hampshire
Blasdon, Philip; 4 Regt Rifles; New Hampshire
Boardby, Samuel; *Fiere Facia*; Baltimore, Maryland
Bodge, Daniel; *Harlequin*; Arundel
Bray, Isacher; *Ida*; Cape Ann
Brien, Lewis; *Hawk*; North Carolina
Brissons, John; *Bunker Hill*; Baltimore, Maryland
Brown, Charles; *Paul Jones*; Virginia
Brown, George; *Ocean*; Pennsylvania
Brown, William; *Ulysses*; New York
Burbidge, Henry; *Greyhound*; Washington
Burleigh, Henry; *Bennett*; Newmarket
Butler, John; *Semiramis*; Pennsylvania
Butts, Joseph; *Fair America*; New York
Campbell, Henry; gave himself up; Delaware
Campbell, James; *Volontaire*; New York
Carson, John; *Fiere Facia*; New Orleans
Carter, Daniel; *Zebra*; Virginia
Cateret, James; *Mary*; Maryland
Chandler, Simon; *Essex*; Massachusetts
Chult, David; *Salvador*; Massachusetts
Clark, Simon; *Snapdragon*; North Carolina
Clerk, William; *Star*; Newport, Rhode Island
Coffee, Ramos; *Portsmouth*; New York
Cole, John; *Adeline*; Baltimore, Maryland
Coleman, William; *Hawk*; North Carolina
Collins, John; *Monmouth*; Philadelphia, Pennsylvania
Compichi (Campichi), St. Yago; *President*; Carthagena
Congdon, James; *Goren*; Rhode Island
Conklin, Ventus; *Herald*; New York
Cook, Benjamin; *Chesapeake*; Baltimore, Maryland
Coombes, James; *Argus*; Wiscasset
Cooper, Thomas; *Union*; Massachusetts
Cornish, Charles; *Chesapeake*; Maryland
Curren, Nathaniel; *Lizard*; Salem, Massachusetts
Cussar, James O.; *Volunteer*; New York

Davenport, John; *Sabine*; Easthaven
Davis, James; *Yorktown*; Savanna, Georgia
Debates, Amos; *Ida*; Hamburg
Denham, Sylas; *Ida*; Boston, Massachusetts
Denning, Joseph; *Ohio*; Massachusetts
Devinas, John; *Ohio*; Salem
Diamond, William; *Mary*; Blockhead, Rhode Island
Dillain, William; *Argus*; New Guernsey
Dilno, Benjamn; *Essex*; Massachusetts
Dyer, Jonathan; *True Blooded Yankee*; Cape Cod, Massachusetts
Edgar, William; *Hepas*; New Jersey
Erwin, William; *Star*; Cumberland
Evans, Edward; *North Star*; Virginia
Fernald, William; *Harpy*; Kiny (?), Maine
Fisher, Charles; *Saratoga*; Delaware
Fletcher, William B.; *Spitfire*; Marblehead, Massachusetts
Flowers, John; *Lion*; Boston
Fogerty, Archibald; *Horatio*; Massachusetts
Fowler, Joshua; *Carnation*; Boston, Massachusetts
Francis, John; *Royal William*; New Hampshire
Freely, Henry; *Pompee*; Pennsylvania
Fulford, Joseph; *Snapdragon*; North Carolina
Gardner, Jeremiah; A Brig; Rhode Island
Gardner, Timothy; *Rolla*; Rhode Island
Gatwood, James; *Bunker Hill*; New Hampshire
Gayler, James; *America*; North Carolina
Gennifon, Michael; *Syren*; Baltimore
Gibson, William; *Rattlesnake*; New York
Gladding, William; *Rattlesnake*; New Jersey
Glodding, Joseph; *Rattlesnake*; Rhode Island
Greaves, Thomas; *Port Mahon*; Boston, Massachusetts
Grey, John; *Paul Jones*; Richmond, Virginia
Gwynn, Josh; *Herald*; Salem, Massachusetts
Hall, Thomas; *Surprize*; Maryland
Harman, Isaac; *Elbridge Gerry*; Massachusetts
Harris, Lamen; *Magdalen*; Massachusetts
Harris, William; *Portsmouth*; New Hampshire
Harrison, Samuel; *Hawk*; North Carolina
Hart, James; *Courier*; Connecticut
Hawley, Frederick; *Royal William*; Wilmington
Haycock, Joseph; *Syren*; Portland
Haywood, John; *SciPion*; Maryland
Henderson, Alexander; *Criterion*; Connecticut
Henry, James; *Argus*; New York
Hentey, Jacob; *Jemmett*; Salem, Massachusetts
Heny, Daniel; *Frolic*; Salem, Massachusetts
Hobday, Francis; *Rattlesnake*; Gloster, Massachusetts
Holbrook, Ebenezer; *Derby*; Massachusetts
Holding, Henry; *Sultan*; Boston, Massachusetts
Holford, Elisha; *Barfleur*; New York
Holstein, Richard; *Baroness Longerville*; Virginia
Hopson, John; *Snapdragon*; North Carolina
Jack, John; *Orontes*; Baltimore
Jackson, Thomas; *Hebrus*; New York
Jackson, Thomas; *Orontes*; New York
Jarvis, Thomas; *Industry*; Marblehead

Jenkins, Nathaniel; *Tom*; Baltimore, Maryland
Jennings, John; *Hawke*; Martha's Vineyard
Johannes, John; *President*; St. Thomas
Johnson, John; *Criterion*; Rhode Island
Johnson, Joseph; *Paul Jones*; Connecticut
Johnson, William; *Antelope*; Philadelphia, Pennsylvania
Johnson, Wm. Alexan.; *William*; Charleston, North Carolina
Jones, George; *Viper*; New Orleans
Jones, Isaac; *Hussar*; Boston, Massachusetts
Jones, James; *Hussar*; New York
Jones, Stephen; *Volunteer*; New York
Jones, Thomas; *Growler*; Baltimore, Maryland
Jose, Emanuel; *David Porter*; Portugal
Joseph, Pedro; *President*; Guadaloupe
Kelley, John; *Alfred*; Marblehead, Massachusetts
King, Uriel; *Dominique*; Massachusetts
Kitre, Dumpy; *Paul Jones*; North Carolina
Knabbs, William; *President*; Baltimore, Maryland
Lackey, Joseph; *Enterprise*; Massachusetts
Lamb, Anthony; *Grand Turk*; Connecticut
Larkin, Amos; *Reynard*; Beverly, Massachusetts
Larkin, Louis; *Young Wasp*; Connecticut
Lawson, James; *Mars*; Africa
Lee, Richard; *Grand Turk*; Marblehead
Lee, Richard Robert; *Amelia*; Massachusetts
Leman, Ambrose; *President*; Carthagena
Lilley, Samuel; *Rattlesnake*; Boston, Massachusetts
Lippart Thomas D.; *Paul Jones*; Pennsylvania
Long, Joseph; *Fame*; Massachusetts
Louis, John; *Hugh Jones*; New Orleans
Lovely, Placid; *Hawk*; New Orleans
Loveridge, William; *Saratoga*; New York
Man, Jabez; *Siro*; Boston, Massachusetts
March, Jesse; *McDonough*; Massachusetts
Marshall, Benjamin; *Minden*; Maine
Marshall, John; *Alchinene*; New Bedford, Massachusetts
Marshall, Solomon; *Mammouth*; Massachusetts
Martin, Manuel; *Paul Jones*; New Orleans
Meads, William; *Snapdragon*; North Carolina
Mendoza, Cesar; *President*; Carthagena
Menillo, John; *Rattlesnake*; Baltimore, Maryland
Miller, Edward; *Mammouth*; New Jersey
Miller, Richard; *Snapdragon*; Pennsylvania
Mills, William; *Zebra*; New Jersey
Mingo, Albert; *Quiz*; New Orleans
Mista, William; *Atlantic*; Virginia
Mitchell, Ezekiel; *Charlotte*; Massachusetts
Mitchell, Reuben; No. 2 Gunboat; Maryland
Monte, Charles; *Fame*; San Antonio, Texas
Montgomery, John; impressed; New York
Moore, George; *Chasseur*; Boston
More, Henry; *Marmion*; New York
Morrell, Jacob; *Fox*; Massachusetts
Murray, James; *Messenger*; Maryland
Nash, Daniel; *Prince*; Vermont
Norton, Edward; *Frolic*; Massachusetts

Osborne, John L.; *Portsmouth*; Newbury Port
Packer, William; *Derby*; Barnstable
Palmer, Joseph; *Ida*; Portsmouth, New Hampshire
Parish, Samuel; *Grand Napoleon*; Virginia
Parker, Thomas; *Domonique*; Delaware
Pass, Samuel; *Dart*; Not Given
Paul, Jonathan; *Hind*; Massachusetts
Peck, Thomas; *Paul Jones*; Connecticut
Perigo, Joel; *Ida*; Connecticut
Perkins, John; *Siro*; Newhampton
Perkins, Joseph; *Lacey*; Massachusetts
Peters, Aaron; *Joel Barlow*; Rhode Island
Peterson, Jacob; *John*; M., Rhode Island
Peterson, John; *Orontes*; Albany
Peterson, Lawrence; *Nonsuch*; Not Given
Pettingall, Joshua; *Enterprise*; Salem, Massachusetts
Pinkham, Jacob; *Monmouth*; Massachusetts
Polland, John; *Ida*; Brazil
Porter, Gideon; *Acteon*; Newport
Potter, John; impressed; Philadelphia, Pennsylvania
Powsland, Edward; *Frolic*; Beverly
Queenwell, Peter; *Walker*; Dartmouth
Ranson, Joseph; *Ned*; Philadelphia
Raysden, John; *Pike*; New York
Read, David; *America*; Wiscasset
Read, William; *Race Horse*; New Hampshire
Rennaben, Benjamin; *Fox*; New Orleans
Ricks, Thomas; *Bristol*; (taken in) New York
Roberson, James; *Price*; Massachusetts
Roberts, John; gave himself up; Baltimore, Maryland
Robinson, Samuel; *Ducornau*; Boston, Massachusetts
Robinson, William; *Plutarch*; Philadelphia
Rogers, Luke; *Fairy*; North Carolina
Romel, Francis; *Chesapeake*; San Sebastian
Roth, James; *Mary*; Connecticut
Rowlinson, Thomas; *Calabria*; Virginia
Salisbury, Joseph; *Jemmett*; Newport
Saul, Francis; *Mercurious*; cannot decipher
Saunders, William; *Mars*; Massachusetts
Sawyer, Jacob; impressed; Providence, Rhode Island
Schew, Richard; *Amiable*; New York
Seapatch, John; *Harlequin*; Massachusetts
Shaw, William; *Argus*; Philadelphia, Pennsylvania
Sheldon, Smith; *Militia*; Rhode Island
Sherriden, Henry; *SciPion*; New York
Simmons, Thomas; *Saratoga*; New Bedford, Massachusetts
Simonds, David; *Enterprise*; Massachusetts
Simonds, Ebenezer; gave himself up; Newburyport, Massachusetts
Simondson, Isaac; *Invincible*; New York
Smart, William; *Elephant*; Virginia
Smides, Rich; *Flash*; New York
Smith, Andrew; *Tom*; Maryland
Smith, Nicholas; *Herald*; Richmond, Virginia
Smith, Richard; *General Kempt*; Salem, Massachusetts

Snell, Shadrach;1st Reg. Rifles; Rhode Island
Squibb, Silus; *Harpy*; New London
Stacey, Stephen; *Ohio*; Marblehead, Massachusetts
Stanwood, Timothy; *Alboukir*; Newburyport, Massachusetts
Steel, John; *Wm. Bayard*; Maryland
Stone, John; *Harlequin*; Arundel
Stove, Lewis; *Tickler*; Connecticut
Strout, John; *Siro*; Portland
Studdy, Richard; *Amelia*; Virginia
Sutton, Martin; *Lion*; New Bedford
Taylor, David; *David Porter*; Philadelphia, Pennsylvania
Thomas, Abraham; *Paul*; Connecticut
Thomas, John; *Elbert Gerry*; Not given
Thompson, Henry; *Prince*; New York
Thompson, Thomas; *Thomas*; New York
Thomson, William; *Siro*; Haiti
Timerman, Matthew; *Tom Thumb*; New York
Toby, Elisha; *True Blooded Yankee*; Massachusetts
Tomkins, Abraham; *Governor*; Shelby, New York
Tophouse, Samuel; taken at Washington; Washington
Tremerin, Joseph; *Mars*; Philadelphia
Tucker, James; *Liberty*; Long Island
Turner, David; *Derby*; Boston, Massachusetts
Turney, John; *Rattlesnake*; Massachusetts
Tuttle, French; *Leo*; Massachusetts
Tyren, William; *Viper*; North Carolina
Vaughan, Nathaniel; *Ducornau*; Newport
Washington, John; *Rolla*; Savannah, Georgia
West, George; gave himself up; Delaware
West, George; *Malta*; Baltimore, Maryland
Whittan, John; *Harlequin*; Portsmouth
Williams, Charles; Pilot; New London, Connecticut
Williams, Edward; out of Russian Ship; Virginia
Williams, John; *Caroline*; Connecticut
Williams, Joseph; *Clorinde*; Martha's Vineyard
Williams, Samuel; *Scorpion*; Massachusetts
Williams, Thomas; *Viper*; Connecticut
Williams, William; impressed; Georgetown
Windyer, Joseph; *Growler*; Marblehead, Massachusetts
Young, William; *Levant*; Massachusetts

Appendix 4: Americans Sailors and Infantry Still Buried in Halifax, Nova Scotia, Canada, since the War of 1812

A total of 195 American soldiers, sailors, and others are listed as being buried in Halifax. The list was discovered late in the 20th century in the records of the British Admiralty in London, transmitted to the U.S. National Archive, and transcribed by Michele Hovey Raymond of Halifax. At first, it was believed that all were buried at Deadman's Island, the cemetery for Melville Island Prison. Some may be buried anonymously, however, in the graveyard of the old naval hospital in Halifax, as noted. They are listed, as given in the Raymond transcription, by name; age; military source and rank; home origin, and cause of death. Where a town is named without a state, the author hasn't presumed to know the state, even if it is obvious.

Abbott, John; Not given; U.S. Army, Private; Not given; Pneumonia
Adams, Peter; 42: *Chesapeake*, Boatswain; Unknown; Wounds*
Alexander, John; Not given; *Romp*; Not given; Not given
Allen, John; Not given; *Cossack*, Master; Massachusetts; Consumption
Allen, Thomas; Not given; *Growler*, Seaman; Not given; Not given
Amos, James; Not given; *Fernandez*, Seaman; Not given; Pneumonia
Asher, Frederick; 42; U.S. Army 14th Reg.; Private; Philadelphia; Dysentry
Baker, Andrew; 27; *Thomas*; Old York, New Hampshire; Mortification of the leg
Banser, Perry; 27; *Ulysses*; Maryland; Inflammation of lungs
Barrington, John; 27; U.S. Army 14th Reg.; Baltimore; Dysentry
Barton, Hiram; Not given; *Ten Brothers*; Not given; Not given
Boggs, Syman; Not given; U.S. Army, Private; Not given; Fever
Boss, Joseph; Not given; *Rolla*, Prize master; Not given; Dysentry
Bowen, Pearce; Not given; U.S. Army, Corporal; Not given; Dysentry
Brooks, Thomas; Not given; *Vixen*, Seaman; Not given; Phthesis
Brown, John; Not given; U.S. Army, Private; Not given; Fever

Brown, Wilson; 28; *Portsmouth Packet*, Master mate; New Hampshire; Consumption
Brownwell, David; Not given; U.S. Army, Private; Not given; Pneumonia
Bryant, David; 18; *Rapid*, Seaman; Soco; Typhus
Buchan, Benjamin; Not given; *Nonsuch*, Seaman; Not given; Not given
Caffet, Moses; Not given; *Julia Simonds*, Master; Not given; Not given
Canon, Daniel; Not given; *Rattlesnake*, Seaman; Not given; Not given
Carleton, John; 26; *Chesapeake*, Seaman; Boston; Pneumonia
Carswell, Samuel; Not given; *Maria*, Seaman; Not given; Dysentry
Carter, Nathaniel; 22; U.S. Army 6th Reg., Private; New Jersey; Disease of Jaw
Cheever, James; 19; *Enterprise*, Seaman; Massachusetts; Consumption
Cleaver, Seth; 32; U.S. Army 14th Reg., Corporal; Philadelphia; Dysentry
Coale, Henry; Not given; U.S. Army, Private; Not given; Dysentry
Coleman, William; Not given; *Montesella*, Seaman; Nantucket; Smallpox
Colley, William; 22; *Packet*, Seaman; Eastport; Typhus/Pneumonia
Combes, Daniel; Not given; *Yankee*, Pilot; Not given; Pneumonia
Cone, Giles; 30; *Chesapeake*, Seaman; Middle Town; Wounds
Cram, Nehemiah; Not given; *Macedonian*, Seaman; Not given; Pneumonia
Crandall, Joshua; Not given; U.S. Army, Private; Not given; Not given
Crutchett, John; 34; *Chesapeake*, Seaman; Cumberland; Wounds
Davis, George; 27; *Gossamer*, Seaman; Portland; Pneumonia
Davis, John; 23; U.S. Army 14th Reg., Private; Pennsylvania; Pneumonia
Davis, Samuel; Not given; *Wave*, Seaman; Not given; Disease of Lungs
Davis, Sheddick; 24; U.S. Army 21st Reg., Private; New York; Wounds
Dawson, Christopher; Not given; Taken on shore, Landsman; Not given; Disease of Lungs
Dixon, William; 22; *Chesapeake*, Marine; Pennsylvania; Wounds*
Domingo, William; 24; *Polly*, Seaman; Salem; Fever
Dotey, Ambrose; Not given; U.S. Army, Private; Not given; Pneumonia
Dowdy, Thomas; Not given; *Perseverence*, Seaman; Not given; Fever
Duffy, Samuel; 30; *Porcupine*, Seaman; New Hampshire; Inflammation of Lungs
Dunkin, William; Unknown; *Catherine*, Seaman; Boston; Killed at Halifax
Dwelly, Lot; 31; *Eldridge Gerey*, Seaman; Boston; Fever
Edwards, Richard; Not given; *Diana*, Seaman; Not given; Fever
Elliot, John; Not given; *Julia Simonds*, Seaman; Not given; Not given
Evelet, Benjamin; Not given; U.S. Army Fencibles, Private; Not given; Fever
Fairfield, Solomon; 27; U.S. Army 22nd Reg., Private; Rhode Island; Smallpox
Farr, Chester; Not given; U.S. Army, Private; Not given; Dysentry
Ferris, Degrass; Not given; *Invincible*, Seaman; Not given; Fever
Foley, Nathaniel; 45; *Porcupine*, Seaman; New York; Astmash (?asthma)
Footman, Mark; 19; *Thomas*, Seaman; New Hampshire; Smallpox
Forbes, Levi; Not given; U.S. Army 14th Reg., Private; Not given; Dysentry
Foster, Charles; Not given; *Essex*, Seaman; Not given; Not given
Fountain, Francis; Not given; *David Porter*, Seaman; Not given; Dysentry
Franklin, George; Not given; U.S. Army, Private; Not given; Not given
Fuller, James; Not given; U.S. Army 23rd Reg., Private; Not given; Dysentry
Fuller, Wm. Oliver; 35; *Portsmouth Packet*, Seaman; District of Maine; Inflammation of Arm
Gaines, Samuel; Not given; *Guerriere*, Seaman; Connecticut; Mania
Gale, John G.; Not given; U.S. Army, Private; Not given; Phthesis
Gooden, Enoch; 26; *Montgomery*, Seaman; Newbury Port; Disease of Chest
Goodwin, Anthony; Not given; *Mary Ann*, Seaman; Not given; Not given
Goodwin, Samuel; 18; *Curlew*, Seaman; Marblehead; Typhus
Goodwin, William; 28; *Hope*, Seaman; Maryland; Fever
Gray, John; 19; *Eldridge Gerey*, Seaman; Massachusetts; Smallpox
Hall, James; 27; *Thomas*, Prize master; Portsmouth; Fever
Hammond, Jesse; Not given; *Nonsuch*, Seaman; Not given; Not given
Hannah, John; Not given; *Financier*, Seaman; Not given; Fever
Harding, Samuel; Not given; *Rambler*, Seaman; Not given; Dysentry
Herring, John; 26; U.S. Army 14th Reg., Private; Maryland; Dysentry
Hicks, John; Not given; *Lukey*, Seaman; Not given; Smallpox
Higby, William; 22; *Revenge*, Seaman; Salem; Apoplexy

Higgins, Seth; Not given; *Three Sisters*, Seaman; Not given; Not given
Hill, James; 26; *Thomas*, Prize master; Pennsylvania; Dysentry
Hill, John; Not given; *Ambition*, Seaman; Not given; Fever
Holmes, Joseph; Not given; *Polly Ann*, Seaman; Not given; Not given
Honeywell, Enoch; 19; U.S. Army 23rd. Reg., Private; New York; Dysentry
Hooper, Thomas; Not given; *Isabella*, Seaman; Not given; Not given
Hopkins, James; 25; *Thomas*, Seaman; Massachusetts; Inflammation of lungs
Horton, Cyrus; Not given; U.S. Army, Private; Not given; Fever
Housten, Christopher; Not given; *Chesapeake*, Seaman; Not given; Wounds*
Howard, Ralph; Not given; U.S. Army, Private; Vermont; Dysentry
Hoyett, Joseph; Not given; *Guerriere*, Seaman; Not given; Consumption
Hunt, Henry; Not given; U.S. Army, Private; Not given; Consumption
Hunter, Joseph; 42; U.S. Army 14th Infantry, Private; Washington; Dysentry
Hutchinson, Elisha; Not given; *Growler*, Seaman; Not given; Not given
Hutchinson, Saul; Not given; U.S. Army, Private; Not given; Disease of Lungs
Istman, Henry; Not given; U.S. Army, Private; Not given; Pneumonia
Jackson, Robert; Not given; *George*, Seaman; Salem; Apoplexy
Jacobs, Samuel; Not given; *Lizard*, Seaman; Not given; Not given
Johnson, David; Not given; U.S. Army, Private; Not given; Fever
Johnson, Isaac; Not given; *Leander*, Seaman; Not given; Not given
Johnson, John; 22; *Chesapeake*, Seaman; New York; Wounds*
Johnson, William; 20; *General Plummer*, Seaman; Boston; Inflammation of Lungs
Jones, David; Not given; *Voador*, Passenger; Not given; Not given
Keith, Robert; 36; *Rolla*, Seaman; New York; Smallpox
Kempton, Daniel; Not given; *Saratoga*, Seaman; Not given; Not given
Lacey, Stephen; Not given; *Hazard*, Mate; Not given; Not given
Lancaster, William; Not given; U.S. Army, Private; Not given; Dysentry
Lane, Jesse; 26; U.S. Army 18th Reg., Private; Virginia; Fever
Lazeler, Benjamin; 25; U.S. Army 23rd Reg., Private; Jersey; Smallpox
Learned, Henry; Not given; U.S. Army, Private; Not given; Not given
Lesley, John; 40; *Porcupine*, Seaman; Salem; Pleurisy
Levii, Henry; 26; U.S. Army 23rd Reg., Corporal; Maryland; Inflammation of Lungs
Lincoln, Hezekiah; Not given; *Nancy*, Seaman; Not given; Not given
Long, Richard; Not given; *Montesella*, Seaman; Not given; Not given
Look, George; Not given; *Diomede*, Seaman; Not given; Not given
Lothrap, Dariah; Not given; U.S. Army, Private; Not given; Fever
Luckey, Samuel; 40; U.S. Army 23rd Reg., Private; New York; Dysentry
Ludlow, A.C.; 24; *Chesapeake*, Lieutenant; North River, New York; Wounds†
Mansell, Marcus; 22; *Chesapeake*, Seaman; Sweden; Wounds*
March, William; 19; U.S. Army 14th Reg., Private; Maryland; Consumption
Martin, Samuel; Not given; *Rolla*, Seaman; Not given; Pneumonia
Mason, Ira; 17; U.S. Army 6th Reg., Private; New York; Smallpox
McCulloch, Robert; Not given; *Vixen*, Seaman; Not given; Not given
McCullogh, Samuel; Not given; U.S. Army, Private; Not given; Not given
Mead, John; 26; *Bunker Hill*, Seaman; Marblehead; Typhus Fever
Messenger, William S.; Not given; U.S. Army, Private; Not given; Fever
Milbank, David; Not given; U.S. Army, Private; Not given; Fever
Miller, Gattet; 19; U.S. Army 14th Reg., Private; Delaware; Dysentry
Moody, Thomas; Not given; *Experiment*, Seaman; Not given; Dysentry
Moore, Milby; Not given; *Jane*, Seaman; Not given; Pneumonia
Morgan, Samuel; Not given; Taken on shore, Landsman; Not given; Not given
Morris, Charles; 36; *York Town*, Seaman; Philadelphia; Rheumatism
Morrison, Moses; Not given; U.S. Army, Private; Not given; Dysentry
Morrison, William; Not given; *Frolic*, Seaman; Not given; Not given
Neill, Robert; Not given; Gunboat #12, Seaman; Not given; Not given
Nelson, John D.; Not given; *Los Dos Ermanos*, Master; Not given; Fever
Newell, James; 27; *Gossamer*, Seaman; Boston; Typhus
Oiler, George; 25; U.S. Army 14th Reg., Private; Maryland; Paraletic
Oliver, Samuel; Not given; *Ulysses*, Seaman; Not given; Not given

Pascall, Ezekial; Not given; U.S. Army Sea Fencibles, Private; Not given; Not given
Perkins, John; Not given; *Friendship*, Master; Not given; Consumption
Phelps, Henry; Not given; U.S. Army, Private; Not given; Dysentry
Phillips, Joseph; Not given; U.S. Army, Private; Not given; Dysentry
Phupp, Mathew; 22; *Ulysses*, Seaman; Boston; Inflammation of Lungs
Poor, John; 52; *Montgomery*, Seaman; Waterford; Disease of Chest
Porter, John; 35; *Montgomery*, Seaman; Salem; Pleurisy
Powers, William; Not given; U.S. Army, Private; Not given; Fever
Proctor, Amos; 35; *Enterprise*, Seaman; Massachusetts; Pleurisy
Read, James; 28; U.S. Army, Private; New York; Pneumonia
Reid, James; Not given; U.S. Army, Private; Not given; Fever
Riche, Aquila; 49; *Friendship*, Master; North Carolina; Pneumonia
Robb, James; Not given; U.S. Army, Private; Not given; Dysentry
Roberts, Charles; Not given; *Hiram*, Seaman; Not given; Not given
Roberts, James; 46; U.S. Army, Militiaman; Essex; Fever
Roberts, William; 25; U.S. Army 14th Reg., Private; Little York, Pennsylvania; Chest Infection
Robins, John; 31; *Montgomery*, Seaman; Mount Desert; Inflammation of Lungs
Robinson, Peter; Not given; *George*, Seaman; Not given; Pneumonia
Rose, Henry; 28; U.S. Army 14th Reg., Private; Virginia; Smallpox
Ross, David; 35; U.S. Army 1st Artillery, Private; Massachusetts; Smallpox
Rumsay, Nathaniel; Not given; Taken on shore, Citizen; Not given; Fever
Schoolman, William; 46; U.S. Army 23rd Reg., Private; New York; Dysentry
Scudder, Henry; Not given; *Enterprise*, Mate; Not given; Not given
Seamorse, George; 26; *Enterprise*, Seaman; Massachusetts; Disease of Scrotum
Shishulk, Sylvester; Not given; *Flash*, Seaman; Not given; Fever
Smith, Jacob; 25; U.S. Army 14th Reg., Private; Germany; Dysentry
Smith, John K.; Not given; *Daedalus*, Seaman; Not given; Consumption
Smith, Thomas (2); 22; *Chesapeake*, Jr. Gunner; Hampton; Syphillis
Snully, Thomas; Not given; U.S. Army, Private; Not given; Not given
Spencer, Andrew; 28; U.S. Army 21st Reg., Private; Salem; Fever/Dysentry
Spergen, Nathaniel; Not given; U.S. Army, Private; Not given; Pneumonia
Stanhope, Curtis; Not given; U.S. Army, Private; Not given; Not given
Stetis, Isaiah; Not given; *Fair American*, Master; Not given; Fever
Stevens, Benjamin W.; Not given; U.S. Army, Private; Not given; Fever
Stewart, Leonard; Not given; *Frolic*, Seaman; Not given; Not given
Strout, Thomas; Not given; *Rattle Snake*, Seaman; Not given; Not given
Swain, John; Not given; *John & James*, Seaman; Not given; Not given
Swenerton, John; Not given; *Snap Dragon*, Seaman; Not given; Not given
Sylvanus, John; Not given; *Essex*, Seaman; Not given; Fever
Taylor, John; Not given; *Surprise*, Seaman; Not given; Fever
Thirsty, Joel; 34; U.S. Army 23rd Reg., Private; Charleston; Dysentry
Thomas, Caleb; Not given; *Flash*, Seaman; Not given; Fever
Thompson, William; Not given; *Nancy*, Seaman; Not given; Fever
Tinker, James; Not given; *Eagle*, Seaman; Not given; Not given
Todd, Samuel; Not given; Taken on shore, Landsman; Not given; Fever
Tower, John; Not given; *Thorn*, Seaman; Not given; Not given
Valiant, William; 24; U.S. Army 14th Reg., Private; Maryland; Smallpox
Vernon, James; 18; *Wasp*, Seaman; Charlestown; Inflammation of Lungs
Veverland, John; 25; U.S. Army 2nd Reg., Private; Pennsylvania; Dysentry
Wallace, Able; Not given; U.S. Army, Private; Not given; Suddenly
Wallace, Edward; Not given; *Wm. & Susan*, Seaman; Not given; Fever
Watson, Henry; 22; *Enterprise*, Seaman; Cape Ann; Typhus
Webber, John; 33; *Ulysses*, Seaman; Portsmouth; Paralysis
West, Jesse; 29; *Eliza*, Seaman; Connecticut; Typhus
White, Cornelius; Not given; U.S. Army, Private; Not given; Suddenly
Wilcox, William; Not given; *Julia*, Seaman; Not given; Not given
Wilkins, James; 22; U.S. Army 6th Reg., Private; Maryland; Fever
Williams, John; Not given; *Vixen*, Seaman; Not given; Fever
Woodman, Jeremiah; Not given; U.S. Army, Private; Not given; Pneumonia

Wright, John; 28; *Chesapeake*, Marine; Pennsylvania; Wounds, etc.
Young, William; 24; U.S. Army 1st Regiment, Private; Boston; Smallpox

*May actually be buried anonymously in the naval hospital cemetery in Halifax. In addition, the following *Chesapeake* sailors not listed above may also be buried in the hospital cemetery:

Dela, Forbes, Quartermaster
Devo, John, Seaman
Lee, Darby, Seaman

Hanscom, Lewis, Ordinary Seaman
Hunt, John, Ordinary Seaman

McNeil, John, Seaman
Symonds, Francis, Seaman

†Lt. A.C. Ludlow was second in command of the *Chesapeake* and was actually buried with Captain James Lawrence in the Old Burial Ground in Halifax. Both bodies were eventually returned to the United States.

SOURCE: H.F. Pullen, *The "**Shannon**" and the "**Chesapeake**" [Toronto, Montreal:* McClelland and Stewart, 1970], 68.

Appendix 5: American Sailors and a Family Member Buried in Port Mahon, Menorca, Spain, from 1825 to the Mid–19th Century

These American sailors, and one wife of a sailor, are buried at the Christian Cemetery at Port Mahon, Menorca, Spain. They are listed by name; age; home origin; year of death; and U.S. Navy ship. The list may not be complete. Their deaths came in the course of normal naval operations and are not associated with any conflict. Information not available is due to initial record keeping or illegibility of tombstones with the passing of time.

Alberger, Robert; 27; na; 1843; USS *Delaware*
Brown, John; na; na; 1832; USS *Java*
Butler, Henry; na; na; 1845; USS *Cumberland*
Croft, John; 31; New York; 1829; USS *Delaware*
Elton, Edward; na; na; na; na
Gillis, Adam; 23; Belfast, Ireland; 1843; USS *Delaware*
Horton, David; 45; Baltimore; 1825; USS *North Carolina*
Howard, Silas; na; na; 1828; USS *Delaware*
Hunter, Mary Griffith; na; na; wife of sailor; na
Johnson, Lester; na; na; na; na
Jones, Henry; na; na; 1826; USS *North Carolina*
Landsley, John; na; na; na; na

Lee, James M.; 19; Philadelphia; 1843; USS *Delaware*
Morton, Samuel; na; na; na; na
M(u/a?)lloy, William; na; Troy, New York; 1829; USS *Delaware*
Patterson, John S.; na; South Carolina; 1842; USS *Congress*
Ri[ ], Jesse; na; na; 1828; USS *Constitution*
Shane, Jacob; 21; Massachusetts; 1843; USS *Delaware*
Smith, James; na; na; 1826; USS *Brandywine*
Smothers, Thomas; 29; Salem, Massachusetts; na; USS *Java*
Zell, Benjamin; 25; Philadelphia; 1843; USS *Delaware*

Appendix 6: American Sailors Buried in Nicaragua since 1859

Two crew members of the USS *Sabine* were killed in accidents in September and October 1859 and are buried in an English cemetery near San Juan Del Norte, Nicaragua.

Burgess, John
Smith, Charles

Appendix 7: American Civil War Casualties Buried in Cherbourg, France, since 1864

These casualties of a battle between the USS *Kearsarge* and the CSS *Alabama* at Cherbourg on June 19, 1864, are believed to be buried in "an ancient hillside cemetery," not currently located, overlooking the harbor.

George Appleby of Liverpool, England, Union Navy
James King of Savannah, Georgia, Confederate Navy
William Robinson of Massacussetts, Confederate Navy

Appendix 8: Punitive Expedition Casualties Buried Near Parral, Mexico, since 1916

The Battle of Parral on April 12, 1916, an event of the Punitive Expedition to Mexico to capture Pancho Villa, resulted in the deaths and burials in Mexico of eight American soldiers. Six were recovered and returned to the United States in 1929, but two were left in a cemetery at Rancho Santa Cruz de Villegas near Parral at GPS coordinates 27° 07° 48° 44° N, 105° 38° 41° 69° W.

Hobert Ledford, Private, hometown unknown (Various accounts give his name as Hobart, Hobert, Robert. Hobert is the name on the grave marker.)
Jay Richley, Sergeant, Saginaw, Michigan

Appendix 9: American Flyers in the Lafayette Flying Corps Buried near Paris, France, 1928–1930

These American pilots of the Lafayette Escadrille and the Lafayette Flying Corps were buried post World War I at the Lafayette Escadrille Memorial at Marnes-la-Coquette, a suburb of Paris. They are listed as given by the Lafayette Flying Corps Memorial Foundation.

ASH, Alan Newton
Sgt BARCLAY, Leif N.
Sgt BAUGHAM, James H.
Sgt. BAYLIES, Frank L.
1st Lt BAYNE, James Alexander
Corp BENNEY, Philip P.
Corp BIDDLE, Julian C.
Sgt BLUETHENTHAL, Arthur
Sgt BOOTH, Veron Jr.
Sgt CAMPBELL, A.C., Jr.
Corp CHADWICK, Oliver
Sgt CHAMBERLAIN, Cyrus F.
1st Lt. CHAPMAN, CW Jr.
Sgt CHAPMAN, Victor
2d Lt CLAPP, Roger Harvey
Capt COLLINS, Phelps
2nd Lt COOKSON, Linn P.
2d Lt DAVIS, Philip Washburn
2d Lt De KRUIJFF, Theodore
Corp DOOLITTLE James R.
DOWD, Dennis
2d Lt DOWD, Meredith L.
Corp DREW, Sidney Rankin Jr.
1st Lt. EDGAR, Stuart Emmet
2d Lt ELY, Dinsmore
Pilot Av FOWLER Eric A.
Sgt GENET, Edmond C.
Sold. 2d cl GRIEB, Norman
1st Lt. GUNDELACH, Andre
Sold. 2d cl HANFORD, Robert M.
1st Lt. HOBBS, Warren Tucker
Sgt HOSKIER, Ronald W.
1st Lt. JOHNSON, Harry F.
Corp LEE, Schuyler

Corp LEHR, Manderson
Sgt LOUGHRAN, Edward J.
Maj LUFBERY, G.R.
Sgt MACMONAGLE, D.
Sgt MCCONNELL, James R.
Sgt MCKERNESS, William
Corp MEEKER, Wiliam Henry
2d Lt MILLER, Walter B.
Sgt NICHOLS, Alan H.
Sgt OVINGTON, Carter L.
Corp PALMER, Henry B.
Sgt PAVELKA, Paul
Sgt PELTON, Alfred D.
Sgt PETERSON, David M.
2nd Lt PRINCE, Norman
1st Lt. PUTNAM, D.E.
Sgt RHENO, Walter D.

Adjutant ROCKWELL, Kiffin Y.
Sgt SCANLAN, Lawrence
Corp SKINNER, Samuel W.
Corp SPENCER, Dumaresq
Sold. 2d cl STARRETT, Frank Elmer
Corp STONE, Donald E.
Sgt TAILER, William Hallet
Ens TAYLOR, Elmer B.
Ens TERRES, Hugh
Corp TRINKARD, Charles
Sgt TUCKER, Dudley G.
Sgt TYSON, Stephen M.
1st Lt. WALCOTT, B.S.
Corp WILSON, Joseph V.
Corp WINTER, Wallace C.
Corp WOODWARD, Houston
Under Lt YORK, Walter R.

Appendix 10: Americans Buried or Memorialized in Commonwealth War Grave Cemeteries since World War I

These American-related casualties who fought with Commonwealth Forces in World War I are buried or memorialized in Commonwealth War Grave Commission cemeteries and memorials in all parts of the world. The vast majority are American born, and a good number are American immigrants. Some were next of kin to American wives or parents, though not necessarily American citizens. This list is distilled in the format given from CWGC records. Where notation about a "true family name" is given, the individual is listed under an alias and a true name, both of which are included in the list. More complete information about origins, age, place and cause of death, related battle action, and next of kin can be found in the name search engine of the Commonwealth War Graves Commission Website.

AUSTRALIA
Fremantle Cemetery, Western Australia
  Trease, Vaughan Gilbert, Driver

AZERBAIJAN
Baku Memorial
  Ralston, John, Private

BELGIUM
Adinkerke Military Cemetery, De Panne, West-Vlaanderen
  Barker, Alexander Watson, Private
Artillery Wood Cemetery, Ieper, West-Vlaanderen
  Felton, F.J., Private
  Saul, T.H., Private
  Wordingham, Vincent Robert, Second Lieutenant
Bedford House Cemetery, Ieper, West-Vlaanderen
  Baldwin, K.G.F., Corporal
  Day, R.G., Private
  Starr, Philip Comfort, Lieutenant
  Wilkinson, Fred, Private
Belgian Battery Corner Cemetery, Ieper, West-Vlaanderen
  Robson, William Telfer, Private
Belgrade Cemetery, Namur, Namur
  Carveth, Frank Alfred, Private
  Ellis, W.H., Gunner
  MacFarland, W.R., Private
  Meehan, Joseph Francis, Private
Berks Cemetery Extension, Comines-Warneton, Hainaut
  Christensen, J., Private
  Clark, Weldon Harry, Private
  Monkman, Herbert Stanley, Captain
  Neal, George, Private
  O'Neil, James Joseph, Private
  Saltsman, John Kline, Private
Bleuet Farm Cemetery, Ieper, West-Vlaanderen
  Duffy, Terence, Sergeant

Brandhoek New Military Cemetery, *Ieper, West-Vlaanderen*
  Johnson, Andrew Rheinold, Sapper
Brandhoek New Military Cemetery No. 3, *Ieper, West-Vlaanderen*
  Holmes, John Alexander, Gunner
  Saunders, Arthur Henry, Gunner
Brussels Town Cemetery, *Evere, Vlaams-Brabant*
  Brown, Robert, Sapper
Buffs Road Cemetery, *Ieper, West-Vlaanderen*
  Hanson, Fred, Gunner
Calvaire (Essex) Military Cemetery, *Comines-Warneton, Hainaut*
  Knight, Arthur, Lieutenant
Canada Farm Cemetery, *Ieper, West-Vlaanderen*
  Gordon, Bertie, Driver
  Henderson, Thomas L., Private
  Mitchell, J., Gunner
Cement House Cemetery, *Langemark-Poelkapelle, West-Vlaanderen*
  Barwick, John Arthur, Gunner
  Hind, Ernest, Private
  Sutcliffe, Geoffrey, Second Lieutenant
Chester Farm Cemetery, *Ieper, West-Vlaanderen*
  Thurston, John Christian, Private
Coxyde Military Cemetery, *Koksijde, West-Vlaanderen*
  Hilton, Herbert, Corporal
  McAuley, Charles John, Sergeant
  Whitehead, Joseph, Private
Cuesmes Communal Cemetery, *Mons, Hainaut*
  Bean, Delbert, Lance Corporal
Dadizeele New British Cemetery, *Moorslede, West-Vlaanderen*
  Sinclair, John Campbell Anderson, Private
Derry House Cemetery No. 2, *Heuvelland, West-Vlaanderen*
  Brand, Stanley Oliver, Lieutenant
Dickebusch New Military Cemetery, *Ieper, West-Vlaanderen*
  Dale, Thomas, Private
  Frogley, H., Lance Corporal
  Green, Walter John, Gunner
  MacDiarmid, George Alexander, Gunner
  Teale, Alfred, Private
Dickebusch New Military Cemetery Extension, *Ieper, West-Vlaanderen*
  Holt, R., Gunner
Divisional Collecting Post Cemetery and Extension, *Ieper, West-Vlaanderen*
  Shay, Albert, Private
  Snowdon, T.H., Private
Dozinghem Military Cemetery, *Poperinge, West-Vlaanderen*
  Cook, Edmund Garretson, Private
  Dicker, E., Bombardier
  Enright, J.H., Private
  Hackett, Frank William, Sergeant
  Harrington, Wayne Francis, Private
  Pettit, H., Private
  Tapp, Theodore Arthur, Captain
  Wardlow, Andrew, Private
  Woodward, S., Captain
  Young, Ernest, Private
Duhallow A.D.S. Cemetery, *Ieper, West-Vlaanderen*
  Angel, William Henry, Private
  Digness, J., Private
  Terry, John, Private
Elouges Communal Cemetery, *Dour, Hainaut*
  Pilling, Frank Clifford, Private
Elzenwalle Brasserie Cemetery, *Ieper, West-Vlaanderen*
  Copson, Arthur Paul, Private
Gijzenzele Churchyard, *Oosterzele, Oost-Vlaanderen*
  Reid, James, Lieutenant
Gwalia Cemetery, *Ieper, West-Vlaanderen*
  Sparkman, Charles Spurgeon, Lance Sergeant
Harlebeke New British Cemetery, *Harelbeke, West-Vlaanderen*
  Hutchins, Alfred John Avalon, Second Lieutenant
  Mercer, James, Private
  Withycombe, Keith Dalston, Driver
Hooge Crater Cemetery, *Ieper, West-Vlaanderen*
  Jeffery, Albert Richard, Lance Corporal
  Lukeis, William, Private
  Reeves, Claude Bailey, Sapper
The Huts Cemetery, *Ieper, West-Vlaanderen*
  Dunlop, Hugh Watt, Driver
  Stevenson, W., Gunner
Huy (La Sarte) Communal Cemetery, *Huy, Leige*
  Corkill, Cecil, Private
  Haverley, Herbert S., Private
Hyde Park Corner (Royal Berks) Cemetery, *Comines-Warneton, Hainaut*
  Gray, Thomas, Rifleman
Jemappes Communal Cemetery, *Mons, Hainaut*
  Thackray, E.W., Private
Kandahar Farm Cemetery, *Heuvelland, West-Vlaanderen*
  Roberts, J.C., Sapper
Kemmel Chateau Military Cemetery, *Heuvelland, West-Vlaanderen*
  Hodsden, Harold K., Private
  Proctor, William Henry, Private
  Ruddock, Richard Fenwick, Second Lieutenant
Kemmel No. 1 French Cemetery, *Heuvelland, West-Vlaanderen*
  MacPherson, W., Lance Corporal
Kezelberg Military Cemetery, *Wevelgem, West-Vlaanderen*
  MacKenzie, Donald Alvin, Lieutenant
Klein-Vierstraat British Cemetery, *Heuvelland, West-Vlaanderen*

Gould, Chalkley Vivian, Major
MacIvor, Norman, Private

Kortrijk (St. Jan) Communal Cemetery, *Kortrijk, West-Vlaanderen*
Cowan, Thomas, Private

La Clytte Military Cemetery, *Heuvelland, West-Vlaanderen*
Heilbron, Louis, Private
Nicholson, Herbert George, Private

La Laiterie Military Cemetery, *Heuvelland, West-Vlaanderen*
Baker, P.I., Private
Bartlett, C.C., Private
Gesner, Ernest Gordon, Private
Peacock, Reginald Fawcett, Lance Corporal

La Plus Douve Farm Cemetery, *Comines-Warneton, Hainaut*
Cuthbert, Robert Lancelot, Private
McCauley, Nathan Mantz, Corporal
Pass, George Vennis, Private
Swann, Louis Harold Hurvey, Lance Corporal

Larch Wood (Railway Cutting) Cemetery, *Ieper, West-Vlaanderen*
Bain, F., Private
Kinney, T.R., Private
McConnell, Harold Jeffrey, Lieutenant
West, John Prout, Lieutenant

Lijssenthoek Military Cemetery, *Poperinge, West-Vlaanderen*
Abbott, Albert Frederick, Sergeant
Allen, M.B., Private
Aston, Walter Douglas, Captain
Berry, George Herbert, Second Lieutenant
Birkbeck, Thomas, Private
Bunniss, William, Lance Corporal
Burdette, Elmer Edgar, Private
Chase, G.F., Private
Christie, Andrew, Gunner
Claggett, Perry Snowden, Private
Coit, Henry Augustus, Private
Currie, Archibald, Private
Daly, Joseph, Private
Denby, W.B., Private
Drew, Harold, Private
Erskine, A., Corporal
Farrington, W., Gunner
Fernald, Leland Wingate, Driver
Garvin, F., Private
Graham, W.B., Sergeant
Hanlon, John, Private
Hawkins, William Sidney, Sergeant
Huot, H., Sapper
Jackson, Thomas, Private
Johnston, Robert Haldane, Corporal
King, Francis Trevor, Sapper
Knowles, William Edward, Private
Landkasky, J.G., Private
Lawrence, Lewis Samuel, Gunner
Lee, Fred, Gunner
Loftin, J.M., Private
Love, John Reginald, Private
Makinson, John, Private
Malone, J., Private
Melvin, Norman Edward, Private
O'Brien, Michael Joseph, Private
Oliver, George Rey, Private
Parnum, John Wescomb, Private
Peltier, Arthur, Private
Petch, J.W.T., Private
Polkinghorn, T., Pioneer
Scobie, W.H., Private
Simpson, H.G., Private
Thorpe, James Stokesbury, Lieutenant
Waring, Gordon MacKenzie, Private
Wolfe, Edwin Thomaswoodyoung, Private

London Rifle Brigade Cemetery, *Comines-Warneton, Hainaut*
Crothers, Samuel, Company Sergeant Major

Maple Copse Cemetery, *Ieper, West-Vlaanderen*
Paul, George William, Private
Thorne, Robert Penoyer, Sergeant

Mendinghem Military Cemetery, *Poperinge, West-Vlaanderen*
Glasgow, Theodore Linscott, Flight Sub-Lieutenant
Mills, Samuel Arthur, Gunner
Ross, Donald Neil Campbell, Second Lieutenant
Ryan, Bliss Wilberforce, Lieutenant

Menin Road South Military Cemetery, *Ieper, West-Vlaanderen*
St. Lawrent, Alfred U., Private

Mons (Bergen) Communal Cemetery, *Mons, Hainaut*
McGrath, James Patrick, Private

Nieuport Memorial, *Nieuwpoort, West-Vlaanderen*
Wager, Willson Stanley, Second Lieutenant

Nine Elms British Cemetery, *Poperinge, West-Vlaanderen*
Anderson, Abner Adolph, Private
Harris, Fred, M.M., Sergeant. Alias. See Schmidt, the true family name.
Hughes, Edgar, Private
Hughes, Edward, Corporal
McIntyre, R., Lieutenant
McKibben, Robert Roy, Private
Miller, C.J., Private
Pask, Edmund, Private
Routledge, Robert, Private
Schmidt, Frederick Adolph, Sergeant
Silvester, A., Private
Simpson, Willard Perry, Private
Sutherland, Willard Perry, Private. Alias. See Simpson, the true family name.
Tressing, Martin Severin, Private
Walters, James Henry, Private

Oosttaverne Wood Cemetery, *Heuvelland, West-Vlaanderen*
- Alt, George Earl, Captain
- Banks, Archie, Private

Oxford Road Cemetery, *Ieper, West-Vlaanderen*
- Newson, Charles Reginald, Gunner
- Sibbald, James Laidlaw, Private

Passchendaele New British Cemetery, *Zonnebeke, West-Vlaanderen*
- Fleming, Robert Emmet, Private
- Hall, M.W., Private
- Herrington, Homer G., Private
- Kline, George Joseph, Private
- McQuaid, J.C., Private
- Parker, G., Private

Perth Cemetery (China Wall), *Ieper, West-Vlaanderen*
- Broadbelt, James Basil Fean, Private
- Sandreich, L., Corporal

Ploegsteert Memorial, *Comines-Warneton, Hainaut*
- Beddow, Maurice, Private
- Finch, George, Private
- Flintham, Joseph Harold, Rifleman
- Goodliffe, John Francis, Private
- Hobbs, William, Private
- Roberts, George Francis, Private
- Warrender, Andrew J., Sergeant

Poelcapelle British Cemetery, *Langemark-Poelkapelle, West-Vlaanderen*
- Liddell, George Kenley, Private
- Smith, Arthur V., Sergeant

Poperinghe New Military Cemetery, *Poperinge, West-Vlaanderen*
- Whiteside, Alexander Forrester, Captain

Poperinghe Old Military Cemetery, *Poperinge, West-Vlaanderen*
- Chivas, Edwin John, Private

Potijze Chateau Grounds Cemetery, *Ieper, West-Vlaanderen*
- Anderson, A., Private
- Douville, Charles George, Private
- Plummer, Alfred John, Gunner

Potijze Chateau Lawn Cemetery, *Ieper, West-Vlaanderen*
- Collins, Herbert James, Private

Potijze Chateau Wood Cemetery, *Ieper, West-Vlaanderen*
- Devlin, John, Private

Quievrain Communal Cemetery, *Quievrain, Hainaut*
- Fennelly, Thomas Francis, Private

Railway Dugouts Burial Ground, *Ieper, West-Vlaanderen*
- Ace, Bernard, Private
- Arnoldi, John Rodger, Gunner
- Berton, Mark Edward, Private
- Cruickshank, William, Private
- Girdner, John Charles Potter, Private
- Herdman, Loudoun Andrew, Private
- Hunter, Robert James Lake, Sergeant
- Layman, Louis, Lance Corporal
- McDowell, Bruce Campbell, Private
- McEntyre, James Monroe, Private
- Nicol, Ewen Cameron, Lieutenant
- Payne, Robert, Lance Corporal
- Stewart, Charles Walter, Major
- Stickland, Alfred Horace, Private
- Woodruff, B., Private

Ramscappelle Road Military Cemetery, *Nieuwpoort, West-Vlaanderen*
- Sawlor, Ray Haliburton, Lieutenant

R.E. Farm Cemetery, *Heuvelland, West-Vlaanderen*
- Hurlbert, R., Private
- Kish, Bert William, Private
- McEneaney, John Arthur, Private

Reninghelst New Military Cemetery, *Poperinge, West-Vlaanderen*
- Collier, Walter Henry Browne, Corporal
- Gorman, Thomas Clarence, Lieutenant
- Hurd, Roy, Gunner

Ridge Wood Military Cemetery, *Ieper, West-Vlaanderen*
- Burns, Thomas Curran, Sapper
- Clarke, Frank, Private
- Mundie, William, Private
- Wolfe, Fred, Private

St. Jean Communal Cemetery, *Kortrijk*
- Cowan, Thomas, Private

St. Quentin Cabaret Military Cemetery, *Heuvelland, West-Vlaanderen*
- MacMaster, William Graham, Lance Corporal
- Morris, Herbert Frank, Private
- Ross, Lorne, Private

Sanctuary Wood Cemetery, *Ieper, West-Vlaanderen*
- Sheppard, Kenneth Geoffrey, Lance Corporal

Strand Military Cemetery, *Comines-Warneton, Hainaut*
- Lewis, Edwin, Gunner

Tournai Communal Cemetery Allied Extension, *Tournai, Hainaut*
- Matteau, A., Private
- Niles, Henry Palmer, Driver
- Russell, Robert Francis, Second Lieutenant

Track "X" Cemetery, *Ieper, West-Vlaanderen*
- McPhee, J.A., Private
- Smith, Laurence Walter, Corporal

Tyne Cot Cemetery, *Zonnebeke, West-Vlaanderen*
- Billard, J., Private
- Brooker, H., Private
- Brown, Hulbert Percy, Private
- Canning, A.H., Lance Corporal
- Fisk, John Knowlton, Private
- Fitzgerald, E.P., Private
- Leslie, Frank, Private
- Martin, William, Private

McCrudden, J., Private
McLean, George Walter, Private
Ounsted, Alfred Judge, Private
Parker, W.C., Private
Pope, F.G., Corporal
Robbins, Mortimer Giberson, Private
Smith, D.E., Lieutenant
Smith, N.C., Lance Corporal
Woodcock, Frank Fremont, Lieutenant

Tyne Cot Memorial, Zonnebeke, West-Vlaanderen
Armstrong, Sidney William, Private
Briggs, Joe, Private
Buckell, Harold Claude, Captain
Cameron, John McGowan, Private
Chivers, Alfred Theodore, Rifleman
Copestake, Reuben, Private
Dowbekin, Harold, Sergeant
Doyle, John, Sergeant
Duffy, John, Sergeant
Heron, Thomas, Private
Hewitson, James, Private
Houghton, Frank, Rifleman
Inwood, Charles Hawkins, Second Lieutenant
Jowett, Wilson, Lance Corporal
La Coste, Charles John Constable, Captain
Lewis, David Morgan, Rifleman
Lewtas, Thomas, Sergeant
Lord, Hugh Cecil, Second Lieutenant
McBurnie, William, Sapper
Millar, Joseph, Private
Miller, George Edward, Private
Morrison, Hugh, Private
Russell, Ernest, Second Lieutenant
Schofield, Frank, Sapper
Smiley, Alexander, Corporal
Tee, Albert Edward, Second Lieutenant
Whitaker, William, Private
Wilson, Rupert Marcellious, Private

Valley Cottages Cemetery, Zillebeke
Nicol, Ewen, Lieutenant

Vlamertinghe Military Cemetery, Ieper, West-Vlaanderen
Chadwick, William Ellison, Gunner
Knapp, W.P., Gunner
Lamontagne, Alfred, Private

Vlamertinghe New Military Cemetery, Ieper, West-Vlaanderen
Coughlin, Kerwin Joseph, Gunner
Harrison, Homer Carbett, Private
MacPherson, Charles Kenneth, Lieutenant
Moyer, O.G., Gunner
Peter, N., Bombardier

Voormezeele Enclosure No. 1 and No. 2, Ieper, West-Vlaanderen
Looker, John Richard, Lance Corporal
Wilkie, J., Private

Voormezeele Enclosure No. 3, Ieper, West-Vlaanderen
Davie, George, Private
Holmes, H., Private
Jardine, John Joseph, Private
Meehan, James, Private

Wavre Communal Cemetery, Wavre, Brabant Wallon
Jamieson, H.C., Private

Westouter Churchyard and Extenstion, Heuvelland
Stevens, William, Gunner

White House Cemetery, St. Jean-les-Ypres, Ieper, West-Vlaanderen
Duplock, Harry Lewis, Private
Maher, Michael, Private
Smith, A.E., Private
Watson, Kenneth Baker, Private

Woods Cemetery, Ieper, West-Vlaanderen
France, Charles Henry, Private
Fraser, Joseph, Private
Lucas, William Harold, Private
Mullen, Robert, Private

Ypres (Menin Gate) Memorial, Ieper, West-Vlaanderen
Anderson, Oscar, Private
Baker, H.I., Private
Banks, Samuel, Private
Barry, Grover Cleveland, Private
Beauchesne, Arthur, Private
Bland, Wilfred Henry, Sapper
Booth, John William, Private
Bouffard, Frank, Lance Corporal
Bowron, Bertram, Private
Boyd, Robert Malcolm, Private
Brewster, William Everett, Private
Briggs, D.H., Lance Corporal
Brodie, Robert Watson, Private
Buxton, John, Private
Carson, George Hastings, Private
Cascadden, John Bryson, Lieutenant
Chapman, Willis Titus, Private
Charlton, Harold Ray, Lance Corporal
Clare, Joseph Henry, Private
Clark, Robert Benjamin, Corporal
Cleal, George Hugh, Private
Conley, Victor Herschel, Sergeant
Connelly, J., Private
Cunningham, Robert, Private
Currie, Edward Campbell, Private
Cutler, Albert, Sergeant
Daniels, Harry Hewitt, Private
Day, Calvin Wellington, Lieutenant
Dewitt, Ralph Edward, Private
Dobry, Louis Anthony, Private
Dochard, John, Private
Douglas, James, Private
Dunbar, Benjamin R., Private
Dunn, Thomas Louis, Private
Dwyer, S., Private
Eykel, William Alfred, Sergeant

Eykelbosch, Frank, Corporal
Fairweather, Charles White, Private
Fitzgerald, Creighton Dewey, Private
Fitzgerald, T.F., Private
Flanagan, Frank, Private
Fletcher, Herbert Harradon, Lance Corporal
Forman, Charles Ian, Corporal
Franklin, Joseph, Lance Corporal
Fraser, John, Lance Corporal
Freeland, Gordon Cameron, Corporal
Friesen, P.W., Private
Goodman, Albert Howard, Private
Graham, L., Private
Haggas, Walter, Private
Hall, A.B., Private
Hallimond, William John, Private
Hamilton, J.C., Private
Hanvey, Ernest, Private
Harbidge, A., Private
Hargrave, Charley Raymond, Private
Harper, MacDonald Francis, Private
Harris, Robert Whinry, Corporal
Harrison, J.F., Private
Haseler, Guy Broadfield, Lance Sergeant
Hass, Albert Fred, Private
Hass, Walter Theodor, Corporal
Hathaway, Carl L., Private
Hawkes, Silvester, Private
Healy, Michael J., Private
Henderson, William Fast, Private
Higgins, James Edward, Private
Hill, Arthur George, Private
Hill, Thomas, Private
Holt, George W., Private
Hughes, Edgar Franklin, Private
Hughes, Edward Samuel, Corporal
Hurry, William Forbes, Private
Jones, L.E., Private
Kaelin, Clarence Daniel, Private
Kiley, John Frank, Private
Kingrey, W.F., Private
Lasoff, S., Private
Lee, Harry R., Private
Lewis, Clifford Henry, Corporal
Lindop, Richard, Private
Lindsay, Peter, Lance Corporal
Little, T.J., Private
Littlewood, Benjamin, Lance Corporal
Lloyd, Osman Ernest Bernard, Private
Long, Thomas E., Private
MacLean, David Ritchie Williamson, Private
MacNeil, John Murdoch, Private
Madden, George Joseph, Sergeant
Mahon, Hugh, Private
Marchant, John Charles, Private
Marshall, Charles Arthur, Sergeant
Matheson, Murdock, Corporal
McArthur, Harry Carruthers, Private
McCleery, William Edward, Private

McColl, Alexander, Private
McCormick, William, Private
McCoy, Roy Lee, Private
McGrayne, George Harold, Private
McIlroy, John, Corporal
McLeod, Donald Henry, Private
McNeil, John, Private
Menard, Sydney Garnet, Private
Menoch, James, Private
Mermet, Henry, Private
Mesick, Andrew Emmett, Private
Methven, Charles, Private
Miller, Samuel Damam, Private
Mitchell, A., Private
Moore, Christopher James, Private
Morgan, Murry A., Private
Moughton, R.B., Private
Mullin, James Smith, Private
Neeson, E.J., Private
Neil, William Campbell, Sergeant
Nelson, E., Private
Nelson, F.A., Sergeant
Niblock, George Foster, Private
Nixon, Samuel J., Private
Northrup, Arthur Ward, Lance Corporal
Odell, William Henry, Private
Olafson, M.J., Private
Patterson, J.W., Private
Paul, James, Sergeant
Perkins, John Burton, Private
Perry, Marshall C., Private
Peterson, Bert Bengmana, Private
Phillips, Earle Merritt, Lance Corporal
Porter, E., Private
Quill, Daniel, Private
Rankin, Richard William, Company Sergeant Major
Rayner, Ernest Robert, Private
Richardson, Blaine, Private
Riddler, James, Private
Rippengale, George, Private
Robson, Matthew Northup, Private
Rushton, Oscar Eugene, Corporal
Russell, Henry Morton Stanley, Sergeant
Sarff, C., Private
Seitsinger, Roy Everette, Private
Sellwood, Herbert, Private
Shoemaker, Joseph Vernier, Private
Simpson, Joseph Carr, Private
Smith, Homer Emmett, Private
Smoker, William, Private
Soberg, Oscar Gustav, Private
Sornberger, Hollis Harris, Private
Spence, Charles Edward, Private
Stephens, W.J., Private
Stevens, Arthur Tyrie, Private
Stewart, William, Private
Stewart, William David, Private
Stoddart, William Arthur, Private

Stokes, Roy George Edward, Private
Suggitt, Francis William, Private
Sullivan, Edward Patrick, Private
Sullivan, James Raphael, Private
Sussemilch, Herbert, Corporal
Swendson, Harry, Lieutenant
Tautz, Lionel John, Private
Taylor, A.H., Private
Tetrault, Joseph Napoleon Adelard, Private
Thomas, Thomas Otway, Private
Thornton, H., Private
Tipples, John, Corporal
Todd, G., Private
Tomory, Alexander Kay, Lance Corporal
Trask, Roscoe Vaughn, Private
Turner, Harry, Private
Wallberg, Martin Tore, Private
Welby, Harry Joseph, Private
Wesson, Arthur Monroe, Private
Wheeler, Edward, Private
White, Joseph Francis Exavier, Private
Wootton, William Osborne, Sapper
Wymond, George Joseph, Private

Ypres Reservoir Cemetery, Ieper, West-Vlaanderen
Berriff, Bruce, Sergeant
Currin, William, Bombardier
Deibert, Martin Mark, Gunner
Merrill, Wainwright, Gunner
Porter, Frederick Charles, Sapper

Zantvoorde British Cemetery, Zonnebeke, West-Vlaanderen
Parsons, Arthur William, Private
Williams, Charles, Private

CANADA

Avondale Cemetery, New Brunswick
Sherwood, Fred W., Corporal

Beamsville (Mount Osborne) Cemetery, Ontario
Hannam, Maurice Rudolph, Private

Blairmore Union Cemetery, Alberta
Olsen, Oscar N., Private

Bocabec Cemetery, New Brunswick
Thomas, Hazen H., Private

Brampton Cemetery, Ontario, Ontario
McCormack, B.P., Private

Brandon Cemetery, Manitoba, Manitoba
Cartwright, George, Private

Brockville (Oakland) Cemetery, Ontario
Anderson, Alex F., Sapper

Burlington (Holy Sepulchre) Cemetery, Ontario
Rostan, Ignatius, Private

Calgary Union Cemetery, Alberta
Allison, Albert A., Corporal
Lovejoy, Alfred, Private
McCuistion, Thomas, Private
Moorhead, A., Private

Cambridge (Mount View) Cemetery, Ontario
Richardson, Richard Stanley, Private

Camp Hughes Cemetery, Manitoba
Barringer, Walter, Private

Canterbury Union Cemetery, York County, New Brunswick
Bickford, Shirley, Private

Castleton Protestant Cemetery, Ontario
Hart, Riley Allen, Private

Chatham (Maple Leaf) Cemetery, Ontario
Holloway, Hubert J., Chief Petty Officer

Cobourg (St. Michael's) Cemetery, Ontario
Cullen, John J., Gunner

Dartmouth (Christ Church) Cemetery, Nova Scotia
Wright, Alan, Private

Eastend (Riverside) Cemetery, Saskatchewan
Fowler, Morris W., Sapper

Edmonton Cemetery, Alberta
Parkes, Arthur Regan, Private

Edmonton (Mount Pleasant) Cemetery, Alberta
Mattson, Charles, Sapper

Edmonton St. Joachim's Roman Catholic Cemetery, Alberta
Reynolds, Fred A., Private

Elma United Church Cemetery, Ontario
Bowman, Charles E., Private

Enfield (St. Bernard's) Cemetery, Nova Scotia
Dwyer, William J., Private

Esquimalt (Veterans') Cemetery, British Columbia
Evans, Henry I., Boy

Fenaghvale (St. Paul's) Cemetery, Ontario
Eaton, Daniel L., Private

Fort Erie (Spears) Cemetery, Ontario
Trice, Gerald A., Private

Fort MacLeod (Union) Cemetery, Alberta
Rhodes, Frederick P., Private

Fredericton Rural Cemetery, New Brunswick
Booker, Delancy, Sapper

Glace Bay (Greenwood) Cemetery, Nova Scotia
Peck, August, Gunner

Granum Cemetery, Alberta
Sammons, Frederick O., Private

Haileybury (Mount Pleasant) Cemetery, Ontario
Croft, Enos Lewis, Private

Halifax (Camp Hill) Cemetery, Nova Scotia
Jackson, Charles W., Private

Halifax (Fairview Lawn) Cemetery, Nova Scotia
Bayers, Louis, Private

Halifax (Fort Massey) Cemetery, Nova Scotia
Lawrence, Fred, Private

Halifax (Mount Olivet) Cemetery, Nova Scotia
Brommitt, George William, Corporal
Hutt, Stanley, Lance Corporal
Malone, John Thomas, Captain

Halifax (St. John's) Cemetery, Nova Scotia
Gibson, John, Corporal

Halifax Memorial, Nova Scotia
  Birmingham, Lorne John, Private
  Cross, J.H., Private
  Farrow, James Graham, Second Mate
  Jackson, William, Corporal
  Jones, Norman, Private
  Jones, Thomas Wheeler, Corporal
  Kitchin, A., Sapper
  Milton, Eddie Thomas, Private
  Newburn, George Monroe, Private
  Ryman, Walter, Private
  Sanderson, R.A., Private
  Skeldon, H., Ordinary Seaman
  Spittal, John, Private
  Tolton, H.B., Private
  Williams, Robert, Private

Hamilton Cemetery, Ontario
  Fletcher, Joseph F., Gunner
  Hinkle, Marion Walter, Corporal
  Smith, Frank L., Private

Kamloops (Pleasant Street) Cemetery, British Columbia
  Ives, Ernest Edward Victor, Quartermaster Sergeant

Kentville (Oak Grove) Cemetery, Nova Scotia
  Thorburn, Wilfred, Private

Kingston (Cataraqui) Cemetery, Ontario
  Harrison, William, Private
  Soltau, Cecil Henry, Sapper

Kingston (St. Mary's) Cemetery, Ontario
  MacDonald, James, Private
  Williams, Kenneth Fenwick, Captain

Kitchener (Mount Hope) Cemetery, Ontario
  Huber, Harry, Private

London (Mount Pleasant) Cemetery, Ontario
  Davies, William Thomas, Private
  Ekstrom, Ernest Sune, Sergeant
  Heald, H., Private
  Mabee, Oliver Roy, Private
  Stanton, Herbert Le Roy, Sapper

London (St. Peter's) Roman Catholic Cemetery, Ontario
  Gibbons, Redmond Joseph, Sapper
  House, Leonard Grant, Private
  Olech, Kasmir, Private

London (Woodland) Cemetery, Ontario
  Taylor, Harry, Private

Medicine Hat (Hillside) Cemetery, Alberta
  Brown, Murdock McDonald, Corporal
  O'Hare, John Thomas, Private

Miami Cemetery, Manitoba
  Wagner, Hugh Christopher, Corporal

Montreal (Mount Royal) Cemetery, Quebec
  Doull, John, Lieutenant Colonel
  Knipe, Leslie Albert, Gunner
  Koehler, William M., Sapper
  Palmer, Alfred D., Lance Corporal
  Roby, Dean, Sapper
  Sage, George, Lieutenant
  Stewart, Irvine, Private
  Sumner, E. Ralph, Cadet
  Watson, William, Private

Montreal (Notre Dame Des Neiges) Cemetery, Quebec
  Aubry, J.H., Lieutenant
  Boulanger, Alfred, Private
  Kelliher, M.J., Private
  Roach, John David, Private
  Walry, Charles, Corporal

Montreal (Hawthorn-Dale) Cemetery, Quebec
  Brown, James Elbert, Sapper
  Williams, George, Private

Morden (Hillside) Cemetery, Manitoba
  Howell, James, Private

Murray River Cemetery, Prince Edward Island
  Bears, George A., Private

Niagara Falls (Drummond Hill) Cemetery, Ontario
  Banks, Robert W., Private

Niagara-on-the-Lake United Church Cemetery, Ontario
  Nisbet, Walter L., Private

North Battleford Cemetery, Saskatchewan
  Griffin, William P., Private

Oshawa Union Cemetery, Ontario
  Moore, Harry, Private

Ottawa (Beechwood) Cemetery, Ontario
  Arnoldi, Ernest Clifton, Lieutenant Colonel
  Atchison, George M., Honorary Captain
  Black, Fergus N., Lieutenant
  Macaulay, George M., Private
  Pelusio, Dominic A., Sergeant
  Steele, Eric C.G., Corporal

Ottawa (Notre Dame) Roman Catholic Cemetery, Ontario
  McLeod, Kenneth Wallace, Sapper
  Poirier, P., Private

Paradise Public Cemetery, Nova Scotia
  Balcom, Harold C., Lieutenant

Picton (Glenwood) Cemetery, Ontario
  Hill, William F., Sapper

Quebec City (Mount Hermon) Cemetery, Quebec
  Dwire, George, Private
  Iler, Eugene P., Private
  Moore, Charles Joseph, Private

The Quebec Memorial, Pointe Claire Field of Honour, Quebec
  Froment, Leo, Sergeant
  Marcotte, Edmond, Private

Robsart General Cemetery, Saskatchewan
  Peterson, Howard L., Private

Sackville Rural Cemetery, New Brunswick
  McCord, George Rankin, Lieutenant

St. John (Fernhill) Cemetery, Saint John County, New Brunswick
   Hall, Ralph Quinton, Private

St. John (St. Joseph's) Roman Catholic Cemetery, Saint John County, New Brunswick
   Whipple, Walter J., Driver

St. Peter's (Catholic) Cemetery, Nova Scotia
   MacDonald, George J., Stoker 1st Class

St. Thomas Cemetery, Elgin County, Ontario
   Cornwall, Ryheo M., Private

Sarnia (Lake View) Cemetery, Ontario
   Simmons, Sylvester Earl, Private

Saskatoon (Woodlawn) Cemetery, Saskatchewan
   Moore, John W., Private

Sherbrooke (St. Peter's) Church Cemetery, Quebec
   Kennison, Francis E., Private

Smith's Falls (Hillcrest) Cemetery, Ontario
   Fox, Thomas F., Private

South Brookfield Protestant Cemetery, Nova Scotia
   Spears, James, Private

Stratford (Avondale) Cemetery, Ontario
   Wenzel, Valentine Stanley, Private

Sydney (Hardwood Hill) Cemetery, Nova Scotia
   Lake, Geoffrey, Lieutenant

Thunder Bay (Riverside) Cemetery, Ontario
   Flynn, James William, Private

Toronto (Mount Hope) Cemetery, Ontario
   Clairmont, Charles David, Gunner
   Healey, John, Private
   Nolan, J.F., Private

Toronto (Mount Pleasant) Cemetery, Ontario
   Dickson, John S., Sapper
   Gregory, James, Sergeant
   Mills, Arthur, Private
   Read, Walter Douglas, Lieutenant
   Touchard, Gustave F., Lieutenant

Toronto Necropolis, Ontario
   Caldwell, Gavin Allen, Air Mechanic 3rd Class
   Russell, Francis J., Private
   White, Augustus, Air Mechanic 3rd Class

Toronto (Park Lawn) Cemetery, Ontario
   Tugman, Ernest, Gunner

Toronto (Prospect) Cemetery, Ontario
   Bloomer, Frederick Boaz, Private
   Clarke, John Walter, Private
   Davidson, Robert Francis, Captain
   Drynan, John, Private
   Hazel, Victor, Private
   Jarvis, Charles, Private
   Louden, Albert, Private
   Oldham, Charles O., Private
   Ross, Charles A., Private
   Sheppard, Frederick, Airman 2nd Class
   Sim, George, Private
   Teck, Peter, Private
   Trevelyan, William, Lieutenant

Toronto (St. John's Norway) Cemetery, Ontario
   Butler, William, Chief Petty Officer
   Chalmers, Donald Bartlette, Private
   Denning, William J., Private
   Mikels, Robert Jacob, Private
   Rolph, Francis, Corporal
   Roy, Stanley, Sergeant
   Schofield, Harry, Private

Toronto (St. Michael's) Roman Catholic Cemetery, Ontario
   Routh, John Cecil, Sapper

Upton (St. Ephrem) Cemetery, Quebec
   Gauthier, Gabriel, Private

Vancouver (Mountain View) Cemetery, British Columbia
   Bailey, Joseph W., Sergeant
   Boot, Edward, Private
   Brown, Frederick A., Sapper
   Chappel, Ernest Clausin, Company Sergeant Major
   Davis, George Allen, Sapper
   Davis, Thomas Edward, Corporal
   Duncan, James C., Private
   Edgecumbe, Sidney R., Private
   Gillissie, Harold G., Captain
   Hughes, Edward Blair, Private
   James, Carl, Private
   Joyal, Eli Felix, Private
   Marpole, Clarence Mawson, Captain
   McArthur, Robert A., Private
   McLean, Daniel H., Lieutenant
   Pitchford, Steven, Private
   Quinton, Edward, Private
   Roche, Charles W., Private
   Rollins, William A., Private
   Tanner, Thomas, Private
   Thomas, William, Sapper
   Thurnham, William Herbert, Sapper
   Western, Gordon Richard, Gunner

Victoria (Ross Bay) Cemetery, British Columbia
   Bowman, Carl Welch, Lieutenant
   Hamilton, James, Private
   Johnston, Clarence Burdett, Petty Officer
   Langille, Edwin R., Private
   Leary, Arthur James, Gunner
   Lismore, Joseph H., Sergeant

Walkerton Cemetery, Ontario
   Rowand, Elmer McLeod, Lieutenant

Waterford (Greenwood) Cemetery, Ontario
   Hayward, Lloyd Stanley Castle, Private

Weston (Riverside) Cemetery, Ontario
   Foster, James, Private

Windsor (Grove) Cemetery, Ontario
   Campbell, Neil Patterson, Corporal

Winnipeg (Brookside) Cemetery, Manitoba
   Brown, Harry, Private
   Cameron, Duncan Lochiel, Private
   Christie, Robert Ross T., Private

Davison, Robert Edward, Sergeant
Dolstrom, Arthur, Private
Govett, Archie, Sapper
Hall, John Courtney Stewart, Private
Kelson, Oscar L., Lance Corporal
King, William, Private
Lowe, Robert, Private
Myers, John Allan, Private
Nicol, John, Corporal
Paget, Alfred, Sergeant
Pollock, Frank Ernest, Private
Saunders, Albert C., Private
Wambolt, Willard, Gunner
Winnipeg (St. Mary's) Cemetery, Manitoba
Lawler, Harry John, Sapper
Parant, Henry Joseph, Private
Patenaude, Napoleon, Private
Rousseau, Louis C., Corporal
Winnipeg (St. James) Cemetery, Manitoba
Moffatt, Athol W., Corporal
Woodstock Methodist Cemetery, New Brunswick
Hull, Wendell Philippe, Sapper
Jacques, Frederick (Fred) Willit, Sergeant
Yarmouth (Mountain) Cemetery, Nova Scotia
Matheson, Charles B., Private

EGYPT

Alexandria (Chatby) Military and War Memorial Cemetery
Newton, Howard, Private
Alexandria (Hadra) War Memorial Cemetery
Kenison, W.G., Private
O'Connor, James, Private
Cairo War Memorial Cemetery
Curtis-Beals, Harry, Second Lieutenant
Matthews, Norman, Driver
Kantara War Memorial Cemetery
Knight, A.H., Private
Lowe, Thomas Percy, Lance Corporal
Sant, Secretary, William Webster
Suez War Memorial Cemetery
Ansbacher, Cyril Louis, Private

FRANCE

Abbeville Communal Cemetery Extension, Somme
Barrett, Leland Kelly Willson, Lieutenant
Hill, J., Private
Lauthers, R., Private
Miller, Gerald, Private
Achicourt Road Cemetery, Achicourt, Pas-de-Calais
Berry, Alfred, Private
Mehring, Rudolph Edwin, Private
Swalles, Arthur Garfield, Private
Achiet-le-Grand Communal Cemetery Extension, Pas-de-Calais
Stanbury, Sidney, Private
Adanac Military Cemetery, Miraumont, Somme
Allen, George, Private

Burdett, Harold Bellamy, Private
Dalzell, R., Private
Hodges, Dudley Howar, Private
Mason, Dorr Lawrence, Private
Ounsted, Paul Frederick, Private
Prax, William, aka Edward Bergen, Private
Renaud, A., Private
Smith, Adon, Private
Sprang, G., Private
Stewart, A.M.W., Private
Agny Military Cemetery, Pas-de-Calais
Corriveau, Joseph William, Private
Germon, Thomas Alexander, Private
Hill, Edgar Harrison, Sergeant
Keast, Wilfred E., Corporal
McDowell, A., Private
McVey, Paul Rutherford, Private
Munro, Harry, Private
Payne, W.J., Driver
Prummer, George Henry, Private
Sewell, Guy Blanchard, Private
Stott, Charlie Henry, Private
Weir, Elgin Frederick, Private
A.I.F. Burial Ground, Flers, Somme
Marr, E., Corporal
McEvoy, Owen, Private
Mildon, B., Private
Tiernan, John Edward, Lance Corporal
Aizecourt-le-Bas Churchyard, Somme
Garlick, Frank Arthur, Second Lieutenant
Albert Communal Cemetery Extension, Somme
Connell, Patrick Joseph, Bombardier
Robertson, Clarence Lewis, Sergeant
Trafford, Albert Clive, Corporal
Wood, R.F., Private
Albuera Cemetery, Bailleul-Sire-Berthoult, Pas-de-Calais
Anderson, J.E., Gunner
Alencon (St. Leonard) Cemetery, Orne
Desrosiers, Oscar, served as Miller, Private
Anneux British Cemetery, Nord
Alward, Wilfrid Forsyth, Private
Amelin, Joseph Samuel, Private
Cartwright, William Baden, Private
Goodwin, Harper, Private
Hendry, John, Private
Lickley, Christian White, Private
Linthwaite, James Ernest, Sergeant
McIntyre, Robert, Private
McKinnon, John Alexander, Sergeant
Reid, Charles, Private
Tolemy, James, Private
Anzin-St. Aubin British Cemetery, Pas-de-Calais
Acre, B.E., 2nd Corporal
Bevan, Thomas Haydn, Sapper
Gordon, George, Private
Haines, R.G., Private
Holwick, Wilford Quayle, Private

Laing, Edward George, Gunner
Morgan, Michael John, Private
Penney, Sidney Stephen, Private
Prince, Thaddeus, Private
Proctor, F.G., Driver
Webster, John Henry, Private

Arneke British Cemetery, *Nord*
Irvine, John, Driver

Arras Flying Services Memorial, *Pas-de-Calais*
Bradley, Harold Bartlett, Lieutenant
Crane, John Wilbur, Captain
Dore, William Henry, Captain
Ferguson, John Shannon, Second Lieutenant
Griggs, Albert, Lieutenant
Irvine, Van Reusselaer Van Tassel, Lieutenant
Johnson, Roland Walker, Second Lieutenant
Korslund, Mils Franklin, Lieutenant
Owen, William Thomas, Lieutenant
Taylor, Edgar, Lieutenant

Arras Memorial, *Pas-de-Calais*
Ariza, Francisco A., Private
Coutts, Alexander, Private
Drew, Albert Jeremiah, Rifleman
Eckersley, Ernest, Private
Greene, Quincy Shaw, Captain
Holloway, William Alma, Corporal
MacLennan, John Alexander, Gunner
Maude, Shepherd, Corporal
Mechan, William, Private
Miller, William Brown, Private
Milton, Peter Ewing, Company Sergeant Major
Morrison, John Edward, Private
Murray, Alister Ian, Lance Corporal
Payne, Thomas, Lance Corporal
Rabbinovitz, Barnett, Rifleman
Riley, Clifford, Rifleman
Smith, Job, Private
Walker, Ernest Edward, Private
Whear, Ralph Morton, Private
Wiles, Sidney, Private
Woulfe, Patrick, Private

Athies Communal Cemetery Extension, *Pas-de-Calais*
Conley, Thomas, Private

Auberchicourt British Cemetery, *Nord*
Brown, Charles W., Private
Ferguson, D.A., Private
Otis, K.R., Sapper
Smith, Irving S., Private

Aubigny Communal Cemetery Extension, *Pas-de-Calais*
Birt, Howard Oscar, Private
Brown, W.J., Private
Dinning, A., Private
Fountain, Thomas, Private
Goodrich, Frank Edward, Captain
Hackworth, Edward Clayborn, Private
Henderson, Andrew, Private
Imrie, Everard Bell, Private
MacDonald, Temple William Faber, Major
McConaughy, Erwin, Private
McEvoy, Frank Richard, Private
McManus, John James, Private
Mooney, George Edmund, Private
Morley, Francis Lehman, Private
Munslow, Stanley, Private
Parsons, Walter Hawkins, Private
Pountney, W.A., Private
Pryke, Herbert Charles, Private
Robinson, William, Private
Sabean, A.C., Private
Sigsworth, E.A., Private
Stafford, Gordon Morcom, Private
Walker, Harry, Private

Auchonvillers Military Cemetery, *Somme*
Hertslet, Harold Cecil, Second Lieutenant
Knight, William, Private

Aulnoy Communal Cemetery, *Nord*
Anderson, N., Private
Bray, W.C., Private
Dunleavy, John, Private
Dunlop, Harry, M.C., Captain
Fawkes, R., Private
Montgomery, William Augustine, Lieutenant
Smith, W.J., Private
Stoney, George Francis, Private
Youngberg, C.F., Private

Authuile Military Cemetery, *Somme*
Curry, H., Private
Wood, James, Private

Aveluy Communal Cemetery Extension, *Somme*
Shaw, Edward Lockhart, Second Lieutenant

Avesnes-le-Comte Communal Cemetery Extension, *Pas-de-Calais*
Coxon, William Lawton, Private

Awoingt British Cemetery, *Nord*
Langdell, George Warren, Private

Bac-du-Sud British Cemetery, Bailleulval, *Pas-de-Calais*
Burns, Leo Fitzmaurice, Private
Gibbons, Arthur Burnham, Lance Corporal
Goldsbrough, Joseph, Private
Murray, Robert Thomas, Private

Bailleul Communal Cemetery (Nord), *Nord*
Godby, Howell Ashbridge, Private
Travis, Herbert Gordon, Private

Bailleul Communal Cemetery Extension (Nord), *Nord*
Blades, R., Private
Drake, G.N., Private
Hetherington, Joseph, Private
May, James, Corporal
Reeves, Frank Gilmore, Private
Smith, Robert Sherman, Private
Van Vatta, Walter, Private
Watkins, Charles, Private

Bailleul Road East Cemetery, St. Laurent-Blangy, *Pas-de-Calais*
Inkster, Andrew James, Lance Corporal

Bapaume Australian Cemetery, *Pas-de-Calais*
Donald, William Austin, Private

Bapaume Post Military Cemetery, Albert, *Somme*
Dixon, E.L., Private

La Baraque British Cemetery, Bellenglise, *Aisne*
Lee, James, Sergeant

Les Baraques Military Cemetery, Sangatte, *Pas-de-Calais*
Johnson, William M., Private

Barlin Communal Cemetery Extension, *Pas-de-Calais*
Butler, Harry Charles, Private
Carley, Samuel Williscraft, Private
Eisenmann, William Christian, Private
Farmer, J. (served as Kirby), Private
Ficht, Herbert Richard, Private
Hillsgrove, Ned Clifton, Private
Homan, Roscoe Earl, Private
Jackson, Norman, Lance Corporal
Plants, Gerald Pembroke, Private
Ray, Arnold O., Private
Rhode, Rolf Viking, Lance Corporal
Swalley, Ralph W., Private
Welsh, John, Sergeant

Barly French Military Cemetery, *Pas-de-Calais*
Brennan, Joseph, Private

Bazentin-le-Petit Communal Cemetery Extension, *Somme*
Daffin, Frederick Charles, Private

Beacon Cemetery, Sailly-Laurette, *Somme*
Taylor, William Edward, Lieutenant

Beaucourt British Cemetery, *Somme*
Bruce, W.J., Private
Dodson, George H., Private
Dunn, Alfred, Private
Lemons, Leon J., served as Beaman, Private
Wright, Daniel Uttley, Lieutenant

Beaumont-Hamel (Newfoundland) Memorial, *Somme*
Blundon, Allen, Leading Seaman
Moss, Daniel, Private

Beauval Communal Cemetery, *Somme*
Thaanum, James Conrad, Second Lieutenant

Becourt Military Cemetery, Becordel-Becourt, *Somme*
Kyle, Austin Carlton, Gunner
Rowell, R., Fitter Staff Sergeant

Beehive Cemetery, Willerval, *Pas-de-Calais*
Desmarais, Joseph, Sergeant
Young, Walter, Private

Bellacourt Military Cemetery, Riviere, *Pas-de-Calais*
Bechtol, Charles Ray, Private
Du Val, Edward William, Lieutenant

Farrar, Percy Earl, Private
Garson, Frederick Hamilton, Gunner
Hannemann, Lionel, Private
Harding, Alexander Claud, Lance Corporal
Hillis, Roger Whitman, Private
Houghton, Frank Wentworth, Private
Larsen, Walter Oswald, Private
McAuliffe, W., Corporal
Scroggie, William H., Lance Corporal

Bellicourt British Cemetery, *Aisne*
Keith, G.T., Private
Simpson, James Wallace, Corporal
Wild, Basil Warren, Lieutenant

Berlaimont Communal Cemetery Extension, *Nord*
O'Donoghue, James, Second Lieutenant

Berles-au-Bois Churchyard Extension, *Pas-de-Calais*
Baker, Archibald John, Private

Bertangles Communal Cemetery, *Somme*
Miller, James Arthur, Second Lieutenant

Bethune Town Cemetery, *Pas-de-Calais*
Jones, P., Private
Mills, John Robert, Private

Beuvry Communal Cemetery, *Pas-de-Calais*
Clark, Charles Loaring, Lieutenant

Beuvry Communal Cemetery Extension, *Pas-de-Calais*
Honey, W.C., Private

Bienvillers Military Cemetery, *Pas-de-Calais*
Beattie, J., Gunner
Gordon, Frederick, Gunner
Norcott, F.B., Gunner
Warner, Frederick Stephen, Corporal

Biganos Communal Cemetery, *Gironde*
Gloster, Sylvester Earle, Private

Blighty Valley Cemetery, Authuile Wood, *Somme*
King, Harry, Captain

Bois-Carre British Cemetery, Thelus, *Pas-de-Calais*
Bow, Clifton Raymond, Private
Jost, Charles Leonard, Private
MacArthur, Arnold Gordon, Private
Morris, Robert, Private
Ross, Leland Stanford, Private
Storey, Creighton R., Private

Bois-Carre Military Cemetery, Haisnes, *Pas-de-Calais*
Coyne, Mark, Private

Bois Guillaume Communal Cemetery, *Seine-Maritime*
Higson, Peter, Private
Sang, Alfred Frederick Joseph, Second Lieutenant
Taylor, Tom, Private

Bouchoir New British Cemetery, *Somme*
Bencraft, Walter Luxton, Private
Foster, W.C., Private
Irving, Archibald, Lance Sergeant

Jauvin, Edward, Private
Kenney, Fredrick M., Private
King, Robert Pollock, Private
Pascoe, A., Private

Boulogne Eastern Cemetery, Pas-de-Calais
Burtch, Homer Pearson, Private
Campbell, George, Private
Guimond, Aurele, Private
Harwood, William, Corporal
Meats, George Henry, Sapper
Nicodemus, Howard, Private
Pickup, W.R.W., Gunner
Pratt, Joseph Burt, Private
Robertson, Charles Gilbert, Private
Smith, Ernest, Private
West, Edward, Private
Whalley, Robert, Private

Bourlon Wood Cemetery, Pas-de-Calais
Arsenault, W., Private
Austin, T., Corporal
Clow, C., Sergeant
Edwards, Dana Dennis, Private
Farrant, E., Private
Ferris, R., Private
Hahn, H., Private
Horsbrugh, Bernard Bethune, Sapper
Kelley, F.J., Lance Corporal

Boves East Communal Cemetery, Somme
Blick, Robert, Private

Boves West Communal Cemetery Extension, Somme
Hughes, W., Farrier Sergeant

Brebieres British Cemetery, Pas-de-Calais
Squires, Frank, Private

Brewery Orchard Cemetery, Bois-Grenier, Nord
Brown, Charles Thomas, Corporal
Tindall, Fredrick, Private

Bronfay Farm Military Cemetery, Bray-sur-Somme, Somme
Wilson, Albert, Gunner

Brown's Copse Cemetery, Roeux, Pas-de-Calais
Allardice, Elihu Sutton, Private
Johnstone, J., Private
Merritt, Frederick Gerald, Private

Brown's Road Military Cemetery, Festubert, Pas-de-Calais
Livingstone, Samuel, Private

Bruay Communal Cemetery Extension, Pas-de-Calais
Harding, William, Private
Hopley, Frederick Joseph, Private
McMillan, Peter Roy, Corporal
Miller, Harry, Private
Rabidue, Willie, Private
Sias, John Francis, Private

Bruay-sur-l'Escaut Communal Cemetery, Nord
Ferris, Howard Robert, Sapper

Bucquoy Road Cemetery, Ficheux, Pas-de-Calais
Black, Robert, Private
Boyle, F.H., Private
Brown, Wilbur Wells, Private
Clark, R., Private
Collins, Maurice Joseph, Private
Good, Herbert James, Private
Green, Roy Leslie, Corporal
Greig, Roderick Douglas, Private
Knight, W.A., Private
Lawson, Gordon, Private
Lightfoot, Charles Murray, Private
MacMillan, Alexander, Lance Sergeant
Massey, Francis Xavier, Private
McCance, John, Private
McEwen, George Arthur, Gunner
Murphy, David Patrick, Private
Noonan, T., Private
Olsen, Frank Theodore, Private
Owings, Samuel Franklin, Private
Pattison, Hugh MacMillan, Lieutenant
Poling, R.V., Private
Rawlins, Harry Parker, Private
Singer, Maurice, Private
Smith, Charles, Private
Swenson, August Waldemar, Private
Swift, William Joshua Greenwood, Private
Thomson, Arthur, Private
White, Vance Smith, Private
Wylie, B., Private

Bully-Grenay Communal Cemetery, British Extension, Pas-de-Calais
Anson, P.A., Private
Hamilton, H.J., Gunner
Hughes, G.A., Lance Corporal
Jones, H.G., Gunner
Knight, George Pine, Private
McKinley, John Herbert, Corporal

Busigny Communal Cemetery Extension, Nord
Daley, Frank, Sapper

Cabaret-Rouge British Cemetery, Souchez, Pas-de-Calais
Bigelow, Braxton, Captain
Boehn, George, Private
Brown, John Stevenson, Private
Clarkin, James Edward, Driver
Curtis, R.B., Private
Gellatly, John Gibb, Private
Hill, Frederick, Private
Lewis, Henry Francis, Lieutenant
Linnell, William, Private
McLeod, A.G., Private
Micks, Davidson Device, Private
Murray, James Sanford, Pioneer
Raymond, Charles Thomas, Private
Reuss, H.H., Private
Ryder, Harold Charles Smedley, Lance Corporal
Taylor, S.H., Private

Vokes, Sidney Vincent, Sergeant
Waters, Harold Percival, Lance Corporal
Winnington, Stanley George, Private

Caix British Cemetery, Somme
Dewar, Gordon William, Sergeant
Doyle, Robert M., Private
Gorman, George Lionel, Gunner
Helmer, Elton Williams, Lieutenant
Laue, Leroy Frank, Private
Lawton, T.C., Private
Mitchell, D., Private
Plato, Major Jason, Private
Power, Edward Victor, Lieutenant
Scott, J.G., Private
Young, Noel, Private

Calais Southern Cemetery, Pas-de-Calais
Ingram, Zeb Vance, Private
Nelson, John Howard, Private

Cambrai East Military Cemetery, Nord
Goodstein, Joseph, Private
McGill, T., Private
Patterson, Colin, Gunner

Cambrai Memorial, Louverval, Nord
Hartley, Charles Fletcher, Second Lieutenant
Knock, George, Private
Lamprell, Harold, Private
McDowell, John, Lance Corporal
Penny, James, Sapper
Simpson, Percy, Lance Sergeant
Thomas, Cyril Gwynne, Private

Cambrin Churchyard Extension, Pas-de-Calais
Lewis, Wilfred John, Lance Corporal
Russell, W., Lance Corporal

Canada Cemetery, Tilloy-les-Cambrai, Nord
Davies, Ernest Clifford, Private
Eyre, Joseph, Lance Sergeant
Haugen, Tean Andrew, Private
Lunn, Robert, Private
Mansfield, Richard Robert, Private
Nelson, J., Lance Corporal
Pick, Cecil Harding, Private
Robinson, R.W., Private
Thomson, James, Private
Watkinson, Wilfred, Private
Wright, Walter Horace, Private

Canadian Cemetery No. 2, Neuville-St. Vaast, Pas-de-Calais
Boucher, Joseph Arthur, Private
Crozier, Herbert Thomas, Lance Corporal
Duncan, George Smith, Private
Humble, Fred, Lance Sergeant
Lyle, Harry, Private
McDonald, Mark, Private
McQuoid, Allen Frederick, Private
Swan, Leonard, Private
Veinotte, Baxter Harris, Private

Cantimpre Canadian Cemetery, Sailly, Nord
Brignell, George Sidney, Private
Caldwell, Clarence James, Private
Chapman, William, Private
Copeland, K.A., Private
Daly, Raymond, Private
French, W.R., Private
Gorham, G.C., Private
Graham, G.H., Private
Grant, Lewis Edward, Private
Grimm, John Seaton, Private
Kingston, Joseph, Private
MacIldowie, James, Private
MacKinnon, James Fabyean, Private
Mooney, James, Private
Noble, James, Private
Preddy, Lewellyn Thompson Pearson, Lance Sergeant
Sandy, Frederick Gayland, Private
Wilmot-Gilbert, Norman Francis, Private
Wright, Ernest Albert, Private

Carnieres Communal Cemetery Extension, Nord
Thomson, Norman Drummond, Private

Carnoy Military Cemetery, Somme
Kemble, Henry Noel, Captain
Wilson, G., Private

Le Cateau Military Cemetery, Nord
Martin, Samuel de Witt, Corporal

Cerisy-Gailly Military Cemetery, Somme
Batt, Francis Joseph, Lieutenant
Pascoe, Edward Bonsal, Private

Chambieres French National Cemetery, Metz, Moselle
Chapin, Elliot Adam, Lieutenant

Chapel Corner Cemetery, Sauchy-Lestree, Pas-de-Calais
Jenkins, William, Private

Charmes Military Cemetery, Essegney, Vosges
Boyd, Henry, Lieutenant
Butcher, Ernest, Private

La Chaudiere Military Cemetery, Vimy, Pas-de-Calais
Andrick, I.C., Private
Boles, David E., Private
Carlson, Clarence, Private
Coddington, Arthur Dudley, Private
Endress, Richard Fuller, Lance Corporal
Good, William James, Private
Gowler, William F., Private
Gurling, S.R., Private
Heal, Daniel, Private
Howe, N.C., Private
Kerr, David, Sergeant
Lake, Arthur Roy, Private
Leland, Clifford Merton, Private
Mitchell, Donald McLean, Private
Monroe, E.E., Lance Corporal
Mosher, Metz Matthew, Private
Schnack, T., Private

Shelters, Earl Arthur, Private
Taberner, William Henry, Private
Webb, Oscar Smith, Private
Whiting, Jack, Private
Wire, Willard Densmore, Private
Yakes, Charles, Lance Corporal

Chocques Military Cemetery, Pas-de-Calais
Devlin, John Edward, Private
Illingworth, Henry, Gunner
Reed, Ray Ralph, Private
Sheridan, Philip T., Private
Tritschler, H.J., Private
Wilson, R., Private

Cite Bonjean Military Cemetery, Armentieres, Nord
Beaver, J., Private
Irish, Howard Otis, Private

City of Paris Cemetery, Pantin, Seine-St-Denis
Clendening, W.J., Signaller
Knowles, Arthur Gordon, Private

Connaught Cemetery, Thiepval, Somme
McIlroy, Samuel, Rifleman

Contalmaison Chateau Cemetery, Somme
Brooks, Charles, Private
McKendrick, A., Private

Contay British Cemetery, Contay, Somme
Andre, G.E.A., Signaller
Gray, Lemon Barney, Sapper
Hill, A.J., Sergeant
Kelly, Thomas Francis, Corporal
Sedgwick, Leon Daniel, Private
Smith, G., Lance Corporal
Welsh, Earl Grames, Corporal

Corbie Communal Cemetery Extension, Somme
Edwards, Ardale Valentine Ernest, Private
Palmer, James Humphrey, Private

Cote 80 French National Cemetery, Etinehem, Somme
Klemm, Alfred, Gunner

Couin New British Cemetery, Pas-de-Calais
Krause, F.L., Private
Rhinesmith, Albert Martin, Second Lieutenant
Ryan, F., Private

Courcelette British Cemetery, Somme
Armstrong, George Harvey, Private
Eccles, Vernon John Lamont, Captain
Howard, Fredrick William, Private
Johnson, Percy S., Lance Corporal
Pitchford, Samuel, Private
Splane, Howard Mylne, Major
Tainer, Arthur Olaf, Private

Crest Cemetery, Fontaine-Notre Dame, Nord
Kelly, John Edward, Private
Maxwell, R.M.M., Private
Plaistow, George William, Private
Shuman, Orville Grant, Private

Croix-Rouge Military Cemetery, Quaedypre, Nord
Hill, Tom Brown, Lance Corporal

Crouy British Cemetery, Crouy-sur-Somme, Somme
Bleil, Albert Edward, Private
Goulette, Raymond, Sergeant
Grande, Anton Ludvik John, Private
Isberg, Henry Oden, Private
Moubray, Arthur Russell St. John, Major
Olson, Herman Leonard, Private

Crucifix Corner Cemetery, Villers-Bretonneux, Somme
Fitzpatrick, Lawrance, Sapper
McCullough, Henry Houston, Private
McMahon, G., Private

Dainville Communal Cemetery, Pas-de-Calais
Marsan, Joseph Damase, Private

Dantzig Alley British Cemetery, Mametz, Somme
Trotter, Alexander William Lewis, Major

Daours Communal Cemetery Extension, Somme
Crone, Daniel, Sergeant
Harvie, John Carson, Gunner
Kelly, Alfred Henry Betham, Private
Otterspoor, John, Private

Delville Wood Cemetery, Longueval, Somme
Peduzzi, James, Private
Smith, Ewart Gladstone, Lance Corporal
Smith, George, Private

Demuin British Cemetery, Somme
Barrett, M., Sergeant

Denain Communal Cemetery, Nord
Chard, Walter Carter, Lance Corporal

Dernancourt Communal Cemetery Extension, Somme
Creasy, Jesse Maxwell, Private

Dive Copse British Cemetery, Sailly-le-Sec, Somme
Harding, George Helliwell, Second Lieutenant

Dominion Cemetery, Hendecourt-les-Cagnicourt, Pas-de-Calais
Bigham, John Stuart, Private
Crawford, James Clarke, Private
Hennessey, Leo M., Private
Hilberg, Harold Oscar, Private
Huntington, Charles Edward, Private
Smith, James McNeill, Private
Warburton, Gregory Augustus, Private
Welch, Thomas, Private

Douai British Cemetery, Cuincy, Nord
Purcell, Donald Roy, Private

Douai Communal Cemetery, Nord
Herbert, George Thomas, Private
Long, R.B., Corporal
Rhyner, A., Private

Doullens Communal Cemetery Extension No. 1, Somme
Barran, R.E., Private

Haughton, Tom Melrose, Private
Kearney, R.P., Private

Drummond Cemetery, Raillencourt, *Nord*
Day, Lewis Aquila, Private
Molan, Harry Julious, Private
Ramage, James Brownlea, Private

Dud Corner Cemetery, Loos, *Pas-de-Calais*
McLaughlin, A., Private

Duisans British Cemetery, Etrun, *Pas-de-Calais*
Barrett, W.E., Private
Boyer, E., Sapper
Brown, William, Private
Castonguay, N.P., Private
Guyette, Michael Edward, Driver
Hamilton, John, Private
Harvey, John Albert, Private
Herd, Fredrick Thomas, Private
Howard, Frank Telford, Private
Johnson, Arthur, Private
Lloyd, John Howard, Private
Morgan, James Francis, Private
Murray, Robert, Lance Corporal
O'Brien, James, Private
O'Neil, John Erwin, Private
Paterson, James, Private
Still, Frank Albert Willis, Private
Tayton, John Henry, Quartermaster Sergeant
Todhunter, Clifford Henry, Corporal
Vercellotti, Anthony, Private

Dunkirk Town Cemetery, *Nord*
Depper, S.G., Chief Petty Officer Mechanic 3rd Grade
Hojel, Jonathan George, Second Lieutenant

Dury Crucifix Cemetery, *Pas-de-Calais*
Appley, Clarence Wasson, Second Lieutenant
Briggs, Thomas, Private
Hershman, R.A., Private
Hodgson, Thomas Nelson, Sergeant
Taylor, Dennis Aloyious, Private

Dury Mill British Cemetery, *Pas-de-Calais*
Borstel, Alexander, Private
Broadford, Robert, Private
Brown, J.W., Private
Coulson, Byard John, Lieutenant
Fallon, Fred, Private
Greenhalgh, Thomas James, Private
Leteux, Albert Francis, Private
Rieger, Ralph Joseph, Lieutenant
Sprackling, Joseph S., Private
Talbott, H.R., Private

Ebblinghem Military Cemetery, *Nord*
Skedden, Charles Edwin Lloyd, Lieutenant

Ecoivres Military Cemetery, Mont-St. Eloi, *Pas-de-Calais*
Allison, James, Private
Bechraft, Thomas C., Lieutenant
Cooney, R.J., Private
Dumas, Joseph Adelard, Private
Goyer, F.J., Private
Holroyd, William, Private
Hopkins, John Oral, Private
Huff, Paul E., Private
King, Henry W., Lance Corporal
Kinsel, William Harrison, Private
Lewis, Julius Opel, Corporal
Mitchell, James George Cooper, Private
Olson, A.J., Private
Poulin, William, Private
Spurling, Walter, Private

Ecoust Military Cemetery, Ecoust-St. Mein, *Pas-de-Calais*
Storey, H., Private

Ecoust-St. Mein British Cemetery, *Pas-de-Calais*
Jordon, Rochy K., Private

Epehy Wood Farm Cemetery, Epehy, *Somme*
Auld, Ebenezer, Lance Corporal
Cregan, John Edward, Private

Esquelbecq Military Cemetery, *Nord*
Vernon, R., Corporal

Estaires Communal Cemetery and Extension, *Nord*
Healy, T., Private
Leventhal, Israel, Private

Estourmel Churchyard, *Nord*
Bowen, Laurance Grant, Lieutenant

Etaples Military Cemetery, *Pas-de-Calais*
Airey, George Ryder, Lieutenant
Bennett, Churchill Edward, Private
Blackwood, James, Lieutenant
Bloor, R., Private
Carter, T.B., Private
Catterson, Monroe, Private
Chamberlain, Frank D., Private
Clarke, Benjamin Otis, Private
Constable, Stanley John, Private
Cutler, William Reynolds, Second Lieutenant
Dean, Floyd Edwin, Driver
Dobbie, Robert Shedden, Second Lieutenant
Flaxington, John, Lance Corporal
Gilbert, John Sidney, Lance Corporal
Green, W.O., Private
Hale, Patrick, Private
Harmon, G.D., Private
Howden, G.W., Sapper
Huseby, Alfred, Lance Corporal
Hutchinson, Reginald Hugh, Private
Jenkins, John, Private
Johnson, Lawrence Wingood, Private
La Monte, Lawrence Dean, Rifleman
Langton, William, Sapper
Lingard, John Joseph, Private
MacKenzie, Robert, Pipe-Major
Mann, E., Private
Marsden, Arthur, Private
McClellan, James William, Private

McRitchie, Wayland Salmon, Gunner
O'Brien, John Thomas, Private
Osmundson, Carl Bernhard, Private
Parisotti, Joseph Bernard Bruno, Private
Puckett, S.L., Private
Robinson, Arthur, Private
Rucker, B.A., Private
Sisson, Frank, Private
Smythe, Henry Hazard, Private
Steele, Morton, Air Mechanic 2nd Class
Stewart, George Arthur, Sapper
Taylor, James Burrows, Private
Wade, Walter George, Driver
Warrington, Alfred George, Private
Wilkinson, H., Private
Wilson, H., Private
Woods, John Henry, Private

Eterpigny British Cemetery, Pas-de-Calais
Elston, Eldon Elon, Private
Hanlon, Clarence Augustine, Private

Eterpigny Communal Cemetery Extension, Somme
Walker, Eric Francis, Private

Faubourg D'amiens Cemetery, Arras, Pas-de-Calais
Becker, Walter Fred, Private
Buttress, Frederick, Lance Corporal
Findlay, George, Private
McLean, Alexander, Private
Stewart, Meno Rossmonde, Private
Wilkinson, Frank, Private

La Ferte-Sous-Jouarre Memorial, Seine-et-Marne
Gidge, Arthur, Private
Smith, James, Private

Feuchy Chapel British Cemetery, Wancourt, Pas-de-Calais
Carrigan, Rupert, Sergeant
Denning, Alven Edward, Private
Farmer, Andrew, Private

Fins New British Cemetery, Sorel-le-Grand, Somme
Pilling, A., Private
Wasserman, D., Private

Five Points Cemetery, Lechelle, Pas-de-Calais
Hesford, William, Private

Flatiron Copse Cemetery, Mametz, Somme
MacFadyen, Jas, Private

Flesquieres Hill British Cemetery, Nord
Cox, William, Private
Spence, Thomas, Private

Fontaine-au-Bois Communal Cemetery, Nord
Fink, L.J., Private

Fosse No. 10 Communal Cemetery Extension, Sains-en-Gohelle, Pas-de-Calais
Dunlop, Daniel Douglas, Corporal
Lee, William James, Sergeant

Fouquescourt British Cemetery, Somme
Cheeseman, Henry Duncan, Private
Spivey, Charles Bartholomew, Private

Tait, James Edward, Lieutenant
Wall, J.B., Private

Franvillers Communal Cemetery Extension, Somme
Miller, Charles Hampden, Corporal

Givenchy-en-Gohelle Canadian Cemetery, Souchez, Pas-de-Calais
Gilroy, L.C., Private
Woodbridge, J., Private

Givenchy Road Canadian Cemetery, Neuville-St. Vaast, Pas-de-Calais
Rossiter, Eli, Private
Vogel, Fredrick Bertrand, Sergeant

Glageon Communal Cemetery Extension, Nord
Wilson, David Miller, Private

Les Gonards Cemetery, Versailles, Yvelines
Barry, J., Private
McDonald, G., Corporal

Gorre British and Indian Cemetery, Pas-de-Calais
Barr, Herbert Carrick, Second Lieutenant
Price, A., Private

Gouzeaucourt New British Cemetery, Nord
Dennis, F., Corporal
McConnell, Harry, Private
Shadbolt, Thomas, Private

Grand Ravine British Cemetery, Havrincourt, Pas-de-Calais
Slaughter, Vivian, Lieutenant

Grevillers (New Zealand) Memorial, Pas-de-Calais
Vaughan, Joseph, Rifleman

Guards' Cemetery, Lesboeufs, Somme
Cawley, Michael Joseph, Private
Finch, Leland John George, Private
Owens, Charles Arnold, Lieutenant
Starr, Dillwyn Parrish, Lieutenant

Guards Cemetery, Windy Corner, Cuinchy, Pas-de-Calais
MacKenzie, James, Lieutenant

Guillemont Road Cemetery, Guillemont, Somme
Skillcorn, John, Lance Corporal (Signaller)

H.A.C. Cemetery, Ecoust-St. Mein, Pas-de-Calais
Ritchey, Cecil Frank, Private

Ham British Cemetery, Muille-Villette, Somme
Goude, F., Sergeant

Hangard Communal Cemetery Extension, Somme
Gregory, Ernest Earl, Private

Hangard Wood British Cemetery, Somme
Lavery, Robert, Private

Happy Valley British Cemetery, Fampoux, Pas-de-Calais
Cullen, Edward, Sergeant

Hargicourt British Cemetery, Aisne
Harper, John Thomas Firm, Private

Hasnon Churchyard, Nord
Fletcher, Charles, Private

Haute-Avesnes British Cemetery, Pas-de-Calais
Wilson, Arthur, Private

***Hawthorn Ridge Cemetery No. 2, Auchonvillers**, Somme*
Rendell, Arthur James, Lance Corporal

***Haynecourt British Cemetery**, Nord*
Bunney, Ben C., Private
Egan, M.J., Private
Finn, W.C., Lieutenant
Hull, Ralph Ray, Private
Johnson, Thomas William, Lieutenant
Lawnsby, Ernest Albert, Private
Littlefield, F., Private
Mansell, Leo West, Private
McAweeney, William Patrie, Private
Nail, Marion Denver, Sergeant
Prince, Joseph Henri George, Private
Smith, E.J., Private
Stevens, Francis Albert, Signaller
Stone, Erik Edward, Private
Tetlow, E., Private

***Hazebrouck Communal Cemetery**, Nord*
Gunn, Frederick Charles, Gunner
Warrington, James Dale, Private

***Heath Cemetery, Harbonnieres**, Somme*
Greppo, Francis, Gunner
Whitworth, Walter Haworth, Second Lieutenant

***Hebuterne Military Cemetery**, Pas-de-Calais*
Moseley, William, Private

***Heilly Station Cemetery, Mericourt-l'Abbe**, Somme*
Cairns, Alan Adam, Private
Hudson, G.G., Lance Corporal
McClean, George J., Private
Simpson, David, Sapper

***Hem Farm Military Cemetery, Hem-Monacu**, Somme*
Landells, C., Private

***Henin Communal Cemetery Extension**, Pas-de-Calais*
Millerson, William Frederick Joseph, Sergeant

***Hermies Hill British Cemetery**, Pas-de-Calais*
Lehman, Glen, Sapper
Mossop, F., Sergeant

***Highland Cemetery, Le Cateau**, Nord*
Torgersen, Cleve Ruben, Private

***Hillside Cemetery, Le Quesnel**, Somme*
Coode, John Griffiths, Private
Pilston, R., Private
West, Robert Ingersoll, Private

***Hinges Military Cemetery**, Pas-de-Calais*
Kellet, Louis McKenzie, Private

***Honnechy British Cemetery**, Nord*
Young, David, Lance Corporal

***Hourges Orchard Cemetery, Domart-sur-la-Luce**, Somme*
Bain, Robert, Private
England, N., Private
Williams, William John, Private

***Huby-St. Leu British Cemetery**, Pas-de-Calais*
Fagan, Thomas Henry, Private
Palardy, Guy, Lieutenant
Townsend, William Henry, Lieutenant

***Humbercamps Communal Cemetery Extension**, Pas-de-Calais*
Davies, Arthur Horace, Gunner

***Lapugnoy Military Cemetery**, Pas-de-Calais*
Best, John Logan, Private
Chapman, Joseph, Private
Cicero, Ralph, Private
Clarke, Richard Kingston, Sergeant
Gammon, Norman West, Private
Grant, Cecil Thomas, Private
Jakobsen, A., Private
Kurtz, Harrison, Private
Marshall, Roy Emerson, Private
Taylor, Ernest, Private
Taylor, Lambert, Gunner

***Laventie Military Cemetery, La Gorgue**, Nord*
Brodie, William Reid, Private
Dalley, Albert, Private

***Lebucquiere Communal Cemetery Extension**, Pas-de-Calais*
Skeens, Walter, Gunner

***Le Cateau Communal Cemetery**, Nord*
Lamb, William Francis, Sapper

***Leval Communal Cemetery**, Nord*
Pennal, Howard Laurence, Second Lieutenant

***Level Crossing Cemetery, Fampoux**, Pas-de-Calais*
Young, Douglas Eldred, Private

***Lichfield Crater, Thelus**, Pas-de-Calais*
Askew, E.R., Private
Feindell, Florus, Private
McKay, William Arthur, Private

***Lievin Communal Cemetery Extension**, Pas-de-Calais*
Conway, Samuel Martin, Private
Hobbs, Charles Herbert, Private
Little, Robert Walter, Gunner

***Ligny-St. Flochel British Cemetery, Averdoingt**, Pas-de-Calais*
Harris-Chubner, Charles Edward, Private
McCallum, W., Private
West, Frank, Private
Williamson, John, Private

***Lillers Communal Cemetery**, Pas-de-Calais*
Andrews, Frederick Russell, Private
Coolidge, Ralph Augustus, Private

***London Cemetery, Neuville-Vitasse**, Pas-de-Calais*
Johnston, Alfred Charles, Private
Yutkovitch, M., Private

***Longuenesse (St. Omer) Souvenir Cemetery**, Pas-de-Calais*
Adams, Briggs Kilburn, Lieutenant
Allan, H., Private

Breese, William Lawrence, Second Lieutenant
Earl, Gladstone Burwash, Private
Lewis, William Heber, Private
Nelson, Howard George, Sapper
Stack, James Charles, Lieutenant

Loos British Cemetery, Pas-de-Calais
Dickson, W., Private
Fayeta, George, Private
Johnson, C., Sergeant
Player, Herbert, Private
Shaw, Kenneth Fleeming, Private

Loos Memorial, Pas-de-Calais
Clayton, John, Private
Cochrane, William, Corporal
Grant, Alexander George William, Lieutenant Colonel
Griffith, John, Corporal
McKendrick, Robert, Private
Newall, Hugh, Private
Nicholls, William Montague, Lieutenant
Peacock, James, Sergeant
Pitkethly, David, Private
Rushton, Harry, Private
Stevenson, Hugh, Private
Sullivan, John Lawrence, Private
Walker, Edward Leonard, Private
Webster, Bruce, Second Lieutenant
Williams, David, Private
Wood, Harold John, Sergeant
Wright, Joseph Sutcliffe, Private

Louez Military Cemetery, Duisans, Pas-de-Calais
Leonard, Herbert Shaw, Sergeant
Lynn, W.H.C., Private
McDonnell, Patrick James, Corporal

Lowrie Cemetery, Havrincourt, Pas-de-Calais
MacLachlan, John Alexander Churchill, Private
Milne, Albert George, Private

Mailly Wood Cemetery, Mailly-Maillet, Somme
Clark, A., Private
Williams, Martin Luther, Private

Manitoba Cemetery, Caix, Somme
Brindley, Charles W., Private
Hawke, Herbert Kitchener, Private
Hood, Horace Stanley, Private
Mason, Edward Leon, Private

Marcoing British Cemetery, Nord
Tobin, James J., Second Lieutenant

Maroc British Cemetery, Grenay, Pas-de-Calais
Barr, W., Private
Hill, V., Private
Olason, Oli, Private
Zapf, George, Private

Maroeuil British Cemetery, Pas-de-Calais
Hardy, George, Private

Maroilles Communal Cemetery, Nord
Shott, Henry Hammond, Captain

Maubeuge-Centre Cemetery, Nord
Mechan, John, Sapper
Peacock, Daniel Marshall, Driver

Mazingarbe Communal Cemetery Extension, Pas-de-Calais
Pepper, Edward Herbert, Second Lieutenant

Merville Communal Cemetery, Nord
Belanger, J., Private
Nilson, Cecil Edgar, Private

Merville Communal Cemetery Extension, Nord
Hurley, Patrick Henry, Driver
Sibley, S.C., Private

Meteren Military Cemetery, Nord
Sammon, J., Private

Mezieres Communal Cemetery Extension, Somme
Allen, Ervin Lewis, Private

Mill Road Cemetery, Thiepval, Somme
Shaw, Horace S., Sergeant

Mill Switch British Cemetery, Tilloy-les-Cambrai, Nord
Colclough, Wilfred George, Private
Dring, Newton Lowell, Private
Miller, Irwin Russel, Private
Mullaney, Michael Joseph, served as Keefe, Private
Payson, Lemuel Wilmot, Private
Toon, George William, Private

Moeuvres Communal Cemetery Extension, Nord
Nixon, James McKinley, Lance Corporal
Shute, A.H., Private

Monchy British Cemetery, Monchy-le-Preux, Pas-de-Calais
Horrocks, H.S., Private
Soden, Arthur Valentine, Gunner

Montay-Neuvilly Road Cemetery, Montay, Nord
Axon, James, Private
Henderson, Peter C., Private

Mont-Bernanchon British Cemetery, Gonnehem, Pas-de-Calais
Kinvig, Herbert, Private

Mont Huon Military Cemetery, Le Treport, Seine-Maritime
Crew, Ralph C., Private
Frank, Frederick William, Gunner
Stout, Clyde Emerson, Private
Tolson, George Lundy, Lance Corporal

Moreuil Communal Cemetery Allied Extension, Somme
Evans, Kenneth George Ogle, Second Lieutenant

Mory Street Military Cemetery, St. Leger, Pas-de-Calais
MacDonald, John, Private

Namps-au-Val British Cemetery, Somme
Lunn, William, Rifleman
Millar, John James, Private

Naves Communal Cemetery Extension, Nord
Beardsell, Herbert, Private
Dayton, Robert Maurice, Private

Deshaies, Oscar J., Private
Marr, G., Driver
Wennevold, John Oscar, Sergeant

La Neuville British Cemetery, Corbie*, Somme*
Simpson, R., Private

Niagara Cemetery, Iwuy*, Nord*
Devereaux, John Joseph, Private
Johnstone, I.W., Private
Wilson, Jacob, Private

Nine Elms Military Cemetery, Thelus*, Pas-de-Calais*
Calder, Alexander Douglas MacDonald, Private
Elrick, Clyde, Corporal
Henderson, I.A., Private
Kingsley, Charles Earlum, Lance Corporal
La Croix, Louis Samuel, Lance Corporal
McGray, Herbert Joyce, Private
Purdy, Walter, Corporal
Robinson, William Matthew, Lance Sergeant
Shipley, Frederick, Sergeant
Smithson, Dwight, Private
Sutherburg, Walford James Wallace, Private

Noeux-les-Mines Communal Cemetery*, Pas-de-Calais*
Holligan, David, Private
Hunter, John William, Private

Noeux-les-Mines Communal Cemetery Extension*, Pas-de-Calais*
Bonach, J., Private
Farquhar, J., Gunner
Fellows, J.T., Gunner
Peck, Charles Henry, Private

Norfolk Cemetery, Becordel-Becourt*, Somme*
Frost, Horace, Corporal
Sadler, Herbert Charles, Private

Noyelles-sur-l'Escaut Communal Cemetery Extension*, Nord*
Tickner, Maurice Edward, Private

Noyon New British Cemetery*, Oise*
Stead, J., Rifleman

Ontario Cemetery, Sains-les-Marquion*, Pas-de-Calais*
Fraser, James Grant, Private
Landreville, F., Private
MacLeod, Alexander K., Private
Metcalf, Milton C., Private
Miller, W.N., Gunner

Orange Hill Cemetery, Feuchy*, Pas-de-Calais*
Crossman, Albert Edwin, Private
Greenwood, Ernest Thomas, Private

Orchard Dump Cemetery, Arleux-en-Gohelle*, Pas-de-Calais*
Apt, William Russell, Private
Mason, Arvid Perry, Private
Steer, Thomas Armstrong, Private
Tait, David Forrest, Corporal

Outtersteene Communal Cemetery Extension, Bailleul*, Nord*
Murray, Howard Weldon, Sapper

Ovillers Military Cemetery*, Somme*
Bareham, R.G., Sergeant

Pernes British Cemetery*, Pas-de-Calais*
Hollebon, William, Sergeant
Howard, Murray Leo, Lieutenant
Pollins, Jay, Second Lieutenant
Wood, William Henry James, Gunner

Peronne Communal Cemetery Extension*, Somme*
Gillespie, Daniel Francies, Lance Corporal
Spooner, Walter Brown, Private

Peronne Road Cemetery, Maricourt*, Somme*
Smith, W.G., Private

Perreuse Chateau Franco British National Cemetery*, Seine-et-Marne*
Beaufort, Francis Henry, Lieutenant

Petit-Vimy British Cemetery*, Pas-de-Calais*
Reedie, John, Private

Philosophe British Cemetery, Mazingarbe*, Pas-de-Calais*
Archibald, James Henry, Private
Egan, John, Private

Plaine French National Cemetery*, Bas-Rhin*
Batty, Horace Walter, Second Lieutenant

Point 110 Old Military Cemetery, Fricourt*, Somme*
Tyrell, Thomas, Private

Point-du-Jour Military Cemetery, Athies*, Pas-de-Calais*
McGrew, Clarence Myvern, Private

Pommereuil British Cemetery*, Nord*
Connor, Cleveland Alexander, Lieutenant

Pont-de-Nieppe Communal Cemetery*, Nord*
Glasspool, Valentine (Cap), Private

Pont-du-Hem Military Cemetery, La Gorgue*, Nord*
Todhunter, Gilbert, Lieutenant (Signalling Officer)

Porte-de-Paris Cemetery, Cambrai*, Nord*
Picard, Narcisse, Lance Sergeant

Pozieres British Cemetery, Ovillers-La Boisselle*, Somme*
Crowder, Thomas, Gunner
Dunwoody, Samuel, Private
Kendall, Joseph Robert, Private
Price, James Sanford, Lieutenant
Russ, Marion Wright, Private
Ryerson, John Egerton, Captain

Pozieres Memorial*, Somme*
Armstrong, Francis S., Private
Fraser-Campbell, William Baillie, Second Lieutenant
Harbison, Alexander, Private
King, Gerald, Sergeant
Ridley, William, Private

Premont British Cemetery*, Aisne*
Leaf, William Henry, Lieutenant

Prospect Hill Cemetery, Gouy*, Aisne*
Brown, Jonathan Martin, D.F.C., Lieutenant

Puchevillers British Cemetery, Somme
  Belisle, Jean Louis, Private
  Garside, Ernest Albert, Corporal
  Hemsley, Arthur, Corporal
  Hewson, H.S., Private
  Tanner, Albert James, Private
  White, Orel, Sergeant
  Williams, Robert Boyd, Corporal
  Wood, George, Private
  Wright, William James, Private

Quarry Cemetery, Marquion, Pas-de-Calais
  Hall, Edward, Private

Quarry Wood Cemetery, Sains-les-Marquion, Pas-de-Calais
  Anderson, Leigh Henry, Gunner (Signaller)
  Bergman, Daniel, Private
  Craig, Lorne Bean, Lieutenant
  Farr, Robert Henry, Private
  Glasford, Merritt Sterling, Lance Corporal
  Hone, James Gordon, Private
  Jackson, Olaf, Private
  MacDonald, Alexander, Sergeant
  McCann, Thomas James, Private
  McGale, Leo, Private
  McIntyre, William Wallace, Private
  Parker, Wilfred, Private
  Robb, T.A., Private
  Williams, Cecil Roy, Private
  Worth, Norman Marshall, Lance Corporal

Quatre-Vents Military Cemetery, Estree-Cauchy, Pas-de-Calais
  Hansen, Arthur Julius, Private
  Little, Joseph Henry, Private
  Sorensen, Norval Alonzo, Private

Queant Communal Cemetery British Extension, Pas-de-Calais
  Jacobson, O., Private
  Nightingale, Harold, Gunner

Queant Road Cemetery, Buissy, Pas-de-Calais
  Copeland, J.H., Private
  Lewis, A., Gunner
  Saunders, F.S., Private
  Speer, Thomas King, Rifleman

Quebec Cemetery, Cherisy, Pas-de-Calais
  Desrosiers, N., Corporal
  George, Joseph, Private
  Lacasse, A.J., Private
  Ryals, John Bryan, Private

Queens Cemetery, Bucquoy, Pas-de-Calais
  Myers, Robert, Private

Le Quesnel Communal Cemetery Extension, Somme
  Chamard, Joseph, Private
  Smith, Edward Eliud, Private

Raillencourt Communal Cemetery Extension, Nord
  Connors, Melvin, Private
  Hill, Walter Elmer, Private
  Jorde, Albert Svan, Private
  Kight, Elton, Sergeant
  Morin, Wilfred, Private
  Patton, John Wiles, Private
  Ryan, Joseph Basil, Private
  Whittle, Frederick, Private

Railway Hollow Cemetery, Hebuterne, Pas-de-Calais
  Owen, Charles Edward, Private

Ramillies British Cemetery, Nord
  Cavanagh, Harry, Private
  Davies, Herbert, Private

Regina Trench Cemetery, Grandcourt, Somme
  Burrow, John James, Private
  Forgerson, Edward, Private
  Metcalf, W.R., Private
  Purdy, F.O., Private
  Sellier, Henry Lucier, Private
  Wallace, John George, Lieutenant

Reumont Churchyard, Nord
  Welsh, John Felter, Private

Ribecourt British Cemetery, Nord
  Purdie, James, Corporal

Ribemont Communal Cemetery Extension, Somme
  Field, G.W., Private
  Michie, David Gordon, Private
  Webdale, W.S.C., Gunner

Roclincourt Military Cemetery, Pas-de-Calais
  Hanson, Sidney Carl, Private

Rocquigny-Equancourt Road British Cemetery, Manancourt, Somme
  Clark, William Muir, Second Lieutenant

Romeries Communal Cemetery Extension, Nord
  Friedman, Israel Joseph, Sapper

Rosieres Communal Cemetery Extension, Somme
  Aitken, George, Private
  Elliott, James Harvey, Private
  Gray, Jay Junius, Private
  Joy, S.B., Private
  Kemp, Kenneth Stephen, Private
  Lauzon, Edward, Private
  Mather, Robert John, Private
  Summers, Victor Lionel, Private

Royal Irish Rifles Graveyard, Laventie, Pas-de-Calais
  Higginson, Tom Arthur, Captain
  Lucas, Robert Henry, Private

Roye New British Cemetery, Somme
  Barker, J., Private

Rue-du-Bois Military Cemetery, Fleurbaix, Pas-de-Calais
  Kelly, Peter, Lance Corporal

Rue-Petillon Military Cemetery, Fleurbaix, Pas-de-Calais
  Murphy, G., Private
  Parker, Robert Vining, Private
  Tenbosch, Christian Peter, Second Lieutenant

Sains-les-Marquion British Cemetery, *Pas-de-Calais*
  Cochran, Alexander, Lance Corporal
  Garrison, Walter Samuel, Private
  Jenson, Jens Anderson, Private

St. Amand British Cemetery, *Pas-de-Calais*
  Hitchcock, George Harry, Driver

St. Andre Communal Cemetery, *Nord*
  Reynolds, Frank, Sapper

St. Aubert British Cemetery, *Nord*
  Feely, Joseph Reilly, Private
  MacPhail, J.W.A., Gunner
  Ramsay, James, Lieutenant

Ste. Catherine British Cemetery, *Pas-de-Calais*
  Chivas, N.J., Bombardier

St. Hilaire Cemetery Extension, Frevent, *Pas-de-Calais*
  Smith, Robert Black, Private
  Turner, Sidney, Private
  Walters, Roy, Private

Ste. Marie Cemetery, Le Havre, *Seine-Maritime*
  Burnett, Arthur (Chick), Volunteer (Driver)
  Driver, Bertie, Private
  Ibbetson, John Henry, Private
  Norton, Alfred, Lance Corporal

St. Martin Calvaire British Cemetery, St. Martin-sur-Cojeul, *Pas-de-Calais*
  Lally, W.J., Private

St. Mary's A.D.S. Cemetery, Haisnes, *Pas-de-Calais*
  Howard, R.J., Second Lieutenant
  Neale, William Edward, Private

St. Nicolas British Cemetery, *Pas-de-Calais*
  Hulme, Henry, Rifleman

St. Olle British Cemetery, Raillencourt, *Nord*
  Bruce, George Lyman, Private
  Delien, August Arthur, Private
  Givens, Frank Russel, Private
  Gleason, P., Private
  Haines, William Albert, Private
  Lannigan, W.H., Private
  Sanderson, Robert Fleming, Private
  Stout, J.P., Private

St. Pierre Cemetery, Amiens, *Somme*
  McDonald, John Cuyler, Private

St. Pol British Cemetery, St. Pol-sur-Ternoise, *Pas-de-Calais*
  Sheflin, Charles Edward, Gunner

St. Pol Communal Cemetery Extension, *Pas-de-Calais*
  McLean, Daniel, Sergeant

St. Riquier British Cemetery, *Somme*
  Hardy, Samuel Bee, Sapper

St. Sever Cemetery, Rouen, *Seine-Maritime*
  Blush, Arthur Roy, Private
  Harrison, Herbert William, Second Lieutenant
  Hocking, William John, Private
  Liggett, William George, Private
  Scott, Albert Frederick, Private
  Telfer, Stephen Vertch, Private

St. Sever Cemetery Extension, Rouen, *Seine-Maritime*
  Adams, Percy John, Private
  Angel, Arthur James, Gunner
  Byers, B.R., Private
  Findlay, Joseph, Private
  Graves, J.E., Corporal
  Griffiths, William Joseph, Sapper
  Knowles, H., Driver
  Lehoux, George Emile, Private
  McDonald, Andrew, Corporal
  Mortimer, Wright, Private
  Nolan, John Herman, Sergeant
  Ralph, Arthur, Private
  Roemers, William, Private
  Walker, P.C., Private

St. Souplet British Cemetery, *Nord*
  Diplock, Douglas Gerard, Second Lieutenant
  Reeves, Robert Herschel, Private

St. Venant-Robecq Road British Cemetery, Robecq, *Pas-de-Calais*
  Kemble, Cyril Stewart, Second Lieutenant

Sancourt British Cemetery, *Nord*
  Beck, Albert Augustus, Private
  Bjerklie, P.J., Private
  Du Boe, John Joseph, Private
  Goodman, W., Private
  Houghton, Tom Hadley, Private
  Jack, A., Private
  Lossen, J., Private
  MacLean, John Lang, Private
  McAleer, Charles, Private
  Miller, Hugh Wilson, Private
  Myevre, Sterling Alcide, Private
  Nason, Alexis Painter, Lieutenant
  Nickerson, Hilbert Austin, Private

Serre Road Cemetery No. 1, *Pas-de-Calais*
  Greenwood, A., Private

Serre Road Cemetery No. 2, *Somme*
  Buckle, Cuthbert Charles Corbett, Second Lieutenant
  Joyce, Patrick, Corporal
  McGregor, Neil Sinclair, Lance Corporal
  Montgomery, Robert Andrew, Private
  Newlands, Sydney Barron, Second Lieutenant
  Patten, Edward, Private
  Ralston, Alexander Cameron, Private
  Reid, Joseph, Private
  Roper, Louis, Private
  Volpe, Pasquale, Private
  Wyman, Frederick Walter, Private

Soissons Memorial, *Aisne*
  Melling, Albert, Private

Milne, William, Corporal
Pells, Cyril Elmore, Second Lieutenant

Somme American Cemetery, Bony, Aisne
Hall, James Grantley, Lieutenant

Stump Road Cemetery, Grandcourt, Somme
Haddock, John Wesley, Private
Smollen, James J., Private

Sucrerie Cemetery, Ablain-St. Nazaire, Pas-de-Calais
Bianche, Charles, Private
Finseth, Iver, Private
McNamara, Edmond, Gunner

Sucrerie Military Cemetery, Colincamps, Somme
Addison, John Baxter, Private

Sun Quarry Cemetery, Cherisy, Pas-de-Calais
Achorn, L.B., Private
Gale, Gerald Gordon, Private
Key, William James, Private
McNett, William Herman, Private
Vincent, Wilfred Joseph, Private

Sunken Road Cemetery, Contalmaison, Somme
Dobson, R.F.H., Private
Wellington, Burton Julian, Private

Supt Churchyard, Jura
Basenach, Frank, Private

Tannay British Cemetery, Thiennes, Nord
Ellis, William Henry, Private

La Targette British Cemetery, Neuville-St. Vaast, Pas-de-Calais
Blanchard, Edward Sherburne, Gunner
Briscoe, H.E., Sergeant
Chapin, Curran Joseph, Private
Graves, Storer Osborn, Bombardier
Hardaker, Tom, Private
Hotton, H.V., Private
McIntyre, Ethan Alexander, Corporal
Norman, Henry Lawrence, Gunner

Terlincthun British Cemetery, Wimille, Pas-de-Calais
Anderson, Mayor Olai, Gunner
Andrews, Miles Beecher, Private
Borsey, James, Private
Bradley, Joseph, Private
Bushaw, Raymond Sylvester, Private
Clingan, Albert James, Lance Corporal
Dalby, John Andrew, Sapper
Dickson, Francis Leslie, Sergeant
Griffin, Frank, Private E11.
Lewis, Thomas, Gunner
MacKintosh, Andrew, Private
Mahan, James William, Sapper
McCleary, John, Gunner
Scott, F.R., Private
Sullivan, Frank Harrington, Second Lieutenant
Thimot, Odelpha, Private
Todd, A.E., Private
Whitney, Silvester, Private

Wilkinson, William, Private
Wolf, Simon, Gunner

Thelus Military Cemetery, Pas-de-Calais
Abbey, Edwin Austin, Lieutenant
Bower, Albert Elmer Eugene, Private
Earles, William Harrison, Private
Forrest, Theodore Wiggins, Private
Goodin, Harry Lester, Private
Lawson, Percy R., Sergeant
Skinner, Albert V., Private
Tulk, O.M., Private
Woodford, H. Clark, Sergeant

Thiepval Memorial, Somme
Adams, Joseph Andrew, Corporal
Allen, William James, Private
Atkin, Allan Oliver, Private
Baker, William Albert Edward, Private
Barker, Harry, Private
Barlow, Lovel Hardwick, Second Lieutenant
Blackshaw, Charles, Rifleman
Blythe, Walter, Private
Bodow, Harry, Rifleman
Bond, Harry, Private
Bradley, John, Private
Brown, James, Private
Brown, Neil, Private
Campbell, Robert, Lance Corporal
Chamberlain, Arthur, Private
Charlton, Alfred Douglas, Lance Corporal
Chittick, Harland Harris, Private
Coutts, James Renwick, Private
Crisp, James, Private
Cunliffe, Fred, Private
Curran, Thomas, Private
De Voney, Frank, Rifleman
Dillon, George Charles Tracey, Second Lieutenant
Drysdale, Charles, Lance Corporal
Eyre, Edwin, Company Sergeant Major
Fleming, Edward, Lance Corporal
Fortman, Albert Frederick, Private
Giles, Frank Eric, Private
Gold, Joseph, Private
Grogan, William, Private
Harris, Clifford Augustus, Sapper
Hatfield, Frank, Lance Corporal
Hearne, Joseph, Private
Hilditch, Harold, Private
Hodge, Roll, Private
Huntington, George Waldorf, Second Lieutenant
Keezer, Benjamin Franklin, Private
Kirton, John James, Private
Lee, Edward, Private
Lillis, John, Private
Lloyd, Alfred Ernest, Private
Manuel, Frank Clifford, Private
Marshall, Charles Frederick, Private

Marson, William Henry, Second Lieutenant
McCarron, Michael, Private
McIlwain, John, Private
McKee, John, Private
Mellor, Clement, Private
Oliver, Robert, Private
Pollock, Charles, Private
Roberts, John Llewellyn, Private
Scollan, John, Private
Surr, Rudolph Vincent, Lieutenant
Swindells, Harry, Private
Taylor, Robert, Private
Thornton, Chester Arthur, served as O'Brien, Private
Tomkins, Walter Richard, Lance Corporal
Tyler, George Henry, Sergeant
Veitch, Francis, Private
Victor, John Ernest, Lance Corporal
Ward, Fred, Private
Ward, Frederic, Private
Wearne, Ivan, Private
Wilkinson, Martin Aloysious, Private
Winkley, Roy, Private

Tigris Lane Cemetery, Wancourt, Pas-de-Calais
O'Neill, R J., Private

Tilloy British Cemetery, Tilloy-les-Mofflaines, Pas-de-Calais
Goodrum, Robert, Private
Taylor, Arthur William, Private

Tincourt New British Cemetery, Somme
Bullion, John, Corporal
Stephens, Richard, Sapper

Toronto Cemetery, Demuin, Somme
Chicoine, E., Private
Giles, Robert Lee, Corporal
Lambe, Albert Edward, Private
Murray, L.M., Private

Le Touret Memorial, Pas-de-Calais
Campbell, William, Lance Sergeant
Cox, Thomas, Private
Cox, William, Private
Digby, Herbert William, Rifleman
Greenhill, John Crerar, Private
Harris, Charles William Henry, Private
Hine, William John, Private
McNamara, Hugh, Lance Corporal
Mulholland, Robert, Private
O'Neill, William, Private
Peel, John, Private
Stevenson, Thomas, Private
Webster, Charles, Private

Tranchee de Mecknes Cemetery, Aix-Noulette, Pas-de-Calais
Forrester, Benjamin Franklin, Private
McRae, A., Private

Trefcon British Cemetery, Caulaincourt, Aisne
Mills, William, Private

Le Treport Military Cemetery, Seine-Maritime
Connolly, John Patrick, Private

Triangle Cemetery, Inchy-en-Artois, Pas-de-Calais
Beaumont, Edwin Forrest, Private

Trois Arbres Cemetery, Steenwerck, Nord
Hoare, Stanley Hubert, Private

Le Trou Aid Post Cemetery, Fleurbaix, Pas-de-Calais
Caithness, R., Private
Hopey, Edmund E., Private

Upton Wood Cemetery, Hendecourt-les-Cagnicourt, Pas-de-Calais
Dine, William Henry, Private
Harrop, Albert Edward, Private
Hellinger, Arthur Ernest, Private
Hinchliffe, Joseph Edward, Private
Lahey, Thomas Anthony, Private
MacDonnell, Hugh Alexander, Private
Maycock, F.G., Private
McGrath, James Michael, Private
McLean, Walter, Private
McRae, G.A., Sapper
Palmer, E., Private
Robinson, Herbert Pollexfen, Private

Valenciennes (St. Roch) Communal Cemetery, Nord
Anderson, John Essley, Private
Carson, J., Sergeant
Clawson, D.A., Private
Lake, William Howard, Private
Lord, Percy Newton, Private
Murphy, John Joseph, 2nd Corporal

Valley Cemetery, Vis-en-Artois, Pas-de-Calais
Lee, Wilfred, Private

Vaulx Hill Cemetery, Pas-de-Calais
Hewett, John Franklin, Lance Corporal
Hill, Horace Sydney, Sergeant

Vermelles British Cemetery, Pas-de-Calais
Atwood, Hubert Leroy, Private
Barney, Montagu Middleton, Second Lieutenant
Cartwright, George Crellin, Captain

Vieille-Chapelle New Military Cemetery, Lacouture, Pas-de-Calais
Hawthorne, Fred, Private
Sim, James, Private

La Ville-Aux-Bois British Cemetery, Aisne
Lewis, Meredith B., Lieutenant

Villers-Bretonneux Memorial, Somme
Cary, Edward Haynes, Private
Quirk, Edward James, Private
Reid, Denis Charles, Lance Corporal

Villers-Bretonneux Military Cemetery, Somme
Bryce, W.R., Private
Forhan, Charles Harold, Private
Higgens, Archibald, Private
King, Lemuel William, Private

Kinney, Frederick, Private
MacDonell, Charles Edward, Sergeant
McDonald, G., Private
Parlee, George William Hugh, Lieutenant
Row, James, Lieutenant
Smith, Anthony, Lieutenant
Washburn, W.A., Private
Watson, Fredrick, Private

Villers Station Cemetery, Villers-au-Bois, Pas-de-Calais
Baker, Thomas Massey, Lieutenant
Brennan, Peter Austin, Lieutenant
Britton, John F., Corporal
Combs, Raymond William, Private
Cotey, Earle, Private
Densmore, Aubrey, Gunner
Dixon, Arthur, Private
Gibbs, Charles Robert, Private
Hewett, Alfred, Private
Hill, James A., Private
Learned, Raymond A., Private
Leslie, W.K., Sergeant
Marshall, Robert Munroe, Private
Matthews, George Collier, Private
McNeill, Gordon, Gunner
McPherson, J.J., Private
Minard, Asa Raymond, Lieutenant
Mondy, James Hiram, Private
Norris, Robert, Private
Revsbech, Rudolph Francis, Gunner
Roberts, John Prendergast, Private
Shaffer, C., Private
Sinclair, H., Private
Swenson, Soren William, Private
Walsh, Edward Christopher, Private
Whitman, Roy Alfred

Vimy Memorial, Pas-de-Calais
Able, Private, Ernest George, Private
Alberg, William, Private
Allan, William Douglas, Private
Ansdell, William Arthur, Private
Archibald, William Johnson, Private
Armstrong, James McDougall, Corporal
Badgley, Frank, Private
Baglien, George, Private
Barrett, George William, Private
Batten, Charles Albert, Private
Beaudoin, William, Private
Beitz, Roy Joseph, Private
Belford, Elmer Henry, Private
Belfountaine, Vincent Louis, Private
Bennett, Roy Newton, Private
Bergquist, Henry, Private
Berthiaume, Armand, Private
Bertrand, Alfred Joseph, Private
Bilton, John, Private
Biron, Auguste, Private
Birtley, Thomas, Private
Bishop, John Albert, Private
Blaney, Richard William, Private
Blashill, Harry Arthur, Private
Blois, Claude, Private
Bonnevie, Hypolite, Corporal
Boucher, Henry, Private
Boudreau, John Angus, Private
Boyland, Alexander Eldrick, Private
Bradt, Russell Ferdinand, Private
Brown, Oliver Perry, Private
Bryson, Robert Palmer, Private
Buchanan, Earl Leroy, Private
Bunch, Charles, Private
Burfield, George, Private
Burnes, William Albert, Corporal
Burns, Tom Joseph, Private
Cameron, Peter Anderson, Private
Campbell, Thomas, Private
Carroll, William Patrick, Private
Carufel, Emile, Private
Casey, Robert, Private
Cavallero, Emilio, Private
Chalmers, Robert, Private
Chatfield, Ernest Coy, Private
Clarke, Richard Halley, Sergeant
Coates, William John, Private
Collins, John, Private
Congdon, Orren John, Private
Coppell, Edward, Lance Corporal
Coughlin, Michael Avery, Private
Cox, Oscar Paul, Private
Craig, William Ernest, Private
Craigen, Charles, Corporal
Crane, Emmett Joseph, Private
Crichton, Robert, Private
Crichton, William, Private
Cunnings, William James, Private
Dalton, Johndean, Sergeant
Dixson, Leonard Charles, Private
Doherty, James Henry, Private
Draker, Albert, Private
Drinkall, Arthur William, Private
Duenkel, William Bernard, Private
Dugas, Ernest, Private
Duncan, Henry, Private
Dunkowski, Stanley, Private
Dunlop, Joseph Sproule, Private
Durrant, Frank Stanley, Private
Edwards, Sidney John, Private
Ellis, Edward Charles, Private
Ellsworth, Ernest, Private
Eng, Robert Ferdinand, Private
Ervin, Henry D., Private
Evans, Alfred, Private
Finlayson, Donald, Private
Flynn, Daniel John Joseph, Private
Foster, Forest Jasper, Private
Fournier, Henry, Private
Fowle, William Owen, Private

Fraser, George, Lance Corporal
Freebairn, Thomas Scott, Private
Gates, John Allison, Private
Gayton, Edmund Patrick, Private
Gendron, Albert, Private
Good, Julius Harry, Private
Graham, Henry Eyres, Corporal
Green, James William, Private
Greenhalgh, Bertrand William, Private
Gregory, William Hugh, Private
Griffin, Lawrence Ambrose, Private
Hague, Augustin, Private
Hamilton, David, Private
Harrison, James, Private
Hemeon, Carl Denlon, Private
Henderson, Alexander, Private
Henderson, George Albert, Private
Henderson, Robert Sime, Private
Hibray, Homer Glen, Corporal
Hodgson, John, Private
Holbrook, Henry Leonard, Private
Hope, James Alfred, Private
Hopper, Gordon Hector, Private
Horner, Frederick George, Private
Hudson, James Leslie, Sapper
Hunt, Ernest Wendover, Corporal
Hunter, James Morrison McKenzie, Private
Irvine, Robert Fraser, Lance Corporal
Jackson, Charles, Private
Jackson, Charles Edward, Private
Jamieson, Frank Cameron, Sergeant
Jessome, John, Private
Joyce, George, Private
Juleff, Henry Clifton, Private
Kelly, John Dennison, Private
Kennedy, James Frederick, Private
King, Robert, Lance Corporal
King, William A., Private
Knowlton, Henry Scott, Private
Lafave, Joseph Edward, Corporal
Lambert, John Edward, Private
Laronge, Frank, Private
Lasante, Arthur, Private
Lavoie, Charles Henri, Private
Lees, James, Private
Levasseur, Benjamin, Private
Levine, Saul, Private
Lightfoot, John Howard, Private
Lowery, George Edward, Private
MacIntyre, Gordon Campbell, Private
MacLean, Alex Stewart, Private
Maille, Joseph Fabien, Private
Maldeis, Harry Bernard, Corporal
Malone, James Gilbert, Private
Martin, Kenneth Lionel, Lance Corporal
Masse, Dieudonne, Private
McAnley, Frank Pancratius, Private
McCaskill, Donald, Private
McClure, David Jason, Private

McCulloch, Thomas, Private
McDonald, Clarence, Private
McDonald, Herbert Lloyd, Private
McEvoy, Timothy, Lance Sergeant
McIntyre, Robert Alexander, Private
McKenna, William Dominick, Private
McKim, William Le Roy, Private
McRae, William Duncan, Private
Mildon, James Rutherford, Sergeant
Miles, Cecil Norman, Private
Mitchell, Alexander, Private
Monroe, Harry, Private
Moody, Robert Thomas, Private
Moore, George McNicol, Private
Murch, Clarence Egbert, Private
Naylor, James, Private
Neelands, Clifford Abraham, Lieutenant
Newman, Joseph Davis, Private
Nicholson, Frank Leslie, Private
Norris, Edward, Private
Nurse, Harry, Private
Oakes, Jack Leonard, Private
O'Brien, Thomas Joseph, Private
O'Meara, Frank, Private
Palmer, James Arthur, Private
Paradis, Alfred, Private
Parry, William, Private
Paulson, Oliver Bennett, Private
Peters, Howard, Private
Philpott, Arthur Edward, Private
Poole, Merton Stanley, Private
Potter, Mark Mills, Private
Purcell, Francis Henry, Private
Quinn, John Martin, Sergeant
Rahn, Herman, Private
Randall, Algernon Claude Burford, Lance Corporal
Ray, Herbert, Corporal
Reynolds, George Alfred Cullen, Lance Corporal
Rigg, Thomas Meldrum, Private
Ripley, Thomas Allan, Private
Rising, Frederick Wilkinson, Sergeant
Risser, Laurie Guston, Private
Roberts, George Dow, Private
Robie, Rea Russel Stanley, Private
Robinson, Chester, Private
Robinson, Fred Milton, Private
Rochon, Ernest Edward, Private
Rogers, Christopher Edgar Wyon, Private
Rogers, Stanley, Private
Rogers, William George, Private
Ross, George Howard, Corporal
Ryan, William Charles, Private
Sambrookes, John, Private
Sampson, Clyde, Private
Schrag, Eliud Joseph, Private
Semple, Joseph, Private
Shortt, Allen, Lieutenant
Simard, Ovila, Private

Smith, Herbert John, Private
Smith, Ola Preston, Private
Smith, Percival, Private
Soden, James Bowden, Private
Somerville, Philip, Private
Soper, Roland Edward Chester, Private
Speck, George Arthur, Private
Starkiss, Samuel George, Private
Steeves, Robert Jacob, Private
Stephenson, James, Private
Steptoe, Sydney Thomas, Private
Stevens, George Manly, Private
Stewart, Holden Delgatie, Private
Stockdale, Harry, Private
Stratton, Darrell Raymond, Private
Stuart, Henry, Private
Swan, John Boyd, Private
Taylor, Edward, Private
Taylor, Harold Harborne, Private
Taylor, John Sanford, Private
Taylor, Roy Alexander, Private
Thieme, Clement Auguste, Private
Thomas, Harry, Private
Thomson, Alexande, Private
Tonge, Joseph Francis, Corporal
Townsley, Hugh Dorsey, Private
Travis, Wallace Irvine, Private
Waddicor, John William, Private
Ward, William Henry, Lance Corporal
Warren, Albert Langston, Private
Watson, James Frederick Trevail, Corporal
Weber, George Roy, Lieutenant
Weir, John Elmer, Private
Welck, Albert Fred, Private
White, Francis Victor, Private
Whitefield, John, Private
Whitehead, Charles, Private
Wiley, George Percy, Lance Corporal
Williams, James Arthur, Private
Willoughby, Frank, Private
Willsey, William Eugene, Private
Wilson, Frederick, Private
Wilson, Henry John, Private
Wilson, Walter Wade, Private
Woods, Charles, Corporal
Wright, Francis Wenman, Private
Younger, Robert, Private

Vis-en-Artois British Cemetery, Haucourt, *Pas-de-Calais*
Adams, Robert Walpole, Private
Allison, Leslie, Private
Biddulph, Cyril, Lieutenant
Bruce, Ernest Alexander, Private
Driscoll, Harvey, Private
Guthrie, Gavin Thomson, Private
Mather, Ernest Oswald, Private
Nichols, A., Private
Nixon, Clyde Jay, Private
Quirion, Alfred, Private
Riley, Frank Lenard, Private
Rogers, James Thomas, Private
Sears, Joseph Millard, Private
Sheppard, Leslie Ernest, Corporal
Tomlin, John Charles, Private
Walsh, G., Private
West, R.E., Private

Vis-en-Artois Memorial, *Pas-de-Calais*
Atherton, Stanley Ernest, Private
Brewer, Cedric Seymour, Private
Hambly, William Robert, Private
Hughes, Arthur Stanley, Private
Mathieson, Robert, Private
Mitchell, Edgar, Corporal
Rogers, Christopher, Private

Wailly Orchard Cemetery, *Pas-de-Calais*
Campbell, T., Private
Doyle, F., Private
Faber, Edwin Fredrick, Private
Gadbois, Edward John, Private
Girouard, George, Private
Malone, J.V., Corporal
McLean, Hugh Francis, Private
Moore, Henry Edwin, Private
O'Hearn, Philip Patrick, Private

Wancourt British Cemetery, *Pas-de-Calais*
Armitage, Robert Mitchell, Private
Baker, Albert Arthur, Private
Bush, Joseph E., Private
Colliver, H.S., Private
Davidson, Dalton M., Private
Dickinson, A., Private
Duguay, A., Private
Fielding, James, Private
Heslop, Henry Gilbert, Private
Krueger, Leo Darwin, Private
Lemay, A., Private
Libby, Paul Everett, Private
O'Neil, P., Private
Parker, Albert, Private
Scott, Grant Robert, Private
Tawse, Peter, Private
Valois, Jean Baptiste, Private

Wanquetin Communal Cemetery Extension, *Pas-de-Calais*
McLean, John Donald, Sapper
Zickan, Frederick William, Private

Warlencourt British Cemetery, *Pas-de-Calais*
Jepps, Walter, Rifleman
Myers, G., Lance Corporal

Warlincourt Halte British Cemetery, Saulty, *Pas-de-Calais*
Fleet, William Alexander, Second Lieutenant

Warloy-Baillon Communal Cemetery Extension, *Somme*
Boisvert, Leon, Private

Harrigan, James Burnett, Gunner
Howarth, George, Private
Murphy, R.T., Gunner
Parsons, George Henry, Private
Sharp, H.C., Private

Warvillers Churchyard Extension, *Somme*
Coss, Henry, Private
McGlone, Felix Wilson, Private
Seal, Gordon Rook, Gunner

Wavans British Cemetery, *Pas-de-Calais*
Miller, Donald, Lieutenant

Wellington Cemetery, Rieux-en-Cambresis, *Nord*
Warrander, G.A., Private

Wimereux Communal Cemetery, *Pas-de-Calais*
Kane, Louis, Lance Corporal
Ross, Angus, Private
Seymour, George Peter, Private
Townsend, Benjamin, Private
Ward, Walter Cyrus, Private

Windmill British Cemetery, Monchy-le-Preux, *Pas-de-Calais*
Corris, Louis William, Sergeant
Loyd, Hugh Arthur, Private
Moody, D.J., Private
Raymond, Hormidas, Private

Woburn Abbey Cemetery, Cuinchy, *Pas-de-Calais*
Adamson, Minto Torrance, Private

Wood Cemetery, Marcelcave, *Somme*
Laine, A., Private
Thomas, William Henry, Lance Corporal

Zouave Valley Cemetery, Souchez, *Pas-de-Calais*
Chatterton, Richard, Private

Zuydcoote Military Cemetery, *Nord*
Kelly, Andrew, Private

GERMANY

Berlin South-Western Cemetery, *Berlin, Brandenburg*
Conheeny, Gerald, M.C.

Cologne Memorial, *Koln (Cologne), Nordrhein-Westfal*
Pulsford, Geoffrey Robert, Private

Cologne Southern Cemetery, *Koln (Cologne), Nordrhein-Westfal*
Bayer, Joseph, Private
Buckle, Peter, Driver

Hamburg Cemetery, *Hamburg, Hamburg*
Davies, Arthur E., Private
Johnson, Herbert, Private

Niederzwehren Cemetery, *Kassel, Hessen*
O'Dea, Andrew, Private
Toovey, Kennedy St. Clair Hamilton, Second Lieutenant

GREECE

Doiran Memorial
Booth, William, Sergeant

Doiran Military Cemetery
Haldane, R.L., Corporal

Karasouli Military Cemetery
Shelly, Daniel Joseph, Private
Wilson, Albert, Corporal

Lahana Military Cemetery
Miller, P., Sergeant

Mikra British Cemetery, Kalamaria
Denley, Frank, Private
Hayward, Edward Ronald, Second Lieutenant

Portianos Military Cemetery, *Lemnos*
Jaggard, Matron, Jessie Brown
McGrath, J., Private

Salonika (Lembet Road) Military Cemetery
Carr, Louis, Driver

Struma Military Cemetery
Collins, C., Private

INDIA

Delhi Memorial (India Gate)
Malone, M.P., Sub-Conductor

Kirkee 1914-1918 Memorial
Hallaran, William, Colonel

IRAQ

Amara War Cemetery
Cooke, J.A., Lance Corporal
Holland, Joseph, Private

Baghdad (North Gate) War Cemetery
Cloute, G., Private
Round, William Ewart, Private

Basra Memorial
Angell, Casaubon Thorold, Private
Commings, Supervisor,
Dennis, Carlton Pardmer, Sapper
Joyce, Patrick, Sapper
McGarry, Hugh, Private
Rabey, F., Gunner
Tucker, Gus, Private

Basra War Cemetery
Clark, Theodore Harvey L., Civilian
Walker, James, Private

IRELAND

Curragh Military Cemetery, *County Kildare*
Staunton, Francis, Sergeant

ISRAEL

Deir El Belah War Cemetery
Barr, James, Private
Greenberg, Phillip, Private
Rae, Alexander, Gunner
Watson, James Brown, Gunner

Gaza War Cemetery
Harvey, Thomas MacNair, Trooper
Holdgate, A.E., Private

Jerusalem War Cemetery
Gillespie, Joseph William, Private
Mulholland, Mitchel Joseph, Rifleman

Ramleh War Cemetery
Armstrong, Henry Tudor, Private
Tight, Charles Robert, Sergeant

JAMAICA

Kingston (Up Park Camp) Military Cemetery
McLean, J., Private

KENYA

Nairobi South Cemetery
Lind, Frants Vilheim, Sergeant

MALAWI

Blantyre Church of Central Africa Presbyterian Cemetery
Goodreau, Bugler, George

Mangochi Town Cemetery, Malawi
Read, S.T., Lieutenant

MALTA

Addolorata Cemetery
McGrath, Thomas, Lance Corporal

Pieta Military Cemetery
Wight, Ronald Toynbee, Private

NETHERLANDS

The Hague General Cemetery, Zuid-Holland
Gordon, Herbert, Lance Corporal

Noordwijk General Cemetery, Zuid-Holland
Lincoln, Fredrick Hugh, Sergeant

NEW ZEALAND

Gisborne (Taruheru) Cemetery, Gisborne District
McLean, Hugh Lyn, Rifleman

Orira Cemetery, Far North District
Wooster, Frank Rupert, Private

Wellington (Karori) Cemetery, Wellington City
Curtin, Denis, Rifleman

Whangarei (Otaika) Public Cemetery, Whangarei District
Chetham, Howard Franklin, Private

RUSSIA

Archangel Memorial
Ross, Thomas, Private

SIERRA LEONE

Freetown (King Tom) Cemetery
King, George Harbord, Chief Petty Officer

SOUTH AFRICA

Durban (Stellawood) Cemetery, Kwazulu Natal
Sanderson, G.W., Driver

SWITZERLAND

Vevey (St. Martin's) Cemetery
Phillips, Harry, Private

TANZANIA

Dar Es Salaam War Cemetery
Daly, E.H., Trooper
Devlin, Francis Cecil Cochran, Lieutenant
Stern, Isser, Driver

TURKEY

Azmak Cemetery, Suvla
Fitzgerald, John, Private

Courtney's and Steel's Post Cemetery
Richards, Lionel, Private

Haidar Pasha Memorial
Axon, Wilfred Taylor, Private

Helles Memorial
Abbott, Charles Henry, Lance Corporal
Bluett, Joseph, Lance Sergeant
Brook, Wilfrid, Private
Denny, John, Private
Dyson, Harry, Private
England, Alex, Private
Gibson, David, Sergeant
Hogan, Patrick, Private
Jacques, Francis Augustus, Lieutenant Colonel
James, Evan, Private
Kilroy, Albert, Private
Kilroy, William, Private
Lynch, Edward, Private
McNulty, John, Private
Pollock, James, Sapper
Sumption, Samuel, Corporal
Sutcliffe, William, Private
Wilson, Matthew, Private

Lancashire Landing Cemetery
Boyd, J., Sapper
Greenwood, Walter, Lance Corporal
Steel, Robert, Private

Lone Pine Cemetery, Anzac
Armstrong, Benjamin Harrison, Private
Lewin, Reginald Arthur, Lance Corporal

Lone Pine Memorial
Allan, James, Sergeant
Bates, John Hugh, Private
Colls, Lisle, Corporal
McGlade, Matthew, Sergeant Major

Redoubt Cemetery, Helles
Page, George, Lance Corporal

Skew Bridge Cemetery
Ferguson, A., Private

Twelve Tree Copse Cemetery
D'arcy, Michael Joseph, Company Quartermaster Sergeant

UNITED KINGDOM

Aberdeen (Allenvale) Cemetery, *Aberdeenshire*
Sazma, Vincent, Private

Abney Park Cemetery, *London*
Gillis, Edwin Gillard, Private

Aldershot Military Cemetery, *Hampshire*
Andersen, A.M., Private
Bunce, John, Private
Connor, P., Private
Hathaway, Frederick, Private
Laing, Arthur Laverne, Private
MacGray, B.H., Private
Miller, Kenneth M., Private
Pillsbury, Frederick Henry, Private
Spencer, John Edwin, Private

Andover Cemetery, *Hampshire*
Slavik, John Frederick, Lieutenant

Aylesbury Cemetery, *Buckinghamshire*
Day, Jeremiah, Private

Barnhill Cemetery, *Angus*
Ramsay, R., Sergeant

Basingstoke (South View or Old) Cemetery, *Hampshire*
Robertson, J., Private

Bath (Locksbrook) Cemetery, *Somerset*
Aldrich, Leo Edwin, Second Lieutenant

Bebington Cemetery, *Cheshire*
Tart, Edmund Graham., Lieutenant

Beckenham Crematorium and Cemetery, *Kent*
Moir, Herbert, Ordinary Seaman

Belfast City Cemetery, *County Antrim*
Millar, Fredrick George, Private

Belfast (Milltown) Roman Catholic Cemetery, *County Antrim*
Donaldson, D., Private

Birkenhead (Flaybrick Hill) Cemetery, *Cheshire*
Lichtenhein, Lawrence James, Private

Birmingham (Lodge Hill) Cemetery, *Warwickshire*
Sickner, Ronald Goldie, Private

Blackpool (Layton) Cemetery, *Lancashire*
Donald, Josiah Alfred, Lance Corporal

Bodelwyddan (St. Margaret) Churchyard, *Flintshire*
Drips, V.P., Private
Johnson, A., Pioneer
Lapine, Joseph Alfred, Private
Waddell, J., Private

Bo'ness Cemetery, *West Lothian*
Mulrine, Signalman, Thomas Joseph

Bordon Military Cemetery, *Hampshire*
Cleghorn, Allen MacKenzie, Captain

Bournemouth East Cemetery, *Hampshire*
Miller, Frederic J., Private

Bradford (Bowling) Cemetery, *Yorkshire*
Armitage, Harry, Sapper

Bramshott (St. Mary) Churchyard, *Hampshire*
Bloomer, John, Private
Carston, Lawrence, Gunner
Dow, Harry William, Private
Ferguson, Aubrey Lee, Private
Findlater, James Ronald, Private
Freeman, Fred McKinly, Private
Glennie, J.R., Sapper
Harvey, John Clunnie, Sapper
Hirssig, Earl Edward, Private
Humphrey, J.H., Private
Krieger, Henry C., Private
Lyseng, Ole K., Private
McKenzie, A., Private
Patriquin, Willard, Private
Pitzer, Lawrence Patrick, Private
Prime, Ernest Valentine, Private
Switzer, Albert Robert, Lieutenant
Throndson, Clarence Andrew, Private
Wallace, Thomas, Private
Wood, Philip Bunte, Private

Bristol (Arnos Vale) Cemetery, *Gloucestershire*
Estey, Hubert William, Private

Bristol (Arnos Vale) Roman Catholic Cemetery, *Gloucestershire*
Hazard, William Edward, Private

Bromley (St. Luke's) Cemetery, *Kent*
Goldstone, Henry Thomas, Gunner

Brookwood Military Cemetery, *Surrey*
Armstrong, E., Acting Bombardier
Bamford, George Washington, Private
Bealer, Harold Van Allen, Lieutenant
Brakhage, Charles, Rifleman
Breen, Patrick John, Private
Chute, Harold R., Sapper
Coleman, Thomas James, Private
Dike, Alton Shirley, Private
Douglass, Judson Alden, Driver
Harris, The Rev. Webster Henry Fanning, Chaplain 4th Class
Hefty, Henry Caspar, Private
Kelly, Thomas Paul, Cadet
McClare, Ernest Ethelbert, Private
Moore, Edward Francis, Sapper
Morton, Grant Melvin, Private
Stewart, Arthur Charles, Driver
Symington, Karl Randolph, Private

Calstock Cemetery, *Cornwall*
Whitford, William Francis, Gunner

Cambridge City Cemetery, *Cambridgeshire*
Buist, Alexander Hall, Private
Paul, H.L., Private
Saxton, Donald Francis, Gunner

Cathcart Cemetery, Renfrewshire
 Diehl, William Henry, Lieutenant
Chapel Hill (St. Mary) Churchyard, Monmouthshire
 Hall, P.B., Private
Chatham Naval Memorial, Kent
 Horn, James Fredrick, Petty Officer 1st Class
Chester (Overleigh) Cemetery, Cheshire
 Nelson, Kenneth Alonzo, Second Lieutenant
Chichester Cemetery, Sussex
 Wyman, Alfred, Lieutenant
Chilton Foliat (St. Mary) Churchyard, Wiltshire
 Cunningham, Lyman Holden, Second Lieutenant
City of London Cemetery and Crematorium, Manor Park, Essex
 Hammond, Vernon John, Captain
Cliveden War Cemetery, Buckinghamshire
 Bray, Probationary Flight Officer, Raymond Earl
 Rhoads, George Arthur, Private
 Russell, Charles Reuben, Private
Consett (Benfieldside) Cemetery, Durham, United Kingdom
 Carr, J.M.M., Private
 Smith, Arthur Nightingale, Driver
Cranwell (St. Andrew) Churchyard, Lincolnshire
 Pitt, Probationary Flight Officer, W.W.
Crowborough Burial Ground, Sussex
 De Morney, Francis Randolph, Sapper
Croydon (Queen's Road) Cemetery, Surrey
 Murphy, Stephen James, Sapper
Doncaster (Christ Church) Churchyard, Yorkshire
 Clarkson, Thomas Cooke, Second Lieutenant
Doncaster (Hyde Park) Cemetery, Yorkshire
 Savage, H.L., Lieutenant
Dover (St. James's) Cemetery, Kent
 Burrows, William, Private
 Cross, Walter Frederick, Private
Drumcree Church of Ireland Churchyard, County Armagh
 Hall, William Victor, Private
Dudley Borough Cemetery, Worcestershire
 Wakelin, Arthur., Sapper
Dundee Eastern Necropolis, Angus
 McIntosh, James, Lance Corporal
Durrington Cemetery, Wiltshire
 Hill, Robert Brinton, Lieutenant
East Boldre (St. Paul) Churchyard, Hampshire
 Blackie, Austin Wyard, Lieutenant
 Kidd, Vernon Monroe, Second Lieutenant
 Vande Water, Malcolm Gifford, Second Lieutenant
East Wemyss Cemetery, Fifeshire
 Campbell, John Aloysius, Private
Eastham (St. Mary) Churchyard, Cheshire
 Murray, Walter Scott, Second Lieutenant

Edinburgh (Comely Bank) Cemetery, Edinburgh
 Farley, O., Private
 Miron, H., Private
Edinburgh (Morningside) Cemetery, Edinburgh
 Clayton, Richard Stopford, Lieutenant
Edinburgh (Piershill) Cemetery, Edinburgh
 Harding, Alfred, Colour Sergeant
Edinburgh (Rosebank) Cemetery, Edinburgh
 White, Robert, Private
Edinburgh (Seafield) Cemetery, Edinburgh
 Valliere, E., Private
Englefield Green Cemetery, Surrey
 Brooks, Charles Albert, Private
 Saunders, Blackden Kenedy, Private
Epsom Cemetery, Surrey
 Bruns, Fredrick, Private
 Corrigan, Albert Victor Ernest, Lance Corporal
 Rhawn, Charles Huhn, Lance Corporal
Exeter Higher Cemetery, Devon
 Quinlan, James, Private
Failsworth Cemetery, Lancashire
 Halliwell, H.H., Sergeant
Figheldean (St. Michael) Churchyard, Wiltshire
 Daly, Joseph James, Lieutenant
Fort Pitt Military Cemetery, Kent
 O'Brien, Roy Oberall, Rifleman
Gillingham (Woodlands) Cemetery, Kent
 Dickson, Almond Colebrook, Private 2nd Class
 Gourlay, Frank Lawrence, Petty Officer
Girvan (Doune) Cemetery, Ayrshire
 McNair, Robert Schermerhorn, Second Lieutenant
Glasgow (Craigton) Cemetery, Glasgow
 Niven, Thomas Munro, Sergeant
Glasgow (Eastwood) Cemetery, Glasgow
 MacKill, Robert, Private
Glasgow (Riddrie Park) Cemetery, Glasgow
 Moir, Robert, Private
 Walker, W.W., Private
Glasgow Western Necropolis, Glasgow
 Carson, William Murray, Private
 Johnston, Ardell Alfred McGill, Private
Golders Green Crematorium, Middlesex
 Hawthorne, Philip Erlam, Lance Corporal
Grayshott (St. Joseph) Roman Catholic Churchyard, Hampshire
 Barraclough, Parker, Private
 Bernard, George Odilon, Private
 Blair, William Parker, Private
 Cotey, W.J., Private
 Hunsberger, F., Private
 Moon, Daniel Charles, Private
 Ryan, George Eathen, Private
Great Crosby (St. Luke) Churchyard, Lancashire
 Hood, Richard Edward, Major

Great Lever (St. Michael) Churchyard, Lancashire
  Stevenson, James, Sapper
Greenwich Cemetery, London
  Alexander, Lee Roy, Private
  Pierce, George Albert, Gunner
Hastings Cemetery, Sussex, Sussex
  Coulter, Douglas Johnstone, Gunner
Hillingdon and Uxbridge Cemetery, Middlesex
  Goodwin, Roy, Sergeant
Hollybrook Memorial, Southampton, Hampshire
  Beer, Jack, Pioneer
  McAlpin, Donald Davis, Second Lieutenant
Hooton (St. Mary of the Angels) Roman Catholic Churchyard, Cheshire
  English, Joseph Patrick Fitzgerald, Second Lieutenant
Hursley (All Saints) Church Cemetery, Hampshire
  George, Leslie, Lieutenant
Inverness (Tomnahurich) Cemetery, Inverness-Shire
  Laing, Wesley Thomas, Private
Ipswich Cemetery, Suffolk
  Cullen, Frank, Private
  Williams, Gilbert Lee, Sapper
Iver Heath (St. Margaret) Churchyard, Buckinghamshire
  Kiburz, Leo Albert, Lieutenant
Kensal Green (All Souls') Cemetery, London
  Fetrol, W., Private
Kensal Green (St. Mary's) Roman Catholic Cemetery, London
  Ames, Peter Ashmun, Lieutenant
  Collins, Daniel Leo, Driver
  Lindsay, Harold Laurance, Private
Kidderminster Cemetery, Worcestershire
  Boraston, William, Private
Leeds (Holbeck) Cemetery, Yorkshire
  Jones, S., Private
Leighterton Church Cemetery, Gloucestershire
  Frederick, Charles Clarence, Cadet
Lenham Cemetery, Kent
  Powell, Roy Victor, Sergeant
Leysdown (St. Clement) Churchyard, Kent
  Smith, Lothrop Lewis de Berniere, Lieutenant
Lincoln (Newport) Cemetery, Lincolnshire
  Crone, Leonard, Second Lieutenant
  Felhauer, Carl Varl, Second Lieutenant
  Heater, Roy Esworth, Second Lieutenant
Liverpool (Allerton) Cemetery, Lancashire
  Benzie, William Robertson, Fireman
Liverpool (Anfield) Cemetery, Lancashire
  Lowe, Michael Joseph, Driver
Liverpool (Broad Green) Jewish Cemetery, Lancashire
  Hymanson, D., Private

Liverpool (Kirkdale) Cemetery, Lancashire, United Kingdo
  Gaba, Joel, Sapper
  Hough, Richard Radcliffe, Private
  McDaniel, Percy, Private
  Merrell, George Clark, Sapper
  Peto, O.K., Private
  Sticker, Thomas Orville, Sapper
Loanhead Cemetery, Midlothian
  Cadzow, J., Private
Lorton (St. Cuthbert) Churchyard, Cumberland
  Benson, John, Private
Lyness Royal Naval Cemetery, Orkney
  Stanley, Leonard, Sub-Lieutenant
Martin (Holy Trinity) Churchyard, Lincolnshire
  Taylor, H., Sapper
Maybole Cemetery, Ayrshire
  Carroll, P., Private
Melcombe Regis Cemetery, Dorset
  Bagshaw, Harry Rendall, Sapper
Minster (Thanet) Cemetery, Kent
  Fitzpatrick, Grant, Sapper
Moneyglass Roman Catholic Cemetery, County Antrim
  McQuaid, J., Sapper
Montrose (Sleepyhillock) Cemetery, Angus
  Fairbairn, Dudley Churchill, Second Lieutenant
Morden Cemetery, Surrey
  McAllister, John, Private
Nairn Cemetery, Nairnshire
  Clark, John, Private
Netley Military Cemetery, Hampshire
  Ferger, John E., Private
  Tyler, Theodore, Private
Nunhead (All Saints) Cemetery, London
  Chant, Arthur Thomas, Private
  Corrie, T.A., Lance Corporal
Orpington (All Saints) Churchyard Extension, Kent
  Anderson, J.A., Sapper
  Armstrong, Francis Herbert, Private
  Watt, J.A., Private
Penrith Cemetery, Cumberland
  Towle, Joseph Frank, Private
Penzance (Paul) Cemetery, Cornwall
  Cloke, Albert Charles, Gunner
Plymouth (Efford) Cemetery, Devon
  Wade, W.F., Private
Plymouth Naval Memorial, Devon
  Barry, John, Sick Berth Steward 2nd Class
  Carbines, William Henry, Leading Seaman
  O'Driscoll, William, Leading Seaman
  Payne, Thomas, Able Seaman
  Toulmin, Stewart Newnham, Surgeon

Plympton (St. Mary) Churchyard, Devon
Rowland, John Henry, Gunner

Portsmouth (Kingston) Cemetery, Hampshire
Maturin, William Henry, Lieutenant

Portsmouth Naval Memorial, Hampshire
Anderson, Andrew Thomas, Engine Room Artificer 3rd Class
Bigsby, Thomas James, Leading Seaman
Knight, Frederick Cyril, Leading Seaman
Learmonth, Deck Hand, Alfred Ian
Taylor, John, Trimmer

Redruth (St. Uny) Churchyard Extension, Cornwall
Hooper, J.T., Signaller

Ripon Cemetery, Yorkshire
Fenn, A.S., Private
Hession, William Joseph, Private

Roslin Cemetery, Midlothian
Brown, A.C., Sapper

Rotherham (Masbrough) Cemetery, Yorkshire
Machin, F., Lance Corporal

Rotherham (Moorgate) Cemetery, Yorkshire
Henry, S., Private

St. Day (Holy Trinity) Churchyard, Cornwall
Simmons, Stephen Washington, Gunner

St. Helens Cemetery, Lancashire
Garland, Alexander, Private

Salisbury (London Road) Cemetery, Wiltshire
Brennan, Lester Luke, Second Lieutenant
Preston, Harry Dennis, Second Lieutenant

Seaford Cemetery, Sussex
Carr, J., Private
Carrick, William Henry, Lance Corporal
Croymans, Henry John, Sapper
Ducharme, Anthony Alexander, Private
Graham, James Booth, Corporal
Hatter, Claude, Sapper
Iodence, Arthur Bryan, Private
Jenkins, Howard Newton, Sapper
Rauffenbart, Walter Ervin, Private
Thomson, Allan Wates, Private
Williams, H.J., Private

Seagoe Cemetery, County Armagh
Dillon, S.G., Private

Shawbury (St. Mary the Virgin) Churchyard, Shropshire
Roper, George, Second Lieutenant

Shorncliffe Military Cemetery, Kent
Arbuckle, Bert, Gunner
Armstrong, George Wheeler, Lieutenant
Bates, George, Private
Gladman, Ottawa Thomas, Private
Gordon, D., Private
Gray, David, Private
Hanson, Charles Johan, Private

McNulty, J.D., Gunner
Ramsdell, John Lucious, Private

Shotley (St. Mary) Churchyard, Suffolk
Harvey, R., Leading Seaman
Taylor, Ernest Edwin, Petty Officer Stoker

Shotwick (St. Michael) Churchyard, Cheshire
Miller, John Jewett, Second Lieutenant
Morange, Leonard Sowersby, Lieutenant
Samuelson, Frank Albert, Second Lieutenant

Southend-on-Sea (Sutton Road) Cemetery, Essex
Sketchley, Stanley, Sergeant

Stanley New Cemetery, Durham
Fryer, Sidney, Gunner

Stourbridge Cemetery, Worcestershire
Smith, R.G., Private

Sunderland (Bishopwearmouth) Cemetery, Durham
Jackson, J.W.A., Private

Sunderland (Southwick) Cemetery, Durham
Forbister, William John, Sapper

Sutton-in-Craven Baptist Burial Ground, Yorkshire
Haggas, W.G., Sapper
Scovil, W.C., Sapper

Torquay Cemetery and Extension, Devon
Caldwell, Robert, Colonel

Tower Hill Memorial, London
Addor, L., Seaman
Allen, W.J., Sailor
Arnesen, M., Seaman
Ashley, C., Fireman and Trimmer
Bennison, Raymond Earl, Surgeon
Birnie, James Alexander, Sailor
Borie, Geo, Oiler
Brown, P.D., Horseman
Brown, Vance, Muleteer
Buckley, Barth, Horseman
Buie, W., Horseman
Burbank, W.A., Sailor
Burchett, W., Muleteer
Byrd, L., Muleteer
Campbell, E.W., Fireman
Clements, William, Fireman
Connelly, Owen, Trimmer
Denis, George, Fireman
Garrity, Joseph, Horseman
Gordon, Ralph, Muleteer
Gray, William, Fireman
Guernsey, William, Muleteer
Hahn, Charles, Muleteer
Harries, Waiter, George Edward
Hazelton, Greaser, Clarence
Hill, John, Muleteer
Holland, John Francis, Ordinary Seaman
House, T.M., Horseman
Jiske, John, Fireman and Trimmer
Jones, Levy, Fireman and Trimmer

Kennewell, Roger William, Sailor
Loy, Thomas, Third Engineer
Mahoney, John, Horseman
Marner, F., Cook
Maydwell, Chas, Ordinary Seaman
McGeehan, John, Horseman
McKee, Henry Taylor, Second Engineer
Newcombe, Robert Irwin Pile, Third Mate
Phelan, J.T., Supercargo
Pitts, William, Able Seaman
Racine, Joseph Charles Edouard, Ship's Cook
Rainwater, C.E., Fireman and Trimmer
Reed, D., Fireman
Robinson, E., Sailor
Robinson, Lewis, Fireman
Scott, David, Muleteer
Scott, John, Muleteer
Shepherd, Edward, Fireman
Shinn, Harry, Fireman
Sinclair, John Ernest, Fourth Engineer Officer
Smith, T., Fireman and Trimmer
Sovig, Neils, Chief Engineer
Strickland, A.L., Fireman
Taylor, Enoch, Muleteer
Taylor, Guy Harry, Fireman and Trimmer
Thomas, Daniel P., Horseman
Thomas, Leonard, Fireman
Thompson, Harry W., Seaman
Walker, Denis, Second Cook
Wallace, Richard, Able Seaman
Warner, Frank H., Seaman
Waters, Lloyd S., Muleteer
Welsh, D., Fireman and Trimmer
Wesley, S.S., Fireman
Wilson, Joe, Muleteer
Wilson, R., Fireman and Trimmer
Wolff, Frederick J., Able Seaman
Wolfunberg, Alfred, Horseman
Zachler, Paul, Sailor

Upavon Cemetery, *Wiltshire*
Misenhimer, William Kay, Second Lieutenant

Upton-cum-Chalvey (St. Mary) Churchyard, Slough, *Buckinghamshire*
Cook, E.A., Second Lieutenant

Wallasey (Rake Lane) Cemetery, *Cheshire*
Snyder, Chester Gordon, Private

Wandsworth (Earlsfield) Cemetery, *London*
McNaughton, Donald, Private

Wandsworth (Putney Vale) Cemetery and Crematorium, *London*
Waterhouse, Joseph, Lieutenant

Warlingham (All Saints) Churchyard, *Surrey*
McAdam, George Wallace, Flight Cadet

Warrington Cemetery, *Lancashire*
Bramhall, William, Sapper
Cadogan, Thomas Francis, Sapper

Whalley (Queen Mary's Hospital) Military Cemetery, *Lancashire*
Horne, J., Private
Johnson, Joseph Sipthus, Sergeant

Winchester (Magdalen Hill) Cemetery, *Hampshire*
Cox, Philip William, Private
Crowson, J., Rifleman
Gill, Ernest, Private

Winchester (West Hill) Old Cemetery, *Hampshire, United Kingdo*
Peel, Wilfred John, Sapper

Withycombe Raleigh (St. John in the Wilderness) Churchyard, *Devon*
Whichelow, C.L.T., Corporal

Witley (Milford) Cemetery, *Surrey*
Convery, Henry William, Driver
Palmer, William, Corporal

Woking (St. John's) Crematorium, *Surrey*
Delay, Aladdin Richard, Second Lieutenant

Wokingham (St. Sebastian) Churchyard, *Berkshire*
Conron, William James, Corporal

Yatesbury (All Saints) Churchyard, *Wiltshire*
Rowe, Marcus, Second Lieutenant

YEMEN

Maala Cemetery
Topping, Peter, Company Quartermaster Sergeant

Appendix 11: American Armed Forces Members Still Buried in Isolated Graves in France Since World War I

These are members of United States forces, most killed during World War I, buried in small communal and military cemeteries across France. In most cases, they were not moved to American cemeteries in Europe or returned home because of decisions made by their families. They fall under the remembrance activities of the Ameican Overseas Memorial Day

Association France (AOMDA), based in Paris, which also performs remembrance activities in the American cemeteries of France. Listings, as given, are by town or village in which the cemetery is located and name(s). Full names, ranks, affiliations and designation as to World War I or World War II are often not given. Where Mr. or Monsieur is used, a noncombatant (ambulance driver, clerk, etc.) may be indicated. More information about a number of these dead can be found by Internet search. Pictures of many of their graves can be found on the "In Memory" Website maintained by Pierre Vandervelden, and each cemetery can be found on this book's Website.

Aignac-le-Duc
  John Johnson
Aix-les-Bains
  Major John Mac Elroy
  Alfred Stout
  Camille Bernard
  Douglas Brown
Appoigny
  Mr. Jocelyn Stephen
  Edgard J. Houseman
Aubepierre-sur-Aube
  Raymond Young
Aulnay-sous-Bois
  Mr. William Goodell
Bagneux
  Michael Lubin
Bar-sur-Aube
  Captain William Kearney
Bavans
  Philippe Schaeffer
Bayeux
  Lieutenant Colonel Peter A. Dewey
Bellerive-sur-Allier
  Colonel Samuel Slater
Bourges
  Corporal Eugene Strengs, 1918
Brassac-les-Mines
  Robert de Lorenzo
Brest
  Freemans
  Squires
  PM Gray
  JP Melhuis
  John William
Calais
  Andrew A. Lavigne
Chatou
  Mr. Lucien Sommer
Chaumont
  John E. Williams
  Frank Schlaich
Clamart
  Julius Snohill

Clermont-en-Argonne
  Craig Harmon Rushnelle, 1916
Garches
  John Dombrowski
  Victor Ehrenzweig
Haut Chinon
  Eugene Strubbe
Hochfelden
  Lieutenant John Grant Rahill
La Neuvillette
  Conrad Kreuter
La Souterraine
  Max Olszewski
Le Château Cambresis
  Kenneth Gow
Le Crotoy
  Roger Sherman Dix
Le Molay Littry
  Howard Dillingham
Les Essarts-le-Roi
  Mr. Roland F. Klein
Les Lilas
  Truffet, na
Luxeuil-les-Bains
  Sergeant K.Y. Rockwell
Marnes-la-Coquette
  Mr. Emory Foster
Meximieux
  LT Harry Burgerman
  George Aubry
Monthureux-sur-Saône
  Antonio Gugudda
Montigny-le-Bretonneux
  Bernie Carroll
Montreuil-sous-Bois
  Lieutenant Laurence A. Pope
Montrichard
  Major William Tyree
Mouzon
  Captain Hamilton Coolidge
Moyenmoutier
  Thomas Rodman Plummer
Nancy
  Lieutenant Richard Banks

Nevers
  Lientenant Herbert Francis Thorpe
Orange
  Thomas H. Condon
Pantin
  Harry Grossmann
  Leopold Kalamanonitz
  Harrison Spencer McKillop
Paris
  Mr. Julius Winter
Perthes
  Monsieur James Dine
  Monsieur Emmett Samford
Remilly
  Norton Kennedy
Romilly-sur-Seine
  Edward M. Stone
  Allen Renkenberger
St.-Germain-en-Laye
  Dennis Dowds
  Stanley Low
  Murphy Hogan
  Hasking
  Sara Clark
  John Read
  Benedicte Legrand
  Diamant
  Addison Armstong
  Colonel Mitchell Bryant
  Davis Hutchins
  Julian Meredith
  James Ross
  Mr. Robinson
Saint-Gervais-en-Forêt
  Gilbert Lerire
  Michel Leconch
Saint-Maur-des-Fosses
  Mr. Alexander G. Stekas
Suippes
  Henri Farnsworth
  Gaston Mayer
Talence
  Edward Simacys
  Abraham Hamde
  Anton Rivas

Charles Carroll
Josesph Bouchard
Thiaucourt-en-Argonne
Charles Hoffecher

Toul
Grace Malloch
Vierville sur Mer
Paul Devaux

Villeparisis
Jules P. Buckmann
George Mac Farland

Appendix 12: American Armed Forces Members of World War I and World War II Still Buried in Isolated Graves in Belgium

These are members of United States forces killed in Belgium in both World War I and World War II who are buried in small communal and military cemeteries. Extensive biographies of each can be found on the American Overseas Memorial Day Association Belgium (AOMDA) Website. In most cases they were not moved to American cemeteries in Europe, returned home or returned from American cemeteries because of decisions made by their families. They fall under the remembrance activities of AOMDA-Belgium, based in Brussels, which also performs remembrance activities in the American cemeteries of Belgium.

WORLD WAR I

Lijssenthoek Commonwealth War Graves Cemetery
Sgt. David Stanley Beattie
105th Infantry Regiment, 27th Division
Killed in action August 31, 1918.
Pfc. Harry King
Troop F, 3rd Cavalry
Died of pneumonia September 20, 1918. Originally buried in the Argonne American cemetery September 1918; reburied in October 1921.
First Lt. James Aaron Pigue
Company A, 117th Infantry Regiment, 30th Division
Killed in action July 18, 1918.

WORLD WAR II

Comblain-la-Tour Church Cemetery
Pfc. Joseph G. Farina
Company B, 526 Armored Infantry Battalion
Killed in action January 3, 1945. Originally buried at Henri-Chapelle American Cemetery on February 25, 1945, and reburied August 5, 1948.

Ganshoren Community Cemetery
Staff Sgt. Gerald E. Sorenson
339th Bomber Squadron, 96th Heavy Bomber Group
Killed in the Belgian Resistance September 3.

Heverlee Commonwealth War Graves Cemetery, near Leuven
First Lt. Donald West
United States Army Air Force
Detached Service, 57 Royal Air Force Squadron.
Killed in action November 3, 1943.

Queue-du-Bois Village Cemetery
Second Lt. Robert Lee Garrett
785th Bomber Squadron, 466 Bomber Group
Killed in action March 23, 1944.
Buried in Queue-de-Bois September 11, 1944; removed to Netherlands American Cemetery on March 4, 1946; reburied at Queue-de-Bois March–April 1949.

Ronse Community Cemetery
Second Lt. Gilbert A. Malrait
719th Bomber Squadron, 449th Bomber Group
Killed in action April 4, 1944.
Born in the United States of immigrant parents, Malrait was eventually buried in his father's hometown of Ronse August 12, 1950.

Appendix 13: Americans Buried or Memorialized in Commonwealth War Grave Cemeteries since World War II

These American-related casualties who fought with Commonwealth Forces in World War II are buried or memorialized in CWGC cemeteries in all parts of the world. The vast majority are American born, and a good number are American immigrants. Some were next of kin to American wives or parents, though not necessarily Amerian citizens. This list is distilled, as given, from CWGC records. More complete information about origins, age, place and cause of death, related battle action, and next of kin can be found in the name search engine of the Commonwealth War Graves Commission Website.

ALGERIA
El Alia Cemetery
  Haven, Roger Wallace, Flying Officer (W.Op./Air Gnr.)

AUSTRALIA
Nowra War Cemetery, New South Wales
  Kennett, Ronald George, Sub-Lieutenant (A)
Townsville War Cemetery, Queensland
  Browne, Robert Stanley, Petty Officer (W/T Mech.)

BAHAMAS
Nassau War Cemetery
  Chouteau, Henri, Captain

BELGIUM
Adegem Canadian War Cemetery, Maldegem, Oost-Vlaanderen
  Agnew, Frank, Private
Brussels Town Cemetery, Evere, Vlaams-Brabant
  Barbour, Stuart Douglas, Flight Lieutenant
  Cochrane, Thomas John, Corporal
  Lovett, William, Corporal
  Warfield, William, Flying Officer (Pilot)
Charleroi Communal Cemetery, Charleroi, Hainaut
  Moore, John Bruce, Sergeant (W.Op./Air Gnr.)
Gosselies Communal Cemetery, Charleroi, Hainaut
  Mead, Robert Frazer, Flight Lieutenant (Pilot)
  Moore, Noel McHenry, Warrant Officer Class I (Pilot)
  Stewart, James Henry, Flying Officer (Pilot)
Heverlee War Cemetery, Leuven, Vlaams-Brabant
  Climie, William Benzie Forbes, Warrant Officer Class II (Air Gnr.)
  Dodge, Stanley Wilbur, Pilot Officer (Pilot)
  Garoutte, Bryon Homer, Warrant Officer Class II (Air Gnr.)
  Gates, Billy Orin, Flight Sergeant (Pilot)
  Johnston, Gerald MacIntoshe, Private
  Mohler, Otis Judson, Warrant Officer Class II (Air Gnr.)

Lanklaar Communal Cemetery, Dilsen-Stokkem, Limburg
  Willson, John Campbell, Flight Sergeant (Air Bomber)
Rekem Communal Cemetery, Lanaken, Limburg
  Park, Thomas Hill, Sergeant (Air Gnr.)

CANADA
Aylmer Cemetery, Ontario
  Seagram, John David, Pilot Officer
Beauceville Cemetery, Quebec
  Poulin, Joseph Jean Louis, Lance Corporal
Burlington (Holy Sepulchre) Cemetery, Ontario
  Livsey, Bernard Mindenhall, Trooper
Burnaby (Forest Lawn) Memorial Park, British Columbia
  Jessee, James Pyle, Flight Lieutenant
Calgary (Burnsland) Cemetery, Alberta
  Baker, John Custance, Flying Officer
  Haggerty, Melville Jerry, Private
  Ricks, Harry Lee, Private
Calgary Jewish Cemetery, Alberta
  Heymans, David Benjamin, Leading Aircraftman
Dartmouth (Mount Hermon) Cemetery, Nova Scotia
  Hook, John Thomas, Flight Lieutenant
Fredericton Rural Cemetery, New Brunswick
  Burse, Russell Ervine, Leading Aircraftman
Gander War Cemetery, Newfoundland and Labrador
  Crymes, Smith Edward, Leading Aircraftman
  Ehrlichman, Rudolph Irwin, Flight Lieutenant
Halifax (Fort Massey) Cemetery, Nova Scotia
  Payne, Edward, Staff Sergeant
Halifax Memorial, Nova Scotia
  Bolin, Gordon Walter, Able Seaman
  Brown, Henry, Able Seaman
  Callow, Alfred, Storekeeper
  Conway, Archibald Henry William, Leading Seaman
  Cumming, Malcolm, Lieutenant (E)
  Davis, Donald, Fireman
  Davis, John, Fireman

Gill, John, Senior Fourth Engineer Officer
King, William Lyon MacKenzie, Surgeon Lieutenant
Taylor, Ernest Francis, Able Seaman
Watson, John Crittenden, Lieutenant (E)
Wells, Reginald Lawrence, Warrant Officer Class II (C.S.M.)
Yonkers, Thomas Trygve, Mess Room Boy

Innisfil (St. Paul's) Cemetery, Ontario
Farrow, Edwin Norman, Private

London (Mount Pleasant) Cemetery, Ontario
Miller, Russell Ainsley, Driver

London (Woodland) Cemetery, Ontario
Wood, Chester Miles, Aircraftman 2nd Class

Milltown Catholic Cemetery, New Brunswick
Burns, William Robinson, Corporal

Montreal (Mount Royal) Cemetery, Quebec
Carson, Hugh Ogilvy, Lieutenant
Lauzon, Norman Leo, Sergeant
Murray, George Black, Sergeant
Smith, Elmer Hawthorne, Lance Corporal
Young, John Russell Dermott, Leading Aircraftman

Montreal (Notre Dame Des Neiges) Cemetery, Quebec
Curtis, Walter Reginald, Corporal
Gaudette, Joseph Emile, Assistant Cook
Labelle, Georges Harry, Captain
Mathieu, Florian Joseph, Private

Niagara-on-the-Lake (St. Mark's) Anglican Cemetery, Ontario
Howarth, Jack Leach, Sergeant

Nictaux (United Baptist) Cemetery, Nova Scotia
Chipman, Lawrence Fairn, Lieutenant (S)

Oshawa Union Cemetery, Ontario
Franklin, Edward Francis, Staff Sergeant

Ottawa (Beechwood) Cemetery, Ontario
Parsons, Edwin Scarritt, Flying Officer
Price, Clarence John, Corporal
Shackleton, Douglas Dennison, Flight Lieutenant

Ottawa Cremation Memorial, Ontario
Bristol, Beverly Ward, Flying Officer
Carvalho, Paul D., Leading Aircraftman
Moody, James Rowland, Leading Aircraftman
Moore, Edward A., Flight Lieutenant
Walker, Ian Paris, Flight Lieutenant

Ottawa Jewish Cemetery, Ontario
Levine, Harry Edgar, Sergeant (Pilot)

Ottawa Memorial, Ontario
Aucoin, Whitney Philip, Flight Sergeant
Bishop, William Mather, Pilot Officer
Bliss, Jack Fenton., Sergeant
Borum, John William, Flying Officer
Burchfield, Lowell Luther, First Officer
Cochran, Robert Hearne, Sergeant
Cox, John Richard, Pilot Officer
Field, Charles William Thomas, Flight Lieutenant
Folk, Robert E., Civilian
Hay, Harry Hilts, Pilot Officer
Hornbrook, Peter Francis, Sergeant
Mansell, Reginald Baynes, Air Vice Marshal
McCarty, Warren Roberts, Flight Sergeant
McCawley, Samuel Howard, Captain
Northgrave, John Milne, Sergeant
Robertson, Ian, Pilot Officer
Schlacks, Albert Redfearn, Flight Lieutenant
Singer, Charles, Civilian

Ottawa (Notre Dame) Roman Catholic Cemetery, Ontario
Blackwell, Dale Lamar, Captain
Enright, Nellie Josephine, Matron
Snider, Lloyd George, Corporal

Owen Sound (Greenwood) Cemetery, Ontario
Somerville, John Henry, Private

Picton (Glenwood) Cemetery, Ontario
Armour, Albert Stewart, Flying Officer

Portage-la-Prairie (Hillside) Cemetery, Manitoba
McIntyre, Peter Douglas, Sergeant

St. Donat Roman Catholic Cemetery, Quebec
Elliott, Franklin Hicks, Sergeant

St. John (Fernhill) Cemetery, Saint John County, New Brunswick
Keeling, Charles, Warrant Engineer

St. John's (Mount Pleasant) Cemetery, Newfoundland and Labrador
Padden, Edwin Joseph, Pilot Officer

Saskatoon (Woodlawn) Cemetery, Saskatchewan
Lindsay, James George Keber, Colonel

Springhill (Hillside) Cemetery, Nova Scotia
Tower, Walter Henry, Private

Sweetsburg (Christ Church) Cemetery, Quebec
Cady, George Clement, Corporal

Thunder Bay (Riverside) Cemetery, Ontario
Gilchrist, Frank Clifford, Lance Corporal
Oag, Thomas, Private

Toronto (Mount Pleasant) Cemetery, Ontario
Harding, Robert Gordon, Corporal

Toronto (Pine Hills) Cemetery, Ontario
Pengelley, Lewis Henry, Warrant Officer Class I (S.M. Instr.)

Toronto (Prospect) Cemetery, Ontario
Doubassoff, Theodore, Flight Lieutenant
Hickey, John James, Trooper
Morton, Hugh Weir, Flight Lieutenant

Toronto (Resthaven) Memorial Garden, Ontario
Matthew, James Smith, Sergeant

Toronto (St. James') Cemetery, Ontario
Corbett, Vaughan Bowerman, Group Captain

Trenton (St. George's) Cemetery, Ontario
Percival, Loriman Samuel, Flying Officer

Valleyfield Protestant Cemetery, Quebec
  Dent, Thomas William., Private

Vancouver (Mountain View) Cemetery, British Columbia
  Cuttle, Charles Roy, Private
  Evans, Norman David, Private
  McDole, Archie John, Lance Corporal

Victoria (Royal Oak) Burial Park, British Columbia
  Dawson, Joseph, Sergeant

Windsor (Grove) Cemetery, Ontario
  Dumond, Leroy, Trooper
  Rees, Ivan Henry, Pilot Officer
  Schneiker, Peter, Gunner

Windsor (Victoria) Memorial Park, Ontario
  Gee, Harold, Corporal
  Naish, Clifford Henry Wesley, Able Seaman

Winnipeg (Brookside) Cemetery, Manitoba
  Murphy, Cornelius Vanderbilt, Company Quartermaster Sergeant
  Wert, Roy Osgood, Lance Corporal

Winnipeg (Elmwood) Cemetery, Manitoba
  Harris, Robert, Private

Yarmouth (Mountain) Cemetery, Nova Scotia
  Maxwell, William James, Leading Aircraftman

CHINA, INCLUDING HONG KONG

Sai Wan Memorial
  Brown, Conrad, Private
  Curtis, Edward Lea, Sergeant
  Donohue, Patrick, Lance Sergeant
  Edgley, Charles, Private
  Greenevitch, Voldemar, Private
  Joseph, H.B., Private
  Prew, Albert George Frith, Private
  Rodgers, Robert Augustus, Private
  White, Nowell Bernard, Lance Corporal

Stanley Military Cemetery
  Scott, Walter Richardson, Deputy Commissioner

CZECH REPUBLIC

Prague War Cemetery
  Shoup, Lambert Laverne, Private

DENMARK

Graasten Cemetery
  Coffey, Robert Ellsworth, Squadron Leader

Kirkeby Churchyard
  Galipeau, Robert Henry, Flight Sergeant (Air Gnr.)

DJIBOUTI

Djibouti New European Cemetery
  Maguire, Lawrence Robert, Pilot Officer (Pilot)

EGYPT

Alamein Memorial
  Cains, Frederick Lighthall Pulsford, Warrant Officer Class II
  Clary, Edgar Leroy, Flying Officer
  Clements, Roger Bentley, Warrant Officer Class II
  Cunningham, Richard Alexander, Flight Sergeant
  Gregory, Forrest June, Flying Officer
  Jackson, Granville Andrew, Flight Sergeant
  Johnston, Hugh Browning, Flight Sergeant
  McArthur, Duncan Harold, Flight Lieutenant
  McClive, Lloyd Peter, Warrant Officer Class II
  Mink, Laurel Louis, Flying Officer
  Mitchell, John Howard, Major
  Palethorpe, Donald Moir, Flight Sergeant
  Prentice, Thomas Walker, Pilot Officer
  Rutkin, Sam, Lieutenant

Alexandria (Hadra) War Memorial Cemetery
  Sheppard, Ernest Edson, Corporal

El Alamein War Cemetery
  Blundell, Peter Charles, Captain
  Stone, Edward Raymond, Captain

Heliopolis War Cemetery
  Burns, Walter William, Flight Sergeant (Pilot)
  Muhart, Sidney Nicholas, Pilot Officer

Port Said War Memorial Cemetery
  Price, George Edward, Sergeant (Air Obs.)

FRANCE

Banneville-la-Campagne War Cemetery, Calvados
  Burden, Joseph Warren, Captain
  Sleep, William Arthur Ernest, Sergeant
  Steiner, Ronald, Private

Bayeux Memorial, Calvados
  McKenzie, Claude Scott, Private

Bayeux War Cemetery, Calvados
  Abrin, Harry Leo, First Officer
  Collins, Kenneth McRoberts, Flying Officer (Pilot)

Beny-sur-Mer Canadian War Cemetery, Reviers, Calvados
  Allman, Leonard Ralph, Flying Officer (Pilot)
  Gosselin, Robert Andrew, Sergeant
  Lewis, William Bruce, Private
  Modeen, George, Rifleman

Boulogne Eastern Cemetery, Pas-de-Calais
  Colloredo-Mansfeld, Count Franz Ferdinand, Squadron Leader (Pilot)

Bretteville-sur-Laize Canadian War Cemetery, Calvados
  Broyles, William Ellsworth, Trooper
  Bunnell, Charles William, Gunner
  Campbell, James, Sergeant
  Daigle, Philibert, Private
  Eldridge, Willoughby, Lance Corporal

Gale, George M., Corporal
Gillis, Calvin Lawrence, Private
Gould, Robert Crossett, Lieutenant
Grieve, Allan C., Lance Corporal
Holiday, Joseph, Private
Jones, William H., Trooper
Kimmel, Spencer Griffith, Flying Officer (Pilot)
Living, Frederick Stevenson, Private
Long, William Eugene Lacour, Trooper
Mayall, Charles J., Private
Murfitt, Herbert Arthur, Corporal
Presnail, William P., Private
Ripley, James, Corporal
Ross, James Aaron, Trooper
Sheldon, Gordon G., Bombardier
Smolkowski, Walter J.C., Private
Waye, Wendell Clifford, Warrant Officer Class II (Air Bomber)
Wolf, Homer Lynn, Flight Lieutenant (Pilot)

Calais Canadian War Cemetery, Leubringhen, Pas-de-Calais
Branch, James David, Lance Corporal
Coleman, Alvero Duane, Bombardier
Collins, Dennis J., Craftsman
Cummings, Robert, Warrant Officer Class II (Air Gnr.)
Downing, Frank Chace, Pilot Officer (Pilot)
Fitzpatrick, Omer J., Private
Lukhmanoff, George Boris, Pilot Officer (W.Op./Obs.)
Mechler, Richard E., Trooper
Morin, Joseph W.H., Trooper
Saulnier, Joseph Helaire, Lance Corporal
Sutherland, Caleb Evert, Lieutenant

Chalons-en-Champagne East Communal Cemetery, Marne
Carruthers, Alexander, Pilot Officer (Pilot)
Gonce, Hugh Bernard, Pilot Officer (Pilot)

Choloy War Cemetery, Meurthe-et-Moselle
Dawson, Grahame George, Air Vice Marshal

Dieppe Canadian War Cemetery, Hautot-sur-Mer, Seine-Maritime
Ballmer, James, Private
Bassett, George Henry, Private
Buchanan, Norman Leslie, Private
Floyd, Walter Lewis, Private
Mignault, Ernest, Corporal
Neale, Eugene Adelbert, Private
Palms, James Chaney, Lieutenant
Richards, Austin Bertram, Private
Schopp, Harold Harrison, Flying Officer (Pilot)
Wysuki, Victor, Private

Dreux Communal Cemetery, Eure-et-Loir
Thomas, Thomas Arthur, Sergeant (W.Op./Air Gnr.)

Dunkirk Memorial, Nord
McVeigh, Daniel, Private

Dunkirk Town Cemetery, Nord
Legge, Preston St Clair, Pilot Officer (W.Op./Air Gnr.)
Mooney, John Joseph, Flight Lieutenant (Pilot)

Grand-Seraucourt British Cemetery, Aisne
Hughes, William Adrian, Flying Officer (Pilot)

Janval Cemetery, Dieppe, Seine-Maritime
Morris, Moran Scott, Pilot Officer (Pilot)

Liesse Communal Cemetery, Aisne
Jonasson, Leonard Norman, Sergeant (Air Gnr.)

Mazargues War Cemetery, Marseilles, Bouches-du-Rhone
Granger, Renaldo, Sergeant

Meharicourt Communal Cemetery, Somme
Walters, Edward Joseph, Warrant Officer (Nav./Bomber)
Weaver, Claud, Pilot Officer (Pilot)

Orleans Main Cemetery, Loiret
Aaron, Elmer Oscar, Flying Officer (Air Bomber)

Oye-Plage Communal Cemetery, Pas-de-Calais
Enfield, Paul Alfred Theodore, Private

Pihen-les-Guines Communal Cemetery, Pas-de-Calais
Frahm, Robert Plimpton, Pilot Officer (Pilot)

Plouescat Communal Cemetery, Finistere
Nash, Robert Arthur, Sub-Lieutenant
Rolls, Raymond Burton, Able Seaman
Watson, Reginald John, Telegraphist

Poix-de-Picardie Churchyard, Somme
Gudmundsen, Dick D., Pilot Officer (Pilot)

St. Cyr-en-Val Communal Cemetery, Loiret
Hillman, Ralph Frithjaf, Sergeant (Air Gnr.)

St. Sever Cemetery Extension, Rouen, Seine-Maritime
Astle, Tyler Levita, Private

Wormhoudt Communal Cemetery, Nord
Dowding, Arthur Denis Caswall, Second Lieutenant

GERMANY

Becklingen War Cemetery, Soltau, Niedersachsen
Bates, David Henderson, Flight Sergeant (Pilot)
Hunter, Donald James, Flight Lieutenant (Pilot)
Jackson, William Brindley, Lieutenant

Berlin 1939-1945 War Cemetery, Berlin
Ackland, William Eric, Flight Sergeant (Air Bomber)
Baroni, Raymond John, Sergeant (Air Gnr.)
Carter, Norman Edward, Pilot Officer (Air Gnr.)
Clay, Harry Charles, Pilot Officer (Air Gnr.)
Hicks, Winford Gordon, Flying Officer (Nav.)
Lamphear, Norman Robert, Pilot Officer (Air Gnr.)
Little, Gordon James, Flying Officer (Air Gnr.)
McElhone, John Joseph, Flying Officer (Air Bomber)

Rossignol, James Louis, Pilot Officer (Pilot)
Travers, Charles, Flying Officer (Air Bomber)
Turner, Claude Sydney, Pilot Officer (Air Gnr.)

***Celle War Cemetery**, Celle, Niedersachsen*
Cook, George Albert, Flying Officer (Pilot)

***Durnbach War Cemetery**, Bad Tolz, Bayern*
Richards, John Edward, Flight Sergeant (Pilot)
Valkenier, William Joseph, Flight Sergeant (W.Op./Air Gnr.)
Waugh, Kenneth Robert, Flight Lieutenant (Pilot)

***Hamburg Cemetery**, Hamburg*
Heffernan, John Anthony Foch, Flying Officer (Pilot)
McGee, Lawrence Edward, Warrant Officer Class II (Pilot)

***Hanover War Cemetery**, Hannover, Niedersachsen*
Dorrell, Jack Wilfred, Flying Officer (W.Op./Air Gnr.)
Douglas, William John, Pilot Officer (Air Gnr.)
Frizzell, Harvey Albert, Pilot Officer (Air Gnr.)
Squibb, Harold Edward, Flight Sergeant (Air Bomber)

***Kiel War Cemetery**, Kiel, Schleswig-Holstein*
Woolford, James, Pilot Officer (Pilot)

***Munster Heath War Cemetery**, Telgte, Nordrhein-Westfalen*
Worth, Lionel Eric, Lieutenant Colonel

***Reichswald Forest War Cemetery**, Kleve, Nordrhein-Westfalen*
Bartlemay, William Arthur, Pilot Officer (W.Op./Air Gnr.)
Brown, Charles Davis, Flying Officer (Air Bomber)
Champion, Frank Desborough, Corporal
Craigie, Charles Cleghorn Brockie, Pilot Officer (W.Op./Air Gnr.)
Grant, Hugh Kerr, Sergeant (Flt. Engr.)
Kinsler, Thomas Francis, Flying Officer (Pilot)
Lochhead, Robert Lachlan, Pilot Officer (Air Gnr.)
Pablo, Daniel Lawrence, Flight Sergeant (Pilot)
Phair, Maurice Andrew, Warrant Officer Class II (Pilot)
Sewell, Vernon Young Hodgson, Sergeant (W.Op./Air Gnr.)
Sleeth, Stewart, Warrant Officer Class II (Nav./Bomber)
Strathern, Kenneth Fairley, Captain
Tanner, Kenneth Boyd, Flight Sergeant (Pilot)
Van Buskirk, Douglas Byrd, Flying Officer (Pilot)
Wood, John Morton Montagu, Captain

***Rheinberg War Cemetery**, Kamp Lintfort, Nordrhein-Westfal*
Bristow, Lester Jack Duncan, Sergeant (Navigator)

Butterworth, Robert Stuart, Flying Officer (Air Bomber)
Philp, Donald Robert, Flight Sergeant (Air Obs.)
Rowsell, Arthur Douglas, Sergeant (Air Gnr.)
Strandberg, Edwin, Warrant Officer Class II (Air Gnr.)

***Sage War Cemetery**, Oldenburg, Niedersachsen*
Gellatly, Charles Dewitt, Flight Sergeant (Air Gnr.)
Herrington, Granite William, Flight Sergeant (Air Gnr.)
Linton, Francis Malcolm, Pilot Officer (Nav.)
Little, Ralph Robert, Flying Officer (Pilot)
Mulhauser, Robert Samuel, Pilot Officer (W.Op./Air Gnr.)
Scheelar, Andrew Frank, Flight Lieutenant (Pilot)

GIBRALTAR

Gibraltar (North Front) Cemetery
Zoul, George, Private

GREECE

Athens Memorial
Rosenstein, Ernest Zeno, Lance Corporal

GUINEA

Kindia Cemetery
Elliott, Lewis, Second Engineer Officer

ICELAND

Reykjavik (Fossvogur) Cemetery
Cann, Allan Parker, Radio Officer

INDIA

Calcutta (Bhowanipore) Cemetery
Butler, John Herbert, Driver

Delhi War Cemetery
Bridges, Frederick Edward, Sergeant

Gauhati War Cemetery
Ryan, Patrick Martindale, Captain

Imphal War Cemetery
Miller, David Johnston, Captain

Kirkee War Cemetery
Dunmore, George Douglas Chamberlain, Sub-Lieutenant
Fassenfeld, Laurence, Private
Harrison, Maurice Guy, Officer Cadet

ISRAEL

Khayat Beach War Cemetery
Macaulay, Thomas Hadley Roderick, Flight Lieutenant (Air Bomber)
Sykes, George Evans Vyner, Lieutenant

Ramleh War Cemetery
Bankier, Lili Stefania, Leading Aircraftwoman
Harrison, A.F., Trooper

ITALY

Agira Canadian War Cemetery, *Sicily*
  Asselin, Maurice, Private
  Petz, Mathew George, Warrant Officer Class II

Arezzo War Cemetery
  Wilson, Alfred, Lance Corporal

Assisi War Cemetery
  Tarling, Bernard Francis, Sergeant

Bari War Cemetery
  Carter, Guy Lloyd, Air Commodore
  Farries, Richard Nelson, Fireman
  Phillips, Floyd J., Flying Officer (Pilot)

Beach Head War Cemetery, *Anzio*
  Fox, Irvine Phillip, Company Sergeant Major

Cassino Memorial
  Richards, Branson, Captain

Cesena War Cemetery
  Cantin, Edmond Lionel, Corporal
  Hayes, George Edward, Private
  Mayes, Thomas Daniel, Corporal

Coriano Ridge War Cemetery
  Burton, Floyd William, Lance Sergeant
  Hansen, Hans Frederic, Lieutenant
  Hutchinson, Kenneth G., Sergeant
  Kenyon, Edward, Private

Florence War Cemetery
  Kinghorn, T.G., Lieutenant

Montecchio War Cemetery
  Hooper, John Jacob, Corporal

Moro River Canadian War Cemetery
  Belliveau, Leonce, Private
  Crosbie, Gordon Alexander, Private
  Doane, Elmer Norman, Lieutenant
  Gunter, Ernest Elmo, Corporal
  Orris, William James, Lance Corporal
  Solman, Arthur S.W., Private
  Sterlin, Mitchell, Lieutenant
  Whittaker, Charles R., Corporal
  Williams, George King, Lance Corporal

Padua War Cemetery
  Williams, Idris, Sergeant (Nav.)

Salerno War Cemetery
  Griffin, Charles Edward, Corporal

Staglieno Cemetery, *Genoa*
  Tyas, Reginald Charles, Flight Sergeant

Villanova Canadian War Cemetery
  Tobin, Clifford Francis, Lieutenant

JAPAN

Yokohama War Cemetery
  Harding, Robert W., Rifleman
  Rowland, Roney, Lance Corporal

KENYA

Eldoret Cemetery
  Petrie, Martin Alfred, Second Lieutenant

MALTA

Malta Memorial
  Barker, Gerald Louis, Flying Officer
  Bellingham, Adam Sidney, Flying Officer
  Breakey, Andrew, Flight Lieutenant
  Cornforth, Stanley, Flying Officer
  Cossette, Roland Adelore, Pilot Officer
  Edgett, Ernest Byron, Flying Officer
  Fox, Harold Joseph, Flight Sergeant
  Jay, David Joseph, Pilot Officer
  Johnson, Carl Lee, Flight Lieutenant
  Kelly, Gardner Hill, Pilot Officer
  Mathews, William Hooker, Flying Officer
  May, Peter Rodriguez, Wing Commander
  Moye, Edwin Dewitt, Flight Sergeant
  Preston, Ian Fraser, Pilot Officer
  Rains, William Frank, Pilot Officer
  Ross, Daniel, Flight Sergeant
  Tew, James Dinsmore, Pilot Officer
  Vanderbeck, Roger Edwin, Warrant Officer Class II

Malta (Capuccini) Naval Cemetery
  Putnam, Hiram Aldine, Pilot Officer (Pilot)

MYANMAR

Rangoon Memorial
  Fullerton, Donald Alexander, Captain

Taukkyan War Cemetery
  Atkinson, Alfred William, Lieutenant
  Keech, Owen Andrew, Pilot Officer
  Laine, Colin, Private
  Thomas, Lloyd Duncan, Flight Lieutenant (Pilot)

NETHERLANDS

Amersfoort (Oud Leusden) General Cemetery, *Utrecht*
  Blake, Frederick Henry, Warrant Officer
  Webber, Rodney, Warrant Officer Class II (Air Gnr.)

Amsterdam New Eastern Cemetery, *Noord-Holland*
  Johnson, Howard Edward, Flight Sergeant (Air Gnr.)
  Prime, Peter, Sergeant (Pilot)
  Simmons, Cecil William, Pilot Officer

Arnhem (Moscowa) General Cemetery, *Gelderland*
  Thorne, James Neale, Pilot Officer (Pilot)

Bergen General Cemetery, *Noord-Holland*
  Russell, Richard Anderson, Flight Sergeant (Pilot)
  Young, Henry Melvin, Squadron Leader (Pilot)

Bergen-op-Zoom Canadian War Cemetery, *Noord-Brabant*
  Bennett, Jack Thomas, Private
  Cook, Spencer Waddy, Flying Officer (Pilot)
  Cullimore, Harvey Edward, Private
  Gall, John, Flying Officer (Nav.)
  Givens, Kenneth Abbot, Private
  Harrington, Thomas Herbert, Private

Lambert, Herbert Owen M., Major
Lillico, William Davidson, Pilot Officer (Air Gnr.)
Malloy, John A., Sergeant
Yates, James William, Signalman

Bergen-op-Zoom War Cemetery, Noord-Brabant
Tyrone, Gordon Louis, Flight Sergeant (Air Gnr.)
Watkins, Vivian Eugene, Flight Lieutenant (Pilot)

Epe General Cemetery, Gelderland
Millen, Frank Severne, Pilot Officer (Pilot)

Flushing (Vlissingen) Northern Cemetery, Zeeland
Olson, Virgil Willis, Pilot Officer

Groesbeek Canadian War Cemetery, Gelderland
Caullay, John, Private
Liston, Robert, Corporal
Mayes, Warren Bretall, Flying Officer (Nav.)
Roberge, Victor Edmund, Lieutenant
Scott, Reginald Thomas Maitland, Lieutenant
Sigley, Vincent Job, Lance Corporal
Slater, Joseph H., Private
Stanley, Austin Costello, Private
Weakley, Lawrence O'Neill, Warrant Officer Class I (Pilot)
West, Philip Geoffrey, Lieutenant
Williams, Joseph Leonard Benedict, Leading Aircraftman
Wood, George Arthur, Pilot Officer (Air Gnr.)

Groesbeek Memorial, Gelderland
Huggins, Stanley A., Driver

Harderwijk General Cemetery, Gelderland
Hicks, Lyle Wilmot, Flight Sergeant (Air Bomber)

Holten Canadian War Cemetery, Overijssel
Bullions, John Alexander, Lance Sergeant
Egan, Joseph Patrick, Gunner
Hubbard, Duane Morris, Corporal
Magill, James K., Rifleman
Perrault, Lawrence E., Private

Jonkerbos War Cemetery, Gelderland
Booth, George Vincent Cyril, Warrant Officer Class II (Air Obs.)
Jost, Burton Norris, Squadron Leader (Pilot)

Noordwijk General Cemetery, Zuid-Holland
Murphy, Edward Warren, Warrant Officer Class I (Pilot)
Neubert, Charles Joseph, Flight Sergeant (Air Gnr.)

Valkenswaard War Cemetery, Noord-Brabant
Ormiston, Robert, Private

Venray War Cemetery, Limburg
Piche, Louis Paul Emile, Flying Officer (Pilot)

Wieringen (Hippolytushoef) General Cemetery, Noord-Holland
Zareikin, Samuel, Pilot Officer (W.Op./Air Gnr.)

NEW CALEDONIA
Bourail Memorial
Leslie, John Christie, Lieutenant

PAKISTAN
Karachi War Cemetery
Smith, Lionel Vernon Osman, Flying Officer (Obs.)

Rawalpindi War Cemetery
Mowatt, Thomas Russell, Captain

POLAND
Poznan Old Garrison Cemetery
Gorak, Theodore, Flying Officer (Pilot)

SINGAPORE
Singapore Memorial
Armstrong, Ronald William, Flight Lieutenant
Ashley, Russell Bradfield, Flight Lieutenant
Barnett, Redmond Lewis, Flying Officer
Besso, Walter Edward, Flying Officer
Cross, Vance Everett, Flying Officer
Dowty, Murray John, Lieutenant
Geffene, Donald, Flying Officer
Holtan, Ralph Henry, Pilot Officer
Marchbanks, Alphonso Calvin, Pilot Officer
Monk, John Wyatt, Flying Officer

SOUTH AFRICA
Johannesburg (West Park) Cemetery, Gauteng
Skinner, Desmond, Aircraftman 2nd Class (Pilot)

SRI LANKA
Kandy War Cemetery
Love, Wilford Clay, Warrant Officer Class II (Pilot)

TUNISIA
Carthage American Military Cemetery
Hemmer, Paul Gordon, Flight Sergeant (Pilot)

Enfidaville War Cemetery
Bittner, Joseph Francois Xavier Jean, Flying Officer (Air Bomber)
Twiss, Albert Roy, Warrant Officer Class II (Air Gnr.)

Medjez-el-Bab Memorial
Wertheim, Gerhard, Private

Medjez-el-Bab War Cemetery
Cowley, Edwin, Sapper

UNITED KINGDOM
Altrincham Bowdon and Hale (Altrincham) Cemetery, Cheshire
Elliott, William Johnston, First Officer
Renicker, Earl Lamar, First Officer

Annan Cemetery, Dumfriesshire
Fattig, Robert Dale, Sergeant (Pilot)
Kennedy, Robert Van, Sergeant (Pilot)
Staley, Charles Wood, Sergeant (Pilot)

Ashton-upon-Mersey (St. Martin) Churchyard, *Cheshire*
Dewhurst, Charles Kenneth, Trooper

Banbury Cemetery, *Oxfordshire*
Booth, Gordon, Flying Officer (Bomb Aimer)

Barmby-on-the-Moor (St. Catherine) Churchyard, *Yorkshire*
Comrie, Wilfrid Phelps (Bill), Warrant Officer Class II (Pilot)
Maxon, James Matthew, Sergeant (Air Gnr.)

Bath (Haycombe) Cemetery, *Somerset*
Babb, Richard Conant, Flight Sergeant (Pilot)
Cooper, Walter Charles, Wing Commander (Pilot)
Grant, William Daniel, Flying Officer (Pilot)
Hall, George Brian, Pilot Officer (Pilot)
L'hommedieu, George Martin, Flight Sergeant (Pilot)
Tanner, Edward Francis, Sergeant (Pilot)

Belfast (Milltown) Roman Catholic Cemetery, *County Antrim*
Holmes, Richard Kevin, Flight Sergeant (Pilot)

Bicester Cemetery, *Oxfordshire*
Templeton, Pat Neff, Flight Sergeant (Pilot)

Biddulph (St. Lawrence) Churchyard, *Staffordshire*
Lowe, Harry, Pilot Officer (Air Bomber)

Birmingham (Brandwood End) Jewish Cemetery, *Warwickshire*
Rosenstein, Simon, Sergeant (Pilot)

Birmingham (Perry Bar) Crematorium, *Warwickshire*
Wolff, Harry, First Officer

Boxgrove (Ss. Mary and Blaise) Churchyard, *Sussex*
Fiske, William Mead Lindsley, Pilot Officer (Pilot)

Bridgwater (Quantock Road) Cemetery, *Somerset*
Andrews, Basil Wilfred, Pilot Officer (Pilot)

Brigg Cemetery, *Lincolnshire*
Goff, Allan Barnes, Sergeant (Pilot)
Mitchell, Morris Randolph, Sergeant (Pilot)

Brookwood Memorial, *Surrey*
Byerly, Robert Bennett, Lieutenant
Scharf, Wilhelm, Driver
Still, Harry, Private

Brookwood Military Cemetery, *Surrey*
Anderson, Paul Roger, Pilot Officer
Andre, John, Lieutenant
Atkinson, Roger Hall, Pilot Officer (Pilot)
Attwood, Walter, Corporal
Baker, Kelts Colfax, Flight Lieutenant
Barrell, Charles Sewell, Pilot Officer
Bolton, Warren Percy, Pilot Officer (Pilot)
Carpenter, Paul John, Lance Corporal
Chatterton, Lawrence Albert, Pilot Officer (Pilot)
Cline, Verle Edmond, Sergeant
Cowie, Robert James, Pilot Officer (Air Gnr.)
Crabb, Allen Peter, Lieutenant
Davis, John Edward, Private
Davis, Philip Meyer, Flight Lieutenant
De Haven, Ben Perry, Pilot Officer
De Louchrey, Bertram, Corporal
Dean, R.A., Sapper
Driver, William Richard, Pilot Officer (Pilot)
Eise, Henry George, Flying Officer
French, Frank Howe, Gunner
Gamble, Frederick Arvon, Pilot Officer
Garvie, Robert Leslie, Flight Lieutenant
Gilliland, Jack Dewberry, Pilot Officer
Haddock, Ieuan, Pilot Officer (W.Op./Air Gnr.)
Hersman, Charles, Lance Corporal
Hill, Harry, Corporal
Hopkins, William Essex, Flight Lieutenant (Pilot)
Hornberger, Henry Lottier, Sergeant
Hyde, Reed Tilton, Flight Lieutenant
Inabinet, William Burness, Pilot Officer (Pilot)
Jackson, George Frederick Radcliffe, Flying Officer
Kelly, Donald Patrick, Flight Lieutenant
Madden, Kitchener Cassius, Gunner
Mamedoff, Andrew B., Flight Lieutenant (Pilot)
Matt, Cleveland Charles, Pilot Officer
McCall, Hugh Harrison, Pilot Officer (Pilot)
McEwen, Ian Donald William Alastair, Guardsman
McGinnis, James Leland, Pilot Officer (Pilot)
Metzger, Eugene, Corporal
Mogk, John Ellsworth, Private
Morgan, Arthur Theodore, Flight Sergeant (Pilot)
Omens, Gilbert Inland, Pilot Officer (Pilot)
Ramsay, John, Sapper
Reed, Robert Burns, Flying Officer
Sanagan, Alan Lewis, Flight Lieutenant (Pilot)
Scarborough, Ross Orden, Pilot Officer (Pilot)
Soares, Walter Gordon., Pilot Officer
Stout, Roy Neal, Pilot Officer
Sullivan, Leroy Means, Flying Officer
Taylor, Kenneth Samson, Pilot Officer (Pilot)
Vatcher, Robert Phillips, Flying Officer
Weir, Jack Wesley, Pilot Officer (Pilot)
White, Ian Rene Gordon, Flying Officer
White, William Joseph, Pilot Officer
Whitney, Gerald Bickle, Pilot Officer
Wilding, John Archibald, Flying Officer (Pilot)

Cambridge American Cemetery, *Cambridgeshire*
Grundstrom, Edwin Allan, First Officer
Trimble, Walter Lee, First Officer
Uhlich, Elmer Edward, First Officer
Watson, Earl Wellington, First Officer
Wetzel, Martin Joseph, First Officer

Cambridge City Cemetery, *Cambridgeshire*
Hutchison, Tom Atwell, Sergeant (Air Gnr.)

Cambridge Crematorium, *Cambridgeshire*
Mahn, Frederick Holbrook, Flight Lieutenant

Carlisle (Dalston Road) Cemetery, Cumberland
  Carver, Herman Joe, Flying Officer (Pilot)
  Spangler, James Bartholomew, Sergeant (Pilot)
Catterick Cemetery, Yorkshire
  Davis, Martin David, Flight Sergeant (Air Gnr.)
Caversfield (St. Laurence) Churchyard, Oxfordshire
  Johnson, William Keith, Pilot Officer (Pilot)
Chatham Naval Memorial, Kent
  Carter, Michael John, Sub-Lieutenant
  Wexham, Robert Martin, Warrant Supply Officer
Chester (Blacon) Cemetery, Cheshire
  Bidwell, Donald David George, Flying Officer (Air Bomber)
  Dunnigan, Vincent James, Sergeant (Pilot)
  Jacobs, Alan Laurie, Flight Sergeant (Pilot)
  Stevens, Paul Bevens, Flying Officer (Pilot U/T)
  Thompson, James Bryan, Flight Lieutenant (Pilot)
  Wedin, Albert Ormond, Sergeant (Air Gnr.)
  Wilcox, Claude Neil, Flying Officer (Pilot)
Chevington Cemetery, Northumberland
  Helbock, Harley Joseph, Flight Sergeant (Pilot)
  Ward, Robert Lawrence (Larry), Sergeant (Air Obs.)
Chichester Cemetery, Sussex
  Koellhoffer, George Thomas, Pilot Officer (Pilot)
Cirencester Cemetery, Gloucestershire
  Marsh, A. James (Jim), Flying Officer (W.Op.)
Cumbernauld Cemetery, Dunbartonshire
  Slaughter, Jane S. (Jean), Private
Drumachose (Christ Church) Church of Ireland Churchyard, County Londonderry
  Fry, William Benjamin, Flight Sergeant (Pilot)
  Matson, Frederick Andrew, Captain (Pilot)
  Norris, Kenneth Allan, Pilot Officer (Pilot)
Dyce Old Churchyard, Aberdeenshire
  Milliken, Roy Alistair, Sergeant
  Morrow, Edgar James, Flight Sergeant (Pilot)
Finningley (Holy Trinity and St. Oswald) Churchyard Extension, Nottinghamshire
  Shadle, Charles Corbett, Pilot Officer (Air Gnr.)
Fort George Military Cemetery, St. Peter Port, Guernsey, Channel Islands
  Biddlecombe, Conrad Peter Vivian, Flight Sergeant (Pilot)
Glasgow (Craigton) Cemetery, Glasgow
  Davey, Hugh Augustine, Pilot Officer (W.Op./Air Gnr.)
Glasgow (St. Kentigern's) Roman Catholic Cemetery, Glasgow
  Parsley, Francis Joseph, Gunner
Glasgow Western Necropolis, Glasgow
  Stewart, Donald Alexander, Private
Grantham Cemetery, Lincolnshire
  Wyatt, Julius Lee, Sergeant (Pilot)

Gravesend Cemetery, Kent
  Reilley, Hugh William, Pilot Officer
Harrogate (Stonefall) Cemetery, Yorkshire
  Healey, Joseph M., Warrant Officer Class I (W.Op./Air Gnr.)
  Mills, Edward Mathis, Warrant Officer Class II (Pilot)
  Zareikin, Joseph M., Pilot Officer (Air Gnr.)
Harwell Cemetery, Berkshire
  Bergsten, Carl Alexis, Flight Sergeant (Pilot)
Haslar Royal Naval Cemetery, Hampshire
  Farnsworth, William Clifford, Sub-Lieutenant (A)
Hawarden Cemetery, Flintshire
  Considine, James Patrick, Pilot Officer (Pilot)
  Crozier, Roger Dennis, Pilot Officer (Pilot)
  Parrott, Joseph Thomas, Pilot Officer (Pilot)
Hawarden (St. Deiniol) Churchyard, Flintshire
  Ensign, Richard Clyde, Pilot Officer (Pilot)
  Womack, Henry Archer (Harry), Sergeant
Heston (St. Leonard) Churchyard, Middlesex
  King, Douglas Stanley, Commander
Hethe (Holy Trinity) Roman Catholic Cemetery, Oxfordshire
  Boggs, William Ferguson, Sergeant (Pilot)
Hixon (St. Peter) Churchyard, Staffordshire
  Hawk, Denzil Clair, Sergeant (Air Gnr)
Honington (All Saints) Churchyard, Suffolk
  Ramey, Warren Thomas, Flight Sergeant (Pilot)
Houghton and Wyton Burial Ground, Huntingdonshire
  Hasekian, Charles Robert, Flight Sergeant (Pilot)
  Todd, David Bryant, Flying Officer (Pilot)
Hove New Cemetery, Sussex
  Robson, George Eyre, Pilot Officer (Pilot)
Hylton (Castletown) Cemetery, Durham
  Avery, William Francis, Pilot Officer (Pilot)
Irvinestown Church of Ireland Churchyard, County Fermanagh
  Bryers, Robert Bruce, Warrant Officer Class II (Air Gnr.)
  Clarke, James William, Flying Officer (Pilot)
Kidlington Burial Ground, Oxfordshire
  Keniston, Robert Leroy, Pilot Officer (Pilot)
Kilbride Old Churchyard, Buteshire
  Duggan, Daniel Joseph, Captain
  King, Watt Miller, Captain
  Wixen, Jack, Captain
Kirkinner Cemetery, Wigtownshire
  Spangler, Harold Leroy, Pilot Officer (Pilot)
Kirknewton (St. Gregory) Churchyard, Northumberland
  MacFadzean, Robert Handley Maxwell, Sergeant (Pilot)
Kirton-in-Lindsey Cemetery, Lincolnshire
  Christine, Wilbert Ronald, Pilot Officer (Pilot)

Leckrone, Philip Howard, Pilot Officer (Pilot)
Whedon, Samuell Fisk, Pilot Officer (Pilot)

Lerwick New Cemetery, *Zetland (Shetland)*
Patterson, John Howard, Pilot Officer (Pilot)

Little Rissington (St. Peter) Churchyard, *Gloucestershire*
Hoese, Bill Ingalls, Sergeant
Lee, James Robert, Pilot Officer (Pilot)

Longside Cemetery, *Aberdeenshire*
Casburn, Robert Hardie, Flying Officer (Pilot)
Jones, William Irving, Pilot Officer (Pilot)

Lossiemouth Burial Ground, *Moray*
Burton, Robert William, Sergeant (Air Gnr.)

Lowestoft Naval Memorial, *Suffolk*
Hancock, Charles Clifford Nelson, Ordinary Telegraphist

Maidenhead Cemetery, *Berkshire*
Acton, Wilbur Washington (Bee, First Officer)

The Maidenhead Register, *Berkshire*
Schatzberg, Seymour Morton, Pilot Officer (Pilot)

Manchester Southern Cemetery, *Lancashire*
Carragher, Francis Dean, First Officer

Marham Cemetery, *Norfolk*
Harvey, Benjamin Campbell, Flight Sergeant (Air Gnr.)
Maskill, Donald Joseph, Flight Sergeant (Pilot)

Merton (St. Mary) Churchyard, *Surrey*
Webb, William Bloomfield, Petty Officer

Middlesbrough (Acklam) Cemetery, *Yorkshire*
Martin, Richard Arthur, Petty Officer

Morpeth (Ss. Mary and James) Churchyard, *Northumberland*
Rossignol, Allen Theodore Lewis, Flying Officer (Pilot)

Moston (St. Joseph's) Roman Catholic Cemetery, *Lancashire*
Stephen, Edward Scott, Sergeant (Nav.)

Newquay (Fairpark) Cemetery, *Cornwall*
Le Mere, Roland Walter, Flight Sergeant (Pilot)

North Cotes (St. Nicholas) Churchyard, *Lincolnshire*
Buckolz, Rollie Ernest, Pilot Officer (Pilot)

Nottingham (Wilford Hill) Jewish Cemetery, *Nottinghamshire*
Kahn, Melvin Samuel, Flight Sergeant (Air Gnr.)

Oldham (Hollinwood) Cemetery, *Lancashire*
McArthur, John, Private

Ollerton Cemetery, *Nottinghamshire*
Smith, Melvin Harry, Sergeant (Pilot)

Orpington (St. Mary Cray) Cemetery, *Kent*
Estes, Willard Noel, First Officer

Oxford (Botley) Cemetery, *Oxfordshire*
Benson, David Howard, Sergeant (Pilot)
Brown, Brian Edward, Flying Officer (Nav)
Duke, Allan Thomas, Flying Officer (Nav.)

Matherly, Jones Monroe, Flying Officer (Pilot)
Nicholls, John Austin Perress, Flying Officer (Pilot)

Paisley (Hawkhead) Cemetery, *Renfrewshire*
York, Frederick Willis, Sergeant (Pilot)

Paisley (Woodside) Cemetery, *Renfrewshire*
Park, Cletus Lloyd, First Officer

Pembroke Dock Military Cemetery, *Pembrokeshire*
Abraham, Heinz-, Corporal

Peterborough (Eastfield) Cemetery, *Northamptonshire*
Huntsinger, Frederick Ray, Sergeant (Pilot)

Plymouth (Weston Mill) Cemetery, *Devon*
Whalen, Harold Fenwick, Flight Sergeant (Pilot)

Plymouth Naval Memorial, *Devon*
Anderson, Robert Douglas, Engine Room Artificer 2nd Class
D'oyly-Hughes, Guy, Captain
Hindle, William Henry, Lance Corporal
Parker, John Stanley, Lieutenant
Priest, William James, Warrant Officer

Portsmouth Naval Memorial, *Hampshire*
Barnes, Thomas, Able Seaman
Binderman, Sidney Lewis, Surgeon Lieutenant
Davies, Charles Edward, Able Seaman
Oates, Leonard Charles, Leading Seaman
Shackell, Gilbert, Able Seaman

Ramsbottom Cemetery, *Lancashire*
Hamer, Harry, Aircraftman 1st Class

Ripon Cemetery, *Yorkshire*
Leckie, Albert Wordie, Flight Sergeant (Air Gnr.)
Parker, James Courtland, Flying Officer (Air Gnr.)

Rugby (Whinfield) Cemetery, *Warwickshire*
Haag, Richard John 5., Sergeant (Pilot)

Runnymede Memorial, *Surrey*
Allen, Ethan, Flying Officer
Arlow, James Henry, Sergeant
Bailey, George Cooley, Flight Lieutenant
Bailey, Robert Gordon, Flight Sergeant
Ballinger, Henry Clasper, Sergeant
Baraw, James Arthur, Pilot Officer
Beach, Carl Adrian, Warrant Officer Class II
Beck, John William, Pilot Officer
Bell, Douglas MacKenzie, Flying Officer
Berney, Richard Bruce, Flight Lieutenant
Bodding, Carl Olaf, Pilot Officer
Bootsma, Donald Hill, Pilot Officer
Brossmer, Robert Vincent, Pilot Officer
Brown, Carlos Manuel, Flight Lieutenant
Brown, Hugh Card, Pilot Officer
Bruce, John Samuel, Flight Lieutenant
Brunette, Louis Raymond, Sergeant
Byrne, Frank Paul, Flying Officer
Connor, James Gibson, Flying Officer
Cowie, James Moore, Flying Officer
Crichton, Cecil Ernest, Pilot Officer
Cronk, George Edward, Pilot Officer

Dale, Gordon James, Flight Sergeant
De Silva, Desmond Michael, Warrant Officer Class II
De Vries, Terence, Flying Officer
Donahue, Arthur Gerald, Flight Lieutenant
Edick, Robert Stanley, Flying Officer
Eichar, Grant Eugene, Pilot Officer
Evans, Brinley Morgan, Sergeant
Evans, Walter Arthur, Flight Sergeant
Fenlaw, Hillard Sidney, Pilot Officer
Flynn, John, Flying Officer
Ford, William Kenneth, Pilot Officer
Freiberg, Ralph William, Pilot Officer
Fulton, Ian Thomson Stirrat, Pilot Officer
Gallagher, Joseph Patrick, Flying Officer
Ganes, Joseph Wayne, Flight Sergeant
Garman, Keith Lavon, Flight Sergeant
Garnett, Francis Campbell, Flight Sergeant
Gillespie, Edward William, Pilot Officer
Glasscock, Seth Shiloh, Flight Sergeant
Godwin, Joseph Erwin, Flying Officer
Gorman, Ralph Ernest, Flight Sergeant
Goulding, Norman James Yates, Sergeant
Gourde, Robert Russell, Flight Sergeant
Green, Leslie Arthur, Flying Officer
Gzowski, Norman Glyn, Flying Officer
Halvorsen, John Detrick, Sergeant
Hanna, Charles Murray, Sergeant
Harwood, Horace Greeley, Pilot Officer
Hooper, Roy Wesley, Flying Officer
Horton, Harold Albert, Flight Sergeant
Houston, Donald, Sergeant
Hovinen, Melvin Olaf, Flying Officer
Hudock, John George, Flight Lieutenant
Hyland, George Albert, Flying Officer
Jenkins, Alger, Warrant Officer Class II
Johnson, Benjamin Peter, Flying Officer
Johnson, Harlow Eugene, Sergeant
Johnson, John William, Warrant Officer Class II
Keough, Vernon Charles, Pilot Officer
Kleinberg, Georges, Flying Officer
Komaiko, William Kadison, Flying Officer
Land, James Edward, Pilot Officer
Lawrence, William Charles, Flying Officer
Leighton, Peter James, Sergeant
Lewis, Howard Clark, Warrant Officer Class II
Luepke, Robert Theodor, Sergeant
Lynch, John Joseph, Warrant Officer Class II
MacArthur, Harry Francis, Sergeant
MacDonald, Gerald Edwin, Pilot Officer
MacDonald, Mado Henry Donald, Pilot Officer
MacGregor, David Alton, Flying Officer
MacPhie, Hugh Douglas, Flight Sergeant
Maisenbacher, William Malcolm, Flight Sergeant
Mann, Joel Brooks, Flying Officer
Marx, Paul Manfred Daniel, Pilot Officer
Masse, George Joseph, Flight Sergeant
Matthews, John Joseph, Flight Sergeant
McCoy, Allan Frank, Warrant Officer Class II
McMillan, Lawrence, Flight Lieutenant
Menish, George Raymond, Sergeant
Morgan, John Gilbert, Sergeant
Mylrea, John Edward, Sergeant
Nadeau, Joseph Albert, Pilot Officer
Neale, William Percival, Flying Officer
Noble, Steven, Pilot Officer
Nugent, Royden Leslie, Flying Officer
O'Hara, Leonard William, Pilot Officer
Palmer, Cyril Dampier, Squadron Leader
Park, Lewis, Flying Officer
Parkyn, Alfred Joseph, Pilot Officer
Pearson, Vernon Lawrence, Pilot Officer
Pickett, Warren Bryan, Sergeant
Priddin, William Edward Ernest, Warrant Officer Class II
Ramsay, John Strachan, Sergeant
Ray, Edmund Rothell, Flying Officer
Reaume, Robert Francis Charles, Flight Sergeant
Redgrave, Charles Derek, Flight Sergeant
Reeves, Jonah Bruce, Flying Officer
Reid, Kenneth Maxime, Pilot Officer
Reid, Wilbert George, Flight Sergeant
Roussel, John Warren, Flying Officer
Shann, Harry Pritchard, Flying Officer
Shelnutt, Barney Walker, Sergeant
Shelnutt, Frank Lee, Warrant Officer Class II
Shelton, Paul Arthur, Flight Lieutenant
Simon, Michael Lemuel, Pilot Officer
Smith, Earl George, Warrant Officer Class II
Spafford, William Marshall, Flight Sergeant
Sponsler, Harry, Warrant Officer Class II
Stillings, John Earl, Flying Officer
Stone, Oscar Wilson, Flight Sergeant
Sutherland, John, Warrant Officer Class II
Taylor, William Douglas, Pilot Officer
Teicheira, George, Pilot Officer
Thibault, Louis Joseph Leo, Flight Lieutenant
Thompson, Frank, Flying Officer
Trippe, Temple Dawson, Flying Officer
Upshur, Robert Alexander, Flight Lieutenant
Vail, Derrick Tilton, Sergeant
Van Buren, Russell Benson, Warrant Officer Class II
Waddell, Woodrow Wilcox, Flight Sergeant
Warren, Robert Orville Orson, Warrant Officer Class II
Wilson, Harry James, Flying Officer
Wilson, Robert Potter, Flight Sergeant
Woolrich, George Dean, Pilot Officer
Zavakos, Frank George, Pilot Officer

Saffron Walden Cemetery, *Essex*
Helgason, Joseph Field, Pilot Officer (Pilot)

Scopwick Church Burial Ground, *Lincolnshire*
Balduff, William, Warrant Officer Class II (Pilot)
Magee, John Gillespie, Pilot Officer (Pilot)
Sweet, Philip Marcus, Pilot Officer (Pilot)
Warner, Kenneth Earle, Flying Officer (Pilot)

Sherborne Cemetery, *Dorset*
  Carlson, Dale Gladstone, Sub-Lieutenant (A)
Stranraer (Glebe) Cemetery, *Wigtownshire*
  Marcus, Jack Allen, Second Officer
Stratford-on-Avon Cemetery, *Warwickshire*
  St. Johns, William Ivan, Pilot Officer (Pilot)
Sutton Bridge (St. Matthew) Churchyard, *Lincolnshire*
  Eves, Elden, Sergeant (Pilot)
  Grove, Fred Ambrose, Pilot Officer (Pilot)
  Pudney, Clinton Landis, Flight Sergeant (Air Gnr.)
  Wilber, Robert Ruggles, Pilot Officer (Pilot)
Topcliffe Church Cemetery, *Yorkshire*
  Kibbe, Donald Kyle, Sergeant (Pilot)
Tower Hill Memorial, *London*
  Bodden, William Crosby, Boatswain (Bosun)
  Boddington, Cyril Harold, Cook
  Carter, Eric Gordon, Able Seaman
  Clarke, James, Able Seaman
  Cockerill, Harry Kingsley, Chief Officer
  Currie, Charles Sime, Chief Engineer Officer
  Ebanks, Willard Charles, Carpenter
  Eglitis, Oskars Richards, First Officer
  Hedley, John William, Carpenter
  Jones, Dennis Gough, Master
  Marchi, Vincent Douglas, Second Radio Officer
  Margitson, John Stuart, Chief Engineer Officer
  McPhillimy, Robert Allison, First Radio Officer
  Thompson, Robert, Master
Tubney (St. Laurence) Churchyard, *Berkshire*
  Brown, Douglas MacGillvary, Pilot Officer (Pilot)
Tunstall (St. John the Baptist) Churchyard, *Lancashire*
  Varley, John Yates, Aircraftman 2nd Class
Warwick Bridge (Our Lady and St. Wilfrid) Roman Catholic Churchyard, *Cumberland*
  Fassino, Stephen D. (Steve), Sergeant (Pilot)
Whitehaven Cemetery, *Cumberland*
  Holcomb, George, First Officer
Winchester (Magdalen Hill) Cemetery, *Hampshire*
  Jenkins, Donald Andrew, Sub-Lieutenant (A)

Appendix 14: Isolated Burials of American Airmen in the Netherlands since World War II

OPIJNEN

American flyers of a B-17 bomber that fell on Opijnen farm fields on July 30, 1943, are buried in the courtyard of the town's Dutch Reformed Church and memorialized in the street names of a nearby neighborhood.

T/Sgt. Douglas V. Blackwood, Radioman
T/Sgt. Americo Cianfichi, Engineer
1st Lt. Robert U. Duggan, Navigator
S/Sgt. George R. Krueger, Waist Gunner
2nd Lt. Daniel V. Ohman, Bombardier
S/Sgt. Mike A. Perrotta, Ball Turret
S/Sgt. Harold R. Sparks, Waist Gunner
S/Sgt. Hermon d. Poling, Tail Gunner

ZOETERMEER

On February 22, 1945, an American B-24 bomber fell on a farm at Zoetermeer. All of its crew survived and either escaped or were captured for short imprisonment near the end of World War II. Aerial gunner John McCormick stayed in Zoetermeer and joined the Dutch Resistance. He was killed by German troops on April 29, 1945. With the consent of his father, he was buried in the courtyard of the Dutch Reformed Church in Zoetermeer, Netherlands, on October 31, 1945.

Staff Sergeant John McCormick, age 23 of Scranton, Pennsylvania

Appendix 15: Isolated Burials of American Airmen in Denmark since World War II

Five World War II American airmen are buried in Denmark. More information about them can be found on the Danish Website "Faldne Allierede Flyvere"— Fallen Allied Airmen.

Marstal Kirkegård — Cemetery, Ærø.
  Staff Sgt. Jack Elwood Wagner; na; Selingsgrove, Pennsylvania
  Killed in action June 20, 1944.

Nykøbing Falster Østre Kirkegård — Cemetery, Guldborgsund
  Second Lt. John R. Vlyman, Jr.; na; na
  Killed in action August 2, 1944.

Øster Starup Kirkegård — Churchyard, Vejle.
  First Lt. Jack Hodge, age 24 of South Carolina
  Killed in action March 11, 1945.

Pedersker Kirkegård — Churchyard, Bornholm
  Sergeant Harry J. Ambrosini, age 24 of Fresno, California
  Killed in action April 29, 1944.

Rødby Kirkegård — Cemetery, Rødby
  Staff Sgt. Charles L. Haswell, gunner; na; na
  Killed in action May 19, 1944.

Appendix 16: American War Dogs Buried in Guam

As elsewhere in the Pacific during World War II, dogs from the United States played an important role in the successful invasion of Guam in 1944. They were used for search, mine detection, messaging, and protection of sleeping soldiers and Marines. They also contributed significantly to morale in battle. Twenty-five dogs were buried near a temporary human cemetery in the course of the invasion, and all were reburied and memorialized at the U.S. Naval Base at Orote Point, Guam, on July 20, 1994. They are named in the order in which they are placed on the memorial.

Kurt	Burch	Arno	Duke	Emmy
Skipper	Yonnie	Pepper	Silver	Max
Nig	Poncho	Koko	Ludwig	Brockie
Missy	Prince	Tubby	Bunkie	Rickey
Blitz	Cappy	Fritz	Hobo	Tam

Chapter Notes

Chapter One

1. Augustus C. Buell and Horace Porter, *Paul Jones, Founder of American Navy*, vol. 2 (New York: Charles Scribner's Sons, 1906), 345.
2. *Ibid.*, 244.
3. Anna De Koven, *The Life and Letters of John Paul Jones*, vol. 2 (New York: Charles Scribner's Sons, 1913), 418.
4. John Paul Jones, *Life and Correspondence of John Paul Jones: From Original Letters and Manuscripts in the Possession of Miss Janette Taylor*, ed. Robert Charles Sands (New York: 1830), 527.
5. M. Elliot Seawell, *Decatur and Sommers* (New York: D. Appleton, 1908), 51.
6. James Fenimore Cooper, *The History of the Navy of the United States of America: Abridged in One Volume* (Philadelphia: Thomas, Cowperthwaite, 1841), 207.
7. *Ibid.*, 214.
8. The location may have been Distress Cove, now St. Bride's, Newfoundland.
9. Andrew Sherburne, *Memoirs of Andrew Sherburne: A Pensioner of the Navy of the Revolution* (Providence, RI: H.M. Brown, 1831), 68.
10. *Ibid.*, 110.
11. Gardner Weld Allen, *A Naval History of the American Revolution*, vol. 2 (Boston and New York: Houghton Mifflin, 1913), 631.
12. Sherburne, *Memoirs of Andrew Sherburne*, 74.
13. *Ibid.*, 81.
14. Francis Abell, *Prisoners of War in Britain 1756 to 1815: A Record of Their Lives, Their Romance and Their Sufferings* (Oxford: Humphrey Milford, Oxford University Press, 1914), 208, 216, 224, 360.
15. Allen, *A Naval History*, vol. 2, 651.

Chapter Two

1. Benjamin Waterhouse, *The Magazine of History with Notes and Queries*, Extra Number — No. 18 (New York: William Abbatt, 1911), 122.
2. John George Brighton, *Admiral Sir P.B.V. Broke: A Memoir* (London: Sampson Low, Son and Marston, 1866), 213.
3. Waterhouse, *The Magazine of History*, 29.
4. *Ibid.*, 18.
5. Benjamin Franklin Palmer, *The Diary of Benjamin F. Palmer, Privateersman* (Philadelphia: Acorn Club, 1914), 232.
6. James Inderwick, *Cruise of the U.S. Brig* Argus *in 1813: Journal of Surgeon James Inderwick* (New York: New York Public Library, 1917), 14.
7. Abell, *Prisoners of War*, 184.
8. Waterhouse, *The Magazine of History*, 54.
9. *Ibid.*, 175.
10. Basil Thomson, *The Story of Dartmoor Prison* (London: William Heineman, 1907), 78.
11. Waterhouse, *The Magazine of History*, 268.

Chapter Three

1. Craig L. Symonds and William J. Clipson, *The Naval Institute Historical Atlas of the U.S. Navy* (Annapolis: Naval Institute Press, 1995), 64.
2. Fletcher Pratt, *The Compact History of the United States Navy* (New York: Hawthorn, 1957), 105. A slightly different version of the poem can be found in *Putnam's Monthly Magazine of American Literature, Science, and Art* 8 (New York: Dix, Edwards, 1857), 483.
3. James Maps, "A Long-Forgotten American Naval Cemetery," *The American Neptune* 25 (Salem, MA: Peabody Museum of Salem) (1965), 157.
4. Gustavus R.B. Horner, *Diseases and Injuries of Seamen* (Philadelphia: Lippincott, Grambo, 1854), 235.
5. Captain Edgar K. Thompson, "Long-Forgotten American Naval Cemetery, a Postscript," *The American Neptune* 26 (Salem, MA: Peabody Museum of Salem) (1966), 218–219.
6. *Ibid.*
7. John L. O'Sullivan, "Annexation," *United States Magazine and Democratic Review* 17, no. 1 (New York: J. & H.G. Langley) (July-August 1845), 5–10,
8. Nathan Covington Brooks, *A Complete History*

of the Mexican War: Its Causes, Conduct, and Consequences (Philadelphia: Grigg, Elliot, 1849), 254.

9. Henry Montgomery, *The Life of Major General Zachary Taylor* (Auburn, MA: Derby, Miller, 1850), 287.

10. "Descendants of Mexican War Veterans, Honoring Our Ancestors," http://www.dmwv.org/honoring/mexcem.htm.

11. "An American Cemetery in Mexico," *The Nation* (March 29, 1866), 392

12. H.R. 3454, U.S. House of Representatives (January 13, 1873).

Chapter Four

1. Bradley R. Hoch, *The Lincoln Trail in Pennsylvania: A History and Guide* (University Park: Pennsylvania State University Press, 2001), 126.

2. *Ibid.*, 129.

3. "Abraham Lincoln's Assassination," http://rogerjnorton.com/Lincoln13.html.

4. Major Lemuel Abijah Abbott, *Civil War Diary 1864* (Burlington, VT: Free Press, 1908), 56.

5. *Ibid.*, 58.

6. *Ibid.*

7. *Ibid.*, 56.

8. General Horace Porter, *Campaigning with Grant* (New York: Century, 1907), 174.

9. "Evolution of the National Cemetery System," http://www.qmfound.com/evolution_of_the_national_cemetery_system_1865_1880.htm.

10. Walt Whitman, *Walt Whitman's Civil War*, ed. Walter Lowenfels (New York: Da Capo, 1961), 6.

11. Walt Whitman, *Specimen Days & Collect* (Philadelphia: David McKay, 1882–83), 247.

12. "Expansion of the National Cemetery System," http://www.qmfound.com/expansion_of_the_national_cemetery_system_1880_1900.htm.

Chapter Five

1. Porter, *Campaigning with Grant*, 129.

2. "Plea for Heroes," *New York Times*, February 14, 1905, 7.

3. Frederick Jackson Bell, *Room to Swing a Cat: Being Some Tales of the Old Navy* (New York: Longmans, Green, 1938), 22.

4. John Henry Sherburne, *The Life and Character of John Paul Jones*, 2nd ed. (New York: Adriance, Sherman, 1851), 370.

5. *Ibid.*, 371.

6. Charles Dickens, "Paul Jones Righted," *All the Year Round* (London), April 2, 1870, 429.

7. "John Paul Jones, The American Patriot," *New York Times*, January 27, 1895, 28.

8. General Horace Porter, "The Recovery of the Body of John Paul Jones," *Century* 70 (1905), 927–955.

9. Buell and Porter, *Paul Jones*, 357.

10. *Ibid.*, 363.

11. "Is It Paul Jones' Body?" *New York Times*, May 21, 1905, 6.

12. "Sigsbee's Squadron Greeted at Cherbourg," *New York Times*, July 1, 1905, 9.

13. "Body of Paul Jones Delivered to the Navy," *New York Times*, July 7, 1905, 3.

14. United States Congress, *John Paul Jones: Commemoration at Annapolis, April 24, 1906* (1906), 19.

15. The Zimmerman telegram, sent from German foreign minister Arthur Zimmermann to the German ambassador to Mexico on January 19, 1917.

Chapter Six

1. "First of American Legion Off for Flanders," *New York Times Magazine*, May 28, 1918.

2. "Thoughts of a Soldier of Justice," http://www.greatwardifferent.com/Great_War/Soldier_Poet/Soldier_Poet_01.htm.

3. "Alan Seeger, Soldier and Poet," *New York Times Book Review*, December 24, 1916.

4. "Thoughts of a Soldier of Justice," http://www.greatwardifferent.com/Great_War/Soldier_Poet/Soldier_Poet_01.htm.

5. *Ibid.*

6. *Ibid.*

7. *Ibid.*

8. *Ibid.*

9. *Ibid.*

10. James Norman Hall, Charles Nordhoff and Edgar G. Hamilton, eds., *The Lafayette Flying Corps*, vol. 1 (Boston: Houghton Mifflin, 1920), 170.

11. "The History of Canada," http://www.linksnorth.com/canada-history/canadaandworldwar1.html.

12. "First of American Legion Off for Flanders," *New York Times Magazine*, May 28, 1916.

13. *Ibid.*

14. "Harvard College," *Report of the Secretary of the Class of 1881 of Harvard College*, no. 7 (Cambridge, MA: University Press, 1921), 222.

15. "All Britain Celebrates Our Advent in War," *New York Times*, April 21, 1917, 1.

16. *Ibid.*

17. Lt. Kenneth Gow, *Letters of a Soldier* (New York: H.B. Covert, 1920).

18. Stephen L. Harris, *Duty, Honor, Privilege: New York's Silk Stocking Regiment and the Breaking of the Hindenburg Line* (Washington, D.C.: Potomac, 2001), 96.

19. *Ibid.*, 105.

20. "Principal Wars in Which the U.S. Participated," http://siadapp.dmdc.osd.mil/personnel/CASUALTY/WCPRINCIPAL.pdf.

21. "Cable Is Awaited for Disposition of 70,000 Graves," *Stars and Stripes*, February 28, 1919, 1.

22. Harris, *Duty, Honor, Privilege*, 186.

23. *Ibid.*, 200.

24. *Ibid.*, 210.

25. *Ibid.*, 289.

26. *Ibid.*, 296.

27. United States War Department, General Staff, *Location of Graves and Disposition of Bodies of American*

Soldiers Who Died Overseas (Washington, D.C.: Government Printing Office, 1920), 5.

28. Letters, photographs and other materials from Archangel soldiers are archived at the Bentley Historical Museum of the University of Michigan, Ann Arbor, and searchable online at http://polarbears.si.umich.edu/.

29. "Assails Command in North Russia," *New York Times*, February 10, 1919, 3.

Chapter Seven

1. "Allied in Homage to America's Dead," *New York Times*, May 31, 1922, 7.
2. *Ibid.*
3. "From a Friend," *Stars and Stripes*, November 29, 1918, 4.
4. "Miss Wilson Sees Loving Hands' Work," *Stars and Stripes*, December 20, 1918, 7.
5. "For the Stranger in a Strange Land," *Journal of the National Dental Association* 6 (Chicago: National Dental Association) (1919), 659.
6. "With All Due Honors: A History of the Quartermaster Graves Registration Mission," http://www.qmfound.com/grave.htm.
7. "O.D. Still in Evidence Up and Down Marne Salient," *Stars and Stripes*, March 21, 1919, 5.
8. "Pershing Opposes Bringing Dead Home," *New York Times*, August 1, 1919, 12.
9. U.S. House of Representatives, Sixty-sixth Congress, vol. 3, November 13, 1919, *Return of Military Dead Buried in France: Hearings before the Committee on Foreign Affairs*, 68.
10. *Ibid.*
11. Eleanor Bradley Peters, "Forgotten Graves—Letter of a Mother Who Saw," *New York Tribune*, September 19, 1919, National Archives.
12. War Department News Bureau, October 9, 1919, National Archives.
13. Gerald F. Jacobson, *History of the 107th Infantry, U.S.A.* (New York: Seventh Regiment Armory, 1920), 165.
14. U.S. House of Representatives, Sixty-sixth Congress, *Return of Military Dead Buried in France*, 81.
15. "Owen Wister Praises Singing Among Soldiers," *New York Times*, May 12, 1918, 58.
16. "Plead for Our Dead in France," *New York Times*, April 15, 1921, 1.
17. "Writers Disagree on Soldier Dead," *New York Times*, April 17, 1921, 20.
18. *Ibid.*

Chapter Eight

1. "Our Soldier Unknown," http://www.qmfound.com/soldier_unknown.htm.
2. *Current History* 15 (New York: New York Times) (1922), iii.
3. Memo from Colonel W.K. Naylor, General Staff to War Department Chief of Staff, December 11, 1923, National Archives.
4. "The American Club of Paris," http://www.americanclubparis.org/history.html.
5. *Europa Yearbook 1928* (London: Europa, 1928), 700.
6. *Europa Yearbook 1929* (London: Europa, 1929), 602.
7. "Memorial Day in Mexico," *New York Times*, June 1, 1897, 12.
8. "To Exhume Soldiers' Bodies," *New York Times*, July 16, 1900, 2.
9. Eileen Welsome, *The General and the Jaguar: Pershing's Hunt for Pancho Villa* (New York: Little, Brown, 2006), 216. Note: Hobert, not Hobart, is the correct spelling of Ledford's given name.
10. *Ibid.*, 215.
11. *Ibid.*, 219.
12. "Six Killed with Pershing in 1916 to Be Reburied Here," *New York Times*, September 10, 1925, 20.
13. Letter from H.C. Bonnycastle, Quartermaster Supply Officer to the Quartermaster General, U.S. Army, Washington, D.C., July 31, 1923, National Archives.
14. *Washington Star*, February 1, 1924, National Archives.
15. Letter from Thomas Hastings to John Weeks, Secretary of War, November 17, 1924, National Archives.
16. Letter from John Weeks, Secretary of War, to Thomas Hastings, December 15, 1924, National Archives.
17. Draft of Act of Congress, July 3, 1926, National Archives.
18. Sixty-ninth Congress, *Congressional Record*, March 15, 1926.
19. *Ibid.*, June 7, 1926.
20. Stephen Kinzer, *Overthrow: America's Century of Regime Change from Hawaii to Iraq* (New York: Times Books, 2006), 59.
21. "Model of Memorial to American Airmen Unveiled," *New York Times*, February 28, 1926, 25.
22. "France Honors Her American Fliers," *New York Times Magazine*, September 4, 1927.
23. Robert L. Willett, *Russian Sideshow: America's Undeclared War, 1918–1920* (Dulles, VA: Brassey's, 2003), 24.
24. Letters, photographs and other materials from Archangel soldiers are archived at the Bentley Historical Museum of the University of Michigan, Ann Arbor, and searchable online at http://polarbears.si.umich.edu/.
25. Knoll, John J., "Crosses," *American Legion*, September 1930, 15–18.
26. *Baltimore Afro-American*, August 23, 1930, 8.

Chapter Nine

1. Mustapha Burchis and Arthur M. Johnson, "Resting Place of Heroes of the Barbary Wars," *Proceedings* (U.S. Naval Institute: Annapolis) (September

1956), 969–973. All quotes and descriptions regarding Mustapha Burchis are throughout the article.

2. American Battle Monument Commission Database, http://www.abmc.gov/search/wwi.php. Statistics of deaths and burials in ABMC and National cemeteries vary in small differences depending on source and date of record. As an example, this page on the same ABMC Website — http://www.abmc.gov/commission/history.php — gives a different figure for World War I and World War II deaths and burials. Reasons for discrepancies are explained in the text of this book over several chapters.

3. "National Cemeteries and Memorials in Global Conflict," http://www.qmfound.com/national_cemeteries_and_memorials_in_global_conflict.htm.

4. Written account of Bart Fromijne, Opijnen, the Netherlands, 1954. Archive of the American Women's Club of Amsterdam.

5. Archive of the American Women's Club of Amsterdam.

6. Airmen remember Comet Line to freedom, http://news.bbc.co.uk/2/hi/europe/988881.stm.

7. *Ibid.*

8. Archive of Janine Parker.

9. Toast at the State Dinner for Prime Minister Poul Schluter of Denmark, http://www.reagan.utexas.edu/archives/speeches/1985/91085c.htm.

10. Jack Waaner, http://www.flensted.eu.com/1944083.shtml; American Airmen, http://www.airmen.dk/c000dkus.htm.

11. James R. Stevens, *Searching for the Hudson Bombers: Lads, Love and Death in World War Two* (Victoria, BC: Trafford, 2004), 37.

12. Daniel Arnstein, "An Ex-Taxi Driver Checks Up on the Famous Burma Road," *Life*, October 6, 1941, 18.

13. Eric Sevareid, "Headhunters Save Airmen in Burma," *New York Times*, August 28, 1943, 5.

14. Bill Gilbert, *Air Power: Heroes and Heroism in American Flight Missions, 1916 to Today* (New York: Kensington, 2004), 82.

15. "U.S. Army Air Force Humplift Operations, April 1942 – September 1945," http://www.sinoam.com/USAAF_HUMP_AIRLIFT_OPERATION.htm.

16. "Graves Registration," http://www.qmfound.com/graves_registration.htm.

17. *Ibid.*

18. "19th Bombardment Group," http://www.armyaircorpsmuseum.org/19th_Bombardment_Group.cfm.

19. 361st LFG, http://www.361fg.com/Hist.htm.

20. "The John McCormick Story," http://www.b24.net/stories/McCormick.htm.

21. Undated, unattributed notes in the archive of the American Women's Club of Amsterdam.

22. "The John McCormick Story," http://www.b24.net/stories/McCormick.htm.

23. *Ibid.*

24. Letter from John McCormick of Scranton, Pennsylvania, to Dr. Joseph Kentgens, Zoetermeer, Netherlands, March 3, 1946, Archive of the American Women's Club of Amsterdam.

Chapter Ten

1. A discussion of the loss statistics of Operation Tidal Wave can be found in James Dugan and Carroll Stewart's *Ploesti: The Great Ground-Air Battle of 1 August, 1943* (New York: Random House, 1962), 222.

2. "Graves Registration Service in the Mediterranean Zone of World War II," *Historical Narrative of American Graves Registration Service in the Mediterranean Zone 1 April 1946–1 October 1947* (Rome: Graves Registration Historical Section, 1947), 130, National Archives.

3. John MacNair Wright, *Captured on Corregidor: Diary of an American P.O.W. in World War II* (Jefferson, NC: McFarland, 1988), 59.

4. Russ Bryant and W. David Perks, *USMC* (St. Paul, MN: Zenith, 2006), 121.

5. General Holland Smith, *Coral and Brass* (Washington, D.C.: Department of the Navy, 1989), 111.

6. "Quartermaster War Dog Program," http://www.qmfound.com/K-9.htm; "Dogs and National Defense," http://www.qmmuseum.lee.army.mil/dogs_and_national_defense.htm.

7. "War Dog Memorial," http://www.findagrave.com/cgi-bin/fg.cgi?GRid=14798700&page=gr.

8. General Dwight D. Eisenhower (Ike), D-day Message, http://www.kansasheritage.org/abilene/ikespeech.html.

9. "1945 US Army WWII Graves Registration Manual," http://www.scribd.com/doc/12981287/1945-US-Army-WWII-Graves-Registration-Manual-62p-FM-1063.

10. Joseph James Shomon, *Crosses in the Wind: The Unheralded Saga of the Men in the American Graves Registration Service in World War II* (Margraten, Holland: Crosses in the Wind Foundation, 1991).

11. Mieke Kirkels and Jo Purnot, *From Farmland to Soldiers Cemetery*, English ed. (Adr. Heijnen, 's-Hertogenbosch, Netherlands: 2009), http://www.akkersvanmargraten.nl/page/24/.

12. "Margraten: The horror of a cemetery," http://www.strijdbewijs.nl/margraten/mareng2.htm.

13. David Anderson, "Grateful Dutch Honor U.S. Heroes," *New York Times*, May 31, 1946, 4.

Chapter Eleven

1. "Allied parachute wedding gown donated to Calgary museum," http://www.cbc.ca/canada/story/2002/03/07/parachute_dress020307.html.

2. Shomon, *Crosses in the Wind*, 135.

3. "Graves Registration," http://www.qmfound.com/graves_registration.htm.

4. Shomon, *Crosses in the Wind*, 135.

5. "Staff Sergeant Gerald E. Sorenson," http://www.aomda.org/htm/graves/sorensen.shtml.

6. "Second Lieutenant Robert Lee Garrett," http://www.aomda.org/htm/graves/garrett.shtml.

7. *Ibid.*

8. "U.S. Memorial in Alsace," *New York Times*, June 8, 1953, 6.

9. Abie Abraham, http://www.us-japandialogueonpows.org/Abraham.htm.
10. *Ibid.*
11. "Ghost of Bataan," http://ghostofbataan.com/bataan/abiemain.html.
12. "Abie Abraham," http://www.us-japandialogueonpows.org/Abraham.htm.
13. "Tragic History," http://www.qmmuseum.lee.army.mil/mortuary/tragic.htm.
14. *Ibid.*
15. Memo from Lt. Colonel Stanford Blunden, QMC to Headquarters, American Graves Registration Service, India-Burma Zone, April 30, 1947, National Archives.
16. *Historical Narrative of American Graves Registration Service in the Mediterranean Zone 1 April 1946–1 October 1947*, Graves Registration Service. National Archive
17. *Ibid.*, 30.
18. *The Living Church* 114 (Living Church Foundation) (March 9, 1947), 11.
19. Commonwealth War Graves Commission, http://www.cwgc.org/.
20. "Bankier, Lili Stefania," http://www.cwgc.org/search/casualty_details.aspx?casualty=2219450.
21. Burchis and Johnson, "Resting Place of Heroes of the Barbary Wars," 973.
22. *The Spoke*, The USS *Spokane*. March 25, 1949, http://www.fulkerson.org/spokane/tripoli.html.
23. Lt. Arthur Miller, Jr., "Tripoli Graves Discovered," *Proceedings* (Annapolis: U.S. Naval Institute) (April 1950), 377.

Chapter Twelve

1. "Operation Glory," http://www.qmmuseum.lee.army.mil/korea/op_glory.htm.
2. "3,600 Korea Missing Now Presumed Dead," *New York Times*, January 1, 1954, 2.
3. See http://www.koreanwar-educator.org/topics/casualties/index.htm. Battle casualty statistics for the Korean War, as with other wars, are subject to interpretation depending on definitions of terms and date of reporting.
4. "A. Peter Dewey," http://www.arlingtoncemetery.net/apdewey.htm.
5. Robert S. McNamara, James G. Blight, and Robert K. Brigham, *Argument Without End: In Search of Answers to the Vietnam Tragedy* (United States: Public Affairs, 1999), 16.
6. "Edges of the Wall," http://thewall-usa.com/literary/edgewall.html. As with casualty statistics, the question of the order of death is subject to interpretation and time.
7. "The History Place presents the Vietnam War–1965," http://www.historyplace.com/unitedstates/vietnam/index-1965.html.
8. *Ibid.*
9. "The History Place presents the Vietnam War–1969," http://www.historyplace.com/unitedstates/vietnam/index-1969.html.
10. "The Vietnam Veterans Memorial," http://thewall-usa.com/summary.asp.

Chapter Thirteen

1. "Brussels Soldiers Thank Belgian Children," http://www.army.mil/-news/2009/05/05/20602-brussels-soldiers-thank-belgian-children/.
2. "Seeger Bell Presented," *New York Times*, May 23, 1922, 13.
3. "Alan Seeger," http://www.npr.org/templates/story/story.php?storyId=1123591&ps=rs.
4. Charles Andrews, *The Prisoners' Memoirs, or Dartmoor Prison: Containing a Complete and Impartial History of the Entire Captivity of the Americans in England* (New York: self-published, 1852), 49, http://www.archive.org/details/prisonersmem00andr.
5. "Minister Church of St. Andrew's," http://www.plymouthdata.info/Churches-Ancient%20Parish-St%20Andrew.htm.
6. "Celebrate Day in Britain," *New York Times*, May 31, 1930, 5.
7. William McDermott, "The U.S. Unknown Soldier," *Rotarian* (November 1945), 11.
8. *Ibid.*
9. Maps, "A Long-Forgotten American Naval Cemetery," 157.
10. Memo from Commander Sixth Fleet to Commander in Chief, U.S. Army, Europe, February 11, 1977.
11. Melba Edmunds, "American Legion Magazine Report," *American Legion*, May 1977.
12. Carlo Sardella, "Hopes Rise for Return of the Bodies of Heroes of the Intrepid," *New York Times*, December 21, 1980, NJ2.
13. "Did Allies Kill GIs in D-day Training Horror?" *Observer* (UK, Guardian), May 16, 2004, http://www.guardian.co.uk/uk/2004/may/16/military.usa.
14. Charles B. MacDonald, "Slapton Sands: The Cover-up That Never Was," *Army* (U.S. Army) (June 1988), 64, http://www.history.navy.mil/faqs/faq20-2.htm.
15. William Marvel, *The "Alabama" & the "Kearsarge": The Sailor's Civil War* (Chapel Hill: University of North Carolina Press, 1996), 260.
16. *Lewiston (ME) Daily Sun*, July 1, 1988, 3.
17. James Brooke, "Halifax Journal: Lively City Lets Ghosts of Deadman's Island Rest," *New York Times World*, March 23, 2000.
18. Chris Dickon, *The Enduring Journey of the USS "Chesapeake"* (Charleston, SC: History Press, 2008), 149, http://www.theusschesapeake.com/Home_Page.html.

Chapter Fourteen

1. Myrna Oliver, "William Putney, 83; Vet Trained War Dogs," *Los Angeles Times*, March 23, 2003, http://articles.latimes.com/2003/mar/23/local/me-putney23.
2. "Defense POW/Missing Personnel Office," http://www.dtic.mil/dpmo/news/Fact_Sheets/korea_factsheet.pdf.
3. Heinz Ahlmeyer Jr., http://www.arlingtoncemetery.net/heinz-ahlmeyer-jr.htm.

4. George F. Horner, "Japanese Losses in Marianas Soar," *New York Times*, June 26, 1944, 7.

5. "Missing Air Crew," http://www.missingaircrew.com/pdf/YapGirvisHaltom.pdf.

6. "What we do at JPAC," http://www.jpac.pacom.mil/index.php?page=mission_overview.

7. Tim Weiner, "Robert S. McNamara, Architect of a Futile War, Dies at 93," *New York Times*, July 7, 2009, A1.

8. *Arizona Republic*, May 26, 2007, http://www.azcentral.com/arizonarepublic/news/articles/0526mexmemorial0526.html?&wired.

9. "Mysterious Graves Shed Light on Dangers Faced by 19th Century Sailors," http://www.navy.mil/search/display.asp?story_id=10134.

10. Letter from Vice Admiral Ronald Hays to Madrid Navy League, June 18, 1981.

11. Newsletter 10, "Working Group on EU Directives and Cultural Heritage," http://www.ablakprofilok.hu/szakirodalom/newsletter_10.pdf.

12. J. Fenimore Cooper, "Richard Somers," *Graham's* 21 no. 4, October 1842, 167.

13. Christopher M. Blanchard, "Libya: Background and U.S. Relations," Congressional Research Service, August 3, 2009, 29.

14. Letter from Admiral Gary Roughead, Chief of Naval Operations to Bill Kelly March 11, 2010, http://remembertheintrepid.blogspot.com/2010_03_01_archive.html.

15. "Memories Must be Fed," http://www.michigansmilitarymuseum.com/manifesto.html.

Chapter Fifteen

1. "L'Escadrille Lafayette," http://www.stratisc.org/Arogers_9.htm.

2. Kirkels and Junot, *From Farmland to Soldiers Cemetery*.

3. "Is the Division of Belgium Inevitable?" http://www.eurotopics.net/en/archiv/archiv_dossier/DOSSIER20292-Is-the-division-of-Belgium-inevitable.

Afterword

1. Defense Prisoner of War/Missing Personnel Office, http://www.dtic.mil/dpmo/http://www.dtic.mil/dpmo/.

2. "161 American Girls Died in World War," *New York Times*, November 11, 1922, 4.

3. American National Red Cross, *History of American Red Cross Nursing*, Part 1 (New York: MacMillan, 1922), 924.

Bibliography

Abbott, Major Lemuel Abijah. *Civil War Diary 1864*. Burlington, VT: Free Press, 1908.

Abell, Francis. *Prisoners of War in Britain 1756 to 1815: A Record of Their Lives, Their Romance and Their Sufferings*. Oxford: Humphrey Milford, Oxford University Press, 1914.

"Alan Seeger, Soldier and Poet." *New York Times Book Review*, December 24, 1916.

"All Britain Celebrates Our Advent in War." *New York Times*, April 21, 1917, 1.

Allen, Gardner Weld. *A Naval History of the American Revolution*. Vol. 2. Boston and New York: Houghton Mifflin, 1913.

"Allied in Homage to America's Dead." *New York Times*, May 31, 1922, 7.

American National Red Cross. *History of American Red Cross Nursing*. Part 1. New York: MacMillan, 1922.

Anderson, David. "Grateful Dutch Honor U.S. Heroes." *New York Times*, May 31, 1946, 4.

Andrews, Charles. *The Prisoners' Memoirs, or Dartmoor Prison, Containing a Complete and Impartial History of the Entire Captivity of the Americans in England*. New York: self-published, 1852. http://www.archive.org/details/prisonersmem00andr.

Arnstein, Daniel. "An Ex-Taxi Driver Checks Up on the Famous Burma Road." *Life*, October 6, 1941, 18.

"Assails Command in North Russia." *New York Times*, February 10, 1919, 3.

Bell, Frederick Jackson. *Room to Swing a Cat: Being Some Tales of the Old Navy*. New York: Longmans, Green, 1938.

"Body of Paul Jones Delivered to the Navy." *New York Times*, July 7, 1905, 3.

Booth, Edwin P. "An American Cemetery Overseas." *The Living Church* 114. (The Living Church Foundation) March 9, 1947.

Brighton, John George. *Admiral Sir P.B.V. Broke: A Memoir*. London: Sampson Low, Son and Marston, 1866.

Brooke, James. *New York Times World*. "Halifax Journal: Lively City Lets Ghosts of Deadman's Island Rest," March 23, 2000.

Brooks, Nathan Covington. *A Complete History of the Mexican War: Its Causes, Conduct, and Consequence*. Philadelphia: Grigg, Elliot, 1849.

Bryant, Russ, and W. David Perks. *USMC*. St. Paul, MN: Zenith, 2006.

Buell, Augustus C., and Horace Porter. *Paul Jones: Founder of American Navy*. Vol. 2. New York: Charles Scribner's Sons, 1906.

Burchis, Mustapha, and Arthur M. Johnson. "Resting Place of Heroes of the Barbary Wars." *Proceedings* (U.S. Naval Institute, Annapolis) (September 1956): 969–973.

"Cable Is Awaited for Disposition of 70,000 Graves." *Stars and Stripes*, February 28, 1919, 1.

Capdevilla, Luc, and Danièle Voldman. *War Dead: Western Societies and the Casualties of War*. Edinburgh University Press, 2006.

"Celebrate Day in Britain." *New York Times*, May 31, 1930, 5.

Congressional Record. March 15, 1926. Sixty-ninth Congress.

Cooper, James Fenimore. *The History of the Navy of the United States of America: Abridged in One Volume*. Philadelphia: Thomas, Cowperthwaite, 1841.

———. "Richard Somers." *Graham's*. 21 no. 4 (October 1842).

Current History 15 (1922). (New York).

De Koven, Anna. *The Life and Letters of John Paul Jones*. Vol. 2. New York: Charles Scribner's Sons, 1913.

Dickens, Charles. "Paul Jones Righted." *All the World Round* (April 2, 1870): 425–430.

Dickon, Chris. *The Enduring Journey of the USS "Chesapeake."* Charleston, SC: History Press, 2008. http://www.theusschesapeake.com/Home_Page.html.

Dugan, James, and Carroll Stewart. *Ploesti: The Great Ground-Air Battle of 1 August 1943*. New York: Random House, 1962.

Edmunds, Melba. "American Legion Magazine Report." *American Legion* (May 1977).

Europa Yearbook, 1928. London: Europa, 1928.

Europa Yearbook, 1929. London: Europa, 1929.

"First of American Legion Off for Flanders." *New York Times Magazine*, May 28, 1916.

"For the Stranger in a Strange Land." *Journal of the National Dental Association* 6 (1919).

"France Honors Her American Fliers." *New York Times Magazine*, September 4, 1927.

"From a Friend." *Stars and Stripes*, November 29, 1918, 4.

Gilbert, Bill. *Air Power: Heroes and Heroism in American Flight Missions, 1916 to Today*. New York: Kensington, 2004.

Gow, Lt. Kenneth. *Letters of a Soldier*. New York: H.B. Covert, 1920.

Graves Registration Service in the Mediterranean Zone of World War II. "Historical Narrative of American Graves Registration Service in the Mediterranean Zone 1 April 1946–1 October 1947." National Archives, Washington, D.C.

Hall, James Norman, Charles Nordhoff and Edgar G. Hamilton, eds. *The Lafayette Flying Corps*. Vol. 1. Boston: Houghton Mifflin, 1920.

Harris, Stephen L. *Duty, Honor, Privilege: New York's Silk Stocking Regiment and the Breaking of the Hindenburg Line*. Washington: Potomac, 2001.

Hawley, Chris. "U.S. heroes are villains at cemetery in Mexico." *Arizona Republic*, May 26, 2007. http://www.azcentral.com/arizonarepublic/news/articles/0526mexmemorial0526.html?&wired.

Hoch, Bradley R. *The Lincoln Trail in Pennsylvania: A History and Guide*. University Park: Pennsylvania State University Press, 2001.

Horner, George F. "Japanese Losses in Marianas Soar." *New York Times*, June 26, 1944, 7.

Horner, Gustavus R.B. *Diseases and Injuries of Seamen*. Philadelphia: Lippincott, Grambo, 1854.

Inderwick, James. *Cruise of the U.S. Brig "Argus" in 1813: Journal of Surgeon James Inderwick*. New York: New York Public Library, 1917.

"Is it Paul Jones' Body?" *New York Times*, May 21, 1905, 6.

Jacobson, Gerald F. *History of the 107th Infantry, U.S.A.* New York: Seventh Regiment Armory, 1920.

John Paul Jones: Commemoration at Annapolis, April 24, 1906. Washington: United States Congress, 1906.

"John Paul Jones, the American Patriot." *New York Times*, January 27, 1895, 28.

Jones, John Paul. *Life and Correspondence of John Paul Jones: From Original Letters and Manuscripts in the Possession of Miss Janette Taylor*, ed. Robert Charles Sands. New York: 1830.

Kinzer, Stephen. *Overthrow: America's Century of Regime Change from Hawaii to Iraq*. New York: Times Books, 2006.

Kirkels, Mieke, and Jo Purnot. *From Farmland to Soldiers Cemetery*. English ed. Adr. Heijnen, 's-Hertogenbosch, Netherlands, 2009.

Knoll, John J. "Crosses." *American Legion* (September 1930), 14–16.

"Lorraine Will Build Monument to First Americans Killed." *New York Times Magazine*, May 26, 1918.

Lowenfels, Walter, ed. *Walt Whitman's Civil War*. New York: Da Capo, 1961.

MacDonald, Charles B. "Slapton Sands: The Coverup That Never Was." *Army* (June 1988). http://www.history.navy.mil/faqs/faq20-2.htm.

Maps, James. "A Long-Forgotten American Naval Cemetery." *American Neptune* 25 (Salem, MA: Peabody Museum of Salem) (1965), 157.

Marvel, William. *The "Alabama" & the "Kearsarge": The Sailor's Civil War*. Chapel Hill: University of North Carolina Press, 1996.

McDermott, William. "The U.S. Unknown Soldier." *Rotarian* (November 1945).

McNamara, Robert S., James G. Blight and Robert K. Brigham. *Argument Without End: In Search of Answers to the Vietnam Tragedy*. United States: Public Affairs, 1999.

"Memorial Day in Mexico." *New York Times*, June 1, 1897, 12.

Miller, Lt. Arthur P., Jr. "Tripoli Graves Discovered." *Proceedings* (U.S. Naval Institute, Annapolis) (April, 1950), 377.

"Miss Wilson Sees Loving Hands' Work." *Stars and Stripes*, December 20, 1918, 7.

"Model of Memorial to American Airmen Unveiled." *New York Times*, February 28, 1926, 25.

Montgomery, Henry. *The Life of Major General Zachary Taylor*. Auburn, MA: Derby, Miller, 1850.

The Nation. "An American Cemetery in Mexico." March 29, 1866, pp. 392–393.

"O.D. Still in Evidence Up and Down Marne Salient." *Stars and Stripes*, March 21, 1919, 5.

Oliver, Myrna. "William Putney, 83; Vet Trained War Dogs." *Los Angeles Times*, March 23, 2003. http://articles.latimes.com/2003/mar/23/local/me-putney23.

"161 American Girls Died in World War." *New York Times*, November 11, 1922, 4.

O'Sullivan, John L. "Annexation." *United States Magazine and Democratic Review* 17, no. 1 (New York: J. & H.G. Langley) (July-August 184), 5–10. http://web.grinnell.edu/courses/HIS/f01/HIS202-01/Documents/OSullivan.html.

"Owen Wister Praises Singing Among Soldiers." *New York Times*, May 12, 1918, 58.

Palmer, Benjamin Franklin. *The Diary of Benjamin F. Palmer, Privateersman*. Philadelphia: Acorn Club, 1914.

"Pershing Opposes Bringing Dead Home." *New York Times*, August 1, 1919, 12.

Peters, Eleanor Bradley. "Forgotten Graves — Letter of a Mother Who Saw." *New York Tribune*, September 19, 1919.

"Plea for Heroes." *New York Times*, February 14, 1905, 7.

"Plead for Our Dead in France." *New York Times*, April 15, 1921, 1.

Porter, General Horace. *Campaigning with Grant*. New York: Century, 1907.

_____. "The Recovery of the Body of John Paul Jones." *Century* 70 (1905), 927–955.

Pratt, Fletcher. *The Compact History of the United States Navy*. New York: Hawthorn, 1957.

Report of the Secretary of the Class of 1881 of Harvard College 7 (Cambridge, MA: University Press) (1921).

Rogers, Joel Augustus. *Baltimore Afro-American*, August 23, 1930, 8.

Sardello, Carlo. "Hopes Rise for Return of the Bodies of Heroes of the Intrepid." *New York Times*, December 21, 1980, NJ2.

Seawell, M. Elliot. *Decatur and Sommers*. New York: D. Appleton, 1908.

"Seeger Bell Presented." *New York Times*, May 23, 1922, 13.

Sevareid, Eric. "Headhunters Save Airmen in Burma." *New York Times*, August 28, 1943, 5.

Sherburne, Andrew. *Memoirs of Andrew Sherburne: A Pensioner of the Navy of the Revolution*. Providence, RI: H.M. Brown, 1831.

Sherburne, John Henry. *The Life and Character of John Paul Jones*. 2nd ed. New York: Adriance, Sherman, 1851.

Shomon, Joseph James. *Crosses in the Wind: The Unheralded Saga of the Men in the American Graves Registration Service in World War II*. Margraten, Holland: Crosses in the Wind Foundation, 1991.

"Sigsbee's Squadron Greeted at Cherbourg." *New York Times*, July 1, 1905, 9.

"Six Killed with Pershing in 1916 to be Reburied Here." *New York Times*, September 10, 1925, 20.

Sledge, Michael. *Soldier Dead*. New York: Columbia University Press, 2005.

Smith, General Holland. *Coral and Brass*. Washington, D.C.: Department of the Navy, 1989.

Stevens, James R. *Searching for the Hudson Bombers: Lads, Love and Death in World War Two*. Victoria, BC: Trafford, 2004.

Symonds, Craig L., and William J. Clipson. *The Naval Institute Historical Atlas of the U.S. Navy*. Annapolis: U.S. Naval Institute Press, 1995.

Thompson, Captain Edgar K. "Long-Forgotten American Naval Cemetery, a Postscript." *American Neptune* 26 (Salem, MA: Peabody Museum of Salem) (1966), 218–219.

Thomson, Basil. *The Story of Dartmoor Prison*. London: William Heineman, 1907.

"3,600 Korea Missing Now Presumed Dead." *New York Times*, January 1, 1954, 2.

"To Exhume Soldiers' Bodies." *New York Times*, July 16, 1900, 2.

Townsend, Mark. "Did Allies kill GIs in D-Day training horror?" *The Observer*, May 16, 2004. http://www.guardian.co.uk/uk/2004/may/16/military.usa.

United States House of Representatives. Committee on Foreign Affairs. Sixty-sixth Congress, Vol. 3, November 13, 1919. *Return of Military Dead Buried in France: Hearings before the Committee on Foreign Affairs*, 81.

United States War Department, General Staff. *Location of Graves and Disposition of Bodies of American Soldiers Who Died Overseas*. Washington, D.C.: Government Printing Office, 1920.

"U.S. Memorial in Alsace." *New York Times*, June 8, 1953, 6.

"USS Spokane to Honor Five Unknown Historians [*sic*] In Tripoli." *The Spoke* (USS *Spokane*), March 25, 1949. http://www.fulkerson.org/spokane/tripoli.html.

Waterhouse, Benjamin. *The Magazine of History, with Notes and Queries*. Extra Number — No. 18. New York: William Abbatt, 1911.

Weiner, Tim. "Robert S. McNamara, Architect of a Futile War, Dies at 93." *New York Times*, July 7, 2009, A1.

Welsome, Eileen. *The General and the Jaguar: Pershing's Hunt for Pancho Villa*. New York: Little, Brown, 2006.

Whitman, Walt. *Specimen Days & Collect*. Philadelphia: David McKay, 1882–83.

Willett, Robert L. *Russian Sideshow: America's Undeclared War, 1918–1920*. Dulles, VA: Brassey's, 2003.

Wright, John MacNair. *Captured on Corregidor: Diary of an American P.O.W. in World War II*. Jefferson, NC: McFarland, 1988.

"Writers Disagree on Soldier Dead." *New York Times*, April 17, 1921, 20.

Index

Numbers in ***bold italics*** indicate pages with photographs.

Abbeville Communal Cemetery Extension, Somme, France 236
Abbot, Lemuel 27–31
Abeels, Arthur 91, 120, 206, ***208***, 214
Abeels, Janine (Jenny) 91, 120, 169–170, 198–199, 206–207, ***208***, 214
Abeels, Roger 91–92, 120, 198–199, 206, ***208***, 214
Aberdeen (Allenvale) Cemetery, Aberdeenshire, United Kingdom 256
Abney Park Cemetery, London, United Kingdom 256
Abraham, SSgt. Abie 123; *Ghost of Bataan* 123
Achicourt Road Cemetery, Achicourt, Pas-de-Calais, France 236
Achiet-Le-Grand Communal Cemetery Extension, Pas-de-Calais, France 236
Act to Establish and to Protect National Cemeteries 33
Adanac Military Cemetery, Miraumont, Somme, France 236
Addolorata Cemetery, Malta 255
Adegem Canadian War Cemetery, Maldegem, Oost-Vlaanderen, Belgium 263
Adinkerke Military Cemetery, De Panne, West-Vlaanderen, Belgium 227
adopted graves 191, 195–197
African Americans ***29***, 113, 197–198
Agira Canadian War Cemetery, Sicily 268
Agny Military Cemetery, Pas-de-Calais, France 236
Ahlmeyer, Healeah 168–169
Ahlmeyer, 2nd Lt. Heinz 168
A.I.F. Burial Ground, Flers, Somme, France 236
Aignac-le-Duc (Cemetery), France 261
Aisne-Marne American Cemetery and Memorial, France 63, 69

Aix-les-Bains (Cemetery), France 261
Aizecourt-Le-Bas Churchyard, Somme, France 236
CSS *Alabama* 160, 213
Alamein Memorial, Egypt 265
Alberger, Robert 21
Albert Communal Cemetery Extension, Somme, France 236
Albuera Cemetery, Bailleul-Sire-Berthoult, Pas-de-Calais, France 236
Aldershot Military Cemetery, Hampshire, United Kingdom 256
Alencon (St. Leonard) Cemetery, Orne, France 236
Alexandria (Chatby) Military and War Memorial Cemetery, Egypt 236
Alexandria (Hadra) War Memorial Cemetery, Egypt 236, 265
Algiers 20; cemetery 263
Allen, Maj. Gen. Henry T. 68
Allen, Lt. William 13, 16, 109, 151
Altrincham Bowdon and Hale (Altrincham) Cemetery, Cheshire, United Kingdom 269
Alvinza, Kretcher 61
Amara War Cemetery, Iraq 254
SS *America* 83
American Battle Monuments Commission (ABMC) 64, 72, 88, 131, 134, 161, 179, 188, 195, 208, 212–213
American Club of Brussels 72
American Club of Paris 71
American Escadrille *see* Lafayette Escadrille
American Field Service (AFS) 47, 83
American Gold Star Mothers Pilgrimages 82–86, ***84***, ***85***
American Legion 67, 84, 88, 122, 152, 156–157, 213
American North Russia Expeditionary Force (ANREF) *see* Polar Bear Expedition

American Overseas Memorial Day Association (AOMDA)—Belgium 2, 72, 120, 149, 169, 198–200, 203–207, ***209***, 214, 262
American Overseas Memorial Day Association (AOMDA)—France 71–72, 123, 188–189, 190, 213, 261; Protestants 5, 24
American Red Cross 130, 213
American University, Brussels 169, 203
American War Mothers 77
American Women's Club of Amsterdam (AWCA) 192–194
Amersfoort (Oud Leusden) General Cemetery, Utrecht, Netherlands 268
Amsterdam New Eastern Cemetery ***135***, 268
Anderson, George Wayne 60
Andover Cemetery, Hampshire, United Kingdom 256
Annan Cemetery, Dumfriesshire, United Kingdom 269
Annapolis Naval Academy 21–22, 36, 40, 51
Anneux British Cemetery, Nord, France 236
Antigua, West Indies 11
Antwerp, Belgium 71, 98, ***132***, 193
Anzin-St. Aubin British Cemetery, Pas-de-Calais, France 236
Appleby, George 160
Appoigny (Cemetery), France 261
Arabian Gulf War ***164***
Archangel, Russia 53–54, ***55–56***, 57, 79–82, 180
Archangel Memorial, Russia 255
Ardennes American Cemetery, Belgium 131, 199–***201***, 208
Arezzo War Cemetery, Italy 268
USS *Argus* 6, 16, 151
Arlington National Cemetery 33, 35, 40, 70, 74, 157, 168
Armed Forces Day (UK) 182
Armistice Day (BE) 182
Armistice Day (US) 70, 201

287

Arneke British Cemetery, Nord, France 237
Arnhem (Moscova) General Cemetery, Gelderland, Nethetrlands 268
Arras, France 63, 97–98, 190–192
Arras Flying Services Memorial, Pas-de-Calais, France 237
Arras Memorial, Pas-de-Calais, France 237
Artillery Wood Cemetery, Ieper, West-Vlaanderen, Belgium 227
Ashton-Upon-Mersey (St. Martin) Churchyard, Cheshire, United Kingdom 270
Assisi War Cemetery, Italy 268
Athens Memorial, Greece 267
Athies Communal Cemetery Extension, Pas-de-Calais, France 237
Aubepierre-sur-Aube (Cemetery), France 261
Auberchicourt British Cemetery, Nord, France 237
Aubigny Communal Cemetery Extension, Pas-de-Calais, France 237
Auchonvillers Military Cemetery, Somme, France 237
Aulnay-sous-Bois (Cemetery), France 261
Aulnoy Communal Cemetery, Nord, France 237
Australia 96–97, 159–161
Authuile Military Cemetery, Somme, France 237
Aveluy Communal Cemetery Extension, Somme, France 237
Avesnes-Le-Comte Communal Cemetery Extension, Pas-de-Calais, France 237
Avondale Cemetery, New Brunswick, Canada 233
Awoingt British Cemetery, Nord, France 237
Aylesbury Cemetery, Buckinghamshire, United Kingdom 256
Aylmer Cemetery, Ontario, Canada 263
Azmak Cemetery, Suvla, Turkey 255

Babinger, Corp. Joseph 54
Bac-Du-Sud British Cemetery, Bailleulval, Pas-de-Calais, France 237
Baghdad (North Gate) War Cemetery, Iraq 254
Bagneux (Cemetery), France 261
Bailleul Communal Cemetery (Nord), Nord, France 237
Bailleul Road East Cemetery, St. Laurent-Blangy, Pas-de-Calais, France 238
Bainbridge, Cdre. William 8
Baku Memorial, Azerbaijan 227
Ballard, 2nd Lt. Clifford 80
Banbury Cemetery, Oxfordshire, United Kingdom 270
Bankier, Lilli Stefania 134

Banneville-La-Campagne War Cemetery, Calvados, France 265
Bapaume Australian Cemetery, Pas-de-Calais, France 238
Bapaume Post Military Cemetery, Albert, Somme, France 238
Bar-sur-Aube (Cemetery), France 261
La Baraque British Cemetery, Bellenglise, Aisne, France 238
Les Baraques Military Cemetery, Sangatte, Pas-de-Calais, France 238
Barbary pirates 5–6, 178
Bari War Cemetery, Italy 268
Barlin Communal Cemetery Extension, Pas-de-Calais, France 238
Barly French Military Cemetery, Pas-de-Calais, France 238
Barmby-on-the-Moor (St. Catherine) Churchyard, Yorkshire, United Kingdom 270
Barnhill Cemetery, Angus, United Kingdom 256
Barron, Capt. James 13
Basingstoke (South View Or Old) Cemetery, Hampshire, United Kingdom 256
Basra Memorial, Iraq 254
Basra War Cemetery, Iraq 254
Bataan Death March 103–104, 123–125, 173
Bath (Haycombe) Cemetery, Somerset, United Kingdom 270
Bath (Locksbrook) Cemetery, Somerset, United Kingdom 256
Battle of Antietam **30**
Battle of Buena Vista 24–25, 73
Battle of Bull Run, first 29, 32
Battle of Chapultepec 25
Battle of Fort Erie 161–162
Battle of Molina del Rey 25
Battle of San Pasqual Valley 24
Battle of Tarawa 104–107, **106**
Battle of the Bulge 115–116, 121
Battle of the Somme 46
Battle of Ypres 49, 150
Bavans (Cemetery), France 261
Bayeux Memorial, Calvados, France 265
Bayeux War Cemetery, Calvados, France 261, 265
Bazentin-Le-Petit Communal Cemetery Extension, Somme, France 238
Beach Head War Cemetery, Anzio, Italy 268
Beacon Cemetery, Sailly-Laurette, Somme, France 238
Beamsville (Mount Osborne) Cemetery, Ontario, Canada 233
Beauceville Cemetery, Quebec, Canada 263
Beaucourt British Cemetery, Somme, France 238
Beaumont-Hamel (Newfoundland) Memorial, Somme, France 238
Beauval Communal Cemetery, Somme, France 238

Bebington Cemetery, Cheshire, United Kingdom 256
Beckenham Crematorium and Cemetery, Kent, United Kingdom 256
Becklingen War Cemetery, Soltau, Niedersachsen, Germany 266
Becourt Military Cemetery, Becordel-Becourt, Somme, France 238
Bedford House Cemetery, Ieper, West-Vlaanderen, Belgium 227
Beehive Cemetery, Willerval, Pas-de-Calais, France 238
Begg, James 149, 199, 204, 206–207
Belfast City Cemetery, County Antrim, United Kingdom 256
Belfast (Milltown) Roman Catholic Cemetery, County Antrim, United Kingdom 256, 270
Belgian Battery Corner Cemetery, Ieper, West-Vlaanderen, Belgium 227
Belgium, political divisions in 203
Belgrade Cemetery, Namur, Namur, Belgium 227
Bellacourt Military Cemetery, Riviere, Pas-de-Calais, France 238
Bellerive-sur-Allier (Cemetery), France 261
Bellicourt British Cemetery, Aisne, France 238
Benn, Carl 162
Beny-Sur-Mer Canadian War Cemetery, Reviers, Calvados, France 265
Bergen General Cemetery, Noord-Holland, Netherlands 269
Bergen-Op-Zoom Canadian War Cemetery, Noord-Brabant, Netherlands 268
Berks Cemetery Extension, Comines-Warneton, Hainaut, Belgium 227
Berlaimont Communal Cemetery Extension, Nord, France 238
Berles-Au-Bois Churchyard Extension, Pas-de-Calais, France 238
Berlin 1939–1945 War Cemetery, Berlin, Germany 266
Berlin South-Western Cemetery, Berlin, Brandenburg, Germany 254
Bertangles Communal Cemetery, Somme, France 238
Bethune Town Cemetery, Pas-de-Calais, France 238
Beuvry Communal Cemetery, Pas-de-Calais, France 238
Bicester Cemetery, Oxfordshire, United Kingdom 256
Biddulph (St. Lawrence) Churchyard, Staffordshire, United Kingdom 270
Bien Hoa, Vietnam 143
Bienvillers Military Cemetery, Pas-de-Calais, France 238
Big Red One 44

Index

Biganos Communal Cemetery, Gironde, France 238
Birkenhead (Flaybrick Hill) Cemetery, Cheshire, United Kingdom 256
Birmingham (Brandwood End) Jewish Cemetery, Warwickshire 270
Birmingham (Lodge Hill) Cemetery, Warwickshire, United Kingdom 256
Birmingham (Perry Bar) Crematorium, Warwickshire, United Kingdom 270
Bisley, Horace 18
"Black Tuesday" 102
Blackpool Cemetery, Lancashire, United Kingdom 256
Blairmore Union Cemetery, Alberta, Canada 233
Blantyre Church Of Central Africa Presbyterian Cemetery, Malawi 255
Blassie, Lt. Michael Joseph 154
Bleuet Farm Cemetery, Ieper, West-Vlaanderen, Belgium 227
Blighty Valley Cemetery, Authuile Wood, Somme, France 238
Bocabec Cemetery, New Brunswick, Canada 233
Bodelwyddan (St. Margaret) Churchyard, Flintshire, United Kingdom 256
Boeing airplanes, various 89, 92, 97, 102, 137–138
Bois-Carre British Cemetery, Thelus, Pas-de-Calais, France 238
Bois-Carre Military Cemetery, Haisnes, Pas-de-Calais, France 238
Bois Guillaume Communal Cemetery, Seine-Maritime, France 238
Boisleux-au-Mont, France 190
Bolsheviks 54–55; government 82
Bo'ness Cemetery, West Lothian, United Kingdom 256
Booth, Sgt. Edwin Bray 127
Booth, Edwin P. 119, 127
Bordon Military Cemetery, Hampshire, United Kingdom 256
Boreham, Peter 183–184
Bouchoir New British Cemetery, Somme, France 238
Boulogne Eastern Cemetery, Pas-de-Calais, France 239, 265
Bourail Memorial, New Zealand 269
Bourdouxhe family 120–121, 205
Bourges (Cemetery), France 261
Bourlon Wood Cemetery, Pas-de-Calais, France 239
Bournemouth East Cemetery, Hampshire, United Kingdom 256
Boves East Communal Cemetery, Somme, France 239
Boves West Communal Cemetery Extension, Somme, France 239

Boxgrove (St. Mary and Blaise) Churchyard, Sussex 270
Boy Scouts of American (BSA) 205, 209
Bozich, Stan 180–181
Bradford (Bowling) Cemetery, Yorkshire, United Kingdom 256
Brampton Cemetery, Ontario, Ontario, Canada 233
Bramshott (St. Mary) Churchyard, Hampshire, United Kingdom 256
Brandhoek New Military Cemetery, Ieper, West-Vlaanderen, Belgium 228
Brandhoek New Military Cemetery No. 3, Ieper, West-Vlaanderen, Belgium 228
Brandon Cemetery, Manitoba, Manitoba, Canada 233
Brassac-les-Mines (Cemetery), France 261
Brebieres British Cemetery, Pas-de-Calais, France 239
Brent, Bishop Charles Henry 50
Brest, France 111–112
Brest (Cemetery), France 261
Bretteville-Sur-Laize Canadian War Cemetery, Calvados 265
Brewery Orchard Cemetery, Bois-Grenier, Nord, France 239
Bridgemon, Rondal 174–175
Bridgemon, Rondal, Jr. 174–*175*
Bridgwater (Quantock Road) Cemetery, Somerset 270
Brigg Cemetery, Lincolnshire, United Kingdom 270
Bring Home the Soldier Dead League 67
Bristol (Arnos Vale) Cemetery, Gloucestershire, United Kingdom 256
Bristol (Arnos Vale) Roman Catholic Cemetery, Gloucestershire, United Kingdom 256
Brittany American Cemetery and Memorial, France 131
Brockville (Oakland) Cemetery, Ontario, Canada 233
Bromley (St. Luke's) cemetery, Kent, United Kingdom 256
Bronfay Farm Military Cemetery, Bray-Sur-Somme, Somme, France 239
USS *Brooklyn* 38
Brooks, Nathan: *A Complete History of the Mexican War: Its Causes, Conduct, and Consequences* 24
Brookwood American Cemetery and Memorial, England 58, 63, 83, 185, *188*, 256, 270
Brown's Copse Cemetery, Roeux, Pas-de-Calais, France 239
Brown's Road Military Cemetery, Festubert, Pas-de-Calais, France 239
Bruay Communal Cemetery Extension, Pas-de-Calais, France 239

Bruay-Sur-L'escaut Communal Cemetery, Nord, France 239
Brussels, Belgium 71, 92
Brussels Town Cemetery, Evere, Vlaams-Brabant, Belgium 228, 263
Bucquoy Road Cemetery, Ficheux, Pas-de-Calais, France *63*, 239
Buffalo, New York 162
Buffs Road Cemetery, Ieper, West-Vlaanderen, Belgium 228
Buis, Maj. Dale 143–144
Bullock, Maj. C. Seymour 48
Bully-Grenay Communal Cemetery, British Extension, Pas-de-Calais, France 239
Bunsen, Lt. Karl von 22
Burchis, Mustapha 87–88, 134, 178
Burgess, John 176
burial at sea *107*
Burlington (Holy Sepulchre) Cemetery, Ontario, Canada 233, 263
Burma 95–96; India-Burma Zone 125–126
Burnaby (Forest Lawn) Memorial Park, British Columbia 263
Busch, Gregg 201–202
Busch, Pfc. Victor 201–*202*
Bush, Wayne J. 199–200
Busigny Communal Cemetery Extension, Nord, France 239

Cabaret-Rouge British Cemetery, Souchez, Pas-de-Calais, France 239
Cairo War Memorial Cemetery, Egypt 236
Caix British Cemetery, Somme, France 240
Calais (Cemetery), France 261
Calais Canadian War Cemetery, Leubringhen, Pas-de-Calais, France 266
Calais Southern Cemetery, Pas-de-Calais, France 240
Calcutta (Bhowanipore) Cemetery, India 267
Calgary (Burnsland) Cemetery, Alberta, Canada 263
Calgary Jewish Cemetery, Alberta, Canada 263
Calgary Union Cemetery, Alberta, Canada 233
Calstock Cemetery, Cornwall, United Kingdom 256
Calvaire (Essex) Military Cemetery, Comines-Warneton, Hainaut, Belgium 228
Cambodia 145–146, 168
Cambrai East Military Cemetery, Nord, France 240
Cambrai Memorial, Louverval, Nord, France 240
Cambridge American Cemetery and Memorial, United Kingdom 110, 131, 159, 270
Cambridge City Cemetery, Cambridgeshire, United Kingdom 256, 270

Cambridge Crematorium, Cambridgeshire, United Kingdom 270
Cambrin Churchyard Extension, Pas-de-Calais, France 240
Camp Hughes Cemetery, Manitoba, Canada 233
Campbell, Pfc. Glenn 196–197
Canada 13, 19, 23, 34, 48–49, 119, 149, 161–165
Canada Cemetery, Tilloy-Les-Cambrai, Nord, France 240
Canada Farm Cemetery, Ieper, West-Vlaanderen, Belgium 228
Canadian Cemetery No. 2, Neuville-St.-Vaast, Pas-de-Calais, France 240
Canal Defense Lights (CDLs) 121
USS *Canberra* 154, **155**
Canterbury Union Cemetery, York County, New Brunswick, Canada 233
Cantimpre Canadian Cemetery, Sailly, Nord, France 240
Carlisle (Dalston Road) Cemetery, Cumberland, United Kingdom 271
Carnieres Communal Cemetery Extension, Nord, France 240
Carnoy Military Cemetery, Somme, France 240
Carter, Pres. Jimmy 157, 168
Carthage American Military Cemetery, Tunisia 269
USS *Casin* 44
Cassino Memorial, Italy 268
Castleton Protestant Cemetery, Ontario, Canada 233
Le Cateau Communal Cemetery, Nord, France 244
Le Cateau Military Cemetery, Nord, France 240
Cathcart Cemetery, Renfrewshire, United Kingdom 257
Catterick Cemetery, Yorkshire, United Kingdom 271
Caversfield (St. Laurence) churchyard, Oxfordshire, United Kingdom 271
Celle War Cemetery, Celle, Niedersachsen, Germany 267
Cement House Cemetery, Langemark-Poelkapelle, West-V., Belgium 228
Cerisy-Gailly Military Cemetery, Somme, France 240
Cesena War Cemetery, Italy 268
Chalons-en-Champagne East Communal Cemetery, Marne, France 266
Chalons-sur-Mer, France 154
Chapel Hill (St. Mary) Churchyard, Monmouthshire, United Kingdom 257
Chaplain's Corps 62
Chapman, Airman Charles Wesley 47–49, 78, 189
Charleroi Communal Cemetery, Charleroi, Hainaut, Belgium 263

Le Château Cambresis (Cemetery), France 261
Chatham, England 12, 16–17, 183
Chatham (Maple Leaf) Cemetery, Ontario, Canada 233
Chatham Naval Memorial, Kent, United Kingdom 257, 271
Chatou (Cemetery), France 261
Chattanooga, Tennessee 33, 74
Chaumont (Cemetery), France 261
Cherbourg, France 40, 83, 159, 226
USS *Chesapeake* 6, 13–14, 16, 162
Chesapeake Affair 13
Chester (Blacon) Cemetery, Cheshire, United Kingdom 271
Chester (Overleigh) Cemetery, Cheshire, United Kingdom 257
Chester Farm Cemetery, Ieper, West-Vlaanderen, Belgium 228
Chevington Cemetery, Northumberland, United Kingdom 271
Chichester Cemetery, Sussex, United Kingdom 257, 271
Chilton Foliat (St. Mary) Churchyard, Wiltshire, United Kingdom 257
China, People's Republic of 138
Chocques Military Cemetery, Pas-de-Calais, France 241
Choloy War Cemetery, Meurthe-et-Moselle, France 266
Christian, Arthur D. 80
Christian, T.J.J., Jr. 97, 190–**191**, 192
Churchill, PM Winston 110
Cirencester Cemetery, Gloucestershire, United Kingdom 271
Cite Bonjean Military Cemetery, Armentieres, Nord, France 241
City of London Cemetery and Crematorium, Manor Park, Essex, United Kingdom 257
City of Paris Cemetery, Pantin, Seine-St-Denis, France 241
Ciudadela, Spain 156
Civil War (American) 27–36, 48; in Australia 159; in France 159
Clamart (Cemetery), France 261
Clermont-en-Argonne (Cemetery), France 261
Cliveden War Cemetery, Buckinghamshire, United Kingdom 257
La Clytte Military Cemetery, Heuvelland, West-Vlaanderen, Belgium 229
Cobourg (St. Michael's) cemetery, Ontario, Canada 233
Cologne Memorial, Koln(Cologne), Nordrhein-Westfal, Germany 254
Cologne Southern Cemetery, Koln (Cologne), Nordrhein-Westfal, Germany 254
Comblain-la-Tour, Belgium 121–122, 205, **207**; church cemetery 262
Comet Line 90, 99, 120, 169, 214
Commonwealth Forces 49, 50
Commonwealth War Graves Commission 62, 93, 133, 185, 190,

192, 204, 206, 227, 263; cemetery at Bucquoy, France **63**
Conference on the Limitation of Armaments 70
Connaught Cemetery, Thiepval, Somme, France 241
Connor, Maj. Gen Fox 61
Consett (Benfieldside) Cemetery, Durham, United Kingdom 257
USS *Constellation* 6
USS *Constitution* 6
Contalmaison Chateau Cemetery, Somme, France 241
Contay British Cemetery, Contay, Somme, France 241
Cooper, James Fenimore: *History of the Navy of the United States of America* 8, 178
Coorevits, Sandrine 205
Corbie Communal Cemetery Extension, Somme, France 241
Coriano Ridge War Cemetery, Italy 268
Corozal American Cemetery and Memorial, Panama 35
Correll, Lucy 192
Cote 80 French National Cemetery, Etinehem, Somme, France 241
Couin New British Cemetery, Pas-de-Calais, France 241
Countess Constance of Caen 84
Courcelette British Cemetery, Somme, France 241
Courtney's and Steel's Post Cemetery, Turkey 255
Coxyde Military Cemetery, Koksijde, West-Vlaanderen, Belgium 228
Craddock, Gen. Bantz J. 201
Cranwell (St. Andrew) Churchyard, Lincolnshire, United Kingdom 257
Crest Cemetery, Fontaine-Notre Dame, Nord, France 241
Cret, Paul Phillipe 72
Crimean War 30
Croix-Rouge Military Cemetery, Quaedypre, Nord, France 241
Crompton, Barry 159–161
Cromwell, Dorothea 213
Cromwell, Gladys 213
Cromwell, William Nelson 78, 189
Cronkite, Walter 144
Le Crotoy (Cemetery), France 261
Crouy British Cemetery, Crouy-Sur-Somme, Somme, France 241
Crowborough Burial Ground, Sussex, United Kingdom 257
HMS *Crown Prince* 12, 17, 183
Croydon (Queen's Road) Cemetery, Surrey, United Kingdom 257
Crucifix Corner Cemetery, Villers-Bretonneux, Somme, France 241
Cuba 34
Cuesmes Communal Cemetery, Mons, Hainaut, Belgium 228
Cumbernauld Cemetery, Dunbartonshire, United Kingdom 271

Curragh Military Cemetery, County Kildare, Ireland 254
Cuzco Beach Cemetery, Cuba 161

D-Day Invasion *see* Normandy Invasion
Dainville Communal Cemetery, Pas-de-Calais, France 241
Da Nang, Vietnam 144
Dantzig Alley British Cemetery, Mametz, Somme, France 241
Daours Communal Cemetery Extension, Somme, France 241
Dar Es Salaam War Cemetery, Tanzania 255
Dartmoor Prison **18**, 58, 151, 184–**186**, 218–221; Dartmoor Massacre 18, 185
Dartmouth (Christ Church) Cemetery, Nova Scotia, Canada 233
Dartmouth (Mount Hermon) Cemetery, Nova Scotia, Canada 263
Daughters of 1812 151–152, 185–**186**, **187**
Daughters of the American Revolution (DAR) 38, 151
Dayton, VADM John H. 79
Deadman's Island, Halifax, Nova Scotia, Canada 1, 162,**163**–165
Dearborn, Michigan 54, 57, 80–82
Decatur, Cdre. Stephen 6–7, 20, 79
Defense Prisoner of War/Missing Personnel Office (DPMO) 168, 179, 212
Deir El Belah War Cemetery, Israel 254
USS *Delaware* 20–21
Delhi Memorial (India Gate), India 254
Delhi War Cemetery, India 267
Delphy, Midshipman Richard 16, 109, 151
Delville Wood Cemetery, Longueval, Somme, France 241
Demuin British Cemetery, Somme, France 241
Denain Communal Cemetery, Nord, France 241
Denegre, Tom 176–177
Denmark 92–93, 130, 213
Deoxyribonucleic acid (DNA) 154, 168, 169, 174
Dernancourt Communal Cemetery Extension, Somme, France 241
Derry House Cemetery No. 2, Heuvelland, West-Vlaanderen, Belgium 228
Detroit, Michigan 54, 57, 80–82
Dewey, Lt.Col. Peter A. 137, 142–143
DeWitt, Maj. Gen J.L. 82–85
Dickebusch New Military Cemetery, Ieper, West-Vlaanderen, Belgium 228
Dickens, Charles: *All the Year Round* 37
Dieppe Canadian War Cemetery, Hautot-Sur-Mer, Seine-Maritime, France 266
Dive Copse British Cemetery, Sailly-Le-Sec, Somme, France 241
Divisional Collecting Post Cemetery and Extension, Ieper, West-Vlaanderen, Belgium 228
Djibouti New European Cemetery 265
Doiran Memorial, Greece 254
Doiran Military Cemetery, Greece 254
Dominion Cemetery, Hendecourt-Les-Cagnicourt, Pas-de-Calais, France 241
Donahue, 2nd Lt. John 99
Doncaster (Christ Church) Churchyard, Yorkshire, United Kingdom 257
Doncaster (Hyde Park) Cemetery, Yorkshire, United Kingdom 257
Douai British Cemetery, Cuincy, Nord, France 241
Douai Communal Cemetery, Nord, France 241
Doullens Communal Cemetery Extension No. 1, Somme, France 241
Dover (St. James's) Cemetery, Kent, United Kingdom 257
Dozinghem Military Cemetery, Poperinge, West-Vlaanderen, Belgium 228
Dreux Communal Cemetery, Eure-et-Loir, France 266
Drumachose (Christ Church) Church Of Ireland Churchyard, County Londonderry, United Kingdom 271
Drumcree Church Of Ireland Churchyard, County Armagh, United Kingdom 257
Drummond Cemetery, Raillencourt, Nord, France 242
Dud Corner Cemetery, LOOS, Pas-de-Calais, France 242
Duggan, Lt. Robert Urquhart 192
Duhallow A.D.S. Cemetery, Ieper, West-Vlaanderen, Belgium 228
Duisans British Cemetery, Etrun, Pas-de-Calais, France 242
Dundee Eastern Necropolis, Angus, United Kingdom 257
Dundon, Walter 80
Dunkirk Memorial, Nord, France 266
Dunkirk Town Cemetery, Nord, France 242, 266
Durban (Stellawood) Cemetery, Kwazule Natal, South Africa 255
Durnbach War Cemetery, Bad Tolz, Bayern, Germany 267
Durrington Cemetery, Wiltshire, United Kingdom 257
Dury Crucifix Cemetery, Pas-de-Calais, France 242
Dury Mill British Cemetery, Pas-de-Calais, France 242
Dutch War Graves Commission 193
Dyce Old Churchyard, Aberdeenshire, United Kingdom 271
Dye, Ira 185

East Boldre (St. Paul) Churchyard, Hampshire, United Kingdom 257
East Wemyss Cemetery, Fifeshire, United Kingdom 257
Eastend (Riverside) Cemetery, Saskatchewan, Canada 233
Eastham (St. Mary) Churchyard, Cheshire 257
Ebblinghem Military Cemetery, Nord, France 242
Ecoivres Military Cemetery, Mont-St. Eloi, Pas-de-Calais, France 242
Ecoust Military Cemetery, Ecoust-St. Mein, Pas-de-Calais, France 242
Ecoust-St. Mein British Cemetery, Pas-de-Calais, France 242
Edinburgh (Comely Bank) Cemetery, Edinburgh, United Kingdom 257
Edinburgh (Morningside) Cemetery, Edinburgh, United Kingdom 257
Edinburgh (Piershill) Cemetery, Edinburgh, United Kingdom 257
Edinburgh (Rosebank) Cemetery, Edinburgh, United Kingdom 257
Edinburgh (Seafield) Cemetery, Edinburgh, United Kingdom 257
Edmonton Cemetery, Alberta, Canada 233
Edmonton (Mount Pleasant) Cemetery, Alberta, Canada 233
Edmonton St. Joachim's Roman Catholic Cemetery, Alberta, Canada 233
Eighty-Fifth Division *see* Polar Bear Expedition
Eisenhower, Dwight D. 110, 123, 143, 154, 199
El Alamein War Cemetery, Egypt 265
El Alia Cemetery, Algiers, Algeria 263
Eldoret Cemetery, Kenya 268
Elma United Church Cemetery, Ontario, Canada 233
Elouges Communal Cemetery, Dour, Hainaut, Belgium 228
Elzenwalle Brasserie Cemetery, Ieper, West-Vlaanderen, Belgium 228
embalming 27, **32**
Enfidaville War Cemetery, Tunisia 269
Enfield (St. Bernard's) Cemetery, Nova Scotia, Canada 233
Englefield Green Cemetery, Surrey, United Kingdom 257
English Cemetery, Mexico 26
English Cemetery, Nicaragua 176, 226

English Cemetery, Spain 21, *22*, 23, 155, 176–*177*
Enright, Thomas 44–45, 52
USS *Enterprise* 6
Eopolucci, John 44–45
Epe General Cemetery, Gelderland, Netherlands 269
Epehy Wood Farm Cemetery, Epehy, Somme, France 242
Epinal American Cemetery and Memorial, France 131
Epsom Cemetery, Surrey, United Kingdom 257
Escadrille Americaine 46–47; *see also* Lafayette Escadrille
Esquelbecq Military Cemetery, Nord, France 242
Esquimalt (Veterans') Cemetery, British Columbia, Canada 233
Les Essarts-le-Roi (Cemetery), France 261
Estaires Communal Cemetery and Extension, Nord, France 242
Estourmel Churchyard, Nord, France 242
Etaples Military Cemetery, Pas-de-Calais, France 242
Eterpigny British Cemetery, Pas-de-Calais, France 243
Eterpigny Communal Cemetery Extension, Somme, France 243
Exeter Higher Cemetery, Devon, United Kingdom 257

Failsworth Cemetery, Lancashire, United Kingdom 257
Farina, PFC Joseph G. 121–122, 169, 205, ***207***
USS *Farragut* 156
Farragut, Adl. David 22, 156
Faubourg d'Ameins Cemetery, Arras, Pas-de-Calais, France 190–*191*, 192, 243
Felix, Lt. Charles William 95
Fenaghvale (St. Paul's) Cemetery, Ontario, Canada 233
La Ferte-Sous-Jouarre Memorial, Seine-et-Marne, France 243
Feuchy Chapel British Cemetery, Wancourt, Pas-de-Calais, France 243
Fields of Margraten Foundation 197
Figheldean (St. Michael) Churchyard, Wiltshire, United Kingdom 257
Finningley (Holy Trinity and St. Oswald) Churchyard Extension, Nottinghamshire, United Kingdom 271
Fins New British Cemetery, Sorel-Le-Grand, Somme, France 243
First Barbary War 6
Five Points Cemetery, Lechelle, Pas-de-Calais, France 243
Flanders Field American Cemetery and Memorial, Belgium 49, 63, 72, *73*, 148, 199, 204, 208–211, ***210***

Flatiron Copse Cemetery, Mametz, Somme, France 243
Flesquieres Hill British Cemetery, Nord, France 243
Florence American Cemetery and Memorial, Italy 131
Florence War Cemetery, Italy 268
Flushing (Vlissingen) Northern Cemetery, Zeeland, Netherlands 269
Foch, Marshall Ferdinand 78
Fontaine-Au-Bois Communal Cemetery, Nord, France 243
Forceville, France 62
Ford, George "Daddy" 59
Fort Erie, Ontario, Canada 161–162
Fort Erie (Spears) Cemetery, Ontario, Canada 233
Fort George Military Cemetery, St. Peter Port, Guernsey, Channel Islands, United Kingdom 271
Fort Lee, Virginia 138
Fort Macleod (Union) Cemetery, Alberta, Canada 233
Fort Pitt Military Cemetery, Kent, United Kingdom 257
Forton Prison, England 11
Fosse No. 10 Communal Cemetery Extension, Sains-En-Gohelle, Pas-de-Calais, France 243
Fouquescourt British Cemetery, Somme, France 243
France 4, 60, 182, 184, 188–189, 203, 212–213, 226, 260–261
Franklin, Benjamin 40, 71
Franvillers Communal Cemetery Extension, Somme, France 243
Fredericton Rural Cemetery, New Brunswick, Canada 233, 263
Freetown (King Tom) Cemetery, Sierra Leone 255
Fremantle Cemetery, Western Australia, Australia 227
French Foreign Legion 45, 65
"From the Halls of Montezuma" (Marine hymn) 25
Fromijne, Bart 89–90, 194

Gadaffi, Col. Muammar 178, 180
Gander War Cemetery, Newfoundland and Labrador, Canada 263
Ganshoren, Belgium 91, 120, 214, 262
Garches (Cemetery), France 261
Garrett, 2nd Lt. Robert Lee 120–121, 205
Gauhati War Cemetery, India 267
Gaverbeek Horse Track and Hippodrome, Belgium 148–149, *150*, 211
Gaza War Cemetery, Israel 255
Gellatly, Charles Dewitt 134
Gibraltar 20; (North Front) Cemetery 267
Gijzenzele Churchyard, Oosterzele, Oost-Vlaanderen, Belgium 228
Gillingham (Woodlands) Cemetery, Kent, United Kingdom 257
Gillis, Adam 20–21

Girvan (Doune) Cemetery, Ayrshire, United Kingdom 257
Gisborne (Taruheru) Cemetery, Gisborne District, New Zealand 255
Givenchy-En-Gohelle Canadian Cemetery, Souchez, Pas-de-Calais, France 243
Givenchy Road Canadian Cemetery, Neuville-St. Vaast, Pas-de-Calais, France 243
Glace Bay (Greenwood) Cemetery, Nova Scotia, Canada 233
Glageon Communal Cemetery Extension, Nord, France 243
Glasgow (Craigton) Cemetery, Glasgow, United Kingdom 257, 271
Glasgow (Eastwood) Cemetery, Glasgow, United Kingdom 257
Glasgow (Riddrie Park) Cemetery, Glasgow, United Kingdom 257
Glasgow (St. Kentigern's) Roman Catholic Cemetery, Glasgow, United Kingdom 271
Glasgow Western Necropolis, Glasgow, United Kingdom 257, 271
Golders Green Crematorium, Middlesex, United Kingdom 257
Les Gonards Cemetery, Versailles, Yvelines, France 243
Google 174
Gorman, Pfc. James **85**
Gorre British and Indian Cemetery, Pas-de-Calais, France 243
Gosselies Communal Cemetery, Charleroi, Hainaut, Belgium 263
Gould, William 27
Gouzeaucourt New British Cemetery, Nord, France 243
Gow, Kenneth 50–53, 65–66, 188
Graasten Cemetery, Denmark 265
Graham, Navy Secy. William 37
Grand Ravine British Cemetery, Havrincourt, Pas-de-Calais, France 243
Grand-Seraucourt British Cemetery, Aisne, France 266
Grant, Gen. Ulysses S. 28–31
Grantham Cemetery, Lincolnshire, United Kingdom 271
Granum Cemetery, Alberta, Canada 233
grave adoption 117, 131
Graves Registration Service 32, 35, 43, 51, 60, 67, 72, 80, 88, 96, 101, 103, 122, 124, 125, 138–139, 141–142, 170, 174, 192; Balkan operations 129; Denmark 130; Mediterranean operations 102, 126–***127***, **128**, 129–130
Gravesend Cemetery, Kent, United Kingdom 271
Grayshott (St. Joseph) Roman Catholic Churchyard, Hampshire, United Kingdom 257
Great Crosby (St. Luke) Churchyard, Lancashire, United Kingdom 257
Great Lever (St. Michael) Church-

yard, Lancashire, United Kingdom 258
Greenwich Cemetery, London, United Kingdom 258
Gresham, James Bethel 44–45
Grevillers (New Zealand) Memorial, Pas-de-Calais, France 243
Grobbel, Clement 181
Grobbel, Mike 180–181
Groesbeek Canadian War Cemetery, Gelderland, Netherlands 269
Groesbeek Memorial, Gelderland, Netherlands 269
Guam Island 107–108
Guards' Cemetery, Lesboeufs, Somme, France 243
Guards Cemetery, Windy Corner, Cuinchy, Pas-de-Calais, France 243
Gwalia Cemetery, Ieper, West-Vlaanderen, Belgium 228

H.A.C. Cemetery, Ecoust-St. Mein, Pas-de-Calais, France 243
The Hague General Cemetery, Zuid-Holland, Netherlands 255
Haidar Pasha Memorial, Turkey 255
Haileybury (Mount Pleasant) Cemetery, Ontario, Canada 233
Halifax, Nova Scotia, Canada 1, 14–15, 162–165, 221–225
Halifax (Camp Hill) Cemetery, Nova Scotia, Canada 233
Halifax (Fairview Lawn) Cemetery, Nova Scotia, Canada 233
Halifax (Fort Massey) Cemetery, Nova Scotia, Canada 233, 263
Halifax Memorial, Nova Scotia, Canada 234, 263
Halifax (Mount Olivet) Cemetery, Nova Scotia, Canada 233
Halifax (St. John's) Cemetery, Nova Scotia, Canada 233
Haltom, 1st Lt. Girvom, Jr. 171
Ham British Cemetery, Muille-Villette, Somme, France 243
Hamburg Cemetery, Hamburg, Hamburg, Germany 254, 267
Hamilton Cemetery, Ontario, Canada 234
Hangard Communal Cemetery Extension, Somme, France 243
Hangard Wood British Cemetery, Somme, France 243
Hanover War Cemetery, Hannover, Niedersachsen, Germany 267
Happy Valley British Cemetery, Fampoux, Pas-de-Calais, France 243
Harbord, Maj. James G. 58
Harderwijk General Cemetery, Gelderland, Netherlands 269
Harding, Pres. Warren G. 70
Hargicourt British Cemetery, Aisne, France 243
Harlebeke New British Cemetery, Harelbeke, West-Vlaanderen, Belgium 228

Harrogate (Stonefall) Cemetery, Yorkshire, United Kingdom 271
Harvard University 45, 49
Harwell Cemetery, Berkshire, United Kingdom 271
Haslar Royal Naval Cemetery, Hampshire, United Kingdom 271
Hasnon Churchyard, Nord, France 243
Hastings, Thomas 75
Hastings Cemetery, Sussex, Sussex, United Kingdom 258
Haut Chinon (Cemetery), France 261
Haute-Avesnes British Cemetery, Pas-de-Calais, France 243
Haven, Roger Wallace 93–94, 133
Le Havre, France 69–70
Hawarden Cemetery, Flintshire, United Kingdom 271
Hawarden (St. Deiniol) Churchyard, Flintshire, United Kingdom 271
Hawthorn Ridge Cemetery No. 2, Auchonvillers, Somme, France 244
Hay, Merle 44–45, 52
Haynecourt British Cemetery, Nord, France 244
Hays, Vadm. Ronald J. 176
Hazebrouck Communal Cemetery, Nord, France 244
Heath Cemetery, Harbonnieres, Somme, France 244
Hebuterne Military Cemetery, Pas-de-Calais, France 244
Heilly Station Cemetery, Mericourt-L'abbe, Somme, France 244
Heliopolis War Cemetery, Egypt 265
Helles Memorial, Turkey 255
Hem Farm Military Cemetery, Hem-Monacu, Somme, France 244
Henin Communal Cemetery Extension, Pas-de-Calais, France 244
Henri Chapelle American Cemetery and Memorial, Belgium 122, 131, 132, 200–*202*, 208
Hermies Hill British Cemetery, Pas-de-Calais, France 244
Herrick, Amb. Meyer 58, 78
Hester, PFC. Rez P. *108*
Heston (St. Leonard) Churchyard, Middlesex, United Kingdom 271
Hethe (Holy Trinity) Roman Catholic Cemetery, Oxfordshire, United Kingdom 271
Heverlee Commonwealth War Graves Cemetery, Leuven, Belgium 262
Heverlee War Cemetery, Leuven, Vlaams-Brabant, Belgium 263
Highland Cemetery, Le Cateau, Nord, France 244
Hillingdon and Uxbridge Cemetery, Middlesex, United Kingdom 258
Hillside Cemetery, Le Quesnel, Somme, France 244

Hindenberg Line 53
Hinges Military Cemetery, Pas-de-Calais, France 244
Hitchings, Robert 196
Hixon (St. Peter) Churchyard, Staffordshire, United Kingdom 271
Ho Chi Min 142, 144
Hoboken, New Jersey 57, 67, 81, 83, 180
Hochfelden, France 123; cemetery 261
Hoffman, Laura 2, 198, 203–*206*, 207, 209, 214
Hollenbeck, Rep. Harold 157
Holmes, Dr. Thomas 32
Holten Canadian War Cemetery, Overijssel, Netherlands 269
Homma, Gen. Masaharu 124
Honington (All Saints) Churchyard, Suffolk, United Kingdom 271
Honnechy British Cemetery, Nord, France 244
Hooge Crater Cemetery, Ieper, West-Vlaanderen, Belgium 228
Hooton (St. Mary of the Angels) Roman Catholic Churchyard, Cheshire, United Kingdom 258
Hoover, Pres. Herbert 84
Horner, Dr. G.R.B.: *Seamen: With Remarks on Their Enlistment, Naval Hygiene and the Duties of Medical Officers* 21
USS *Hornet* 14
Hosteter, Theodore Rickey 66
Houdon, Jean-Antoine 38, *40*
Houghton and Wyton Burial Ground, Huntingdonshire, United Kingdom 271
Hourges Orchard Cemetery, Domart-Sur-La-Luce, Somme, France 244
Hove New Cemetery, Sussex, United Kingdom 271
Howard, John 10–11
Huby-St. Leu British Cemetery, Pas-de-Calais, France 244
Huijnen, Robin 196–197
Humbercamps Communal Cemetery Extension, Pas-de-Calais, France 244
Hursley (All Saints) Church Cemetery, Hampshire, United Kingdom 258
The Huts Cemetery, Ieper, West-Vlaanderen, Belgium 228
Huy (La Sarte) Communal Cemetery, Huy, Leige, Belgium 228
Hyde Park Corner (Royal Berks) Cemetery, Comines-Warneton, Hainaut, Belgium 228
Hylton (Castletown) Cemetery, Durham, United Kingdom 271

Imphal War Cemetery, India 267
impressment 3, 12
Inderwick, James: *Cruise of the U.S. Brig "Argus" in 1813* 16
Ingram, Osmand 44–45

Innisfil (St. Paul's) Cemetery, Ontario 264
International Business Machine Company (IBM) 141
International Red Cross 31
Internet 169, 185, 196, 214
USS *Intrepid* 7–8, 87, 135, 157, 177–180
Inverness (Tomnahurich) Cemetery, Inverness-shire, United Kingdom 258
Ipswich Cemetery, Suffolk, United Kingdom 258
Irvinestown Church Of Ireland Churchyard, County Fermanagh, United Kingdom 271
Iver Heath (St. Margaret) Churchyard, Buckinghamshire, United Kingdom 258

Jale, Veuve A. 59
Jamestown Exposition 51
Janson, Martinus 98, 194
Janval Cemetery, Dieppe, Seine-Maritime, France 266
Japan 95–96, 103–107, 170; postwar 125, 138–139; prisoner of war camps 124, 173
Jefferson, Pres. Thomas 5, 6, 13, 136
Jemappes Communal Cemetery, Mons, Hainaut, Belgium 228
HMS *Jersey* 9–**10**
Jerusalem War Cemetery, Israel 255
Johannesburg (West Park) Cemetery, Gauteng, South Africa 269
Johnson, Pres. Lyndon 144
Joint Field Activities (JFAs), Korea 168
The Joint POW/MIA Accounting Command (JPAC) 168, 171–173
Jones, Adl. John Paul 3, **4**, 5, 36–42, **40**, 156, 179, 213; as Pavel Dzhones 4
de Jongh, Andree 87, 90
Jonkerbos War Cemetery, Gelderland, Netherlands 269
Joy, Ron 19, 184–**186**

Kamiomi, Japan 125
Kamloops (Pleasant Street) Cemetery, British Columbia, Canada 234
Kandahar Farm Cemetery, Heuvelland, West-Vlaanderen, Belgium 228
Kandy War Cemetery, Sri Lanka 269
Kantara War Memorial Cemetery, Egypt 236
Karachi War Cemetery, Pakistan 269
Karamanli, Yusuf 6
Karasouli Military Cemetery, Greece 254
USS *Kearsarge* 160, 213
Kelly, William 178–180
Kemmel Chateau Military Cemetery, Heuvelland, West-Vlaanderen, Belgium 228

Kemmel No. 1 French Cemetery, Heuvelland, West-Vlaanderen, Belgium 228
Kennedy, Pres. John F. 144
Kensal Green (All Souls') Cemetery, London, United Kingdom 258
Kensal Green (St. Mary's) Roman Catholic Cemetery, London, United Kingdom 258
Kentgens, Dr. Joseph 99–101
Kentville (Oak Grove) Cemetery, Nova Scotia, Canada 234
Kezelberg Military Cemetery, Wevelgem, West-Vlaanderen, Belgium 228
Khayat Beach War Cemetery, Israel 267
Kidderminster Cemetery, Worcestershire, United Kingdom 258
Kidlington Burial Ground, Oxfordshire, United Kingdom 271
Kiel War Cemetery, Kiel, Schleswig-Holstein, Germany 267
Kilbride Old Churchyard, Buteshire, United Kingdom 271
Kindia Cemetery, Guinea 267
King, General Edward P. 103
King, James 160
King, William 161
Kingston (Cataraqui) Cemetery, Ontario, Canada 234
Kingston (St. Mary's) Cemetery, Ontario, Canada 234
Kingston (Up Park Camp) Military Cemetery, Jamaica 255
Kipling, Rudyard 62
Kirkeby Churchyard, Denmark 265
Kirkee 1914–1918 Memorial, India 254
Kirkee War Cemetery, India 267
Kirkels, Mieke 112; *From Farmland to Soldiers Cemetery* 112, 197–198
Kirkinner Cemetery, Wigtownshire, United Kingdom 271
Kirknewton (St. Gregory) Churchyard, Northumberland, United Kingdom 271
Kirton-in-Lindsey Cemetery, Lincolnshire, United Kingdom 271
Kitchener (Mount Hope) Cemetery, Ontario, Canada 234
Klein-Vierstraat British Cemetery, Heuvelland, West-Vlaanderen, Belgium 228
de Koch, Hendrik 90, 194
Korean War 137–142, **139**, **140**; postwar 168
Kortrijk (St. Jan) Communal Cemetery, Kortrijk, West-Vlaanderen, Belgium 229

La Baraque British Cemetery, Bellenglise, Aisne, France 238
La Clytte Military Cemetery, Heuvelland, West-Vlaanderen, Belgium 229
Lafayette Escadrille Memorial/Foundation, France 78, **189**–190

Lafayette (Flying) Escadrille 46, 78, 189
La Ferte-Sous-Jouarre Memorial, Seine-et-Marne, France 243
Lahana Military Cemetery, Greece 254
La Laiterie Military Cemetery, Heuvelland, West-Vlaanderen, Belgium 229
SS *Lake Daraga* 57, 180
Lancashire Landing Cemetery, Turkey 255
Landricourt-Sous-Coucy, France 151
La Neuville British Cemetery, Corbie, Somme, France 246
La Neuvillette (Cemetery), France 261
de Langhe, Secy. Guido 210
Lanklaar Communal Cemetery, Dilsen-Stokkem, Limburg, Belgium 263
Laos 168
La Plus Douve Farm Cemetery, Comines-Warneton, Hainaut, Belgium 229
Lapugnoy Military Cemetery, Pas-de-Calais, France 244
Larch Wood (Railway Cutting) Cemetery, Ieper, West-Vlaanderen, Belgium 229
La Souterraine (Cemetery), France 261
Last Known Alive (LKA) 168
La Targette British Cemetery, Neuville-St. Vaast, Pas-de-Calais, France 249
Laventie Military Cemetery, La Gorgue, Nord, France 244
La Ville-Aux-Bois British Cemetery, Aisne, France 250
Lawrence, Capt. James 14–15
Lawrence, James Daniel Pablo 133
Lebucquiere Communal Cemetery Extension, Pas-de-Calais, France 244
Le Cateau Communal Cemetery, Nord, France 244
Le Cateau Military Cemetery, Nord, France 240
Le Château Cambresis (Cemetery), France 261
Le Crotoy (Cemetery), France 261
Ledford, Hobert 74, 174–**175**
Leeds (Holbeck) Cemetery, Yorkshire, United Kingdom 258
Le Havre, France 69–70
Leighterton Church Cemetery, Gloucestershire, United Kingdom 258
Le Molay Littry (Cemetery), France 261
Lenham Cemetery, Kent, United Kingdom 258
HMS *Leopard* 13, 16
Le Quesnel Communal Cemetery Extension, Somme, France 247
Lerwick New Cemetery, Zetland (Shetland), United Kingdom 272

Les Baraques Military Cemetery, Sangatte, Pas-de-Calais, France 238
Les Essarts-le-Roi (Cemetery), France 261
Les Gonards Cemetery, Versailles, Yvelines, France 243
Les Lilas (Cemetery), France 261
Le Touret Memorial, Pas-de-Calais, France 250
Le Treport Military Cemetery, Seine-Maritime, France 250
Le Trou Aid Post Cemetery, Fleurbaix, Pas-de-Calais, France 250
Leval Communal Cemetery, Nord, France 244
Level Crossing Cemetery, Fampoux, Pas-de-Calais, France 244
Leysdown (St. Clement) churchyard, Kent, United Kingdom 258
Liberation Day (NL) 182
Lichfield Crater, Thelus, Pas-de-Calais, France 244
Liesse Communal Cemetery, Aisne, France 266
Lievin Communal Cemetery Extension, Pas-de-Calais, France 244
Ligny-St. Flochel British Cemetery, Averdoingt, Pas-de-Calais, France 244
Lihons, France Commonwealth War Graves Cemetery 151
Lijssenthoek Military Cemetery, Poperinge, West-Vlaanderen, Belgium 66, 68, 204, **206**, 214, 229, 262
Les Lilas (Cemetery), France 261
Lillers Communal Cemetery, Pas-de-Calais, France 244
Lincoln, Pres. Abraham 27, 32, 33
Lincoln (Newport) Cemetery, Lincolnshire, United Kingdom 258
Lindbergh, Charles 72, **73**, 209
Little, Lt. William K 102–103, ***104***
Little Rissington (St. Peter) Churchyard, Gloucestershire, United Kingdom 272
Liverpool (Anfield) Cemetery, Lancashire, United Kingdom 258
Liverpool (Broad Green) Jewish Cemetery, Lancashire, United Kingdom 258
Liverpool (Kirkdale) Cemetery, Lancashire, United Kingdom 258
Loanhead Cemetery, Midlothian, United Kingdom 258
London, England 50, 58, 72, 83
London Cemetery, Neuville-Vitasse, Pas-de-Calais, France 244
London (Mount Pleasant) Cemetery, Ontario, Canada 234, 264
London Rifle Brigade Cemetery, Comines-Warneton, Hainaut, Belgium 229
London (St. Peter's) Roman Catholic Cemetery, Ontario, Canada 234
London (Woodland) Cemetery, Ontario, Canada 234, 264

Lone Pine Cemetery, Anzac, Turkey 255
Lone Pine Memorial, Anzac, Turkey 255
Longside Cemetery, Aberdeenshire, United Kingdom 272
Longuenesse (St. Omer) Souvenir Cemetery, Pas-de-Calais, France 244
Loos British Cemetery, Pas-de-Calais, France 245
Loos Memorial, Pas-de-Calais, France 245
Lorraine American Cemetery, France 123, 131
Lorton (St. Cuthbert) churchyard, Cumberland, United Kingdom 258
Lossiemouth Burial Ground, Moray, United Kingdom 272
Louez Military Cemetery, Duisans, Pas-de-Calais, France 245
Lowestoft Naval Memorial, Suffolk, United Kingdom 272
Lowrie Cemetery, Havrincourt, Pas-de-Calais, France 245
Ludington, Quartermaster Gen. Marshall 34
RMS *Lusitania* 49
Luxembourg American Cemetery, Luxembourg 131
Luxeuil-les-Bains (Cemetery), France 261
Luxford, Pat 109, 183
Lyness Royal Naval Cemetery, Orkney, United Kingdom 258
Lyrea, Hughe 162

Macalla, Michael 79–81
MacArthur, Gen. Douglas 103, 123–124, 125, 170
MacDonald, Betty: *The Egg and I* 193
Machine Records Units (MRUs) 141
MacLean, Guy 163–165
MacLeish, Archibald: "The Young Dead Soldiers Do Not Speak" 214
Maidenhead Cemetery, Berkshire, United Kingdom 272
The Maidenhead Register, Berkshire, United Kingdom 272
Mailly Wood Cemetery, Mailly-Maillet, Somme, France 245
USS *Maine* 34
Malrait, Gilbert 204, 214
Malta (Capuccini) Naval Cemetery 268
Malta Memorial 268
Manchester Southern Cemetery, Lancashire, United Kingdom 272
Mangochi Town Cemetery, Malawi 255
Manifest Destiny 23, 162
Manila American Cemetery and Memorial, Philippines 126, 131
Manitoba Register, CAIX, Somme, France 245
Maple Copse Cemetery, Ieper, West-Vlaanderen, Belgium 229

Maps, Jim 154–156
Marcoing British Cemetery, Nord, France 245
Margraten, Netherlands 112–***118***, 121, 127–129, 130–132, ***134***, 195–198
Marham Cemetery, Norfolk, United Kingdom 272
Marnes-la-Coquette (Cemetery), France 226–227, 261
Maroc British Cemetery, Grenay, Pas-de-Calais, France 245
Maroeuil British Cemetery, Pas-de-Calais, France 245
Maroilles Communal Cemetery, Nord, France 245
Marshall, Gen. George C. 141
Marstal Kirkegård — Cemetery, Ærø, Denmark 275
Martin, Cdr.Gen. Gregory S. 189
Martin, Mary Morgan 96
Martin (Holy Trinity) Churchyard, Lincolnshire, United Kingdom 258
Maubeuge-Centre Cemetery, Nord, France 245
SS *Mayaguez* 146
Maybole Cemetery, Ayrshire, United Kingdom 258
Mazargues War Cemetery, Marseilles, Bouches-du-Rhone, France 266
Mazingarbe Communal Cemetery Extension, Pas-de-Calais, France 245
McAdoo, Navy Secy. William 37
McBride, Nettie Grace 213
McCormick, S/Sgt. John 2, 98–101, 194–195
McCormick, John 101
McCullough, TSgt. John R. 170–171
McDermott, William F. 152–154
McDonald, Charles 159
McKinley, Pres. William 34–35
McManaman, TSgt. Bernard 91–92, 137, 169
McManaman, Janine Parker 137, 166, 169, 198
McNamara, Robert 172
McRae, Dr. John: "In Flanders Fields" 149–151, 209, 215
Medicine Hat (Hillside) Cemetery, Alberta, Canada 234
Mediteranean Sea 6, 20
Medjez-El-Bab Memorial, Tunisia 269
Medjez-El-Bab War Cemetery, Tunisia 269
Meharicourt Communal Cemetery, Somme, France 266
Meigs, Quartermaster Gen. Montgomery 33
Melcombe Regis Cemetery, Dorset, United Kingdom 258
Melville Island, Halifax, Nova Scotia, Canada 1, 14–15, 162, 183
Memorial Day (FR) 182
Memorial Day (US) 58, ***64–65***, 68, 71, 72, ***73***, 103, 117–118, 130,

134, 148–*150*, 152, 161, 165, 174, 176, 181, 182, 185, 188–*189*, 190, 192, *193*–194, 195, 198, *199*, *200*–*202*, 203–*206*, *207*, *208*, 209, *210*–214
Mendinghem Military Cemetery, Poperinge, West-Vlaanderen, Belgium 229
Menin Road South Military Cemetery, Ieper, West-Vlaanderen, Belgium 229
Merton (St. Mary) Churchyard, Surrey, United Kingdom 272
Merville Communal Cemetery, Nord, France 245
Meteren Military Cemetery, Nord, France 245
Meuse-Argonne American Cemetery and Memorial, France 63, 69, 70
Mexican-American War 24, 157
Mexican Revolution 42
Mexico 23–27, 42–43, 48, 72–74, 174–175, 226
Mexico City [US] National Cemetery 23–27, 35, 64, 72, 174
Meximieux (Cemetery), France 261
Mezieres Communal Cemetery Extension, Somme, France 245
Miami Cemetery, Manitoba, Canada 234
Michigan's Own Military and Space Museum 180–181
Middlesbrough (Acklam) Cemetery, Yorkshire, United Kingdom 272
Mikra British Cemetery, Kalamaria, Greece 254
Mill Road Cemetery, Thiepval, Somme, France 245
Mill Switch British Cemetery, Tilloy-Les-Cambrai, Nord, France 245
Millbay Prison *see* Old Mill Prison
Milltown Catholic Cemetery, New Brunswick, Canada 264
Minster (Thanet) Cemetery, Kent, United Kingdom 258
Moeuvres Communal Cemetery Extension, Nord, France 245
Le Molay Littry (Cemetery), France 261
Monchy British Cemetery, Monchy-Le-Preux, Pas-de-Calais, France 245
Moneyglass Roman Catholic Cemetery, County Antrim, United Kingdom 258
Monroe Doctrine 20
Mons (Bergen) Communal Cemetery, Mons, Hainaut, Belgium, 229
Mont-Bernanchon British Cemetery, Gonnehem, Pas-de-Calais, France 245
Mont Huon Military Cemetery, Le Treport, Seine-Maritime, France 245
Montay-Neuvilly Road Cemetery, Montay, Nord, France 245

Montecchio War Cemetery, Italy 268
Montgomery, Gen. Bernard 110
Monthureux-sur-Saône (Cemetery), France 261
Montigny-le-Bretonneux (Cemetery), France 261
Montreal (Hawthorn-Dale) Cemetery, Quebec, Canada 234
Montreal (Mount Royal) Cemetery, Quebec, Canada 234, 264
Montreal (Notre Dame Des Neiges) Cemetery, Quebec, Canada 234, 264
Montreuil-sous-Bois (Cemetery), France 261
Montrichard (Cemetery), France 261
Montrose (Sleepyhillock) Cemetery, Angus, United Kingdom 258
Moody, Rev. Paul 67
Morden Cemetery, Surrey, United Kingdom 258
Morden (Hillside) Cemetery, Manitoba, Canada 234
Moreuil Communal Cemetery Allied Extension, Somme, France 245
Morgan, Lt. George E. 96
Moro River Canadian War Cemetery, Italy 268
Morpeth (Ss. Mary and James) Churchyard, Northumberland, United Kingdom 272
Mory Street Military Cemetery, St. Leger, Pas-de-Calais, France 245
Moston (St. Joseph's) Roman Catholic Cemetery, Lancashire, United Kingdom 272
Mouzon (Cemetery), France 261
Moyenmoutier (Cemetery), France 261
Munster Heath War Cemetery, Telgte, Nordrhein-Westfalen, Germany 267
Murray River Cemetery, Prince Edward Island, Canada 234

Nairn Cemetery, Nairnshire, United Kingdom 258
Nairobi South Cemetery, Kenya 255
Namps-Au-Val British Cemetery, Somme, France 245
Nancy (Cemetery), France 261
Napoleonic Wars 13, 183
Nassau War Cemetery 263
National Association for the Advancement of Colored People (NAACP) 84
National War Dog Cemetery, Guam 166–*167*, 275
Native Americans 84
Naves Communal Cemetery Extension, Nord, France 245
Navy League of the United States, Madrid Council 156, 176–177
Netherlands American Cemetery, Netherlands 112, *118*, 127- 129, 132, *133*, *134*, 195, 198; *see also* Margraten, Netherlands

Netley Military Cemetery, Hampshire, United Kingdom 258
Neupré, Belgium 198–*199*
La Neuville British Cemetery, Corbie, Somme, France 246
La Neuvillette (Cemetery), France 261
Nevers (Cemetery), France 261
New Guinea 96, 173
New Zealand 161
Newell, SN. James 15
Newquay (Fairpark) Cemetery, Cornwall, United Kingdom 272
Niagara Cemetery, Iwuy, Nord, France 246
Niagara Falls (Drummond Hill) Cemetery, Ontario, Canada 234
Niagara-on-the-Lake United Church Cemetery, Ontario, Canada 234, 264
Nicaragua 78; English cemetery 225
Nictaux (United Baptist) Cemetery, Nova Scotia, Canada 264
Niederzwehren Cemetery, Kassel, Hessen, Germany 254
Nieuport Memorial, Nieuwpoort, West-Vlaanderen, Belgium 229
Nightingale, Florence 30
Nine Elms British Cemetery, Poperinge, West-Vlaanderen, Belgium 229
Nine Elms Military Cemetery, Thelus, Pas-de-Calais, France 246
960th Quartermaster Service Company 197
94th Aero Squadron 47
Nixon, Pres. Richard 145
No Place Field, England 183
Noah, Mark (History Flight organization proprietor) 172–173, 181
Noeux-Les-Mines Communal Cemetery, Pas-de-Calais, France 246
Noordwijk General Cemetery, Zuid-Holland, Netherlands 255, 269
Norfolk, Virginia 13, 79; public library 196
Norfolk Cemetery, Becordel-Becourt, Somme, France 246
Normandy American Cemetery and Memorial, France 132
Normandy Invasion 97, 109, 111, 188
North Africa American Cemetery and Memorial, Tunisia 132, *135*
North Battleford Cemetery, Saskatchewan, Canada 234
North Cotes (St. Nicholas) Churchyard, Lincolnshire, United Kingdom 272
Norway 213
Nottingham (Wilford Hill) Jewish Cemetery, Nottinghamshire, United Kingdom 272
Nowra War Cemetery, New South Wales, Australia 263

Noyelles-Sur-L'escaut Communal Cemetery Extension, Nord, France 246
Noyon New British Cemetery, Oise, France 246
Nunhead (All Saints) Cemetery, London, United Kingdom 258
Nurses: Army, Red Cross, YMCA 213–214
Nykøbing Falster Østre Kirkegård — Cemetery, Guldborgsund, Denmark 275

Oakland, California 144
Odell, Derek 185
Office of Strategic Services (OSS) 143
USS *Ohio* 161
Oise-Aisne American Cemetery and Memorial, France 64, 67
Old Mill Prison, England 10, 14, 151
Oldham (Hollinwood) Cemetery, Lancashire, United Kingdom 272
Olivo, Maj. Carlos L. 175–176
Ollerton Cemetery, Nottinghamshire, United Kingdom 272
USS *Olympia* 69–70
164th Civil Engineering Squadron, Tennessee Air National Guard 164
Ontario Cemetery, Sains-Les-Marquion, Pas-de-Calais, France 246
Oosttaverne Wood Cemetery, Heuvelland, West-Vlaanderen, Belgium 230
Operation Bodyguard 110
Operation Glory 142, 168
Operation Overlord 110–111, 121
Operation Tidal Wave 102
Operation Tiger 109–110, 157–159
Opijnen, Netherlands 89–90, 112, 192, **193**, 194, 274
Orange (Cemetery), France 261
Orange Hill Cemetery, Feuchy, Pas-de-Calais, France 246
Orchard Dump Cemetery, Arleux-En-Gohelle, Pas-de-Calais, France 246
Orders in Council 13, 19
Orira Cemetery, Far North District, New Zealand 255
Orleans Main Cemetery, Loiret, France 266
Orpington (All Saints) Churchyard Extension, Kent, United Kingdom 258
Orpington (St. Mary Cray) Cemetery, Kent, United Kingdom 272
Oshawa Union Cemetery, Ontario, Canada 234, 264
Øster Starup Kirkegård — Churchyard, Vejle, Denmark 275
O'Sullivan, John O. 23
Ottawa (Beechwood) Cemetery, Ontario, Canada 234
Ottawa Cremation Memorial, Ontario, Canada 264
Ottawa Jewish Cemetery, Ontario, Canada 264

Ottawa Memorial, Ontario, Canada 264
Ottawa (Notre Dame) Roman Catholic Cemetery, Ontario, Canada 234, 264
Outtersteene Communal Cemetery Extension, Bailleul, Nord, France 246
Ovillers Military Cemetery, Somme, France 246
Ovnand, Msgt. Chester 143
Owen Sound (Greenwood) Cemetery, Ontario 264
Oxford (Botley) Cemetery, Oxfordshire, United Kingdom 272
Oxford Road Cemetery, Ieper, West-Vlaanderen, Belgium 230
Oye-Plage Communal Cemetery, Pas-de-Calais, France 266
Ozdarski, Joseph S. 80

Pachiotti family 121–122, 205, **207**
Padua War Cemetery, Italy 268
Paisley (Hawkhead) Cemetery, Renfrewshire, United Kingdom 272
Paisley (Woodside) Cemetery, Renfrewshire, United Kingdom 272
Palmer, Privateersman Benjamin 15
Panama Canal 51, 78
Pancho Villa 42, 48, 226
Panmunjon, Korea 142, 168
Pantin (Cemetery), France 261
Paradise Public Cemetery, Nova Scotia, Canada 234
Paris, France 4–5, 37, 78, 86, 111, 226, 261
Parral, Mexico 42, 73, 174–175, 226
Passchendaele New British Cemetery, Zonnebeke, West-Vlaanderen, Belgium 230
Patton, Gen. George 43, 99
Pearl Harbor 94, 103
Pedersker Kirkegård — Churchyard, Bornholm, Denmark 275
Peiper, Col. Joachim 121
Pembroke Dock Military Cemetery, Pembrokeshire, United Kingdom 272
Pembroke Prison, England 11
Penrith Cemetery, Cumberland, United Kingdom 258
Penzance (Paul) Cemetery, Cornwall, United Kingdom 258
Pernes British Cemetery, Pas-de-Calais, France 246
Peronne Communal Cemetery Extension, Somme, France 246
Peronne Road Cemetery, Maricourt, Somme, France 246
Perreuse Chateau Franco British National Cemetery, Seine-et-Marne, France 246
Pershing, Gen. John 42–43, 45, 48, 50, 60, 64, 73
Perth Cemetery (China Wall), Ieper, West-Vlaanderen, Belgium 230
Perthes (Cemetery), France 261
Peterborough (Eastfield) Cemetery,

Northamptonshire, United Kingdom 272
Peters, Eleanor Bradley 61
Petit-Vimy British Cemetery, Pas-de-Calais, France 246
USS *Philadelphia* 6–8
Philippine Islands 103–104
Philippine War 34
Philosophe British Cemetery, Mazingarbe, Pas-de-Calais, France 246
Picton (Glenwood) Cemetery, Ontario, Canada 234, 264
Pieta Military Cemetery, Malta 255
Pigue, Edward H. 66–68, 71, 204
Pigue, Lt. James A. 51–52, 66–68, 71, 169, 204, **206**, 214
Pihen-Les-Guines Communal Cemetery, Pas-de-Calais, France 266
Placentia, Newfoundland, Canada 8
Plaine French National Cemetery, Bas-Rhin, France 246
Ploegsteert Memorial, Comines-Warneton, Hainaut, Belgium 230
Ploiesti, Romania 102–103, **104**
Plombieres, Belgium 201–203
Plouescat Communal Cemetery, Finistere, France 266
La Plus Douve Farm Cemetery, Comines-Warneton, Hainaut, Belgium 229
Plymouth, England 2, 9–10, 16, 58, 109, 151–152, 182–183, 218; *see also* No Place Field, Old Mill Prison, Stray Park
Plymouth (Efford) Cemetery, Devon, United Kingdom 258
Plymouth Naval Memorial, Devon, United Kingdom 258, 272
Plymouth (Weston Mill) Cemetery, Devon, United Kingdom 272
Plympton (St. Mary) Churchyard, Devon, United Kingdom 259
Poelcapelle British Cemetery, Langemark-Poelkapelle, West-V., Belgium 230
Point-Du-Jour Military Cemetery, Athies, Pas-de-Calais, France 246
Point 110 Old Military Cemetery, Fricourt, Somme, France 246
Poix-De-Picardie Churchyard, Somme, France 266
Polar Bear Expedition 54–57, **55**, **56**, 79, 81, 180–181
Polar Bear Memorial Association 80, 180
Polk, Pres. James L. 24
Pommereuil British Cemetery, Nord, France 246
Ponopy, Hines 61
Pont-De-Nieppe Communal Cemetery, Nord, France 246
Poperinghe New Military Cemetery, Poperinge, West-Vlaanderen, Belgium 230

Poperinghe Old Military Cemetery, Poperinge, West-Vlaanderen, Belgium 230
Port Mahon, Menorca, Spain 21–23, 79, 154–156, 176–177, 255
Port Said War Memorial Cemetery, Egypt 265
Portage-La-Prairie (Hillside) Cemetery, Manitoba, Canada 264
Portchester Castle, England 16
Porte-De-Paris Cemetery, Cambrai, Nord, France 246
Porter, Cdr. David 22
Porter, Gen. Horace: *Campaigning with Grant* 31, 36–40, 179
Portianos Military Cemetery, Lemnos, Greece 254
USS *Portland* 156
Portsmouth, England 11, 16–17, 58; *see also* Forton Prison, Portchester castle
Portsmouth, Virginia 13
Portsmouth (Kingston) Cemetery, Hampshire, United Kingdom 259
Portsmouth Naval Memorial, Hampshire, United Kingdom 259, 272
Posey, SMSgt. Henry 164–65
Potijze Chateau Grounds Cemetery, Ieper, West-Vlaanderen, Belgium 230
Potijze Chateau Wood Cemetery, Ieper, West-Vlaanderen, Belgium 230
Powers, Lt. Ralph 55–56
Pozieres British Cemetery, Ovillers-La Boisselle, Somme, France 246
Pozieres Memorial, Somme, France 246
Poznan Old Garrison Cemetery, Poland 269
Prague War Cemetery, Czechoslovakia 265
Preble, Cdre. Edward 6–8
Premont British Cemetery, Aisne, France 246
SS *President Roosevelt* 81
Prince William 186
Princetown, England 18, 58, 151–152, 184, *187*
prison hulks 9–11, 18, 183–184
Prison Ships Martyrs Monument, New York 11
Prospect Hill Cemetery, Gouy, Aisne, France 246
Protestant Cemetery, Libya 88, 177–*180*
Prysten House, Plymouth, England 152–*153*
Puchevillers British Cemetery, Somme, France 247
Punchbowl Cemetery and Memorial, Hawaii 126, 168
Punitive Expedition 42, 51, 73, 82
Putney, Dr. William 166

Quarry Cemetery, Marquion, Pas-de-Calais, France 247
Quarry Wood Cemetery, Sains-Les-Marquion, Pas-de-Calais, France 247
Quartermaster Burial Corps 35, 62, 112
Quartermaster General 120, 193
Quatre-Vents Military Cemetery, Estree-Cauchy, Pas-de-Calais, France 247
Queant Communal Cemetery British Extension, Pas-de-Calais, France 247
Queant Road Cemetery, Buissy, Pas-de-Calais, France 247
Quebec Cemetery, Cherisy, Pas-de-Calais, France 247
Quebec City (Mount Hermon) Cemetery, Quebec, Canada 234
The Quebec Memorial, Pointe Claire Field Of Honour, Quebec, Canada 234
Queen Elizabeth II 186
Queen Marie, Romania 84
Queens Cemetery, Bucquoy, Pas-de-Calais, France 247
Le Quesnel Communal Cemetery Extension, Somme, France 247
Queue-du-Bois, Belgium 120–121, 205, 262
Quievrain Communal Cemetery, Quievrain, Hainaut, Belgium 230

Rahill, 2nd Lt. John 122–123, 188
Raillencourt Communal Cemetery Extension, Nord, France 247
railroads 23, 27, 35
Railway Dugouts Burial Ground, Ieper, West-Vlaanderen, Belgium 229
Railway Hollow Cemetery, Hebuterne, Pas-de-Calais, France 247
USS *Raleigh* 79
Ramleh War Cemetery, Israel 255, 267
Ramsbottom Cemetery, Lancashire, United Kingdom 272
Ramscappelle Road Military Cemetery, Nieuwpoort, West-Vlaanderen, Belgium 230
Ranfranz, Pat 170–173, 181
Rangoon Memorial, Burma/Myanmar 268
Rawalpindi War Cemetery, Pakistan 269
R.E. Farm cemetery, Heuvelland, West-Vlaanderen, Belgium 229
Reagan, Pres. Ronald 93, 157
Redoubt Cemetery, Helles, Turkey 255
Redruth (St. Uny) Churchyard Extension, Cornwall, United Kingdom 259
Regina Trench Cemetery, Grandcourt, Somme, France 247
Reichswald Forest War Cemetery, Kleve, Nordrhein-Westfalen, Germany 267
Rekem Communal Cemetery, Lanaken, Limburg, Netherlands 263
Remembrance Day (UK) 182
Remembrance of the Dead Day (NL) 182, *193*
Remilly (Cemetery), France 261
Reninghelst New Military Cemetery, Poperinge, West-Vlaanderen, Belgium 230
SS *Republic* 83
Resistance, Belgian 91–92, 121, 169, 202, 206
Resistance, Dutch 2, 91, 99, 120, 194–195
Reumont Churchyard, Nord, France 247
Revolutionary War 4, 8–13, 16, 50, 71, 151
Reykjavik (Fossvogur) Cemetery, Iceland 267
Rhea, Col. Mike 175–176
Rhone American Cemetery and Memorial, France 132
Ribecourt British Cemetery, Nord, France 247
Ribemont Communal Cemetery Extension, Somme, Somme, France 247
Richley, Jay 74, 174–*175*
Richter, Sp.4 Ruediger *145*
Rico *167*
Ridge Wood Military Cemetery, Ieper, West-Vlaanderen, Belgium 230
Ripon Cemetery, Yorkshire, United Kingdom 259, 272
River Medway, England *17*, 183–184
Robinson 183
Robinson, William 160
Robsart General Cemetery, Saskatchewan, Canada 234
Roclincourt Military Cemetery, Pas-de-Calais, France 247
Rocquigny-Equancourt Road British Cemetery, Manancourt, Somme, France 247
Rødby Kirkegård — Cemetery, Rødby, Denmark 275
Rogers, Joel Augustus 86
Romeries Communal Cemetery Extension, Nord, France 247
Romilly-sur-Seine (Cemetery), France 261
Ronse Community Cemetery, Belgium 262
Roosevelt, Pres. Franklin D. 103, 135
Roosevelt, Quentin 59
Roosevelt, Pres. Theodore 36, 40, *41*, 67, 88, 179
Rose, John 183
Rosieres Communal Cemetery Extension, Somme, France 247
Roslin Cemetery, Midlothian, United Kingdom 259
Rotherham (Masbrough) Cemetery, Yorkshire, United Kingdom 259
Roughead, Adm. Gary 179

Royal Canadian Air Force 93
Royal Irish Rifles Graveyard, Laventie, Pas-de-Calais, France 247
Roye New British Cemetery, Somme, France 247
Rue-Du-Bois Military Cemetery, Fleurbaix, Pas-de-Calais, France 247
Rue-Petillon Military Cemetery, Fleurbaix, Pas-de-Calais, France 247
Rugby (Whinfield) Cemetery, Warwickshire, United Kingdom 272
Runnymede Memorial, Surrey, United Kingdom 272
Rush, Amb. Richard 37
Russian Expeditionary Force (ANREF) *see* Polar Bear Expedition
Russian Revolution 53

USS *Sabine* 176
Sackville Rural Cemetery, New Brunswick, Canada 234
Saffron Walden Cemetery, Essex, United Kingdom 273
Sage War Cemetery, Oldenburg, Niedersachsen, Germany 267
Sai Wan Memorial, China 265
Saigon, Vietnam 144
Sains-Les-Marquion British Cemetery, Pas-de-Calais, France 248
St. Amand British Cemetery, Pas-de-Calais, France 248
St. Andre Communal Cemetery, Nord, France 248
St. Andrews Church, Plymouth, England 16, 152
St. Aubert British Cemetery, Nord, France 248
Ste. Catherine British Cemetery, Pas-de-Calais, France 248
St. Cyr-en-Val Communal Cemetery, Loiret, France 266
St. Day (Holy Trinity) Churchyard, Cornwall, United Kingdom 258
St. Donat Roman Catholic Cemetery, Quebec, Canada 264
St. Germain-en-Laye (Cemetery), France 261
Saint-Gervais-en-Forêt (Cemetery), France 261
St. Helens Cemetery, Lancashire, United Kingdom 258
St. Hilaire Cemetery Extension, Frevent, Pas-de-Calais, France 248
St. Jean Communal Cemetery, Kortrijk, Belgium 230
St. John (Fernhill) Cemetery, Saint John County, New Brunswick, Canada 235, 264
St. John (St. Joseph's) Roman Catholic Cemetery, Saint John County, New Brunswick, Canada 235
St. John's (Mount Pleasant) Cemetery, Newfoundland and Labrador, Canada 264

St. Louis Cemetery, Paris, France 4–5, 37
Ste. Marie Cemetery, Le Havre, Seine-Maritime, France 248
St. Martin Calvaire British Cemetery, St. Martin-Sur-Cojeul, Pas-de-Calais, France 248
St. Mary's A.D.S. Cemetery, Haisnes, Pas-de-Calais, France 248
St. Mary's Island, England 183
Saint-Maur-des-Fosses (Cemetery), France 261
St. Michael's Church, England 151–152, 184, **187**
St. Mihiel American Cemetery and Memorial, France 64, 69
St. Nicolas British Cemetery, Pas-de-Calais, France 248
St. Olle British Cemetery, Raillencourt, Nord, France 248
St. Peter's (Catholic) Cemetery, Nova Scotia, Canada 235
St. Pierre Cemetery, Amiens, Somme, France 248
St. Pol British Cemetery, St. Pol-Sur-Ternoise, Pas-de-Calais, France 248
St. Pol Communal Cemetery Extension, Pas-de-Calais, France 248
St. Quentin Cabaret Military Cemetery, Heuvelland, West-Vlaanderen, Belgium 230
St. Riquier British Cemetery, Somme, France 248
St. Sever Cemetery, Rouen, Seine-Maritime, France 248, 266
St. Souplet British Cemetery, Nord, France 65–66, 248
St. Thomas Cemetery, Elgin County, Ontario, Canada 235
St. Venant-Robecq Road British Cemetery, Robecq, Pas-de-Calais, France 248
Salerno War Cemetery, Italy 268
Salisbury (London Road) Cemetery, Wiltshire, United Kingdom 259
Salonika (Lembet Road) Military Cemetery, Greece 254
Saltash, England 183
Salvatore, Dr. John 183
Sancourt British Cemetery, Nord, France 248
Sanctuary Wood Cemetery, Ieper, West-Vlaanderen, Belgium 230
San Diego, California 24
San Juan del Norte, Nicaragua 175
Santa Anna, Gen. A.L. 24
Santa Cruz de Villegas, Mexico 74, **174**
Sarnia (Lake View) Cemetery, Ontario, Canada 235
Saskatoon (Woodlawn) Cemetery, Saskatchewan, Canada 235, 264
Schuck, PFC. Alfred **55**
Schue, Pvt. Clarence 54
Scopwick Church Burial Ground, Lincolnshire, United Kingdom 273

Seaford Cemetery, Sussex, United Kingdom 258
Seagoe Cemetery, County Armagh, United Kingdom 259
Seeger, Alan 44–46, 49, 151; "I Have a Rendezvous with Death" 46, 51; "Ode in Memory of the American Volunteers Fallen for France" 65
Seeger, Pete 151
Seekings, Dorothy 159
Serre Road Cemetery No. 1, Pas-de-Calais, France 248
Serre Road Cemetery No. 2, Somme, France 248
Seventh New York Regiment *see* Silk Stocking Regiment
Severaid, Eric 95
HMS *Shannon* 14, 162
Shawbury (St. Mary the Virgin) Churchyard, Shropshire, United Kingdom 259
Shea, Iris 163
CSS *Shenandoah* 160
Sherborne Cemetery, Dorset, United Kingdom 274
Sherbrooke (St. Peter's) Church Cemetery, Quebec, Canada 235
Sherburne, Andrew: *Memoirs of Andrew Sherburne: A Pensioner of the Navy of the Revolution, Written by Himself* 3, 8–10, 11, 12
Sherburne, Col. John 37
Sheridan, Jerry 2, 169, 198, 203–209, **206–207**, 215
Sherman, Gen. William 33
Sherman Tank **158**
Sherry, Patrick 161
Shomon, Lt. Col. James J. 112–117; *Crosses in the Wind* 112–113, 119, 128, 197–198
Shorncliffe Military Cemetery, Kent, United Kingdom 259
Shotley (St. Mary) Churchyard, Suffolk, United Kingdom 259
Shotwick (St. Michael) Churchyard, Cheshire, United Kingdom 259
Sicily-Rome American Cemetery and Memorial, Italy 126, 132
Siebold, Grace 82
Siegfried Line 98
Silk Stocking Regiment 50, 53
Sims, Christopher 149, 208–209
Singapore Memorial 269
611th Quartermaster Graves Registration Company 111–117
Skew Bridge Cemetery, Turkey 255
Slapton Sands, England 109, 157–159; *see also* Operation Tiger
Small, Ken 157–159
smallpox 17
Smith, Bryan 185
Smith, Charles 176
Smith, PFC. Harry W. 61
Smith, Gen. Holland 105
Smith, James 22
Smith's Falls (Hillcrest) Cemetery, Ontario, Canada 235
Soissons Memorial, Aisne, France 248

Soller, PO2 Blake *167*
USS *Somers* 157, 161
Somers Point, New Jersey 6, 157, 177–180
Somers, Lt. Richard 6–8, 20, 87, 157, 177–179, 218
Somme American Cemetery and Memorial, Bony, Aisne, France 64, 65, 69, 249
Sorenson, SSgt. Gerald 91–92, 120, 169, 198, 206, **208**, 214
Sorenson, Nora 91, 120, 206
La Souterraine (Cemetery), France 261
South Brookfield Protestant Cemetery, Nova Scotia, Canada 235
Southend-On-Sea (Sutton Road) Cemetery, Essex, United Kingdom 259
Spanish-American War 34, 43; National Spanish American War Gravesite Recording Project 161
Spanish Civil War 79, 155
Speicher, Lt.Cdr. Michael Scott *164*
Spencer, Sgt. Daniel *145*
USS *Spokane* 135–136
Springhill (Hillside) Cemetery, Nova Scotia, Canada 264
Staglieno Cemetery, Genoa, Italy 268
Stanley Military Cemetery, Hong-Kong, China 265
Stanley New Cemetery, Durham, United Kingdom 259
"Star Spangled Banner" 50, 58
Starr, Lt. Philip Comfort 49, 62
Stourbridge Cemetery, Worcestershire, United Kingdom 259
Strand Military Cemetery, Comines-Warneton, Hainaut, Belgium 230
Stranraer (Glebe) Cemetery, Wigtownshire, United Kingdom 274
Stratford (Avondale) Cemetery, Ontario, Canada 235
Stratford-on-Avon Cemetery, Warwickshire, United Kingdom 274
Stray Park Burial Ground, England 183
Struma Military Cemetery, Greece 254
Stump Road Cemetery, Grandcourt, Somme, France 249
Sucrerie Cemetery, Ablain-St. Nazaire, Pas-de-Calais, France 249
Sucrerie Military Cemetery, Colincamps, Somme, France 249
Suez War Memorial Cemetery, Egypt 236
Suippes (Cemetery), France 261
Sullivan, Vadm. William J. 199
Summit, New Jersey 50
Sun Quarry Cemetery, Cherisy, Pas-de-Calais, France 249
Sunderland (Bishopwearmouth) Cemetery, Durham, United Kingdom 259
Sunderland (Southwick) Cemetery, Durham, United Kingdom 259

Sunken Road Cemetery, Contalmaison, Somme, France 249
Supt Churchyard, Jura, France 249
Suresnes American Cemetery and Memorial, France **64–65**, 132
Sutton Bridge (St. Matthew) Churchyard, Lincolnshire, United Kingdom 274
Sutton-in-Craven Baptist Burial Ground, Yorkshire, United Kingdom 259
Sweden 213
Sweetsburg (Christ Church) Cemetery, Quebec, Canada 264
Sydney (Hardwood Hill) Cemetery, Nova Scotia, Canada 235

Talence (Cemetery), France 261
Tan Son Nhut, Vietnam 145
Tannay British Cemetery, Thiennes, Nord, France 249
Tarawa 173; *see also* Battle of Tarawa
La Targette British Cemetery, Neuville-St. Vaast, Pas-de-Calais, France 249
Taukkyan War Cemetery, Burma/Myanmar 268
Taylor, Pres. Zachary 24
Teeuwise, Johann 99
temporary cemeteries: Korea 138; World War I 51, 52, 53, 59, 60, 63, 64; World War II 126–127, 129–30
Terlincthun British Cemetery, Wimille, Pas-de-Calais, France 249
Thelus Military Cemetery, Pas-de-Calais, France 249
Thiaucourt-en-Argonne (Cemetery), France 262
Thiepval Memorial, Somme, France 249
13th Bombardment Squadron (Light-Night Intruder) 137
Thirteenth Cavalry, Troop M 73
Thompson, Barbie 2, 109, 182–*186*
Thompson, Capt. Edgar K. 23
392nd Bombing Group 98
361st Fighter group 97
Thunder Bay (Riverside) Cemetery, Ontario, Canada 235, 264
Tigris Lane Cemetery, Wancourt, Pas-de-Calais, France 250
Tilloy British Cemetery, Tilloy-Les-Mofflaines, Pas-de-Calais, France 250
Tincourt New British Cemetery, Somme, France 250
Tison, Annette 98
HMS *Titanic* 163
Tomb of the Unknown Soldier *see* Unknown Soldier
Topcliffe Church Cemetery, Yorkshire, United Kingdom 274
Toronto Cemetery, Demuin, Somme, France 250
Toronto (Mount Hope) Cemetery, Ontario, Canada 235

Toronto (Mount Pleasant) Cemetery, Ontario, Canada 235, 264
Toronto Necropolis, Ontario, Canada 235
Toronto (Park Lawn) Cemetery, Ontario, Canada 235
Toronto (Pine Hills) Cemetery, Ontario, Canada 264
Toronto (Prospect) Cemetery, Ontario, Canada 235, 264
Toronto (Resthaven) Memorial Garden, Ontario 264
Toronto (St. James') Cemetery, Ontario 264
Toronto (St. John's Norway) Cemetery, Ontario, Canada 235
Toronto (St. Michael's) Roman Catholic Cemetery, Ontario, Canada 235
Torquay Cemetery and Extension, Devon, United Kingdom 259
Toul (Cemetery), France 262
Le Touret Memorial, Pas-de-Calais, France 250
Tournai Communal Cemetery Allied Extension, Tournai, Hainaut, Belgium 230
Tower Hill Memorial, London, United Kingdom 259, 274
Townsville War Cemetery, Queensland, Australia 263
Track "X" Cemetery, Ieper, West-Vlaanderen, Belgium 230
Tranchee De Mecknes Cemetery, Aix-Noulette, Pas-de-Calais, France 250
Treaty of Guadeloupe Hidalgo 24
Treaty of Versailles 53
Trefcon British Cemetery, Caulaincourt, Aisne, France 250
Trenton (St. George's) Cemetery, Ontario, Canada 264
Le Treport Military Cemetery, Seine-Maritime, France 250
Triangle Cemetery, Inchy-En-Artois, Pas-de-Calais, France 250
Trinity Churchyard, New York, United States 16
Tripoli, Libya 5–8, 87–88, 135–136, 156, 177, 218
Tripolitan War *see* First Barbary War
Trois Arbres Cemetery, Steenwerck, Nord, France 250
Le Trou Aid Post Cemetery, Fleurbaix, Pas-de-Calais, France 250
Truman, Harry 138
Tubney (St. Laurence) Churchyard, Berkshire, United Kingdom 274
Tunstall (St. John The Baptist) Churchyard, Lancashire, United Kingdom 274
Twelve Tree Copse Cemetery, Turkey 256
Tyne Cot Cemetery, Zonnebeke, West-Vlaanderen, Belgium 230
Tyne Cot Memorial, Zonnebeke, West-Vlaanderen, Belgium 231
typhus 17

Ulrich, Adm. Harry 176
United Nations Cemetery Pusan, Korea **140**, 141
USS *United States* 16
U.S. Army Central Identification Laboratory in Hawaii (CILH) 173
U.S. Army Quartermaster Foundation 70
U.S. National Defense Authorization Act, FY 2010 173
U.S. Naval Academy 36, **40**, **51**; *see also* Annapolis, Maryland
U.S. Veteran's Administration 165
Unknown Soldier: Korean War 154; Vietnam War 154; World War I 69–71, 74–78, 154; World War II 154–**155**
Upavon Cemetery, Wiltshire, United Kingdom 260
Upton (St. Ephrem) Cemetery, Quebec, Canada 235
Upton Wood Cemetery, Hendecourt-Les-Cagnicourt, Pas-de-Calais, France 250

Valenciennes (St. Roch) Communal Cemetery, Nord, France 250
Valkenswaard War Cemetery, Noord-Brabant, Netherlands 269
Valley Cemetery, Vis-En-Artois, Pas-de-Calais, France 250
Valley Cottages Cemetery, Zillebeke, Belgium 231
Valleyfield Protestant Cemetery, Quebec, Canada 265
Vancouver (Mountain View) Cemetery, British Columbia, Canada 235, 265
Vandervelden, Pierre 63, 191
van Laar, Joseph 113
van Metre, Peter 189–190
van Rij, Jacob 99–101
Vaulx Hill Cemetery, Pas-de-Calais, France 250
Venray War Cemetery, Limburg, Netherlands 269
Vermelles British Cemetery, Pas-de-Calais, France 250
Vermuelen, Ton 2, 194–195
Veterans of Foreign Wars 80
Vevey (St. Martin's) Cemetery, Switzerland 255
Victoria (Ross Bay) Cemetery, British Columbia, Canada 235
Victoria (Royal Oak) Burial Park, British Columbia, Canada 265
Vieille-Chapelle New Military Cemetery, Lacouture, Pas-de-Calais, France 250
Vierville sur Mer (Cemetery), France 262
Viet Nam War 142–146, **145**; postwar 168, 172
Villanova Canadian War Cemetery, Italy 268
La Ville-Aux-Bois British Cemetery, Aisne, France 250

Villeparisis (Cemetery), France 262
Villers-Bretonneux Memorial, Somme, France 250
Villers-Bretonneux Military Cemetery, Somme, France 250
Villers Station Cemetery, Villers-Au-Bois, Pas-de-Calais, France 251
Vimy Memorial, Pas-de-Calais, France 251
Vis-En-Artois British Cemetery, Haucourt, Pas-de-Calais, France 253
Vis-En-Artois Memorial, Pas-de-Calais, France 253
Vlamertinghe Military Cemetery, Ieper, West-Vlaanderen, Belgium 231
Vlamertinghe New Military Cemetery, Ieper, West-Vlaanderen, Belgium 231
Voormezeele Enclosure No. 1 and No. 2, Ieper, West-Vlaanderen, Belgium 231
Voormezeele Enclosure No. 3, Ieper, West-Vlaanderen, Belgium 231

Wadsworth, Sen. James, Jr. 57
Wagner, Sgt. Jack Elwood 93, 130
Walkerton Cemetery, Ontario, Canada 235
Wallasey (Rake Lane) Cemetery, Cheshire, United Kingdom 260
Wancourt British Cemetery, Pas-de-Calais, France 253
Wandsworth (Earlsfield) Cemetery, London, United Kingdom 260
Wandsworth (Putney Vale) Cemetery and Crematorium, London, United Kingdom 260
Wanquetin Communal Cemetery Extension, Pas-de-Calais, France 253
War Dogs 105–**108**, 166, 275
War of 1812 9, 11, 12, 15–20, 23, 40, 104, 152, 161–162, 183–185
Ware, Cora Willis 83
Ware, Sir Fabian 62
Waregem, Belgium 63, 72, 148–150, 203–204, 210
Warlencourt British Cemetery, Pas-de-Calais, France 253
Warlincourt Halte British Cemetery, Saulty, Pas-de-Calais, France 253
Warlingham (All Saints) Churchyard, Surrey, United Kingdom 260
Warloy-Baillon Communal Cemetery Extension, Somme, France 253
Warrington Cemetery, Lancashire, United Kingdom 260
Warvillers Churchyard Extension, Somme, France 254
Warwick Bridge (Our Lady and St. Wilfrid) Roman Catholic Churchyard, Cumberland, United Kingdom 274

Waterford (Greenwood) Cemetery, Ontario, Canada 235
Waterhouse, Benjamin: *A Journal of a Young Man of Massachusetts* 12, 14, 16–19, 183
Wavans British Cemetery, Pas-de-Calais, France 254
Wavre Communal Cemetery, Wavre, Brabant Wallon, Belgium 231
Weeks, War Dept. Secy. John 75
Wellington Cemetery, Rieux-En-Cambresis, Nord, Nord, France 254
Wellington (Karori) Cemetery, Wellington City, New Zealand 255
West Point 33
Weston (Riverside) Cemetery, Ontario, Canada 235
Westouter Churchyard Extension, Heuvelland, Belgium 231
Whalley (Queen Mary's Hospital) Military Cemetery, Lancashire, United Kingdom 260
Whangarei (Otaika) Public Cemetery, Whangarei District, New Zealand 255
White Chapel Memorial Cemetery, United States 81–82, 180–181
White House Cemetery, St. Jean-Les-Ypres, Ieper, West-Vlaanderen, Belgium 231
Whitehaven Cemetery, Cumberland, United Kingdom 274
Whitman, Walt 28; *Specimen Days and Collect* 34
Wiart, Laurent 191–192
Wieringen (Hippolytushoef) General Cemetery, Noord-Holland, Netherlands 269
Wiggins, Jeff 197
Wilson, Margaret 59
Wilson, Pres. Woodrow 42, 48–49, 54, 70
Wimereux Communal Cemetery, Pas-de-Calais, France 254
Winchester (Magdalen Hill) Cemetery, Hampshire, United Kingdom 260
Winchester (West Hill) Old Cemetery, Hampshire, United Kingdom 260, 274
Windsor (Grove) Cemetery, Ontario, Canada 235, 265
Windsor (Victoria) Memorial Park, Ontario 265
Winnipeg (Brookside) Cemetery, Manitoba, Canada 235, 265
Winnipeg (Elmwood) Cemetery, Manitoba, Canada 265
Winnipeg (St. James) Cemetery, Manitoba, Canada 236
Winnipeg (St. Mary's) Cemetery, Manitoba, Canada 236
Winter, Wallace Charles 78
Wister, Owen 58, 67
Withycombe Raleigh (St. John in the Wilderness) Churchyard, Devon, United Kingdom 260

Witley (Milford) Cemetery, Surrey, United Kingdom 260
Woburn Abbey Cemetery, Cuinchy, Pas-de-Calais, France 254
Woking (St. John's) Crematorium, Surrey, United Kingdom 260
Wokingham (St. Sebastian) Churchyard, Berkshire, United Kingdom 260
Women's Auxilliary Air Force 132
Wood Cemetery, Marcelcave, Somme, France 254
Woods Cemetery, Ieper, West-Vlaanderen, Belgium 231
Woodstock Methodist Cemetery, New Brunswick, Canada 236
Wormhoudt Communal Cemetery, Nord, France 266

Yap, Micronesian Islands *170*–173
Yarmouth (Mountain) Cemetery, Nova Scotia, Canada 236, 265
Yatesbury (All Saints) Churchyard, Wiltshire, United Kingdom 260
Yokohama, Japan 125, 139; War Cemetery 268
Young, Sgt. Edward 79
Younger, Sgt. Edward F. 70, 148, 154
Ypres, Belgium 49, 51–52
Ypres (Menin Gate) Memorial, Ieper, West-Vlaanderen, Belgium 231
Ypres Reservoir Cemetery, Ieper, West-Vlaanderen, Belgium 233

Zantvoorde British Cemetery, Zonnebeke, West-Vlaanderen, Belgium 233
Zimmerman Telegram 43, 49
Zoetermeer, Netherlands 2, 98, *101*, 112, 119, 194–195, 274
Zouave Valley Cemetery, Souchez, Pas-de-Calais, France 254
Zuydcoote Military Cemetery, Nord, France 254

www.ingramcontent.com/pod-product-compliance
Lightning Source LLC
Chambersburg PA
CBHW081541300426
44116CB00015B/2707